ALSO BY MARISABINA RUSSO

PICTURE BOOKS

The Line Up Book
Why Do Grown-Ups Have All the Fun?
The Big Fat Worm by Nancy Van Laan
Only Six More Days
A Week of Lullabies compiled and edited by Helen Plotz
Waiting for Hannah
When Summer Ends by Susi Gregg Fowler
Where Is Ben?
A Visit to Oma
Alex Is My Friend
Trade-In Mother
It Begins with an A by Stephanie Calmenson
I Don't Want to Go Back to School
Time to Wake Up!
Bear E. Bear by Susan Straight
Good-bye, Curtis by Kevin Henkes
Grandpa Abe
Swim! by Eve Rice
Under the Table
When Mama Gets Home
Hannah's Baby Sister
Mama Talks Too Much
The Big Brown Box
Come Back, Hannah!
The Trouble with Baby
Always Remember Me: How One Family Survived World War II
The Bunnies Are Not in Their Beds
A Very Big Bunny
I Will Come Back for You: A Family in Hiding During World War II
Peter Is Just a Baby
Sophie Sleeps Over
Little Bird Takes a Bath

ILLUSTRATED BOOKS FOR OLDER READERS

Vacation Time: Poems for Children by Nikki Giovanni
Vegetables: An Illustrated History with Recipes by Elizabeth Burton Brown
Easy-to-Make Spaceships That Really Fly by Mary and Dewey Blocksma

NOVELS

House of Sports
A Portrait of Pia

WHY IS EVERYBODY YELLING?

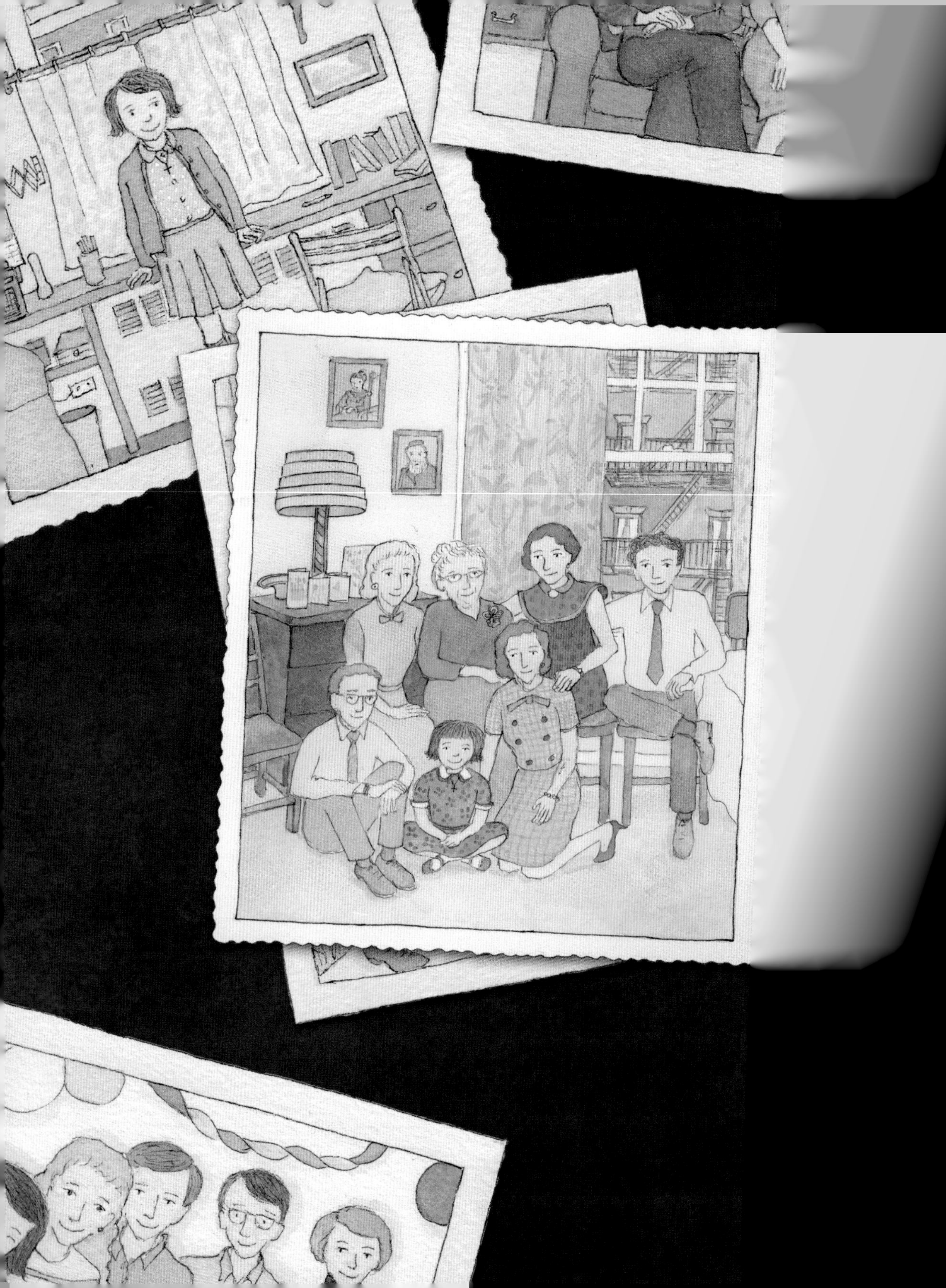

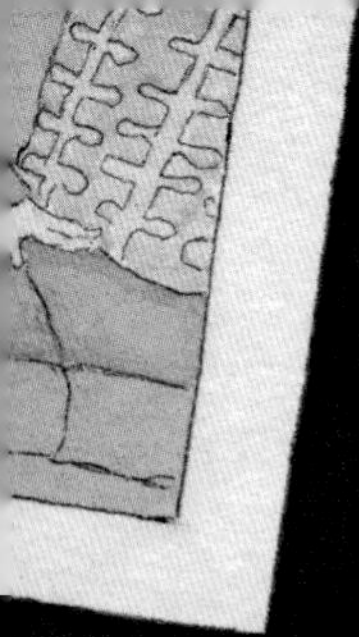
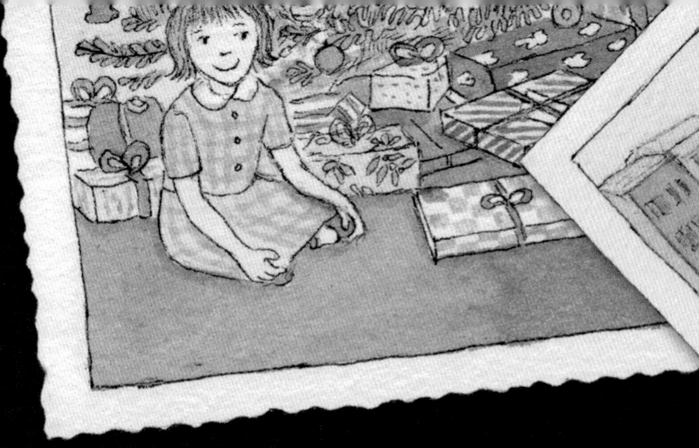
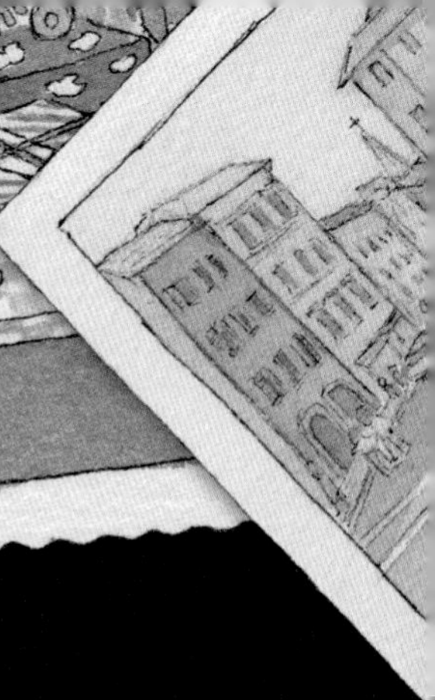

WHY IS EVERYBODY YELLING?

Growing Up in My Immigrant Family

MARISABINA RUSSO

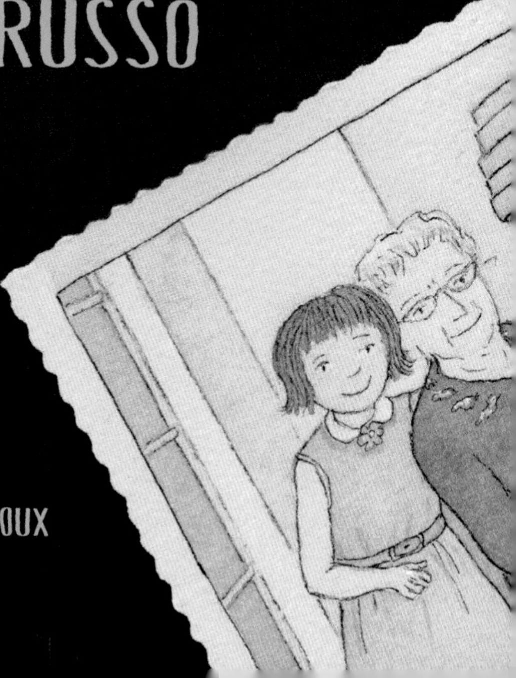

FARRAR STRAUS GIROUX
NEW YORK

For Jackson, Travis, Audrey, and Camilla

Farrar Straus Giroux Books for Young Readers
An imprint of Macmillan Publishing Group, LLC
120 Broadway, New York, NY 10271

Copyright © 2021 by Marisabina Russo
Printed in China by RR Donnelley Asia Printing Solutions Ltd., Dongguan City, Guangdong Province
Designed by Kirk Benshoff and Sunny Lee
First edition, 2021
1 3 5 7 9 10 8 6 4 2

fiercereads.com

Library of Congress Cataloging-in-Publication Data is available
ISBN 978-0-374-30383-9

Our books may be purchased in bulk for promotional, educational, or business use.
Please contact your local bookseller or the Macmillan Corporate and Premium Sales Department at
(800) 221-7945, ext. 5442, or by email at MacmillanSpecialMarkets@macmillan.com.

CONTENTS

ONE

God's Grace

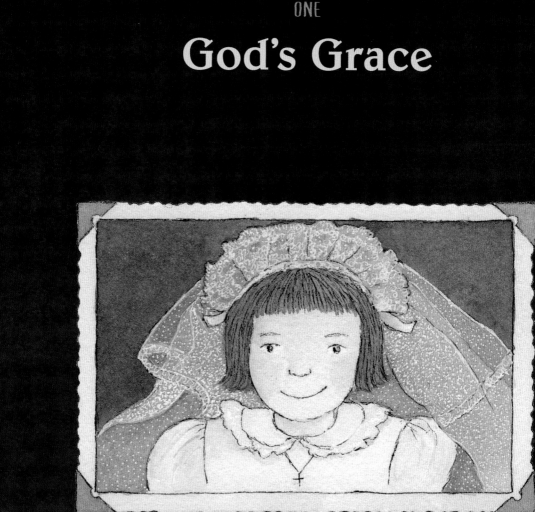

1957

WHEN I WAS A LITTLE GIRL, I TOOK CATHOLICISM VERY SERIOUSLY.

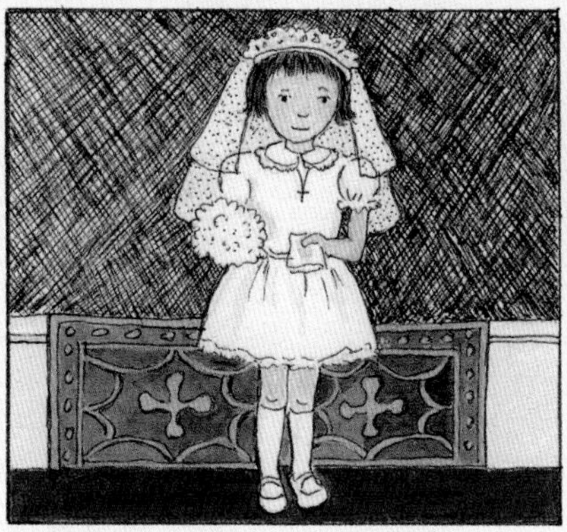

THERE WAS NOTHING I DIDN'T LIKE ABOUT THE CATHOLIC CHURCH.

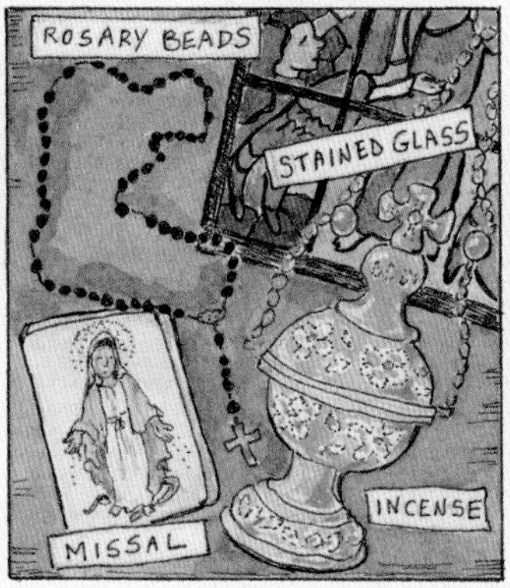
ROSARY BEADS
STAINED GLASS
MISSAL
INCENSE

I THOUGHT MY TEACHER, SISTER JOSEPH GERARD, WAS BEAUTIFUL EVEN IN HER HABIT.

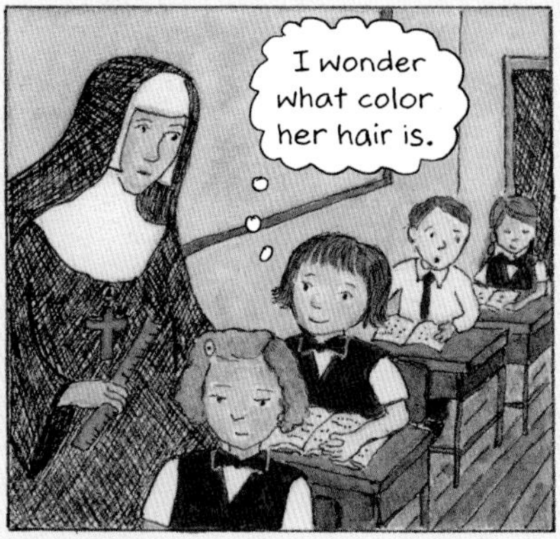
I wonder what color her hair is.

DESPITE THE FACT THAT MY RELATIVES SPOKE YIDDISH, ATE HERRING, AND DRANK SELTZER, IT NEVER OCCURRED TO ME THAT I MIGHT ACTUALLY BE JEWISH.

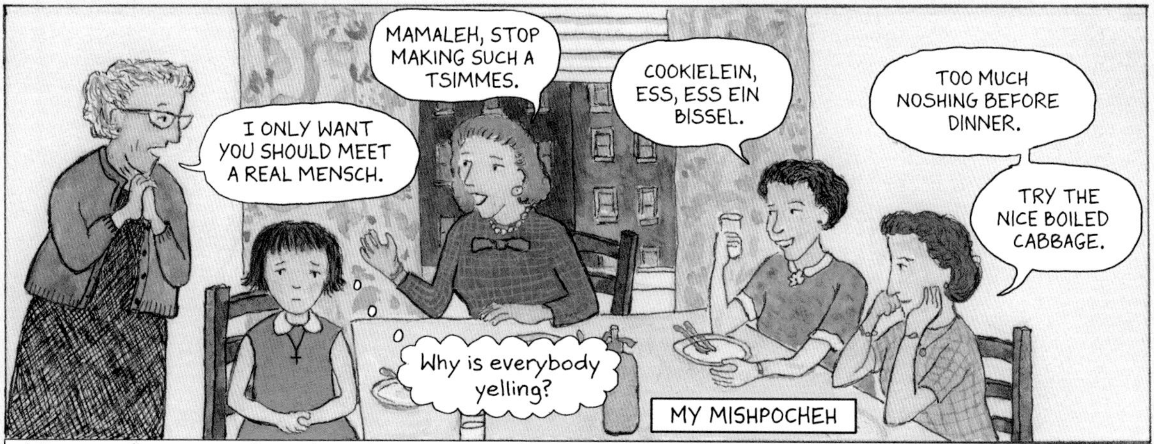
I ONLY WANT YOU SHOULD MEET A REAL MENSCH.
MAMALEH, STOP MAKING SUCH A TSIMMES.
COOKIELEIN, ESS, ESS EIN BISSEL.
TOO MUCH NOSHING BEFORE DINNER.
TRY THE NICE BOILED CABBAGE.
Why is everybody yelling?
MY MISHPOCHEH

tsimmes—*fuss* ***mensch***—*a decent person* ***Cookielein***—*Cookie dear* ***ess, ess ein bissel***—*eat, eat a little*
noshing—*snacking* ***mishpocheh***—*clan, extended family*

MY DREAM WAS TO BECOME A NUN SO THAT I COULD LIVE A CALM AND ORDERLY LIFE FAR FROM THE FERMISHT TUMMEL OF MY OWN FAMILY.

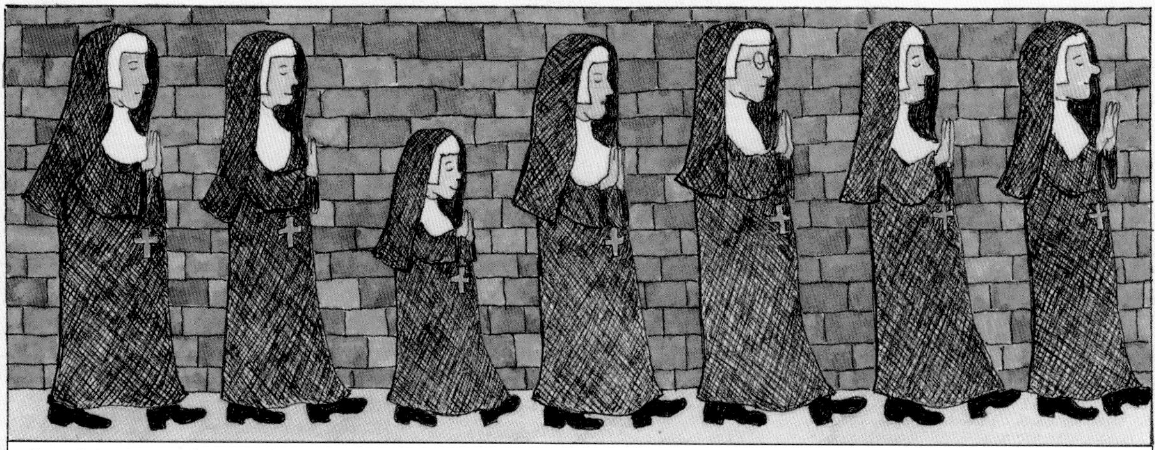

fermisht tummel—*mixed-up commotion*

THERE WAS A LOT ABOUT MY FAMILY'S HISTORY THAT I DIDN'T UNDERSTAND. ALL I KNEW FOR SURE WAS THAT MY MOTHER HAD ONCE BEEN JEWISH BUT BECAME A CATHOLIC WHEN SHE LIVED IN ITALY DURING THE WAR, AND IT WAS A TERRIBLE "SHANDA" OR DISGRACE, ACCORDING TO MY TANTES EMMY AND ANNY.

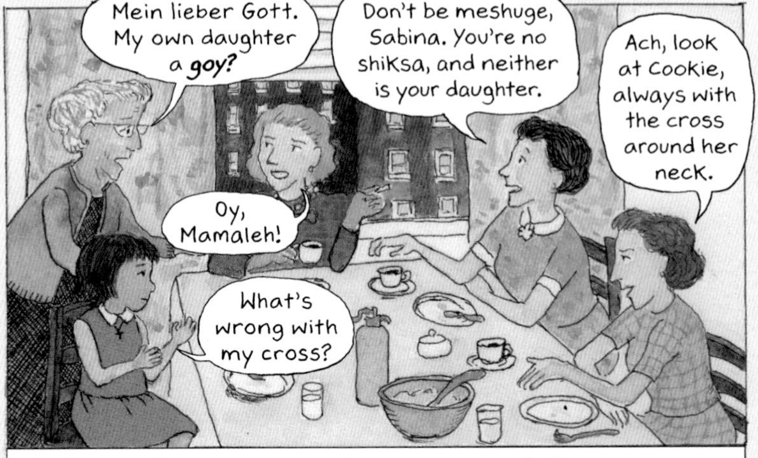

Mein lieber Gott. My own daughter a **goy?**
Don't be meshuge, Sabina. You're no shiksa, and neither is your daughter.
Ach, look at Cookie, always with the cross around her neck.
Oy, Mamaleh!
What's wrong with my cross?

Mein lieber Gott—*Dear God* ***goy***—*Gentile* ***meshuge***—*foolish* ***shiksa***—*a non-Jewish woman*

BUT WHEN I WAS SEVEN, MY MOTHER BEGAN TO QUESTION HER DECISION TO SEND ME TO PAROCHIAL SCHOOL.

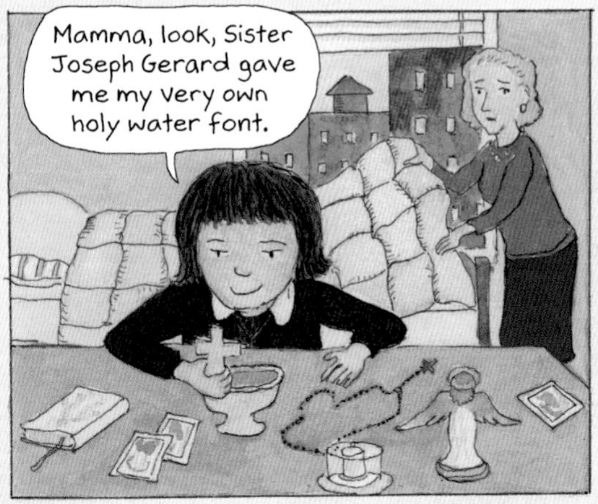

Mamma, look, Sister Joseph Gerard gave me my very own holy water font.

I THINK IT MIGHT HAVE BEEN MY HOMEMADE WIMPLE THAT PUSHED HER OVER THE EDGE.

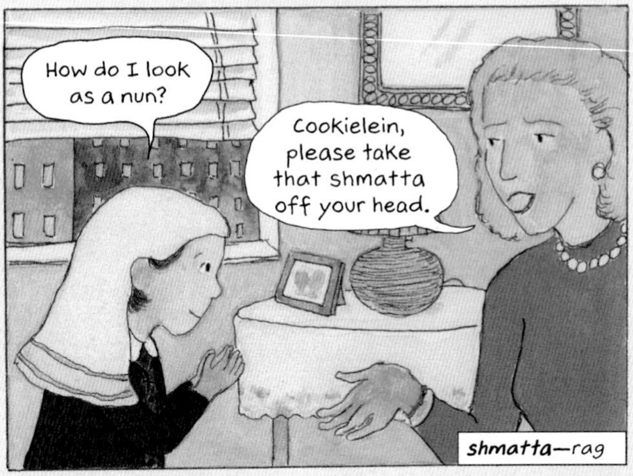

How do I look as a nun?
Cookielein, please take that shmatta off your head.

shmatta—*rag*

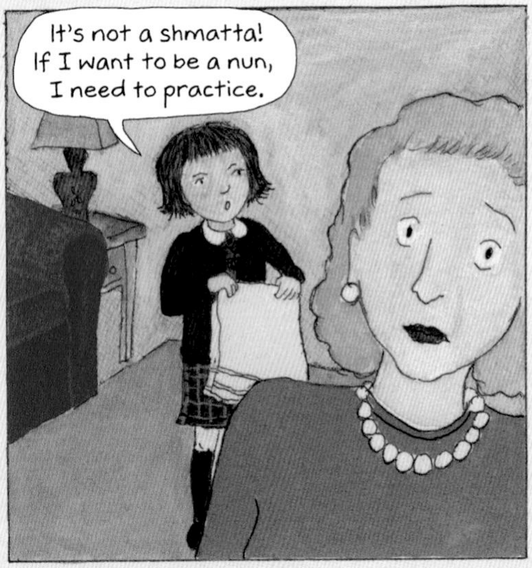

It's not a shmatta! If I want to be a nun, I need to practice.

ONE SATURDAY MY MOTHER SUGGESTED WE GO OUT FOR CHEESEBURGERS.

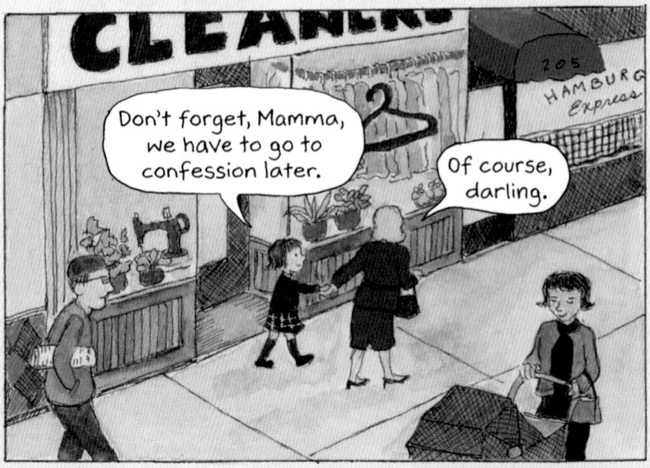

CLEANERS
205
HAMBURG Express
Don't forget, Mamma, we have to go to confession later.
Of course, darling.

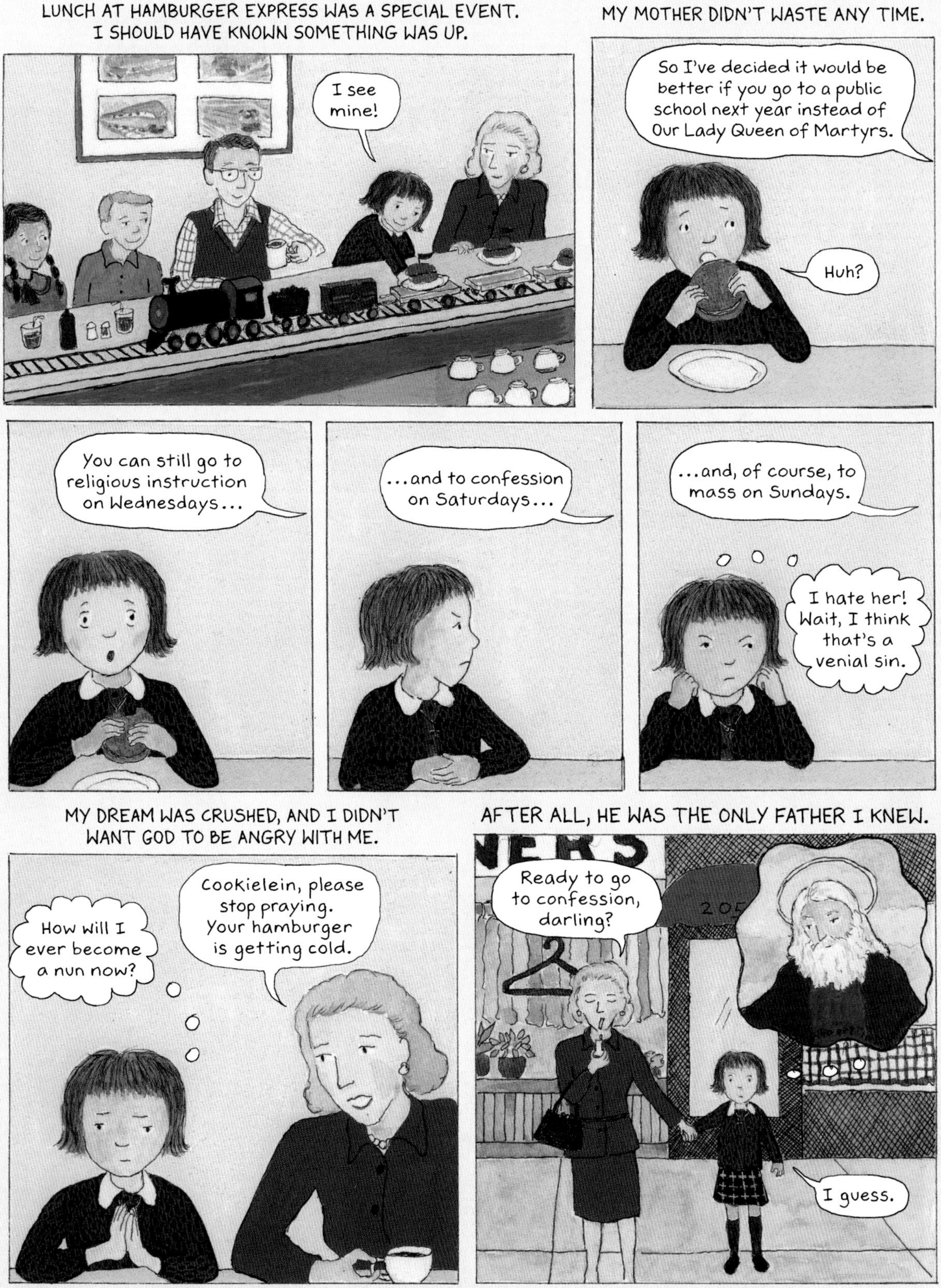
LUNCH AT HAMBURGER EXPRESS WAS A SPECIAL EVENT. I SHOULD HAVE KNOWN SOMETHING WAS UP.
I see mine!
MY MOTHER DIDN'T WASTE ANY TIME.
So I've decided it would be better if you go to a public school next year instead of Our Lady Queen of Martyrs.
Huh?
You can still go to religious instruction on Wednesdays...
...and to confession on Saturdays...
...and, of course, to mass on Sundays.
I hate her! Wait, I think that's a venial sin.
MY DREAM WAS CRUSHED, AND I DIDN'T WANT GOD TO BE ANGRY WITH ME.
How will I ever become a nun now?
Cookielein, please stop praying. Your hamburger is getting cold.
AFTER ALL, HE WAS THE ONLY FATHER I KNEW.
Ready to go to confession, darling?
I guess.

THE WALK TO CHURCH TOOK US PAST
MY BELOVED, SOON-TO-BE EX-SCHOOL.

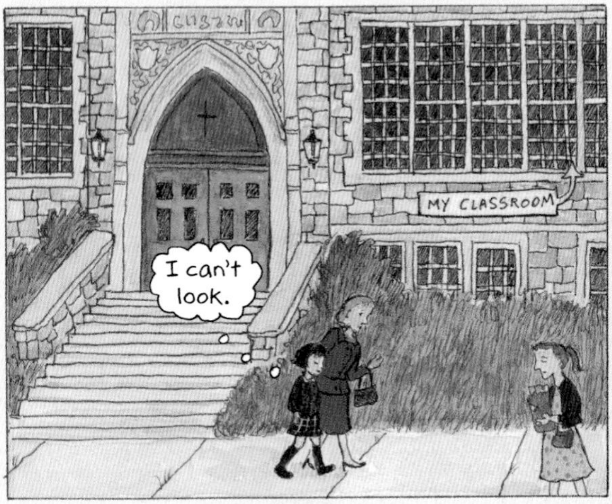
MY CLASSROOM
I can't look.

MY MOTHER NEVER MADE HER OWN
CONFESSION. SHE WOULD WAIT FOR ME
IN THE BACK PEW. I ALWAYS ASSUMED
IT WAS BECAUSE SHE HAD NO SINS.

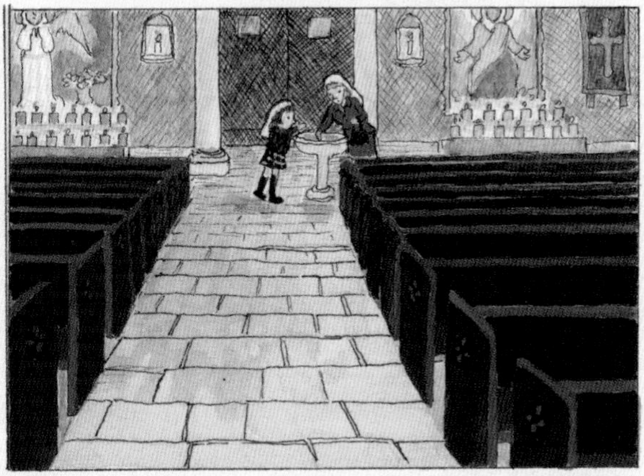

BUT TODAY SHE CROSSED HERSELF WITH HOLY WATER, GENUFLECTED, AND MARCHED
STRAIGHT DOWN THE CENTER AISLE TO THE CONFESSIONAL BOOTHS.

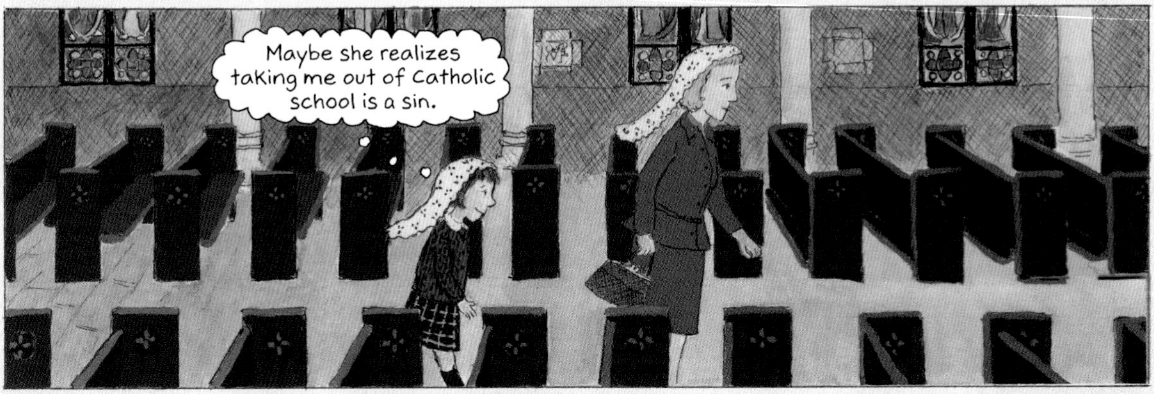
Maybe she realizes taking me out of Catholic school is a sin.

WHILE WE WAITED WITH THE OTHER SINNERS,
MY MIND DRIFTED TO MY MOTHER'S
UNEXPECTED CONFESSION.

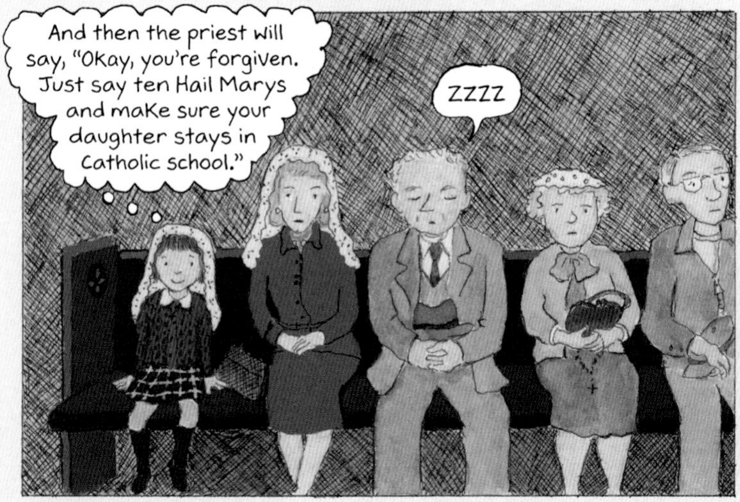
And then the priest will say, "Okay, you're forgiven. Just say ten Hail Marys and make sure your daughter stays in Catholic school."
ZZZZ

AT LAST IT WAS MY MOTHER'S
TURN. I PROUDLY WATCHED HER
ENTER THE BOOTH.

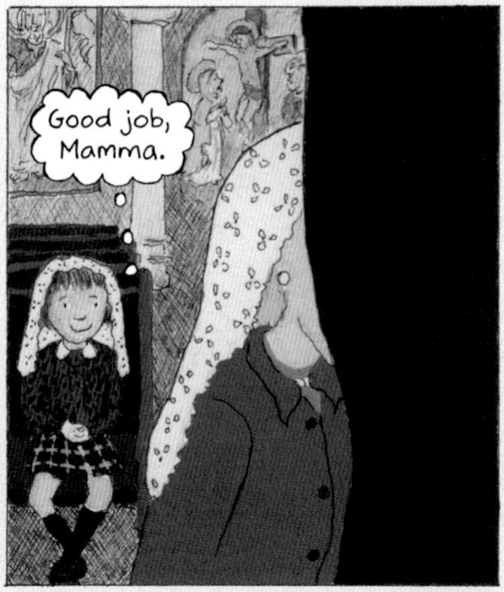
Good job, Mamma.

I LISTENED TO THE USUAL MURMURS COMING FROM BEHIND THE HEAVY RED CURTAIN.

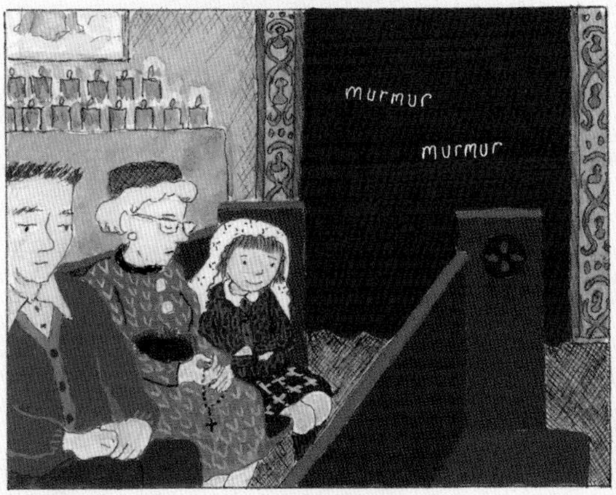
murmur
murmur

BUT THEN...THE VOICES BECAME LOUDER...

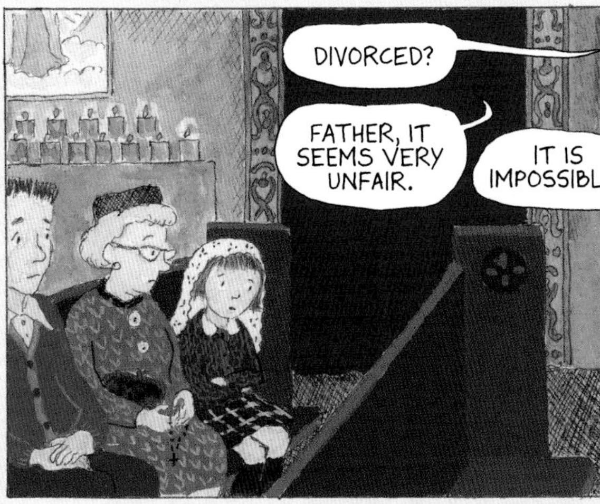
DIVORCED?
FATHER, IT SEEMS VERY UNFAIR.
IT IS IMPOSSIBLE.

...AND LOUDER!

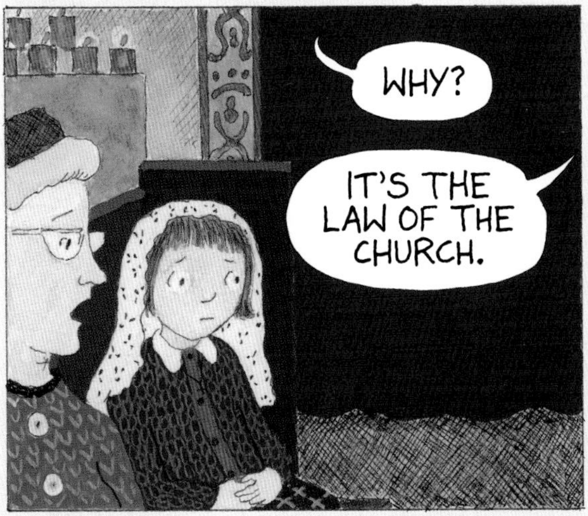
WHY?
IT'S THE LAW OF THE CHURCH.

MY MOTHER WAS ARGUING WITH THE PRIEST!

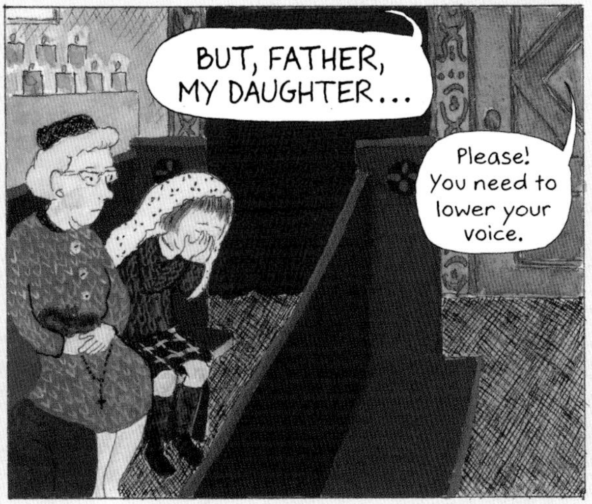
BUT, FATHER, MY DAUGHTER...
Please! You need to lower your voice.

FINALLY, MY MOTHER EMERGED FROM THE CONFESSIONAL BOOTH, HER RAGE BARELY CONCEALED.

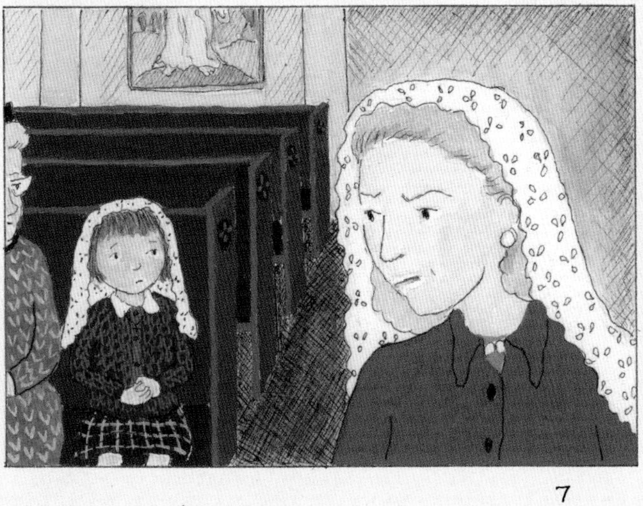

SHE DIDN'T APPROACH THE ALTAR TO SAY PENANCE. INSTEAD SHE SAT DOWN IN THE FIRST PEW.

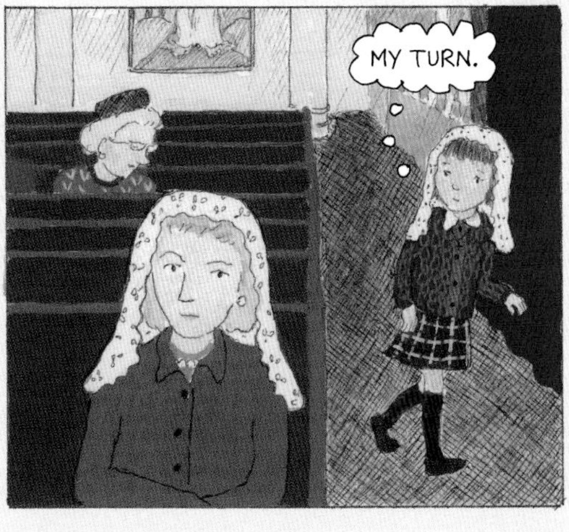
MY TURN.

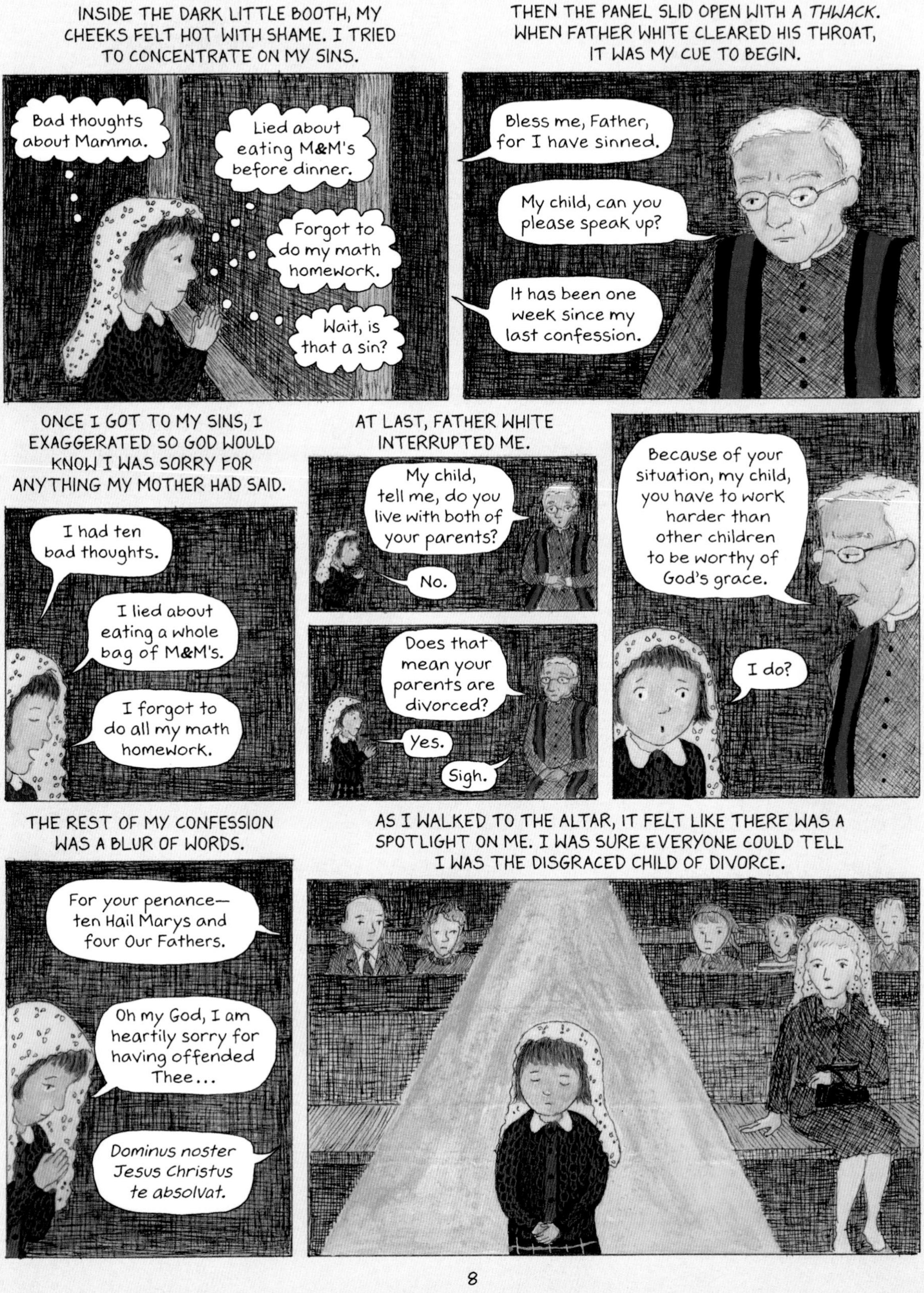
INSIDE THE DARK LITTLE BOOTH, MY CHEEKS FELT HOT WITH SHAME. I TRIED TO CONCENTRATE ON MY SINS.
Bad thoughts about Mamma.
Lied about eating M&M's before dinner.
Forgot to do my math homework.
Wait, is that a sin?
THEN THE PANEL SLID OPEN WITH A *THWACK*. WHEN FATHER WHITE CLEARED HIS THROAT, IT WAS MY CUE TO BEGIN.
Bless me, Father, for I have sinned.
My child, can you please speak up?
It has been one week since my last confession.
ONCE I GOT TO MY SINS, I EXAGGERATED SO GOD WOULD KNOW I WAS SORRY FOR ANYTHING MY MOTHER HAD SAID.
I had ten bad thoughts.
I lied about eating a whole bag of M&M's.
I forgot to do all my math homework.
AT LAST, FATHER WHITE INTERRUPTED ME.
My child, tell me, do you live with both of your parents?
No.
Does that mean your parents are divorced?
Yes.
Sigh.
Because of your situation, my child, you have to work harder than other children to be worthy of God's grace.
I do?
THE REST OF MY CONFESSION WAS A BLUR OF WORDS.
For your penance— ten Hail Marys and four Our Fathers.
Oh my God, I am heartily sorry for having offended Thee...
Dominus noster Jesus Christus te absolvat.
AS I WALKED TO THE ALTAR, IT FELT LIKE THERE WAS A SPOTLIGHT ON ME. I WAS SURE EVERYONE COULD TELL I WAS THE DISGRACED CHILD OF DIVORCE.

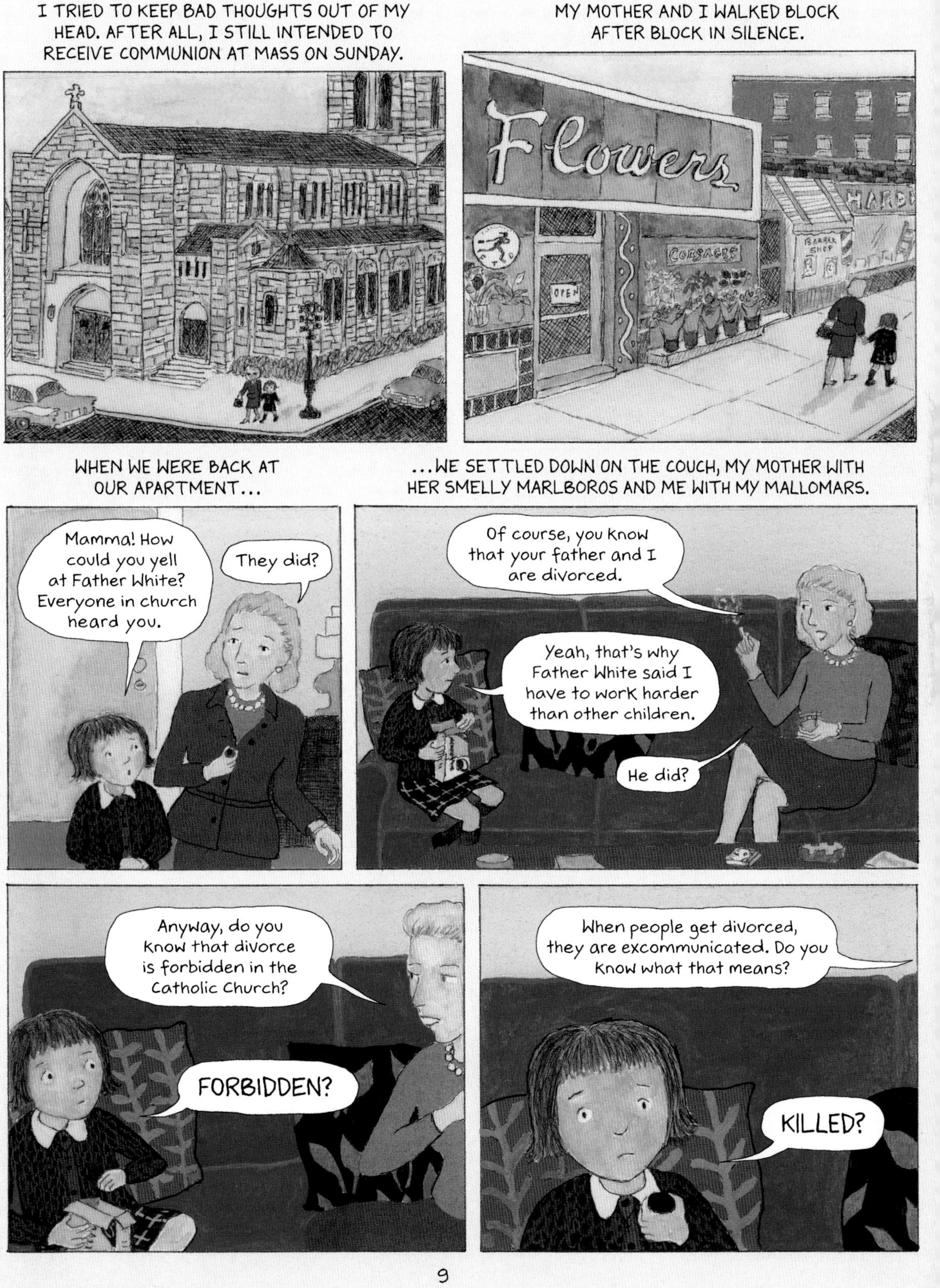
I TRIED TO KEEP BAD THOUGHTS OUT OF MY HEAD. AFTER ALL, I STILL INTENDED TO RECEIVE COMMUNION AT MASS ON SUNDAY.
MY MOTHER AND I WALKED BLOCK AFTER BLOCK IN SILENCE.
Flowers
CORSAGES
OPEN
BARBER SHOP
WHEN WE WERE BACK AT OUR APARTMENT...
Mamma! How could you yell at Father White? Everyone in church heard you.
They did?
...WE SETTLED DOWN ON THE COUCH, MY MOTHER WITH HER SMELLY MARLBOROS AND ME WITH MY MALLOMARS.
Of course, you know that your father and I are divorced.
Yeah, that's why Father White said I have to work harder than other children.
He did?
Anyway, do you know that divorce is forbidden in the Catholic Church?
FORBIDDEN?
When people get divorced, they are excommunicated. Do you know what that means?
KILLED?

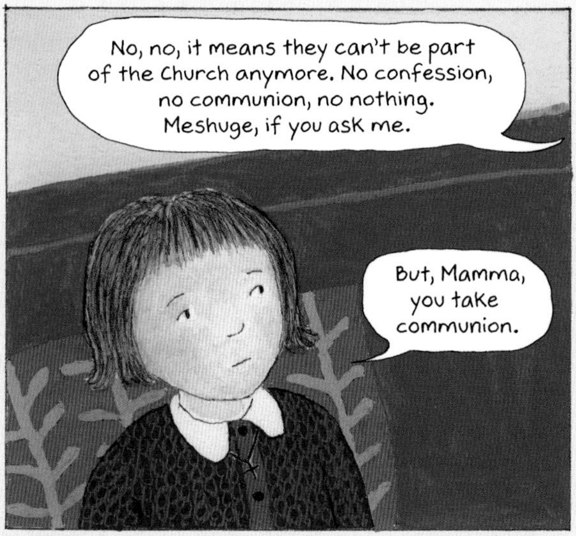
No, no, it means they can't be part of the Church anymore. No confession, no communion, no nothing. Meshuge, if you ask me.
But, Mamma, you take communion.

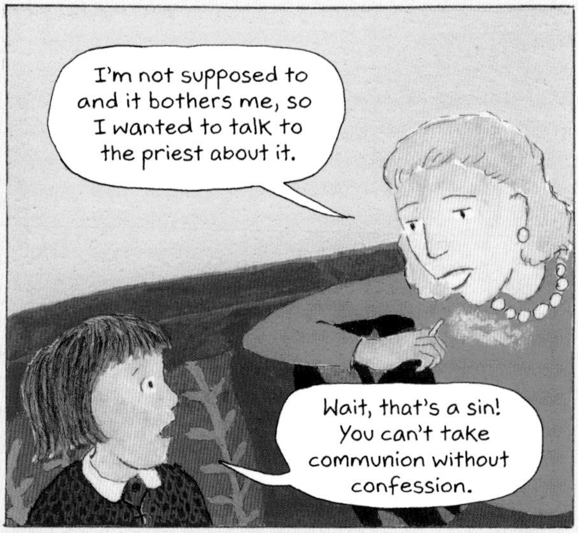
I'm not supposed to and it bothers me, so I wanted to talk to the priest about it.
Wait, that's a sin! You can't take communion without confession.

THIS WAS WORSE THAN I THOUGHT.

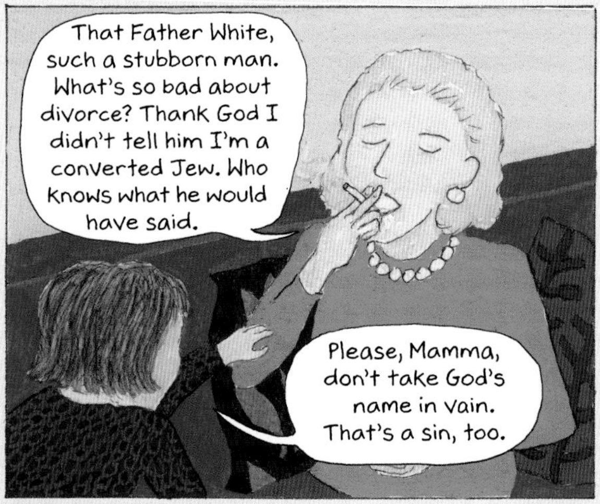
That Father White, such a stubborn man. What's so bad about divorce? Thank God I didn't tell him I'm a converted Jew. Who knows what he would have said.
Please, Mamma, don't take God's name in vain. That's a sin, too.

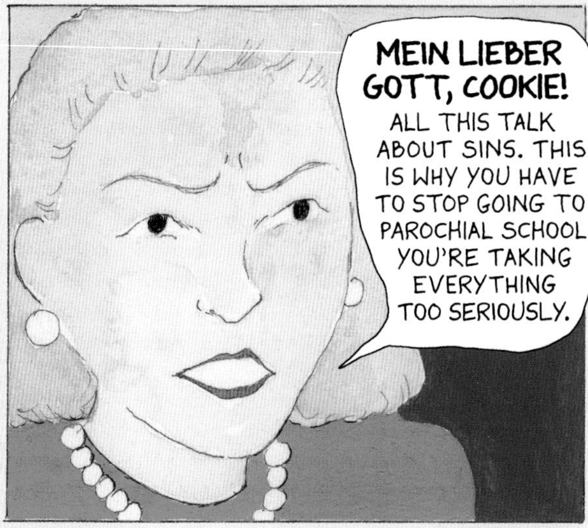
MEIN LIEBER GOTT, COOKIE! ALL THIS TALK ABOUT SINS. THIS IS WHY YOU HAVE TO STOP GOING TO PAROCHIAL SCHOOL. YOU'RE TAKING EVERYTHING TOO SERIOUSLY.

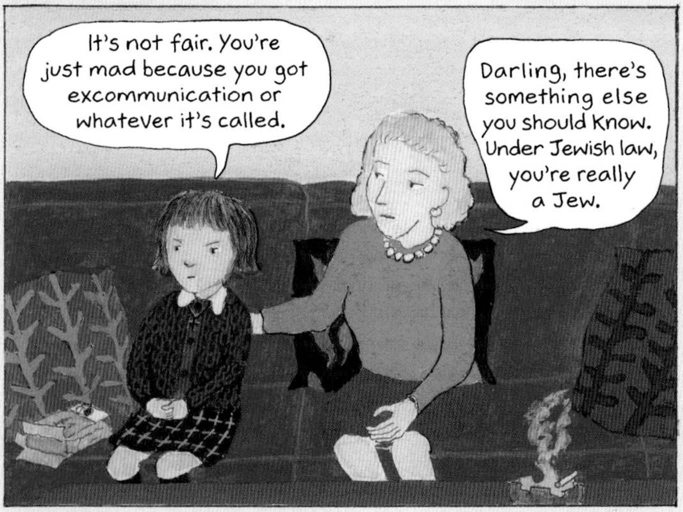
It's not fair. You're just mad because you got excommunication or whatever it's called.
Darling, there's something else you should know. Under Jewish law, you're really a Jew.

WHAT WAS MY MOTHER TALKING ABOUT? I HAD JUST HAD MY FIRST COMMUNION. HOW COULD I BE . . .

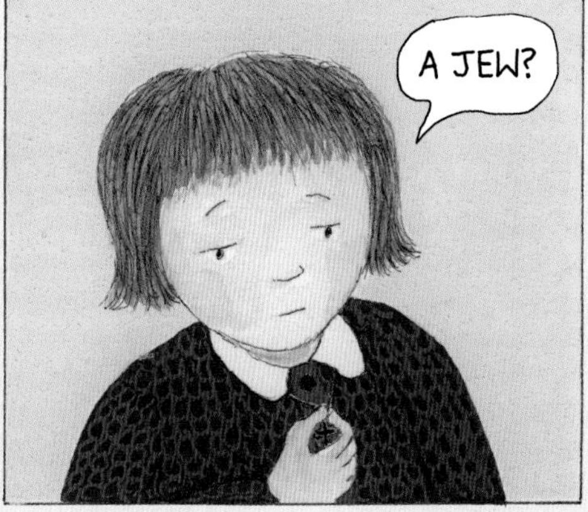
A JEW?

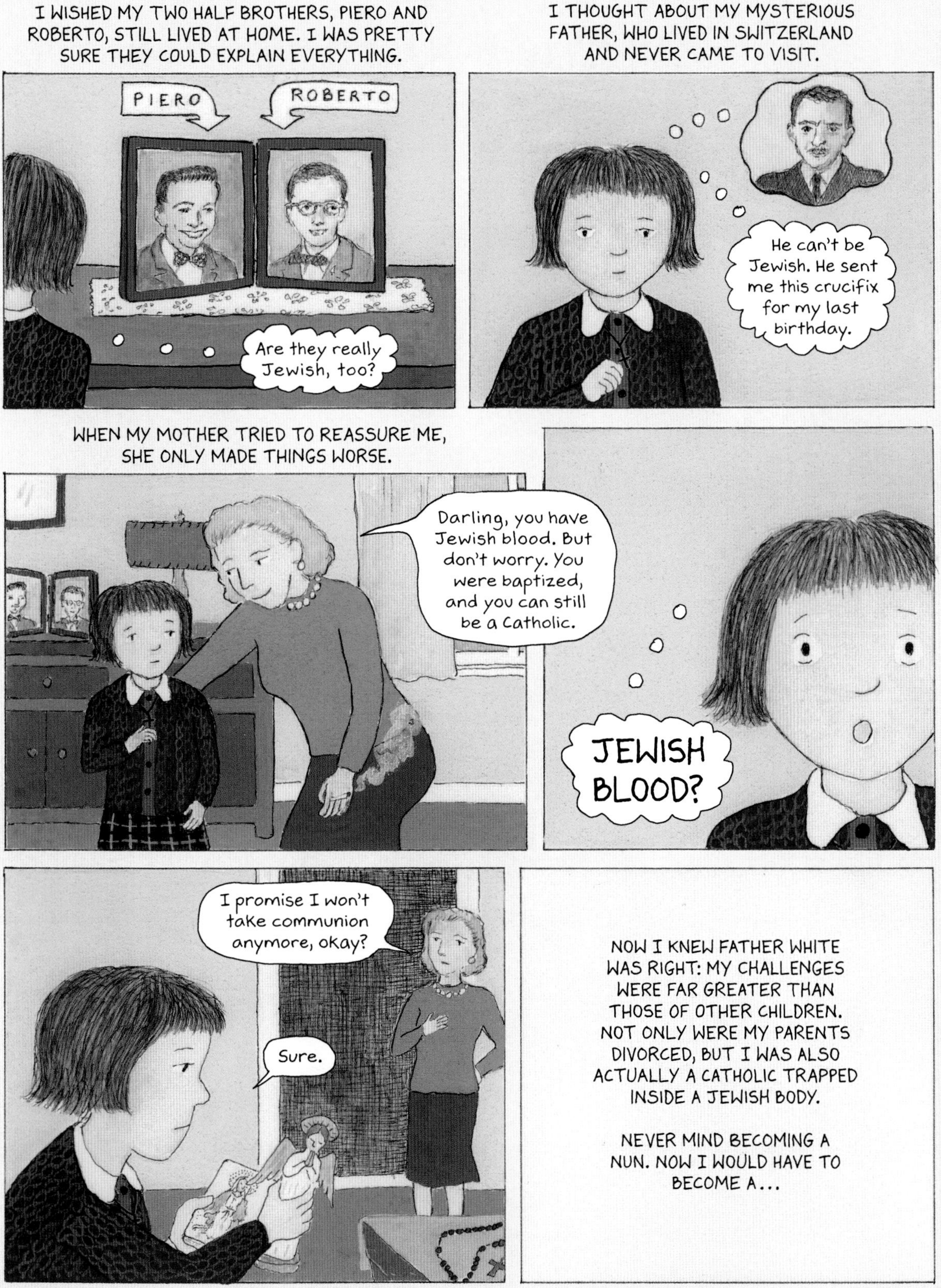
I WISHED MY TWO HALF BROTHERS, PIERO AND ROBERTO, STILL LIVED AT HOME. I WAS PRETTY SURE THEY COULD EXPLAIN EVERYTHING.
PIERO
ROBERTO
Are they really Jewish, too?
I THOUGHT ABOUT MY MYSTERIOUS FATHER, WHO LIVED IN SWITZERLAND AND NEVER CAME TO VISIT.
He can't be Jewish. He sent me this crucifix for my last birthday.
WHEN MY MOTHER TRIED TO REASSURE ME, SHE ONLY MADE THINGS WORSE.
Darling, you have Jewish blood. But don't worry. You were baptized, and you can still be a Catholic.
JEWISH BLOOD?
I promise I won't take communion anymore, okay?
Sure.
NOW I KNEW FATHER WHITE WAS RIGHT: MY CHALLENGES WERE FAR GREATER THAN THOSE OF OTHER CHILDREN. NOT ONLY WERE MY PARENTS DIVORCED, BUT I WAS ALSO ACTUALLY A CATHOLIC TRAPPED INSIDE A JEWISH BODY.
NEVER MIND BECOMING A NUN. NOW I WOULD HAVE TO BECOME A...

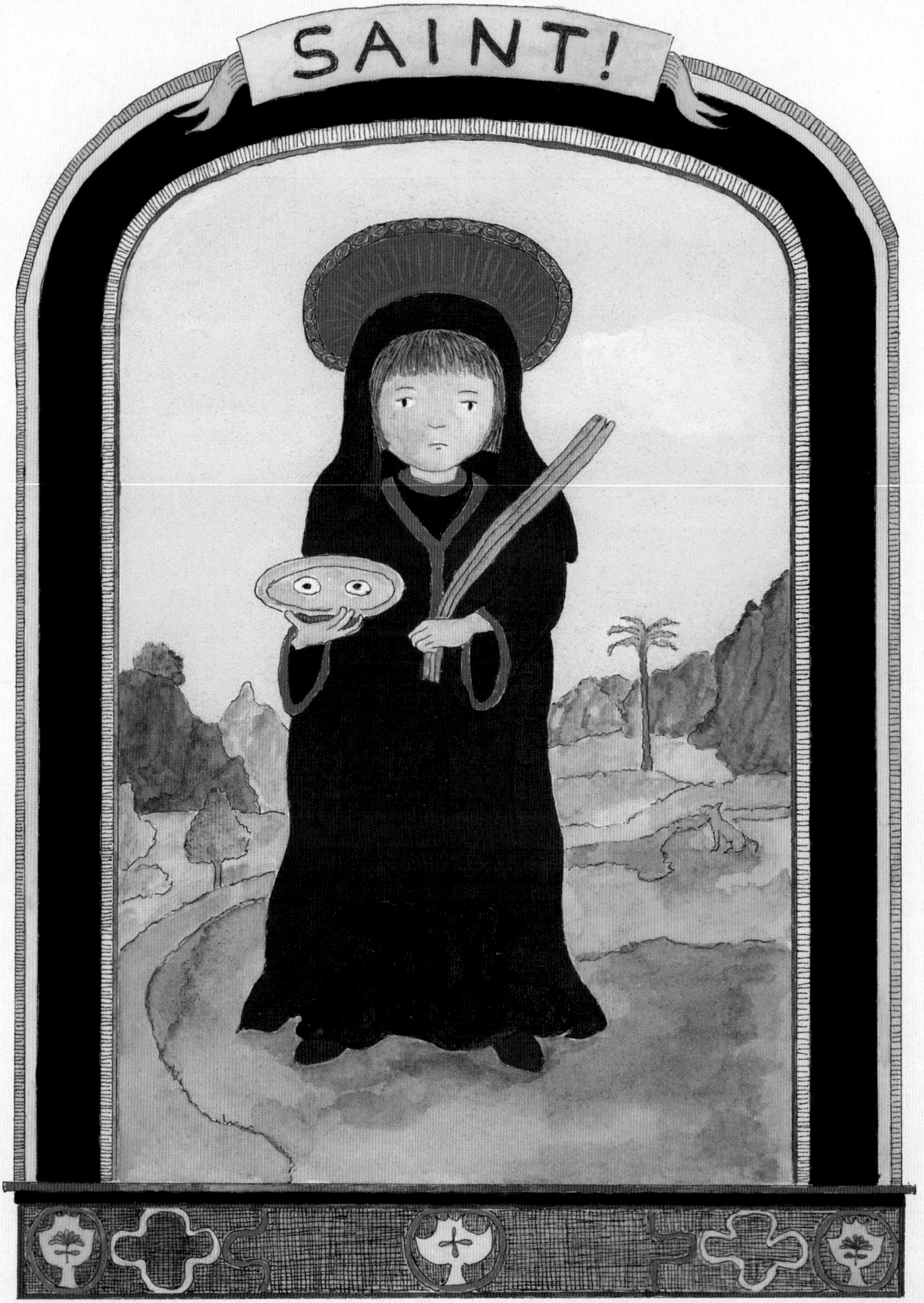
SAINT!

TWO

Language Barrier

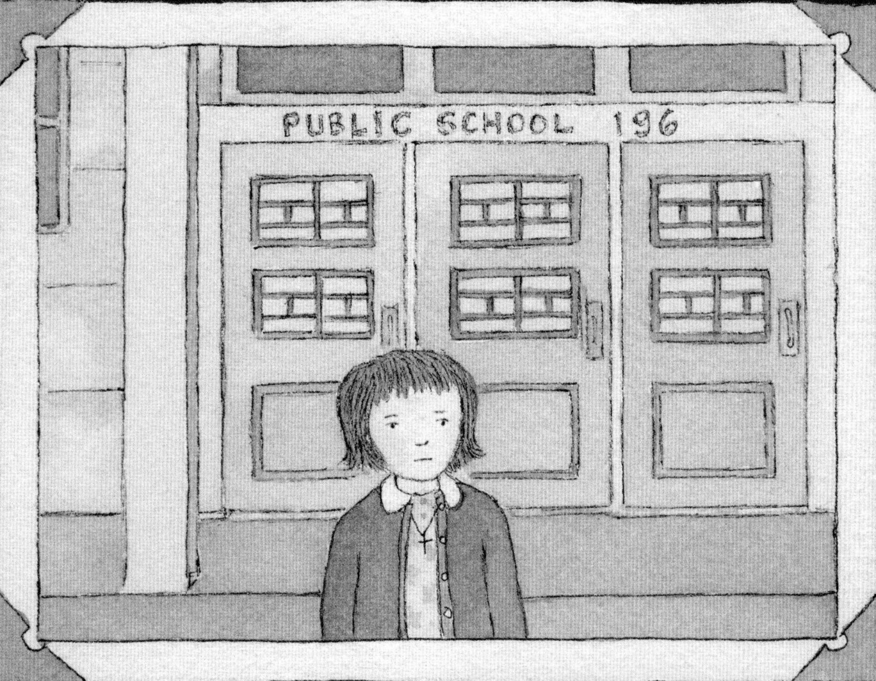
PUBLIC SCHOOL 196

1957

MY MOTHER DECIDED THAT P.S. 196 IN FOREST HILLS, A NEARBY NEIGHBORHOOD, WOULD BE THE PERFECT PLACE FOR ME TO KICK MY ADDICTION TO CATHOLICISM.

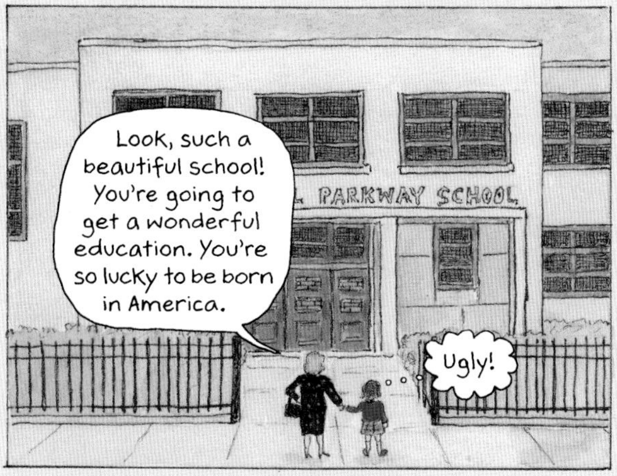
L PARKWAY SCHOOL
Look, such a beautiful school! You're going to get a wonderful education. You're so lucky to be born in America.
Ugly!

SHE ACTED AS IF MY WHOLE LIFE DEPENDED ON MY INTERVIEW WITH THE PRINCIPAL.

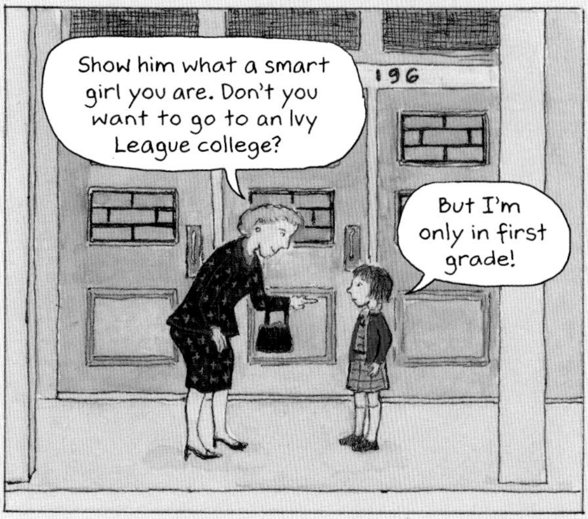
196
Show him what a smart girl you are. Don't you want to go to an Ivy League college?
But I'm only in first grade!

I HAD TO SKIP SCHOOL AND MAMMA MISSED WORK FOR THIS IMPORTANT MEETING.

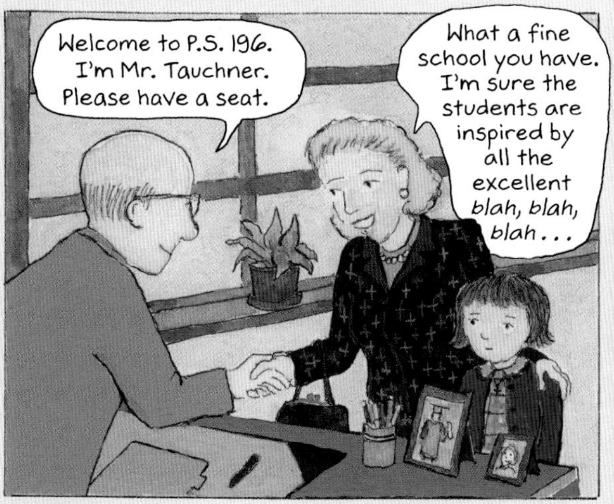
Welcome to P.S. 196. I'm Mr. Tauchner. Please have a seat.
What a fine school you have. I'm sure the students are inspired by all the excellent *blah, blah, blah* . . .

MY MOTHER KNEW HOW TO TURN ON THE CHARM.

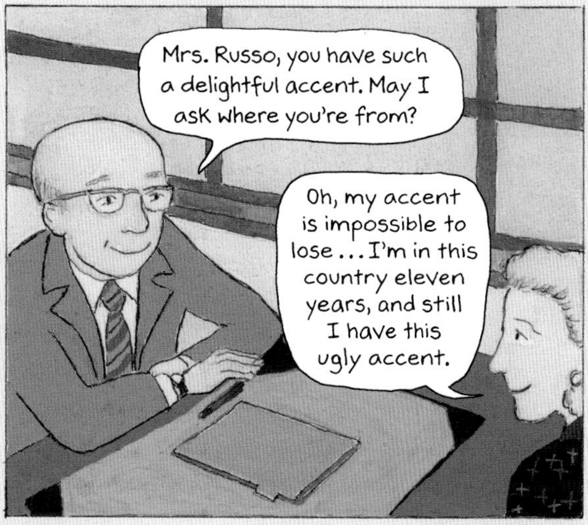
Mrs. Russo, you have such a delightful accent. May I ask where you're from?
Oh, my accent is impossible to lose . . . I'm in this country eleven years, and still I have this ugly accent.

BUT SHE WAS ALSO CAREFUL NOT TO REVEAL TOO MUCH.

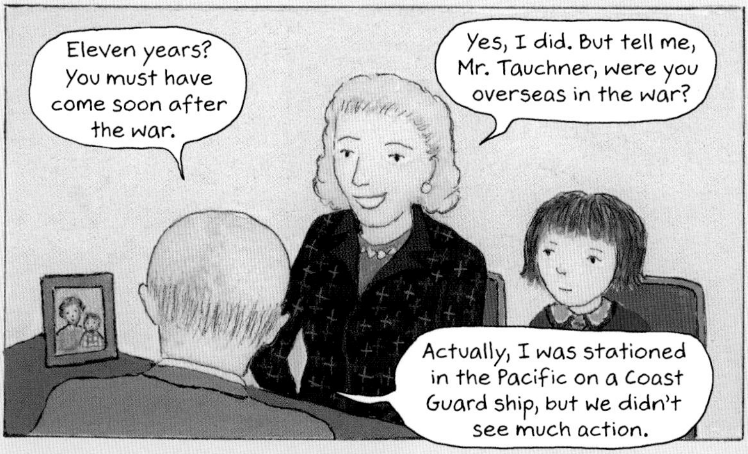
Eleven years? You must have come soon after the war.
Yes, I did. But tell me, Mr. Tauchner, were you overseas in the war?
Actually, I was stationed in the Pacific on a Coast Guard ship, but we didn't see much action.

UNFORTUNATELY, I WAS MUCH LESS ADEPT AT KEEPING FAMILY SECRETS.

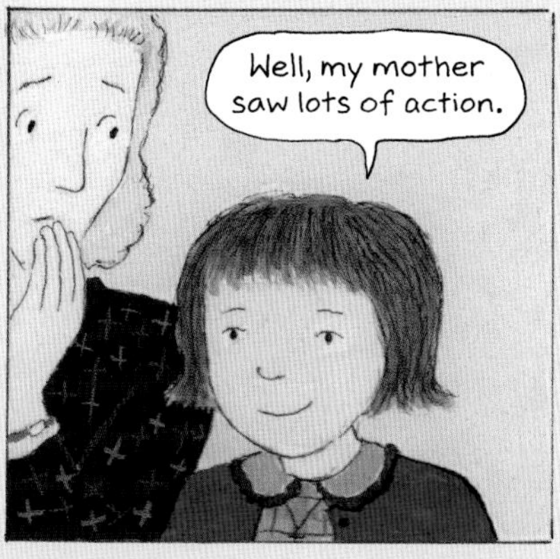
Well, my mother saw lots of action.

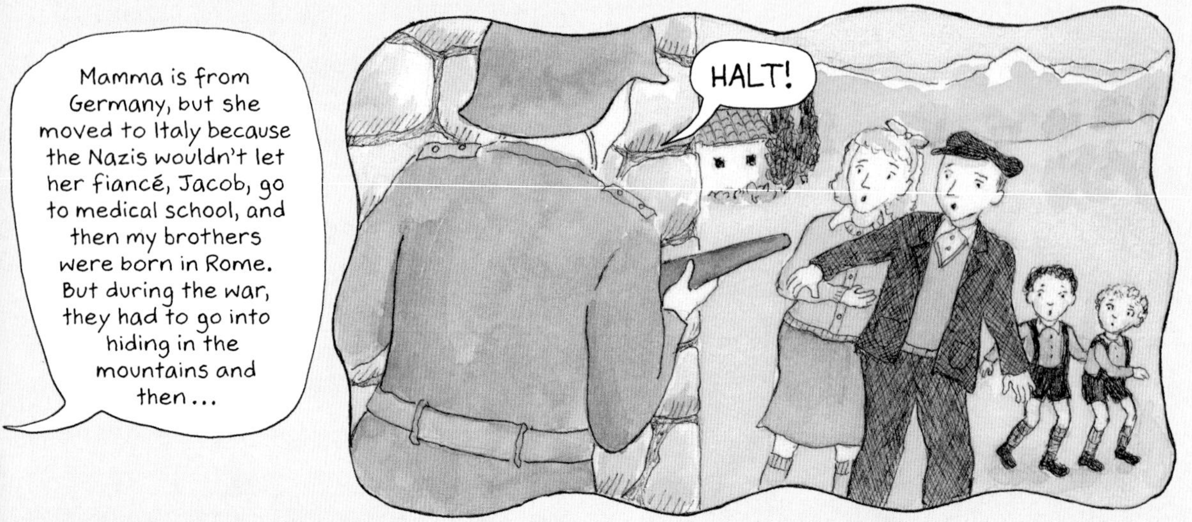
Mamma is from Germany, but she moved to Italy because the Nazis wouldn't let her fiancé, Jacob, go to medical school, and then my brothers were born in Rome. But during the war, they had to go into hiding in the mountains and then...
HALT!

I WAS VERY PROUD OF MAMMA'S WARTIME BRAVERY, AND I NEVER TIRED OF HER FAMILY STORIES. SHE ALWAYS SAID I WAS HER BEST AUDIENCE.

IN THE 1920S, MY MOTHER AND MY AUNTS WERE JEWISH GIRLS GROWING UP AMONG A LARGE EXTENDED FAMILY IN LEIPZIG, GERMANY.

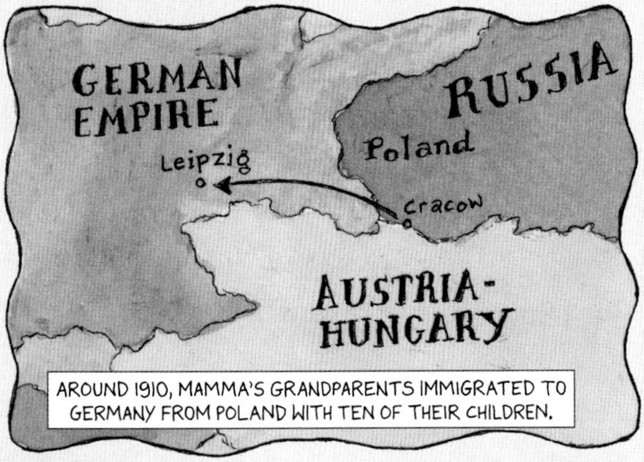
GERMAN EMPIRE
RUSSIA
Poland
Leipzig
Cracow
AUSTRIA-HUNGARY

AROUND 1910, MAMMA'S GRANDPARENTS IMMIGRATED TO GERMANY FROM POLAND WITH TEN OF THEIR CHILDREN.

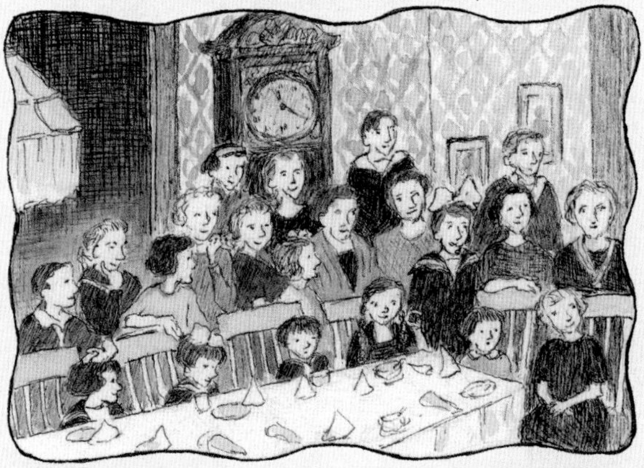

BUT IN THE 1930S, WITH THE RISE OF HITLER AND THE NAZIS, THE FAMILY WAS TORN APART.

MAMMA ELOPED TO ITALY WITH HER FIANCÉ. HE BECAME A DOCTOR. MY BROTHERS WERE BORN. UNFORTUNATELY, WHEN ITALY ENTERED WORLD WAR II ON THE GERMAN SIDE, FOREIGN JEWISH MEN LIKE JACOB WERE SENT TO INTERNMENT CAMPS OR ENFORCED RESIDENCES.

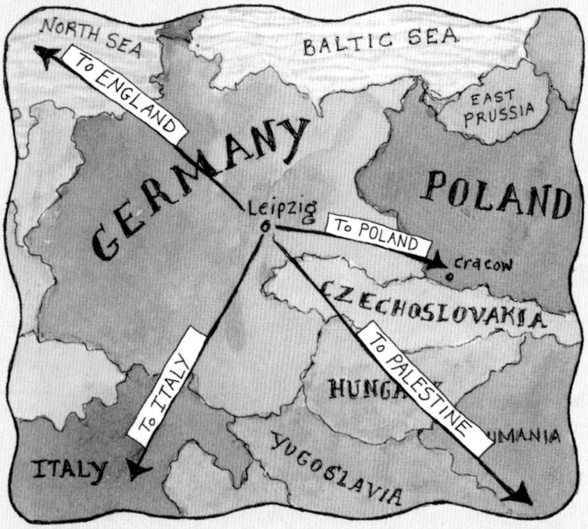
NORTH SEA
BALTIC SEA
EAST PRUSSIA
To ENGLAND
GERMANY
POLAND
Leipzig
To POLAND
Cracow
CZECHOSLOVAKIA
To ITALY
To PALESTINE
ITALY
YUGOSLAVIA

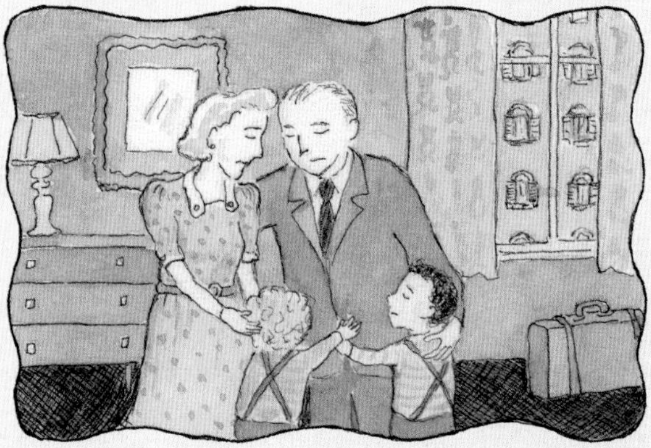

MAMMA AND MY BROTHERS WERE ALLOWED TO VISIT ON WEEKENDS, BUT THEN JACOB HEARD HE WAS ABOUT TO BE SENT TO A CONCENTRATION CAMP. HE ESCAPED INTO THE MOUNTAINS BEFORE THE NEXT DAY'S ROLL CALL.

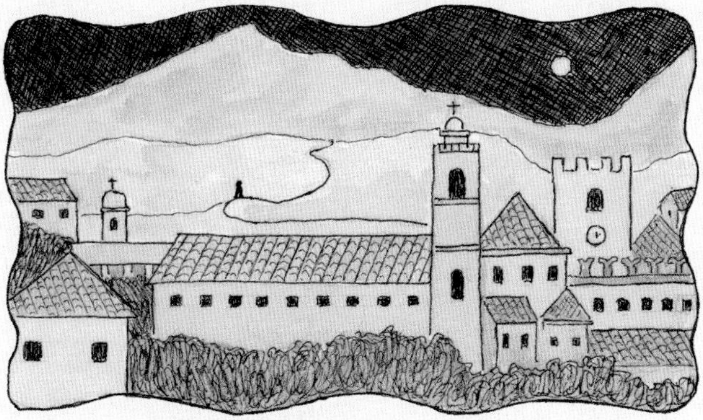

MY MOTHER SOON FOLLOWED WITH PIERO AND ROBERTO. THEY HID WITH FARMERS, SLEEPING IN BARNS AND HELPING WITH CHORES.

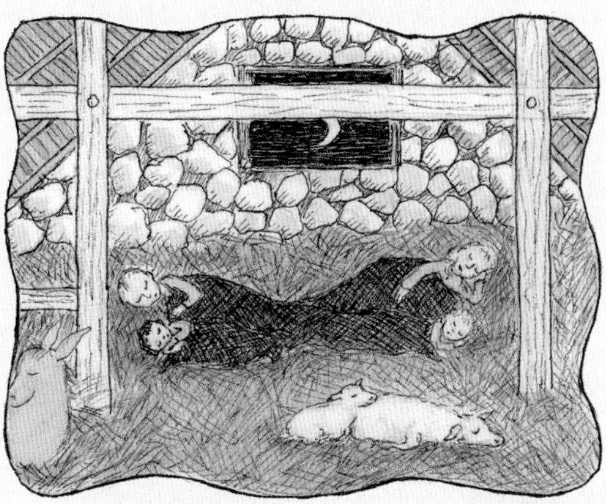

MAMMA AND JACOB JOINED THE PARTISANS, A LOCAL GROUP OF RESISTANCE FIGHTERS. MAMMA RAN THE HAM RADIO. JACOB TREATED WOUNDED BRITISH NAVY MEN WHO WERE RESCUED IN NEARBY SAN BENEDETTO DEL TRONTO.

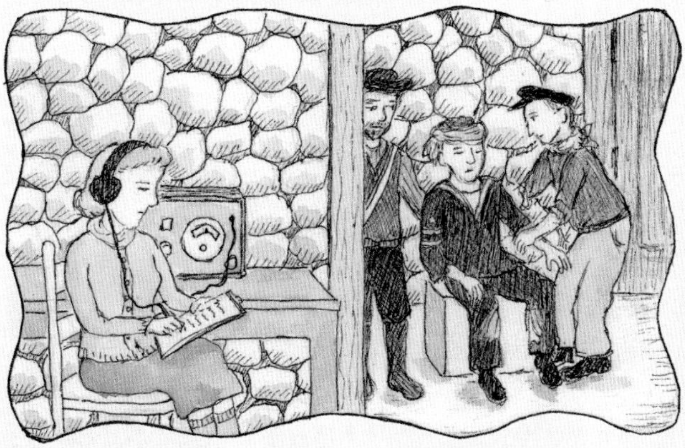

BUT THE GERMANS DISCOVERED THEIR HIDING PLACE. MAMMA WAS SHOT IN THE KNEE. JACOB WAS DRAGGED OFF. MY BROTHERS SAW THE WHOLE THING.

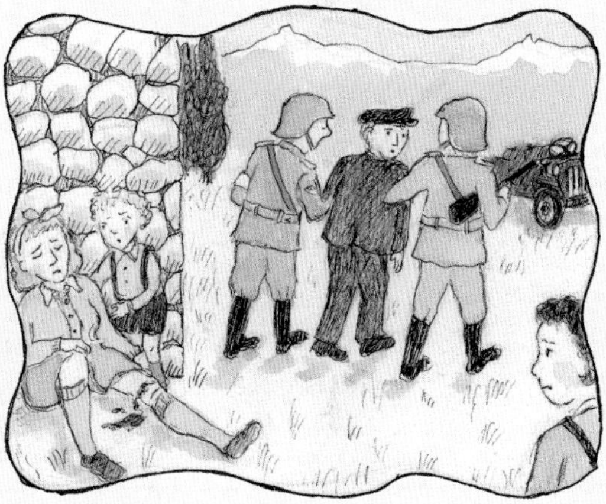

MY MOTHER WAS SENT TO A HOSPITAL RUN BY NUNS. A GERMAN SOLDIER GUARDED HER SO SHE WOULDN'T ESCAPE. MY BROTHERS STAYED IN THE HOSPITAL ORPHANAGE.

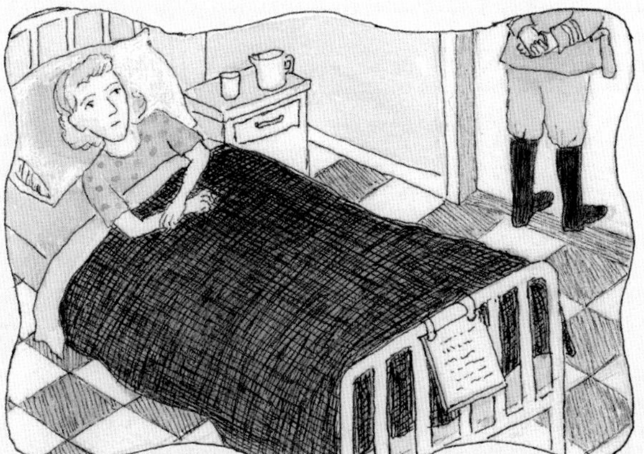

THEN CAME NEWS THAT JACOB, AFTER DAYS OF INTERROGATION AND TORTURE, HAD BEEN MURDERED BY THE NAZIS.

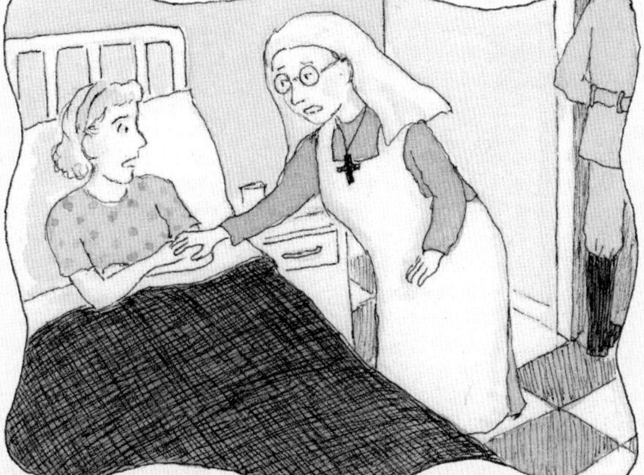

ONE NIGHT DURING A COMMOTION WITH A PATIENT DOWN THE HALL, THE NUNS CARRIED MY MOTHER TO THE HOSPITAL BASEMENT, WHERE THEY HID HER WITH MY BROTHERS UNTIL THE WAR WAS OVER.

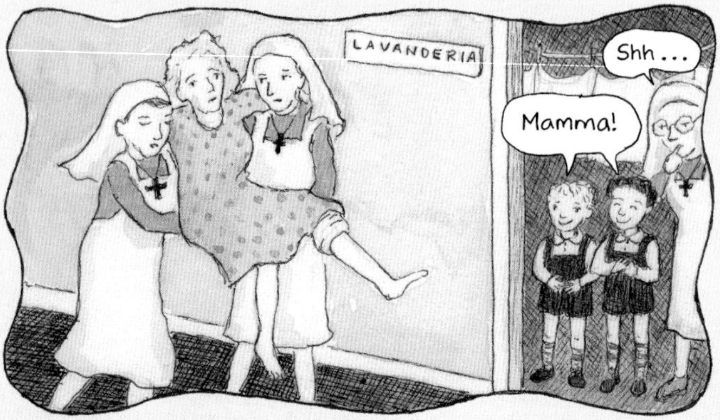
LAVANDERIA
Shh...
Mamma!

WHEN SHE WAS FINALLY ABLE TO WALK AGAIN, MY MOTHER, PIERO, AND ROBERTO GOT A RIDE BACK TO ROME IN A JEEP WITH AN AMERICAN SOLDIER.

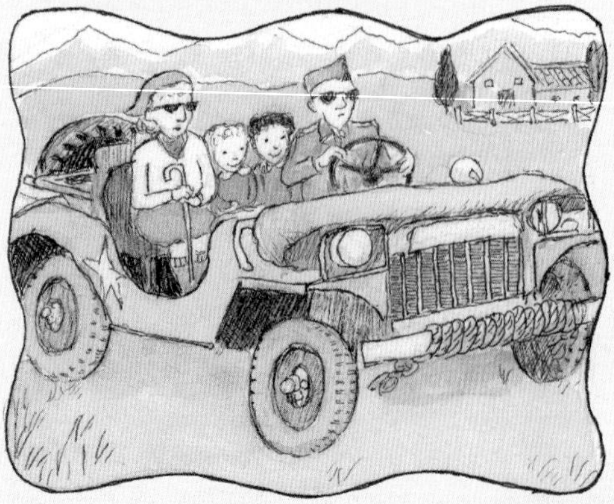

WHILE I WANTED TO TELL MY NEW PRINCIPAL ALL THESE DETAILS, I HAD ALREADY SAID MORE THAN ENOUGH AS FAR AS MAMMA WAS CONCERNED.

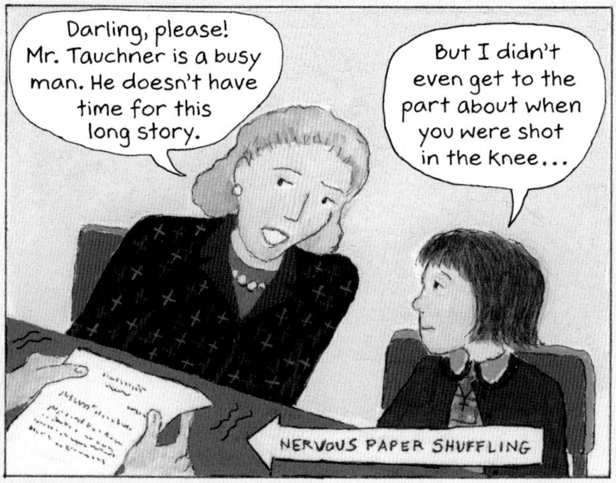
Darling, please! Mr. Tauchner is a busy man. He doesn't have time for this long story.
But I didn't even get to the part about when you were shot in the knee...
NERVOUS PAPER SHUFFLING

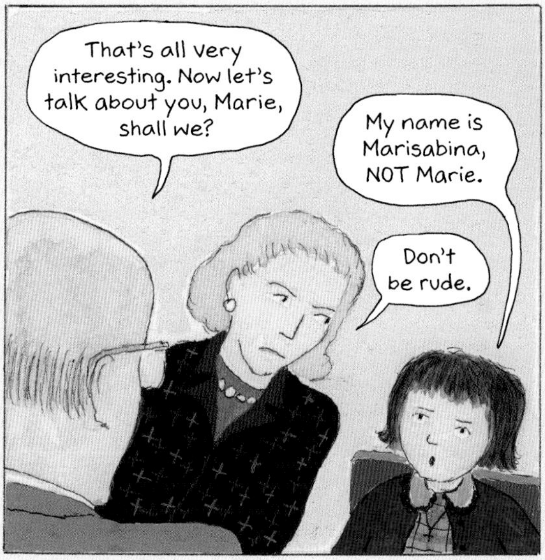
That's all very interesting. Now let's talk about you, Marie, shall we?
My name is Marisabina, NOT Marie.
Don't be rude.

EVEN THOUGH I DIDN'T WANT TO GO TO P.S. 196...

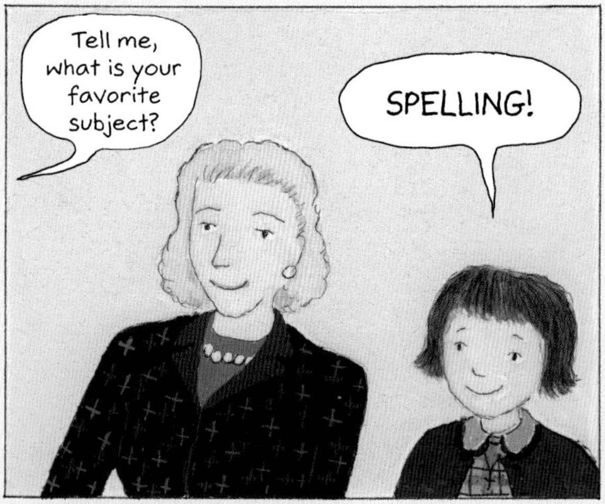
Tell me, what is your favorite subject?
SPELLING!

...I WAS DETERMINED TO MAKE MAMMA PROUD.

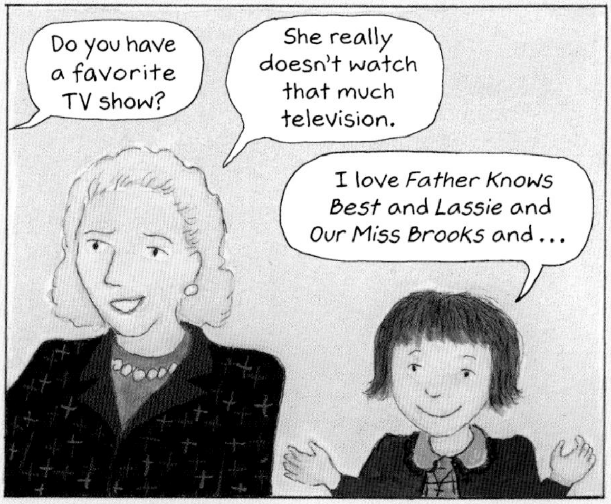
Do you have a favorite TV show?
She really doesn't watch that much television.
I love *Father Knows Best* and *Lassie* and *Our Miss Brooks* and...

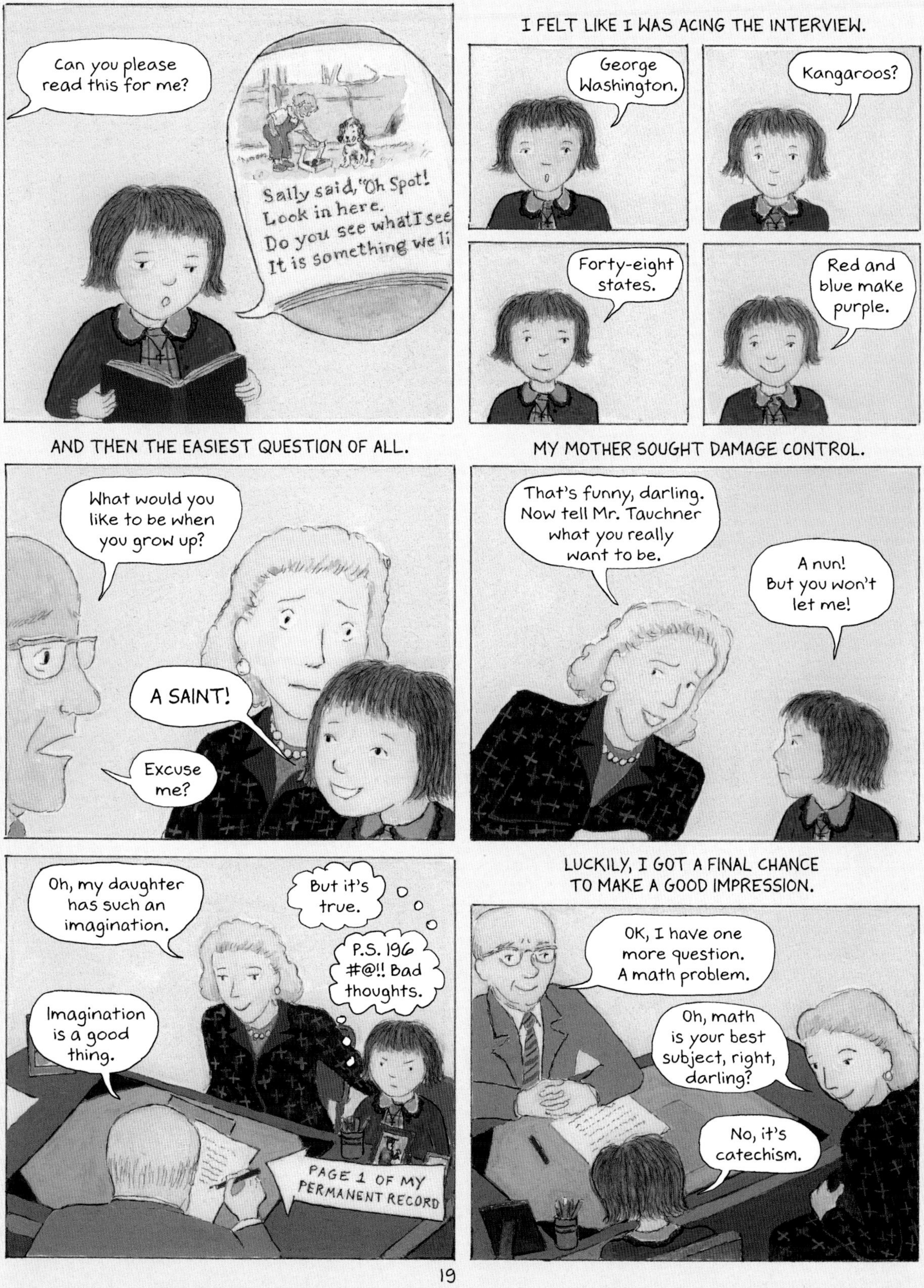
Can you please read this for me?
Sally said, "Oh Spot! Look in here. Do you see what I see? It is something we li
I FELT LIKE I WAS ACING THE INTERVIEW.
George Washington.
Kangaroos?
Forty-eight states.
Red and blue make purple.
AND THEN THE EASIEST QUESTION OF ALL.
What would you like to be when you grow up?
A SAINT!
Excuse me?
MY MOTHER SOUGHT DAMAGE CONTROL.
That's funny, darling. Now tell Mr. Tauchner what you really want to be.
A nun! But you won't let me!
Oh, my daughter has such an imagination.
But it's true.
P.S. 196 #@!! Bad thoughts.
Imagination is a good thing.
PAGE 1 OF MY PERMANENT RECORD
LUCKILY, I GOT A FINAL CHANCE TO MAKE A GOOD IMPRESSION.
OK, I have one more question. A math problem.
Oh, math is your best subject, right, darling?
No, it's catechism.

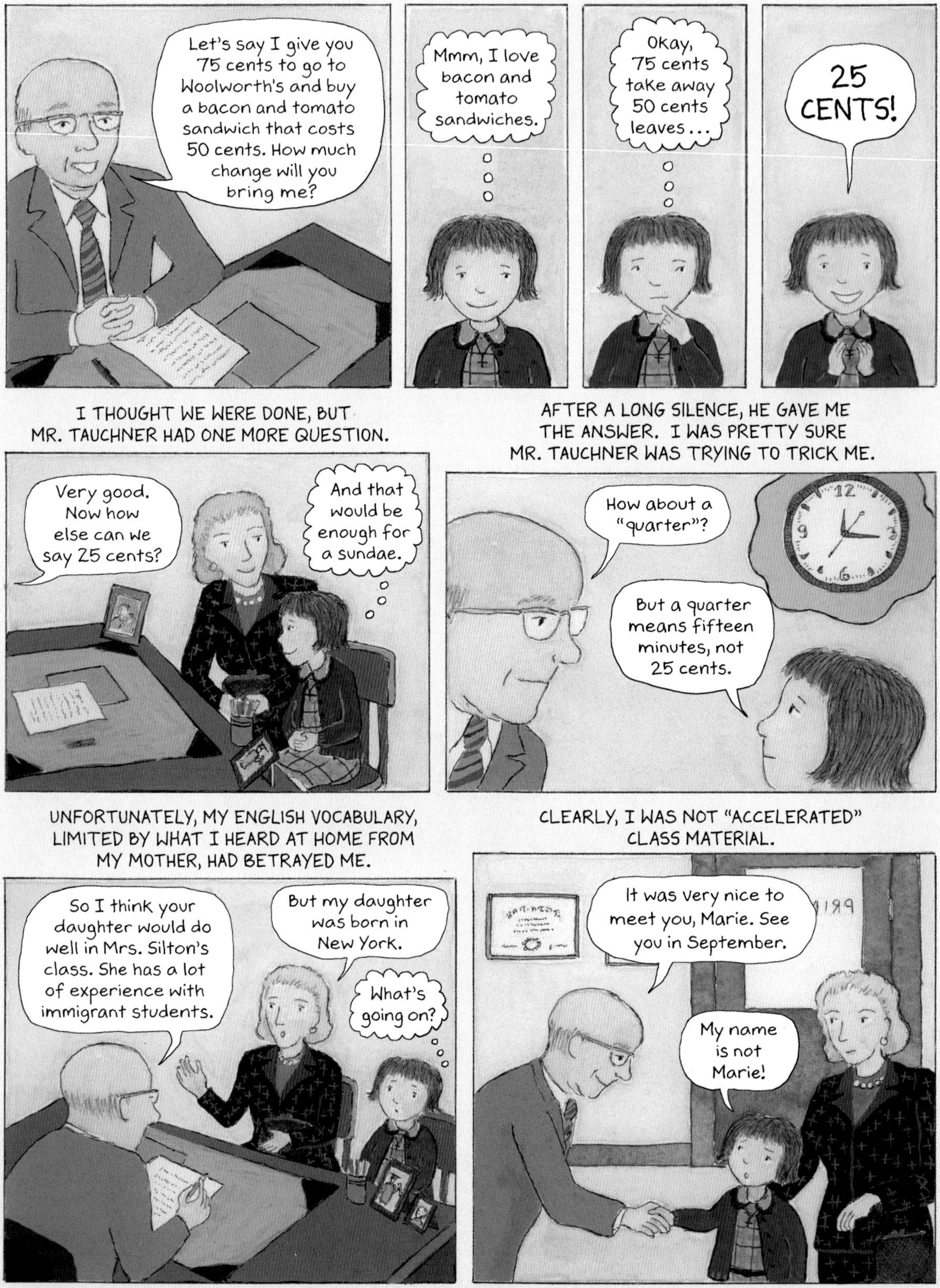

Let's say I give you 75 cents to go to Woolworth's and buy a bacon and tomato sandwich that costs 50 cents. How much change will you bring me?
Mmm, I love bacon and tomato sandwiches.
Okay, 75 cents take away 50 cents leaves . . .
25 CENTS!
I THOUGHT WE WERE DONE, BUT MR. TAUCHNER HAD ONE MORE QUESTION.
Very good. Now how else can we say 25 cents?
And that would be enough for a sundae.
AFTER A LONG SILENCE, HE GAVE ME THE ANSWER. I WAS PRETTY SURE MR. TAUCHNER WAS TRYING TO TRICK ME.
How about a "quarter"?
But a quarter means fifteen minutes, not 25 cents.
UNFORTUNATELY, MY ENGLISH VOCABULARY, LIMITED BY WHAT I HEARD AT HOME FROM MY MOTHER, HAD BETRAYED ME.
So I think your daughter would do well in Mrs. Silton's class. She has a lot of experience with immigrant students.
But my daughter was born in New York.
What's going on?
CLEARLY, I WAS NOT "ACCELERATED" CLASS MATERIAL.
It was very nice to meet you, Marie. See you in September.
My name is not Marie!

I HAD LET MY MOTHER DOWN. AS WE WALKED UP THE BLOCK, HER DISAPPOINTMENT WAS PALPABLE. I TRIED TO CHEER HER UP WITH A STORY FROM THE BIBLE.

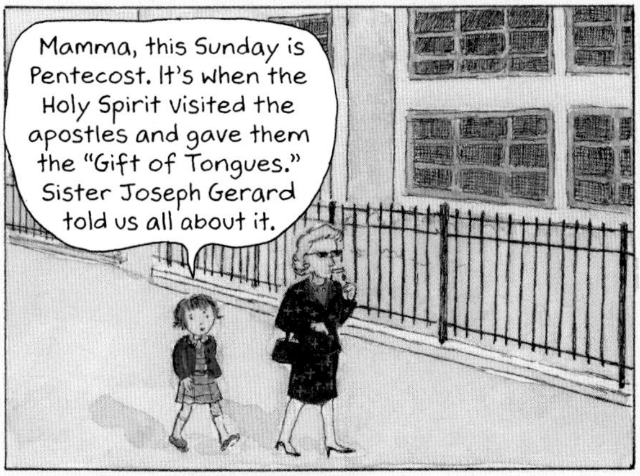
Mamma, this Sunday is Pentecost. It's when the Holy Spirit visited the apostles and gave them the "Gift of Tongues." Sister Joseph Gerard told us all about it.

BUT I COULD TELL MY MOTHER WASN'T LISTENING. SHE WAS PROBABLY THINKING ABOUT MY TWO OVERACHIEVING HALF BROTHERS.

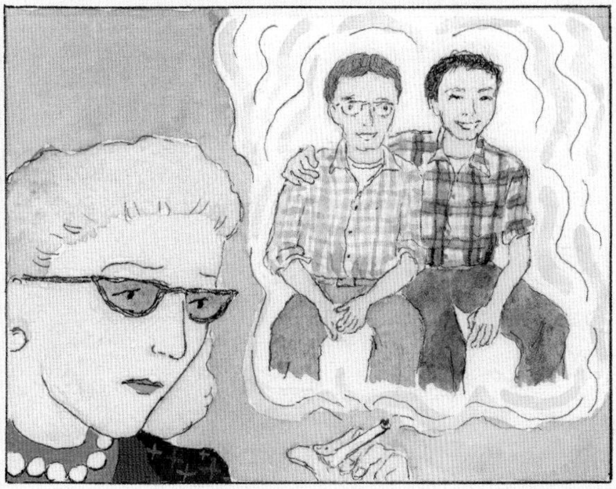

MY TWO OVERACHIEVING HALF BROTHERS WHOSE BRAVE FATHER HAD BEEN KILLED BY THE NAZIS JUST BEFORE THE WAR ENDED.

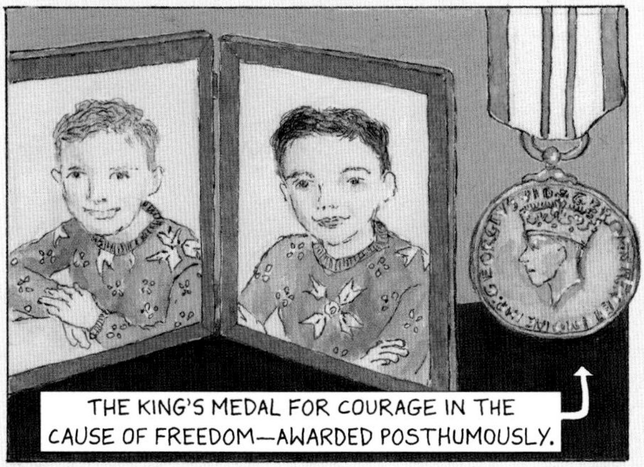
THE KING'S MEDAL FOR COURAGE IN THE CAUSE OF FREEDOM—AWARDED POSTHUMOUSLY.

MY TWO OVERACHIEVING HALF BROTHERS WHO HAD SURVIVED THE SAME TERRIBLE WAR AND IMMIGRATED TO THIS COUNTRY NOT SPEAKING A WORD OF ENGLISH YET STILL MANAGED TO WIN SCHOLARSHIPS TO A BOARDING SCHOOL AND THEN TO HARVARD AND CORNELL. AND EVEN THOUGH PIERO HAD BEEN EXPELLED FROM HARVARD, HE *HAD* GOTTEN IN, AND MY MOTHER STILL BELIEVED HE'D RETURN AND GRADUATE SOMEDAY.

THE UNSPOKEN QUESTION HUNG IN THE AIR:

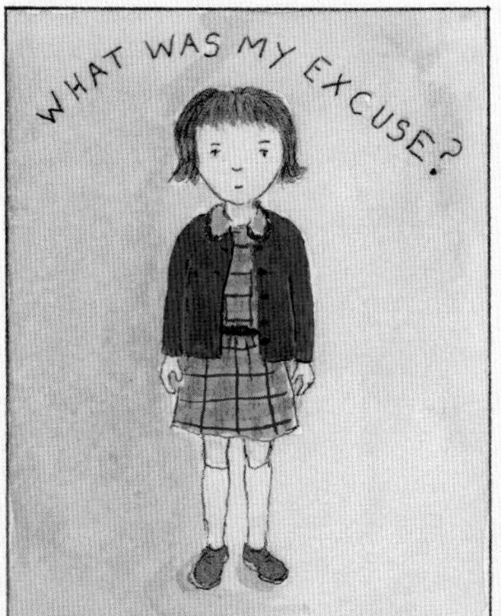
WHAT WAS MY EXCUSE?

OBVIOUSLY, JEWISH OR NOT, THE REST OF MY FAMILY WAS ALREADY WORTHY OF GOD'S GRACE. I, ON THE OTHER HAND, HAD A LONG, LONG WAY TO GO.

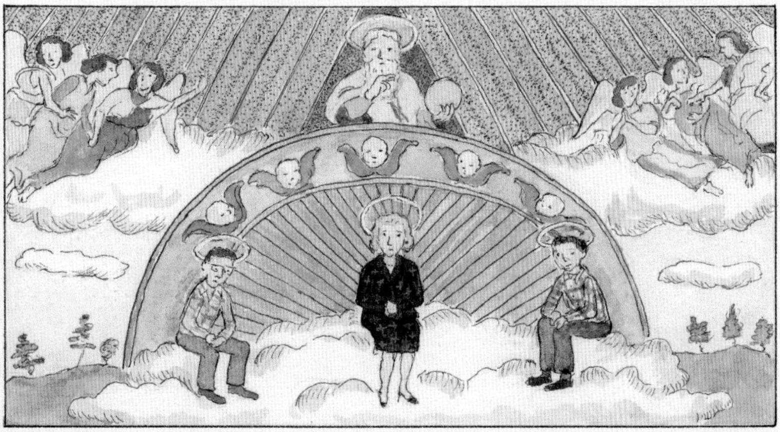

THREE

Piccolo Pucci

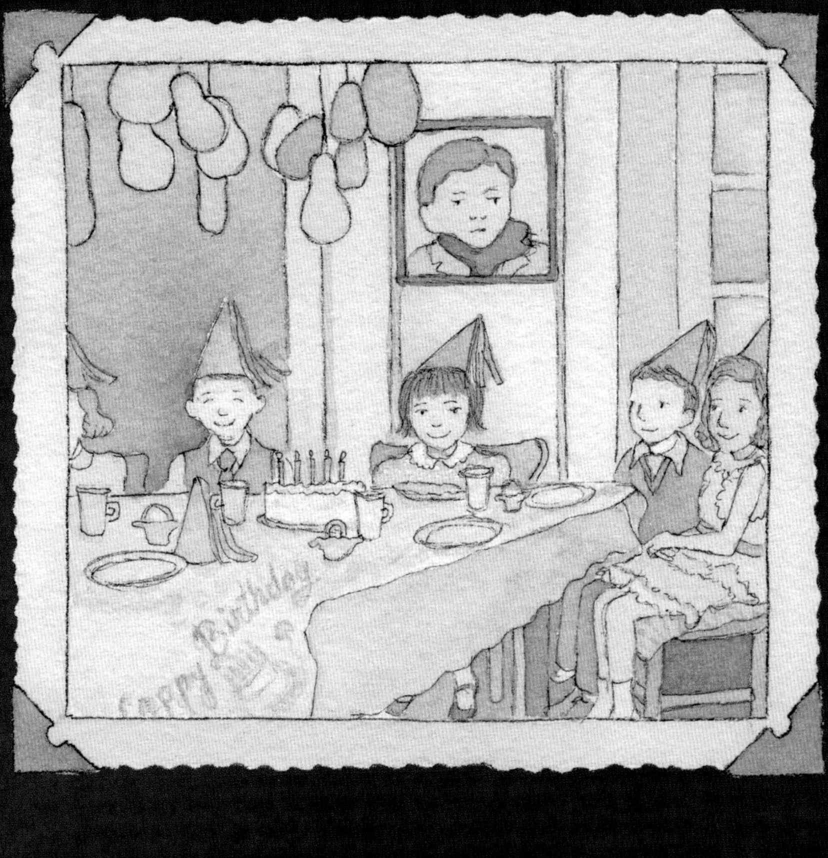
Happy Birthday

1957

MY ELDEST BROTHER, PIERO, WAS HANDSOME, BRILLIANT, AND CHARISMATIC.

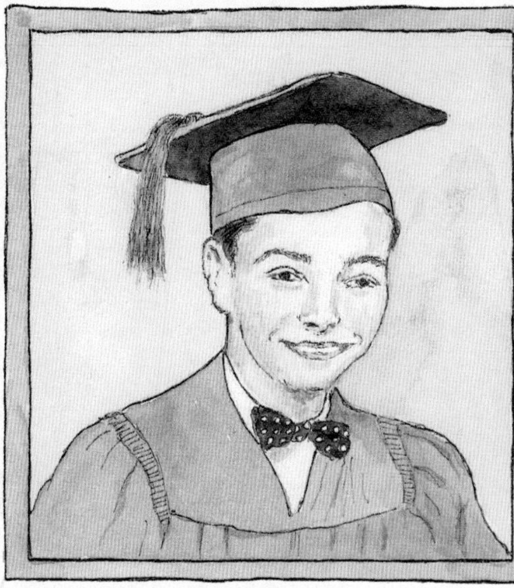

IN FACT, WHEN PIERO WAS A LITTLE BOY LIVING IN ITALY, HE HAD BEEN A MOVIE STAR. ACCORDING TO FAMILY LORE, HE HAD GONE TO A CASTING CALL WHERE THE DIRECTOR, AUGUSTO GENINA, WAS LOOKING FOR THE "TYPICAL ITALIAN BOY."

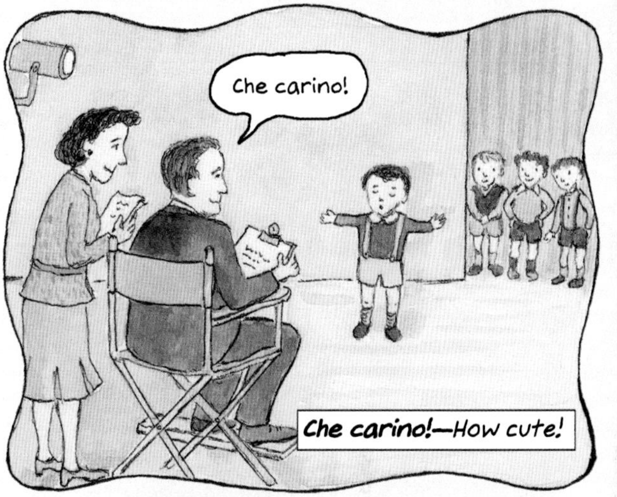
Che carino!
Che carino!—How cute!

SURPRISINGLY, PIERO WON THE PART EVEN THOUGH HIS PARENTS WERE BOTH JEWISH IMMIGRANTS. HIS SCREEN NAME WAS PICCOLO PUCCI.

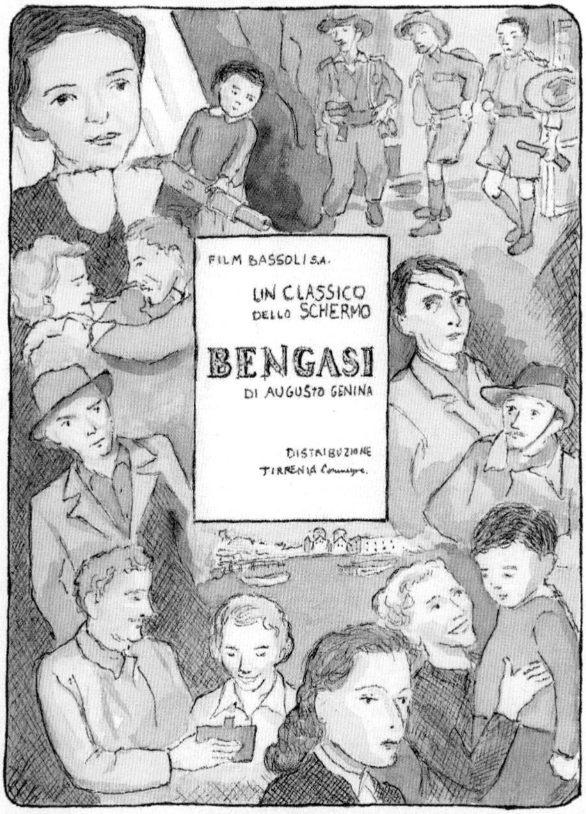
FILM BASSOLI S.A.
UN CLASSICO DELLO SCHERMO
BENGASI
DI AUGUSTO GENINA
DISTRIBUZIONE
TIRRENIA

THE FILM, *BENGASI*, WAS SHOWN AT THE TENTH VENICE FILM FESTIVAL, PRESIDED OVER BY NONE OTHER THAN IL DUCE, BENITO MUSSOLINI, THE DICTATOR WHO RULED ITALY AND WAS AN ALLY OF THE NAZI LEADER, ADOLF HITLER, RULER OF GERMANY.

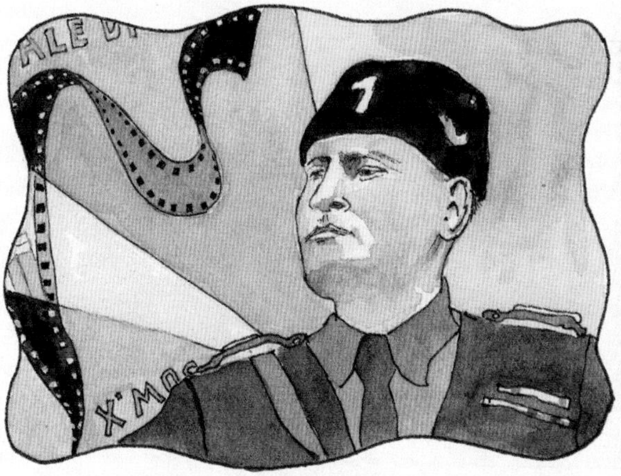

IT WON THE MUSSOLINI CUP FOR BEST ITALIAN FILM OF 1942.

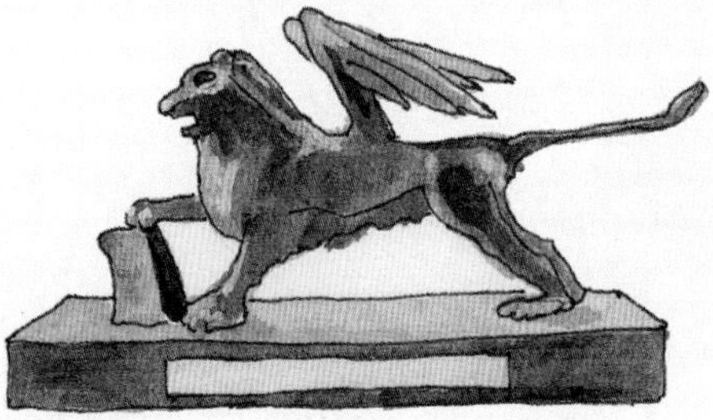

BUT AS I LATER LEARNED, THIS TURN OF EVENTS WAS NO HELP TO PIERO OR THE REST OF THE FAMILY WHEN THEY WERE FORCED INTO HIDING IN THE MOUNTAINS THE VERY NEXT YEAR.

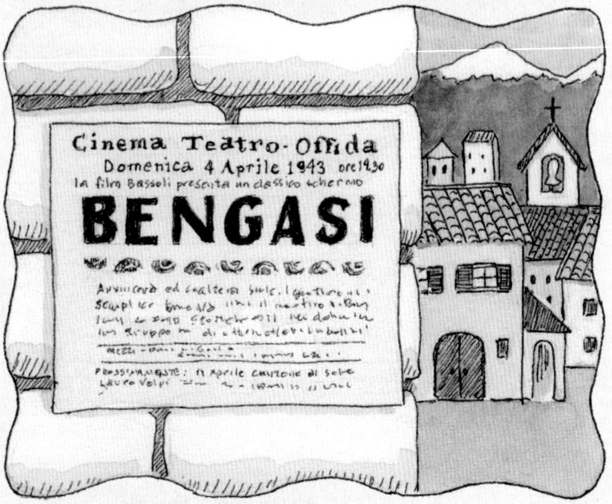
Cinema Teatro-Offida
Domenica 4 Aprile 1943
BENGASI

NOR DID IT HELP MY WIDOWED MOTHER TAKE CARE OF HER SONS WHEN THEY RETURNED TO WAR-TORN ROME, WHERE SQUATTERS WERE LIVING IN THEIR APARTMENT AND FOOD WAS IN SHORT SUPPLY.

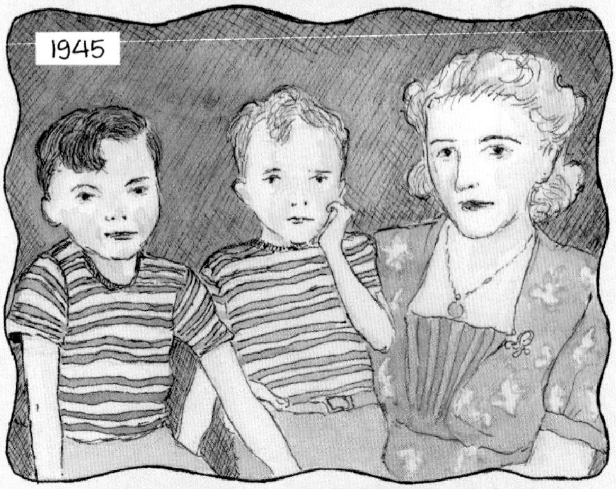
1945

A YEAR LATER, SHE MANAGED TO SECURE A JOB IN WASHINGTON, D.C., SO SHE PACKED UP PIERO AND ROBERTO AND SAILED FOR THE UNITED STATES TO REUNITE . . .

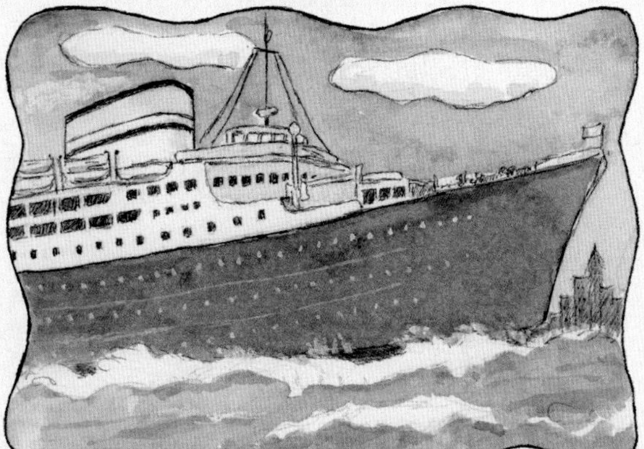

. . . FIRST WITH HER SISTER EMMY, WHO HAD ESCAPED FROM EUROPE BEFORE THE WAR . . .

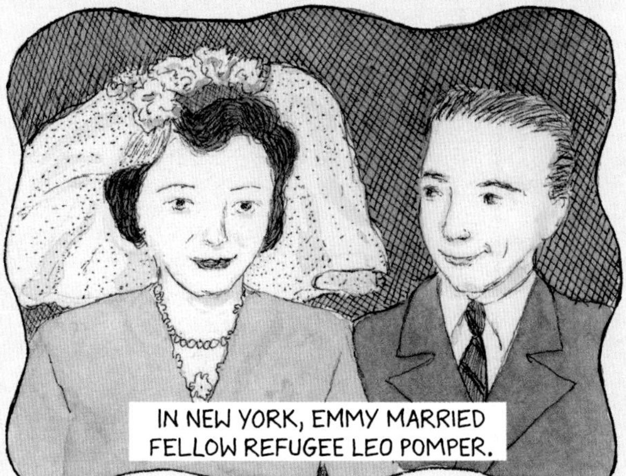
IN NEW YORK, EMMY MARRIED FELLOW REFUGEE LEO POMPER.

. . . AND LATER WITH HER OTHER SISTER, ANNY, WHO HAD SURVIVED AUSCHWITZ.

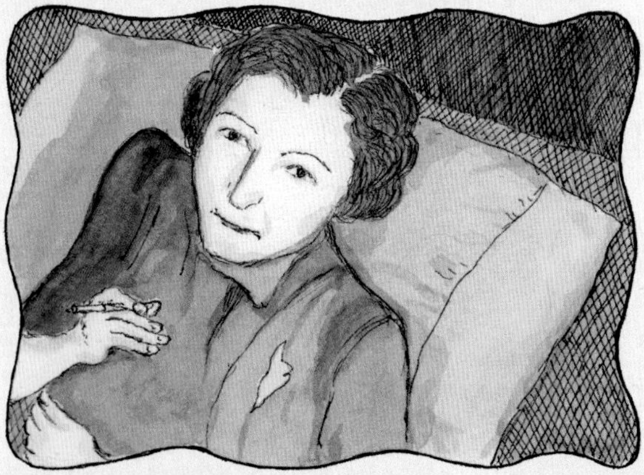

THEIR MOTHER, MY OMA, WHO HAD SURVIVED A DIFFERENT CONCENTRATION CAMP, WAS THE LAST TO OBTAIN A VISA AND LEAVE GERMANY. SHE FINALLY MADE IT TO NEW YORK IN 1948.

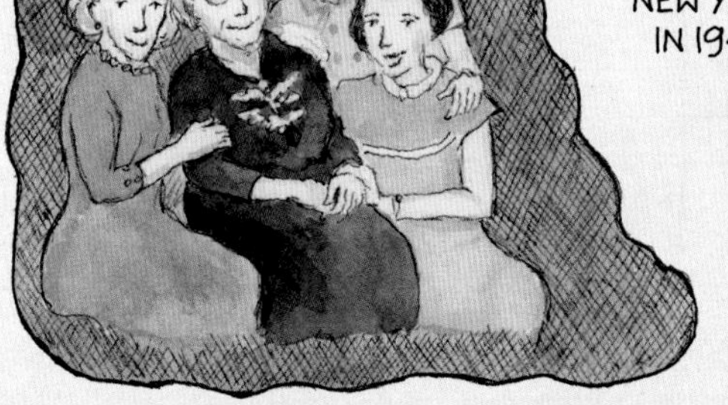

FOR AS LONG AS I COULD REMEMBER, A LARGE PORTRAIT OF PIERO DOMINATED ONE WALL OF OUR APARTMENT IN KEW GARDENS.

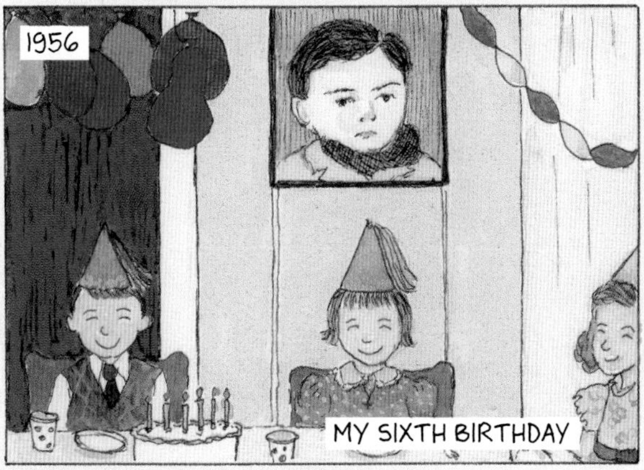
1956
MY SIXTH BIRTHDAY

IT WAS A CONSTANT REMINDER OF HIS STAR POWER.

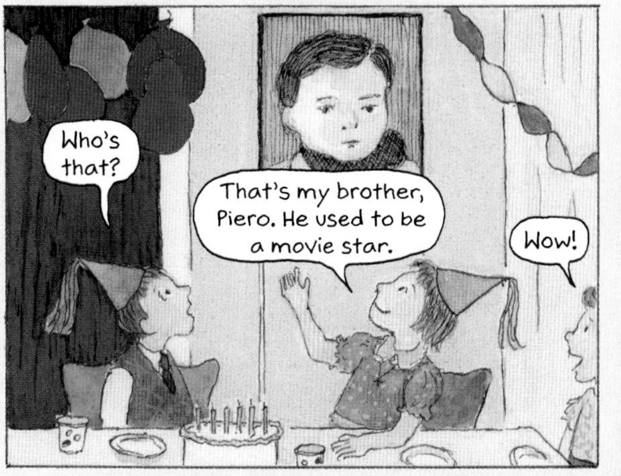
Who's that?
That's my brother, Piero. He used to be a movie star.
Wow!

AND IF I NEEDED MORE EVIDENCE, ALL I HAD TO DO WAS FLIP THROUGH AN OLD PHOTO ALBUM.

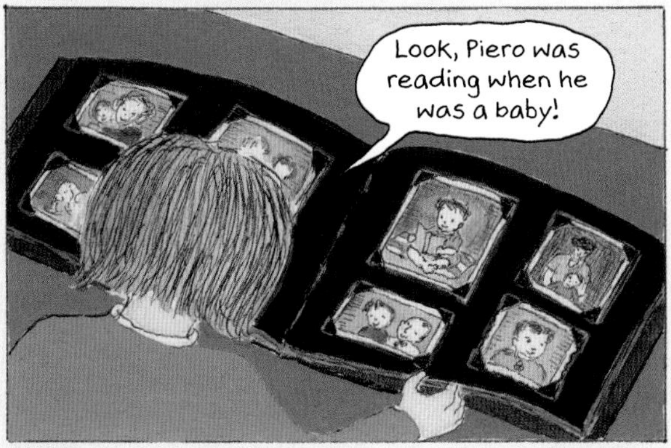
Look, Piero was reading when he was a baby!

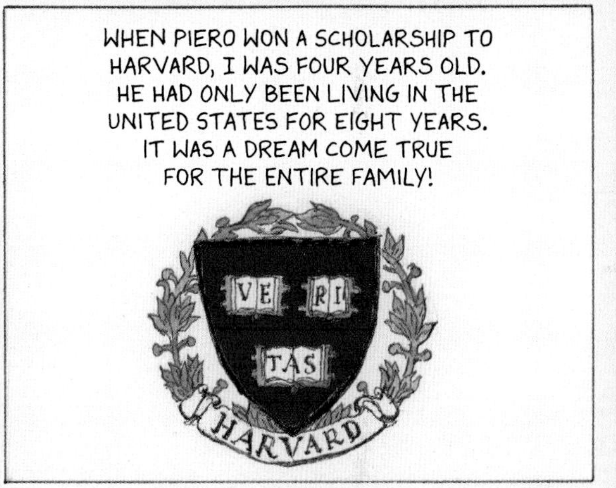
WHEN PIERO WON A SCHOLARSHIP TO HARVARD, I WAS FOUR YEARS OLD. HE HAD ONLY BEEN LIVING IN THE UNITED STATES FOR EIGHT YEARS. IT WAS A DREAM COME TRUE FOR THE ENTIRE FAMILY!
VE RI TAS
HARVARD

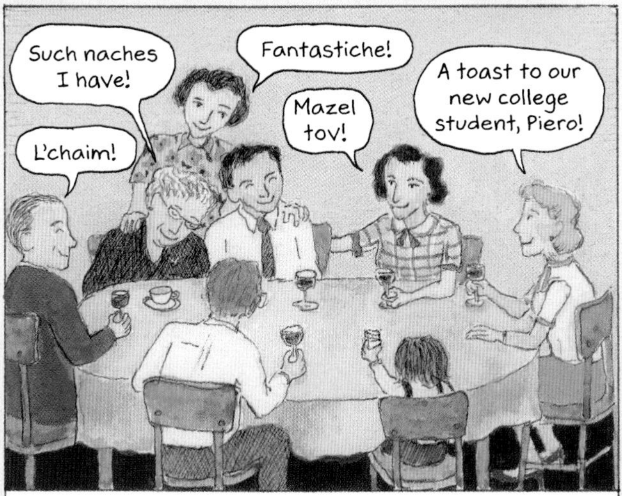
Such naches I have!
Fantastiche!
A toast to our new college student, Piero!
Mazel tov!
L'chaim!

naches—*joyful pride* ***L'chaim!***—*To life!*
Fantastiche!—*Fantastic!* ***Mazel tov!***—*Congratulations!*

WELL, ALMOST.

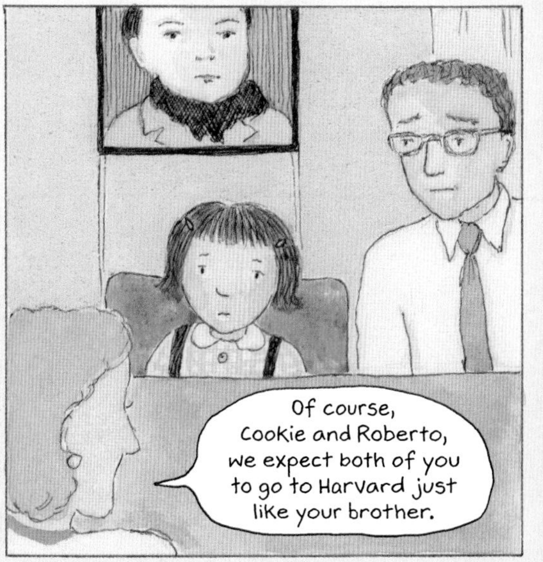
Of course, Cookie and Roberto, we expect both of you to go to Harvard just like your brother.

AT FIRST, PIERO SEEMED TO ADAPT EASILY TO COLLEGE LIFE.

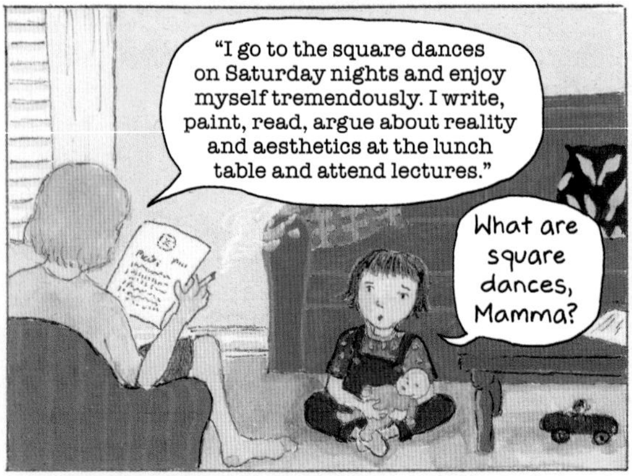
"I go to the square dances on Saturday nights and enjoy myself tremendously. I write, paint, read, argue about reality and aesthetics at the lunch table and attend lectures."
What are square dances, Mamma?

BUT THEN HE STOPPED WEARING A TIE TO CLASS AND GREW A THICK BLACK BEARD. AT HARVARD IN 1955, THIS WAS SHOCKING BEHAVIOR.

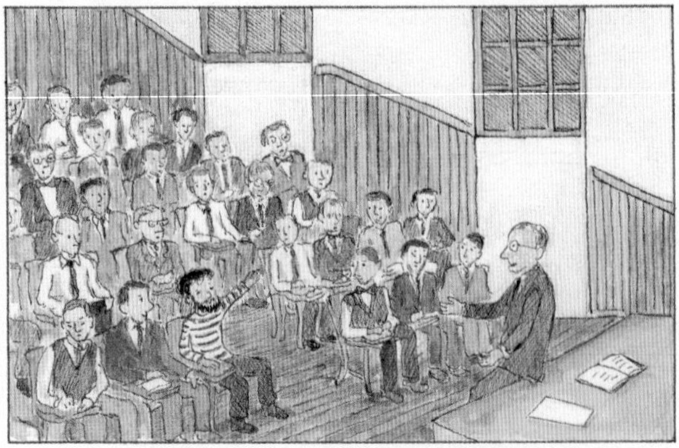

DURING HIS SOPHOMORE YEAR, PIERO TOOK A PRICELESS BUST FROM HARVARD'S FOGG MUSEUM AND SET IT ON THE FIREPLACE MANTEL IN HIS DORM ROOM.

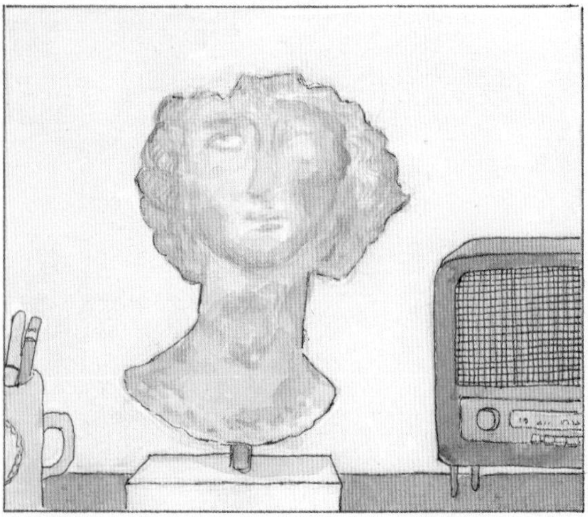

HE DIDN'T SEE ANYTHING WRONG WITH BORROWING THE BUST, BUT HARVARD DID, AND HE WAS ASKED TO LEAVE.

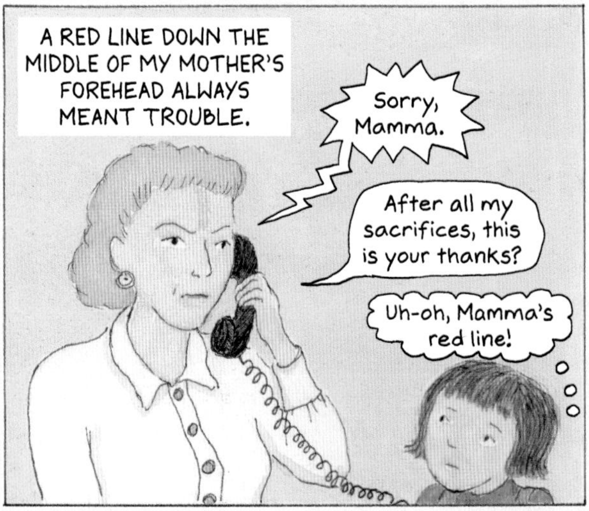
A RED LINE DOWN THE MIDDLE OF MY MOTHER'S FOREHEAD ALWAYS MEANT TROUBLE.
Sorry, Mamma.
After all my sacrifices, this is your thanks?
Uh-oh, Mamma's red line!

STILL, MY MOTHER NEVER GAVE UP HOPE THAT PIERO WOULD STRAIGHTEN HIMSELF OUT.

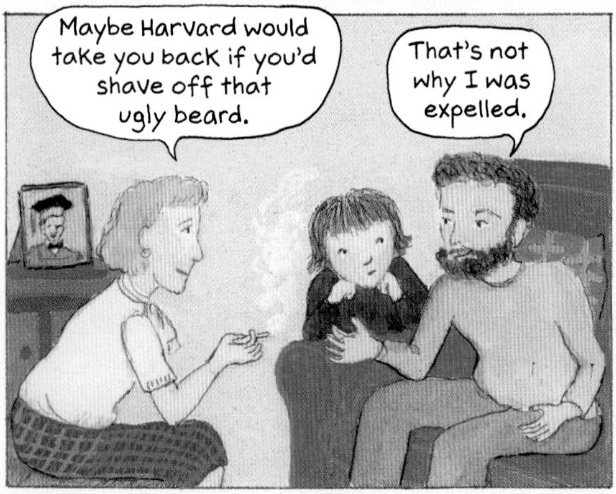
Maybe Harvard would take you back if you'd shave off that ugly beard.
That's not why I was expelled.

EVEN WHEN HE UNEXPECTEDLY BOARDED A SHIP BOUND FOR ITALY...

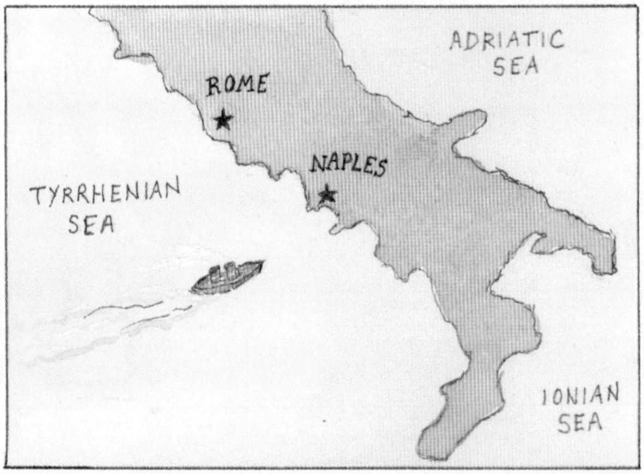
ADRIATIC SEA
ROME
NAPLES
TYRRHENIAN SEA
IONIAN SEA

...AND LATER JUMPED INTO THE BAY OF NAPLES AS THE SHIP APPROACHED THE HARBOR (SOMETHING SHE ONLY DISCOVERED ONE MORNING WHILE RIDING THE TRAIN TO WORK).

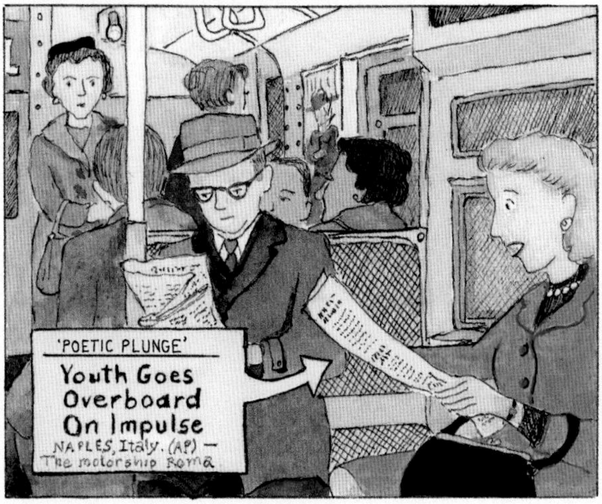
'POETIC PLUNGE'
Youth Goes Overboard On Impulse
NAPLES, Italy. (AP) — The motorship Roma

A FEW MONTHS LATER, PIERO MOVED BACK TO CAMBRIDGE, NOT TO STUDY, BUT TO MODEL FOR ART CLASSES AND WORK ON HIS NOVEL.

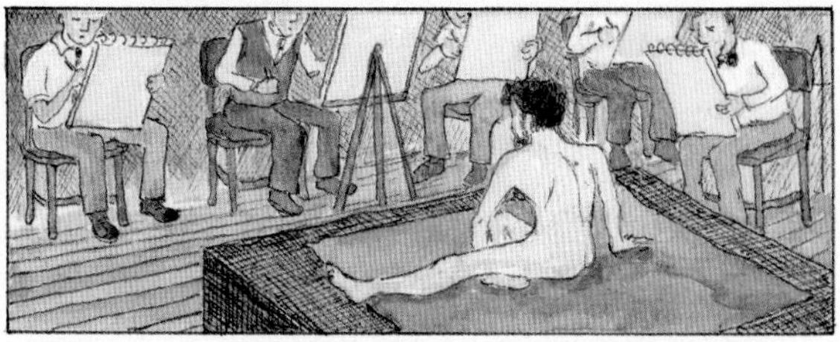

AND SOON AFTER THAT, HE TOOK OFF FOR MEXICO WITH HIS HIGH SCHOOL FRIEND ANGUS.

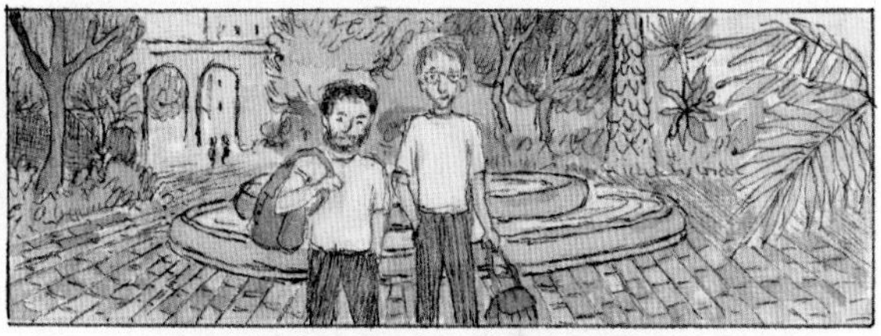

MY MOTHER'S FAITH IN PIERO SEEMED JUSTIFIED WHEN AT LAST HE RETURNED TO NEW YORK. BUT THEN SOMETHING HAPPENED THAT UPSET HER SO MUCH SHE DECIDED TO CALL THE POLICE, AND PIERO WAS TAKEN TO THE KINGS COUNTY MENTAL HOSPITAL. HE WAS LATER MOVED TO ANOTHER HOSPITAL, THIS TIME IN WESTCHESTER. NO ONE EVER TOLD ME WHAT HAPPENED.

WE VISITED HIM ON SUNDAYS AFTER CHURCH. TANTE ANNY AND HER BOYFRIEND, WOLFGANG, PICKED US UP FOR THE RIDE NORTH TO THE HOSPITAL.

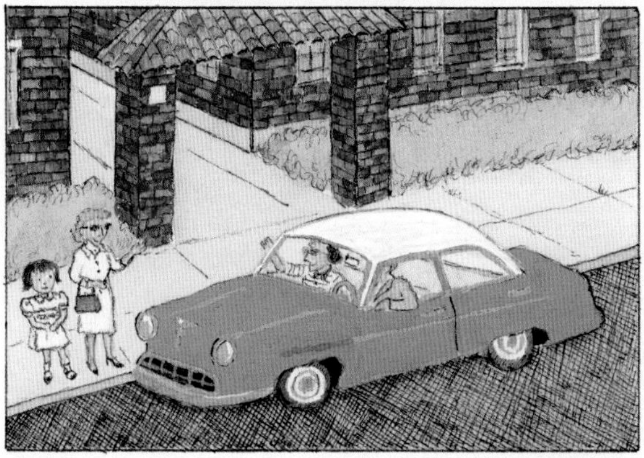

WE HEADED ACROSS THE WHITESTONE BRIDGE AND UP THE HUTCHINSON RIVER PARKWAY.

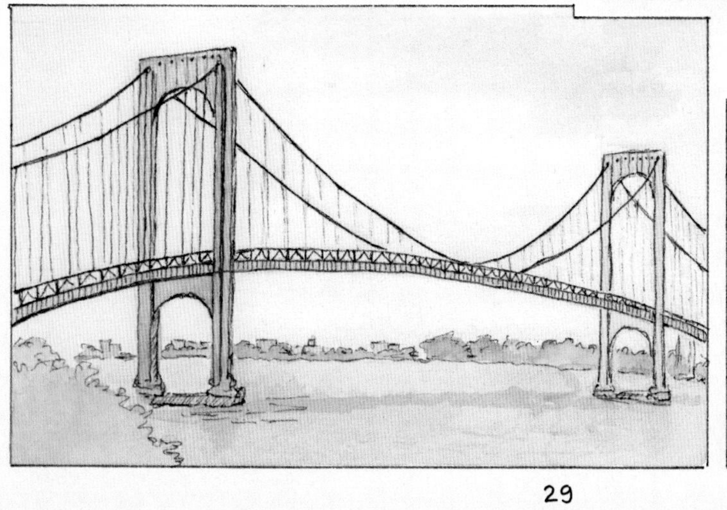

WOLFGANG GAVE ME THE CREEPS, BUT HE WAS THE ONLY PERSON WE KNEW WHO OWNED A CAR.

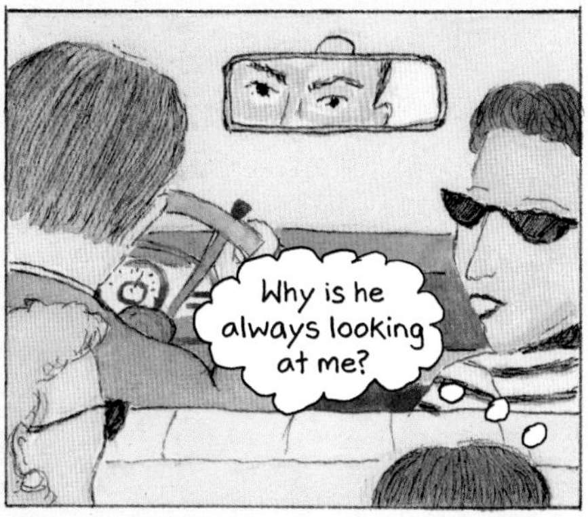
Why is he always looking at me?

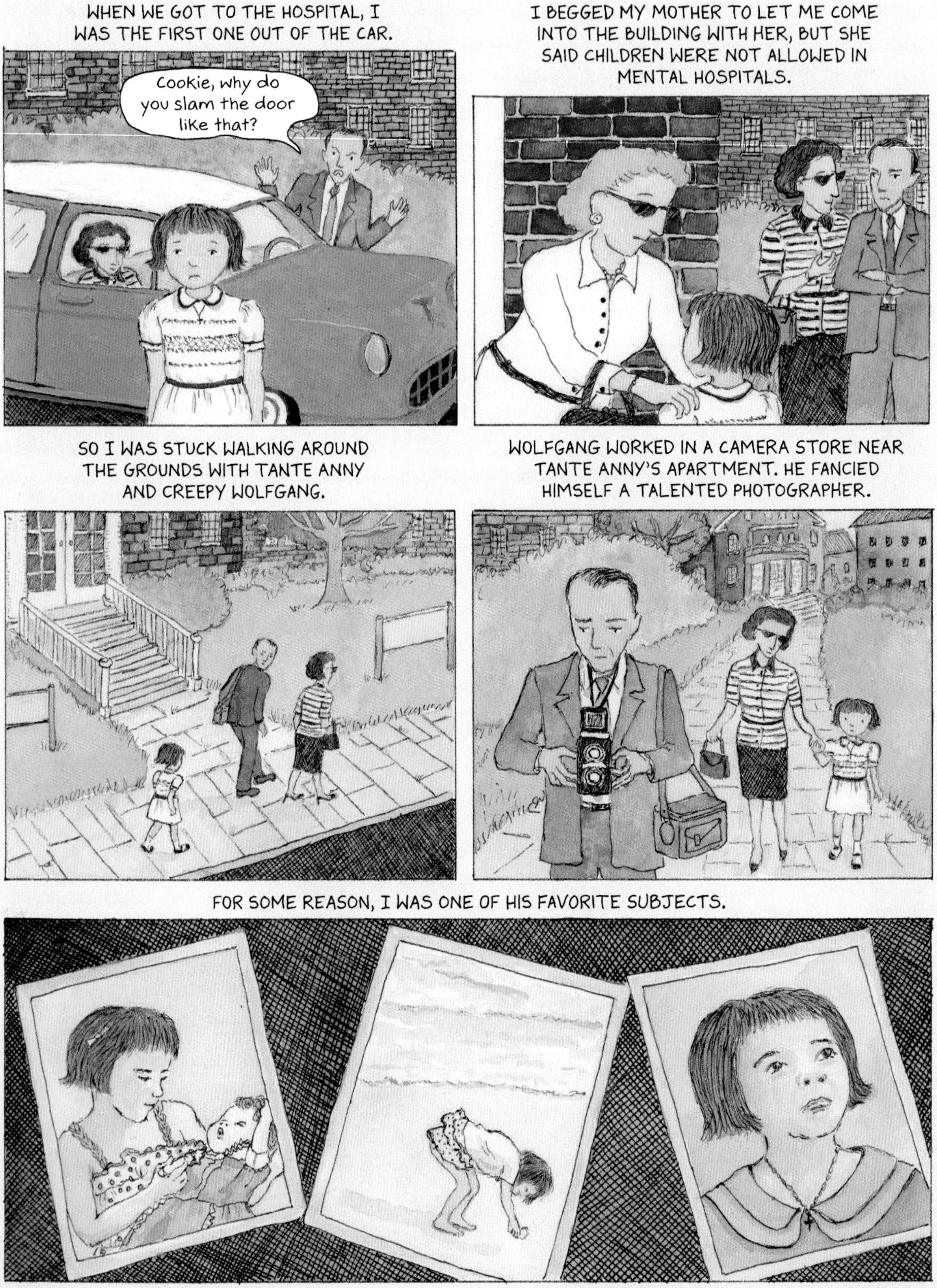
WHEN WE GOT TO THE HOSPITAL, I WAS THE FIRST ONE OUT OF THE CAR.
Cookie, why do you slam the door like that?
I BEGGED MY MOTHER TO LET ME COME INTO THE BUILDING WITH HER, BUT SHE SAID CHILDREN WERE NOT ALLOWED IN MENTAL HOSPITALS.
SO I WAS STUCK WALKING AROUND THE GROUNDS WITH TANTE ANNY AND CREEPY WOLFGANG.
WOLFGANG WORKED IN A CAMERA STORE NEAR TANTE ANNY'S APARTMENT. HE FANCIED HIMSELF A TALENTED PHOTOGRAPHER.
FOR SOME REASON, I WAS ONE OF HIS FAVORITE SUBJECTS.

AS I TRUDGED ALONG THE BRICK PATHS, I TRIED NOT TO HAVE BAD THOUGHTS. AFTER ALL, I'D ONLY RECEIVED COMMUNION A FEW HOURS AGO.

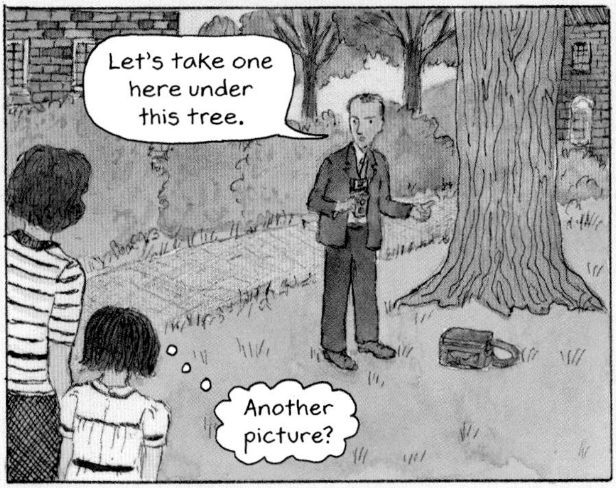
Let's take one here under this tree.
Another picture?

I COULDN'T UNDERSTAND WHAT TANTE ANNY SAW IN WOLFGANG, BUT SHE SEEMED TO ENJOY BEING HIS STYLIST.

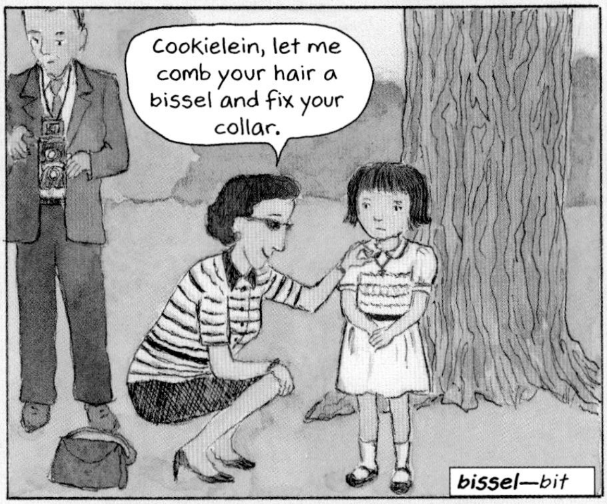
Cookielein, let me comb your hair a bissel and fix your collar.
bissel—*bit*

TANTE ANNY HAD A LINE OF BLUE NUMBERS AND A TRIANGLE TATTOOED ON HER LEFT ARM. MY MOTHER WARNED ME NOT TO ASK HER ABOUT THEM. SHE SAID IT HAD TO DO WITH SOMETHING TERRIBLE THAT HAD HAPPENED TO MY AUNT DURING THE WAR AT A PLACE CALLED AUSCHWITZ.

BUT SOMETIMES I FOUND IT HARD NOT TO STARE AT THEM.

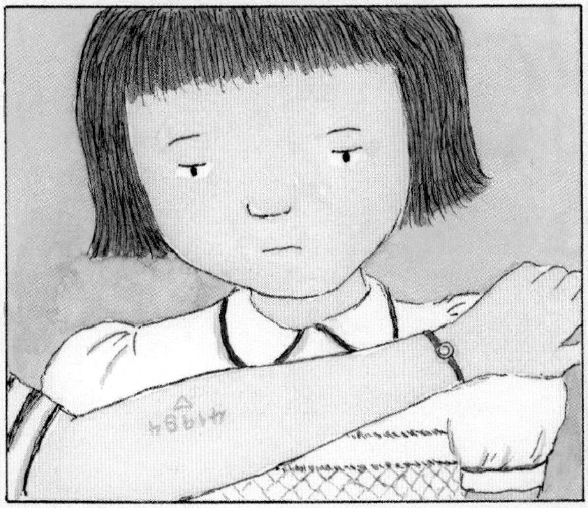

WHEN MY MOTHER FINALLY REAPPEARED, I RUSHED TO HUG HER.

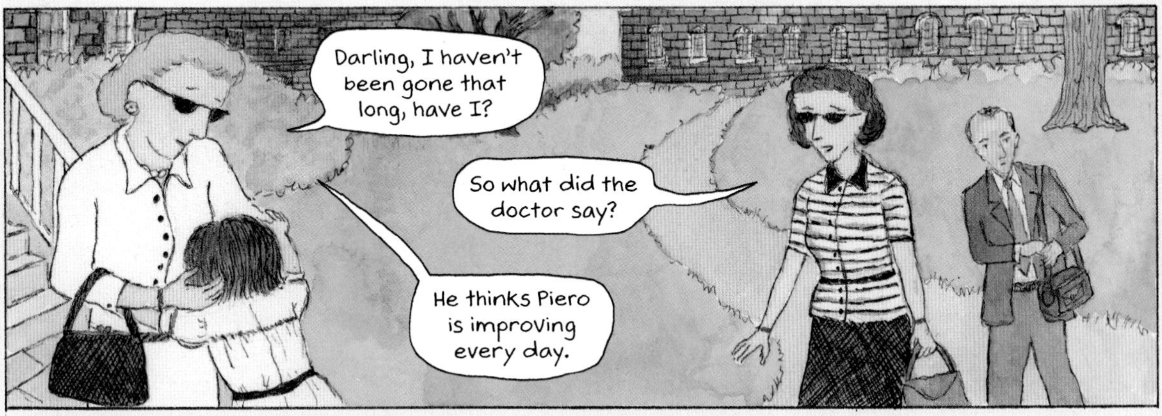
Darling, I haven't been gone that long, have I?
So what did the doctor say?
He thinks Piero is improving every day.

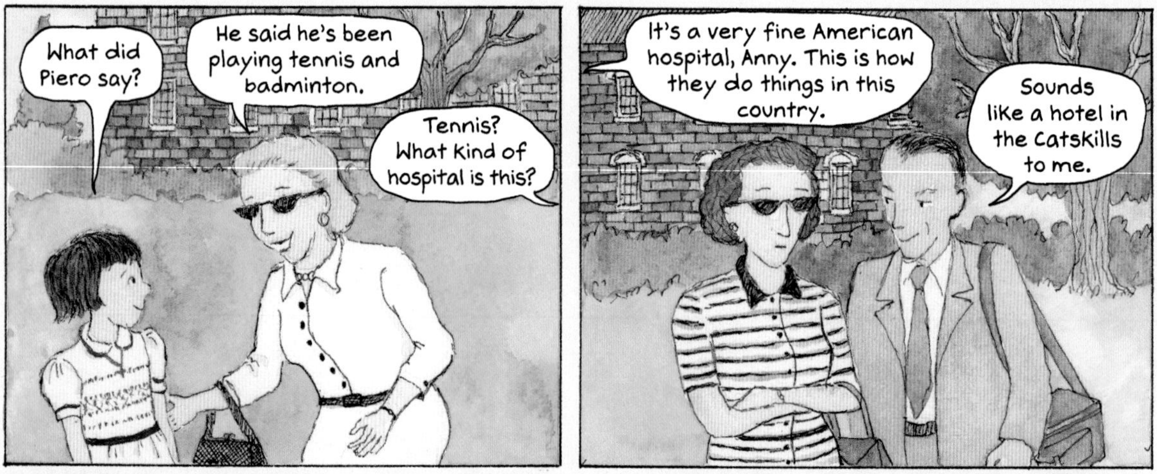
What did Piero say?
He said he's been playing tennis and badminton.
Tennis? What kind of hospital is this?
It's a very fine American hospital, Anny. This is how they do things in this country.
Sounds like a hotel in the Catskills to me.

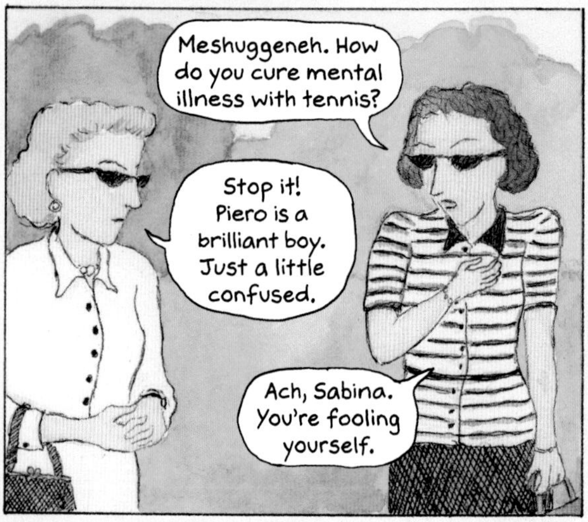
Meshuggeneh. How do you cure mental illness with tennis?
Stop it! Piero is a brilliant boy. Just a little confused.
Ach, Sabina. You're fooling yourself.

ONCE WE WERE IN THE CAR, THEY SWITCHED TO GERMAN. THE ARGUING CONTINUED ALL THE WAY BACK TO THE CITY.

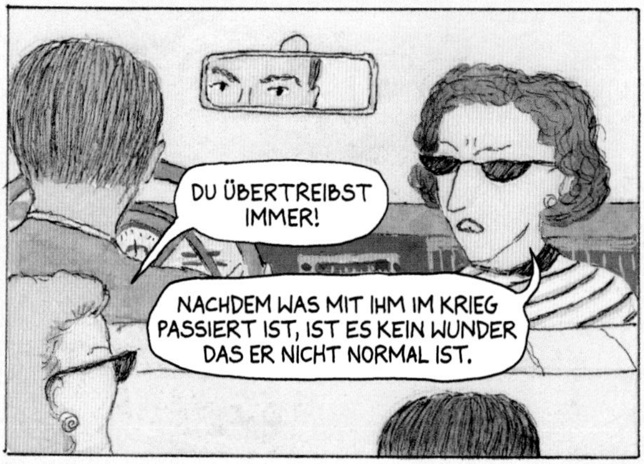
DU ÜBERTREIBST IMMER!
NACHDEM WAS MIT IHM IM KRIEG PASSIERT IST, IST ES KEIN WUNDER DAS ER NICHT NORMAL IST.

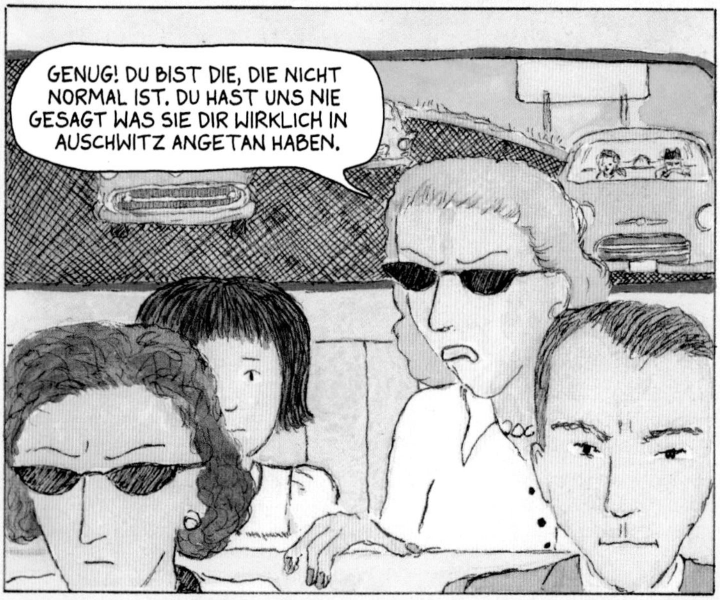
GENUG! DU BIST DIE, DIE NICHT NORMAL IST. DU HAST UNS NIE GESAGT WAS SIE DIR WIRKLICH IN AUSCHWITZ ANGETAN HABEN.

Du übertreibst immer!—
You always exaggerate!

Nachdem was mit ihm im Krieg passiert ist, ist es kein Wunder das er nicht normal ist.—
After what happened to him in the war, it's no wonder he's not normal.

Genug! Du bist die, die nicht normal ist. Du hast uns nie gesagt was sie dir wirlich in Auschwitz angetan haben.—
Enough! You're the one who's not normal. You've never told us what they really did to you in Auschwitz.

ON THE WAY HOME TO QUEENS, WE'D STOP IN WASHINGTON HEIGHTS IN THE NORTHERN PART OF MANHATTAN TO SEE TANTE EMMY, UNCLE LEO, AND OMA.

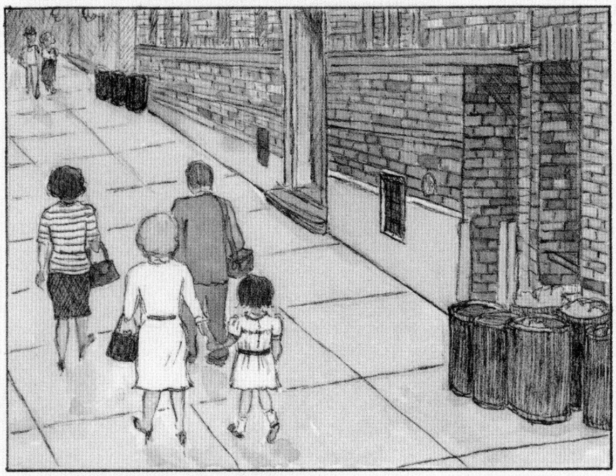

I WAS HAPPY TO GET AWAY FROM WOLFGANG'S STARE AND MY MOTHER AND TANTE ANNY'S INCESSANT ARGUING.

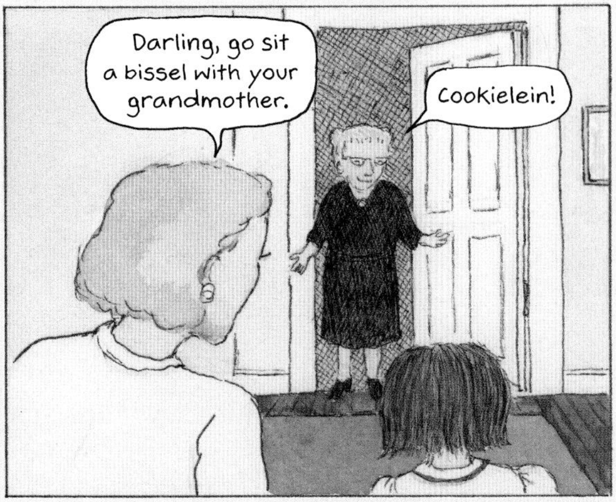
Darling, go sit a bissel with your grandmother.
Cookielein!

OMA HAD A ROOM OF HER OWN AT THE END OF A HALL. SHE HAPPILY CHATTED IN YIDDISH. IT DIDN'T BOTHER EITHER OF US THAT I COULD NOT UNDERSTAND HALF OF HER WORDS.

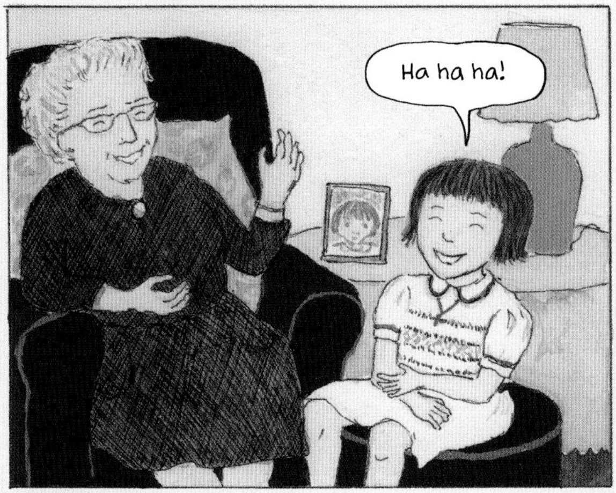
Ha ha ha!

SHE OFFERED ME JELLIED FRUIT SLICES AND NONPAREILS AND GAVE ME SILVER DOLLARS THAT WERE ALWAYS HIDDEN IN HER POCKETS.

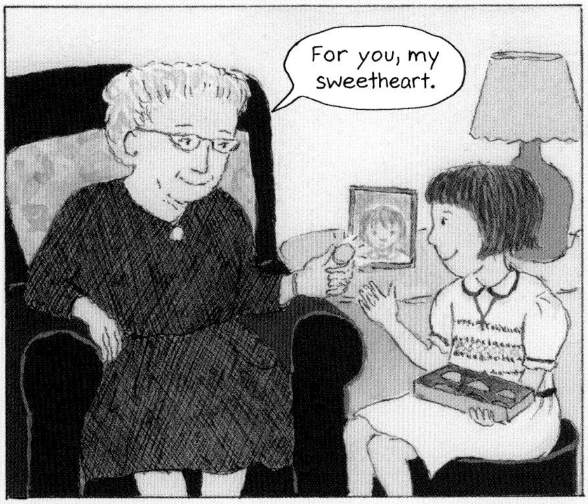
For you, my sweetheart.

SITTING IN MY GRANDMOTHER'S COZY BEDROOM, FAR FROM THE AGITATED VOICES OF THE REST OF THE FAMILY, WAS ALWAYS THE BEST PART OF SUNDAY.

SOON ENOUGH WE WOULD BOTH BE CALLED TO DINNER AND BACK INTO THE FERMISHT TUMMEL.

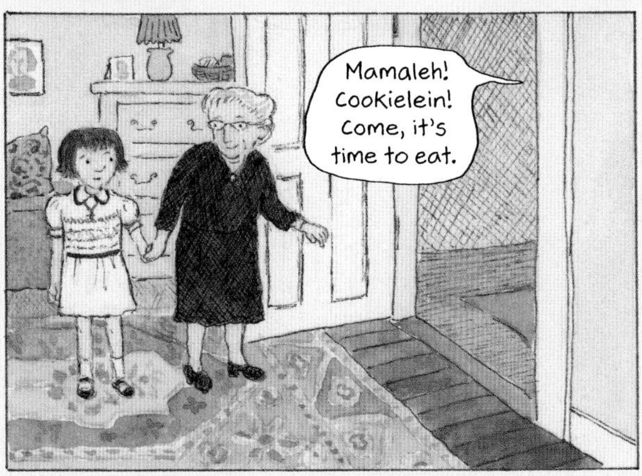
Mamaleh! Cookielein! Come, it's time to eat.

FOUR

Sans Souci

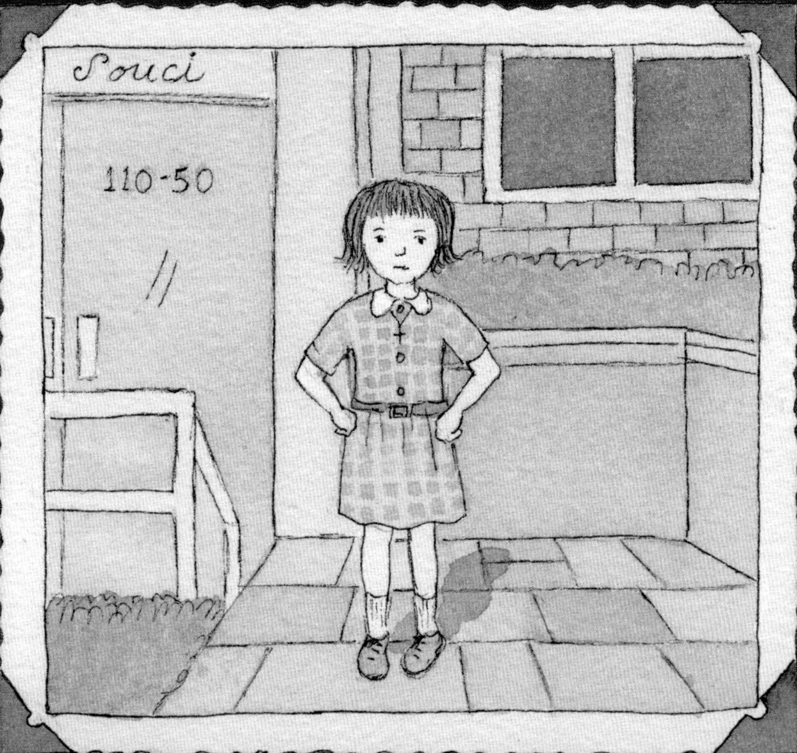
Souci
110-50

1957

IN ORDER FOR ME TO GO TO P.S. 196, WE HAD TO MOVE FROM KEW GARDENS TO FOREST HILLS. MY MOTHER FOUND A BRAND-NEW APARTMENT BUILDING ONLY ONE BLOCK AWAY FROM MY NEW SCHOOL.

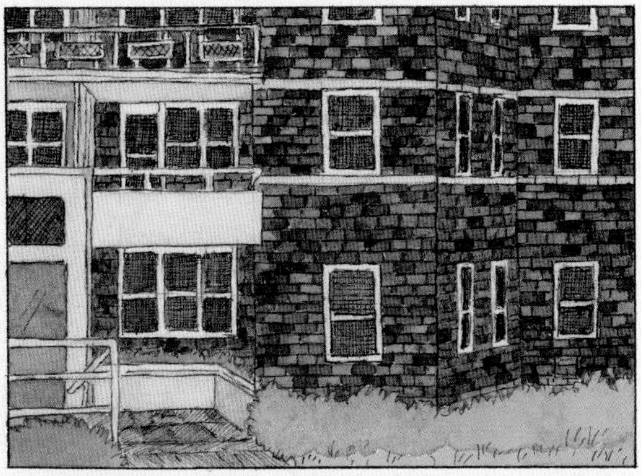

UNLIKE OTHER BUILDINGS IN THE NEIGHBORHOOD WITH THEIR STUFFY BRITISH NAMES, OURS WAS CALLED THE SANS SOUCI.

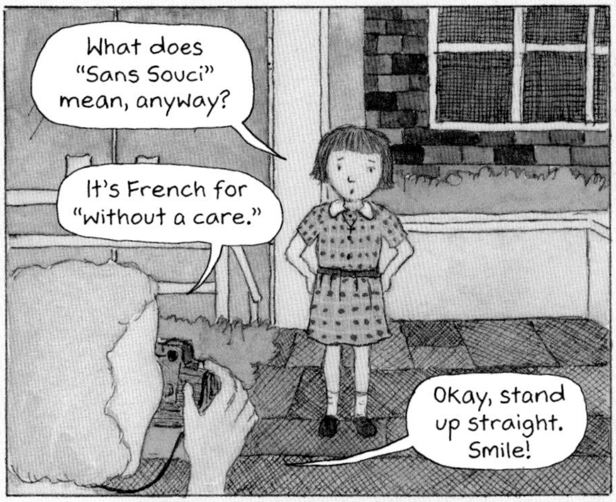
What does "Sans Souci" mean, anyway?
It's French for "without a care."
Okay, stand up straight. Smile!

FOR MY MOTHER, THE MOVE REPRESENTED A STEP UP THE LADDER OF AMERICAN PROMISE AND AWAY FROM THE RUBBLE OF EUROPE.

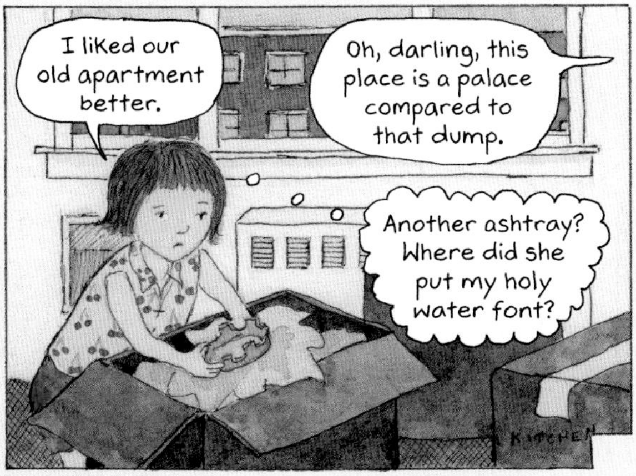
I liked our old apartment better.
Oh, darling, this place is a palace compared to that dump.
Another ashtray? Where did she put my holy water font?

OF COURSE, MY MOTHER WAS RIGHT. THE SANS SOUCI WAS A BIG IMPROVEMENT.

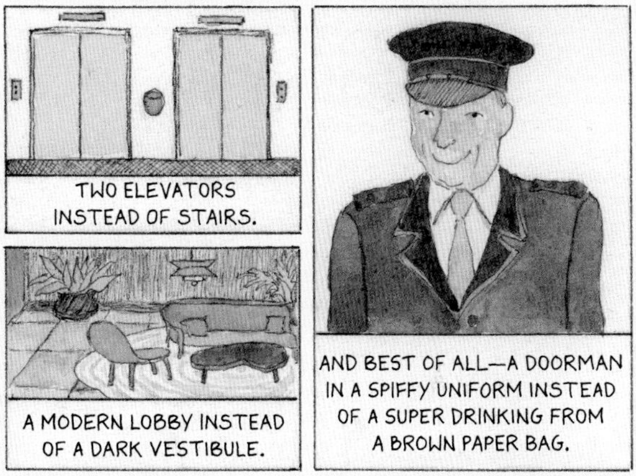
TWO ELEVATORS INSTEAD OF STAIRS.
A MODERN LOBBY INSTEAD OF A DARK VESTIBULE.
AND BEST OF ALL—A DOORMAN IN A SPIFFY UNIFORM INSTEAD OF A SUPER DRINKING FROM A BROWN PAPER BAG.

DURING THE DAY THE DOORMAN WAS STEFAN, A COURTLY MAN FROM VIENNA.

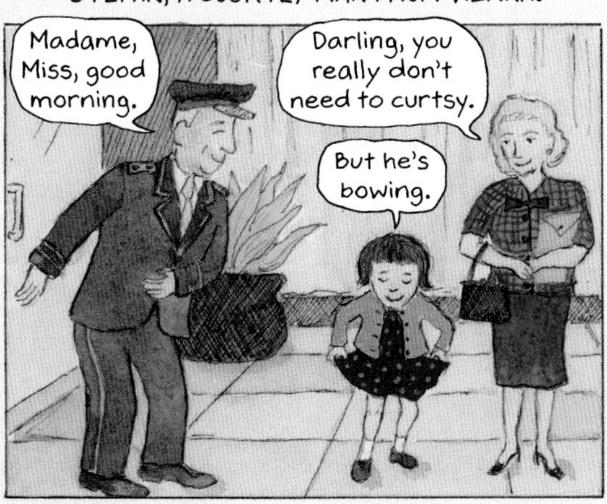
Madame, Miss, good morning.
Darling, you really don't need to curtsy.
But he's bowing.

TO MY AUNTS AND GRANDMOTHER, THE MOVE TO THE SANS SOUCI WAS YET ANOTHER OF MY MOTHER'S WILD SCHEMES, LIKE ELOPING TO ITALY WITH HER POLISH FIANCÉ AND CONVERTING TO CATHOLICISM A FEW YEARS LATER.

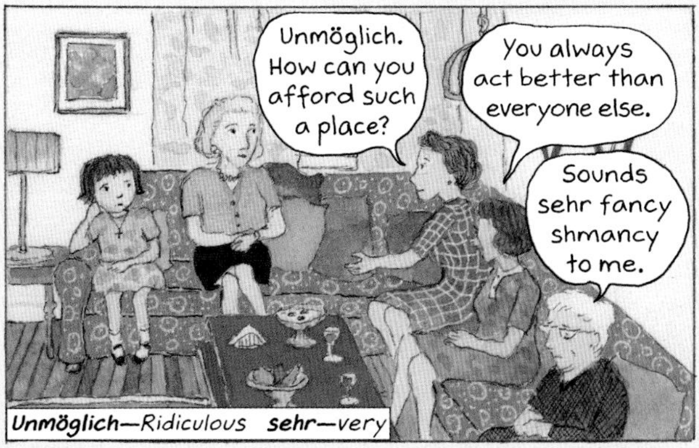
Unmöglich. How can you afford such a place?
You always act better than everyone else.
Sounds sehr fancy shmancy to me.
Unmöglich—Ridiculous sehr—very

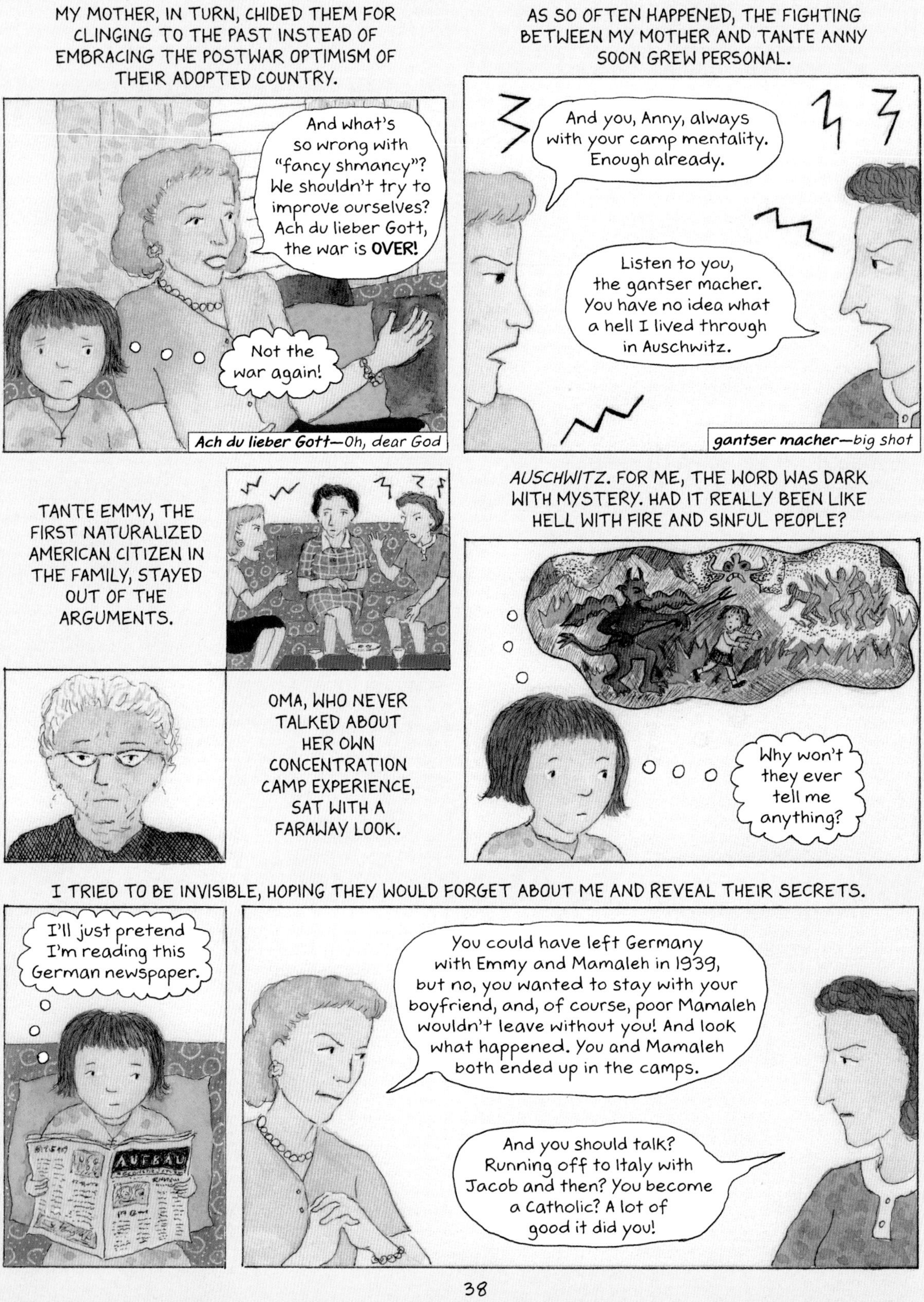
MY MOTHER, IN TURN, CHIDED THEM FOR CLINGING TO THE PAST INSTEAD OF EMBRACING THE POSTWAR OPTIMISM OF THEIR ADOPTED COUNTRY.
And what's so wrong with "fancy shmancy"? We shouldn't try to improve ourselves? Ach du lieber Gott, the war is **OVER!**
Not the war again!
Ach du lieber Gott—*Oh, dear God*
AS SO OFTEN HAPPENED, THE FIGHTING BETWEEN MY MOTHER AND TANTE ANNY SOON GREW PERSONAL.
And you, Anny, always with your camp mentality. Enough already.
Listen to you, the gantser macher. You have no idea what a hell I lived through in Auschwitz.
gantser macher—*big shot*
TANTE EMMY, THE FIRST NATURALIZED AMERICAN CITIZEN IN THE FAMILY, STAYED OUT OF THE ARGUMENTS.
OMA, WHO NEVER TALKED ABOUT HER OWN CONCENTRATION CAMP EXPERIENCE, SAT WITH A FARAWAY LOOK.
AUSCHWITZ. FOR ME, THE WORD WAS DARK WITH MYSTERY. HAD IT REALLY BEEN LIKE HELL WITH FIRE AND SINFUL PEOPLE?
Why won't they ever tell me anything?
I TRIED TO BE INVISIBLE, HOPING THEY WOULD FORGET ABOUT ME AND REVEAL THEIR SECRETS.
I'll just pretend I'm reading this German newspaper.
AUFBAU
You could have left Germany with Emmy and Mamaleh in 1939, but no, you wanted to stay with your boyfriend, and, of course, poor Mamaleh wouldn't leave without you! And look what happened. You and Mamaleh both ended up in the camps.
And you should talk? Running off to Italy with Jacob and then? You become a Catholic? A lot of good it did you!

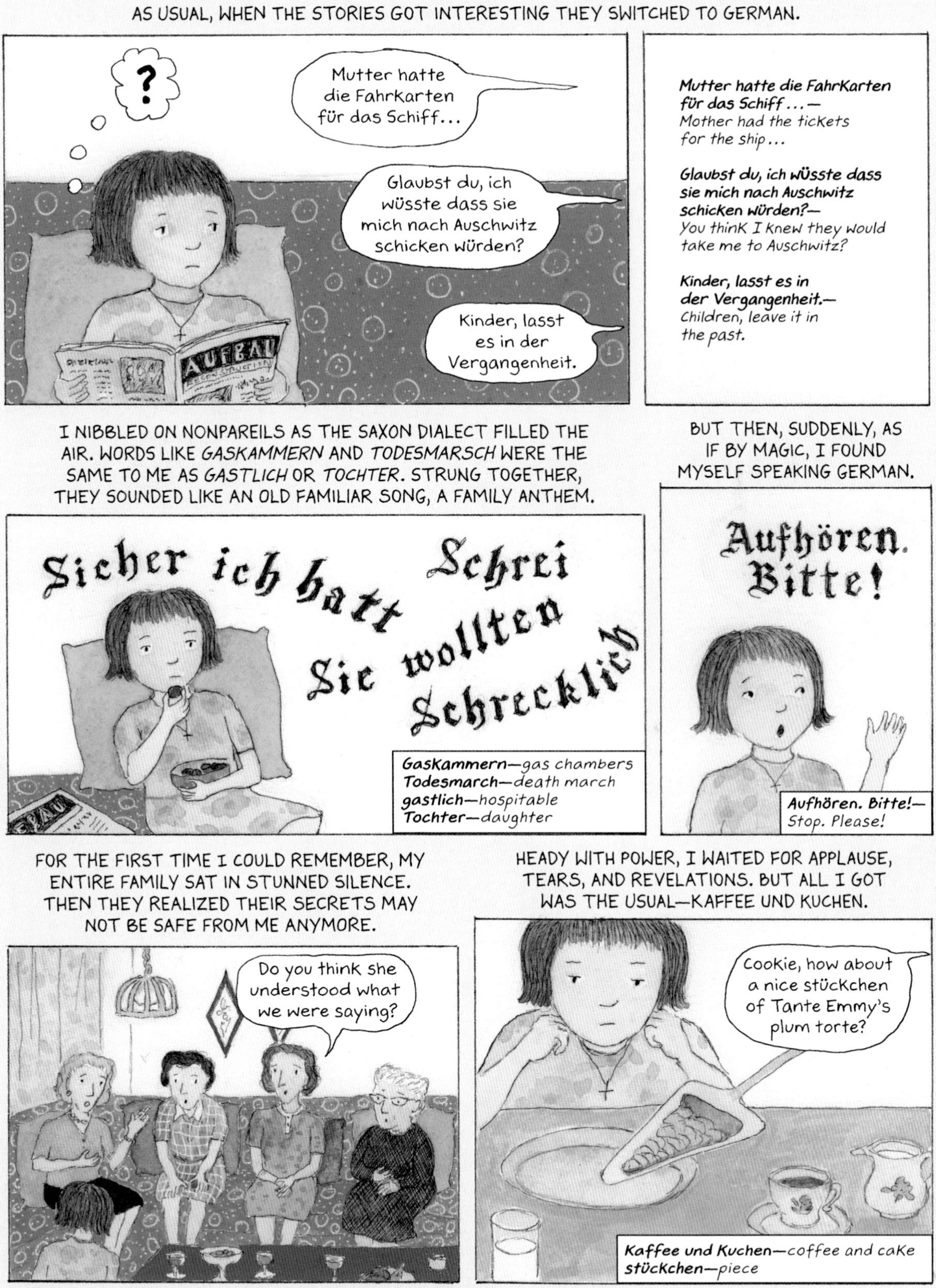
AS USUAL, WHEN THE STORIES GOT INTERESTING THEY SWITCHED TO GERMAN.
?
Mutter hatte die FahrKarten für das Schiff...
Glaubst du, ich wüsste dass sie mich nach Auschwitz schicken würden?
Kinder, lasst es in der Vergangenheit.
AUFBAU
Mutter hatte die FahrKarten für das Schiff . . .—*Mother had the tickets for the ship . . .*
Glaubst du, ich wüsste dass sie mich nach Auschwitz schicken würden?—*You think I knew they would take me to Auschwitz?*
Kinder, lasst es in der Vergangenheit.—*Children, leave it in the past.*
I NIBBLED ON NONPAREILS AS THE SAXON DIALECT FILLED THE AIR. WORDS LIKE *GASKAMMERN* AND *TODESMARSCH* WERE THE SAME TO ME AS *GASTLICH* OR *TOCHTER*. STRUNG TOGETHER, THEY SOUNDED LIKE AN OLD FAMILIAR SONG, A FAMILY ANTHEM.
Sicher ich hatt Schrei Sie wollten Schrecklich
GasKammern—*gas chambers*
Todesmarch—*death march*
gastlich—*hospitable*
Tochter—*daughter*
BUT THEN, SUDDENLY, AS IF BY MAGIC, I FOUND MYSELF SPEAKING GERMAN.
Aufhören. Bitte!
Aufhören. Bitte!—*Stop. Please!*
FOR THE FIRST TIME I COULD REMEMBER, MY ENTIRE FAMILY SAT IN STUNNED SILENCE. THEN THEY REALIZED THEIR SECRETS MAY NOT BE SAFE FROM ME ANYMORE.
Do you think she understood what we were saying?
HEADY WITH POWER, I WAITED FOR APPLAUSE, TEARS, AND REVELATIONS. BUT ALL I GOT WAS THE USUAL—KAFFEE UND KUCHEN.
Cookie, how about a nice stücKchen of Tante Emmy's plum torte?
Kaffee und Kuchen—*coffee and caKe*
stücKchen—*piece*

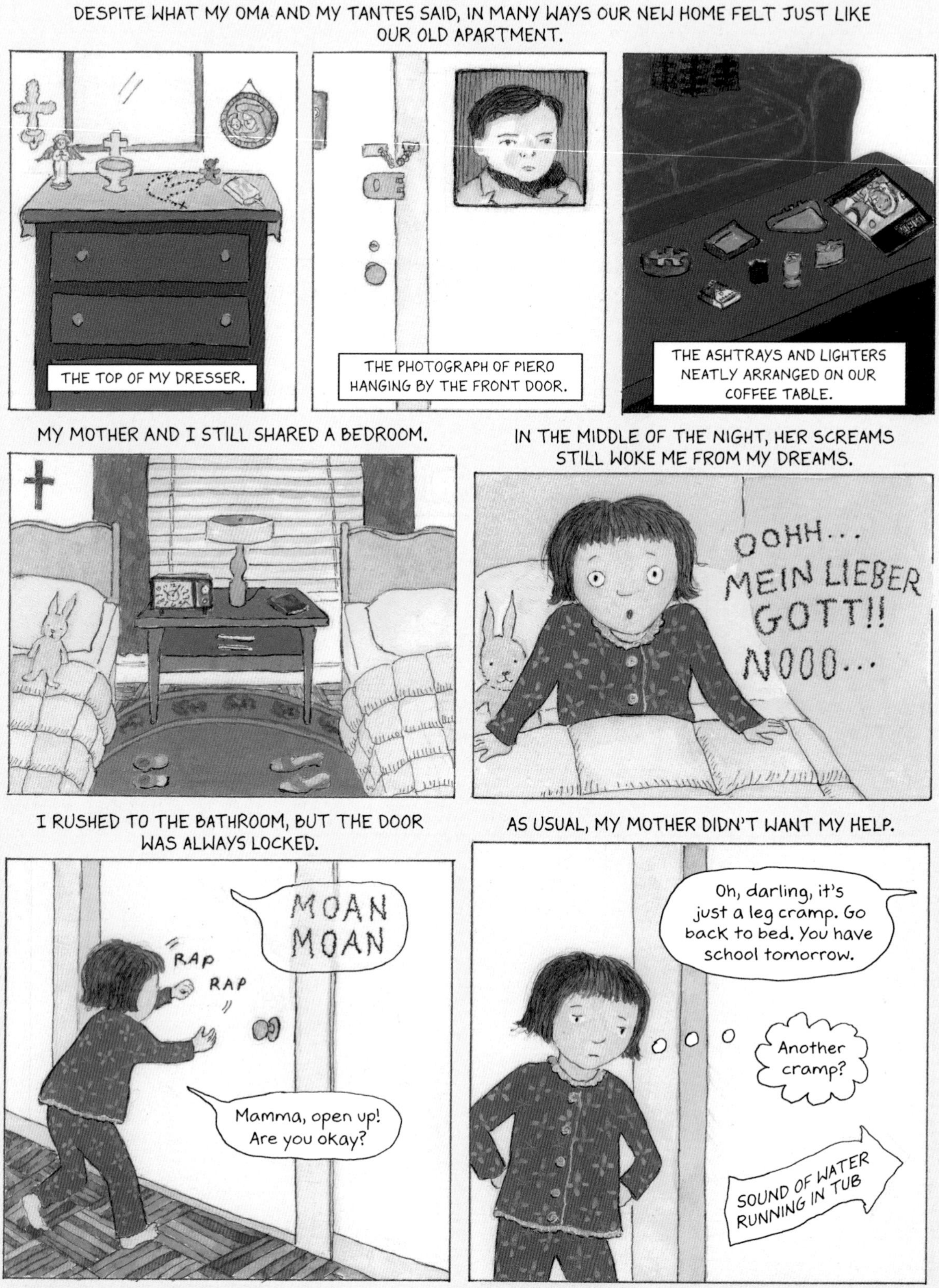
DESPITE WHAT MY OMA AND MY TANTES SAID, IN MANY WAYS OUR NEW HOME FELT JUST LIKE OUR OLD APARTMENT.
THE TOP OF MY DRESSER.
THE PHOTOGRAPH OF PIERO HANGING BY THE FRONT DOOR.
THE ASHTRAYS AND LIGHTERS NEATLY ARRANGED ON OUR COFFEE TABLE.
MY MOTHER AND I STILL SHARED A BEDROOM.
IN THE MIDDLE OF THE NIGHT, HER SCREAMS STILL WOKE ME FROM MY DREAMS.
OOHH... MEIN LIEBER GOTT!! NOOO...
I RUSHED TO THE BATHROOM, BUT THE DOOR WAS ALWAYS LOCKED.
MOAN MOAN
RAP RAP
Mamma, open up! Are you okay?
AS USUAL, MY MOTHER DIDN'T WANT MY HELP.
Oh, darling, it's just a leg cramp. Go back to bed. You have school tomorrow.
Another cramp?
SOUND OF WATER RUNNING IN TUB

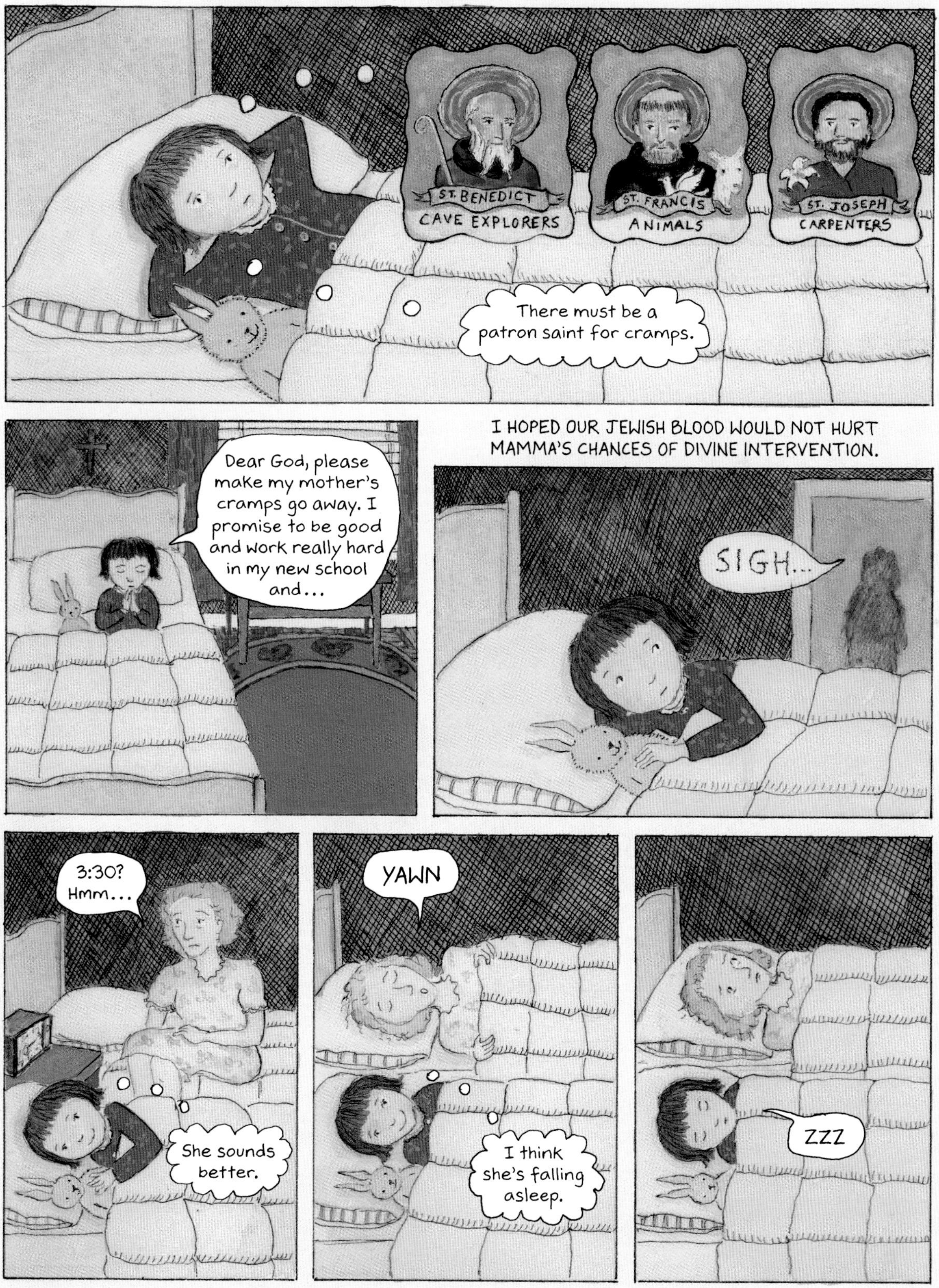
ST. BENEDICT
CAVE EXPLORERS
ST. FRANCIS
ANIMALS
ST. JOSEPH
CARPENTERS
There must be a patron saint for cramps.
Dear God, please make my mother's cramps go away. I promise to be good and work really hard in my new school and...
I HOPED OUR JEWISH BLOOD WOULD NOT HURT MAMMA'S CHANCES OF DIVINE INTERVENTION.
SIGH...
3:30? Hmm...
She sounds better.
YAWN
I think she's falling asleep.
ZZZ

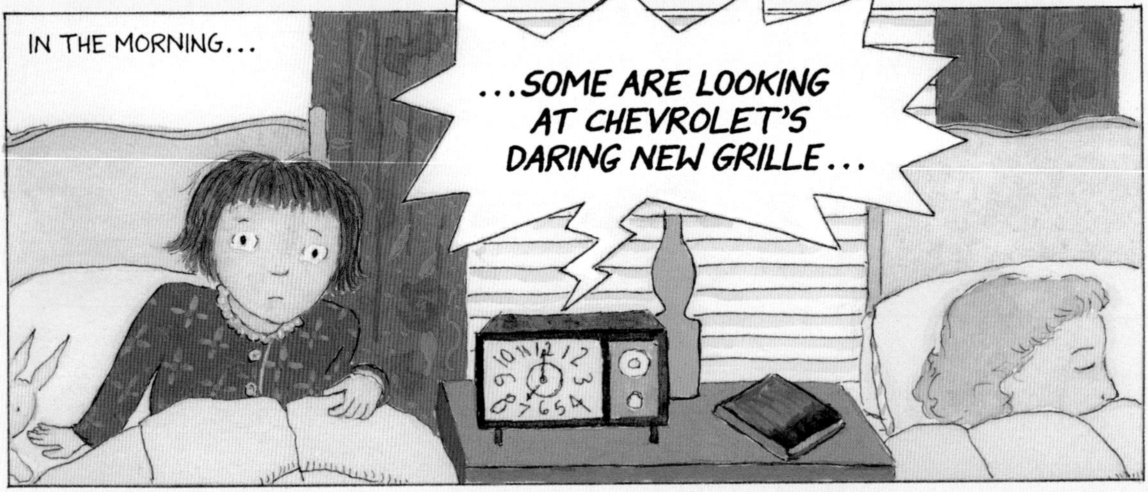
IN THE MORNING...
...SOME ARE LOOKING AT CHEVROLET'S DARING NEW GRILLE...

GETTING MY MOTHER UP ON TIME FOR WORK WAS AN ENORMOUS RESPONSIBILITY.

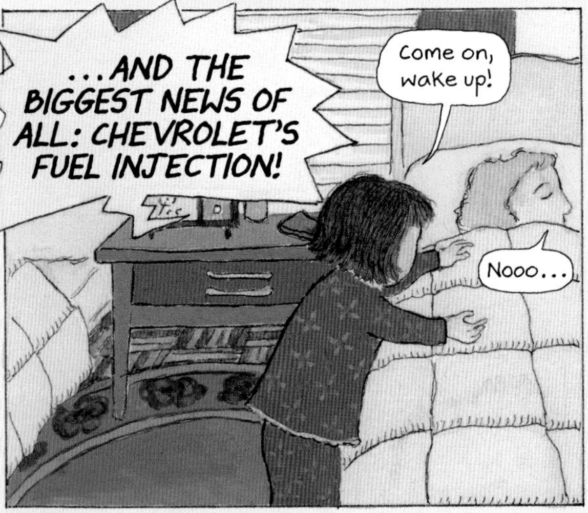
...AND THE BIGGEST NEWS OF ALL: CHEVROLET'S FUEL INJECTION!
Come on, wake up!
Nooo...

AFTER ALL, SHE HAD ALREADY BEEN FIRED FROM TWO SECRETARIAL JOBS FOR BEING LATE.

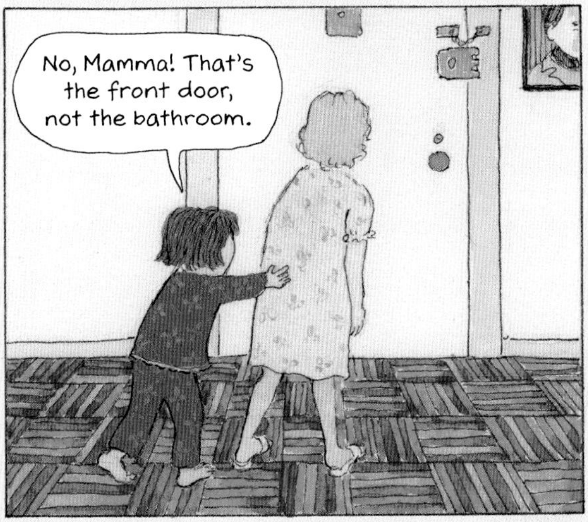
No, Mamma! That's the front door, not the bathroom.

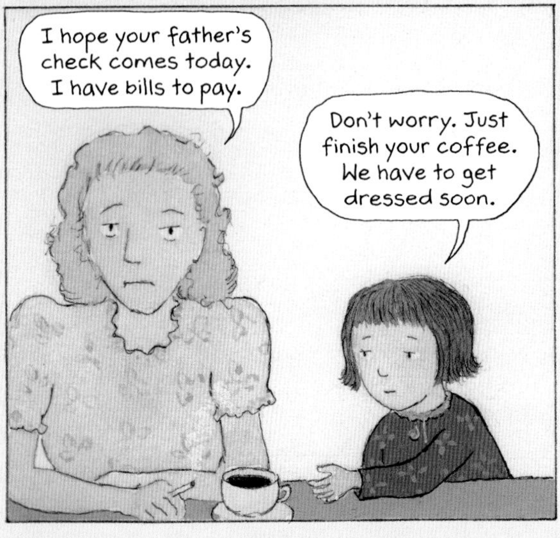
I hope your father's check comes today. I have bills to pay.
Don't worry. Just finish your coffee. We have to get dressed soon.

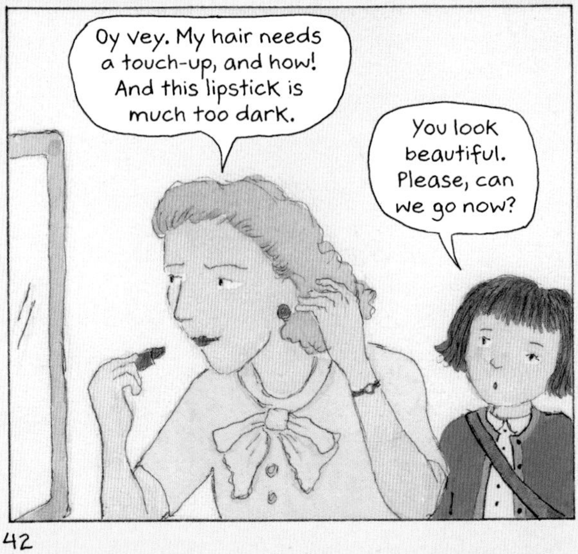
Oy vey. My hair needs a touch-up, and how! And this lipstick is much too dark.
You look beautiful. Please, can we go now?

AT LAST, ON THE SIDEWALK IN FRONT OF THE SANS SOUCI, MY MOTHER WAS READY TO GIVE ME HER DAILY ADMONITIONS.

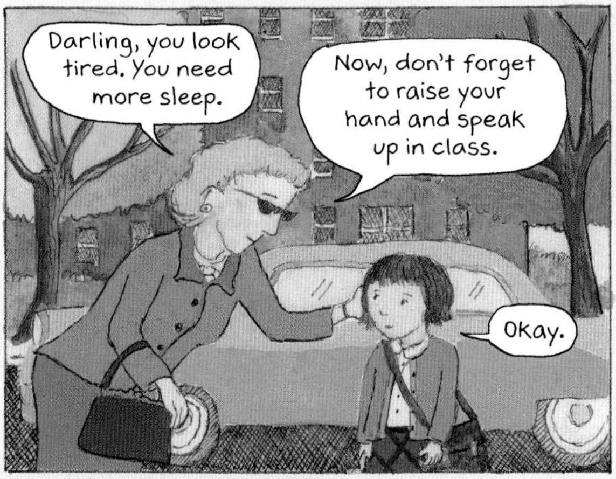
Darling, you look tired. You need more sleep.
Now, don't forget to raise your hand and speak up in class.
Okay.

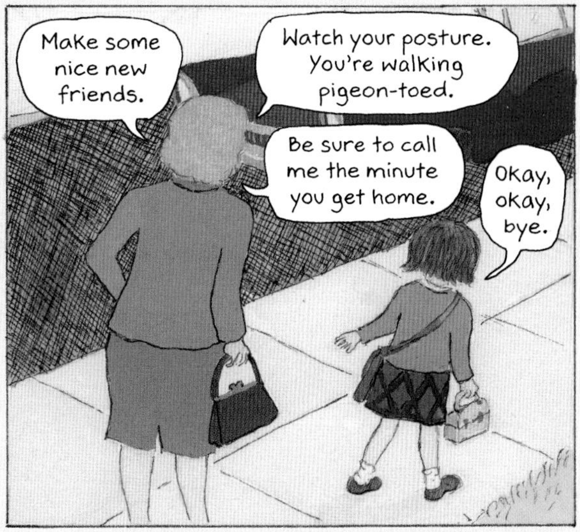
Make some nice new friends.
Watch your posture. You're walking pigeon-toed.
Be sure to call me the minute you get home.
Okay, okay, bye.

BUT IT WASN'T EASY MAKING FRIENDS IN MY NEW SCHOOL.

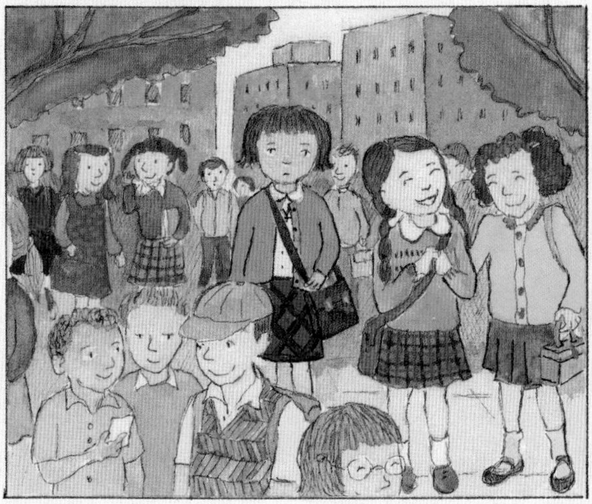

THEN AGAIN, HAD I MADE ANY FRIENDS AT OUR LADY QUEEN OF MARTYRS? BEAUTIFUL AS SHE WAS, SISTER JOSEPH GERARD HAD NOT ENCOURAGED SOCIAL INTERACTION.

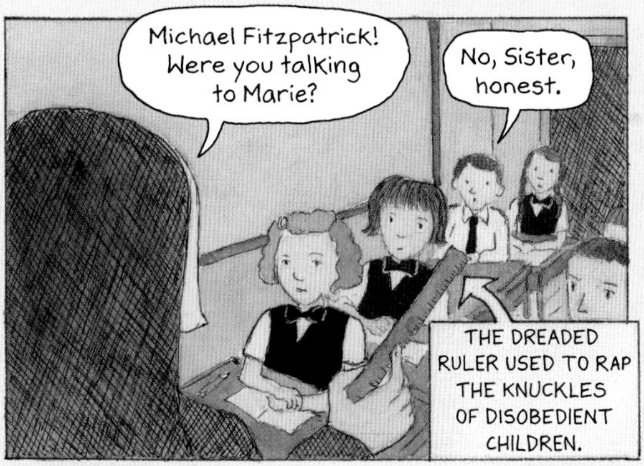
Michael Fitzpatrick! Were you talking to Marie?
No, Sister, honest.
THE DREADED RULER USED TO RAP THE KNUCKLES OF DISOBEDIENT CHILDREN.

EVEN THOUGH I WAS NOW IN PUBLIC SCHOOL, I FOUND IT HARD TO BREAK OLD HABITS.

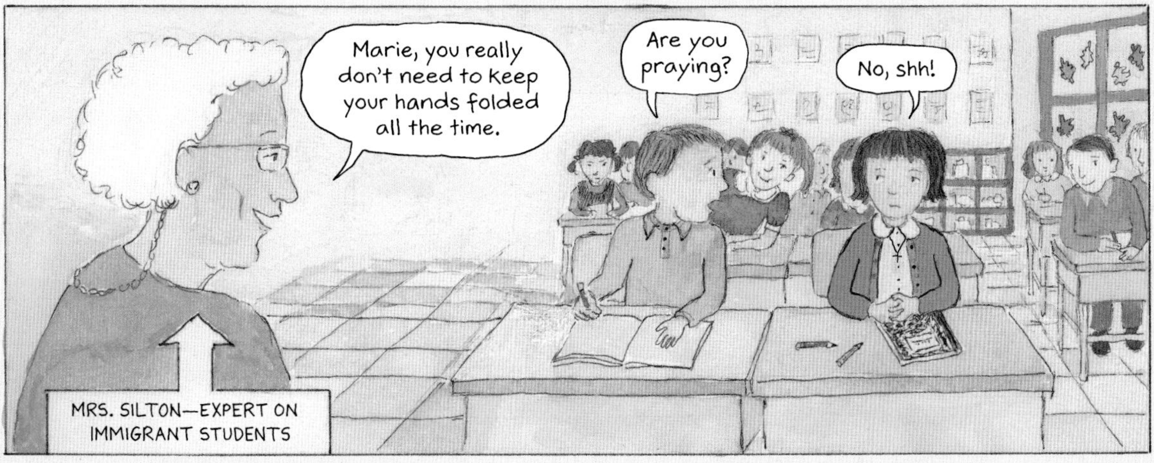
Marie, you really don't need to keep your hands folded all the time.
Are you praying?
No, shh!
MRS. SILTON—EXPERT ON IMMIGRANT STUDENTS

AT SHOW-AND-TELL, I REALIZED NONE OF MY NEW CLASSMATES WERE CATHOLIC.

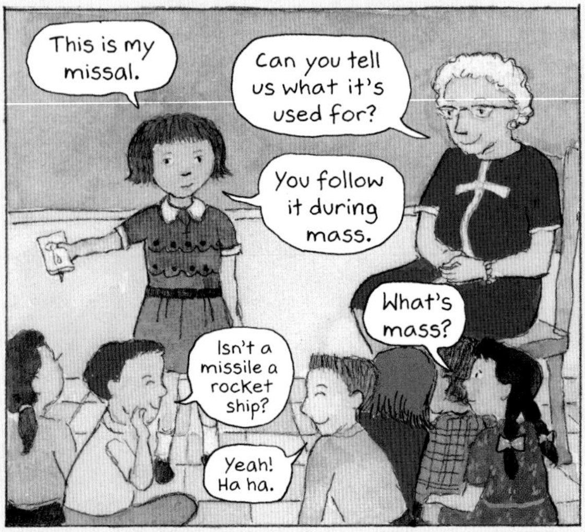
This is my missal.
Can you tell us what it's used for?
You follow it during mass.
What's mass?
Isn't a missile a rocket ship?
Yeah! Ha ha.

I WAS THE ONLY ONE WHO LEFT SCHOOL EARLY ON WEDNESDAYS TO GO TO RELIGIOUS INSTRUCTION. I WALKED WITH A BOY FROM A DIFFERENT CLASS AND HIS MOTHER.

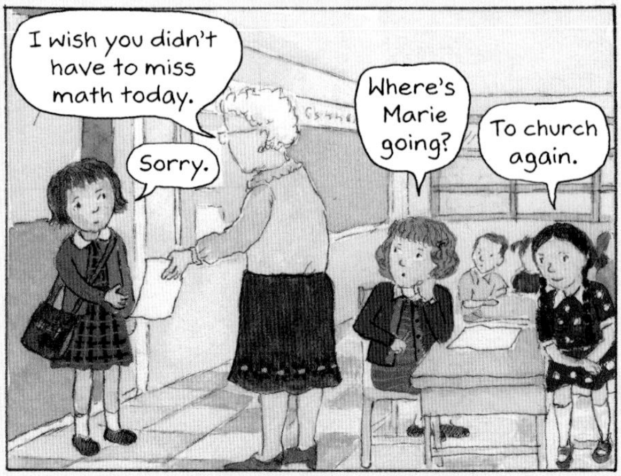
I wish you didn't have to miss math today.
Sorry.
Where's Marie going?
To church again.

ON JEWISH HOLIDAYS MOST OF MY CLASS WAS ABSENT.

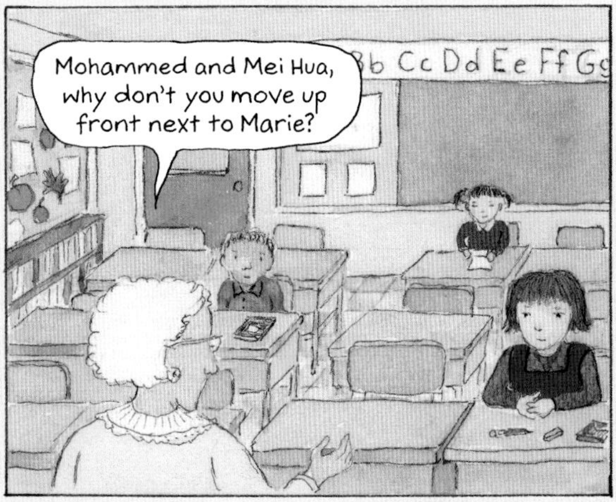
Mohammed and Mei Hua, why don't you move up front next to Marie?

IT ONLY SEEMED FAIR THAT I WOULD GET TO CELEBRATE CATHOLIC HOLIDAYS BY STAYING HOME, BUT MY MOTHER HAD A DIFFERENT OPINION.

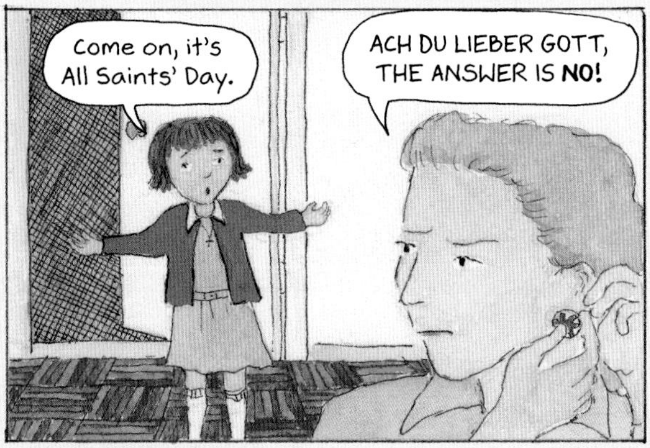
Come on, it's All Saints' Day.
ACH DU LIEBER GOTT, THE ANSWER IS NO!

THERE WAS LITTLE CHANCE OF MAKING NEW FRIENDS AFTER SCHOOL BECAUSE I HAD TO HURRY HOME...

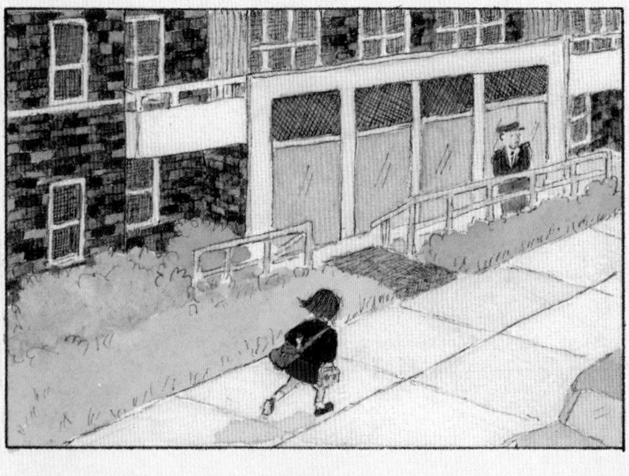

...AND CALL MY MOTHER THE MINUTE I WAS SAFELY LOCKED IN OUR APARTMENT.

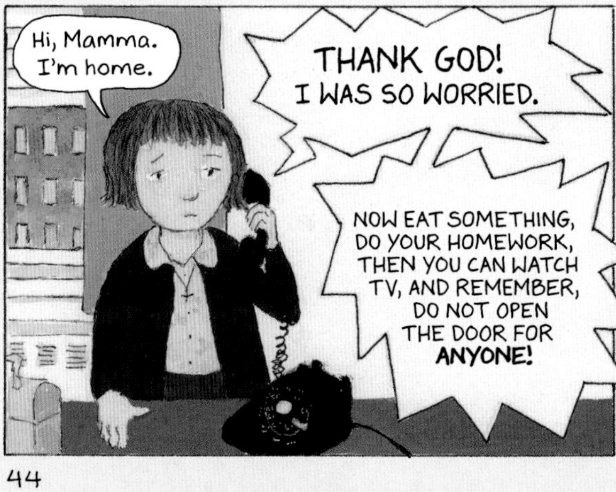
Hi, Mamma. I'm home.
THANK GOD! I WAS SO WORRIED.
NOW EAT SOMETHING, DO YOUR HOMEWORK, THEN YOU CAN WATCH TV, AND REMEMBER, DO NOT OPEN THE DOOR FOR ANYONE!

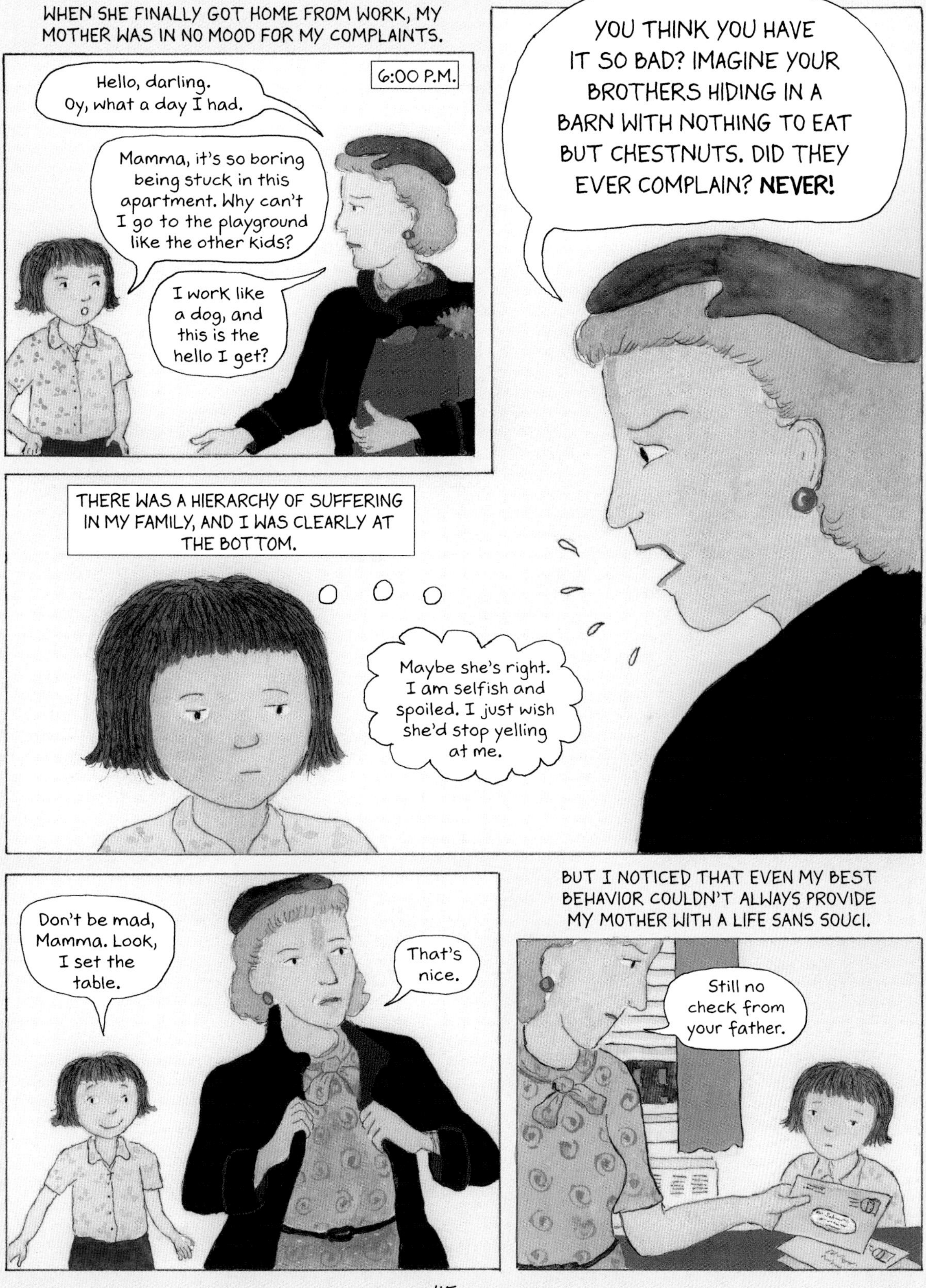
WHEN SHE FINALLY GOT HOME FROM WORK, MY MOTHER WAS IN NO MOOD FOR MY COMPLAINTS.
6:00 P.M.
Hello, darling. Oy, what a day I had.
Mamma, it's so boring being stuck in this apartment. Why can't I go to the playground like the other kids?
I work like a dog, and this is the hello I get?
YOU THINK YOU HAVE IT SO BAD? IMAGINE YOUR BROTHERS HIDING IN A BARN WITH NOTHING TO EAT BUT CHESTNUTS. DID THEY EVER COMPLAIN? NEVER!
THERE WAS A HIERARCHY OF SUFFERING IN MY FAMILY, AND I WAS CLEARLY AT THE BOTTOM.
Maybe she's right. I am selfish and spoiled. I just wish she'd stop yelling at me.
Don't be mad, Mamma. Look, I set the table.
That's nice.
BUT I NOTICED THAT EVEN MY BEST BEHAVIOR COULDN'T ALWAYS PROVIDE MY MOTHER WITH A LIFE SANS SOUCI.
Still no check from your father.

FIVE

Real-Life Christmas

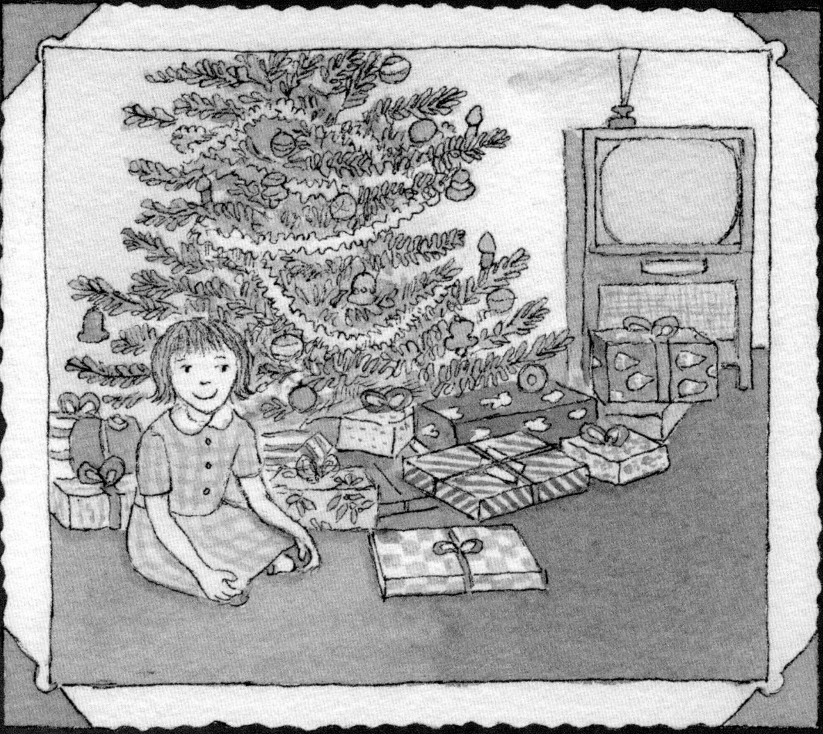

ONE AFTERNOON, AS I WAS RUSHING THROUGH THE LOBBY, STEFAN STOPPED ME.

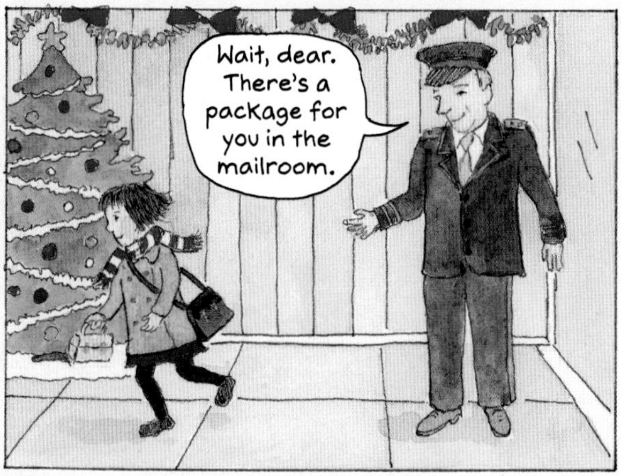

Wait, dear. There's a package for you in the mailroom.

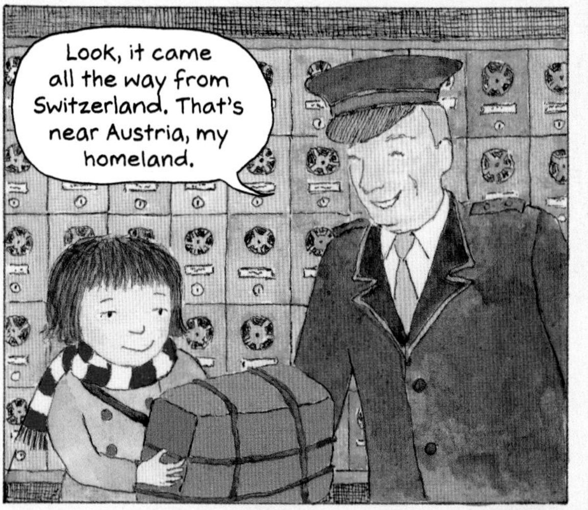

Look, it came all the way from Switzerland. That's near Austria, my homeland.

IT WAS FROM MY FATHER. ALTHOUGH HE WAS ITALIAN, HE LIVED IN GENEVA BECAUSE OF HIS WORK. HE NEVER CALLED OR CAME TO VISIT, CHOOSING INSTEAD TO WRITE ME LETTERS IN ITALIAN THAT MY MOTHER HAD TO TRANSLATE. THEY ALWAYS ENDED WITH A PROMISE THAT WE WOULD SEE EACH OTHER SOON. TWICE A YEAR HE SENT ME GIFTS: FOR MY BIRTHDAY AND FOR CHRISTMAS.

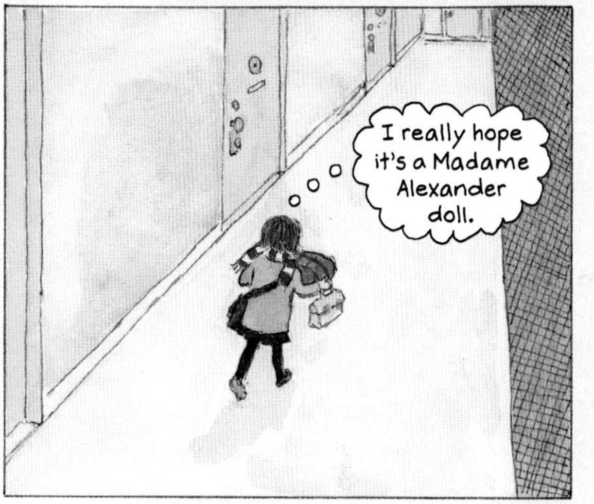

I really hope it's a Madame Alexander doll.

UNFORTUNATELY, HIS GIFTS WERE USUALLY DISAPPOINTING, TENDING TOWARD JEWELRY OR USEFUL CLOTHING.

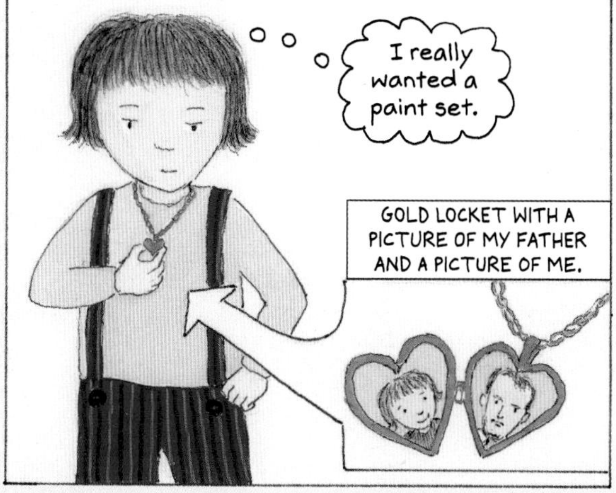

I really wanted a paint set.
GOLD LOCKET WITH A PICTURE OF MY FATHER AND A PICTURE OF ME.

MY MOTHER AND FATHER HAD MET IN WASHINGTON, D.C., AFTER THE WAR WHEN SHE GOT A JOB THERE WORKING FOR THE ITALIAN TRADE COMMISSION.

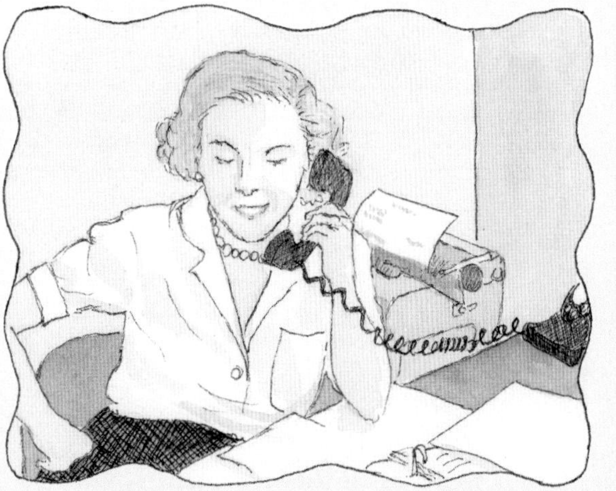

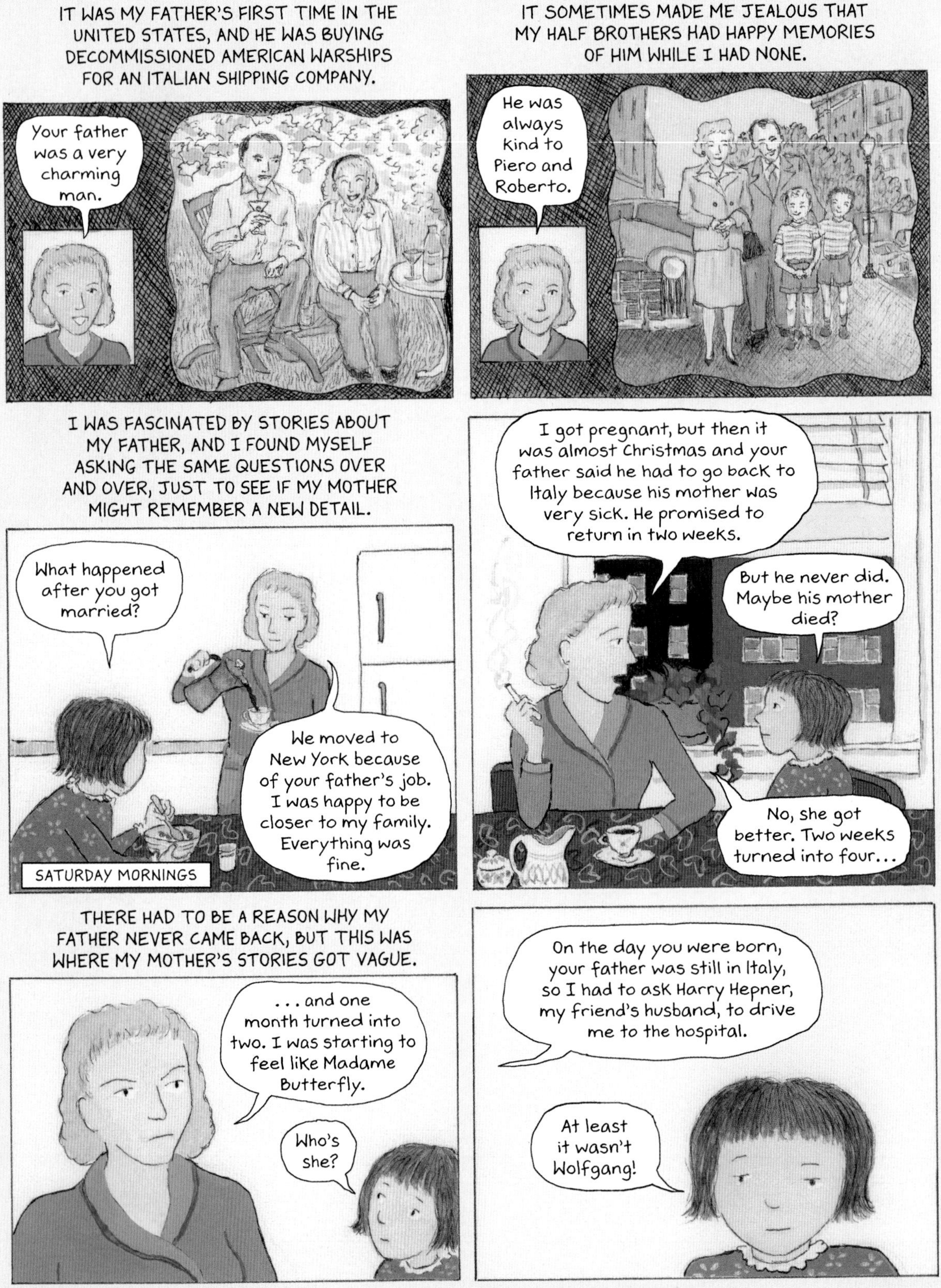
IT WAS MY FATHER'S FIRST TIME IN THE UNITED STATES, AND HE WAS BUYING DECOMMISSIONED AMERICAN WARSHIPS FOR AN ITALIAN SHIPPING COMPANY.
Your father was a very charming man.
IT SOMETIMES MADE ME JEALOUS THAT MY HALF BROTHERS HAD HAPPY MEMORIES OF HIM WHILE I HAD NONE.
He was always kind to Piero and Roberto.
I WAS FASCINATED BY STORIES ABOUT MY FATHER, AND I FOUND MYSELF ASKING THE SAME QUESTIONS OVER AND OVER, JUST TO SEE IF MY MOTHER MIGHT REMEMBER A NEW DETAIL.
What happened after you got married?
We moved to New York because of your father's job. I was happy to be closer to my family. Everything was fine.
SATURDAY MORNINGS
I got pregnant, but then it was almost Christmas and your father said he had to go back to Italy because his mother was very sick. He promised to return in two weeks.
But he never did. Maybe his mother died?
No, she got better. Two weeks turned into four...
THERE HAD TO BE A REASON WHY MY FATHER NEVER CAME BACK, BUT THIS WAS WHERE MY MOTHER'S STORIES GOT VAGUE.
...and one month turned into two. I was starting to feel like Madame Butterfly.
Who's she?
On the day you were born, your father was still in Italy, so I had to ask Harry Hepner, my friend's husband, to drive me to the hospital.
At least it wasn't Wolfgang!

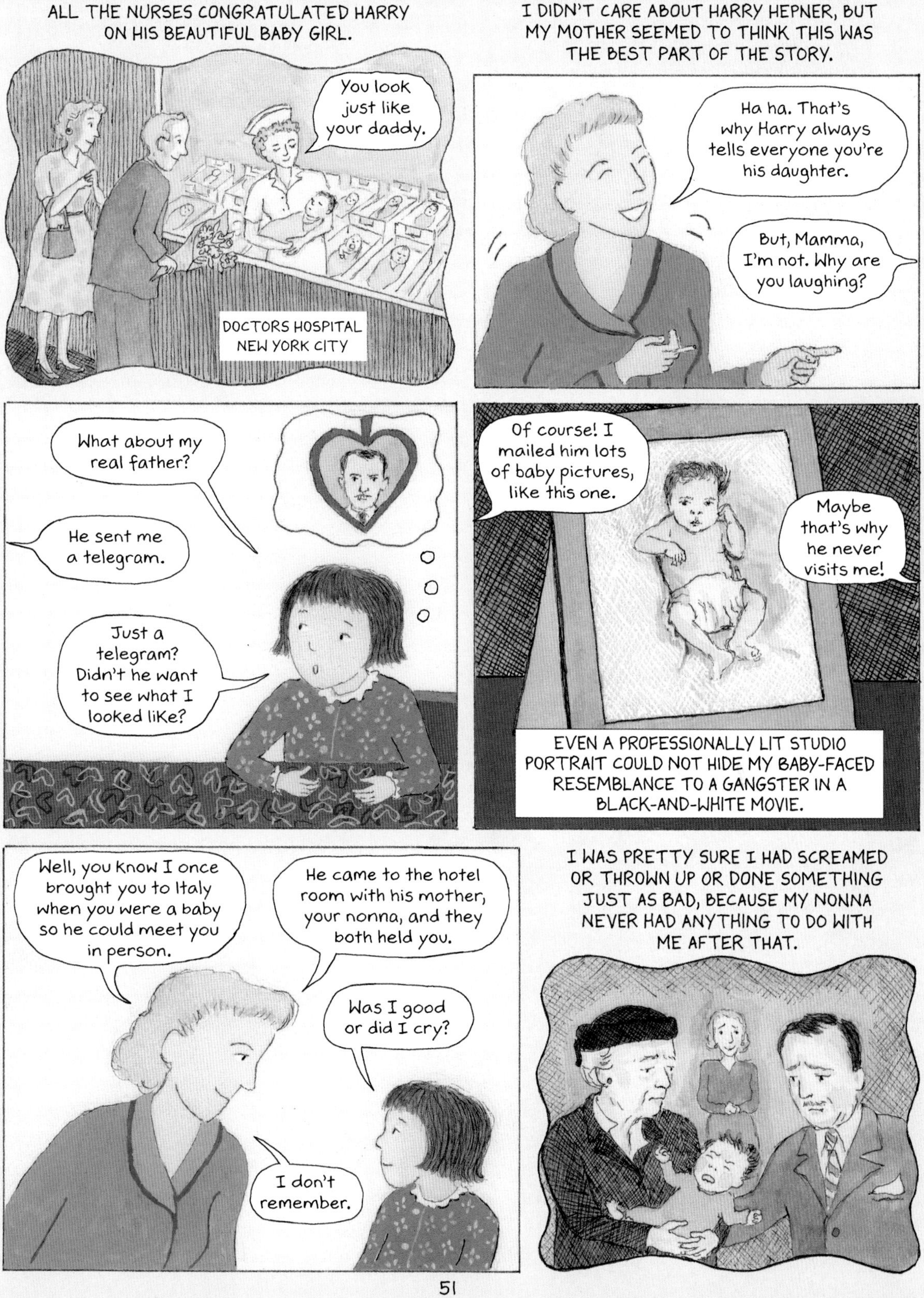

ALL THE NURSES CONGRATULATED HARRY ON HIS BEAUTIFUL BABY GIRL.
You look just like your daddy.
DOCTORS HOSPITAL NEW YORK CITY
I DIDN'T CARE ABOUT HARRY HEPNER, BUT MY MOTHER SEEMED TO THINK THIS WAS THE BEST PART OF THE STORY.
Ha ha. That's why Harry always tells everyone you're his daughter.
But, Mamma, I'm not. Why are you laughing?
What about my real father?
He sent me a telegram.
Just a telegram? Didn't he want to see what I looked like?
Of course! I mailed him lots of baby pictures, like this one.
Maybe that's why he never visits me!
EVEN A PROFESSIONALLY LIT STUDIO PORTRAIT COULD NOT HIDE MY BABY-FACED RESEMBLANCE TO A GANGSTER IN A BLACK-AND-WHITE MOVIE.
Well, you know I once brought you to Italy when you were a baby so he could meet you in person.
He came to the hotel room with his mother, your nonna, and they both held you.
Was I good or did I cry?
I don't remember.
I WAS PRETTY SURE I HAD SCREAMED OR THROWN UP OR DONE SOMETHING JUST AS BAD, BECAUSE MY NONNA NEVER HAD ANYTHING TO DO WITH ME AFTER THAT.

MY MOTHER'S EYES WOULD GROW CLOUDY AT THIS POINT IN THE STORY. THEN SHE ALWAYS FOUND A WAY TO CHANGE THE SUBJECT.

Oy, look at the time! I'm going to be late for the beauty parlor.

DESPITE THE LINGERING MYSTERY OF MY FATHER'S RETURN TO EUROPE, I WAS GLAD HE REMEMBERED TO SEND ME GIFTS. SAFELY LOCKED IN THE APARTMENT, I PUT HIS PACKAGE UNDER OUR CHRISTMAS TREE, RIGHT NEXT TO THE CRÈCHE.

THE CRÈCHE WAS ONE OF THE FEW THINGS MY MOTHER HAD RETRIEVED FROM HER APARTMENT IN ROME AFTER THE WAR.

EVEN THOUGH JOSEPH'S NOSE WAS CHIPPED AND THE COW WAS MISSING AN EAR, I THOUGHT THE CRÈCHE WAS BEAUTIFUL.

ESPECIALLY BABY JESUS, SWADDLED IN A PIECE OF FELT AND SLEEPING IN A CARDBOARD MANGER.

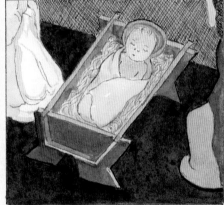

FOR ME, THE CRÈCHE WAS MY OWN LITTLE THEATER WHERE I COULD REENACT THE STORY OF CHRISTMAS OVER AND OVER.

When Mary and Joseph got to Bethlehem, they had to sleep in a barn, and then Baby Jesus was born! He was crying, "Wah, wah," and the sheep were going, "Baa, baa." Then Mary wrapped Jesus in a blanket and put him in the manger and...look, here come the Three Wise Men...

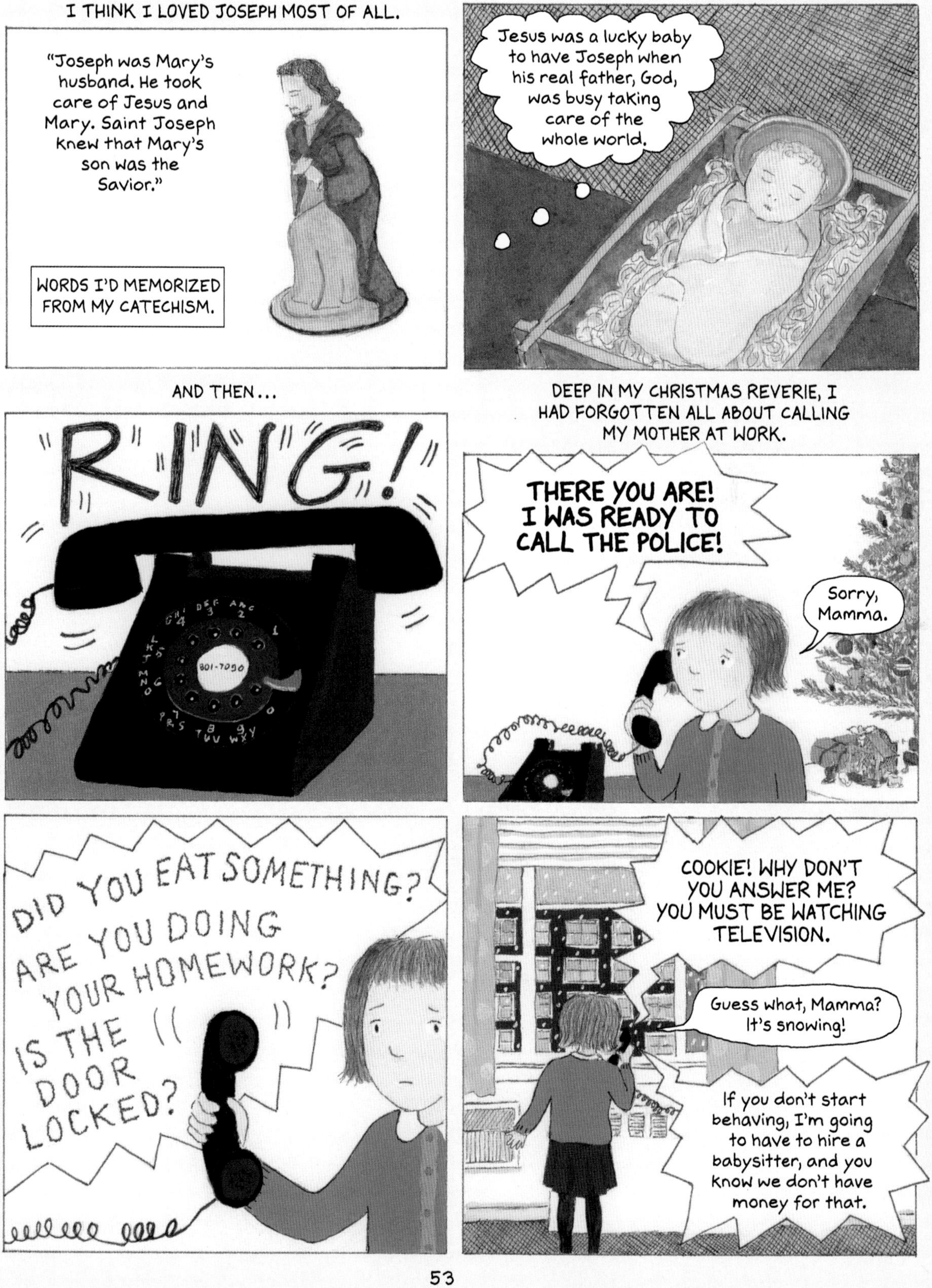
I THINK I LOVED JOSEPH MOST OF ALL.
"Joseph was Mary's husband. He took care of Jesus and Mary. Saint Joseph knew that Mary's son was the Savior."
WORDS I'D MEMORIZED FROM MY CATECHISM.
Jesus was a lucky baby to have Joseph when his real father, God, was busy taking care of the whole world.
AND THEN...
RING!
801-7090
DEEP IN MY CHRISTMAS REVERIE, I HAD FORGOTTEN ALL ABOUT CALLING MY MOTHER AT WORK.
THERE YOU ARE! I WAS READY TO CALL THE POLICE!
Sorry, Mamma.
DID YOU EAT SOMETHING? ARE YOU DOING YOUR HOMEWORK? IS THE DOOR LOCKED?
COOKIE! WHY DON'T YOU ANSWER ME? YOU MUST BE WATCHING TELEVISION.
Guess what, Mamma? It's snowing!
If you don't start behaving, I'm going to have to hire a babysitter, and you know we don't have money for that.

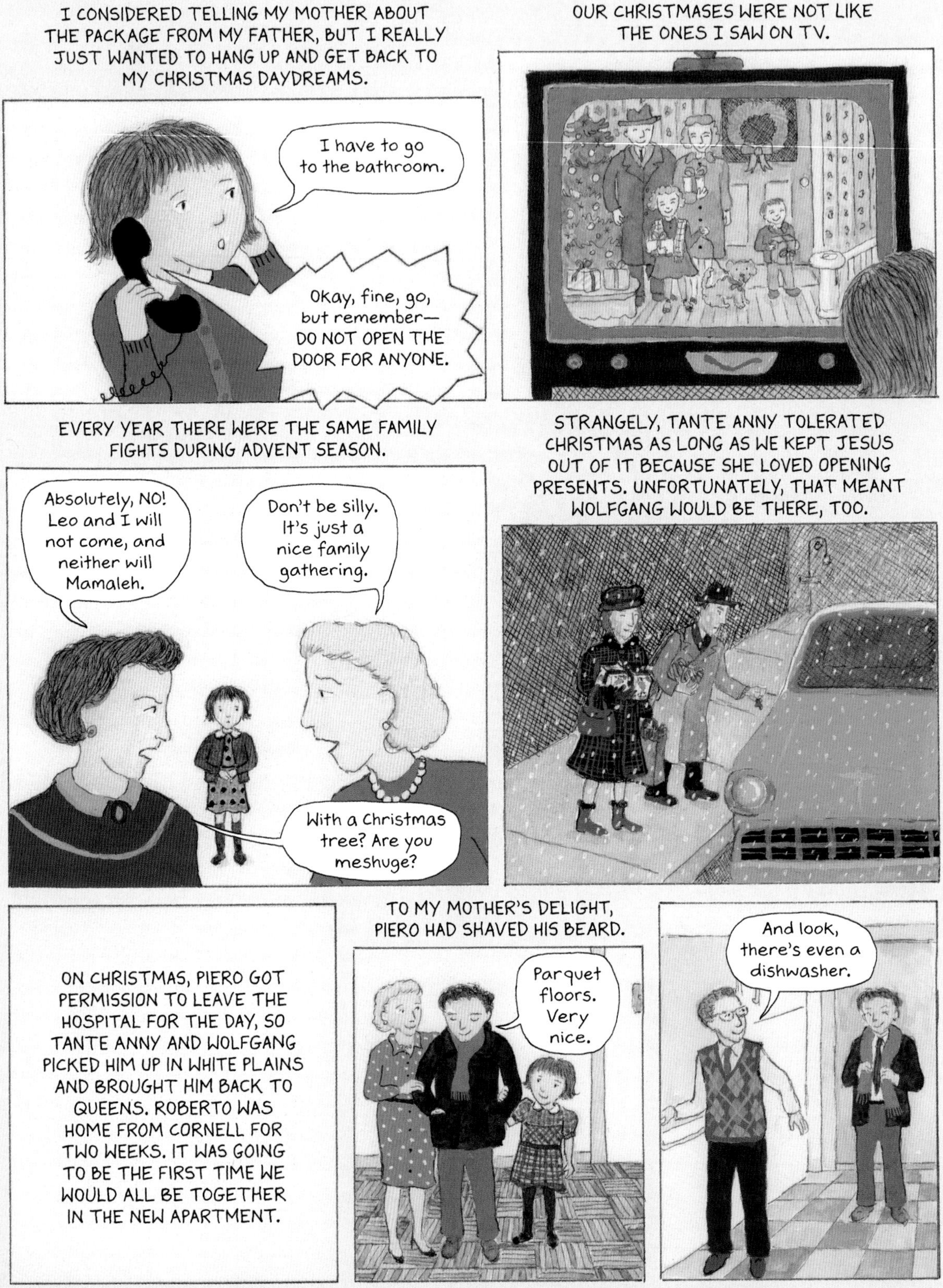
I CONSIDERED TELLING MY MOTHER ABOUT THE PACKAGE FROM MY FATHER, BUT I REALLY JUST WANTED TO HANG UP AND GET BACK TO MY CHRISTMAS DAYDREAMS.
I have to go to the bathroom.
Okay, fine, go, but remember— DO NOT OPEN THE DOOR FOR ANYONE.
OUR CHRISTMASES WERE NOT LIKE THE ONES I SAW ON TV.
EVERY YEAR THERE WERE THE SAME FAMILY FIGHTS DURING ADVENT SEASON.
Absolutely, NO! Leo and I will not come, and neither will Mamaleh.
Don't be silly. It's just a nice family gathering.
With a Christmas tree? Are you meshuge?
STRANGELY, TANTE ANNY TOLERATED CHRISTMAS AS LONG AS WE KEPT JESUS OUT OF IT BECAUSE SHE LOVED OPENING PRESENTS. UNFORTUNATELY, THAT MEANT WOLFGANG WOULD BE THERE, TOO.
ON CHRISTMAS, PIERO GOT PERMISSION TO LEAVE THE HOSPITAL FOR THE DAY, SO TANTE ANNY AND WOLFGANG PICKED HIM UP IN WHITE PLAINS AND BROUGHT HIM BACK TO QUEENS. ROBERTO WAS HOME FROM CORNELL FOR TWO WEEKS. IT WAS GOING TO BE THE FIRST TIME WE WOULD ALL BE TOGETHER IN THE NEW APARTMENT.
TO MY MOTHER'S DELIGHT, PIERO HAD SHAVED HIS BEARD.
Parquet floors. Very nice.
And look, there's even a dishwasher.

WE OPENED GIFTS. I SAVED THE ONE FROM MY FATHER FOR LAST.

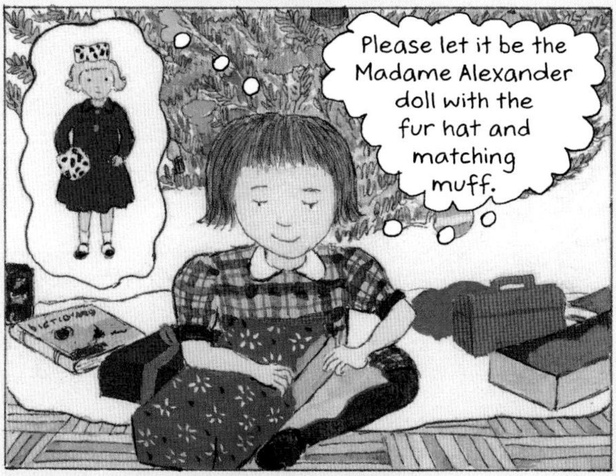
Please let it be the Madame Alexander doll with the fur hat and matching muff.

IT WAS A WINTER COAT.

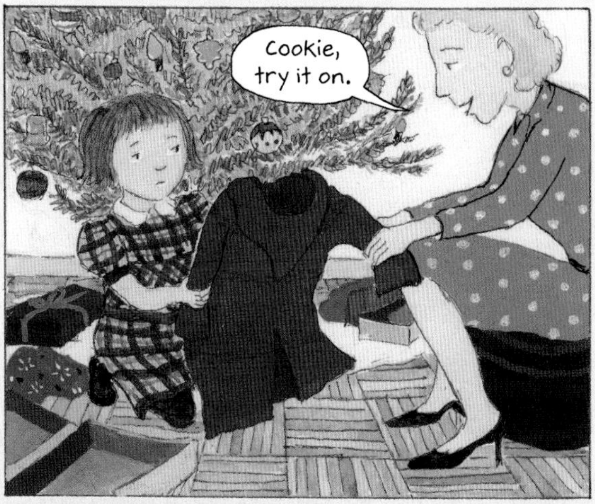
Cookie, try it on.

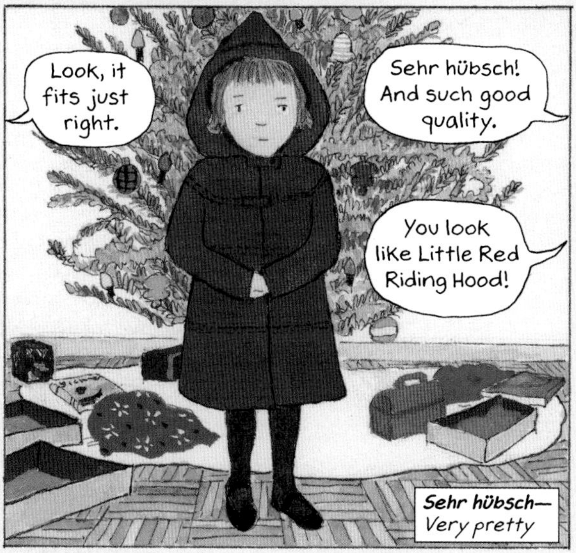
Look, it fits just right.
Sehr hübsch! And such good quality.
You look like Little Red Riding Hood!

Sehr hübsch—
Very pretty

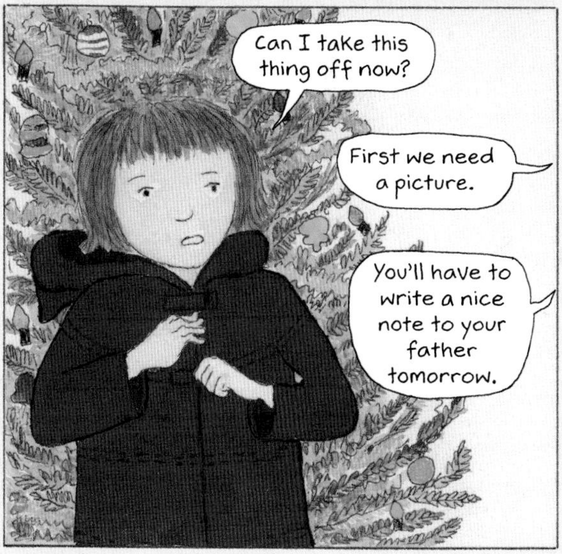
Can I take this thing off now?
First we need a picture.
You'll have to write a nice note to your father tomorrow.

OVER DINNER, PIERO HAD AN ANNOUNCEMENT TO MAKE.

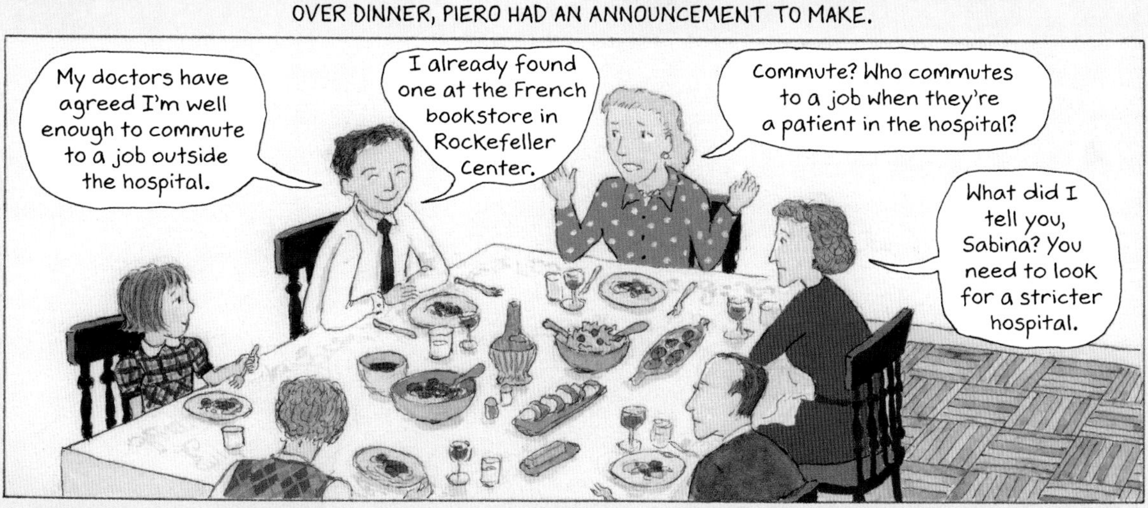
My doctors have agreed I'm well enough to commute to a job outside the hospital.
I already found one at the French bookstore in Rockefeller Center.
Commute? Who commutes to a job when they're a patient in the hospital?
What did I tell you, Sabina? You need to look for a stricter hospital.

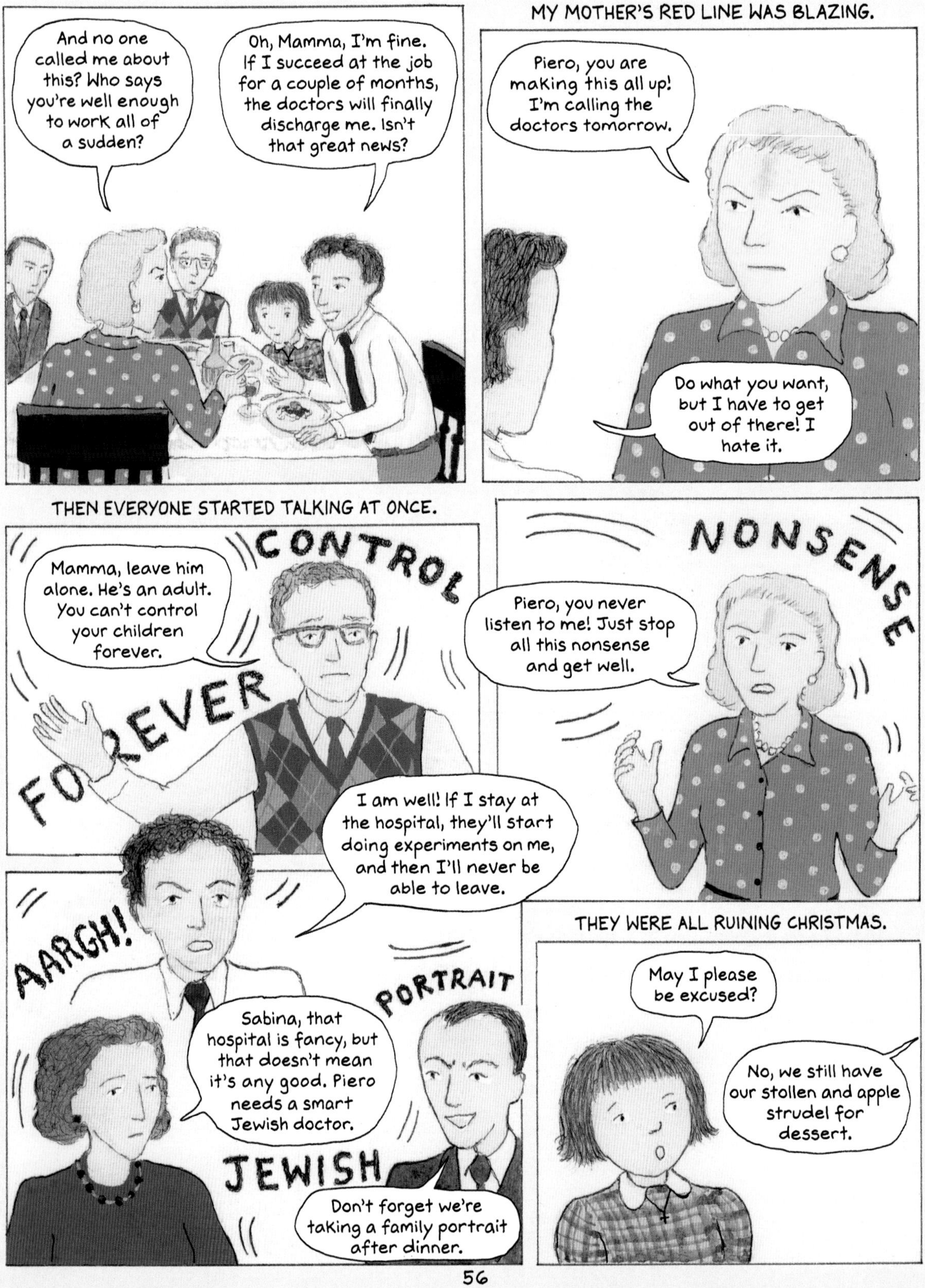
And no one called me about this? Who says you're well enough to work all of a sudden?
Oh, Mamma, I'm fine. If I succeed at the job for a couple of months, the doctors will finally discharge me. Isn't that great news?
MY MOTHER'S RED LINE WAS BLAZING.
Piero, you are making this all up! I'm calling the doctors tomorrow.
Do what you want, but I have to get out of there! I hate it.
THEN EVERYONE STARTED TALKING AT ONCE.
CONTROL
Mamma, leave him alone. He's an adult. You can't control your children forever.
FOREVER
NONSENSE
Piero, you never listen to me! Just stop all this nonsense and get well.
I am well! If I stay at the hospital, they'll start doing experiments on me, and then I'll never be able to leave.
AARGH!
PORTRAIT
Sabina, that hospital is fancy, but that doesn't mean it's any good. Piero needs a smart Jewish doctor.
JEWISH
Don't forget we're taking a family portrait after dinner.
THEY WERE ALL RUINING CHRISTMAS.
May I please be excused?
No, we still have our stollen and apple strudel for dessert.

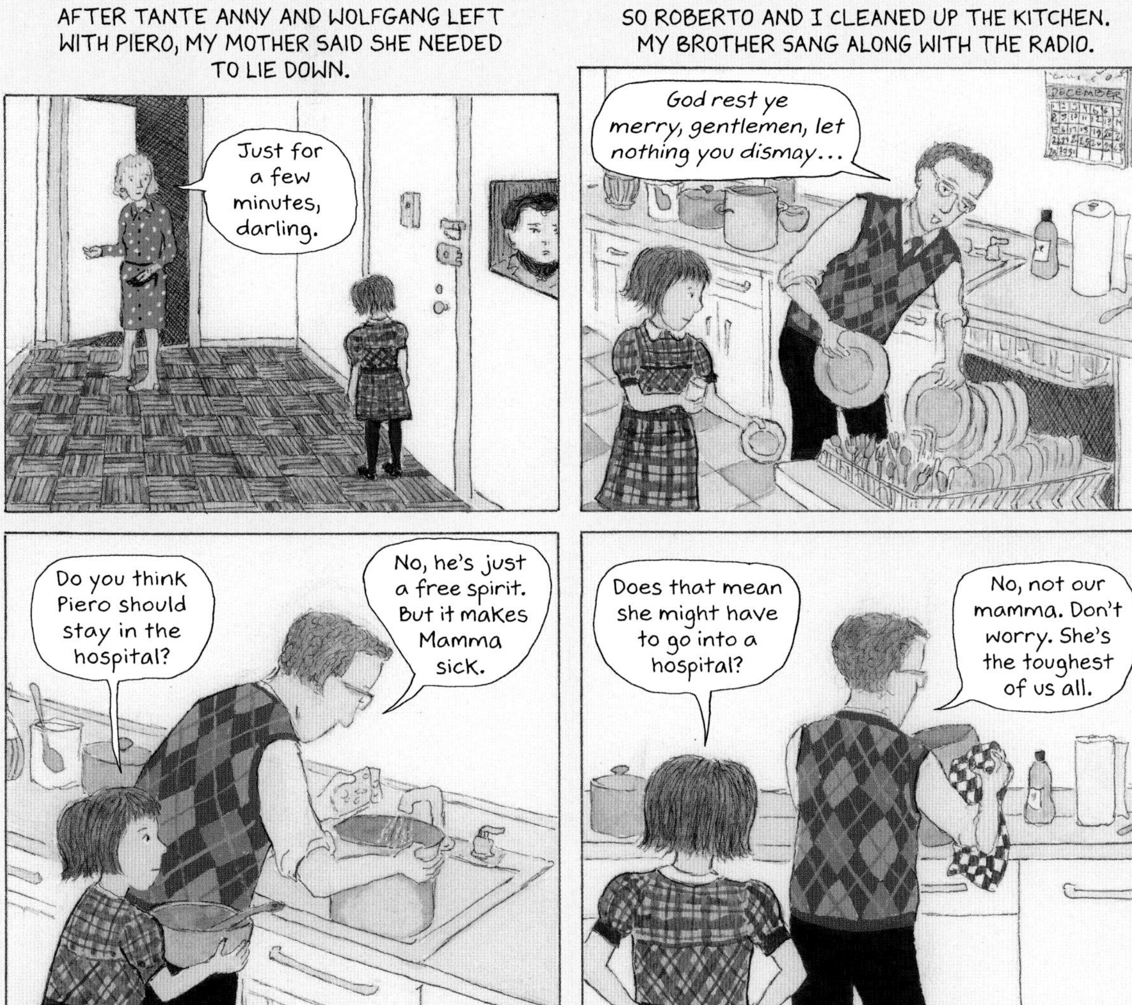
AFTER TANTE ANNY AND WOLFGANG LEFT WITH PIERO, MY MOTHER SAID SHE NEEDED TO LIE DOWN.
Just for a few minutes, darling.
SO ROBERTO AND I CLEANED UP THE KITCHEN. MY BROTHER SANG ALONG WITH THE RADIO.
God rest ye merry, gentlemen, let nothing you dismay…
Do you think Piero should stay in the hospital?
No, he's just a free spirit. But it makes Mamma sick.
Does that mean she might have to go into a hospital?
No, not our mamma. Don't worry. She's the toughest of us all.
But why does she always get so upset about everything? Why does everyone in our family have to yell all the time? No one ever yells like that on *Father Knows Best* or *Lassie*.
Cookie, those are TV shows! They're just make-believe stories someone dreamed up.
This, on the other hand, is real life.

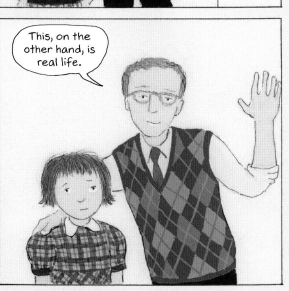

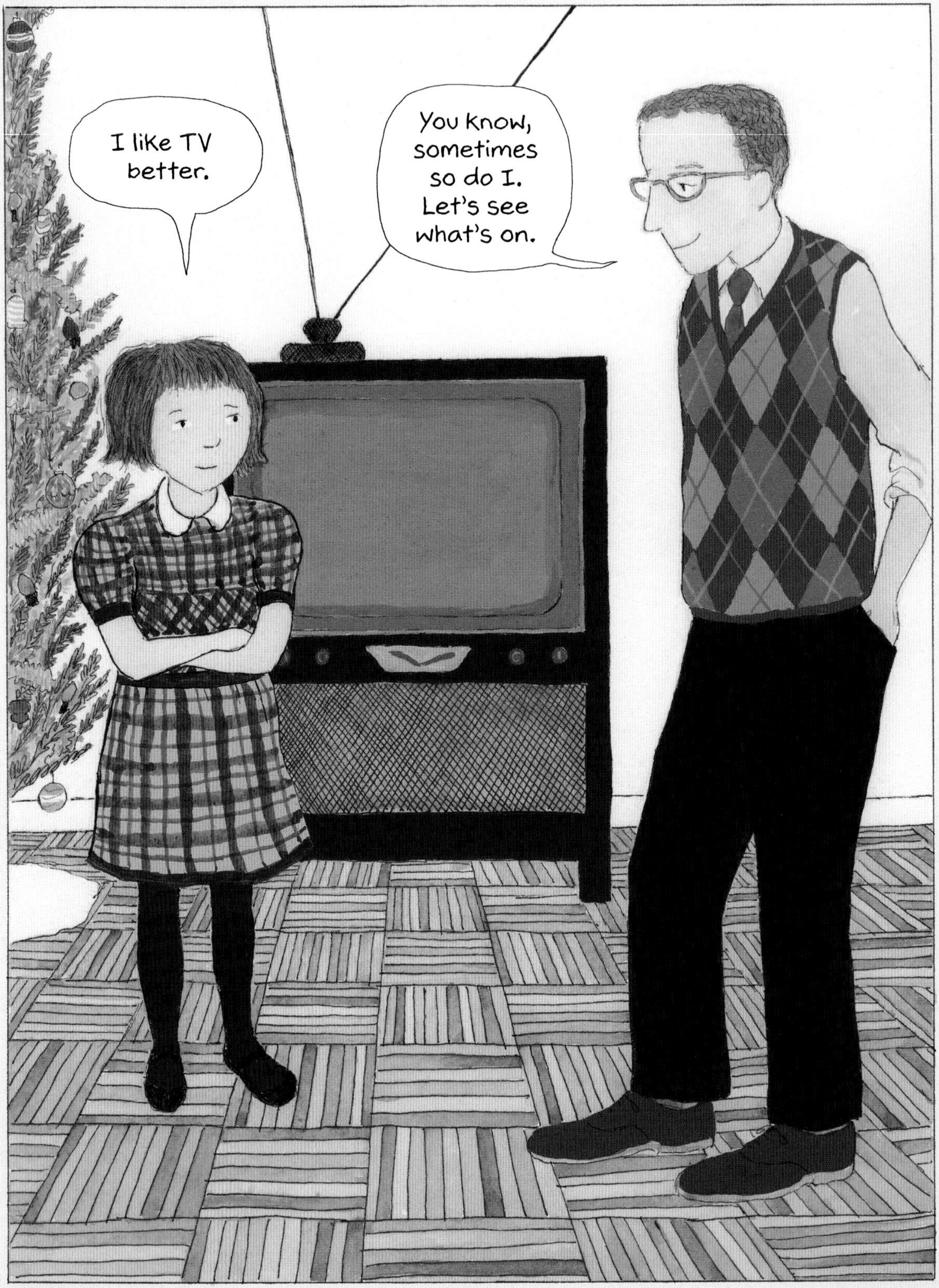
I like TV better.
You know, sometimes so do I. Let's see what's on.

SIX

Command Performance

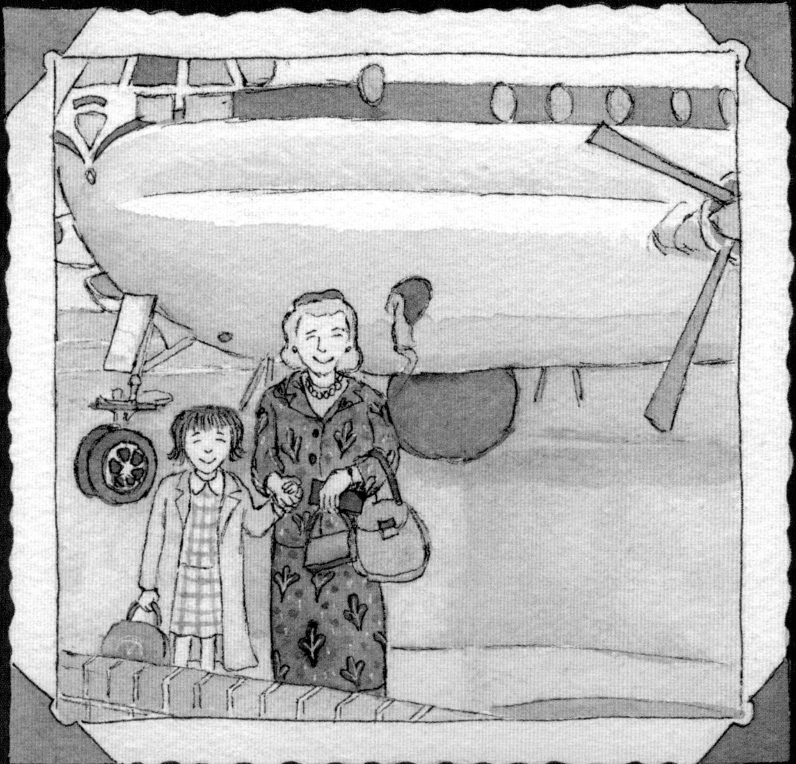

1958

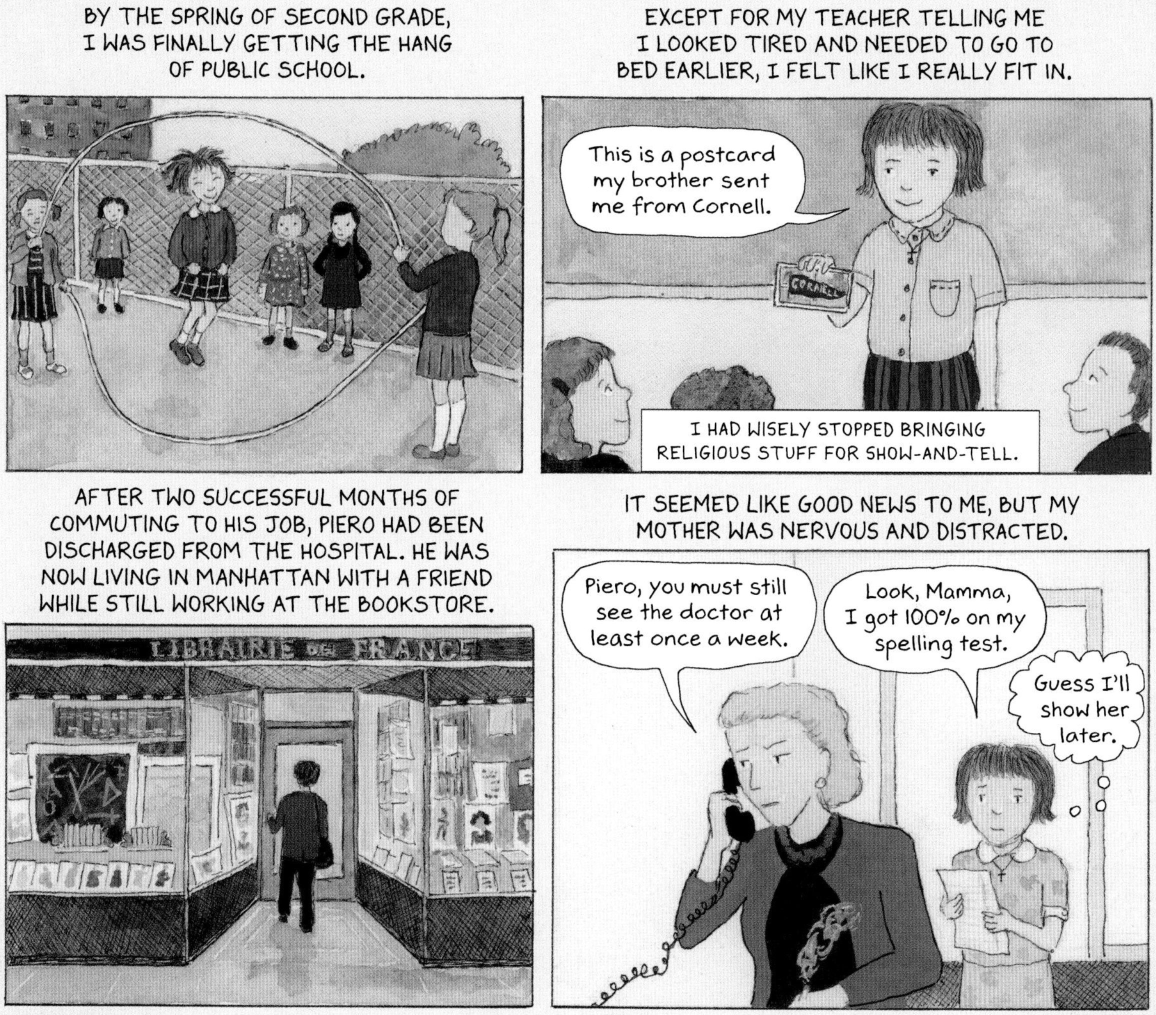
BY THE SPRING OF SECOND GRADE, I WAS FINALLY GETTING THE HANG OF PUBLIC SCHOOL.
EXCEPT FOR MY TEACHER TELLING ME I LOOKED TIRED AND NEEDED TO GO TO BED EARLIER, I FELT LIKE I REALLY FIT IN.
This is a postcard my brother sent me from Cornell.
CORNELL
I HAD WISELY STOPPED BRINGING RELIGIOUS STUFF FOR SHOW-AND-TELL.
AFTER TWO SUCCESSFUL MONTHS OF COMMUTING TO HIS JOB, PIERO HAD BEEN DISCHARGED FROM THE HOSPITAL. HE WAS NOW LIVING IN MANHATTAN WITH A FRIEND WHILE STILL WORKING AT THE BOOKSTORE.
LIBRAIRIE DE FRANCE
IT SEEMED LIKE GOOD NEWS TO ME, BUT MY MOTHER WAS NERVOUS AND DISTRACTED.
Piero, you must still see the doctor at least once a week.
Look, Mamma, I got 100% on my spelling test.
Guess I'll show her later.
THEN WITHOUT TELLING ANYONE, PIERO LEFT NEW YORK ON A FREIGHTER BOUND FOR EUROPE. I WAS THE FIRST TO FIND OUT.
Look, Mamma!
I got this card from Piero today. He's in Paris!
What? Your brother has no sense. He lives in a dream world. When I think of how he promised his father he'd follow in his footsteps and become a doctor, too.
Piero also sent a feather for my birthday. He says it came from an angel who reminded him of me.
Hmm...

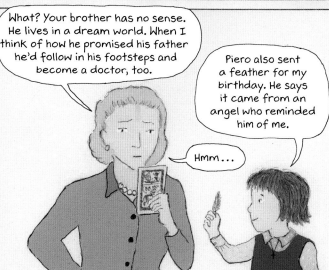

MORE OF PIERO'S LETTERS BEGAN TO ARRIVE FROM PARIS, BUT MY MOTHER FOUND LITTLE IN THEM TO EASE HER MIND.

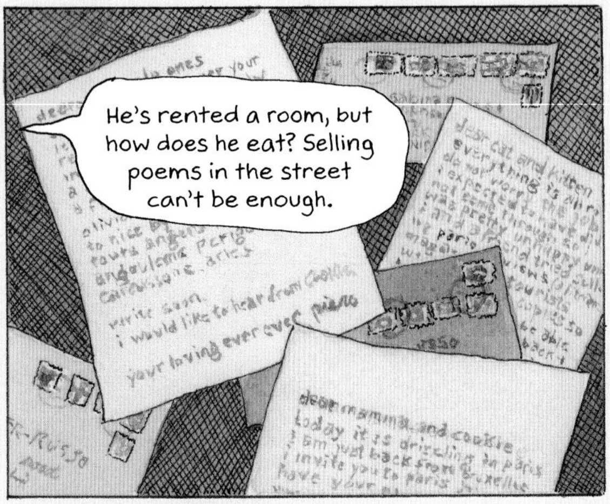
He's rented a room, but how does he eat? Selling poems in the street can't be enough.

AROUND THE SAME TIME, OMA HAD A STROKE. SHE WAS IN A HOSPITAL AND WOULD HAVE TO GO TO A NURSING HOME IN A FEW WEEKS.

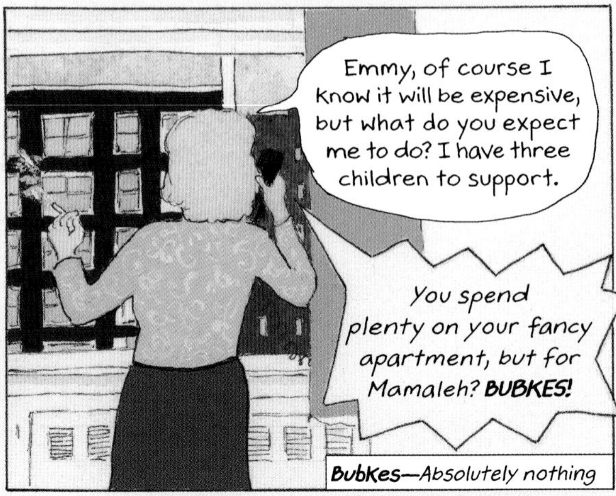
Emmy, of course I know it will be expensive, but what do you expect me to do? I have three children to support.
You spend plenty on your fancy apartment, but for Mamaleh? **BUBKES!**

Bubkes—*Absolutely nothing*

MY MOTHER'S NIGHTLY CRAMPS SEEMED TO GROW WORSE AND WORSE. IN THE MORNING IT WAS HARDER THAN EVER TO WAKE HER UP.

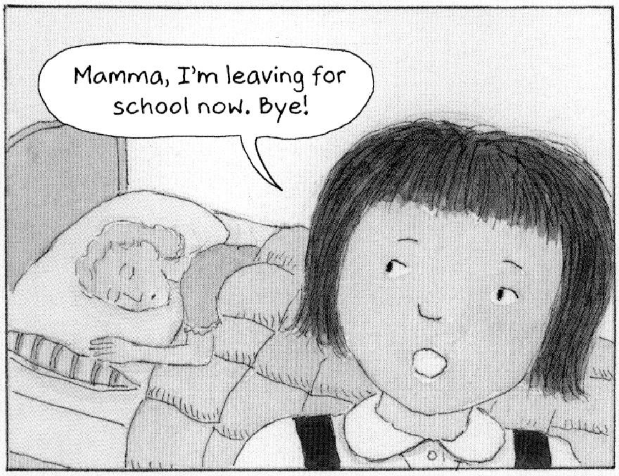
Mamma, I'm leaving for school now. Bye!

FINALLY, HER CHRONIC LATENESS GOT HER FIRED FROM ANOTHER SECRETARIAL JOB. AS USUAL, IN TIMES OF TROUBLE, I TURNED TO GOD.

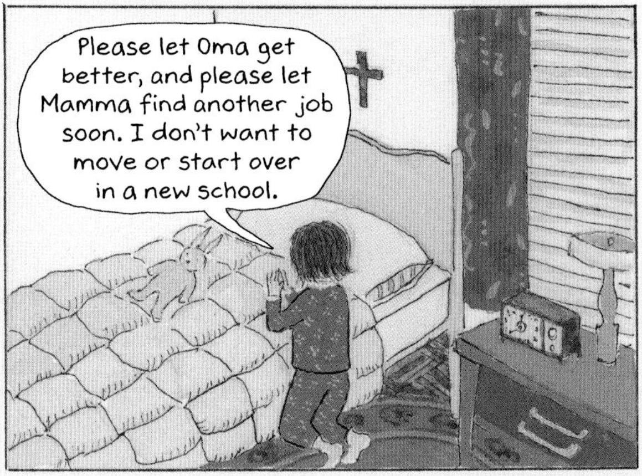
Please let Oma get better, and please let Mamma find another job soon. I don't want to move or start over in a new school.

MY MOTHER STUDIED THE CLASSIFIEDS AND WENT ON INTERVIEWS. SHE WROTE TO MY FATHER TO SEE IF HE COULD HELP OUT WITH A LITTLE EXTRA MONEY.

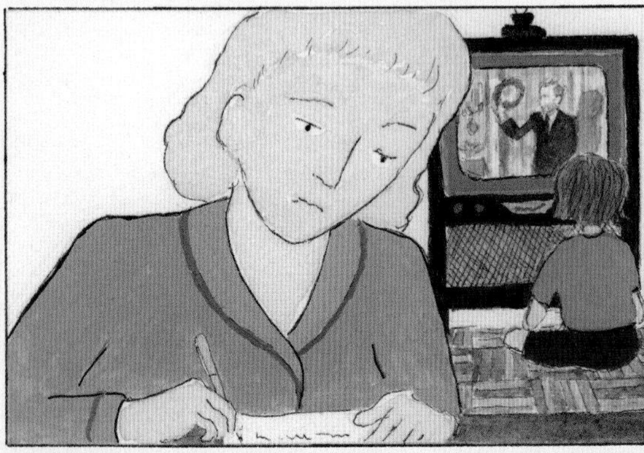

HIS RESPONSE CAME AS A BIG SURPRISE.

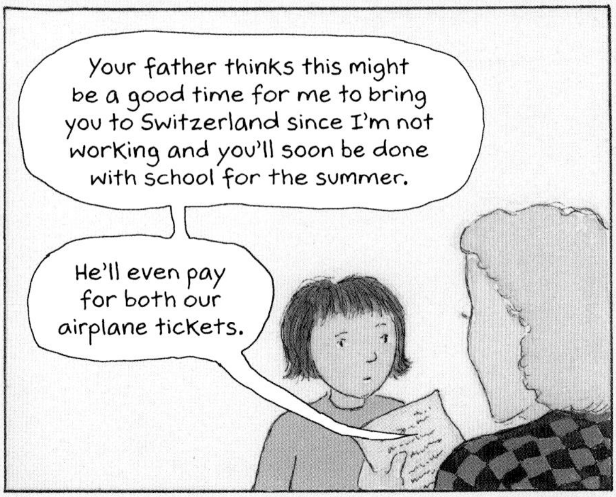
Your father thinks this might be a good time for me to bring you to Switzerland since I'm not working and you'll soon be done with school for the summer.
He'll even pay for both our airplane tickets.

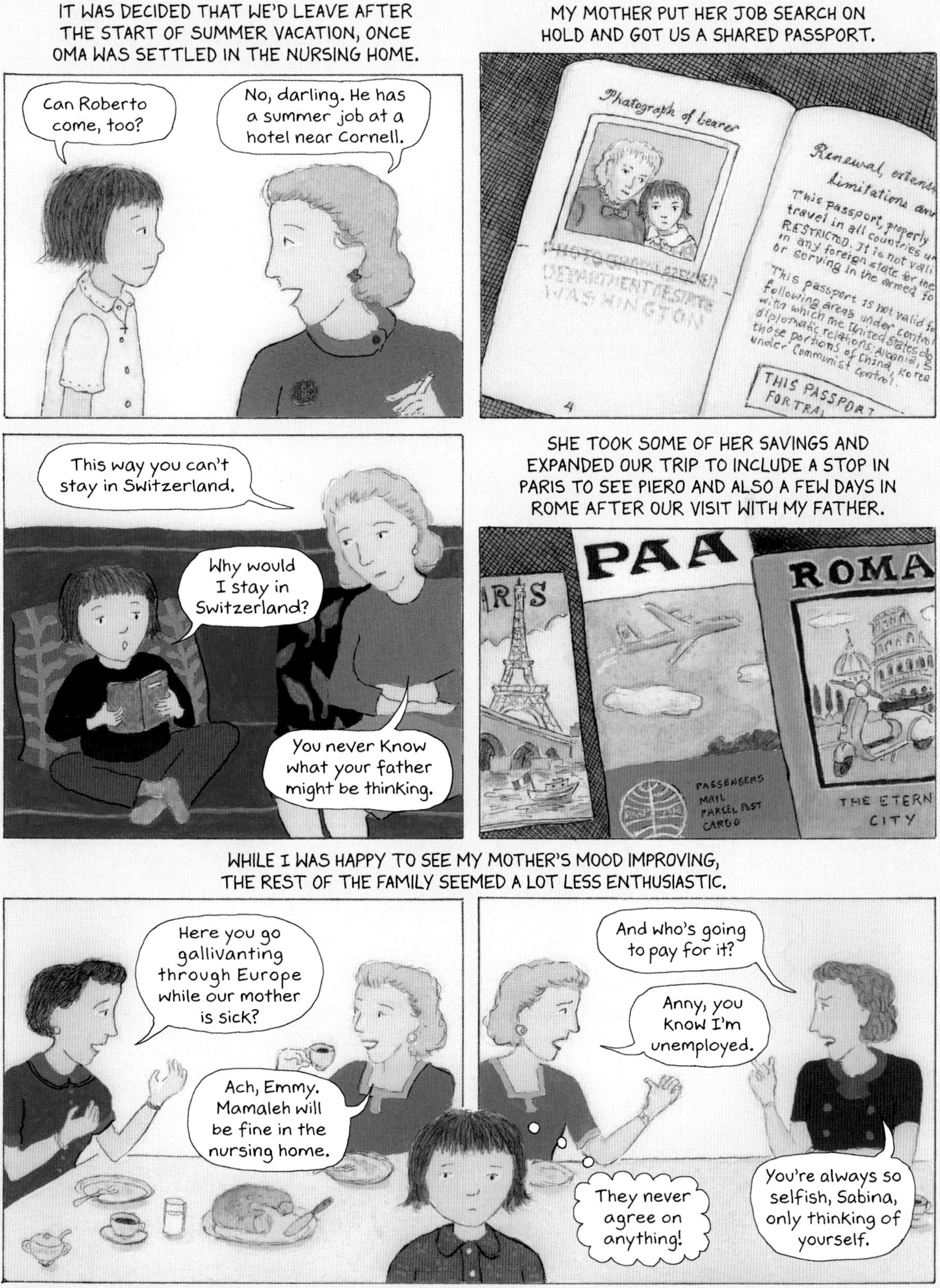
IT WAS DECIDED THAT WE'D LEAVE AFTER THE START OF SUMMER VACATION, ONCE OMA WAS SETTLED IN THE NURSING HOME.
Can Roberto come, too?
No, darling. He has a summer job at a hotel near Cornell.
MY MOTHER PUT HER JOB SEARCH ON HOLD AND GOT US A SHARED PASSPORT.
Photograph of bearer
This way you can't stay in Switzerland.
Why would I stay in Switzerland?
You never know what your father might be thinking.
SHE TOOK SOME OF HER SAVINGS AND EXPANDED OUR TRIP TO INCLUDE A STOP IN PARIS TO SEE PIERO AND ALSO A FEW DAYS IN ROME AFTER OUR VISIT WITH MY FATHER.
PAA
ROMA
PASSENGERS MAIL PARCEL POST CARGO
THE ETERN CITY
WHILE I WAS HAPPY TO SEE MY MOTHER'S MOOD IMPROVING, THE REST OF THE FAMILY SEEMED A LOT LESS ENTHUSIASTIC.
Here you go gallivanting through Europe while our mother is sick?
Ach, Emmy. Mamaleh will be fine in the nursing home.
And who's going to pay for it?
Anny, you know I'm unemployed.
They never agree on anything!
You're always so selfish, Sabina, only thinking of yourself.

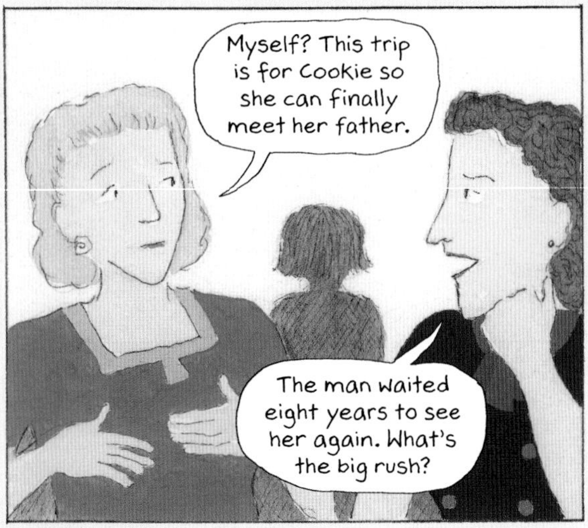
Myself? This trip is for Cookie so she can finally meet her father.
The man waited eight years to see her again. What's the big rush?

I HAD TO AGREE WITH TANTE ANNY. WHY WAS MY FATHER SUDDENLY SO EAGER TO SEE ME?

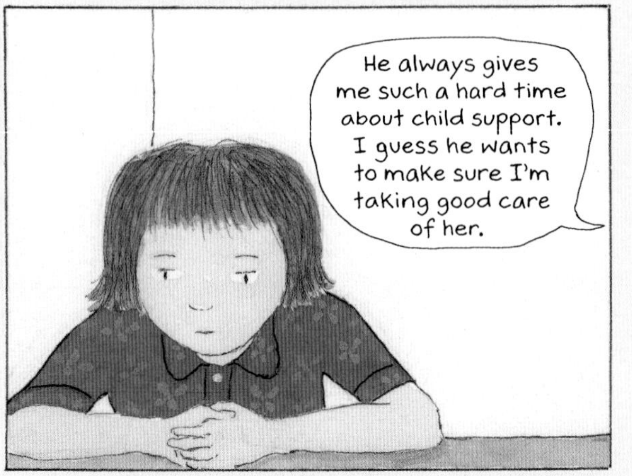
He always gives me such a hard time about child support. I guess he wants to make sure I'm taking good care of her.

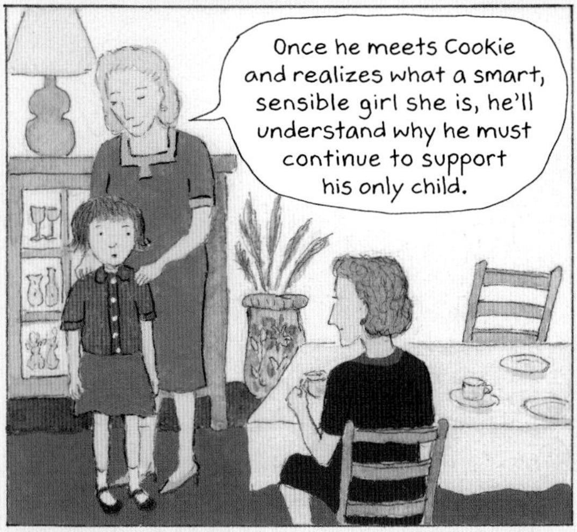
Once he meets Cookie and realizes what a smart, sensible girl she is, he'll understand why he must continue to support his only child.

ALL OF A SUDDEN, THE SUCCESS OF OUR TRIP SEEMED TO HINGE ON MY PERFORMANCE. IT REMINDED ME OF MY INTERVIEW AT P.S. 196. WHAT IF I DIDN'T LIVE UP TO MY FATHER'S EXPECTATIONS? OR MAMMA'S? WHAT THEN?

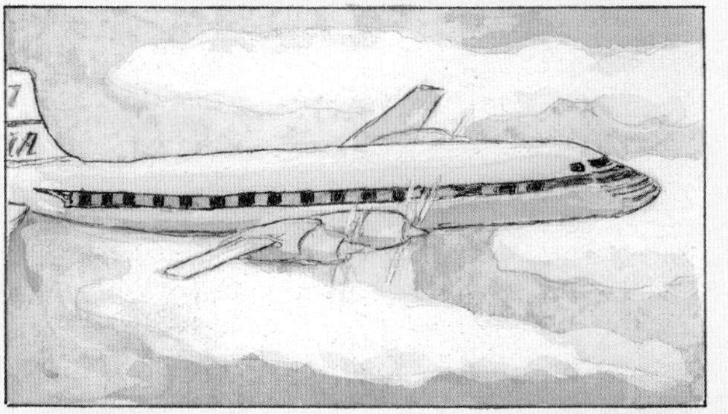

ON THE DAY WE ARRIVED IN PARIS, I WAS SICK. WHEN PIERO AND HIS GIRLFRIEND, OLIVIA, CAME TO OUR HOTEL, I WAS IN BED.

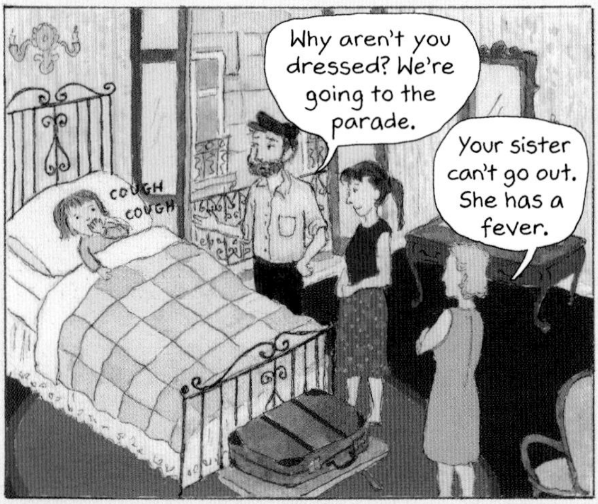
Why aren't you dressed? We're going to the parade.
COUGH
COUGH
Your sister can't go out. She has a fever.

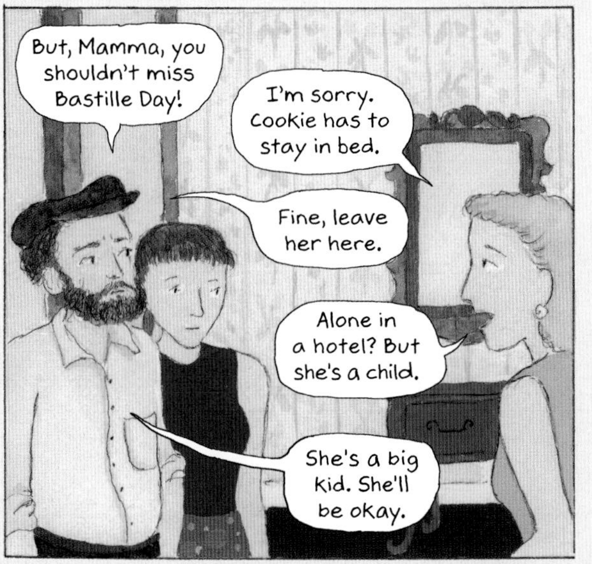
But, Mamma, you shouldn't miss Bastille Day!
I'm sorry. Cookie has to stay in bed.
Fine, leave her here.
Alone in a hotel? But she's a child.
She's a big kid. She'll be okay.

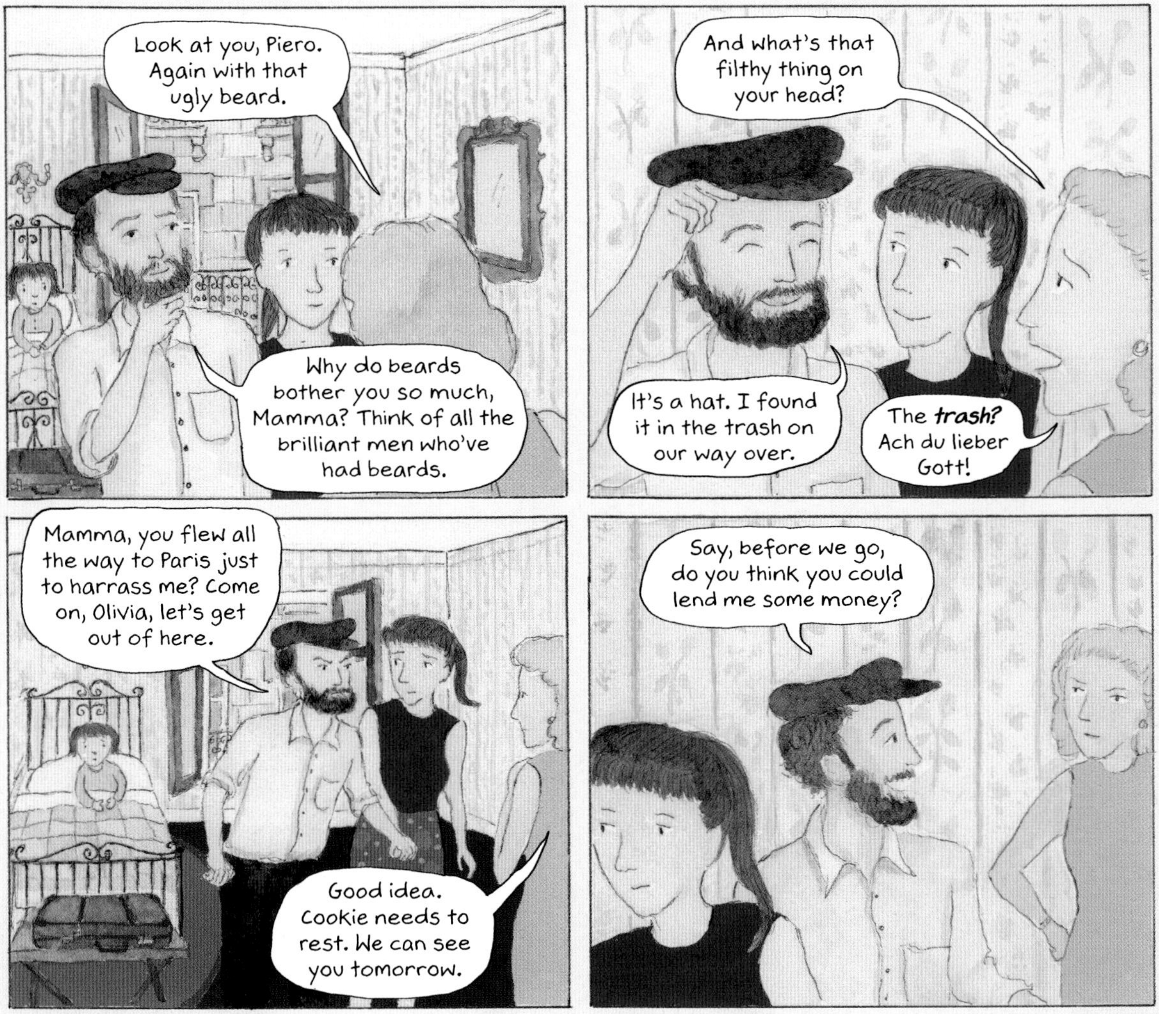
Look at you, Piero. Again with that ugly beard.
Why do beards bother you so much, Mamma? Think of all the brilliant men who've had beards.
And what's that filthy thing on your head?
It's a hat. I found it in the trash on our way over.
The ***trash?*** Ach du lieber Gott!
Mamma, you flew all the way to Paris just to harrass me? Come on, Olivia, let's get out of here.
Good idea. Cookie needs to rest. We can see you tomorrow.
Say, before we go, do you think you could lend me some money?

THE NEXT MORNING MY FEVER WAS GONE, SO MY MOTHER AND I TOOK A TAXI TO RUE DESCARTES.

PIERO LIVED ON THE TOP FLOOR.

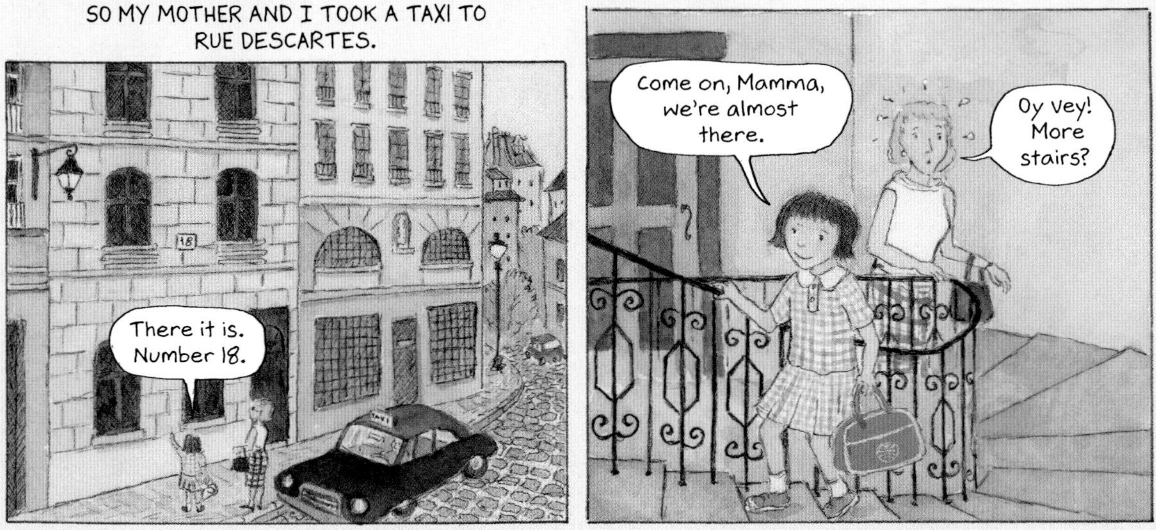
18
There it is. Number 18.
TAXI
Come on, Mamma, we're almost there.
Oy vey! More stairs?

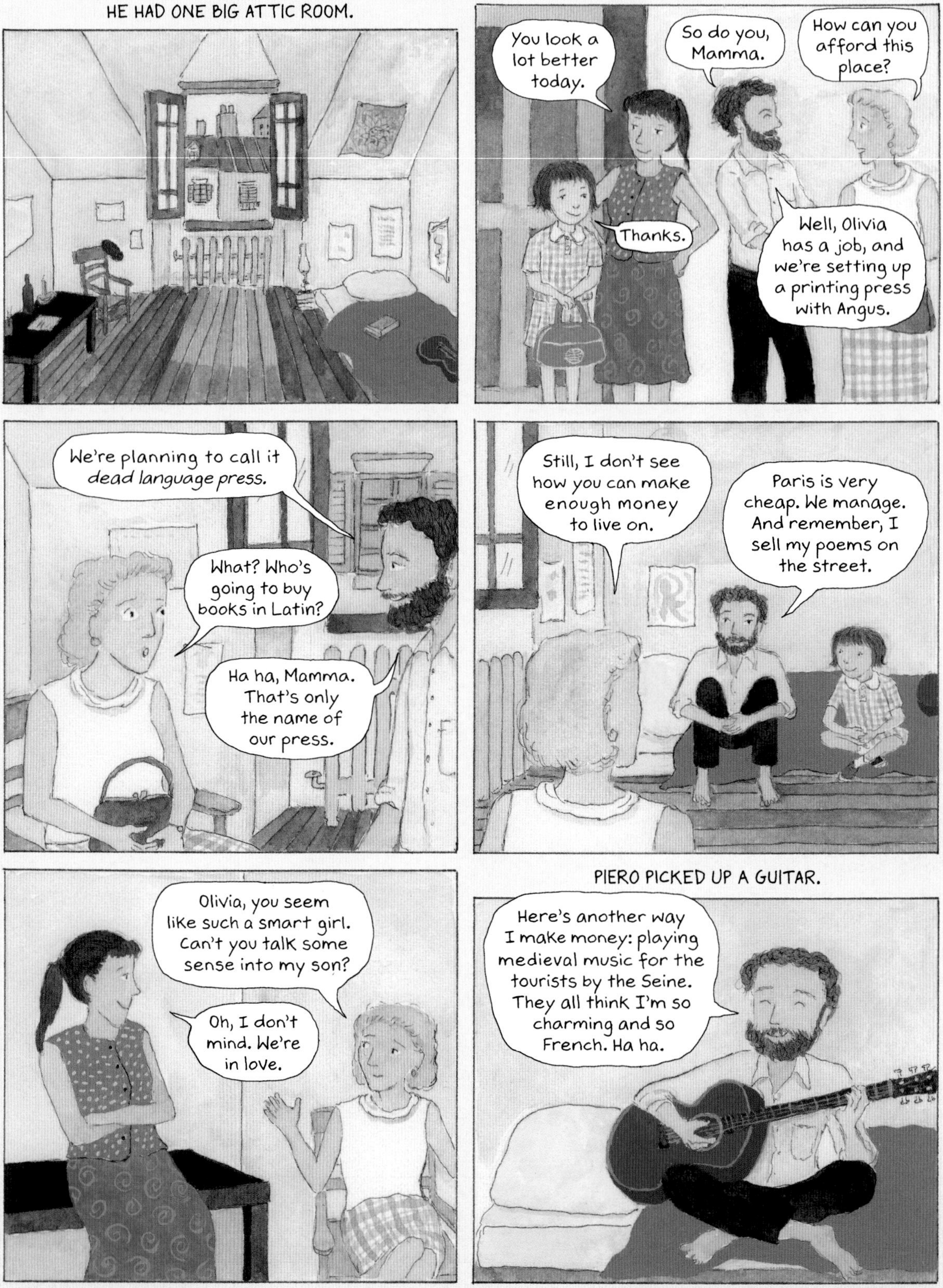
HE HAD ONE BIG ATTIC ROOM.
You look a lot better today.
So do you, Mamma.
How can you afford this place?
Thanks.
Well, Olivia has a job, and we're setting up a printing press with Angus.
We're planning to call it *dead language press.*
What? Who's going to buy books in Latin?
Ha ha, Mamma. That's only the name of our press.
Still, I don't see how you can make enough money to live on.
Paris is very cheap. We manage. And remember, I sell my poems on the street.
Olivia, you seem like such a smart girl. Can't you talk some sense into my son?
Oh, I don't mind. We're in love.
PIERO PICKED UP A GUITAR.
Here's another way I make money: playing medieval music for the tourists by the Seine. They all think I'm so charming and so French. Ha ha.

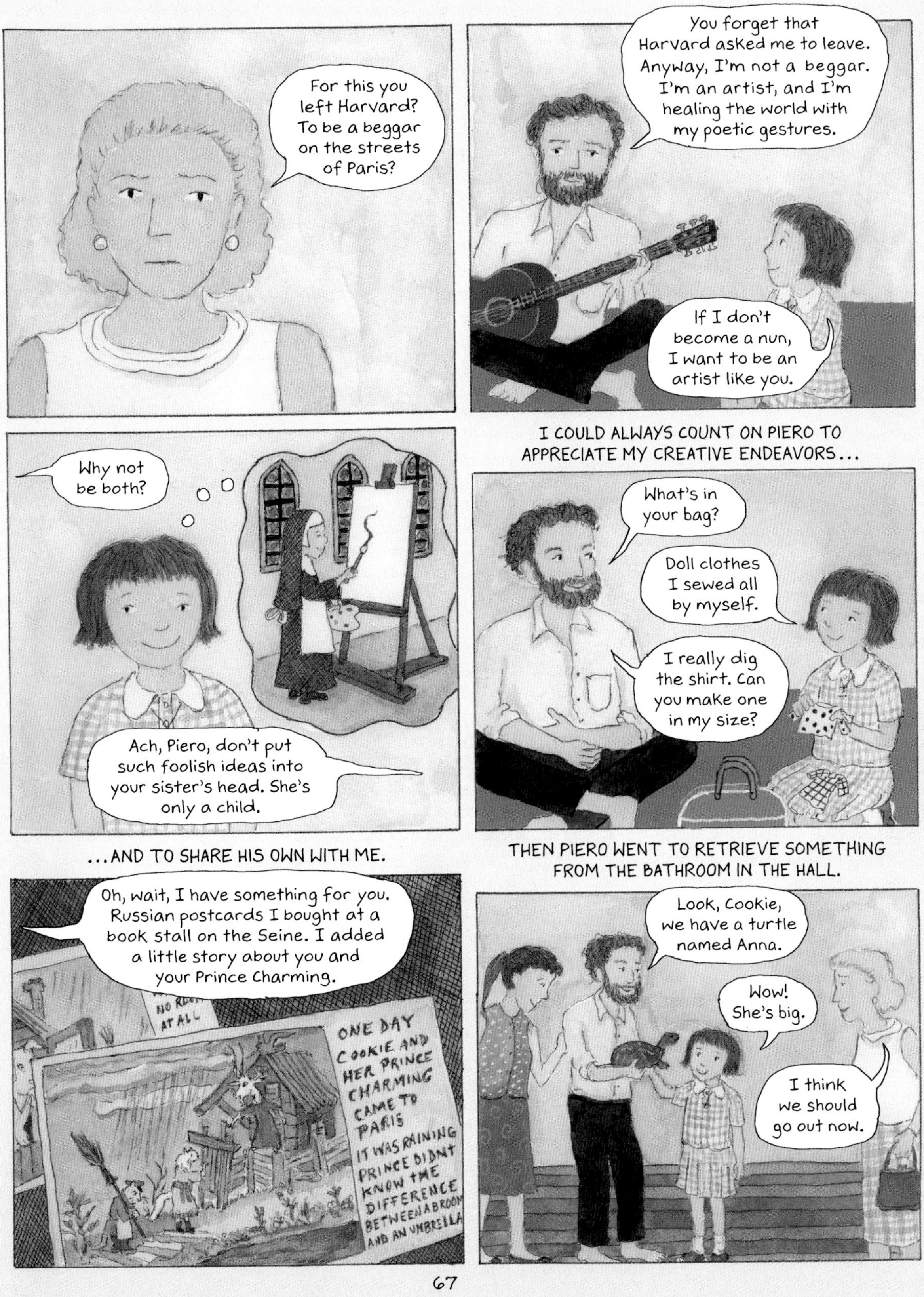
For this you left Harvard? To be a beggar on the streets of Paris?
You forget that Harvard asked me to leave. Anyway, I'm not a beggar. I'm an artist, and I'm healing the world with my poetic gestures.
If I don't become a nun, I want to be an artist like you.
Why not be both?
Ach, Piero, don't put such foolish ideas into your sister's head. She's only a child.
I COULD ALWAYS COUNT ON PIERO TO APPRECIATE MY CREATIVE ENDEAVORS...
What's in your bag?
Doll clothes I sewed all by myself.
I really dig the shirt. Can you make one in my size?
...AND TO SHARE HIS OWN WITH ME.
Oh, wait, I have something for you. Russian postcards I bought at a book stall on the Seine. I added a little story about you and your Prince Charming.
ONE DAY COOKIE AND HER PRINCE CHARMING CAME TO PARIS
IT WAS RAINING PRINCE DIDNT KNOW THE DIFFERENCE BETWEEN A BROOM AND AN UMBRELLA
THEN PIERO WENT TO RETRIEVE SOMETHING FROM THE BATHROOM IN THE HALL.
Look, Cookie, we have a turtle named Anna.
Wow! She's big.
I think we should go out now.

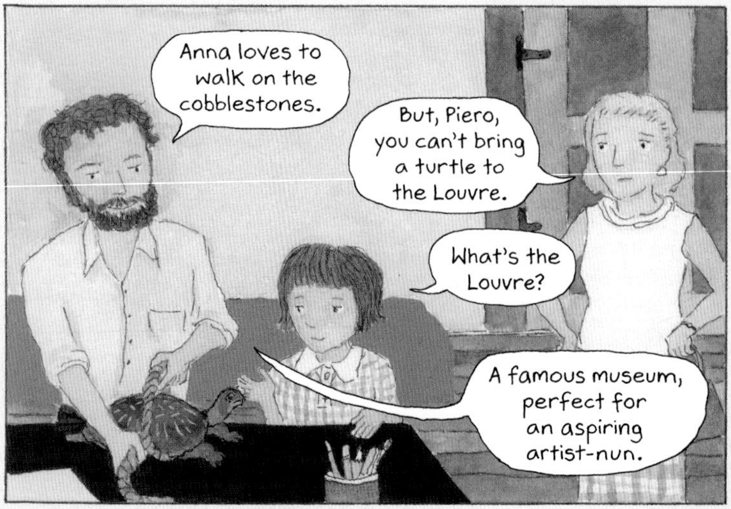
Anna loves to walk on the cobblestones.
But, Piero, you can't bring a turtle to the Louvre.
What's the Louvre?
A famous museum, perfect for an aspiring artist-nun.

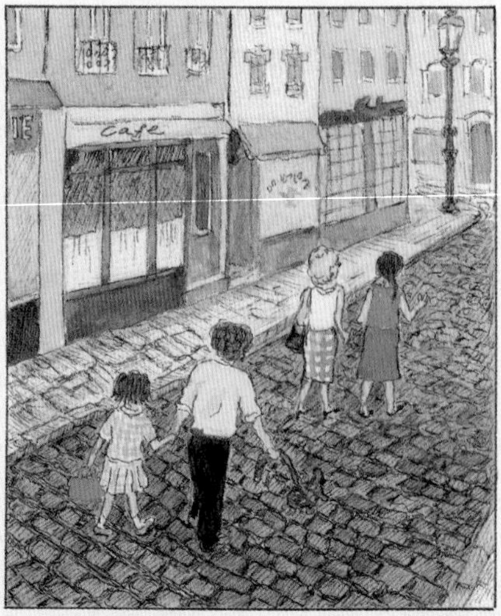
Cafe

AT THE LOUVRE:

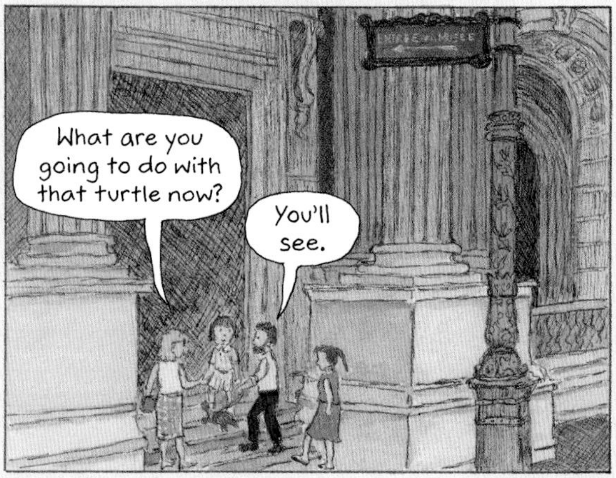
What are you going to do with that turtle now?
You'll see.

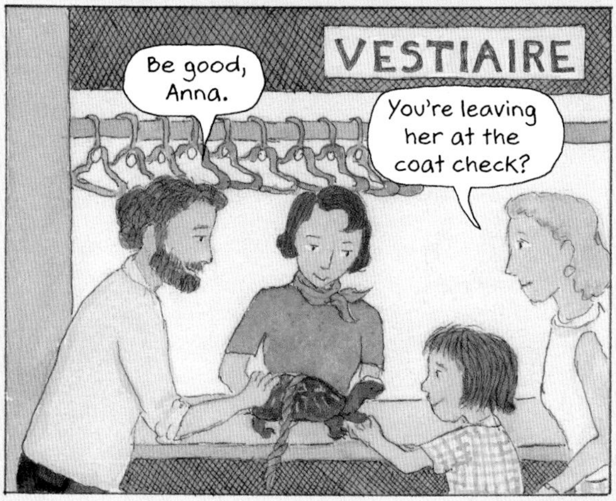
VESTIAIRE
Be good, Anna.
You're leaving her at the coat check?

MY BROTHER LED US TO THE GRANDE GALERIE. ALL AROUND, PEOPLE WERE TALKING IN WHISPERS.

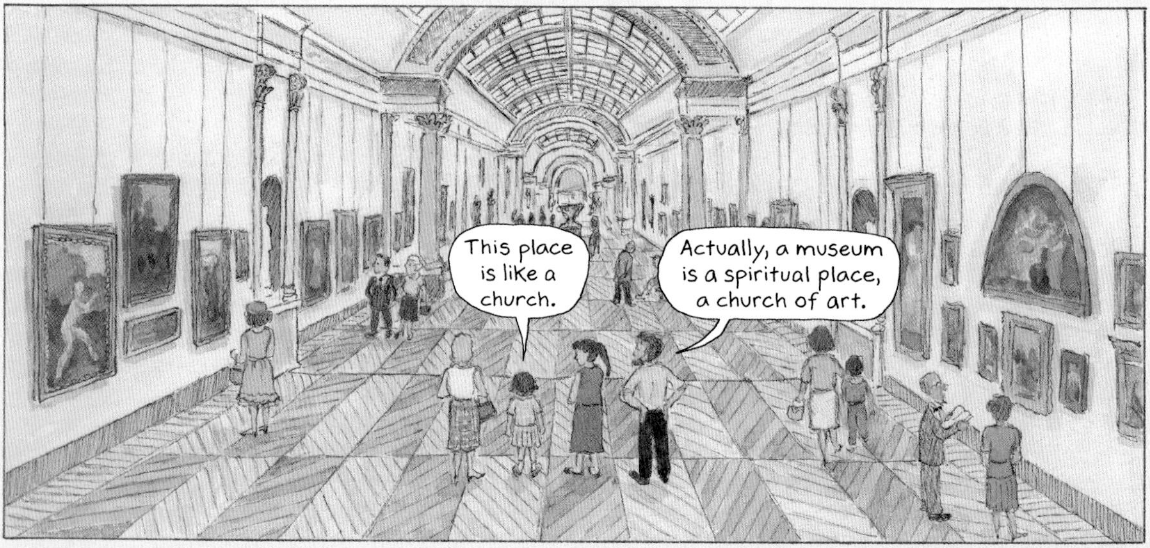
This place is like a church.
Actually, a museum is a spiritual place, a church of art.

MOVING FROM PAINTING TO PAINTING, MY BROTHER AND I ATTRACTED A SMALL AUDIENCE.

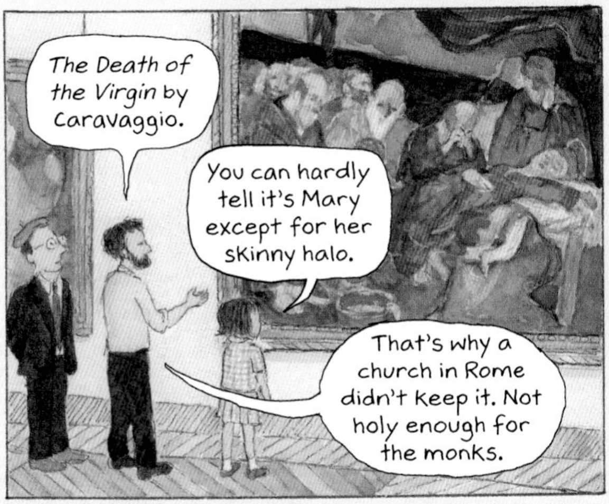

The Death of the Virgin by Caravaggio.
You can hardly tell it's Mary except for her skinny halo.
That's why a church in Rome didn't keep it. Not holy enough for the monks.

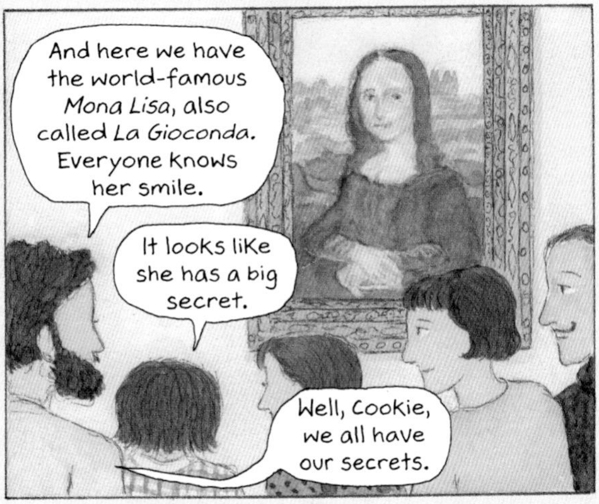

And here we have the world-famous *Mona Lisa*, also called *La Gioconda*. Everyone knows her smile.
It looks like she has a big secret.
Well, Cookie, we all have our secrets.

PIERO WAS OBVIOUSLY THE SMARTEST PERSON IN THE WHOLE MUSEUM.

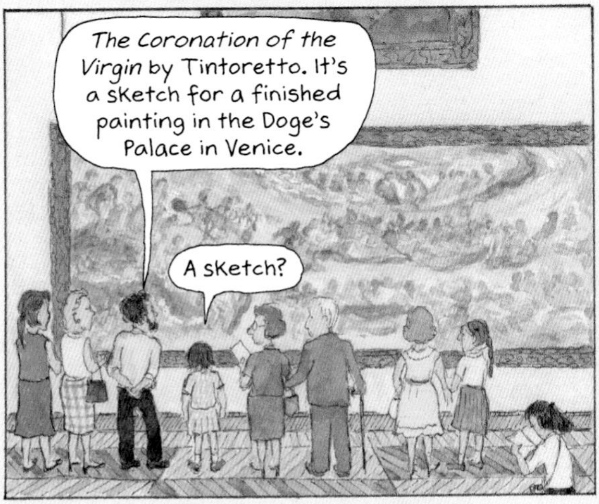

The Coronation of the Virgin by Tintoretto. It's a sketch for a finished painting in the Doge's Palace in Venice.
A sketch?

AND HE MADE ME FEEL PRETTY SMART, TOO.

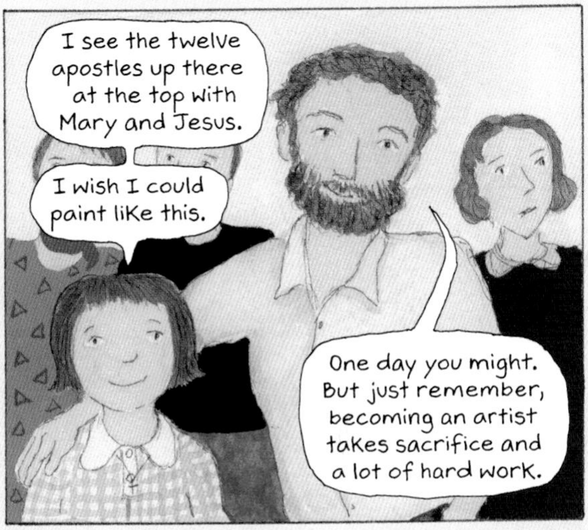

I see the twelve apostles up there at the top with Mary and Jesus.
I wish I could paint like this.
One day you might. But just remember, becoming an artist takes sacrifice and a lot of hard work.

I WONDERED WHY WE COULDN'T JUST SKIP GENEVA AND ROME, AND SPEND THE REST OF THE SUMMER IN PARIS.

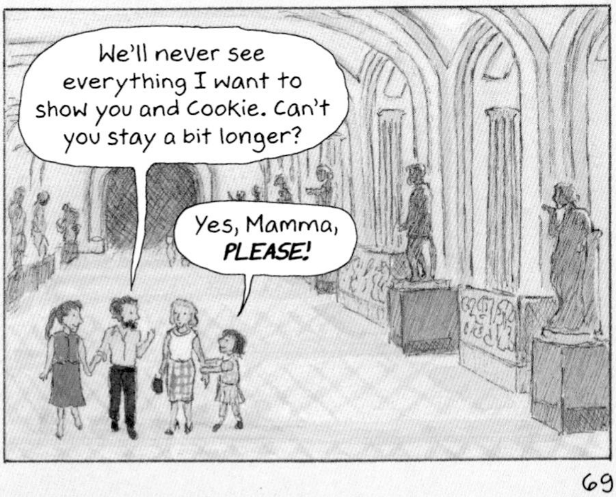

We'll never see everything I want to show you and Cookie. Can't you stay a bit longer?
Yes, Mamma, ***PLEASE!***

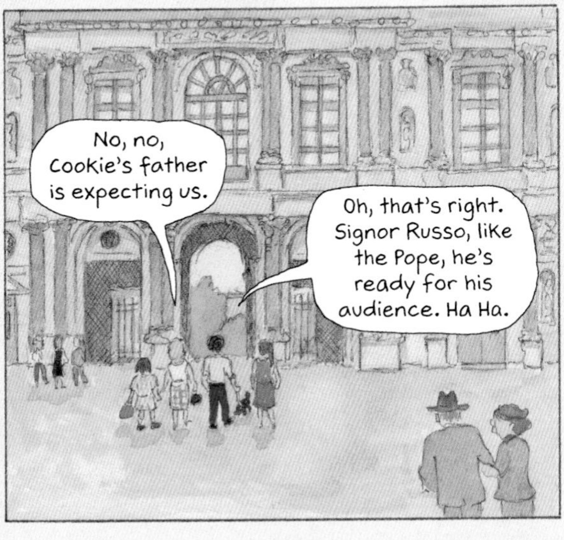

No, no, Cookie's father is expecting us.
Oh, that's right. Signor Russo, like the Pope, he's ready for his audience. Ha Ha.

AND SO THE NEXT WEEKEND WE WERE ON A PLANE HEADING TO SWITZERLAND.
IT WAS FINALLY TIME FOR MY COMMAND PERFORMANCE.

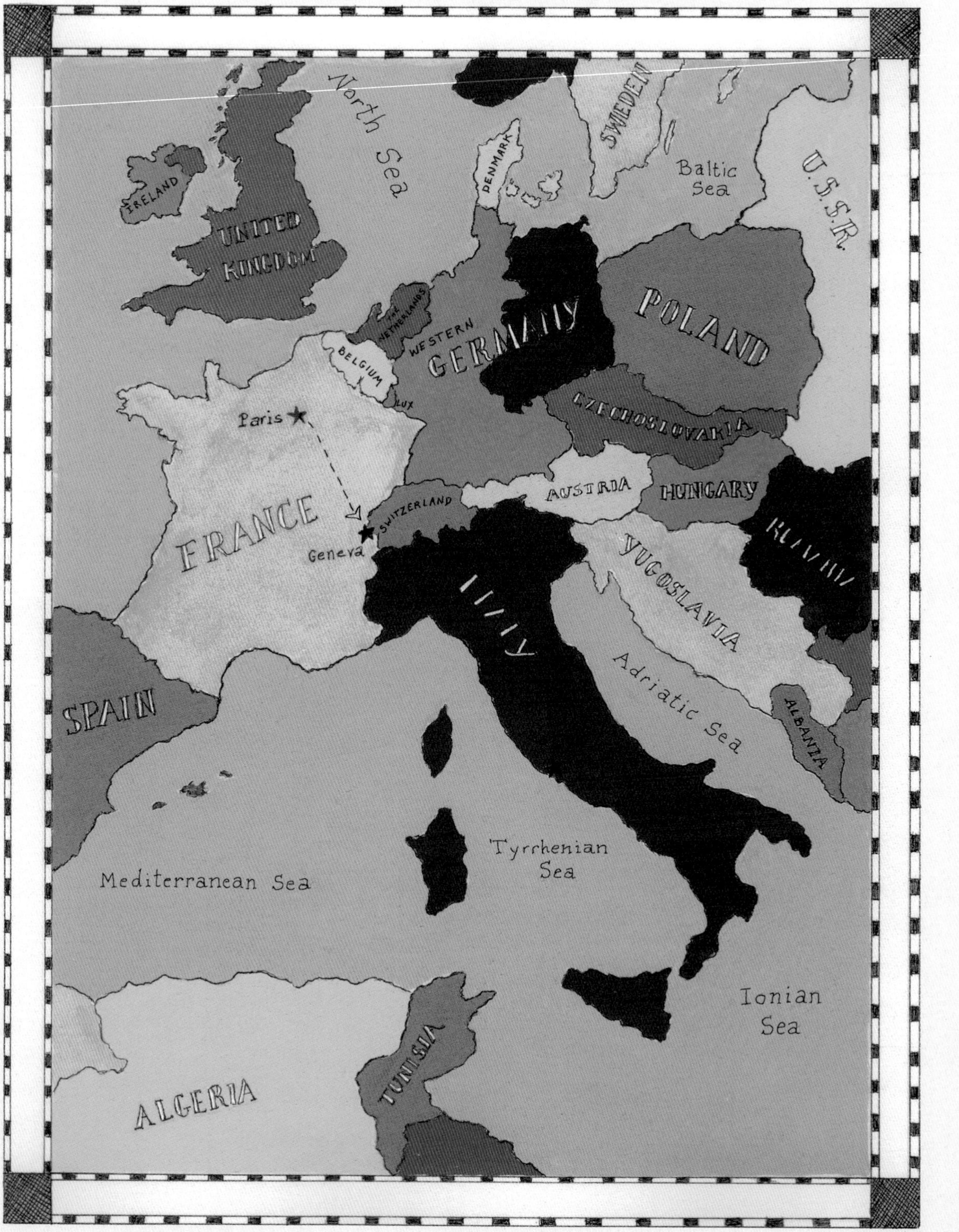
North Sea
SWEDEN
DENMARK
Baltic Sea
U.S.S.R.
IRELAND
UNITED KINGDOM
THE NETHERLANDS
BELGIUM
LUX
WESTERN GERMANY
POLAND
CZECHOSLOVAKIA
Paris
FRANCE
Geneva
SWITZERLAND
AUSTRIA
HUNGARY
YUGOSLAVIA
Adriatic Sea
ALBANIA
SPAIN
Mediterranean Sea
Tyrrhenian Sea
Ionian Sea
TUNISIA
ALGERIA

SEVEN

The Man in the Gray Suit

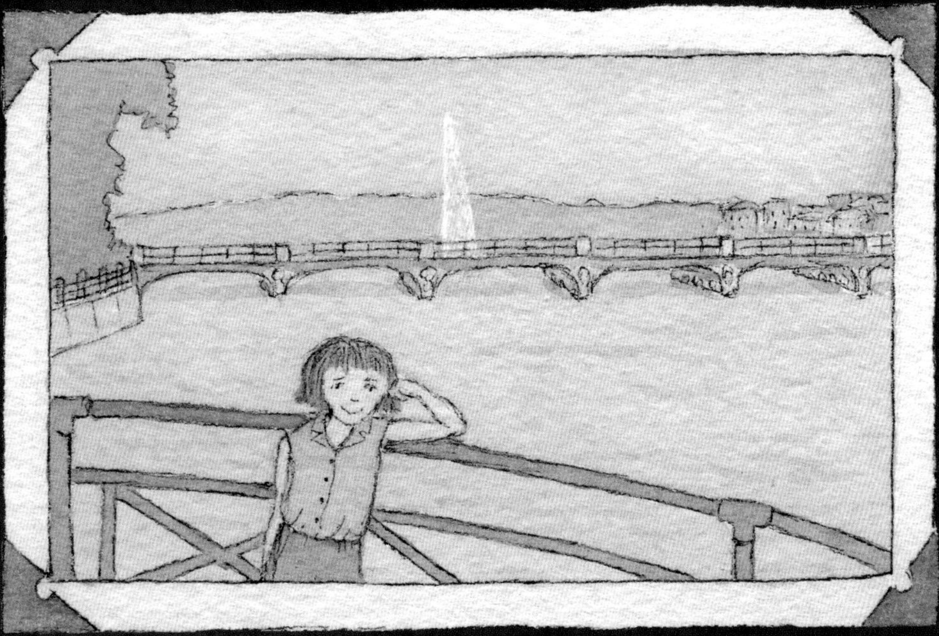

1958

WE ARRIVED IN GENEVA.

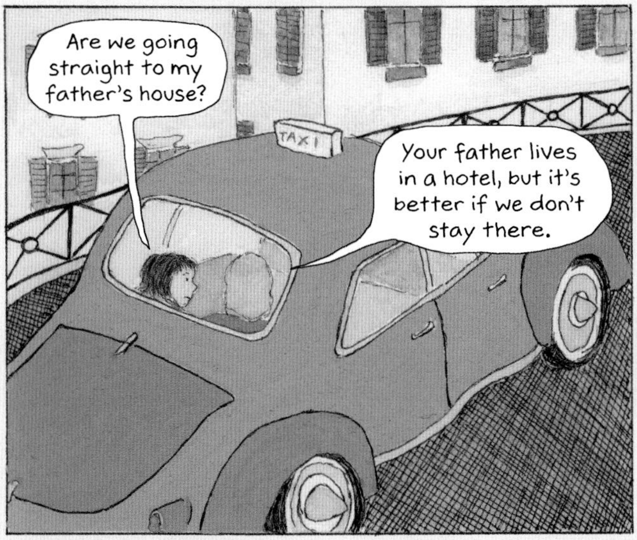
Are we going straight to my father's house?
TAXI
Your father lives in a hotel, but it's better if we don't stay there.

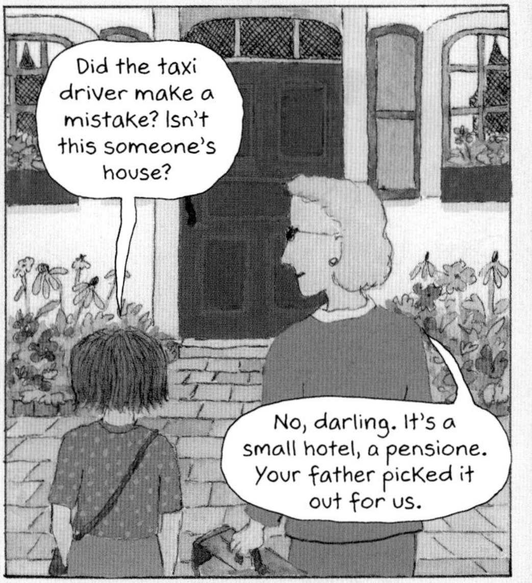
Did the taxi driver make a mistake? Isn't this someone's house?
No, darling. It's a small hotel, a pensione. Your father picked it out for us.

A CHEERY WOMAN MET US AT THE DOOR.

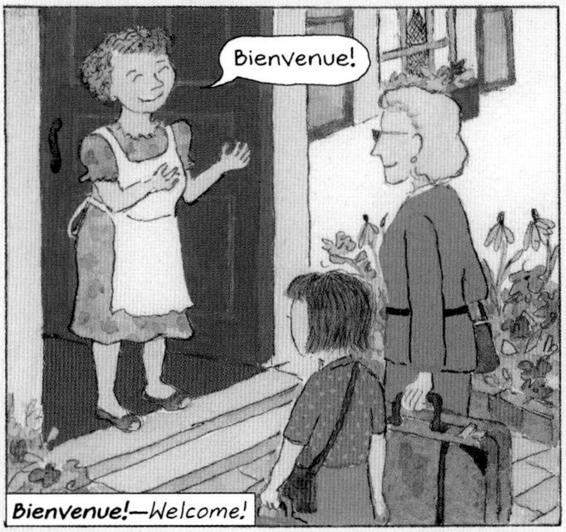
Bienvenue!

Bienvenue!—*Welcome!*

SHE USHERED US INTO A LIVING ROOM.

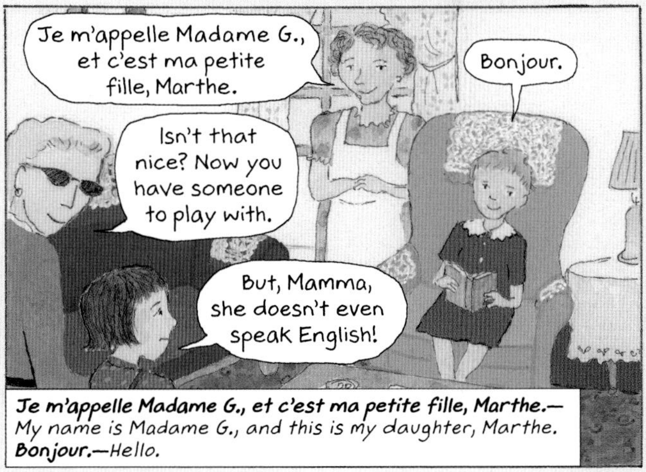
Je m'appelle Madame G., et c'est ma petite fille, Marthe.
Bonjour.
Isn't that nice? Now you have someone to play with.
But, Mamma, she doesn't even speak English!

Je m'appelle Madame G., et c'est ma petite fille, Marthe.—
My name is Madame G., and this is my daughter, Marthe.
Bonjour.—*Hello.*

THE NEXT MORNING AT BREAKFAST:

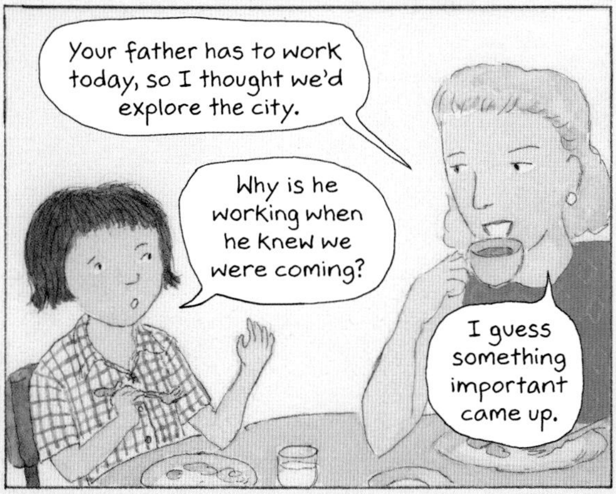
Your father has to work today, so I thought we'd explore the city.
Why is he working when he knew we were coming?
I guess something important came up.

TO MY CHAGRIN, MY MOTHER INVITED MARTHE TO JOIN US FOR OUR TOUR OF GENEVA.

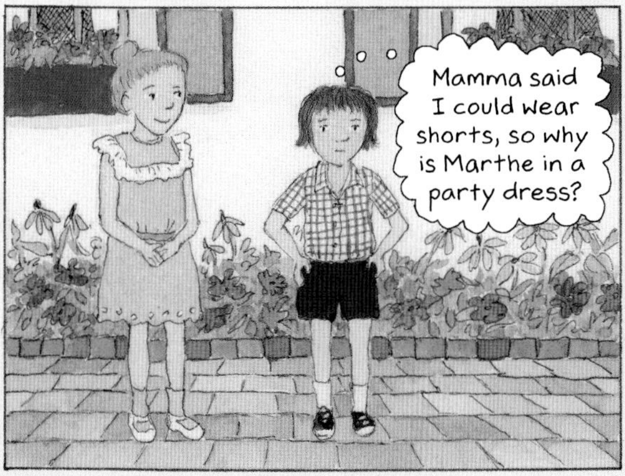
Mamma said I could wear shorts, so why is Marthe in a party dress?

ON THE TROLLEY, MY MOTHER AND MARTHE CHATTED AWAY IN FRENCH AS IF I WASN'T EVEN THERE.

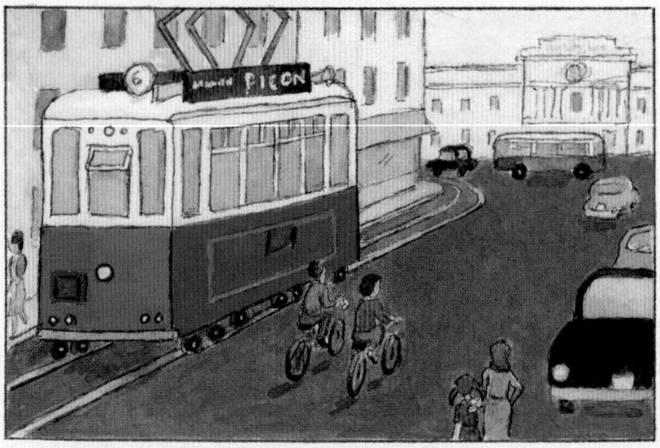
PICON

MARTHE WAS THE KIND OF CHILD MY MOTHER MOST ADMIRED—WELL GROOMED, POLITE, A YOUNG LADY. IN OTHER WORDS, EUROPEAN.

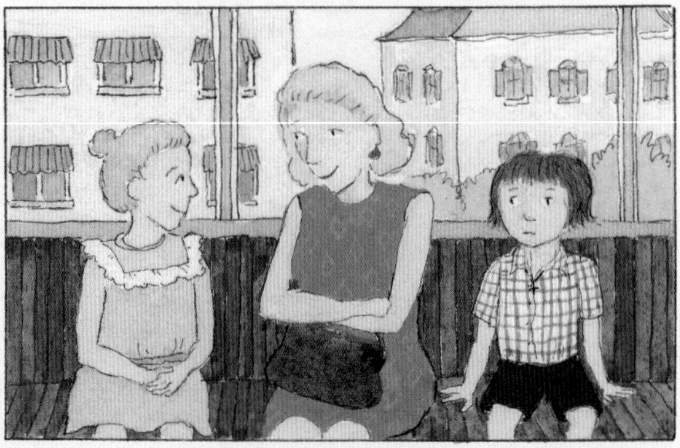

I COULD TELL SHE THOUGHT MARTHE WOULD BE A "GOOD INFLUENCE" ON ME. MY MOTHER WAS ALWAYS ON THE LOOKOUT FOR GOOD INFLUENCES.

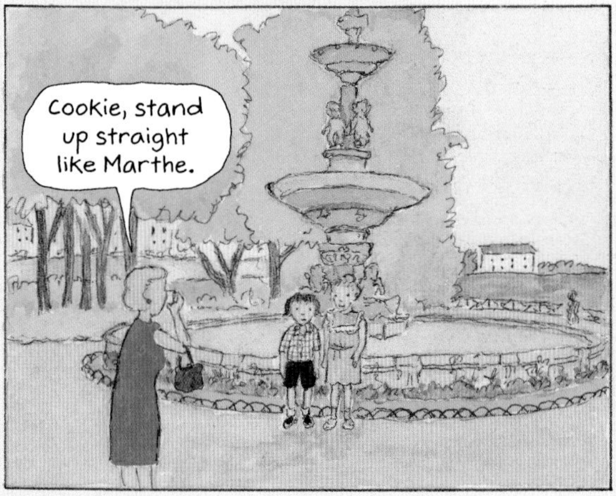
Cookie, stand up straight like Marthe.

MAYBE THIS WAS A LAST-DITCH EFFORT TO GROOM ME FOR MY UPCOMING ENCOUNTER WITH MY FATHER?

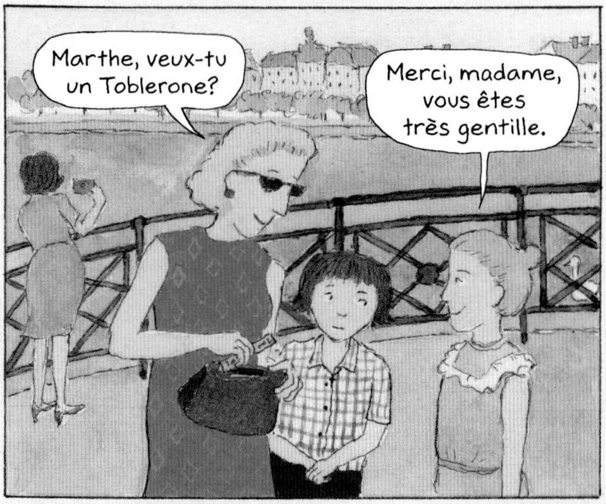
Marthe, veux-tu un Toblerone?
Merci, madame, vous êtes très gentille.

IF SO, I WAS FAILING MISERABLY.

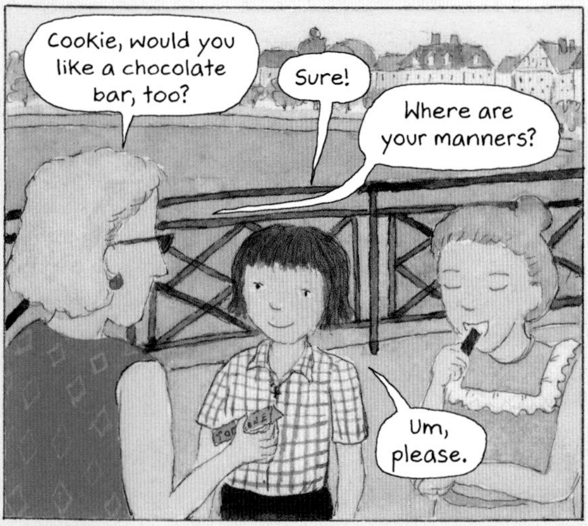
Cookie, would you like a chocolate bar, too?
Sure!
Where are your manners?
Um, please.

THE DAY DRAGGED ON AND ON.

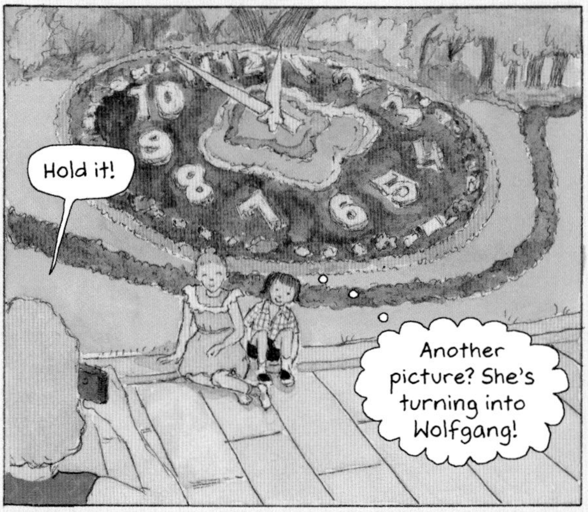
Hold it!
Another picture? She's turning into Wolfgang!

I STARTED TO THINK MARTHE SHOULD MEET MY FATHER AND PRETEND TO BE ME.

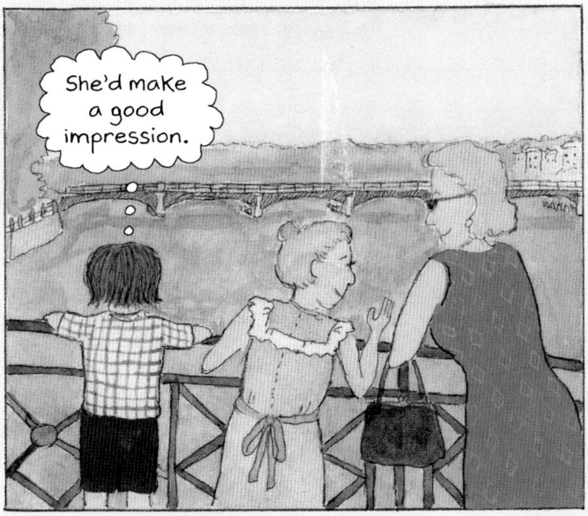

She'd make a good impression.

BUT THE NEXT DAY IT WAS MARTHE WHO WAS OUTSIDE HELPING HER MOTHER IN THE GARDEN WHILE I WAS THE ONE PREPARING FOR THE ARRIVAL OF MY FATHER.

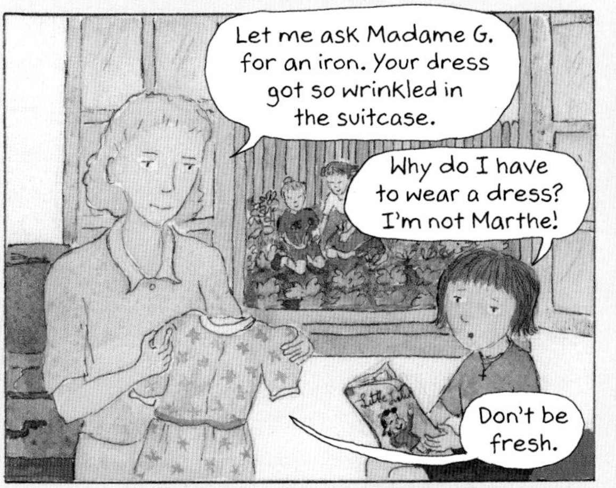

Let me ask Madame G. for an iron. Your dress got so wrinkled in the suitcase.
Why do I have to wear a dress? I'm not Marthe!
Don't be fresh.

IT SEEMED TO TAKE ALL AFTERNOON TO GET READY.

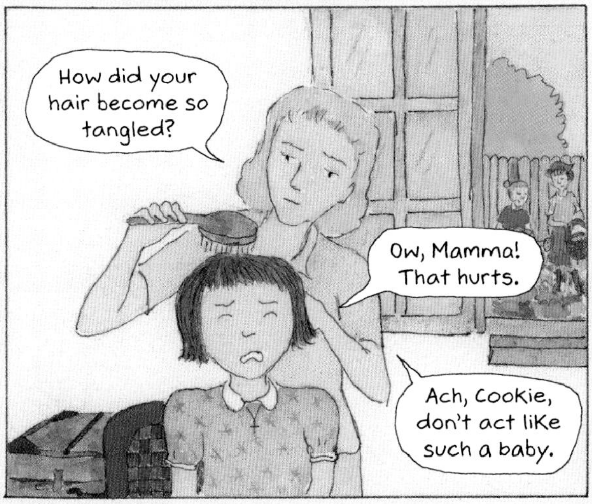

How did your hair become so tangled?
Ow, Mamma! That hurts.
Ach, Cookie, don't act like such a baby.

ONCE MY MOTHER WAS DONE WITH ME, SHE BEGAN HER OWN INTRICATE BEAUTY RITUAL.

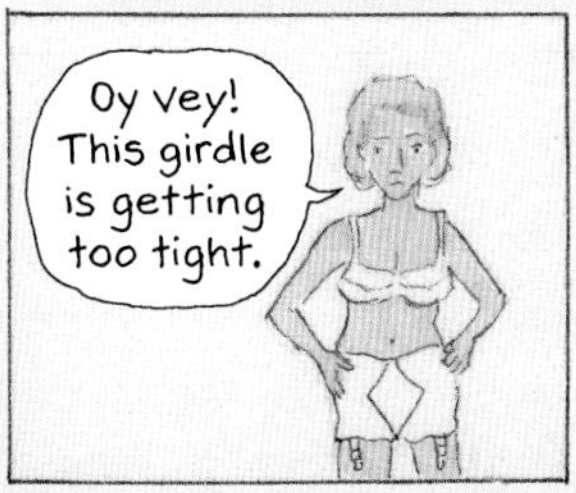

Oy vey! This girdle is getting too tight.

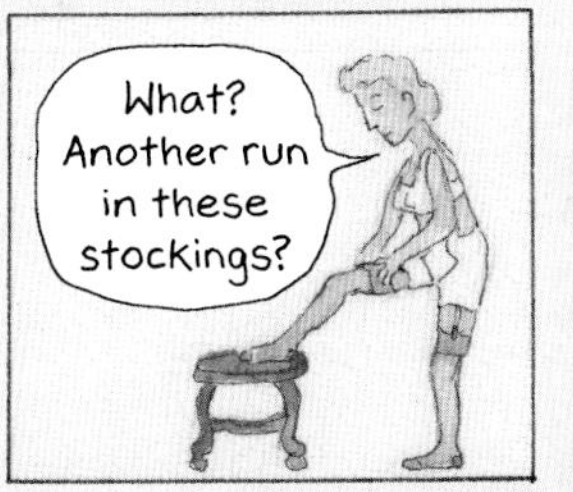

What? Another run in these stockings?

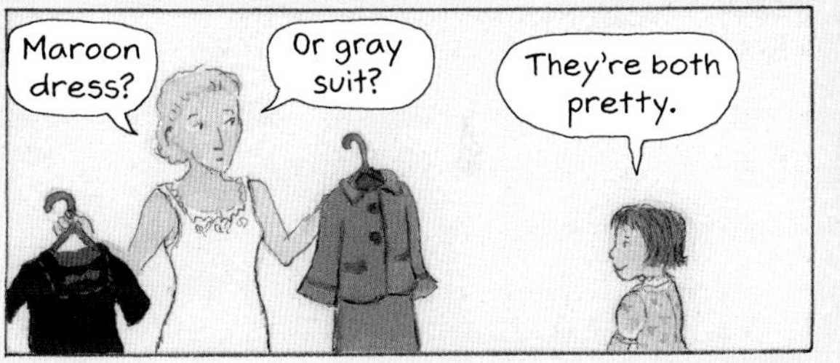

Maroon dress?
Or gray suit?
They're both pretty.

AS USUAL, MY MOTHER TOOK GREAT PRIDE IN HER APPEARANCE. SHE NEVER WENT ANYWHERE, EVEN IF IT WAS JUST TO THE GROCERY STORE ON SATURDAY MORNING, WITHOUT POWDER AND LIPSTICK. NORMALLY, APPLYING HER MAKEUP WAS NO BIG DEAL, BUT TODAY WAS DIFFERENT.

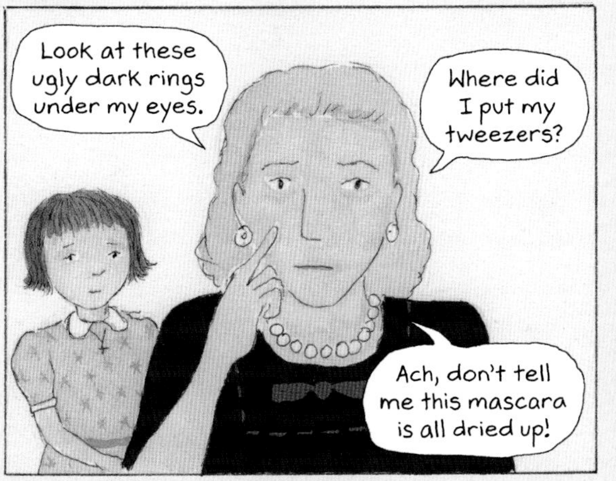

Look at these ugly dark rings under my eyes.
Where did I put my tweezers?
Ach, don't tell me this mascara is all dried up!

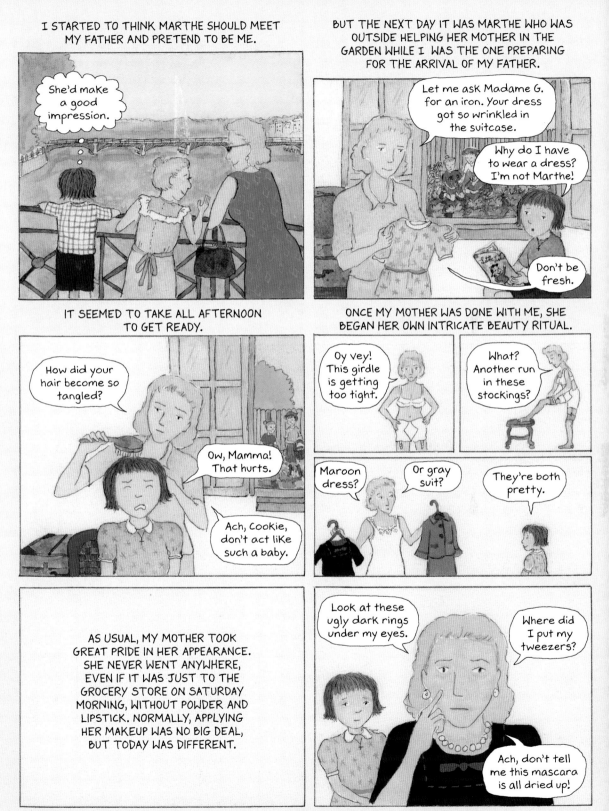

AT LAST, WHEN WE WERE BOTH READY, I SAT ON A CHAIR IN THE PENSIONE LIVING ROOM TRYING NOT TO WRINKLE MY DRESS WHILE MY MOTHER PACED BY THE WINDOW.

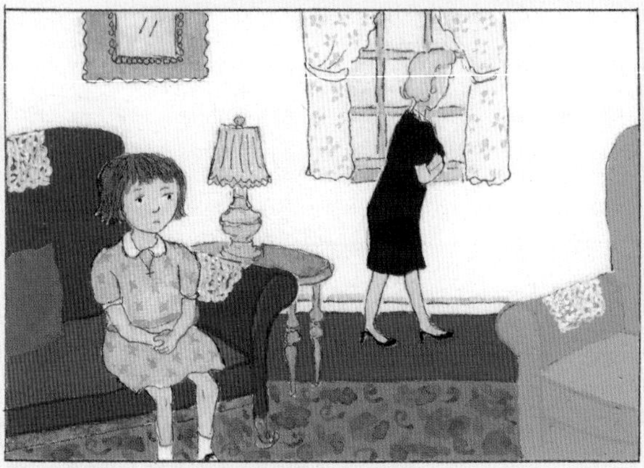

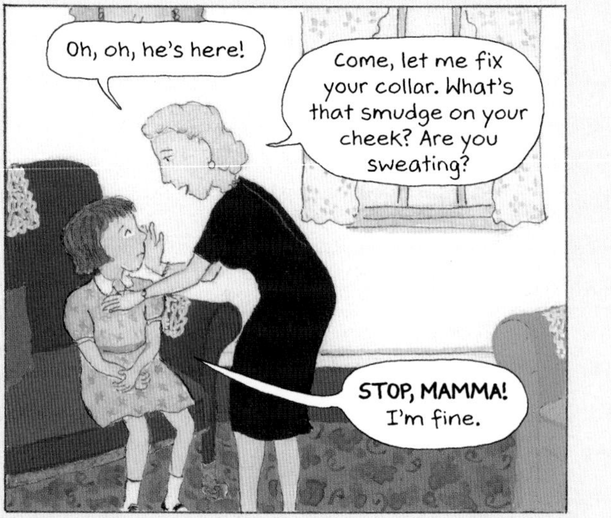
Oh, oh, he's here!
Come, let me fix your collar. What's that smudge on your cheek? Are you sweating?
STOP, MAMMA! I'm fine.

A MAN IN A GRAY SUIT AND BLACK TIE APPEARED IN THE DOORWAY. EVEN THOUGH MY MOTHER RUSHED TO GREET HIM, I WAS SURE THERE HAD TO BE SOME MISTAKE.

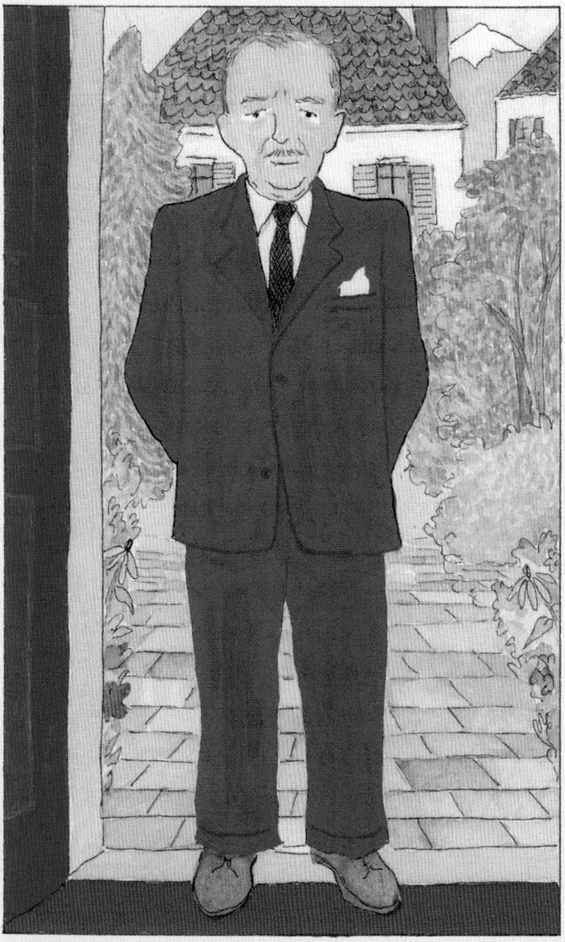

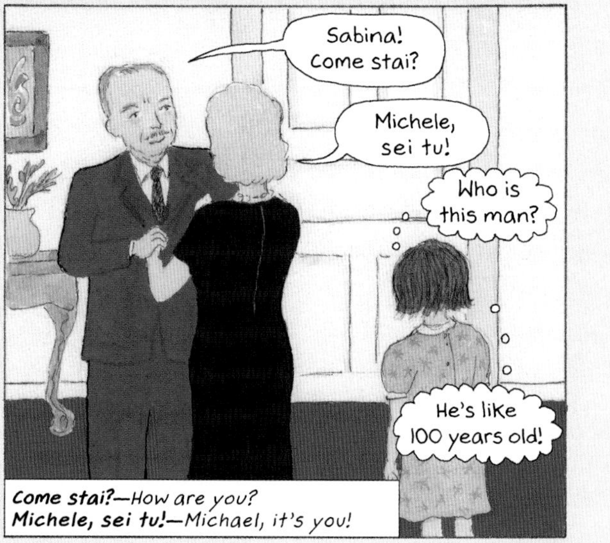
Sabina! Come stai?
Michele, sei tu!
Who is this man?
He's like 100 years old!

Come stai?—*How are you?*
Michele, sei tu!—*Michael, it's you!*

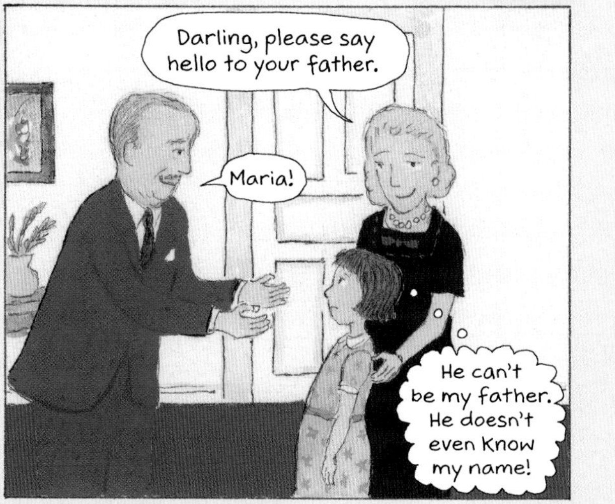
Darling, please say hello to your father.
Maria!
He can't be my father. He doesn't even know my name!

FOR AN INSTANT, I PICTURED
MY FAVORITE TV DADS.

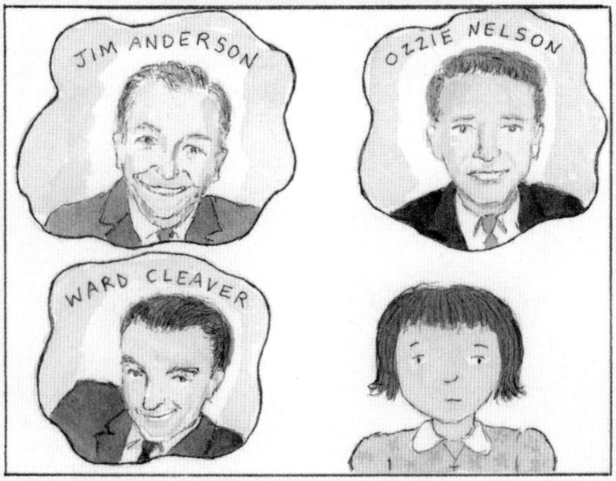
JIM ANDERSON
OZZIE NELSON
WARD CLEAVER

IT WAS EASY TO SEE THIS MAN BORE
NO RESEMBLANCE TO ANY OF THEM.

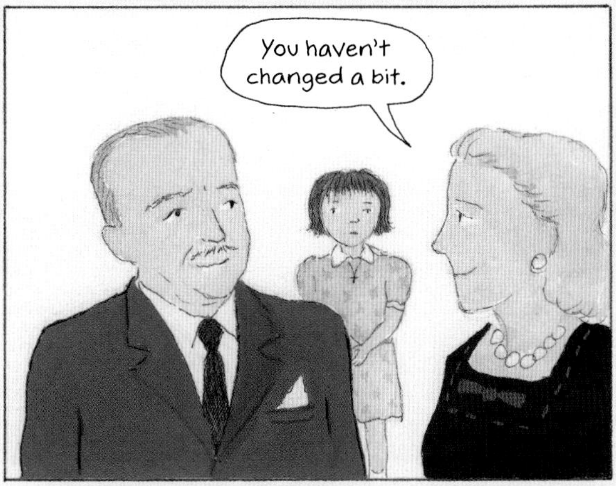
You haven't changed a bit.

ON TOP OF THAT, HE COULD
BARELY SPEAK ENGLISH.

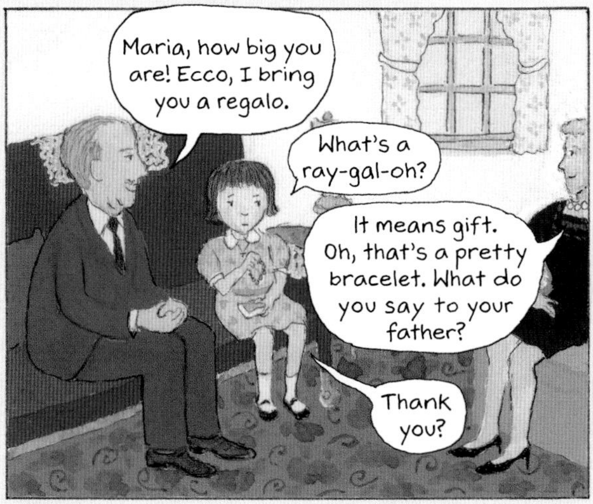
Maria, how big you are! Ecco, I bring you a regalo.
What's a ray-gal-oh?
It means gift. Oh, that's a pretty bracelet. What do you say to your father?
Thank you?

HE OFFERED MY MOTHER A CIGARETTE OUT
OF A SLEEK GOLD CASE. EVEN THOUGH THEY
WERE SPEAKING IN ITALIAN, I WAS PRETTY
SURE THEY WERE TALKING ABOUT ME.

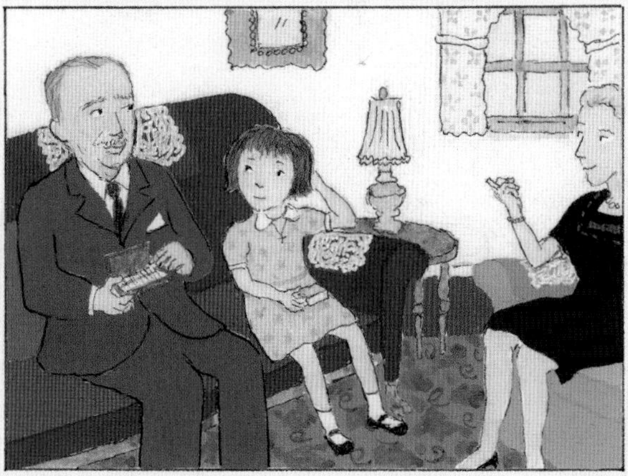

AND THEN, AS IF HE'D JUST REMEMBERED SOMETHING VERY IMPORTANT,
MY FATHER CLAPPED HIS HANDS AND STOOD UP.

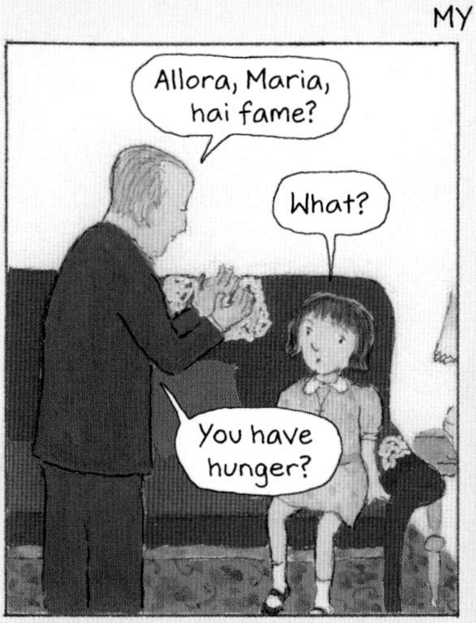
Allora, Maria, hai fame?
What?
You have hunger?

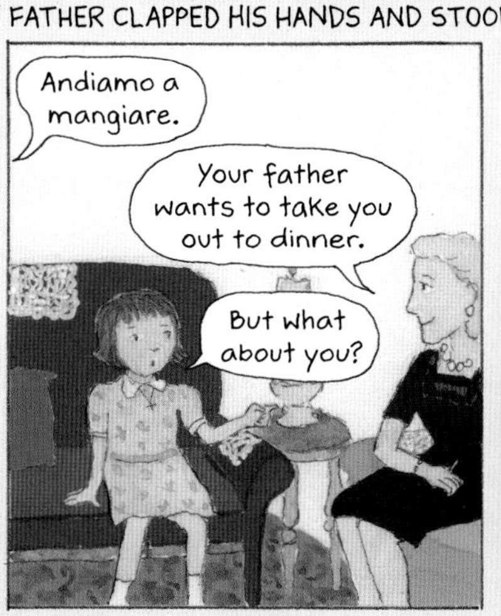
Andiamo a mangiare.
Your father wants to take you out to dinner.
But what about you?

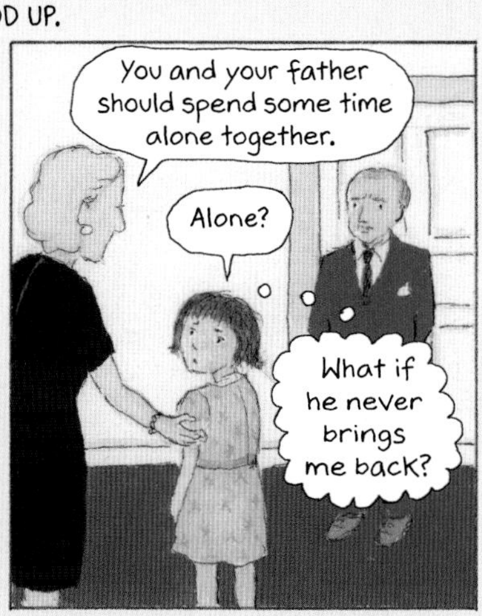
You and your father should spend some time alone together.
Alone?
What if he never brings me back?

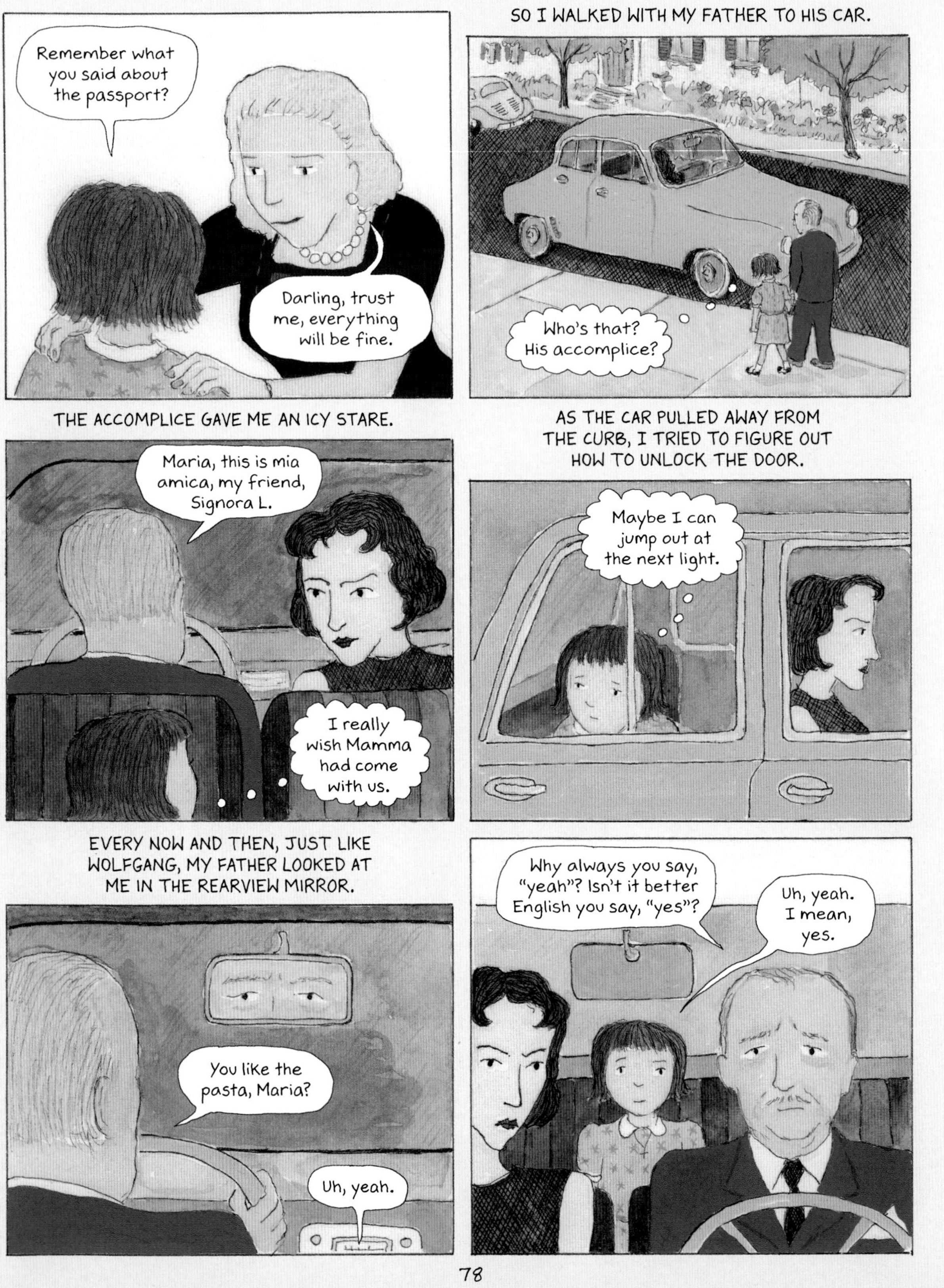
Remember what you said about the passport?
Darling, trust me, everything will be fine.
SO I WALKED WITH MY FATHER TO HIS CAR.
Who's that? His accomplice?
THE ACCOMPLICE GAVE ME AN ICY STARE.
Maria, this is mia amica, my friend, Signora L.
I really wish Mamma had come with us.
AS THE CAR PULLED AWAY FROM THE CURB, I TRIED TO FIGURE OUT HOW TO UNLOCK THE DOOR.
Maybe I can jump out at the next light.
EVERY NOW AND THEN, JUST LIKE WOLFGANG, MY FATHER LOOKED AT ME IN THE REARVIEW MIRROR.
You like the pasta, Maria?
Uh, yeah.
Why always you say, "yeah"? Isn't it better English you say, "yes"?
Uh, yeah. I mean, yes.

THE RESTAURANT WAS VERY ELEGANT. AS SOON AS WE WERE SEATED, MY FATHER TURNED ALL HIS ATTENTION TO ME WHILE THE ACCOMPLICE SILENTLY STUDIED THE MENU.

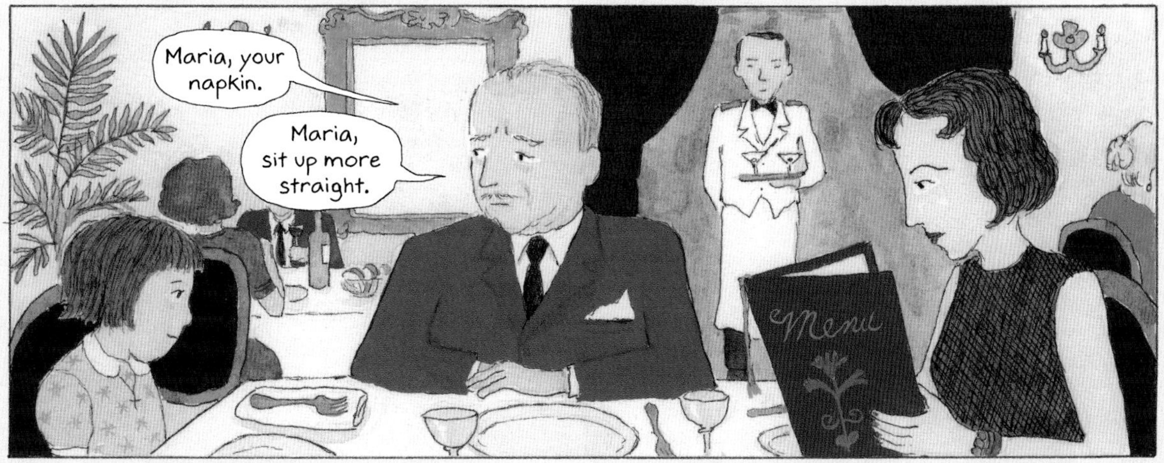
Maria, your napkin.
Maria, sit up more straight.
Menu

MY FATHER HAD LOTS OF QUESTIONS, NOT ALWAYS EASY TO DECIPHER.

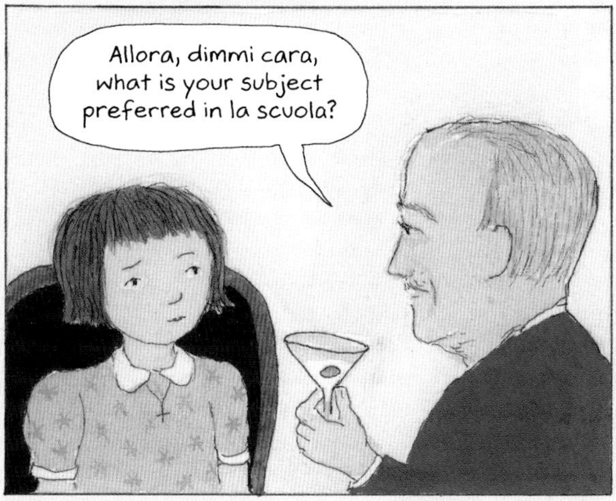
Allora, dimmi cara, what is your subject preferred in la scuola?

IT WAS A LOT LIKE BEING INTERVIEWED BY MR. TAUCHNER, ONLY IN A FOREIGN LANGUAGE.

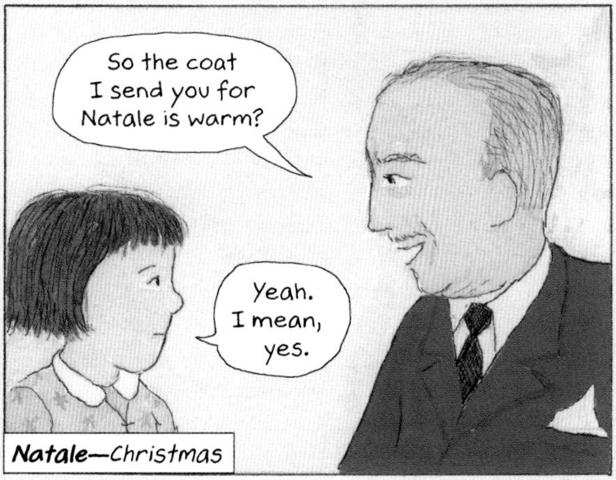
So the coat I send you for Natale is warm?
Yeah. I mean, yes.

Natale—Christmas

WAS MY FATHER CONSIDERING ME FOR AN ACCELERATED CLASS OR JUST FOR THE POSITION AS HIS DAUGHTER?

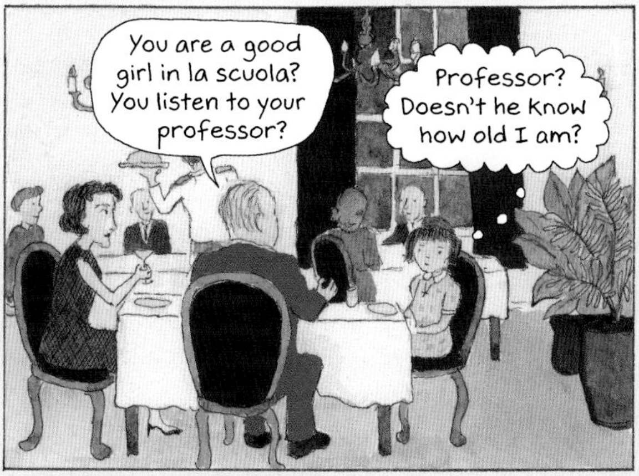
You are a good girl in la scuola? You listen to your professor?
Professor? Doesn't he know how old I am?

WHEN THE FOOD ARRIVED, I GOBBLED IT UP. I JUST WANTED THE WHOLE EVENING TO BE OVER AS FAST AS POSSIBLE.

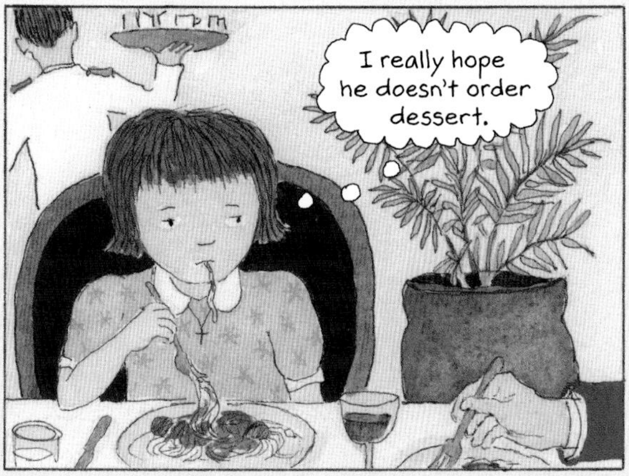
I really hope he doesn't order dessert.

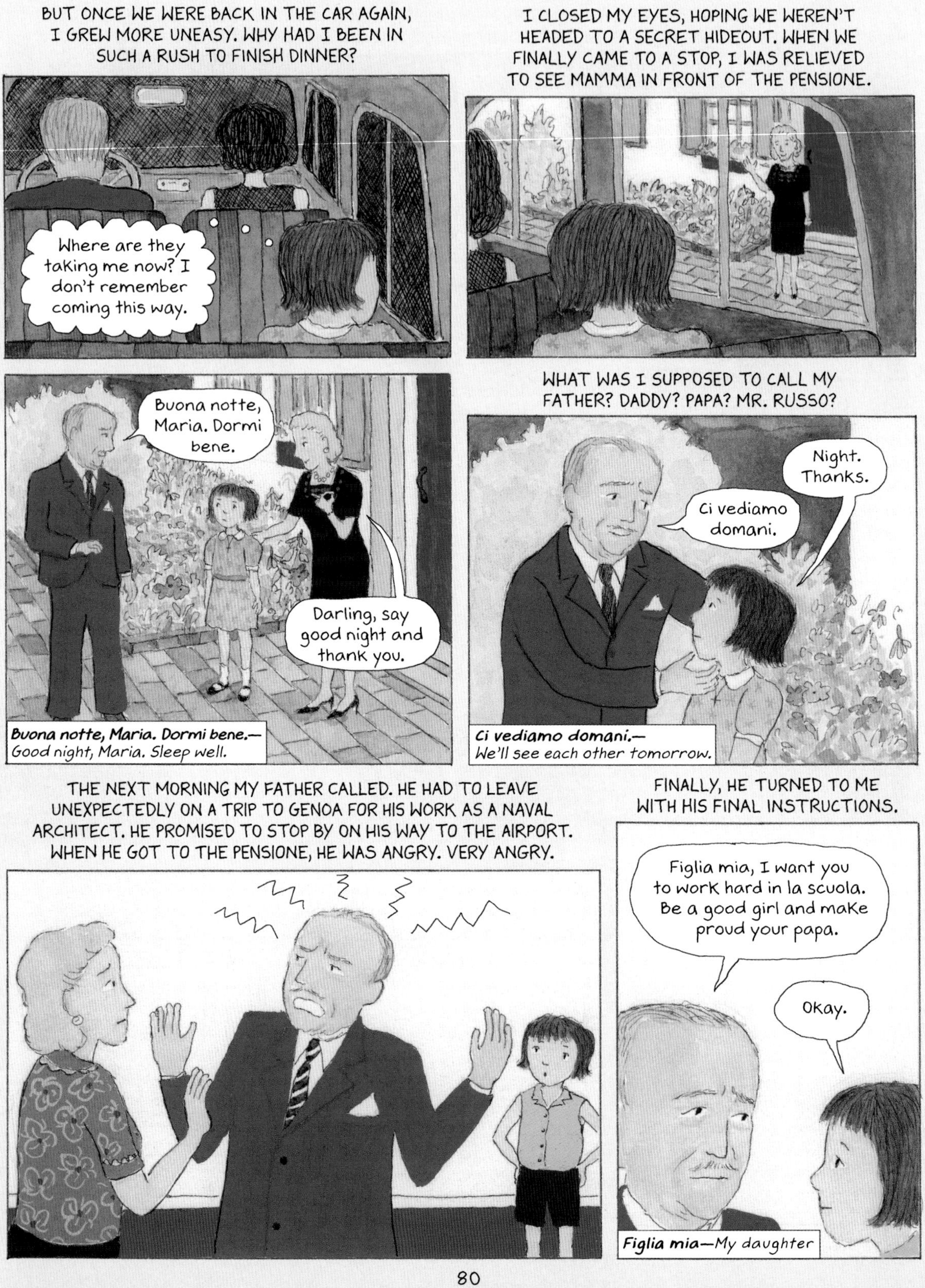
BUT ONCE WE WERE BACK IN THE CAR AGAIN, I GREW MORE UNEASY. WHY HAD I BEEN IN SUCH A RUSH TO FINISH DINNER?
Where are they taking me now? I don't remember coming this way.
I CLOSED MY EYES, HOPING WE WEREN'T HEADED TO A SECRET HIDEOUT. WHEN WE FINALLY CAME TO A STOP, I WAS RELIEVED TO SEE MAMMA IN FRONT OF THE PENSIONE.
Buona notte, Maria. Dormi bene.
Darling, say good night and thank you.
Buona notte, Maria. Dormi bene.—
Good night, Maria. Sleep well.
WHAT WAS I SUPPOSED TO CALL MY FATHER? DADDY? PAPA? MR. RUSSO?
Ci vediamo domani.
Night. Thanks.
Ci vediamo domani.—
We'll see each other tomorrow.
THE NEXT MORNING MY FATHER CALLED. HE HAD TO LEAVE UNEXPECTEDLY ON A TRIP TO GENOA FOR HIS WORK AS A NAVAL ARCHITECT. HE PROMISED TO STOP BY ON HIS WAY TO THE AIRPORT. WHEN HE GOT TO THE PENSIONE, HE WAS ANGRY. VERY ANGRY.
FINALLY, HE TURNED TO ME WITH HIS FINAL INSTRUCTIONS.
Figlia mia, I want you to work hard in la scuola. Be a good girl and make proud your papa.
Okay.
Figlia mia—My daughter

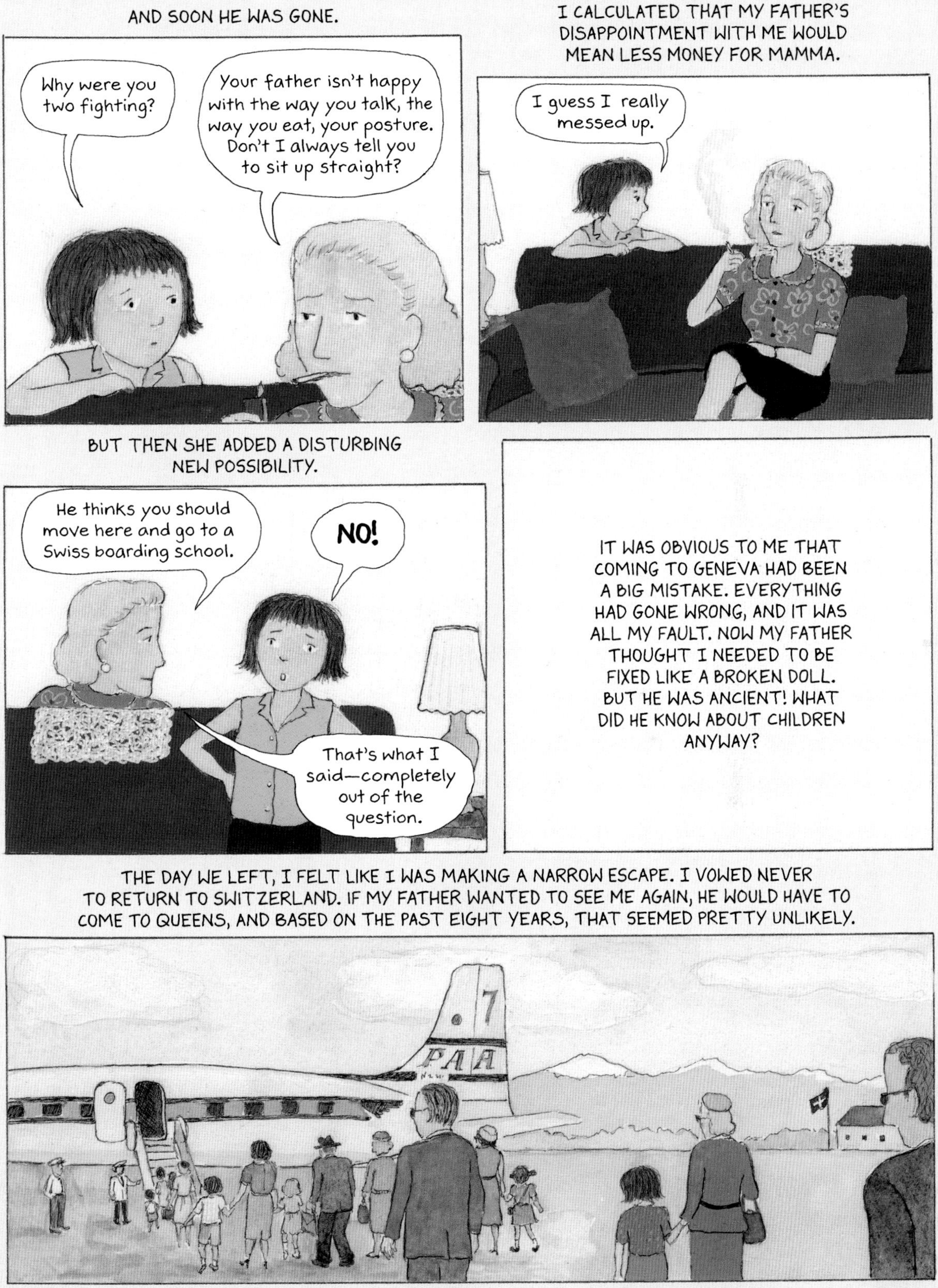
AND SOON HE WAS GONE.
Why were you two fighting?
Your father isn't happy with the way you talk, the way you eat, your posture. Don't I always tell you to sit up straight?
I CALCULATED THAT MY FATHER'S DISAPPOINTMENT WITH ME WOULD MEAN LESS MONEY FOR MAMMA.
I guess I really messed up.
BUT THEN SHE ADDED A DISTURBING NEW POSSIBILITY.
He thinks you should move here and go to a Swiss boarding school.
NO!
That's what I said—completely out of the question.
IT WAS OBVIOUS TO ME THAT COMING TO GENEVA HAD BEEN A BIG MISTAKE. EVERYTHING HAD GONE WRONG, AND IT WAS ALL MY FAULT. NOW MY FATHER THOUGHT I NEEDED TO BE FIXED LIKE A BROKEN DOLL. BUT HE WAS ANCIENT! WHAT DID HE KNOW ABOUT CHILDREN ANYWAY?
THE DAY WE LEFT, I FELT LIKE I WAS MAKING A NARROW ESCAPE. I VOWED NEVER TO RETURN TO SWITZERLAND. IF MY FATHER WANTED TO SEE ME AGAIN, HE WOULD HAVE TO COME TO QUEENS, AND BASED ON THE PAST EIGHT YEARS, THAT SEEMED PRETTY UNLIKELY.
7
PAA

AS WE FLEW TO ROME, I WONDERED IF I WOULD EVER SEE MY FATHER AGAIN.

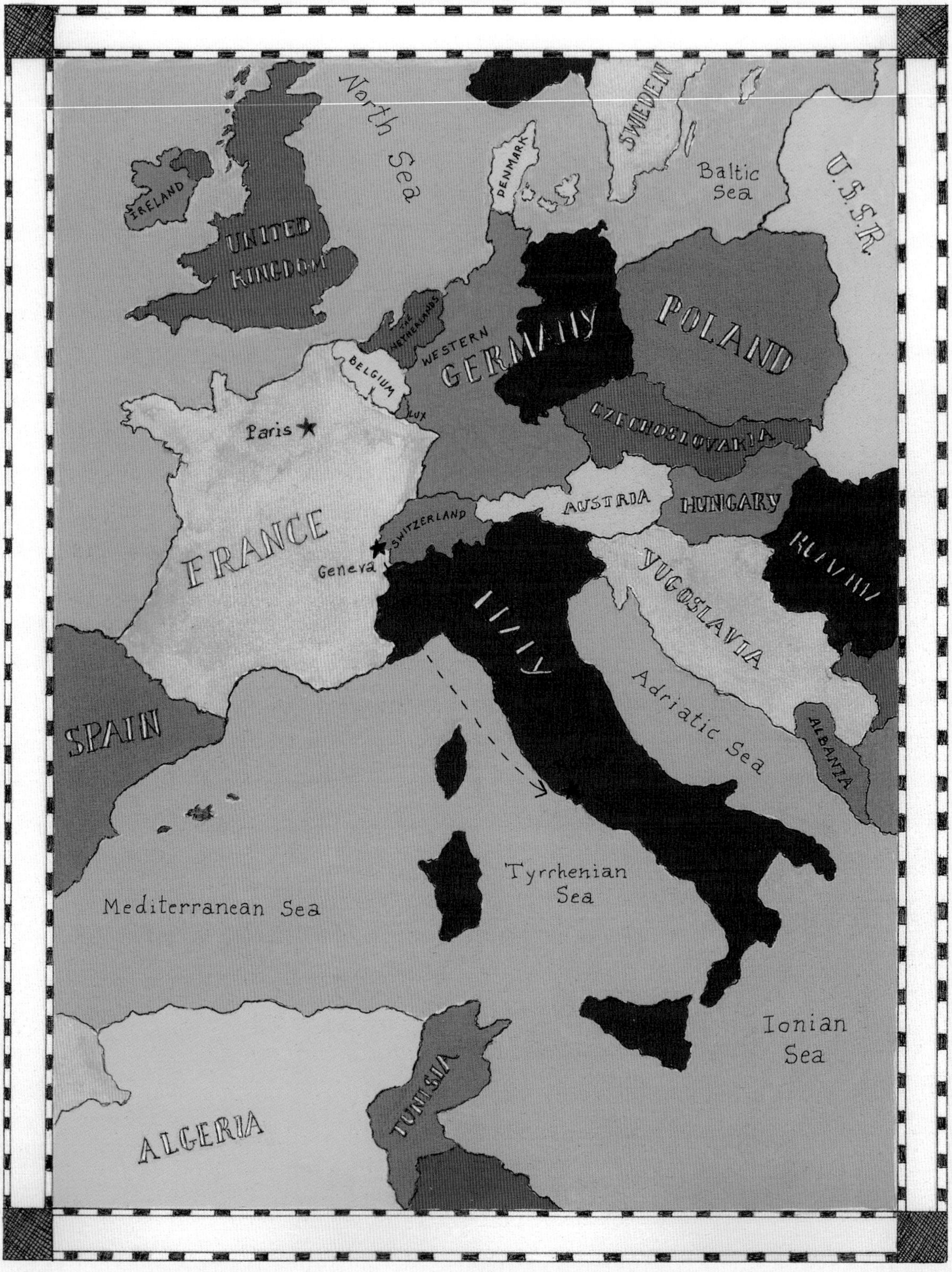

North Sea
SWEDEN
DENMARK
Baltic Sea
U.S.S.R.
IRELAND
UNITED KINGDOM
THE NETHERLANDS
WESTERN GERMANY
GERMANY
POLAND
BELGIUM
LUX
Paris
CZECHOSLOVAKIA
AUSTRIA
HUNGARY
SWITZERLAND
FRANCE
Geneva
YUGOSLAVIA
ITALY
Adriatic Sea
ALBANIA
SPAIN
Tyrrhenian Sea
Mediterranean Sea
Ionian Sea
TUNISIA
ALGERIA

EIGHT

Roman Holiday

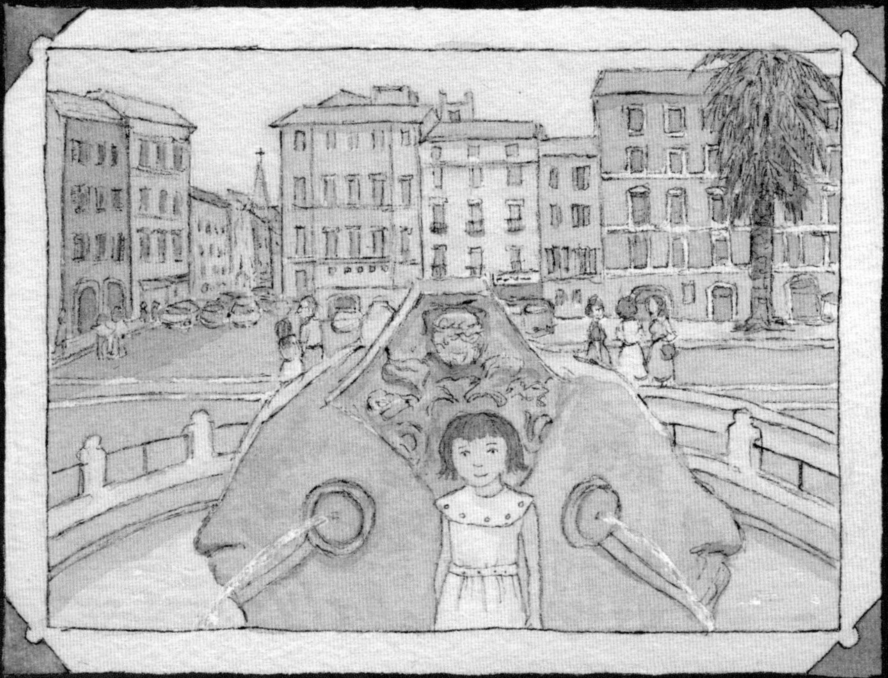

1958

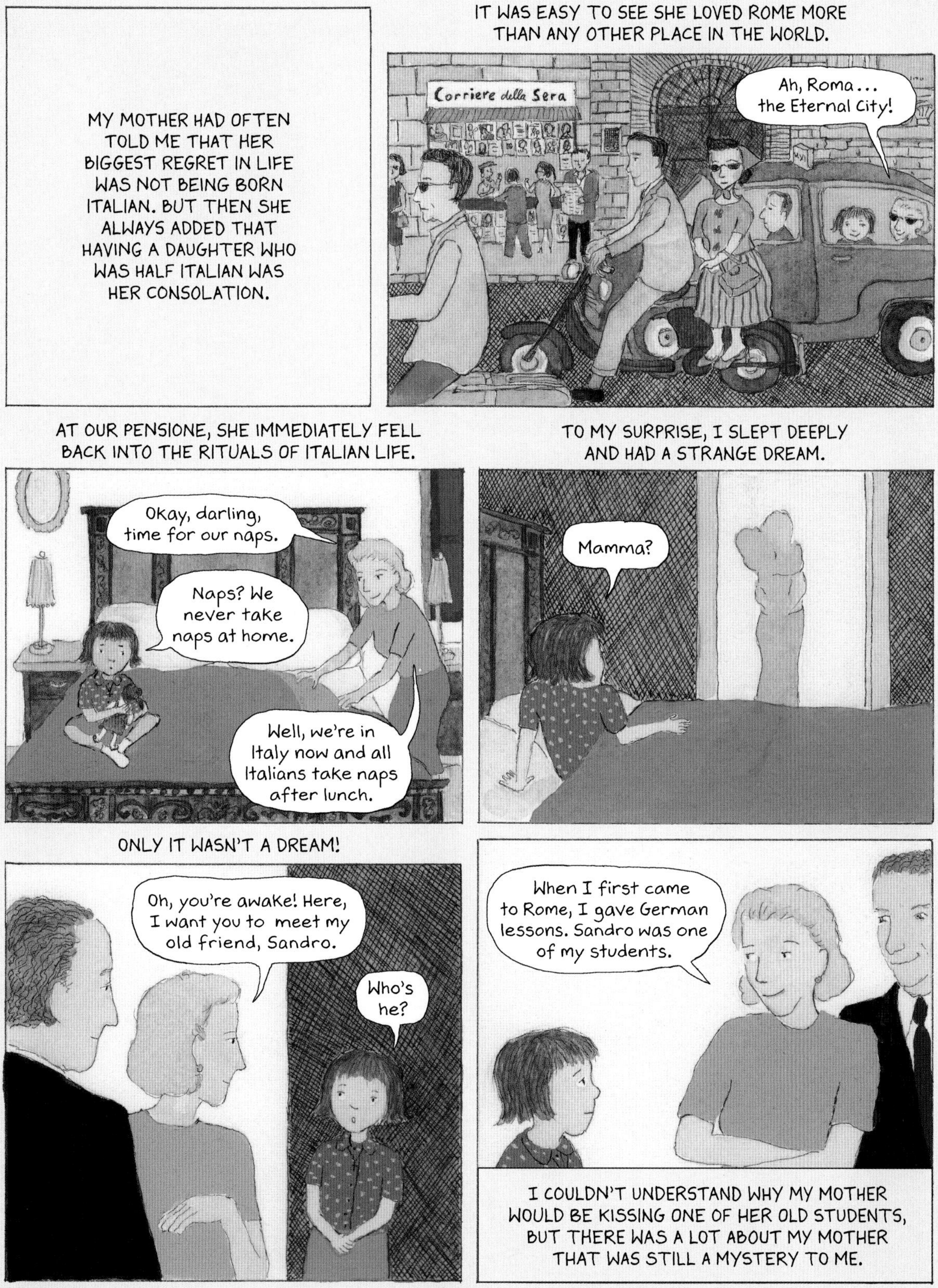
MY MOTHER HAD OFTEN TOLD ME THAT HER BIGGEST REGRET IN LIFE WAS NOT BEING BORN ITALIAN. BUT THEN SHE ALWAYS ADDED THAT HAVING A DAUGHTER WHO WAS HALF ITALIAN WAS HER CONSOLATION.
IT WAS EASY TO SEE SHE LOVED ROME MORE THAN ANY OTHER PLACE IN THE WORLD.
Corriere della Sera
Ah, Roma... the Eternal City!
AT OUR PENSIONE, SHE IMMEDIATELY FELL BACK INTO THE RITUALS OF ITALIAN LIFE.
Okay, darling, time for our naps.
Naps? We never take naps at home.
Well, we're in Italy now and all Italians take naps after lunch.
TO MY SURPRISE, I SLEPT DEEPLY AND HAD A STRANGE DREAM.
Mamma?
ONLY IT WASN'T A DREAM!
Oh, you're awake! Here, I want you to meet my old friend, Sandro.
Who's he?
When I first came to Rome, I gave German lessons. Sandro was one of my students.
I COULDN'T UNDERSTAND WHY MY MOTHER WOULD BE KISSING ONE OF HER OLD STUDENTS, BUT THERE WAS A LOT ABOUT MY MOTHER THAT WAS STILL A MYSTERY TO ME.

WHEN SANDRO TOOK US OUT TO DINNER, I LEARNED ABOUT A FEW OTHER ITALIAN CUSTOMS.

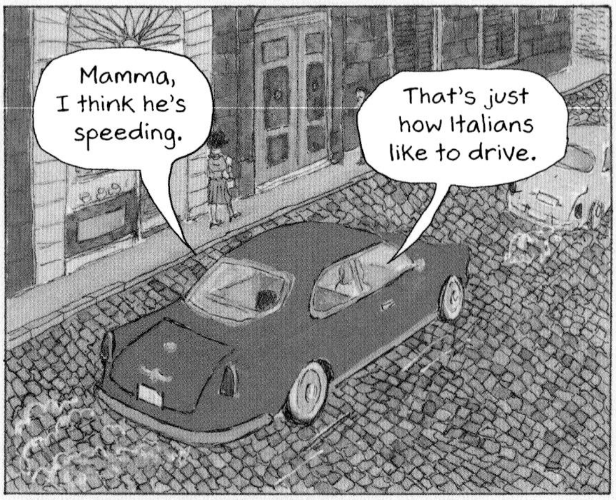
Mamma, I think he's speeding.
That's just how Italians like to drive.

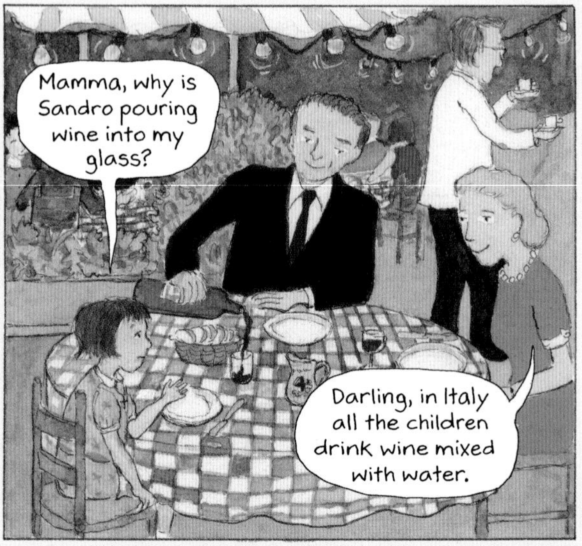
Mamma, why is Sandro pouring wine into my glass?
Darling, in Italy all the children drink wine mixed with water.

MY MOTHER AND SANDRO SLIPPED EASILY INTO CONVERSATION, ALL BUT FORGETTING I WAS THERE.

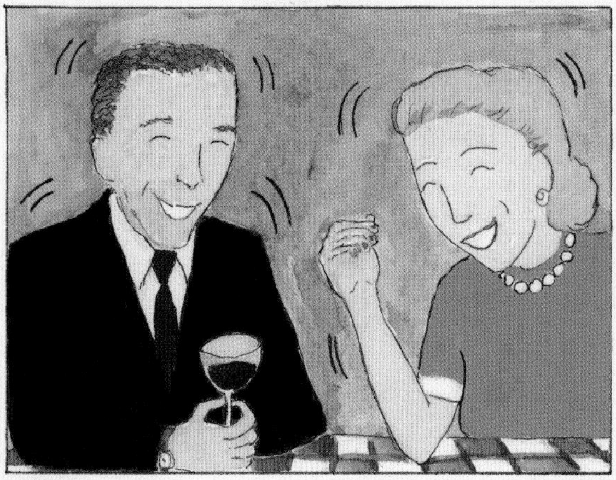

IT WAS A RELIEF NOT TO BE THE CENTER OF ATTENTION, NO CRITICISMS OF MY POSTURE OR MANNERS.

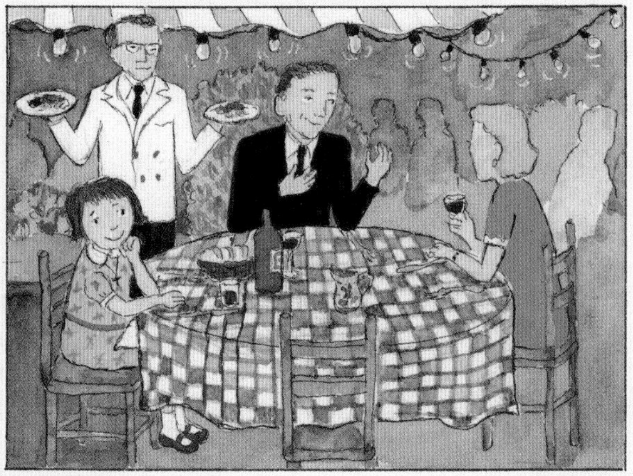

LATER, BACK AT THE PENSIONE...

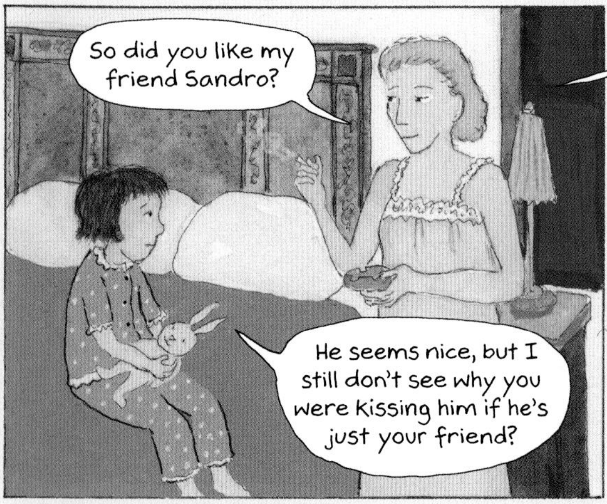
So did you like my friend Sandro?
He seems nice, but I still don't see why you were kissing him if he's just your friend?

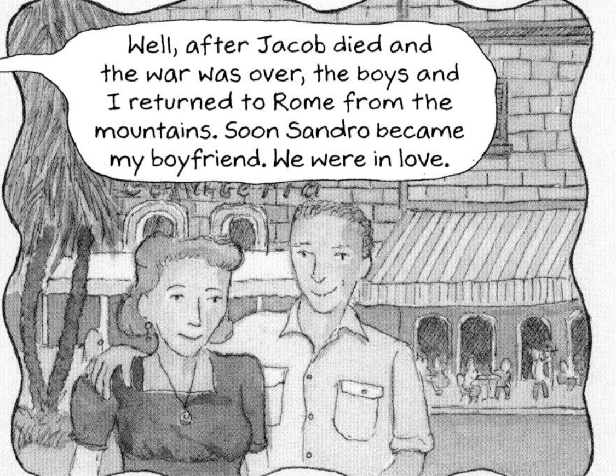
Well, after Jacob died and the war was over, the boys and I returned to Rome from the mountains. Soon Sandro became my boyfriend. We were in love.

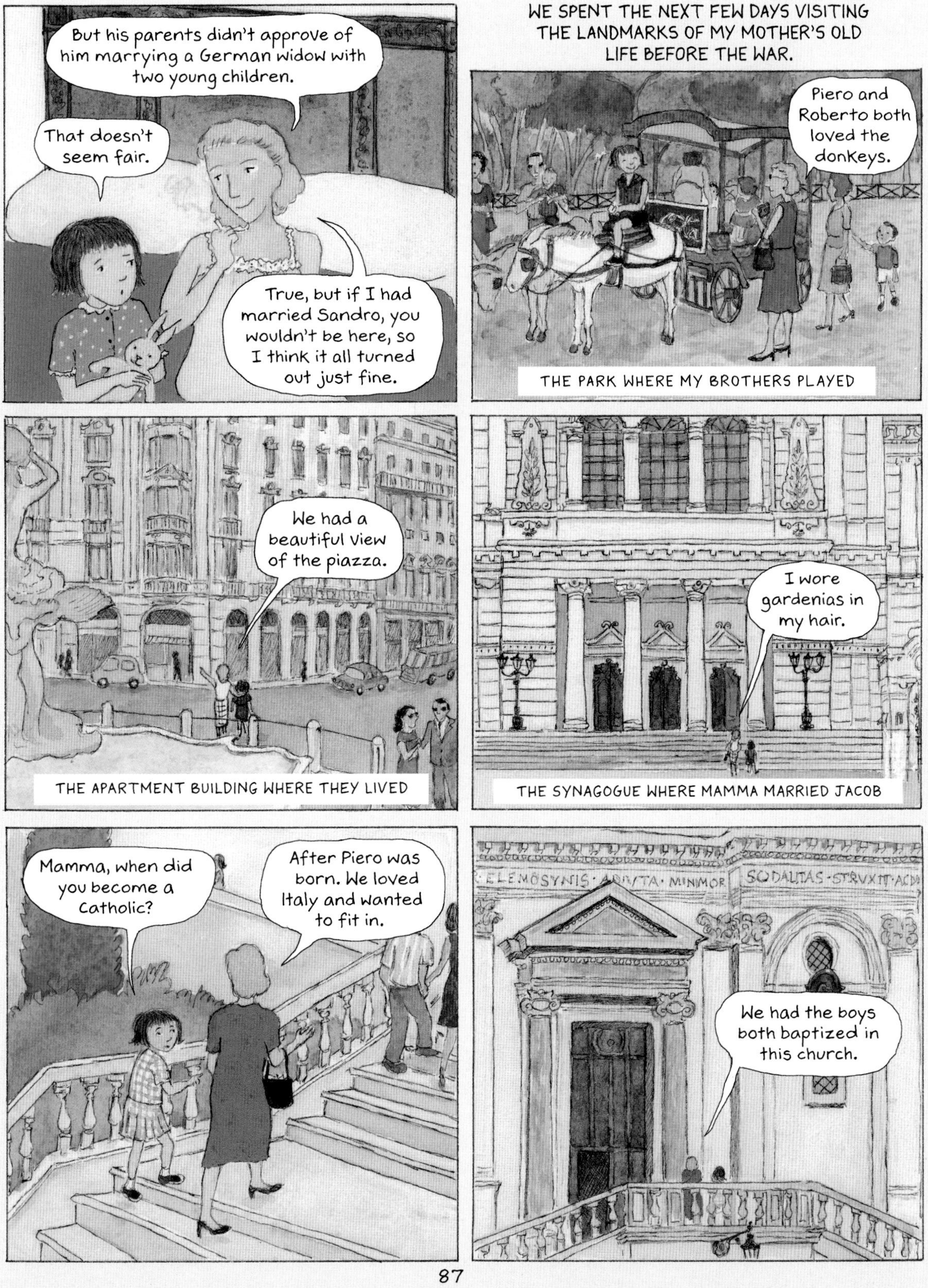
But his parents didn't approve of him marrying a German widow with two young children.
That doesn't seem fair.
True, but if I had married Sandro, you wouldn't be here, so I think it all turned out just fine.
WE SPENT THE NEXT FEW DAYS VISITING THE LANDMARKS OF MY MOTHER'S OLD LIFE BEFORE THE WAR.
Piero and Roberto both loved the donkeys.
THE PARK WHERE MY BROTHERS PLAYED
We had a beautiful view of the piazza.
THE APARTMENT BUILDING WHERE THEY LIVED
I wore gardenias in my hair.
THE SYNAGOGUE WHERE MAMMA MARRIED JACOB
Mamma, when did you become a Catholic?
After Piero was born. We loved Italy and wanted to fit in.
ELEMOSYNIS · ADIVTA · MINIMOR
SODALITAS · STRVXIT · ACD
We had the boys both baptized in this church.

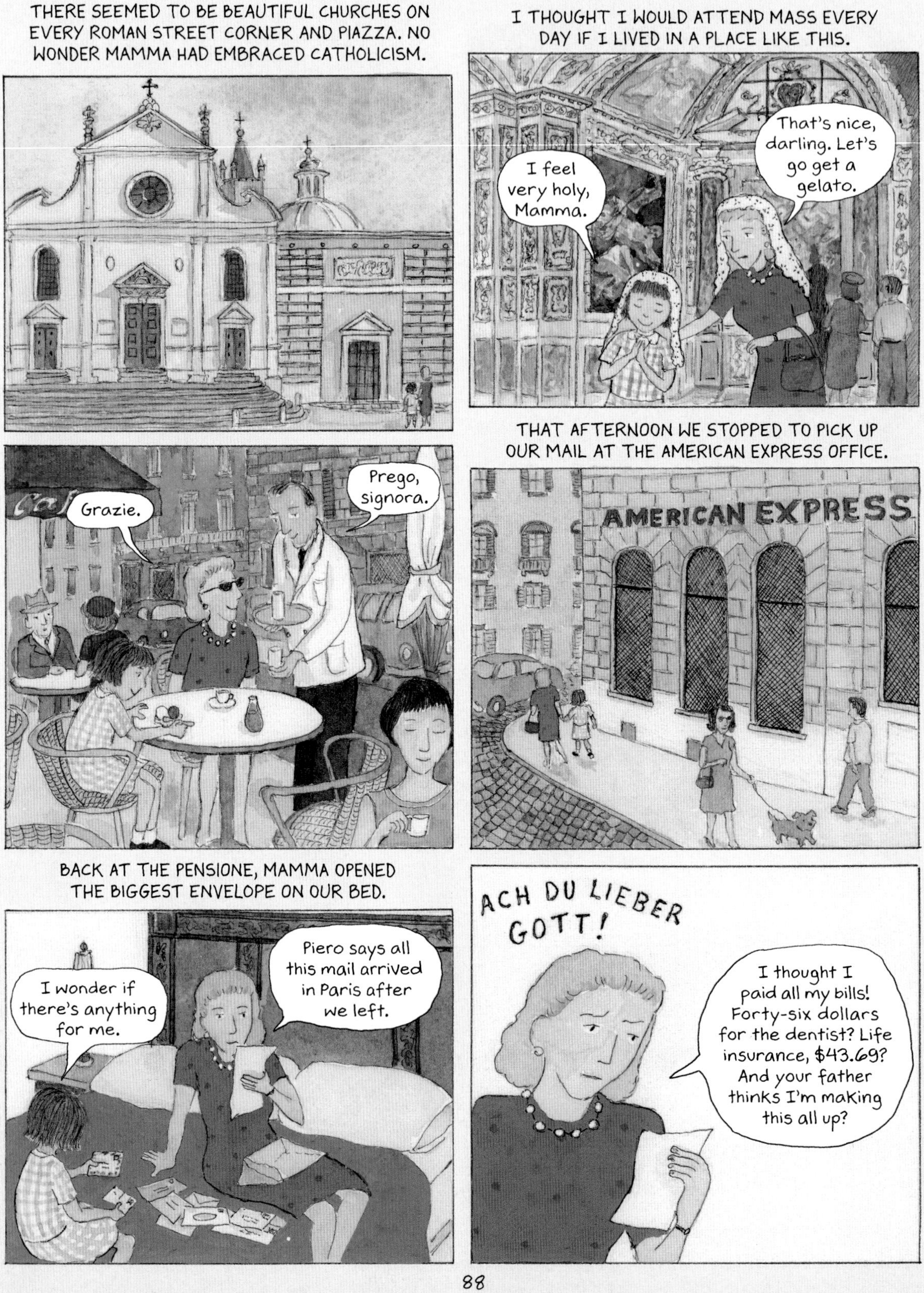
THERE SEEMED TO BE BEAUTIFUL CHURCHES ON EVERY ROMAN STREET CORNER AND PIAZZA. NO WONDER MAMMA HAD EMBRACED CATHOLICISM.
I THOUGHT I WOULD ATTEND MASS EVERY DAY IF I LIVED IN A PLACE LIKE THIS.
I feel very holy, Mamma.
That's nice, darling. Let's go get a gelato.
Grazie.
Prego, signora.
THAT AFTERNOON WE STOPPED TO PICK UP OUR MAIL AT THE AMERICAN EXPRESS OFFICE.
AMERICAN EXPRESS
BACK AT THE PENSIONE, MAMMA OPENED THE BIGGEST ENVELOPE ON OUR BED.
I wonder if there's anything for me.
Piero says all this mail arrived in Paris after we left.
ACH DU LIEBER GOTT!
I thought I paid all my bills! Forty-six dollars for the dentist? Life insurance, $43.69? And your father thinks I'm making this all up?

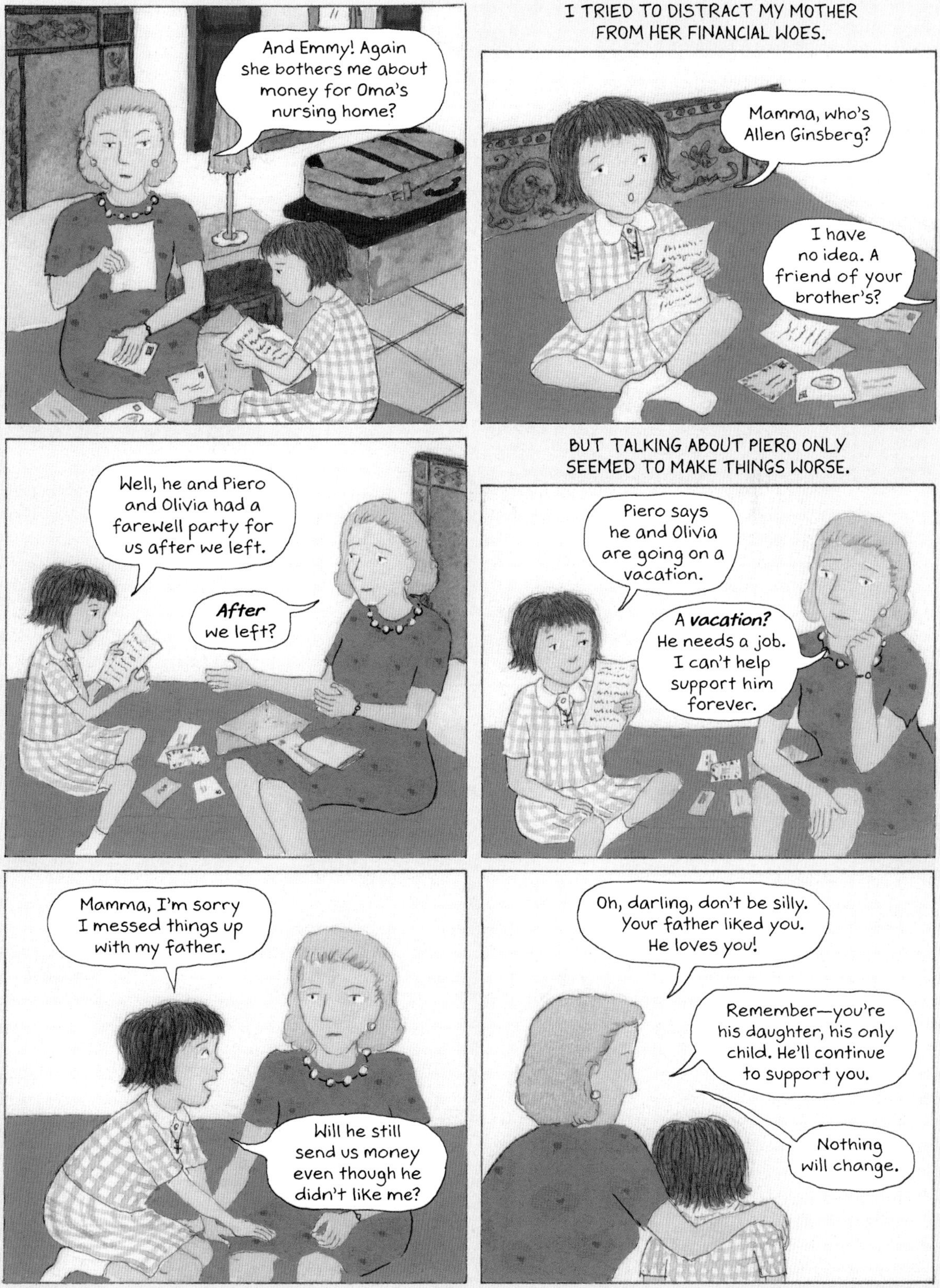
And Emmy! Again she bothers me about money for Oma's nursing home?
I TRIED TO DISTRACT MY MOTHER FROM HER FINANCIAL WOES.
Mamma, who's Allen Ginsberg?
I have no idea. A friend of your brother's?
Well, he and Piero and Olivia had a farewell party for us after we left.
After we left?
BUT TALKING ABOUT PIERO ONLY SEEMED TO MAKE THINGS WORSE.
Piero says he and Olivia are going on a vacation.
A vacation? He needs a job. I can't help support him forever.
Mamma, I'm sorry I messed things up with my father.
Will he still send us money even though he didn't like me?
Oh, darling, don't be silly. Your father liked you. He loves you!
Remember—you're his daughter, his only child. He'll continue to support you.
Nothing will change.

IT WAS OBVIOUS TO ME THAT THINGS WOULD BE BETTER FOR EVERYONE IF MY FATHER AND I STAYED FAR APART. NO MORE TRIPS TO SWITZERLAND, NO VISITS TO NEW YORK. OF COURSE, I WOULD CONTINUE TO WRITE MY POLITE LETTERS AND SEND MY SCHOOL PICTURES, AND HE WOULD CONTINUE TO WRITE HIS BORING ITALIAN LETTERS AND SEND HIS DISAPPOINTING GIFTS. THAT WOULD BE ENOUGH.

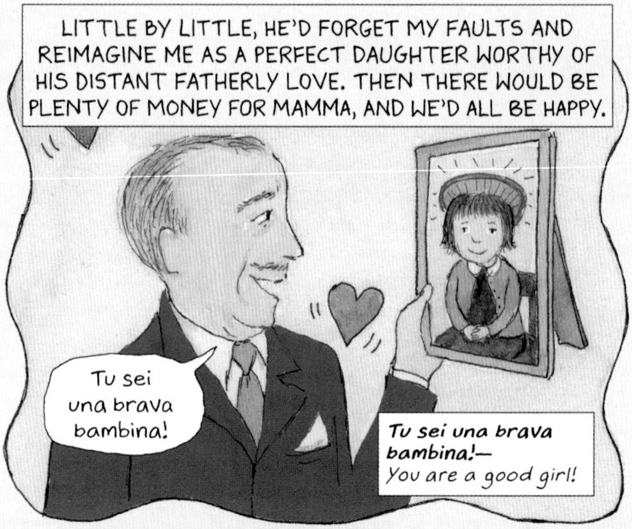
LITTLE BY LITTLE, HE'D FORGET MY FAULTS AND REIMAGINE ME AS A PERFECT DAUGHTER WORTHY OF HIS DISTANT FATHERLY LOVE. THEN THERE WOULD BE PLENTY OF MONEY FOR MAMMA, AND WE'D ALL BE HAPPY.
Tu sei una brava bambina!
Tu sei una brava bambina!— *You are a good girl!*

THE DAY WE LEFT ROME AND HEADED FOR NEW YORK, I WAS RELIEVED OUR TRIP WAS FINALLY OVER. IT WAS TIME TO GET BACK TO THE SANS SOUCI, BACK TO P.S. 196, BACK TO MY REGULAR LIFE.

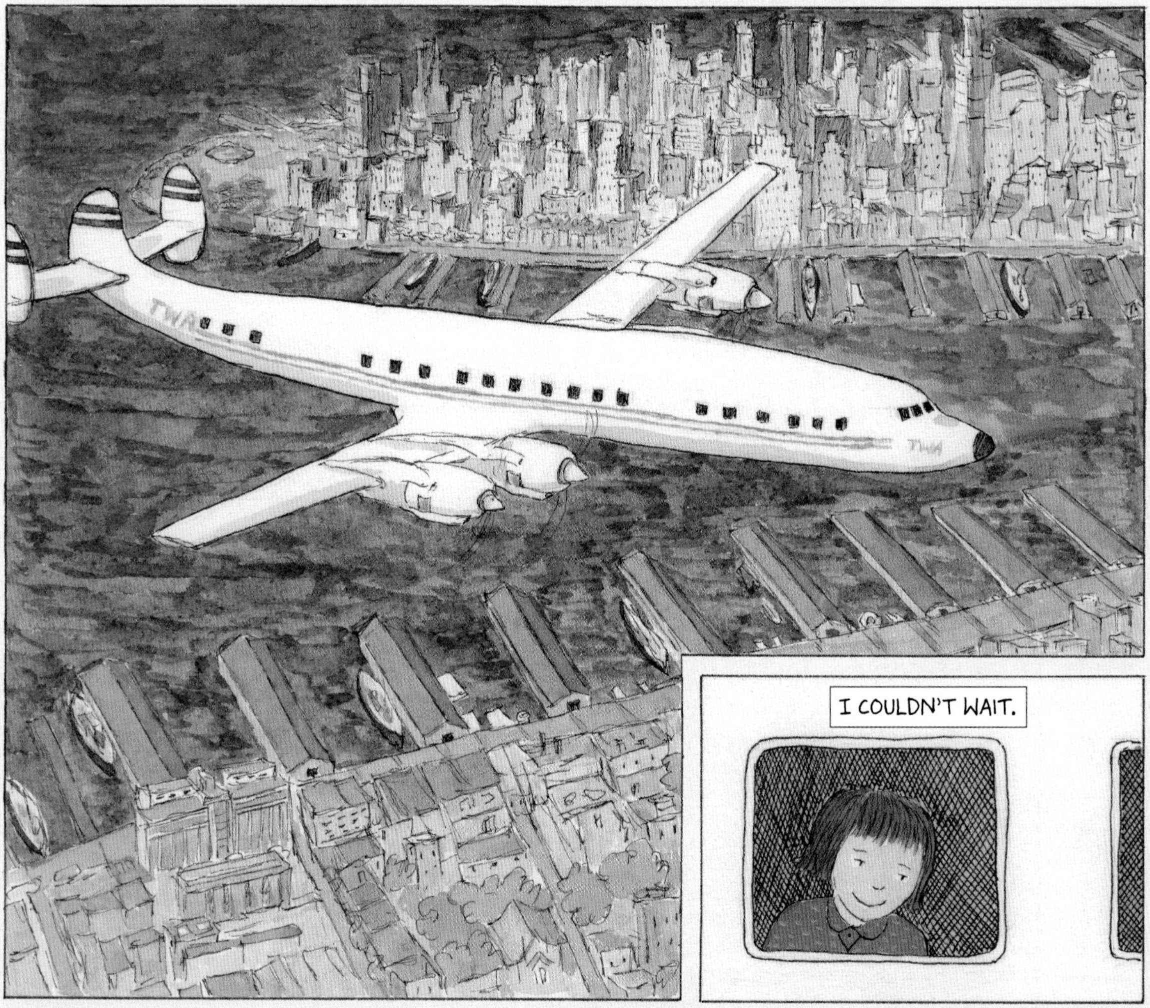
TWA
TWA
I COULDN'T WAIT.

NINE

Oma's Miracle

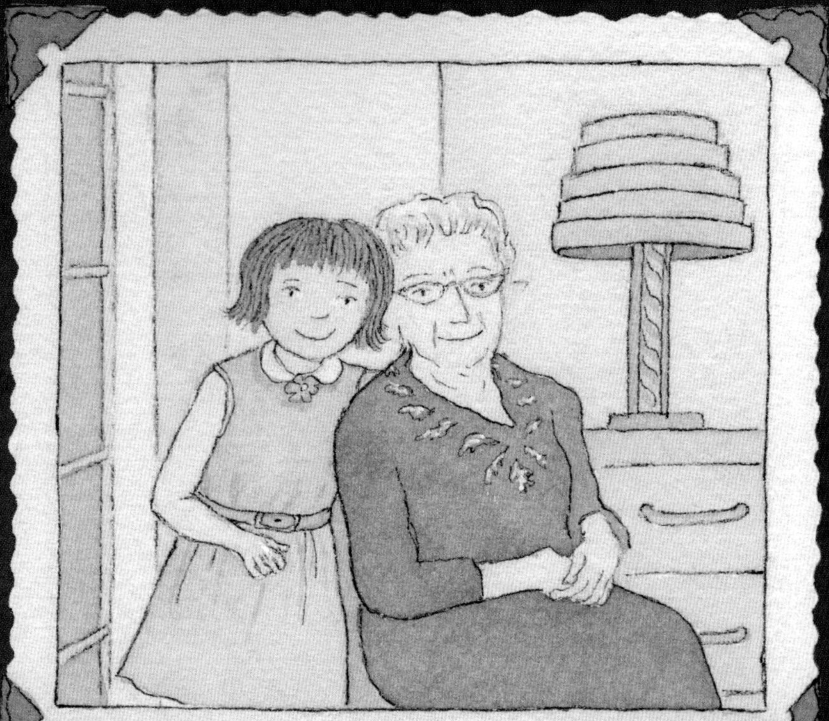

1958

WHEN WE GOT BACK FROM EUROPE, THE FIRST THING WE DID WAS VISIT OMA IN THE NURSING HOME. I HAD NOT SEEN HER SINCE HER STROKE.

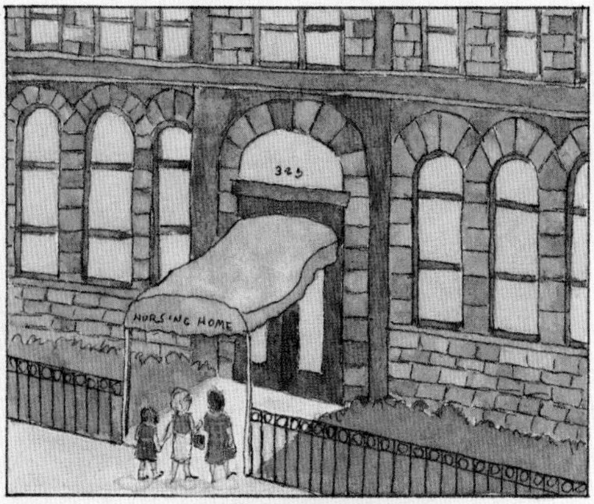
345
NURSING HOME

WE WALKED DOWN LONG HALLS FULL OF OLD PEOPLE. THE PLACE WAS KIND OF CREEPY.

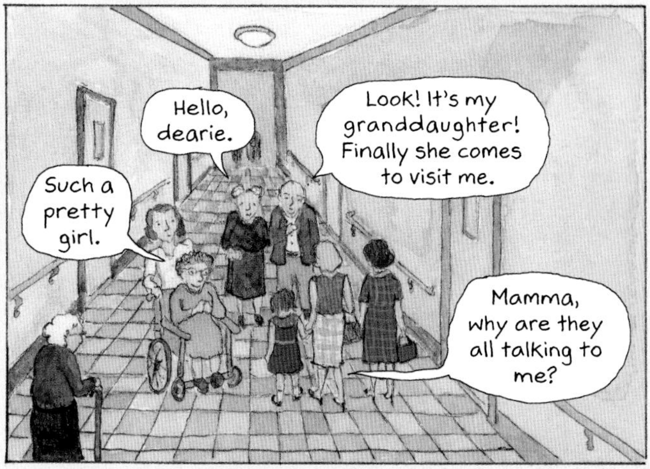
Hello, dearie.
Look! It's my granddaughter! Finally she comes to visit me.
Such a pretty girl.
Mamma, why are they all talking to me?

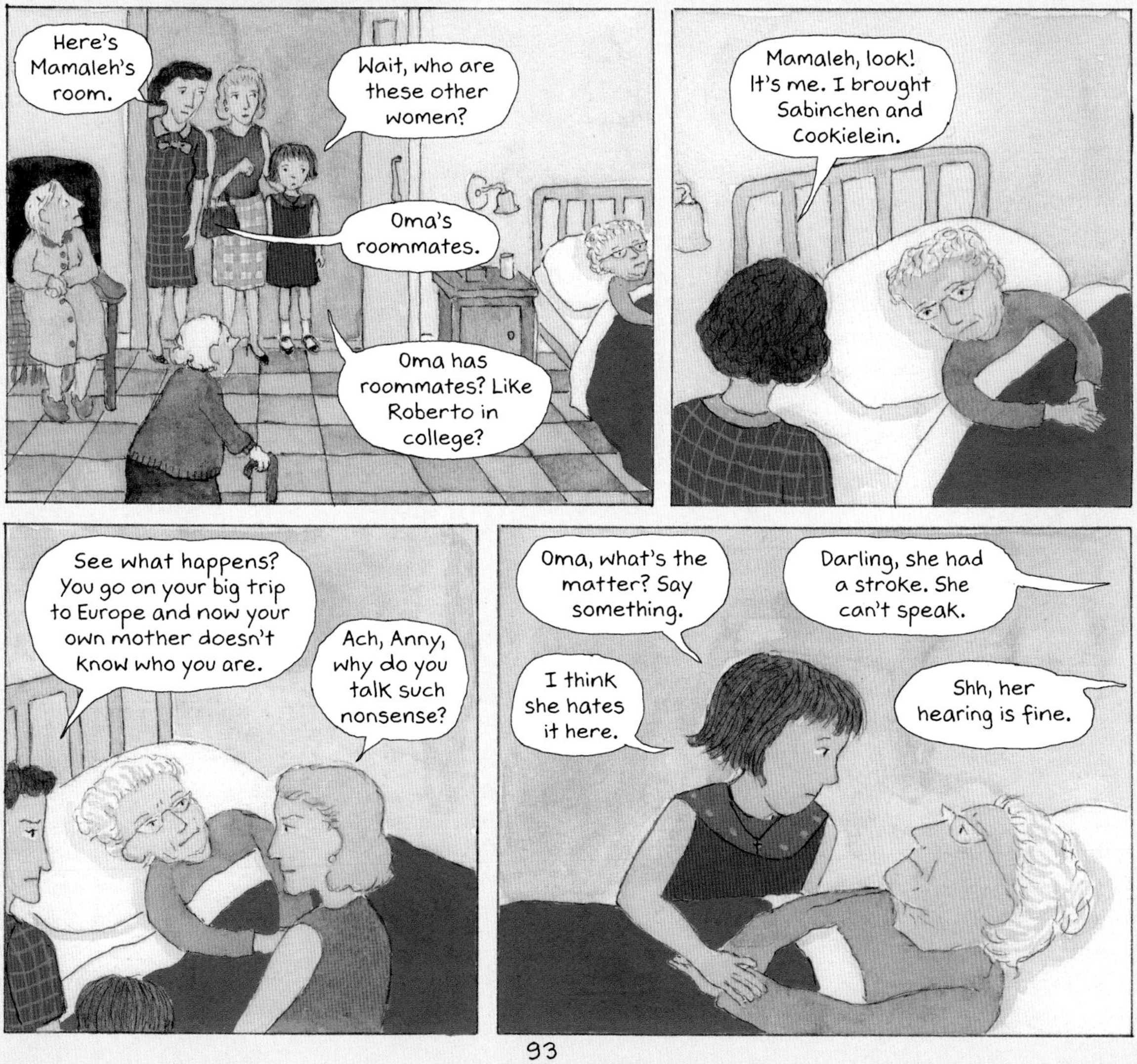
Here's Mamaleh's room.
Wait, who are these other women?
Oma's roommates.
Oma has roommates? Like Roberto in college?
Mamaleh, look! It's me. I brought Sabinchen and Cookielein.
See what happens? You go on your big trip to Europe and now your own mother doesn't know who you are.
Ach, Anny, why do you talk such nonsense?
Oma, what's the matter? Say something.
Darling, she had a stroke. She can't speak.
I think she hates it here.
Shh, her hearing is fine.

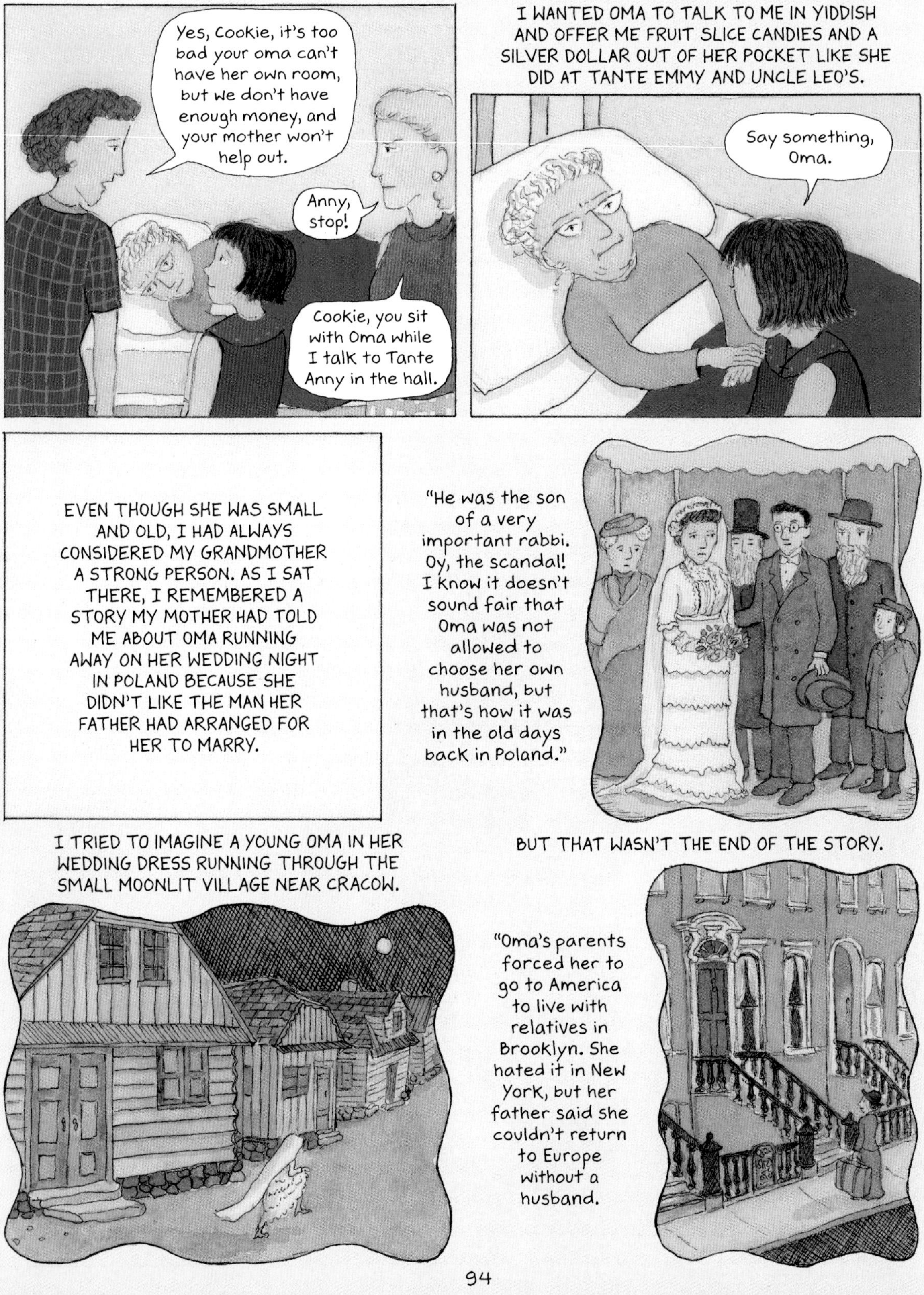
Yes, Cookie, it's too bad your oma can't have her own room, but we don't have enough money, and your mother won't help out.
Anny, stop!
Cookie, you sit with Oma while I talk to Tante Anny in the hall.
I WANTED OMA TO TALK TO ME IN YIDDISH AND OFFER ME FRUIT SLICE CANDIES AND A SILVER DOLLAR OUT OF HER POCKET LIKE SHE DID AT TANTE EMMY AND UNCLE LEO'S.
Say something, Oma.
EVEN THOUGH SHE WAS SMALL AND OLD, I HAD ALWAYS CONSIDERED MY GRANDMOTHER A STRONG PERSON. AS I SAT THERE, I REMEMBERED A STORY MY MOTHER HAD TOLD ME ABOUT OMA RUNNING AWAY ON HER WEDDING NIGHT IN POLAND BECAUSE SHE DIDN'T LIKE THE MAN HER FATHER HAD ARRANGED FOR HER TO MARRY.
"He was the son of a very important rabbi. Oy, the scandal! I know it doesn't sound fair that Oma was not allowed to choose her own husband, but that's how it was in the old days back in Poland."
I TRIED TO IMAGINE A YOUNG OMA IN HER WEDDING DRESS RUNNING THROUGH THE SMALL MOONLIT VILLAGE NEAR CRACOW.
BUT THAT WASN'T THE END OF THE STORY.
"Oma's parents forced her to go to America to live with relatives in Brooklyn. She hated it in New York, but her father said she couldn't return to Europe without a husband.

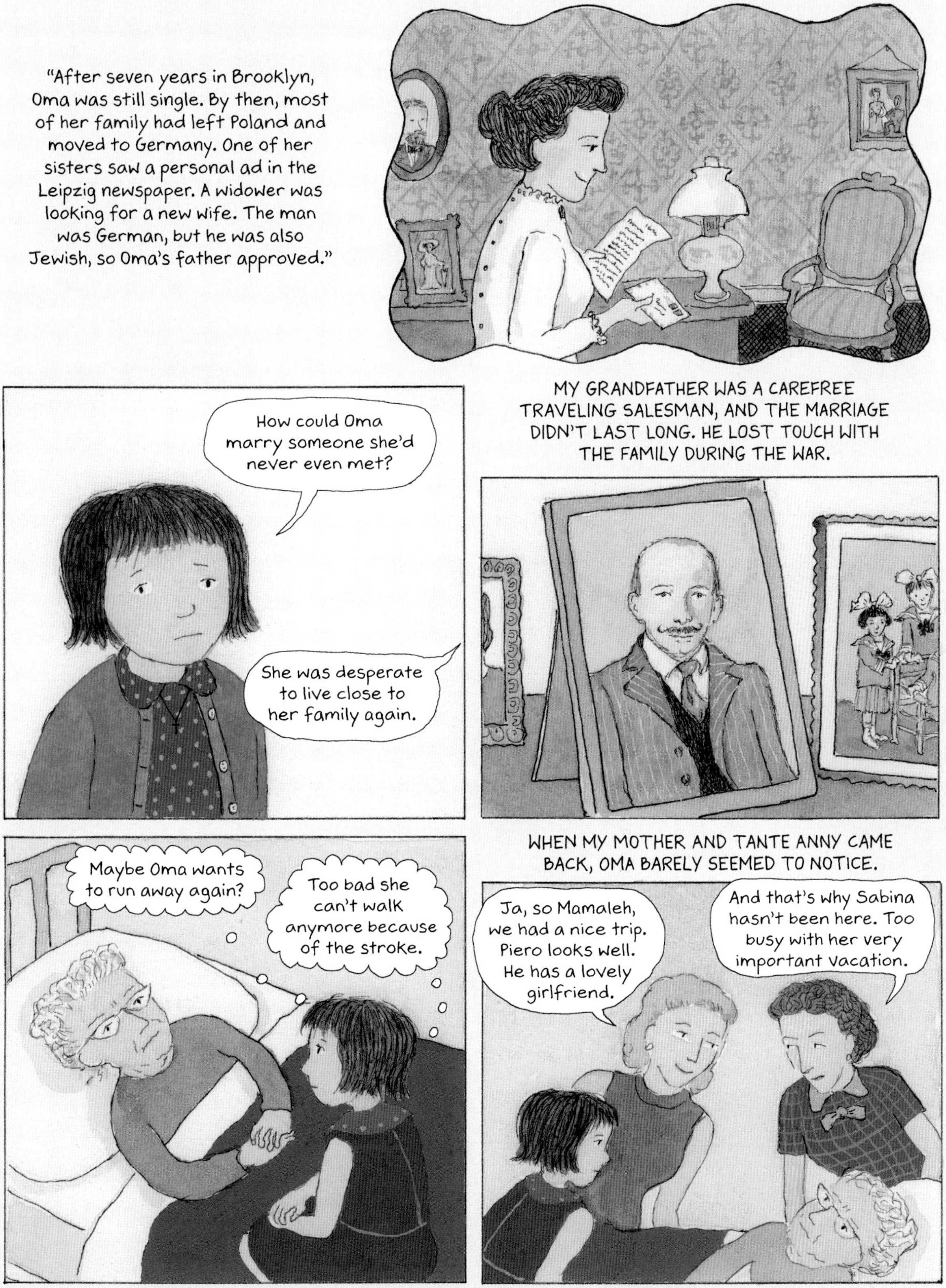
"After seven years in Brooklyn, Oma was still single. By then, most of her family had left Poland and moved to Germany. One of her sisters saw a personal ad in the Leipzig newspaper. A widower was looking for a new wife. The man was German, but he was also Jewish, so Oma's father approved."
How could Oma marry someone she'd never even met?
She was desperate to live close to her family again.
MY GRANDFATHER WAS A CAREFREE TRAVELING SALESMAN, AND THE MARRIAGE DIDN'T LAST LONG. HE LOST TOUCH WITH THE FAMILY DURING THE WAR.
Maybe Oma wants to run away again?
Too bad she can't walk anymore because of the stroke.
WHEN MY MOTHER AND TANTE ANNY CAME BACK, OMA BARELY SEEMED TO NOTICE.
Ja, so Mamaleh, we had a nice trip. Piero looks well. He has a lovely girlfriend.
And that's why Sabina hasn't been here. Too busy with her very important vacation.

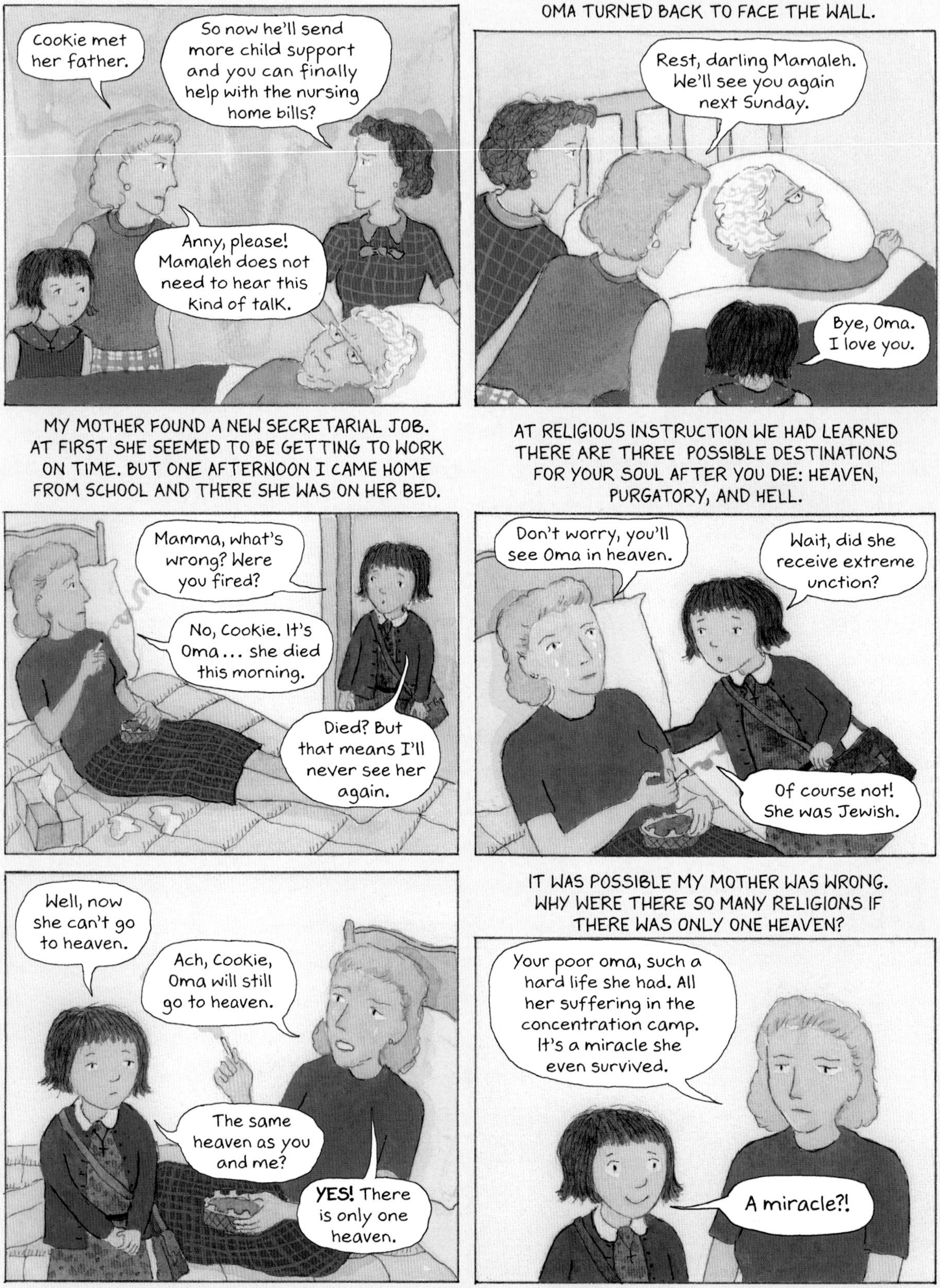

Cookie met her father.
So now he'll send more child support and you can finally help with the nursing home bills?
Anny, please! Mamaleh does not need to hear this kind of talk.
OMA TURNED BACK TO FACE THE WALL.
Rest, darling Mamaleh. We'll see you again next Sunday.
Bye, Oma. I love you.
MY MOTHER FOUND A NEW SECRETARIAL JOB. AT FIRST SHE SEEMED TO BE GETTING TO WORK ON TIME. BUT ONE AFTERNOON I CAME HOME FROM SCHOOL AND THERE SHE WAS ON HER BED.
Mamma, what's wrong? Were you fired?
No, Cookie. It's Oma... she died this morning.
Died? But that means I'll never see her again.
AT RELIGIOUS INSTRUCTION WE HAD LEARNED THERE ARE THREE POSSIBLE DESTINATIONS FOR YOUR SOUL AFTER YOU DIE: HEAVEN, PURGATORY, AND HELL.
Don't worry, you'll see Oma in heaven.
Wait, did she receive extreme unction?
Of course not! She was Jewish.
Well, now she can't go to heaven.
Ach, Cookie, Oma will still go to heaven.
The same heaven as you and me?
YES! There is only one heaven.
IT WAS POSSIBLE MY MOTHER WAS WRONG. WHY WERE THERE SO MANY RELIGIONS IF THERE WAS ONLY ONE HEAVEN?
Your poor oma, such a hard life she had. All her suffering in the concentration camp. It's a miracle she even survived.
A miracle?!

I NEEDED TO KNOW MORE ABOUT THIS MIRACLE BECAUSE IT MIGHT BE ENOUGH TO GET OMA INTO CATHOLIC HEAVEN.

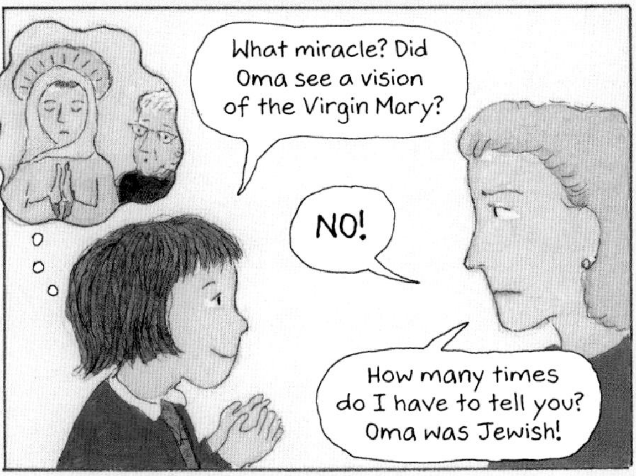
What miracle? Did Oma see a vision of the Virgin Mary?
NO!
How many times do I have to tell you? Oma was Jewish!

THE FUNERAL TOOK PLACE THE NEXT DAY. OMA WAS BURIED IN A JEWISH CEMETERY IN NEW JERSEY. I WASN'T ALLOWED TO ATTEND.

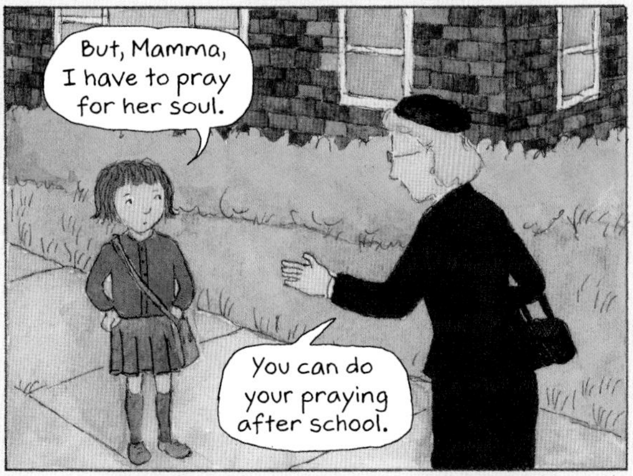
But, Mamma, I have to pray for her soul.
You can do your praying after school.

THEN THERE WAS SOME KIND OF SECRET WEEKLONG JEWISH RITUAL CALLED "SITTING SHIVA" THAT I ALSO WASN'T ALLOWED TO ATTEND.

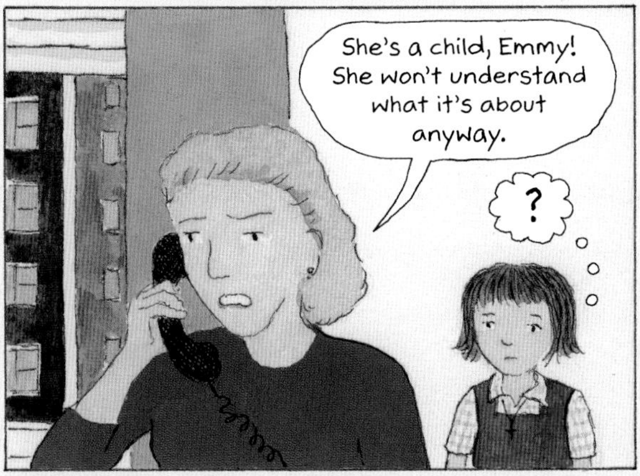
She's a child, Emmy! She won't understand what it's about anyway.
?

AND SO MY GRANDMOTHER WAS GONE WITHOUT A TRACE. THE NEXT SATURDAY AFTER CONFESSION, I ASKED MAMMA IF WE COULD LIGHT A VOTIVE CANDLE FOR OMA.

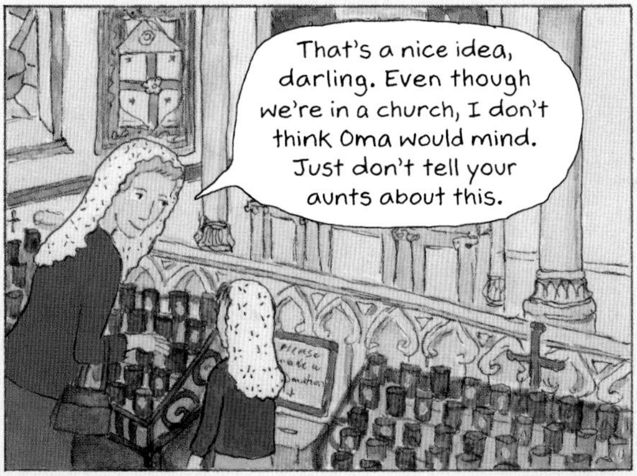
That's a nice idea, darling. Even though we're in a church, I don't think Oma would mind. Just don't tell your aunts about this.

IF MY FAMILY WAS NOT GOING TO LET ME MOURN WITH THEM, I'D HAVE TO DO IT ON MY OWN.

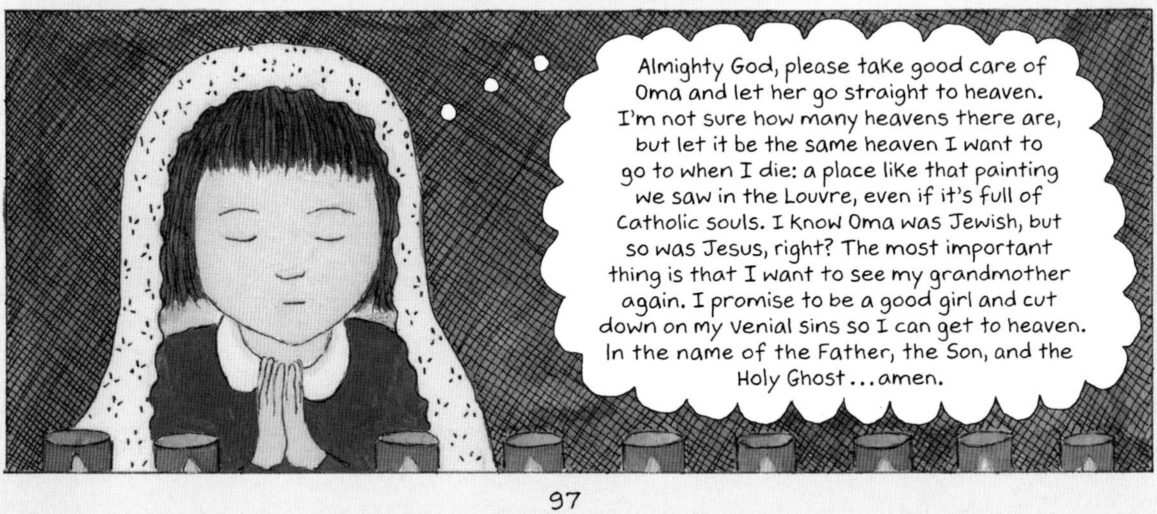
Almighty God, please take good care of Oma and let her go straight to heaven. I'm not sure how many heavens there are, but let it be the same heaven I want to go to when I die: a place like that painting we saw in the Louvre, even if it's full of Catholic souls. I know Oma was Jewish, but so was Jesus, right? The most important thing is that I want to see my grandmother again. I promise to be a good girl and cut down on my venial sins so I can get to heaven. In the name of the Father, the Son, and the Holy Ghost . . . amen.

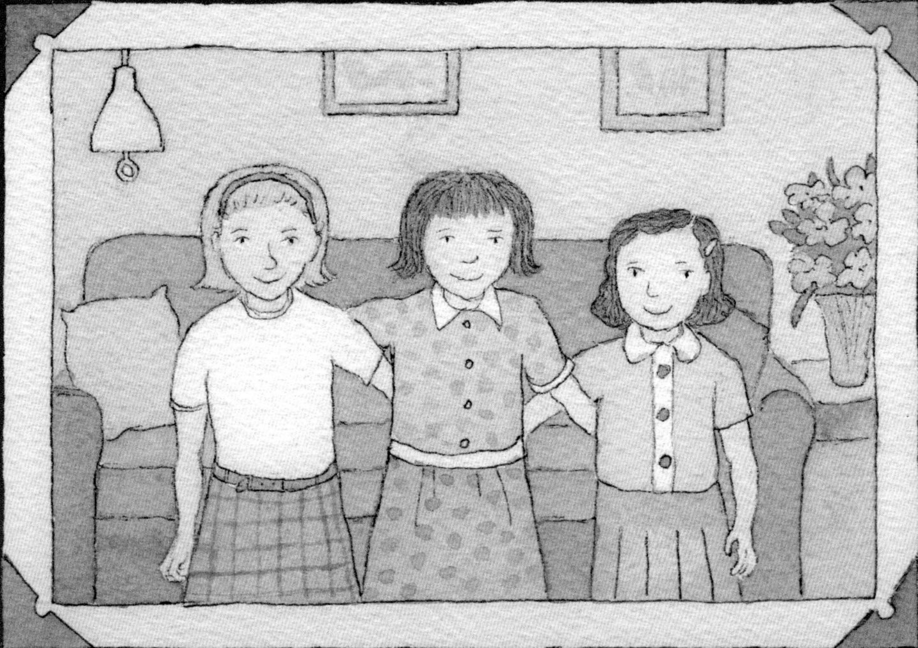

1958-59

EVEN THOUGH I WAS NOW IN THIRD GRADE, MY MOTHER HADN'T LOOSENED ANY OF HER RULES.

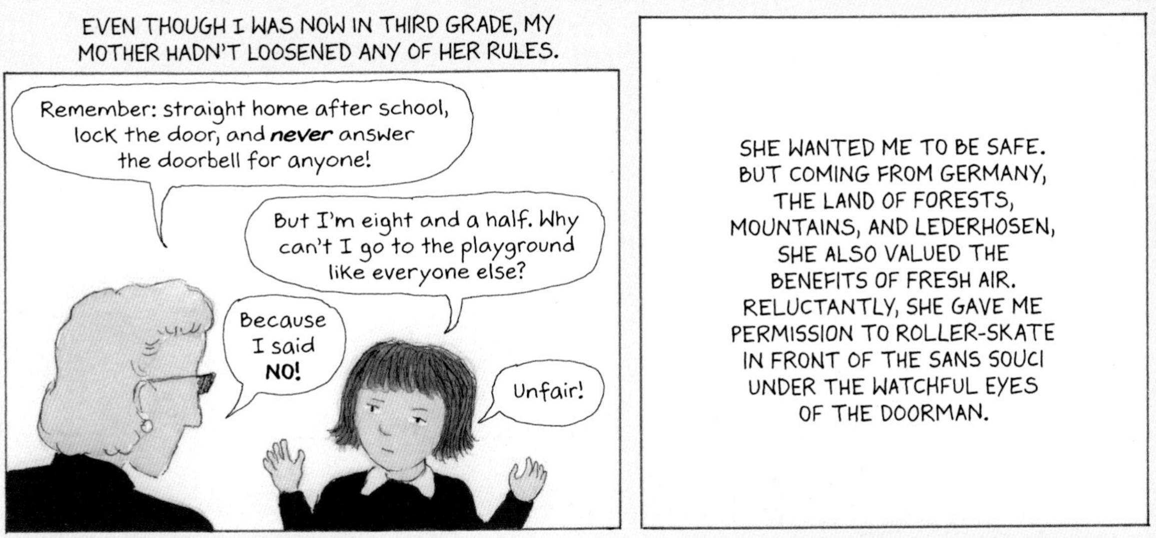
Remember: straight home after school, lock the door, and **never** answer the doorbell for anyone!
But I'm eight and a half. Why can't I go to the playground like everyone else?
Because I said **NO!**
Unfair!

SHE WANTED ME TO BE SAFE. BUT COMING FROM GERMANY, THE LAND OF FORESTS, MOUNTAINS, AND LEDERHOSEN, SHE ALSO VALUED THE BENEFITS OF FRESH AIR. RELUCTANTLY, SHE GAVE ME PERMISSION TO ROLLER-SKATE IN FRONT OF THE SANS SOUCI UNDER THE WATCHFUL EYES OF THE DOORMAN.

I HAD A TWENTY-MINUTE DAILY TIME LIMIT, AND I MADE THE MOST OF IT.

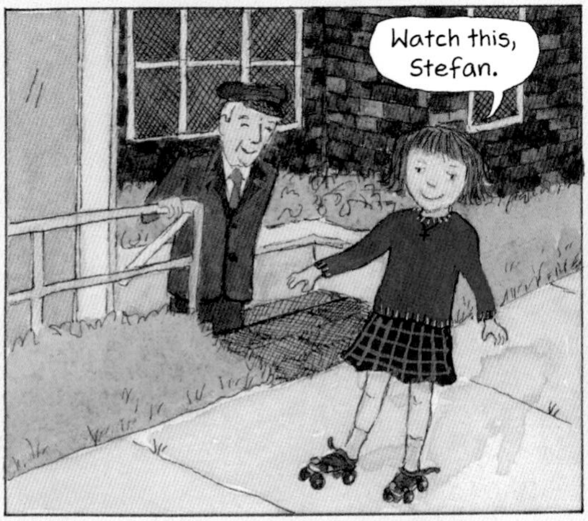
Watch this, Stefan.

BUT THEN MY MOTHER RECEIVED AN ANGRY LETTER FROM OUR LANDLORD WHO, DESPITE BEING A GERMAN REFUGEE HIMSELF, DIDN'T SEEM TO APPRECIATE A CHILD'S NEED FOR OUTDOOR PLAY.

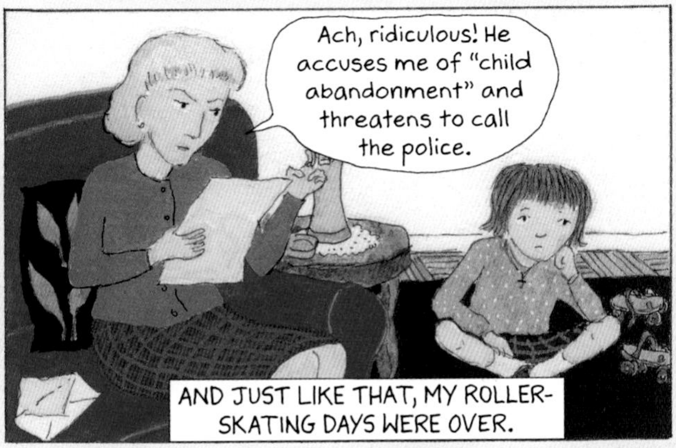
Ach, ridiculous! He accuses me of "child abandonment" and threatens to call the police.
AND JUST LIKE THAT, MY ROLLER-SKATING DAYS WERE OVER.

MY EVER-RESOURCEFUL MOTHER HATCHED A NEW PLAN.

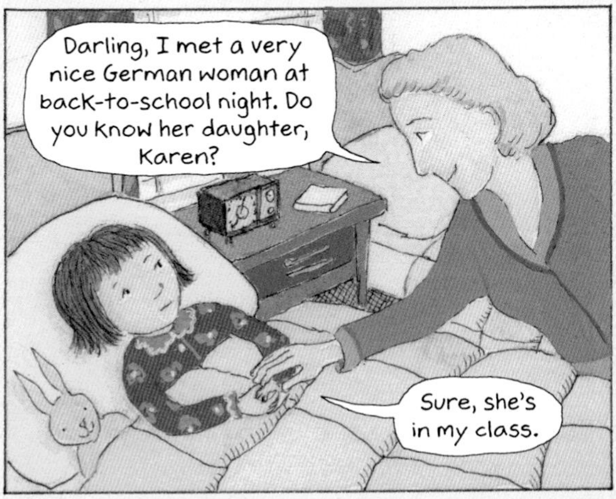
Darling, I met a very nice German woman at back-to-school night. Do you know her daughter, Karen?
Sure, she's in my class.

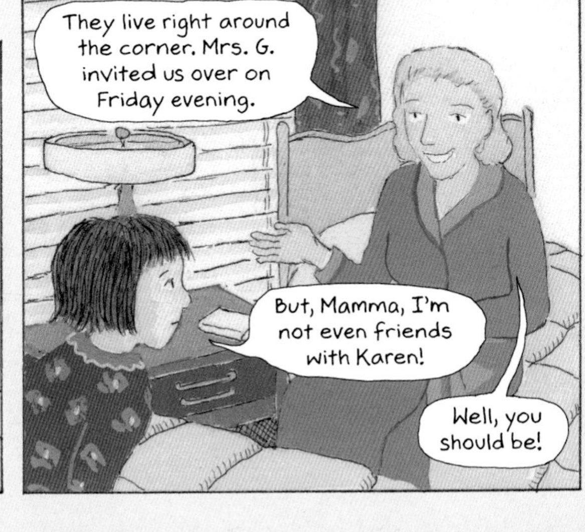
They live right around the corner. Mrs. G. invited us over on Friday evening.
But, Mamma, I'm not even friends with Karen!
Well, you should be!

AT KAREN'S APARTMENT, HER PARENTS WERE READY WITH KAFFEE UND KUCHEN.

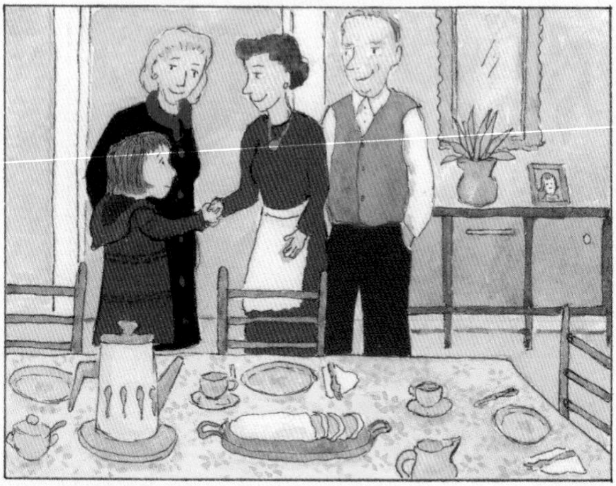

KAREN WAS BUSY GIVING HER DOLL A BATH AND DIDN'T SEEM TO BE EXPECTING ME.

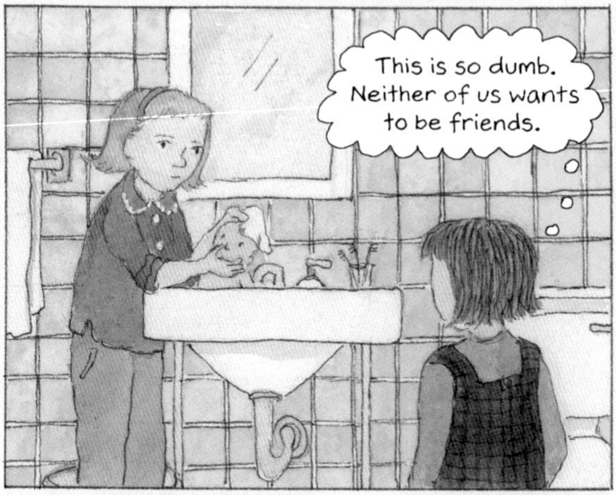
This is so dumb. Neither of us wants to be friends.

WHEN IT WAS FINALLY TIME TO GO HOME:

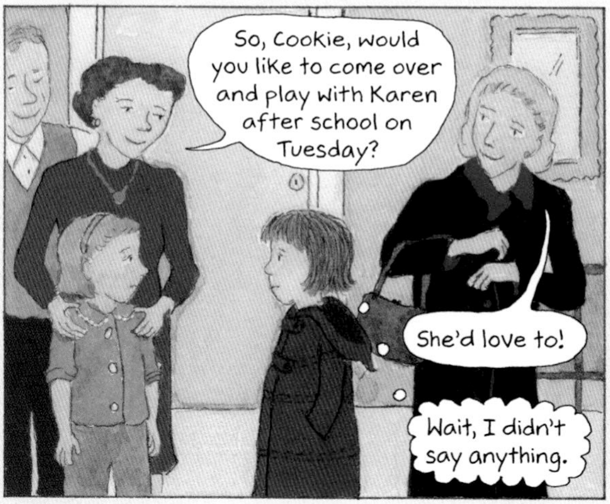
So, Cookie, would you like to come over and play with Karen after school on Tuesday?
She'd love to!
Wait, I didn't say anything.

MY MOTHER'S MOTIVES SOON BECAME CLEAR.

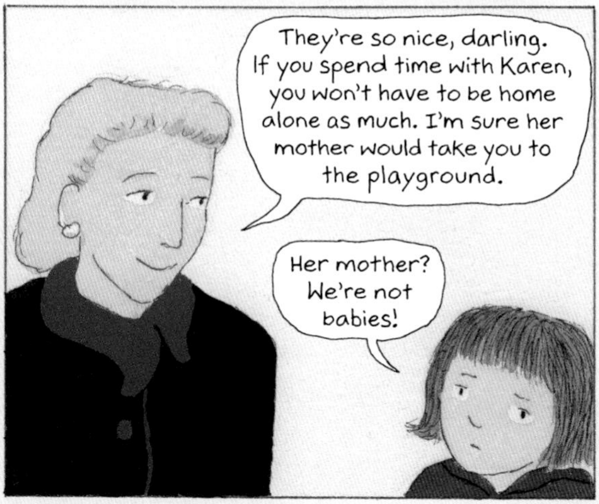
They're so nice, darling. If you spend time with Karen, you won't have to be home alone as much. I'm sure her mother would take you to the playground.
Her mother? We're not babies!

TO MY RELIEF, I DISCOVERED THAT MRS. G. HAD NO INTEREST IN ACCOMPANYING US ANYWHERE.

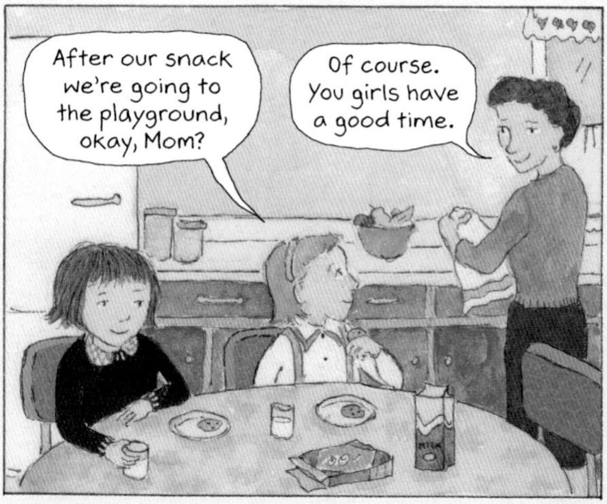
After our snack we're going to the playground, okay, Mom?
Of course. You girls have a good time.

KAREN AND I BONDED AS WE WANDERED FARTHER AND FARTHER FROM HER BUILDING.

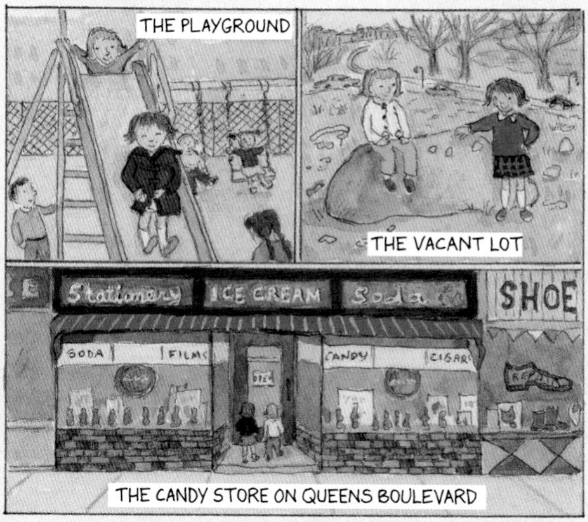
THE PLAYGROUND
THE VACANT LOT
Stationery
ICE CREAM
Soda
SHOE
SODA
FILMS
CANDY
CIGARS
THE CANDY STORE ON QUEENS BOULEVARD

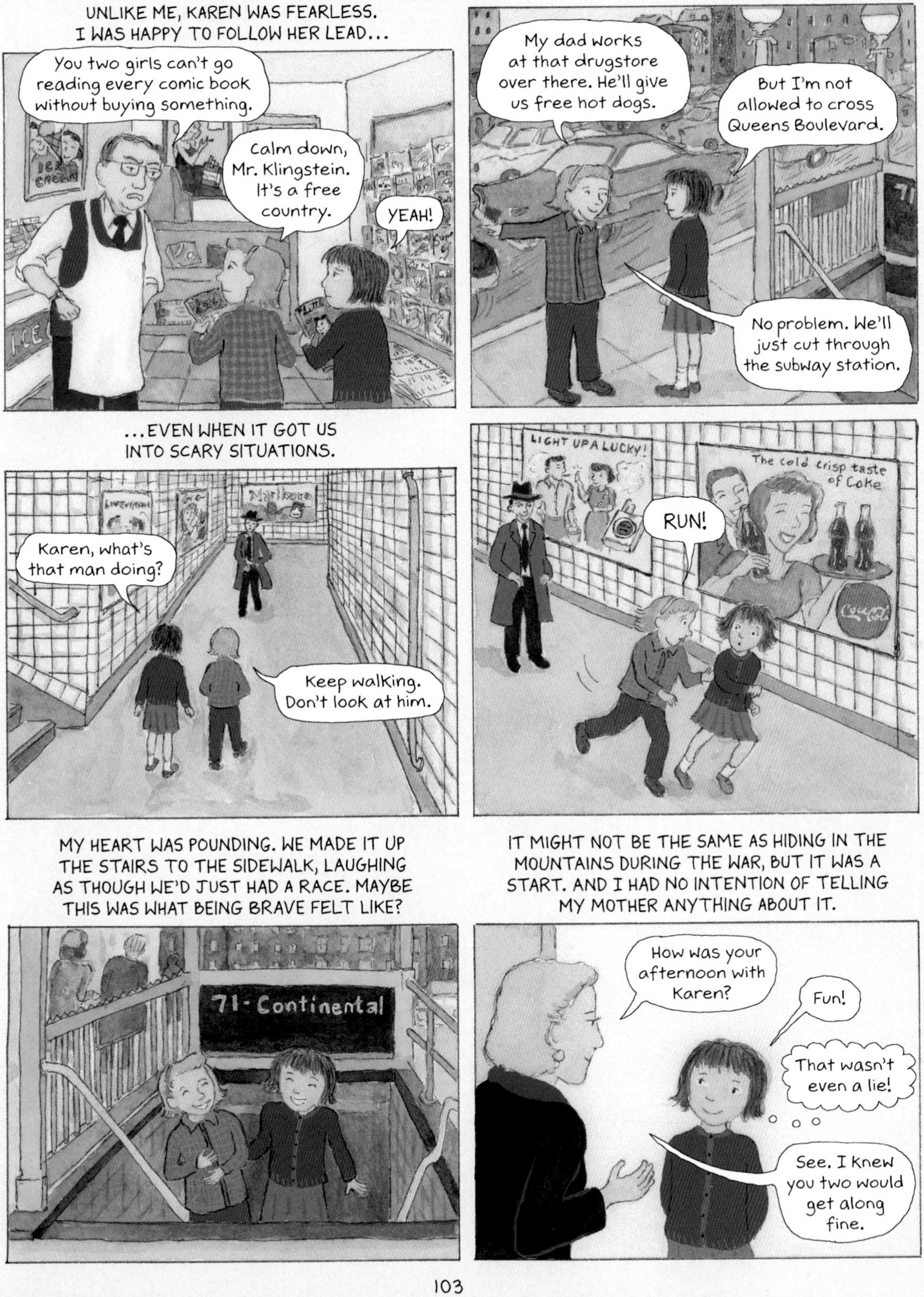
UNLIKE ME, KAREN WAS FEARLESS.
I WAS HAPPY TO FOLLOW HER LEAD...
You two girls can't go reading every comic book without buying something.
Calm down, Mr. Klingstein. It's a free country.
YEAH!
My dad works at that drugstore over there. He'll give us free hot dogs.
But I'm not allowed to cross Queens Boulevard.
No problem. We'll just cut through the subway station.
...EVEN WHEN IT GOT US INTO SCARY SITUATIONS.
Karen, what's that man doing?
Keep walking. Don't look at him.
LIGHT UP A LUCKY!
The cold crisp taste of Coke
RUN!
MY HEART WAS POUNDING. WE MADE IT UP THE STAIRS TO THE SIDEWALK, LAUGHING AS THOUGH WE'D JUST HAD A RACE. MAYBE THIS WAS WHAT BEING BRAVE FELT LIKE?
71 - Continental
IT MIGHT NOT BE THE SAME AS HIDING IN THE MOUNTAINS DURING THE WAR, BUT IT WAS A START. AND I HAD NO INTENTION OF TELLING MY MOTHER ANYTHING ABOUT IT.
How was your afternoon with Karen?
Fun!
That wasn't even a lie!
See. I knew you two would get along fine.

BUOYED BY HER SUCCESS WITH KAREN, MY MOTHER MATCHED ME UP WITH ANOTHER GIRL. SHE LIVED IN THE SANS SOUCI, AND HER NAME WAS ROBERTA.

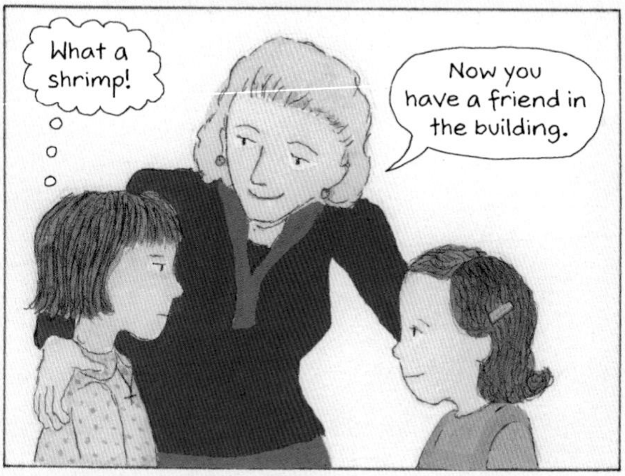
What a shrimp!
Now you have a friend in the building.

ROBERTA WAS TWO YEARS YOUNGER THAN I WAS, BUT NO MATTER, HER PARENTS WERE ITALIAN! BETTER YET, THEY WERE NEAPOLITAN LIKE MY FATHER.

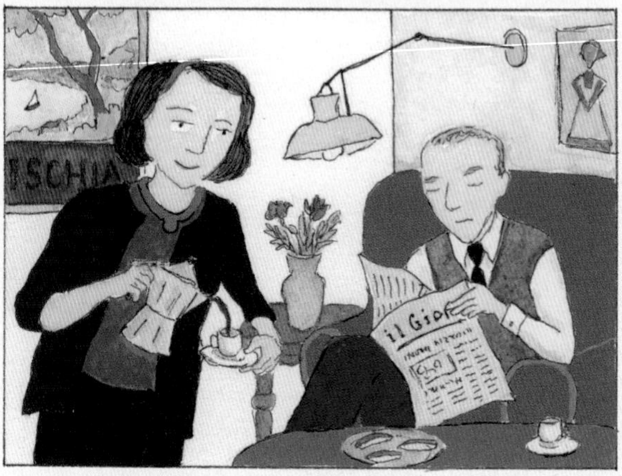

IN A WAY, ROBERTA WAS MORE OF A LITTLE SISTER THAN A REAL FRIEND.

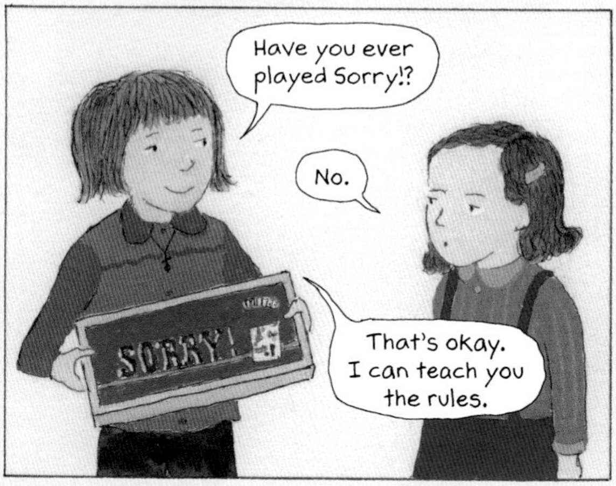
Have you ever played Sorry!?
No.
SORRY!
That's okay. I can teach you the rules.

BUT HADN'T I ALWAYS WANTED A LITTLE SISTER?

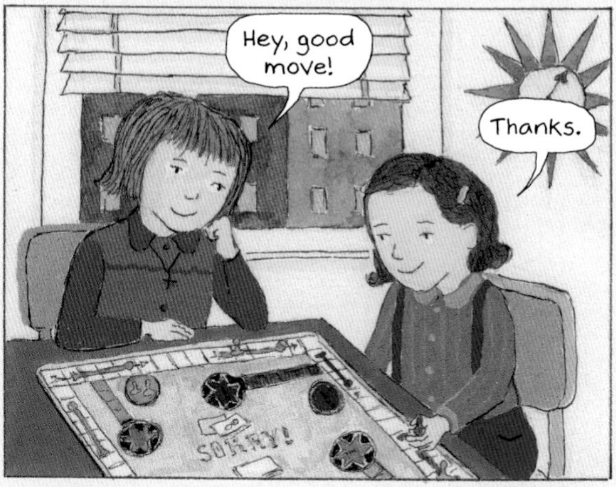
Hey, good move!
Thanks.
SORRY!

HER FATHER, A SUCCESSFUL BUSINESSMAN, SOON MOVED THE FAMILY TO A BIG DUTCH COLONIAL A FEW BLOCKS AWAY.

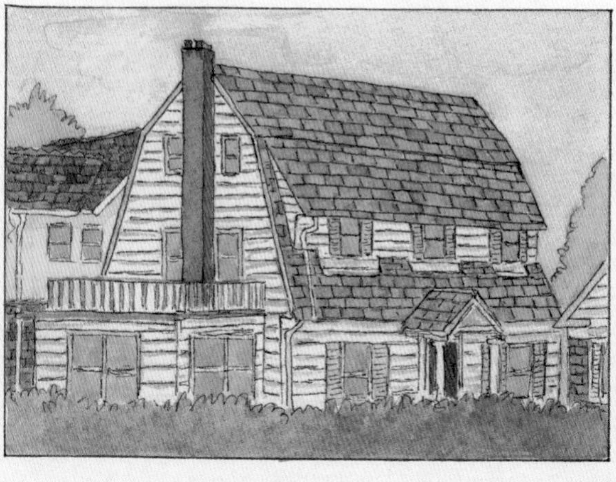

ROBERTA BECAME THE FIRST PERSON I'D EVER KNOWN WHO LIVED IN A REAL HOUSE, NOT AN APARTMENT BUILDING. I WAS KIND OF JEALOUS.

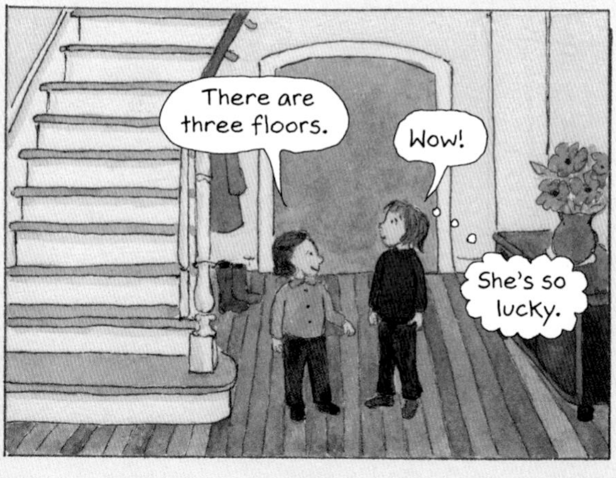
There are three floors.
Wow!
She's so lucky.

I LOVED SPENDING TIME THERE. IT WAS LIKE AN ITALIAN VERSION OF *FATHER KNOWS BEST.*

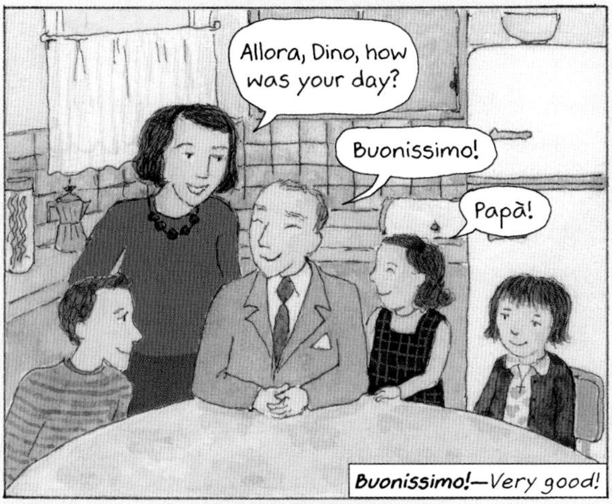
Allora, Dino, how was your day?
Buonissimo!
Papà!
Buonissimo!—*Very good!*

ONLY MRS. F., ROBERTA'S MOTHER, WASN'T A HOMEMAKER. SHE WAS AN ARTIST WITH A STUDIO IN THE ATTIC.

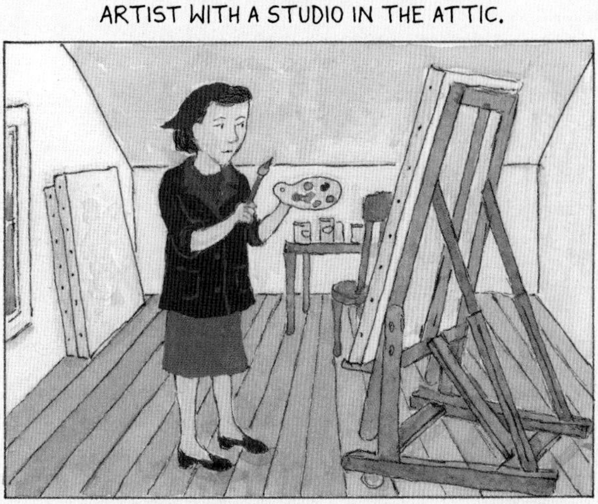

SHE ALSO GAVE ART LESSONS TO NEIGHBORHOOD CHILDREN. KAREN AND I BOTH SIGNED UP.

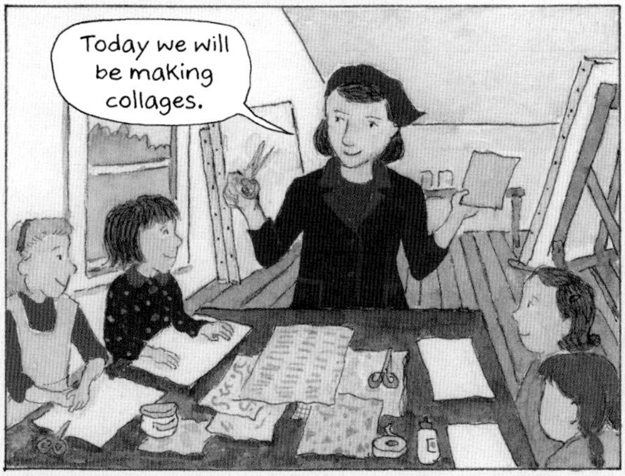
Today we will be making collages.

SATURDAY MORNINGS IN MRS. F.'S ATTIC STUDIO MADE ME THINK ABOUT PIERO IN HIS GARRET ON RUE DESCARTES.

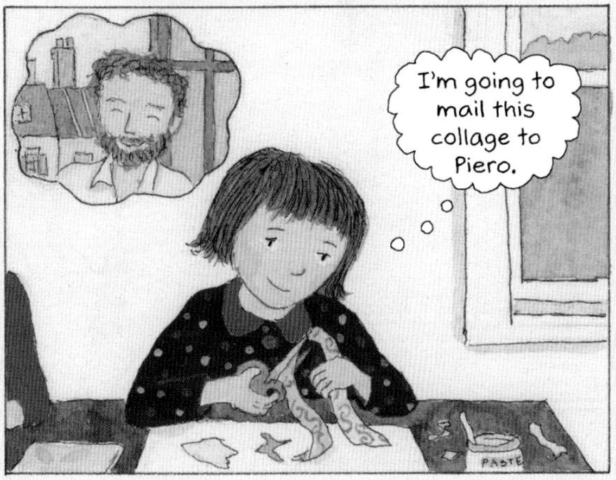
I'm going to mail this collage to Piero.
PASTE

THIRD GRADE WAS TURNING OUT TO BE A VERY GOOD YEAR, WITH ART LESSONS EVERY WEEK...

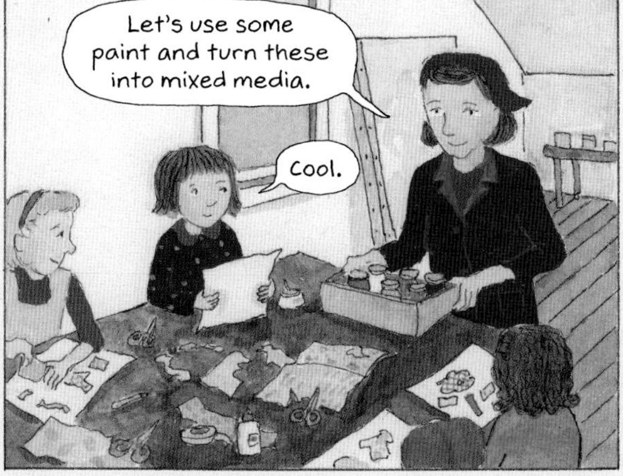
Let's use some paint and turn these into mixed media.
Cool.

...AND FREEDOM TO WANDER THE NEIGHBORHOOD AFTER SCHOOL.

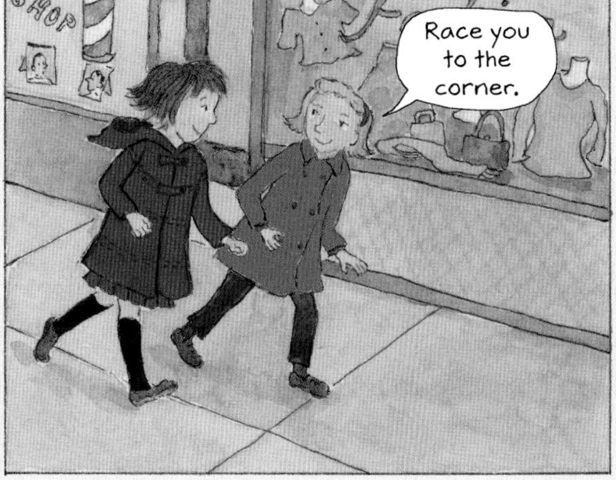
SHOP
Race you to the corner.

MY MOTHER PROBABLY DIDN'T REALIZE THAT THE TWO NEW FRIENDS SHE HAD SO CAREFULLY CHOSEN FOR ME WERE OPENING UP MY WORLD.

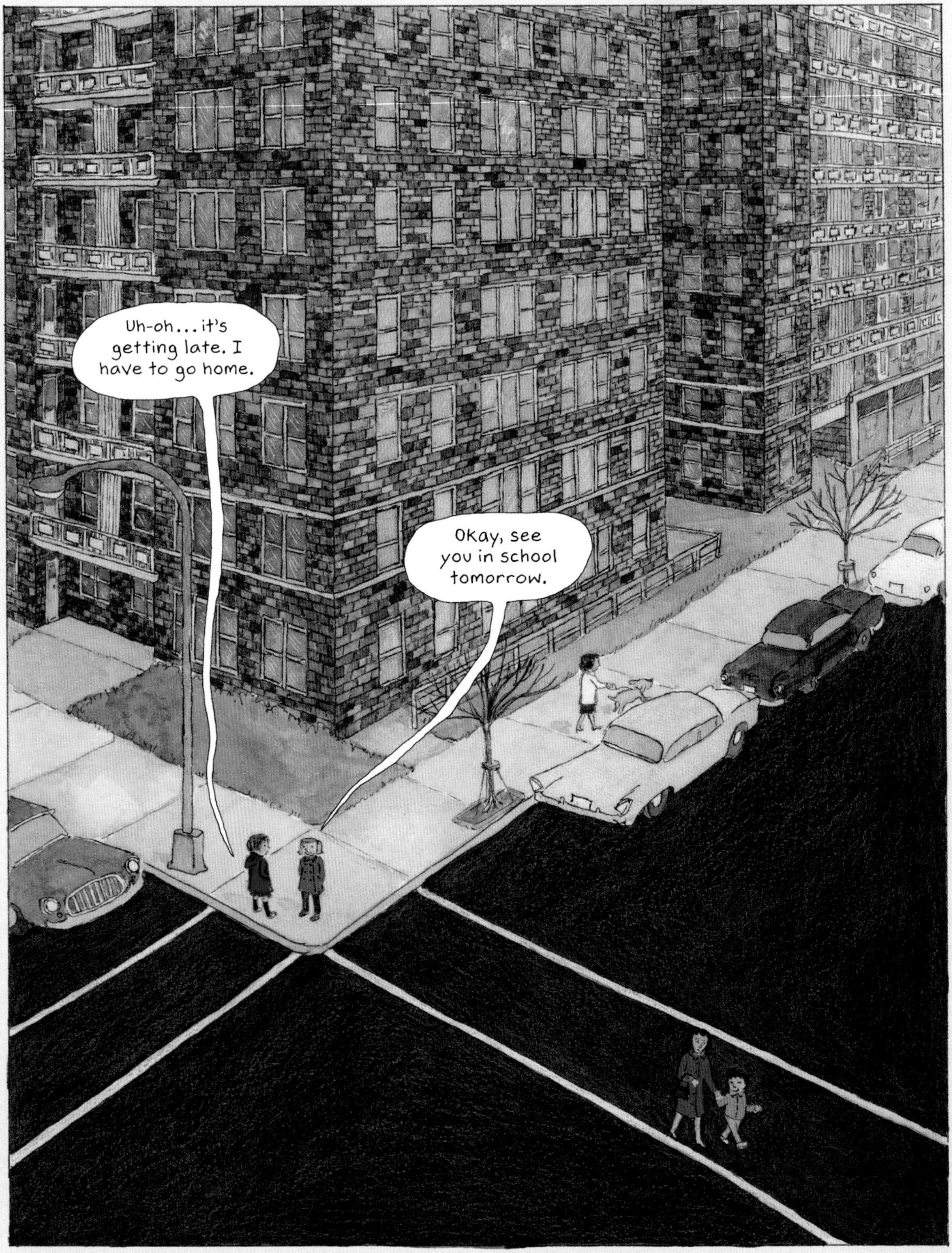
Uh-oh... it's getting late. I have to go home.
Okay, see you in school tomorrow.

ELEVEN

A Room of My Own

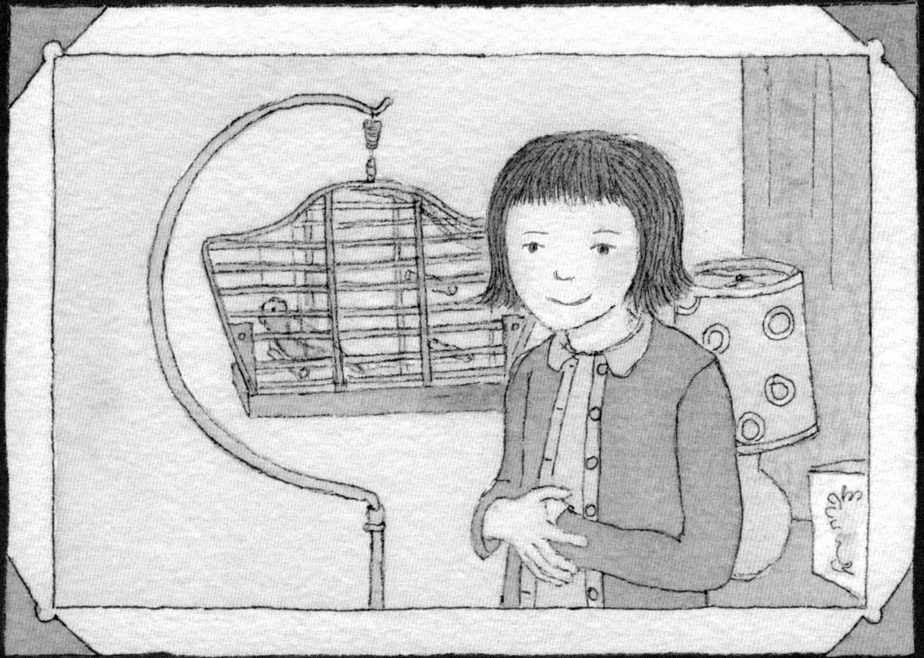

1958-59

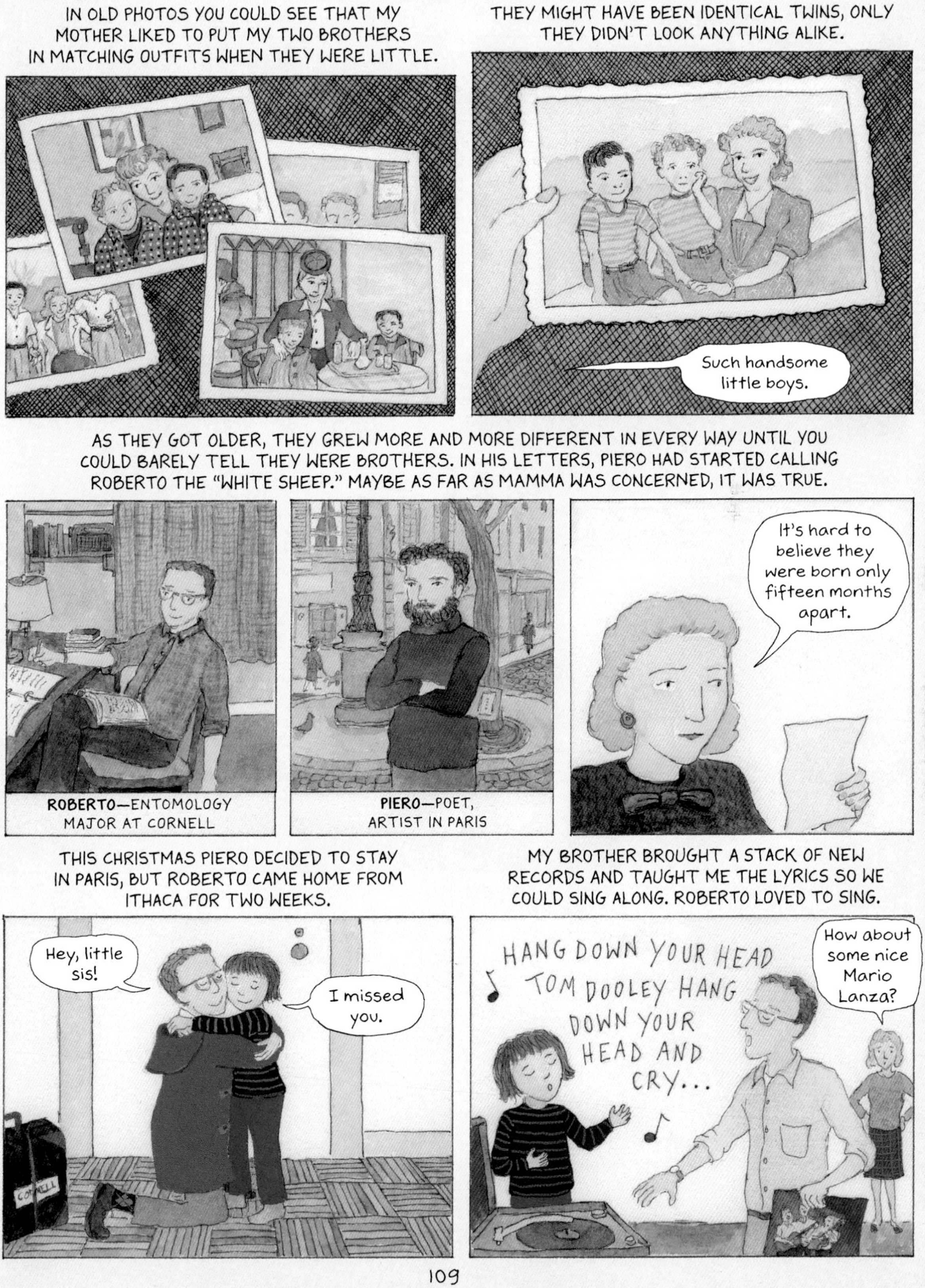
IN OLD PHOTOS YOU COULD SEE THAT MY MOTHER LIKED TO PUT MY TWO BROTHERS IN MATCHING OUTFITS WHEN THEY WERE LITTLE.
THEY MIGHT HAVE BEEN IDENTICAL TWINS, ONLY THEY DIDN'T LOOK ANYTHING ALIKE.
Such handsome little boys.
AS THEY GOT OLDER, THEY GREW MORE AND MORE DIFFERENT IN EVERY WAY UNTIL YOU COULD BARELY TELL THEY WERE BROTHERS. IN HIS LETTERS, PIERO HAD STARTED CALLING ROBERTO THE "WHITE SHEEP." MAYBE AS FAR AS MAMMA WAS CONCERNED, IT WAS TRUE.
ROBERTO—ENTOMOLOGY MAJOR AT CORNELL
PIERO—POET, ARTIST IN PARIS
It's hard to believe they were born only fifteen months apart.
THIS CHRISTMAS PIERO DECIDED TO STAY IN PARIS, BUT ROBERTO CAME HOME FROM ITHACA FOR TWO WEEKS.
Hey, little sis!
I missed you.
CORNELL
MY BROTHER BROUGHT A STACK OF NEW RECORDS AND TAUGHT ME THE LYRICS SO WE COULD SING ALONG. ROBERTO LOVED TO SING.
HANG DOWN YOUR HEAD TOM DOOLEY HANG DOWN YOUR HEAD AND CRY...
How about some nice Mario Lanza?

MY FAVORITE TIME WITH ROBERTO WAS WHEN MAMMA WENT OUT FOR THE EVENING.

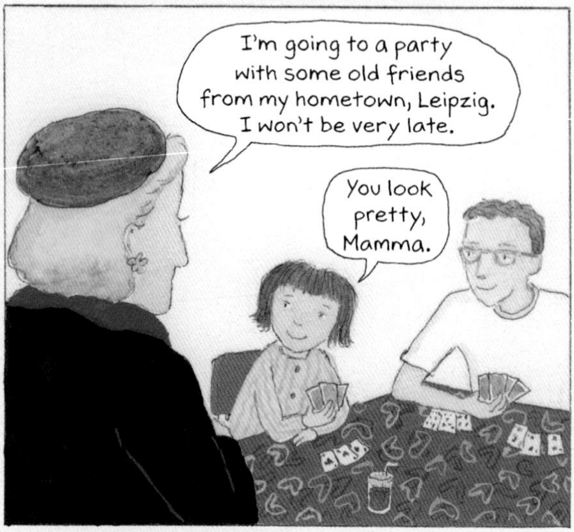
I'm going to a party with some old friends from my hometown, Leipzig. I won't be very late.
You look pretty, Mamma.

HE WAS MUCH MORE FUN THAN THE ELDERLY GERMAN WOMAN WHO SOMETIMES BABYSAT.

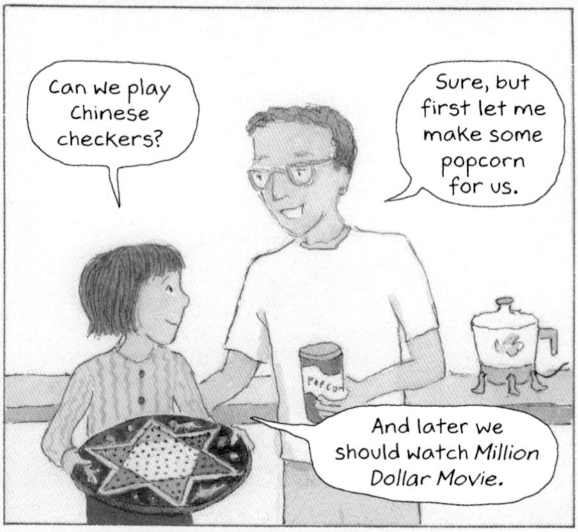
Can we play Chinese checkers?
Sure, but first let me make some popcorn for us.
And later we should watch *Million Dollar Movie.*

IT SEEMED LIKE MAMMA MADE PLANS TO GO OUT EVERY NIGHT OF MY BROTHER'S VISIT.

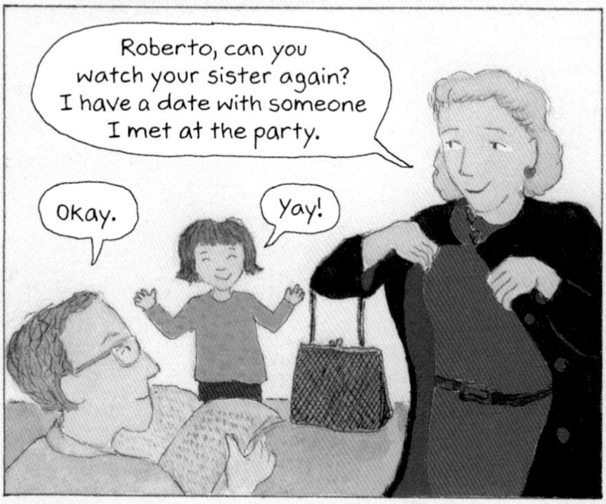
Roberto, can you watch your sister again? I have a date with someone I met at the party.
Okay.
Yay!

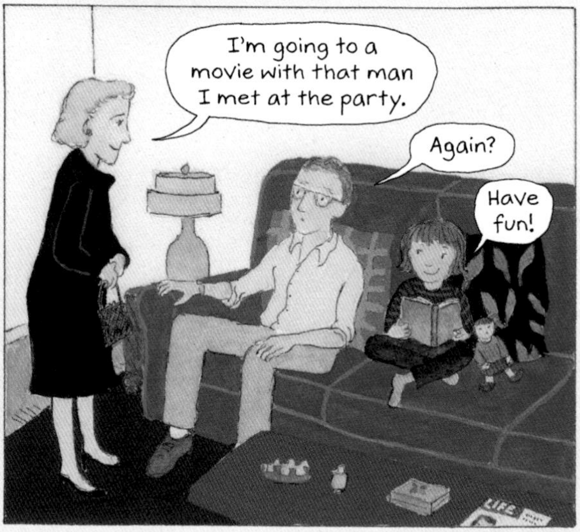
I'm going to a movie with that man I met at the party.
Again?
Have fun!
LIFE

WHILE MY MOTHER WENT OUT ON PLENTY OF DATES, SHE HAD NEVER BROUGHT ANYONE HOME TO MEET MY BROTHERS AND ME. BUT THAT ALL CHANGED ONE EVENING BEFORE ROBERTO RETURNED TO COLLEGE WHEN SHE BROUGHT HOME THE MAN FROM THE PARTY. EVEN THOUGH SHE SAID HE WAS POLISH, HE HAD THE IMPROBABLE NAME SOL WEDGEWOOD.

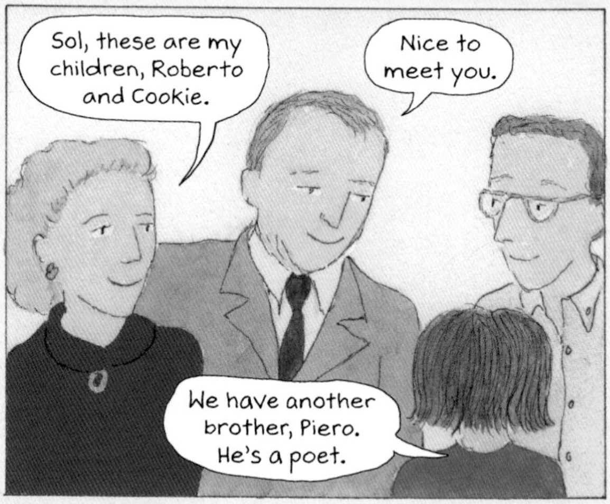
Sol, these are my children, Roberto and Cookie.
Nice to meet you.
We have another brother, Piero. He's a poet.

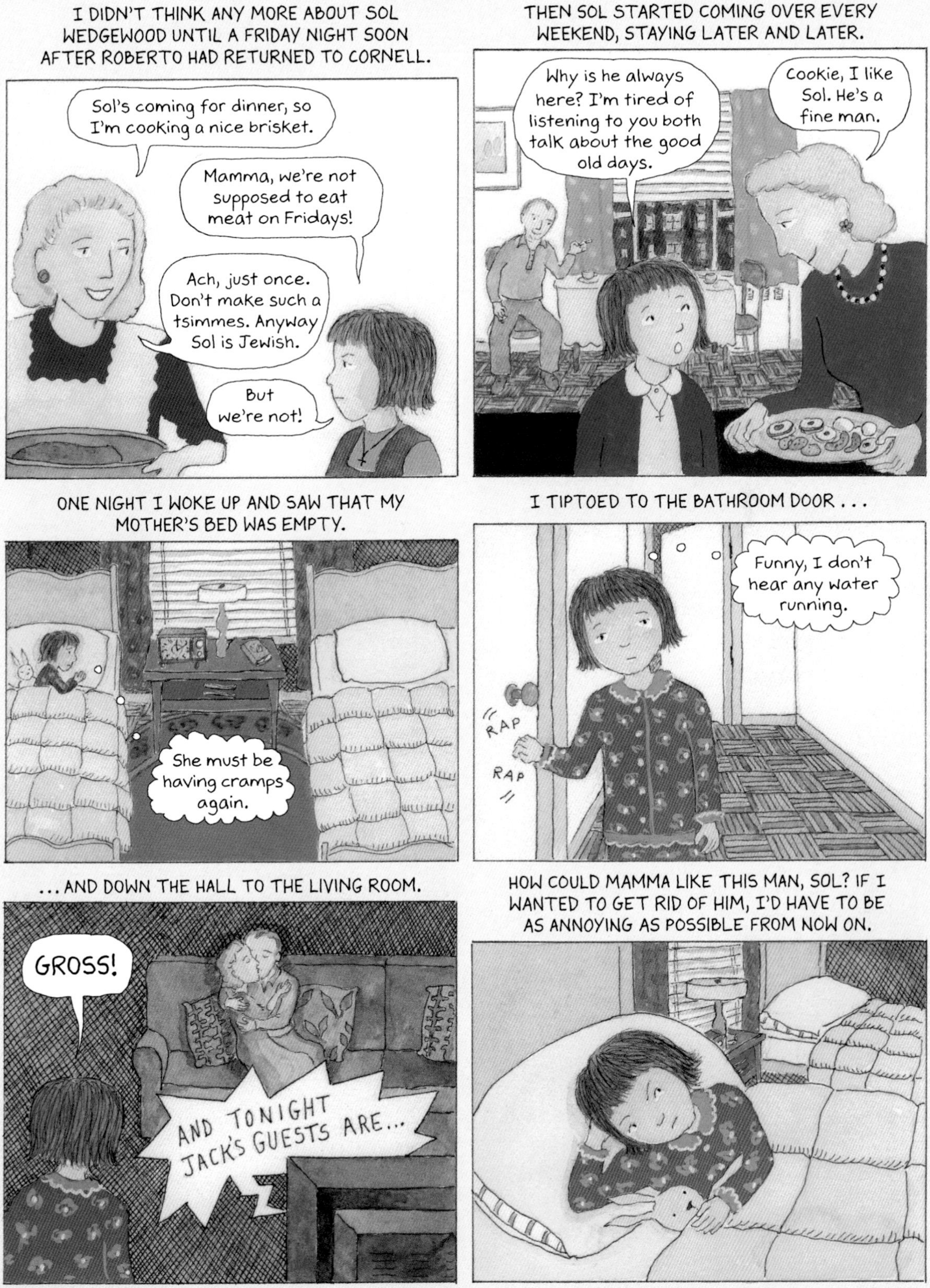
I DIDN'T THINK ANY MORE ABOUT SOL WEDGEWOOD UNTIL A FRIDAY NIGHT SOON AFTER ROBERTO HAD RETURNED TO CORNELL.
Sol's coming for dinner, so I'm cooking a nice brisket.
Mamma, we're not supposed to eat meat on Fridays!
Ach, just once. Don't make such a tsimmes. Anyway Sol is Jewish.
But we're not!
THEN SOL STARTED COMING OVER EVERY WEEKEND, STAYING LATER AND LATER.
Why is he always here? I'm tired of listening to you both talk about the good old days.
Cookie, I like Sol. He's a fine man.
ONE NIGHT I WOKE UP AND SAW THAT MY MOTHER'S BED WAS EMPTY.
She must be having cramps again.
I TIPTOED TO THE BATHROOM DOOR . . .
Funny, I don't hear any water running.
RAP
RAP
. . . AND DOWN THE HALL TO THE LIVING ROOM.
GROSS!
AND TONIGHT JACK'S GUESTS ARE . . .
HOW COULD MAMMA LIKE THIS MAN, SOL? IF I WANTED TO GET RID OF HIM, I'D HAVE TO BE AS ANNOYING AS POSSIBLE FROM NOW ON.

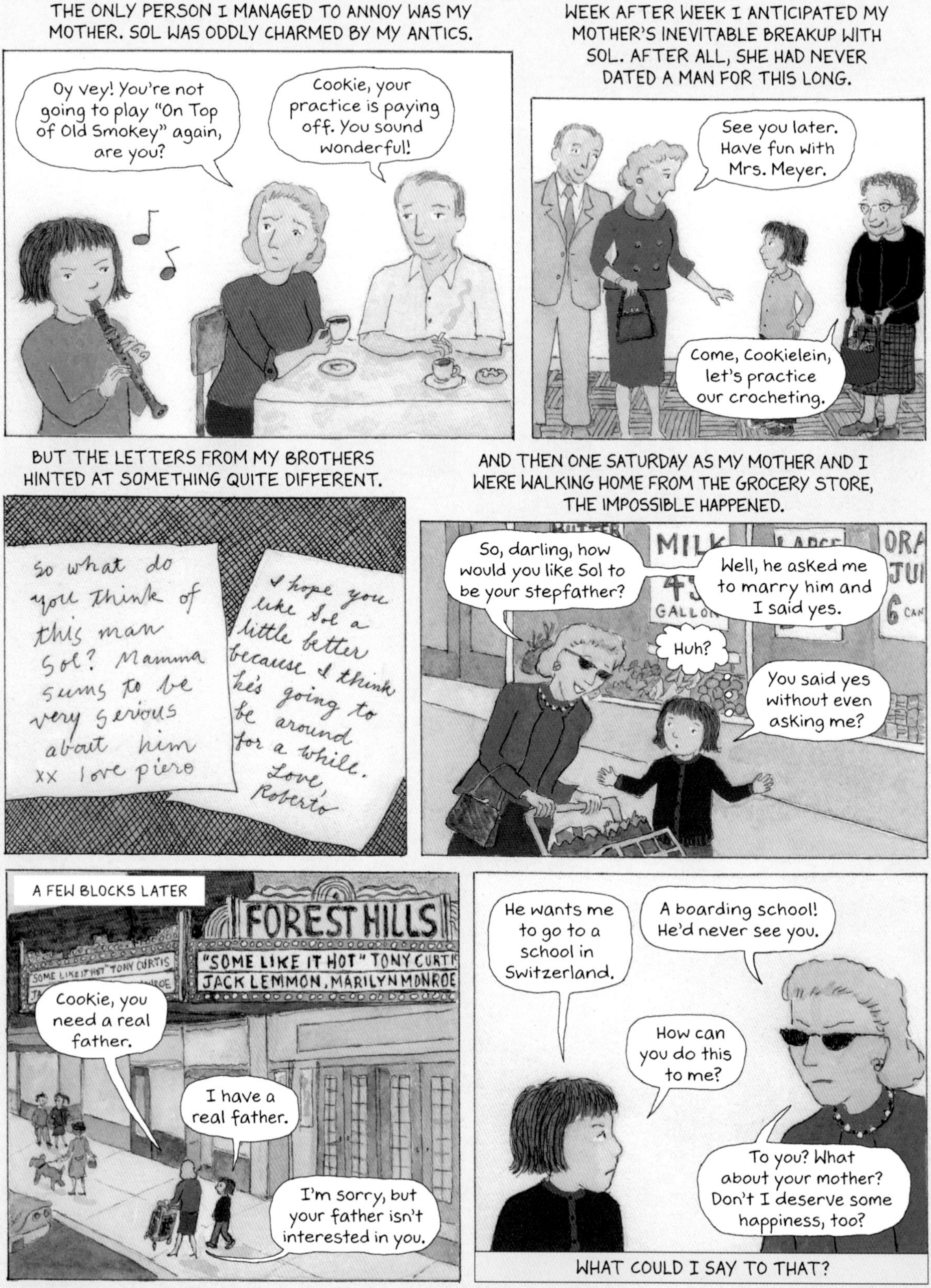
THE ONLY PERSON I MANAGED TO ANNOY WAS MY MOTHER. SOL WAS ODDLY CHARMED BY MY ANTICS.
Oy vey! You're not going to play "On Top of Old Smokey" again, are you?
Cookie, your practice is paying off. You sound wonderful!
WEEK AFTER WEEK I ANTICIPATED MY MOTHER'S INEVITABLE BREAKUP WITH SOL. AFTER ALL, SHE HAD NEVER DATED A MAN FOR THIS LONG.
See you later. Have fun with Mrs. Meyer.
Come, Cookielein, let's practice our crocheting.
BUT THE LETTERS FROM MY BROTHERS HINTED AT SOMETHING QUITE DIFFERENT.
So what do you think of this man Sol? Mamma seems to be very serious about him xx love piero
I hope you like Sol a little better because I think he's going to be around for a while. Love, Roberto
AND THEN ONE SATURDAY AS MY MOTHER AND I WERE WALKING HOME FROM THE GROCERY STORE, THE IMPOSSIBLE HAPPENED.
MILK
So, darling, how would you like Sol to be your stepfather?
Well, he asked me to marry him and I said yes.
Huh?
You said yes without even asking me?
A FEW BLOCKS LATER
FOREST HILLS
"SOME LIKE IT HOT" TONY CURTIS
JACK LEMMON, MARILYN MONROE
Cookie, you need a real father.
I have a real father.
I'm sorry, but your father isn't interested in you.
He wants me to go to a school in Switzerland.
A boarding school! He'd never see you.
How can you do this to me?
To you? What about your mother? Don't I deserve some happiness, too?
WHAT COULD I SAY TO THAT?

SO THE WEDDING WAS PLANNED. THEY GOT MARRIED AT CITY HALL ONE DAY WHILE I WAS AT SCHOOL AND THEN HAD A FEW PEOPLE OVER THAT EVENING. HARRY HEPNER AND HIS WIFE WERE THERE.

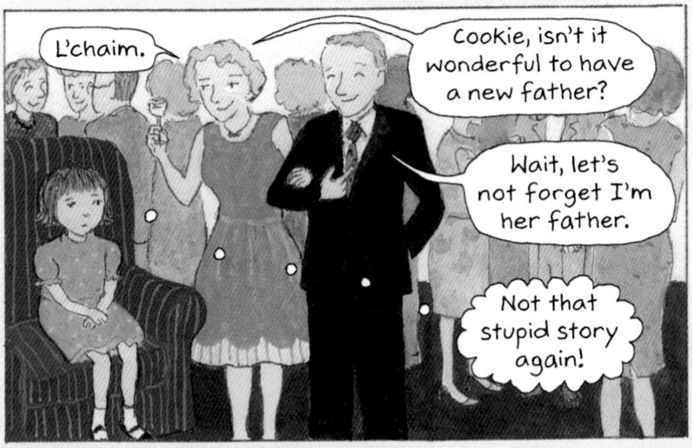
L'chaim.
Cookie, isn't it wonderful to have a new father?
Wait, let's not forget I'm her father.
Not that stupid story again!

FOR THEIR HONEYMOON, THEY BOOKED A TRIP TO MIAMI.

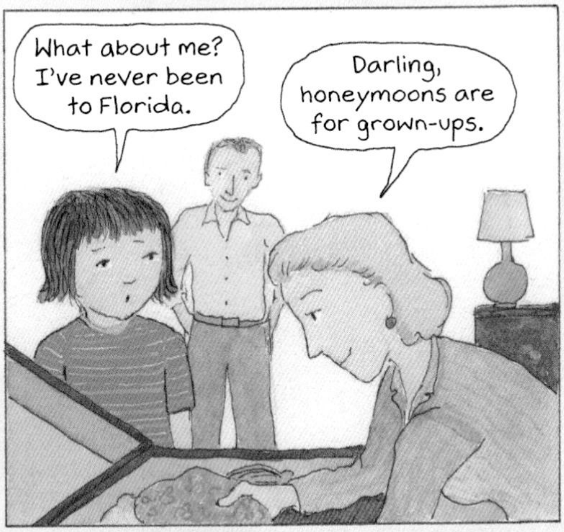
What about me? I've never been to Florida.
Darling, honeymoons are for grown-ups.

I STAYED WITH KAREN. AT FIRST IT WAS KIND OF FUN, LIKE A NEVER-ENDING SLUMBER PARTY.

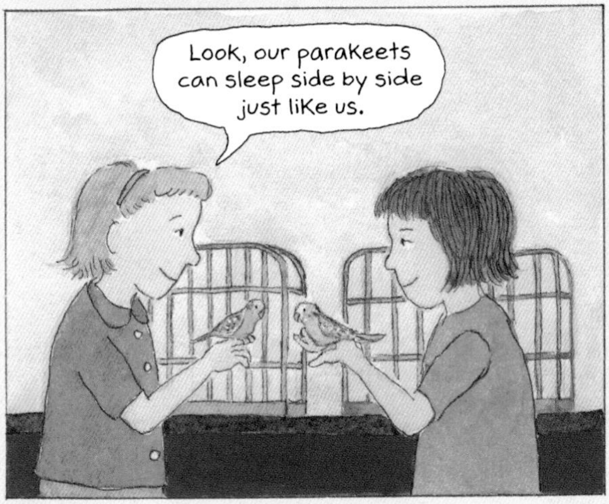
Look, our parakeets can sleep side by side just like us.

BUT AFTER A COUPLE OF NIGHTS, I STARTED HAVING TROUBLE FALLING ASLEEP.

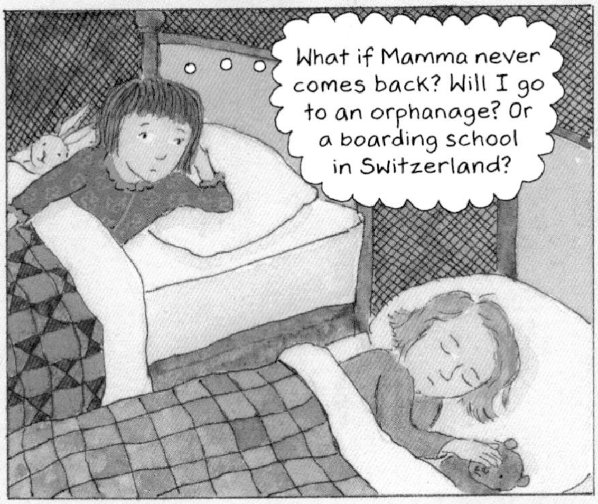
What if Mamma never comes back? Will I go to an orphanage? Or a boarding school in Switzerland?

A WEEK LATER THE NEWLYWEDS RETURNED LOOKING TAN AND RELAXED WHILE I HAD DARK RINGS UNDER MY EYES.

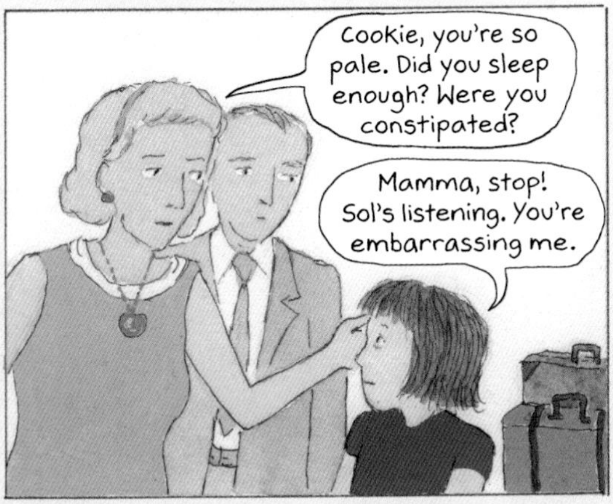
Cookie, you're so pale. Did you sleep enough? Were you constipated?
Mamma, stop! Sol's listening. You're embarrassing me.

FOR THE FIRST TIME IN MY LIFE, I WOULDN'T BE SHARING A BEDROOM WITH MY MOTHER BECAUSE SHE AND SOL WERE SLEEPING IN THE LIVING ROOM. I SHOULD HAVE BEEN HAPPY TO HAVE A ROOM OF MY OWN, BUT INSTEAD...

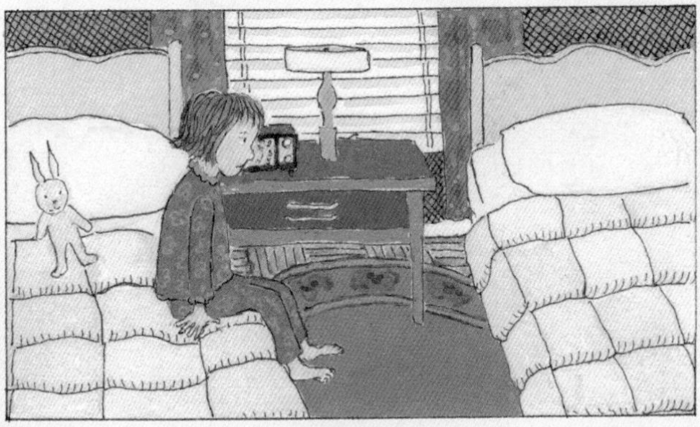

...I BECAME A NINE-YEAR-OLD INSOMNIAC.

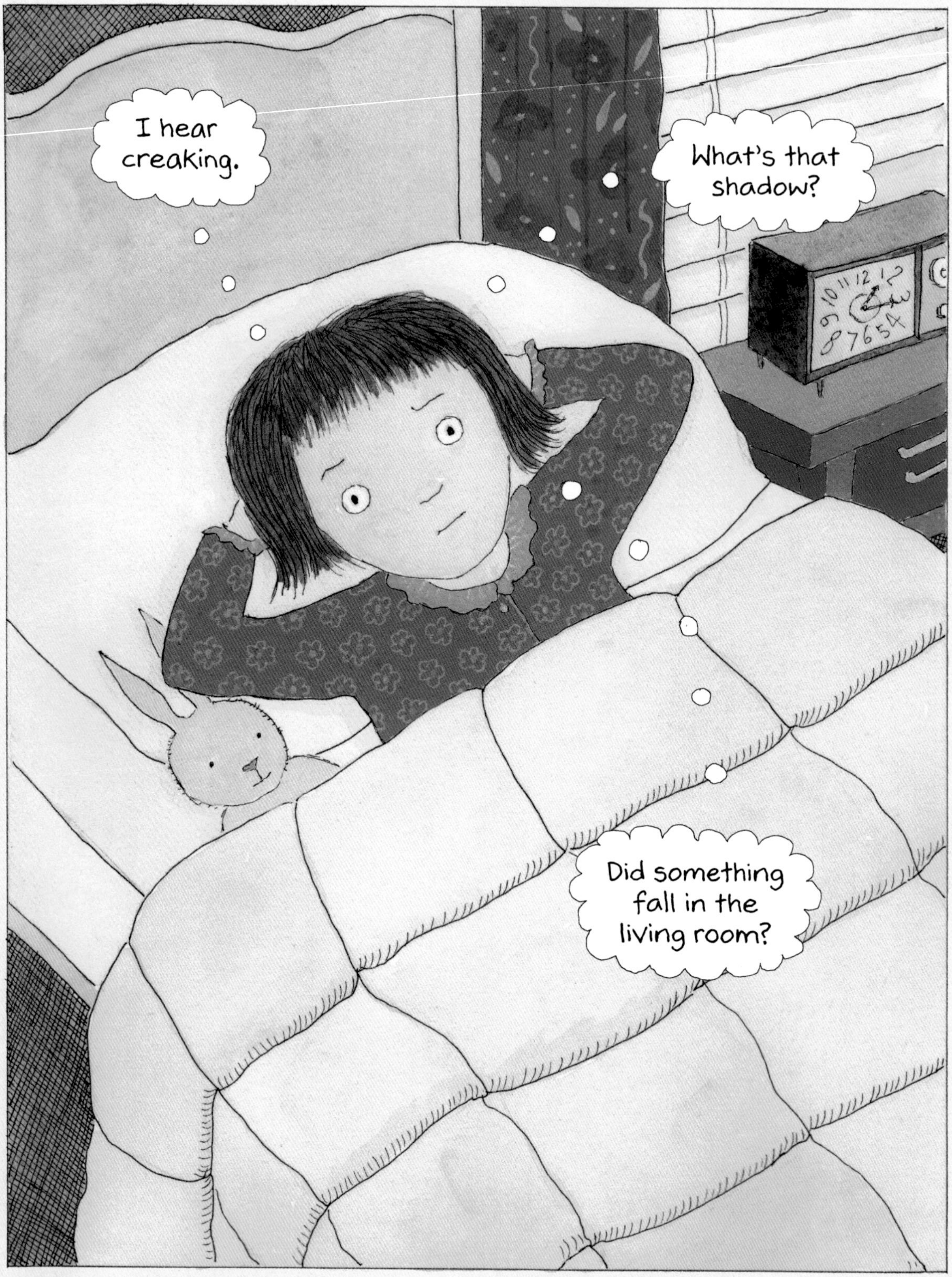
I hear creaking.
What's that shadow?
Did something fall in the living room?

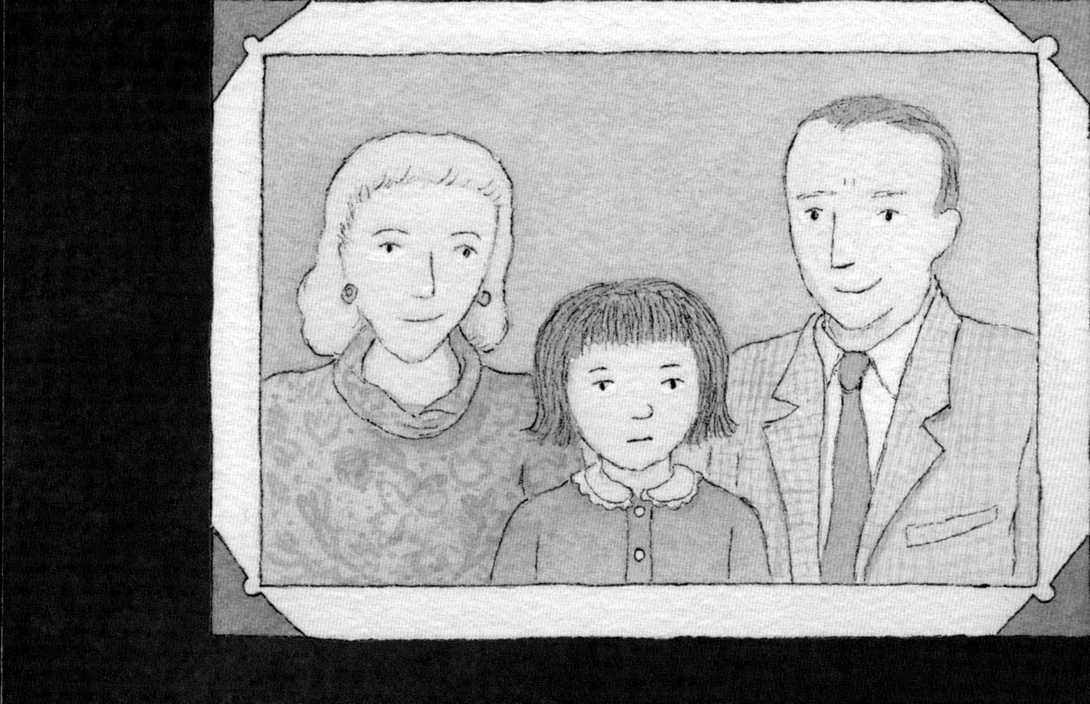

1959

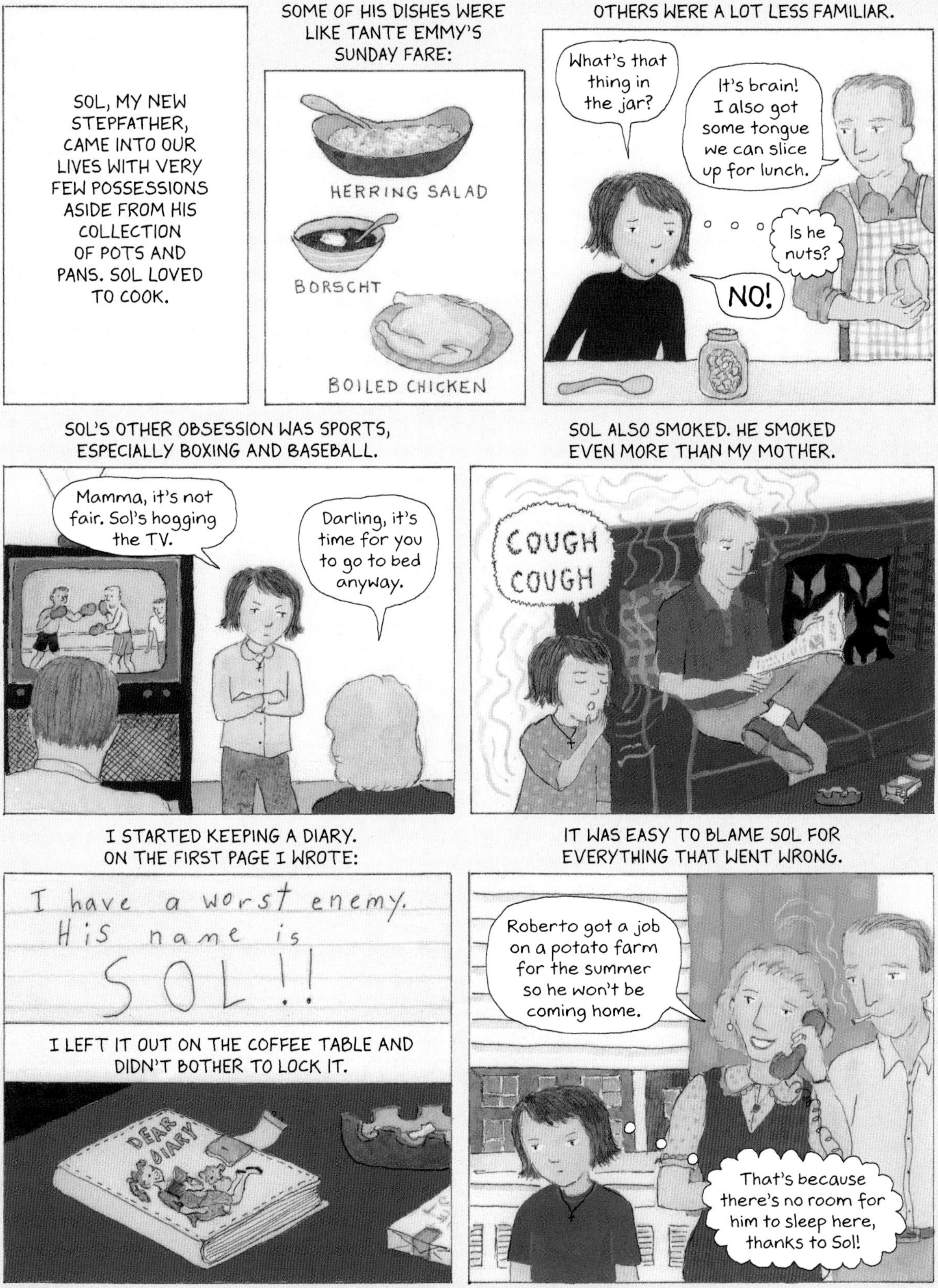
SOL, MY NEW STEPFATHER, CAME INTO OUR LIVES WITH VERY FEW POSSESSIONS ASIDE FROM HIS COLLECTION OF POTS AND PANS. SOL LOVED TO COOK.
SOME OF HIS DISHES WERE LIKE TANTE EMMY'S SUNDAY FARE:
HERRING SALAD
BORSCHT
BOILED CHICKEN
OTHERS WERE A LOT LESS FAMILIAR.
What's that thing in the jar?
It's brain! I also got some tongue we can slice up for lunch.
Is he nuts?
NO!
SOL'S OTHER OBSESSION WAS SPORTS, ESPECIALLY BOXING AND BASEBALL.
Mamma, it's not fair. Sol's hogging the TV.
Darling, it's time for you to go to bed anyway.
SOL ALSO SMOKED. HE SMOKED EVEN MORE THAN MY MOTHER.
COUGH COUGH
I STARTED KEEPING A DIARY. ON THE FIRST PAGE I WROTE:
I have a worst enemy. His name is SOL!!
I LEFT IT OUT ON THE COFFEE TABLE AND DIDN'T BOTHER TO LOCK IT.
DEAR DIARY
IT WAS EASY TO BLAME SOL FOR EVERYTHING THAT WENT WRONG.
Roberto got a job on a potato farm for the summer so he won't be coming home.
That's because there's no room for him to sleep here, thanks to Sol!

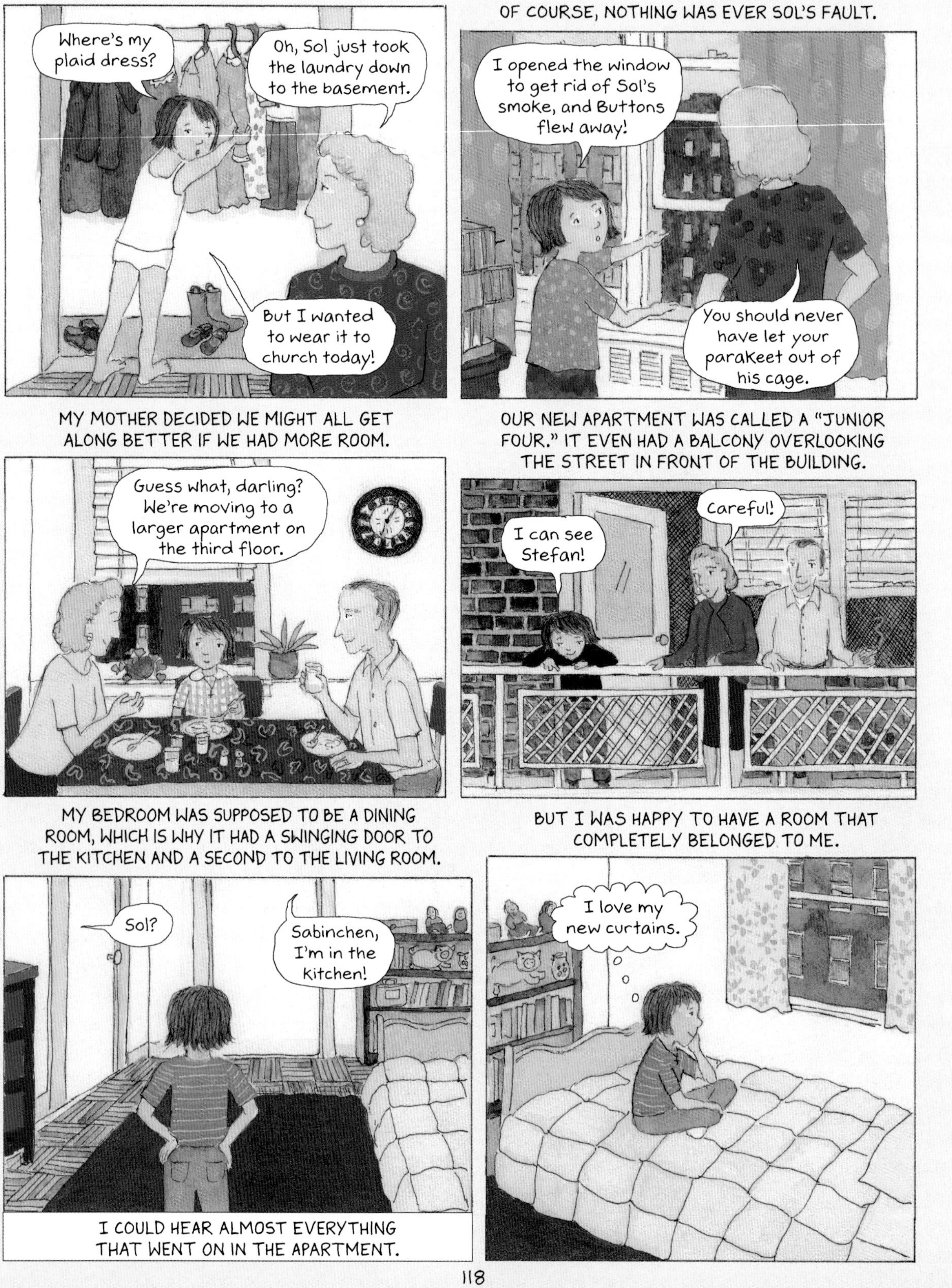
Where's my plaid dress?
Oh, Sol just took the laundry down to the basement.
But I wanted to wear it to church today!
OF COURSE, NOTHING WAS EVER SOL'S FAULT.
I opened the window to get rid of Sol's smoke, and Buttons flew away!
You should never have let your parakeet out of his cage.
MY MOTHER DECIDED WE MIGHT ALL GET ALONG BETTER IF WE HAD MORE ROOM.
Guess what, darling? We're moving to a larger apartment on the third floor.
OUR NEW APARTMENT WAS CALLED A "JUNIOR FOUR." IT EVEN HAD A BALCONY OVERLOOKING THE STREET IN FRONT OF THE BUILDING.
I can see Stefan!
Careful!
MY BEDROOM WAS SUPPOSED TO BE A DINING ROOM, WHICH IS WHY IT HAD A SWINGING DOOR TO THE KITCHEN AND A SECOND TO THE LIVING ROOM.
Sol?
Sabinchen, I'm in the kitchen!
I COULD HEAR ALMOST EVERYTHING THAT WENT ON IN THE APARTMENT.
BUT I WAS HAPPY TO HAVE A ROOM THAT COMPLETELY BELONGED TO ME.
I love my new curtains.

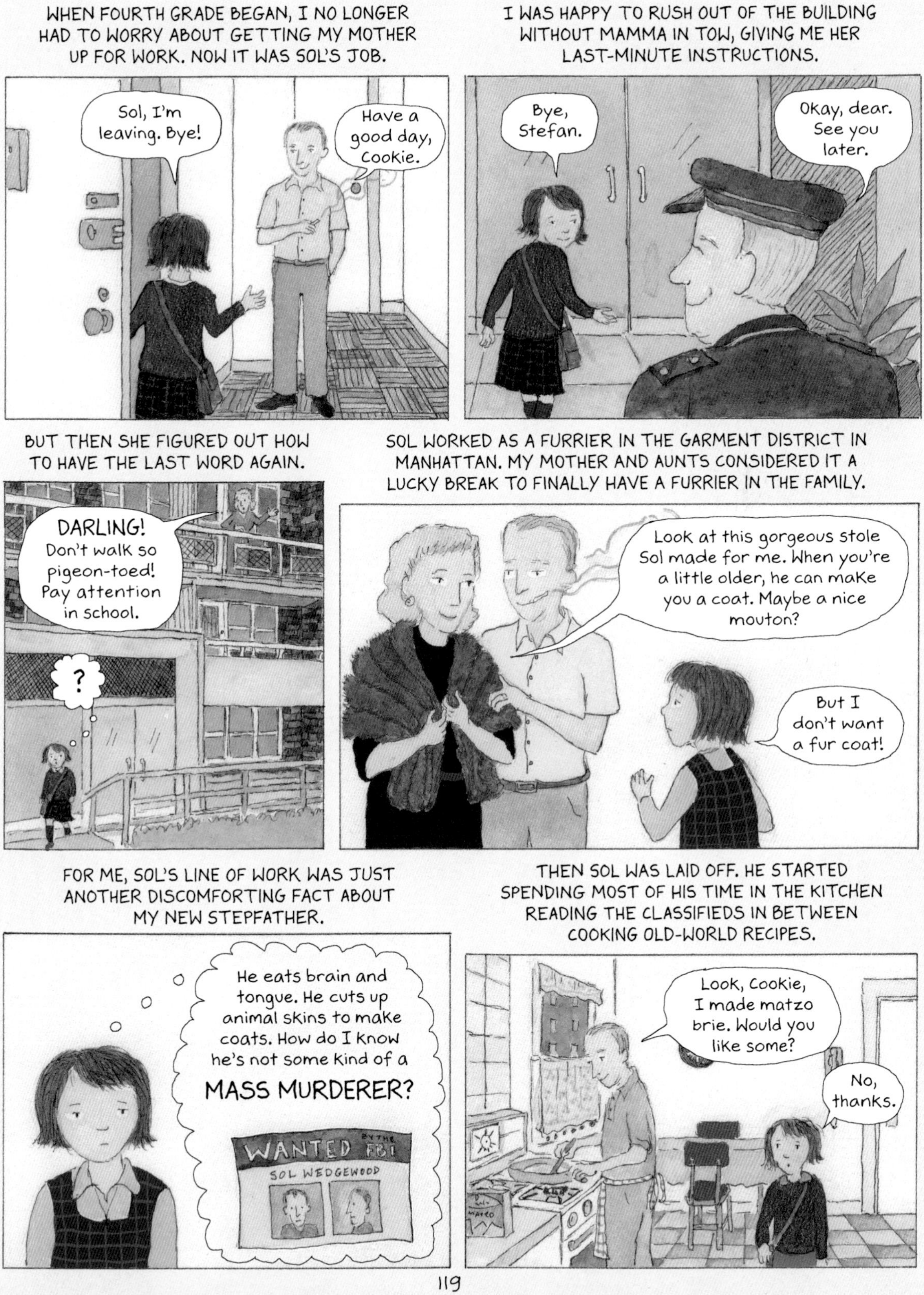
WHEN FOURTH GRADE BEGAN, I NO LONGER HAD TO WORRY ABOUT GETTING MY MOTHER UP FOR WORK. NOW IT WAS SOL'S JOB.
Sol, I'm leaving. Bye!
Have a good day, Cookie.
I WAS HAPPY TO RUSH OUT OF THE BUILDING WITHOUT MAMMA IN TOW, GIVING ME HER LAST-MINUTE INSTRUCTIONS.
Bye, Stefan.
Okay, dear. See you later.
BUT THEN SHE FIGURED OUT HOW TO HAVE THE LAST WORD AGAIN.
DARLING! Don't walk so pigeon-toed! Pay attention in school.
?
SOL WORKED AS A FURRIER IN THE GARMENT DISTRICT IN MANHATTAN. MY MOTHER AND AUNTS CONSIDERED IT A LUCKY BREAK TO FINALLY HAVE A FURRIER IN THE FAMILY.
Look at this gorgeous stole Sol made for me. When you're a little older, he can make you a coat. Maybe a nice mouton?
But I don't want a fur coat!
FOR ME, SOL'S LINE OF WORK WAS JUST ANOTHER DISCOMFORTING FACT ABOUT MY NEW STEPFATHER.
He eats brain and tongue. He cuts up animal skins to make coats. How do I know he's not some kind of a MASS MURDERER?
WANTED BY THE FBI
SOL WEDGEWOOD
THEN SOL WAS LAID OFF. HE STARTED SPENDING MOST OF HIS TIME IN THE KITCHEN READING THE CLASSIFIEDS IN BETWEEN COOKING OLD-WORLD RECIPES.
Look, Cookie, I made matzo brie. Would you like some?
No, thanks.
MATZO

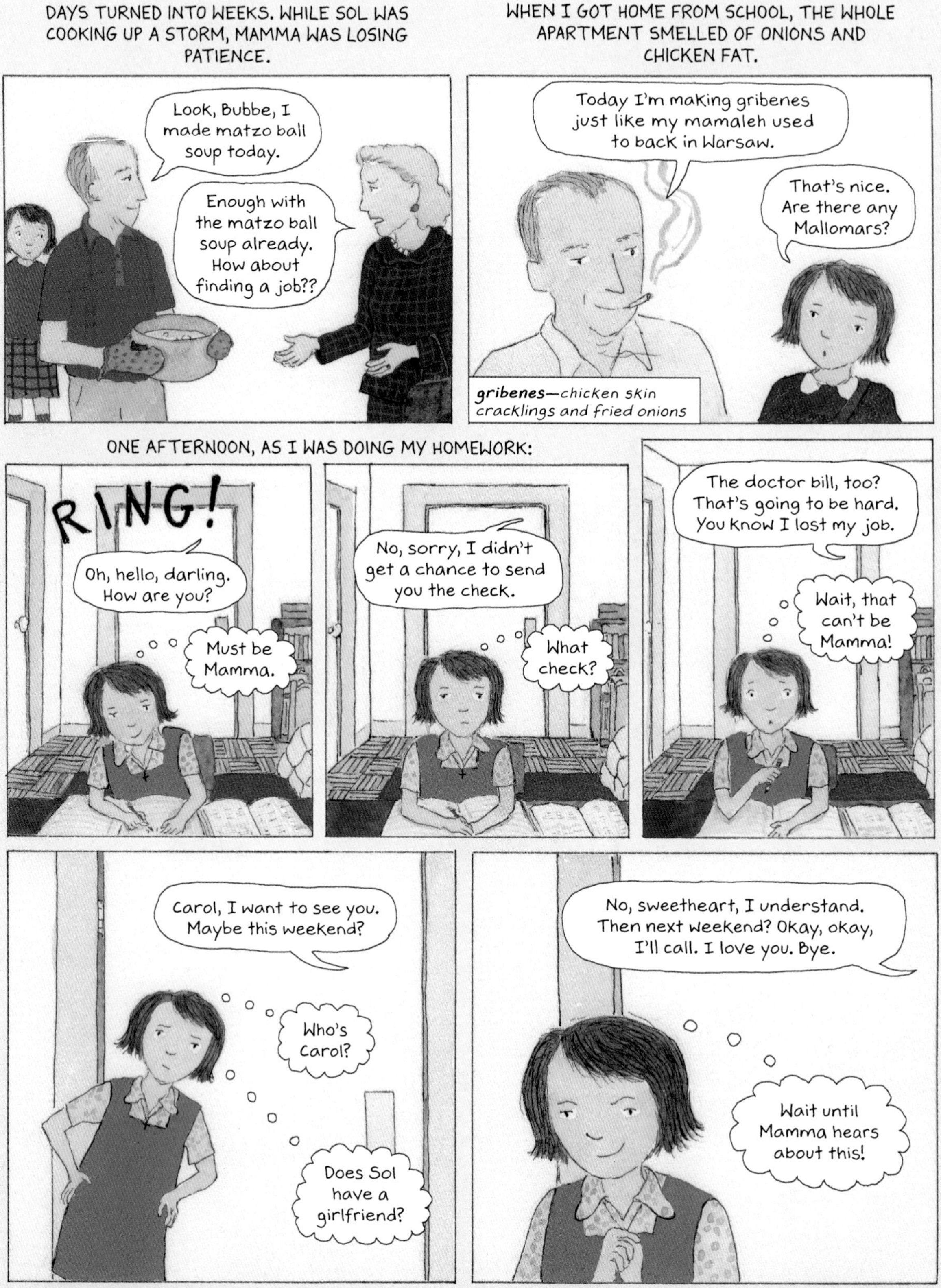
DAYS TURNED INTO WEEKS. WHILE SOL WAS COOKING UP A STORM, MAMMA WAS LOSING PATIENCE.
Look, Bubbe, I made matzo ball soup today.
Enough with the matzo ball soup already. How about finding a job??
WHEN I GOT HOME FROM SCHOOL, THE WHOLE APARTMENT SMELLED OF ONIONS AND CHICKEN FAT.
Today I'm making gribenes just like my mamaleh used to back in Warsaw.
That's nice. Are there any Mallomars?
gribenes—chicken skin cracklings and fried onions
ONE AFTERNOON, AS I WAS DOING MY HOMEWORK:
RING!
Oh, hello, darling. How are you?
Must be Mamma.
No, sorry, I didn't get a chance to send you the check.
What check?
The doctor bill, too? That's going to be hard. You know I lost my job.
Wait, that can't be Mamma!
Carol, I want to see you. Maybe this weekend?
Who's Carol?
Does Sol have a girlfriend?
No, sweetheart, I understand. Then next weekend? Okay, okay, I'll call. I love you. Bye.
Wait until Mamma hears about this!

I WAS SURE MY BOMBSHELL REVELATION WOULD LEAD TO SOL'S IMMINENT DEPARTURE.

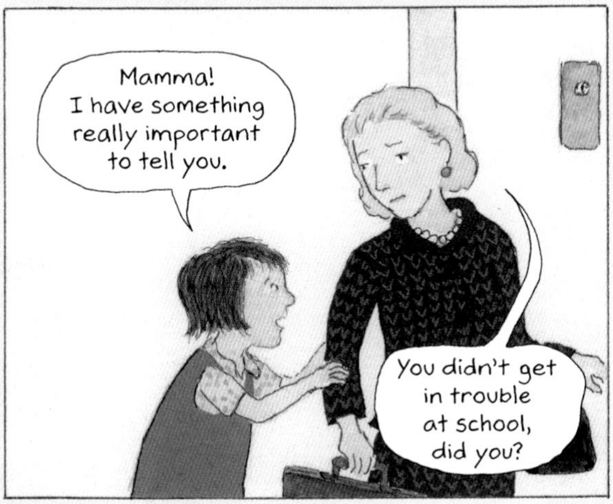

Mamma! I have something really important to tell you.
You didn't get in trouble at school, did you?

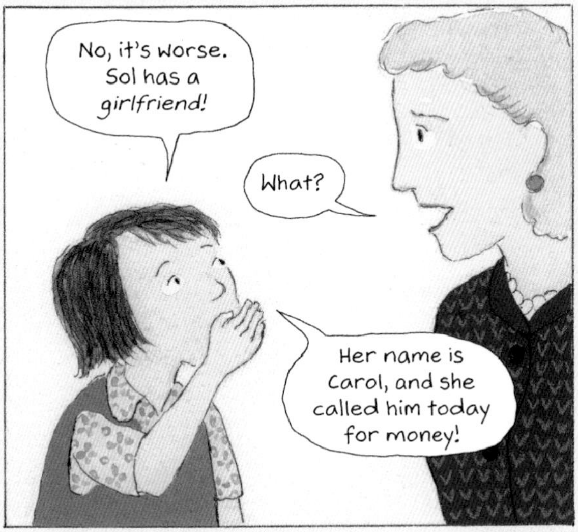

No, it's worse. Sol has a *girlfriend!*
What?
Her name is Carol, and she called him today for money!

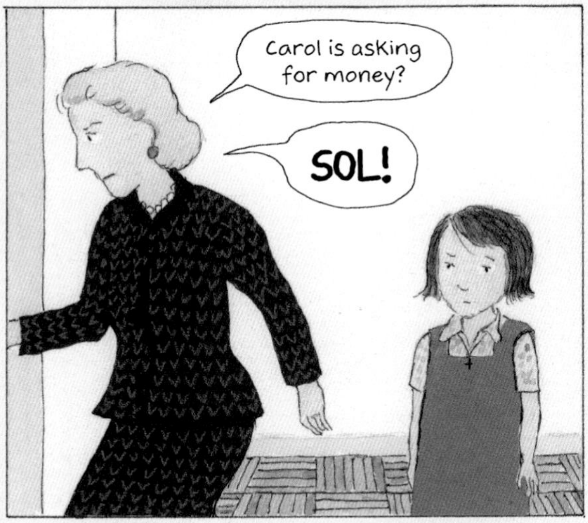

Carol is asking for money?
SOL!

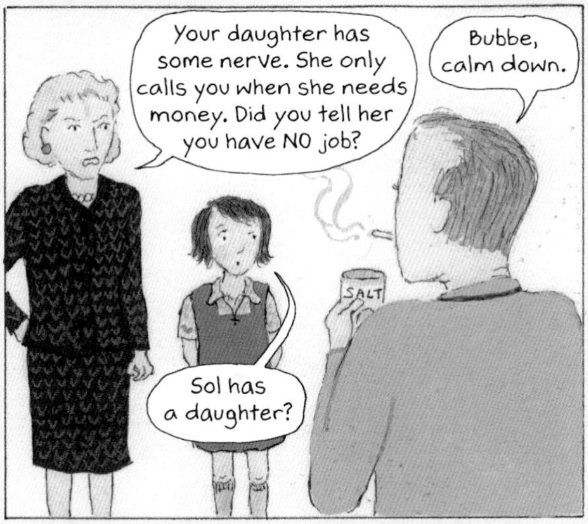

Your daughter has some nerve. She only calls you when she needs money. Did you tell her you have NO job?
Bubbe, calm down.
SALT
Sol has a daughter?

IT TURNED OUT THAT SOL HAD NOT ONE BUT TWO DAUGHTERS. LIKE MY FATHER, HE HAD TO PAY CHILD SUPPORT.

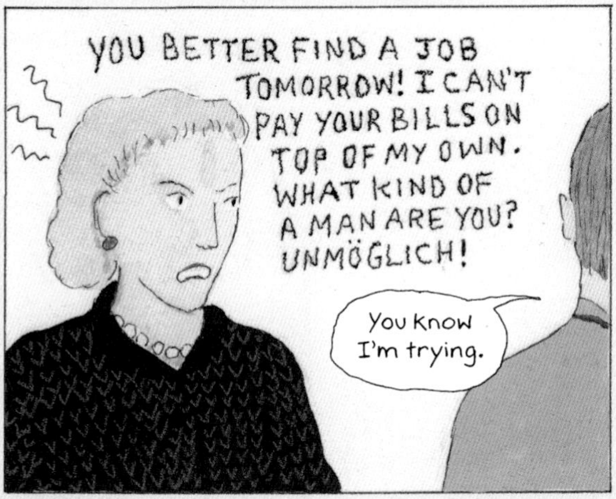

YOU BETTER FIND A JOB TOMORROW! I CAN'T PAY YOUR BILLS ON TOP OF MY OWN. WHAT KIND OF A MAN ARE YOU? UNMÖGLICH!
You know I'm trying.

AS I LISTENED TO MY MOTHER BROWBEAT SOL, I HAD MIXED FEELINGS. ON ONE HAND, I WAS RELIEVED TO SEE MY MOTHER'S RAGE DIRECTED AT SOMEONE ELSE INSTEAD OF ME.

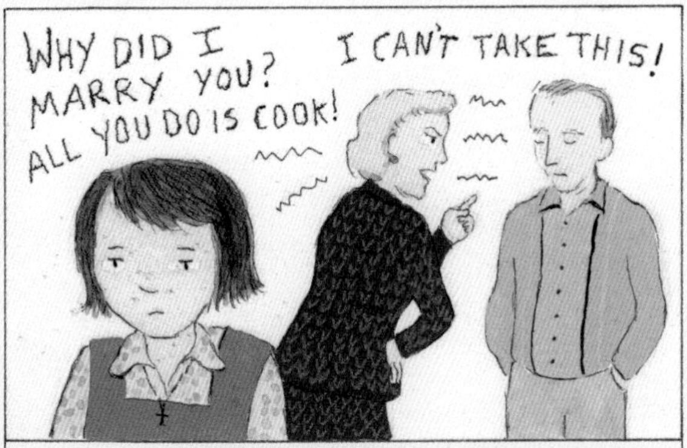

WHY DID I MARRY YOU? ALL YOU DO IS COOK!
I CAN'T TAKE THIS!

BUT ON THE OTHER, I KIND OF FELT SORRY FOR SOL.

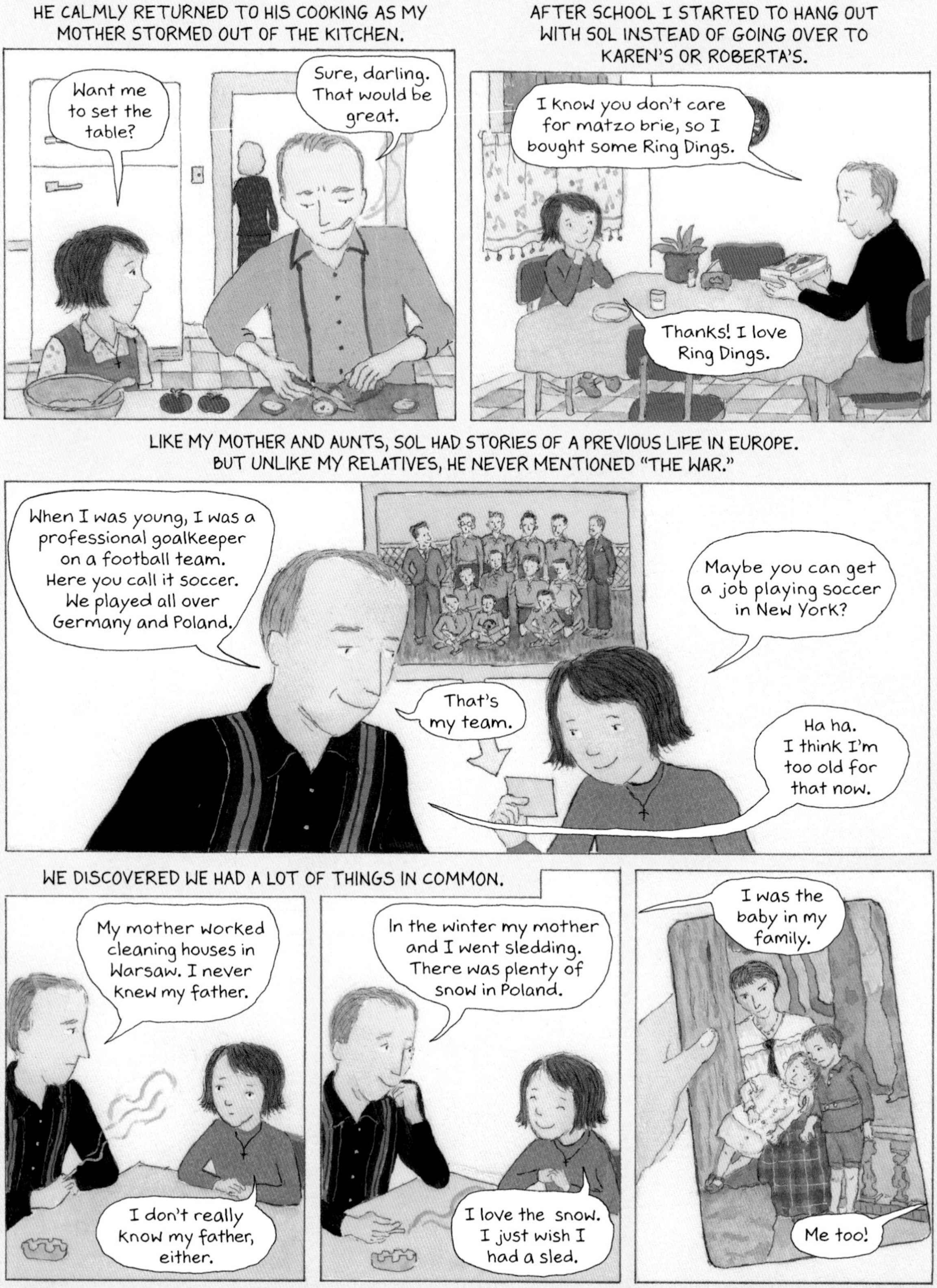
HE CALMLY RETURNED TO HIS COOKING AS MY MOTHER STORMED OUT OF THE KITCHEN.
Want me to set the table?
Sure, darling. That would be great.
AFTER SCHOOL I STARTED TO HANG OUT WITH SOL INSTEAD OF GOING OVER TO KAREN'S OR ROBERTA'S.
I know you don't care for matzo brie, so I bought some Ring Dings.
Thanks! I love Ring Dings.
LIKE MY MOTHER AND AUNTS, SOL HAD STORIES OF A PREVIOUS LIFE IN EUROPE. BUT UNLIKE MY RELATIVES, HE NEVER MENTIONED "THE WAR."
When I was young, I was a professional goalkeeper on a football team. Here you call it soccer. We played all over Germany and Poland.
That's my team.
Maybe you can get a job playing soccer in New York?
Ha ha. I think I'm too old for that now.
WE DISCOVERED WE HAD A LOT OF THINGS IN COMMON.
My mother worked cleaning houses in Warsaw. I never knew my father.
I don't really know my father, either.
In the winter my mother and I went sledding. There was plenty of snow in Poland.
I love the snow. I just wish I had a sled.
I was the baby in my family.
Me too!

BUT AS SOON AS MY MOTHER GOT HOME FROM WORK, THE CALM WAS SHATTERED.

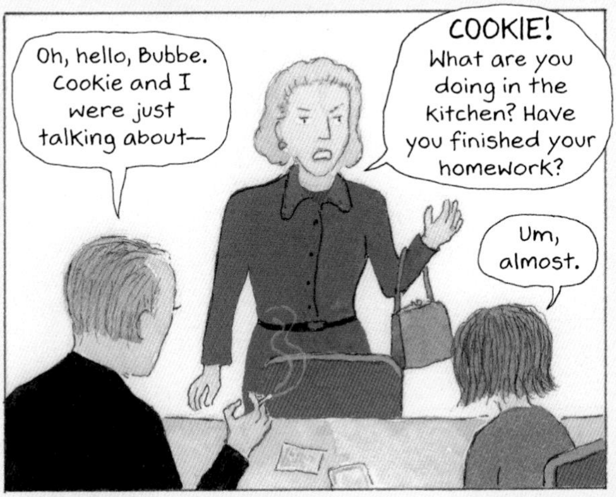
Oh, hello, Bubbe. Cookie and I were just talking about—
COOKIE! What are you doing in the kitchen? Have you finished your homework?
Um, almost.

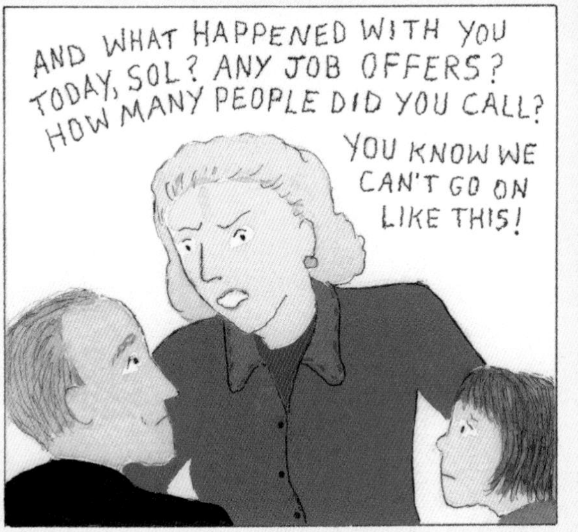
AND WHAT HAPPENED WITH YOU TODAY, SOL? ANY JOB OFFERS? HOW MANY PEOPLE DID YOU CALL?
YOU KNOW WE CAN'T GO ON LIKE THIS!

AFTER A FEW UNEMPLOYED MONTHS, SOL FINALLY FOUND A NEW JOB. NOT AS A FURRIER OR A SOCCER PLAYER, BUT AS A REAL ESTATE AGENT; A QUESTIONABLE CAREER MOVE, MY MOTHER WAS QUICK TO POINT OUT.

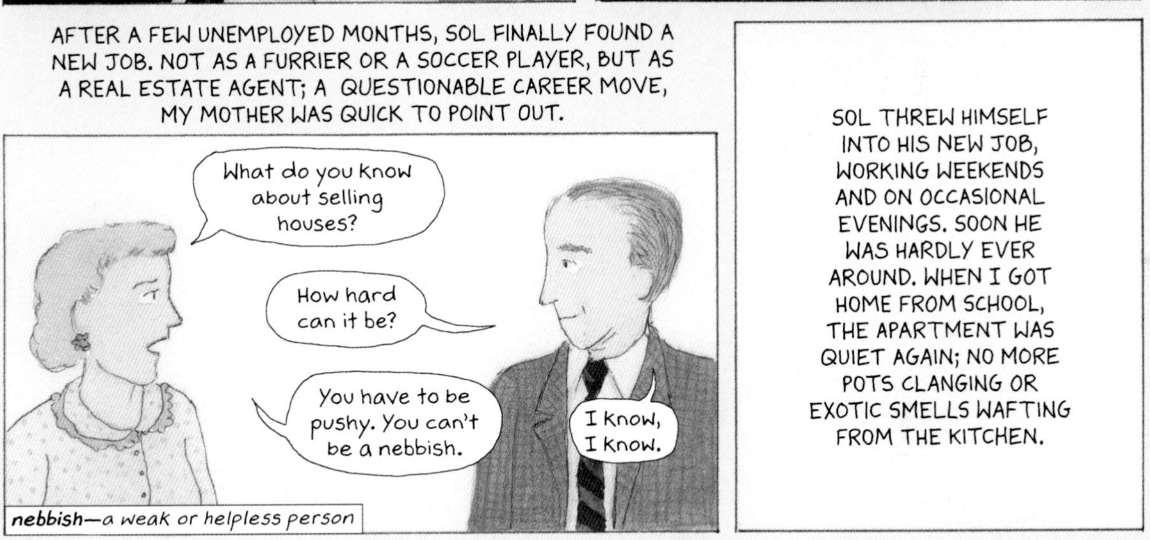
What do you know about selling houses?
How hard can it be?
You have to be pushy. You can't be a nebbish.
I know, I know.

nebbish—*a weak or helpless person*

SOL THREW HIMSELF INTO HIS NEW JOB, WORKING WEEKENDS AND ON OCCASIONAL EVENINGS. SOON HE WAS HARDLY EVER AROUND. WHEN I GOT HOME FROM SCHOOL, THE APARTMENT WAS QUIET AGAIN; NO MORE POTS CLANGING OR EXOTIC SMELLS WAFTING FROM THE KITCHEN.

AFTER CHECKING IN WITH MY MOTHER AT HER OFFICE, I ATE MY MALLOMARS AND WROTE IN MY DIARY.

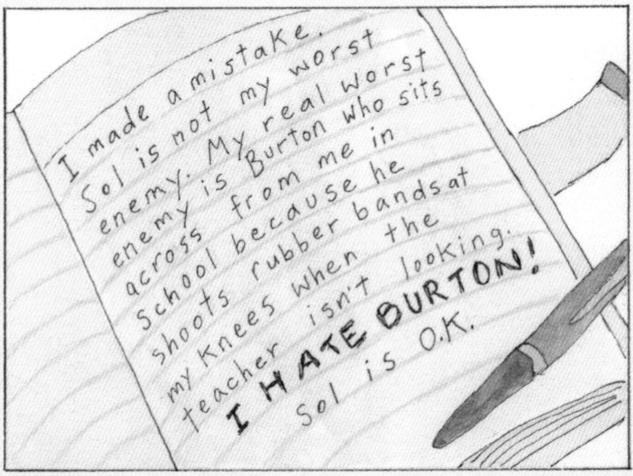
I made a mistake. Sol is not my worst enemy. My real worst enemy is Burton who sits across from me in school because he shoots rubber bands at my knees when the teacher isn't looking.
I HATE BURTON!
Sol is O.K.

THEN I CALLED KAREN TO SEE IF SHE WANTED TO GO TO THE PLAYGROUND.

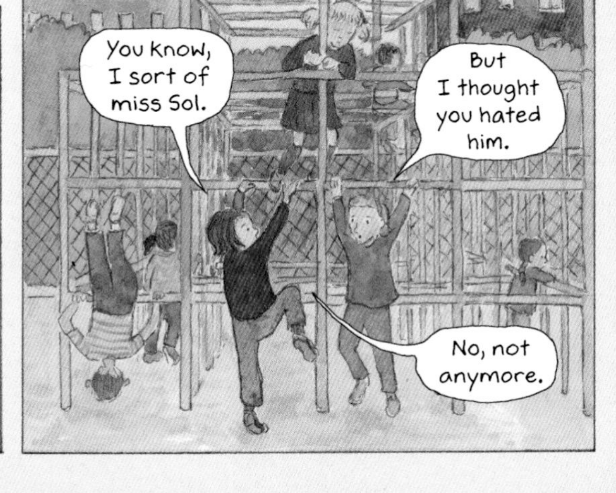
You know, I sort of miss Sol.
But I thought you hated him.
No, not anymore.

THIRTEEN

Camp

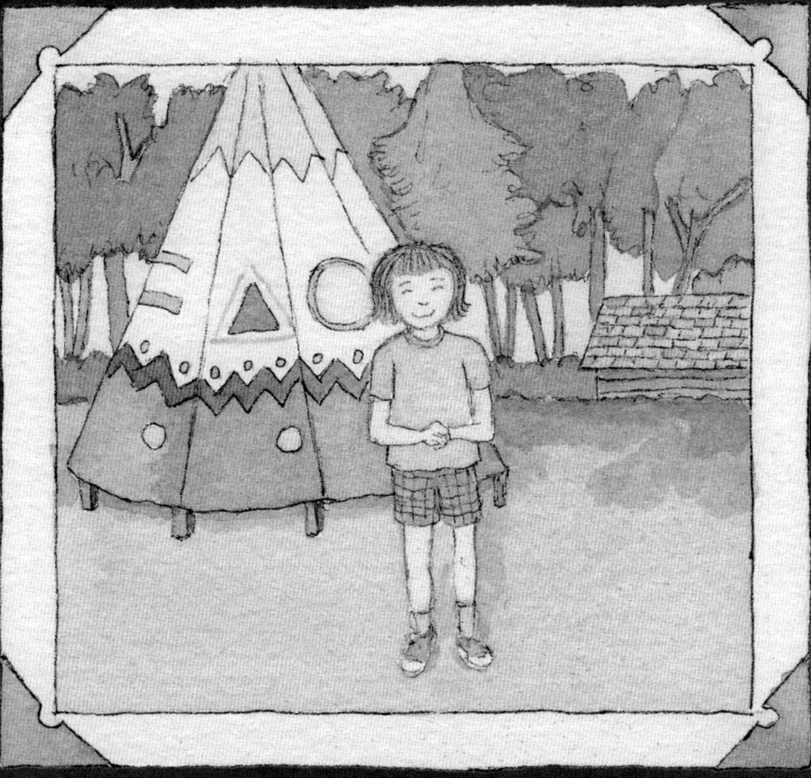

1960

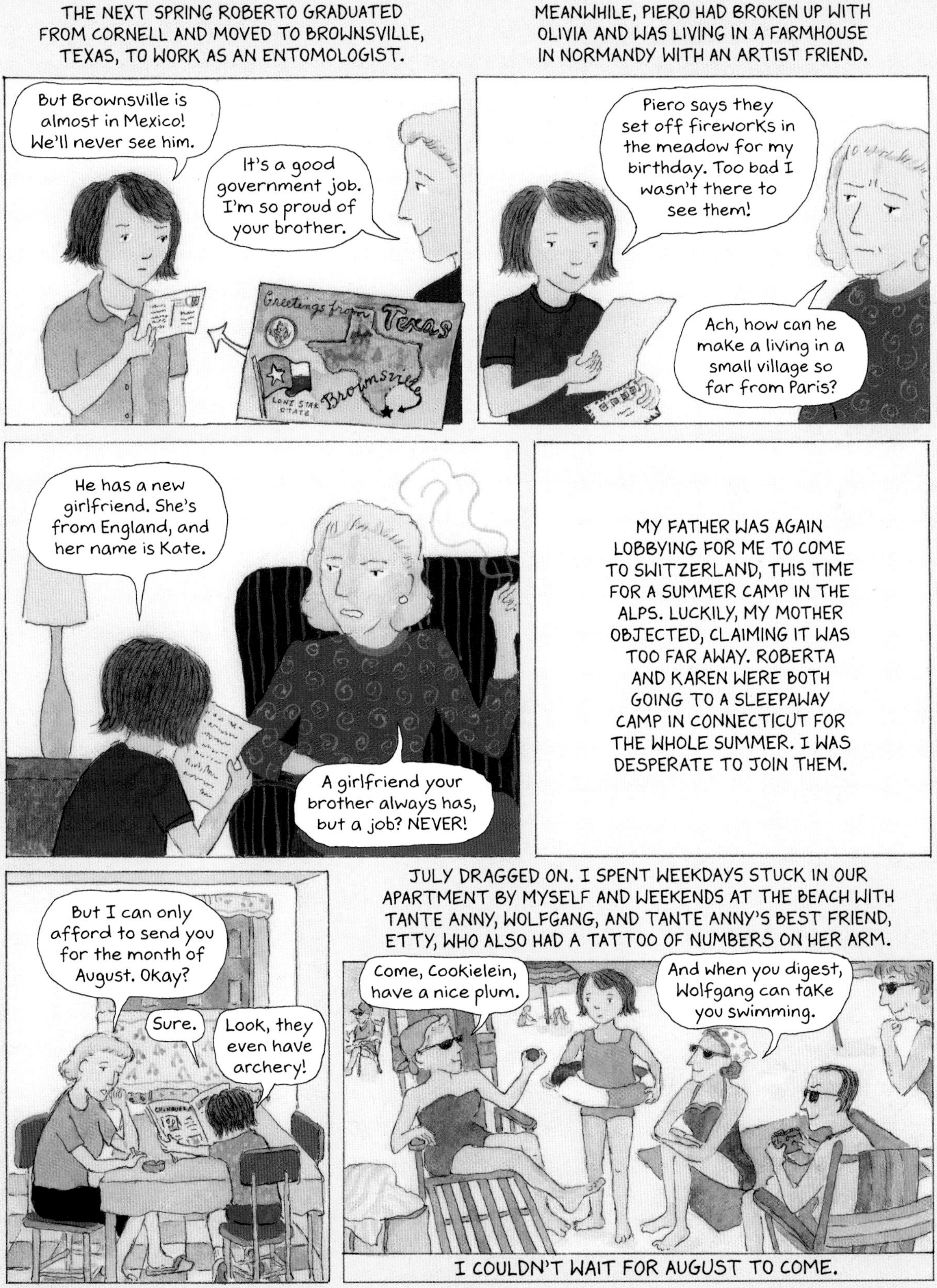
THE NEXT SPRING ROBERTO GRADUATED FROM CORNELL AND MOVED TO BROWNSVILLE, TEXAS, TO WORK AS AN ENTOMOLOGIST.
But Brownsville is almost in Mexico! We'll never see him.
It's a good government job. I'm so proud of your brother.
Greetings from Texas
Brownsville
LONE STAR STATE
MEANWHILE, PIERO HAD BROKEN UP WITH OLIVIA AND WAS LIVING IN A FARMHOUSE IN NORMANDY WITH AN ARTIST FRIEND.
Piero says they set off fireworks in the meadow for my birthday. Too bad I wasn't there to see them!
Ach, how can he make a living in a small village so far from Paris?
He has a new girlfriend. She's from England, and her name is Kate.
A girlfriend your brother always has, but a job? NEVER!
MY FATHER WAS AGAIN LOBBYING FOR ME TO COME TO SWITZERLAND, THIS TIME FOR A SUMMER CAMP IN THE ALPS. LUCKILY, MY MOTHER OBJECTED, CLAIMING IT WAS TOO FAR AWAY. ROBERTA AND KAREN WERE BOTH GOING TO A SLEEPAWAY CAMP IN CONNECTICUT FOR THE WHOLE SUMMER. I WAS DESPERATE TO JOIN THEM.
But I can only afford to send you for the month of August. Okay?
Sure.
Look, they even have archery!
JULY DRAGGED ON. I SPENT WEEKDAYS STUCK IN OUR APARTMENT BY MYSELF AND WEEKENDS AT THE BEACH WITH TANTE ANNY, WOLFGANG, AND TANTE ANNY'S BEST FRIEND, ETTY, WHO ALSO HAD A TATTOO OF NUMBERS ON HER ARM.
Come, Cookielein, have a nice plum.
And when you digest, Wolfgang can take you swimming.
I COULDN'T WAIT FOR AUGUST TO COME.

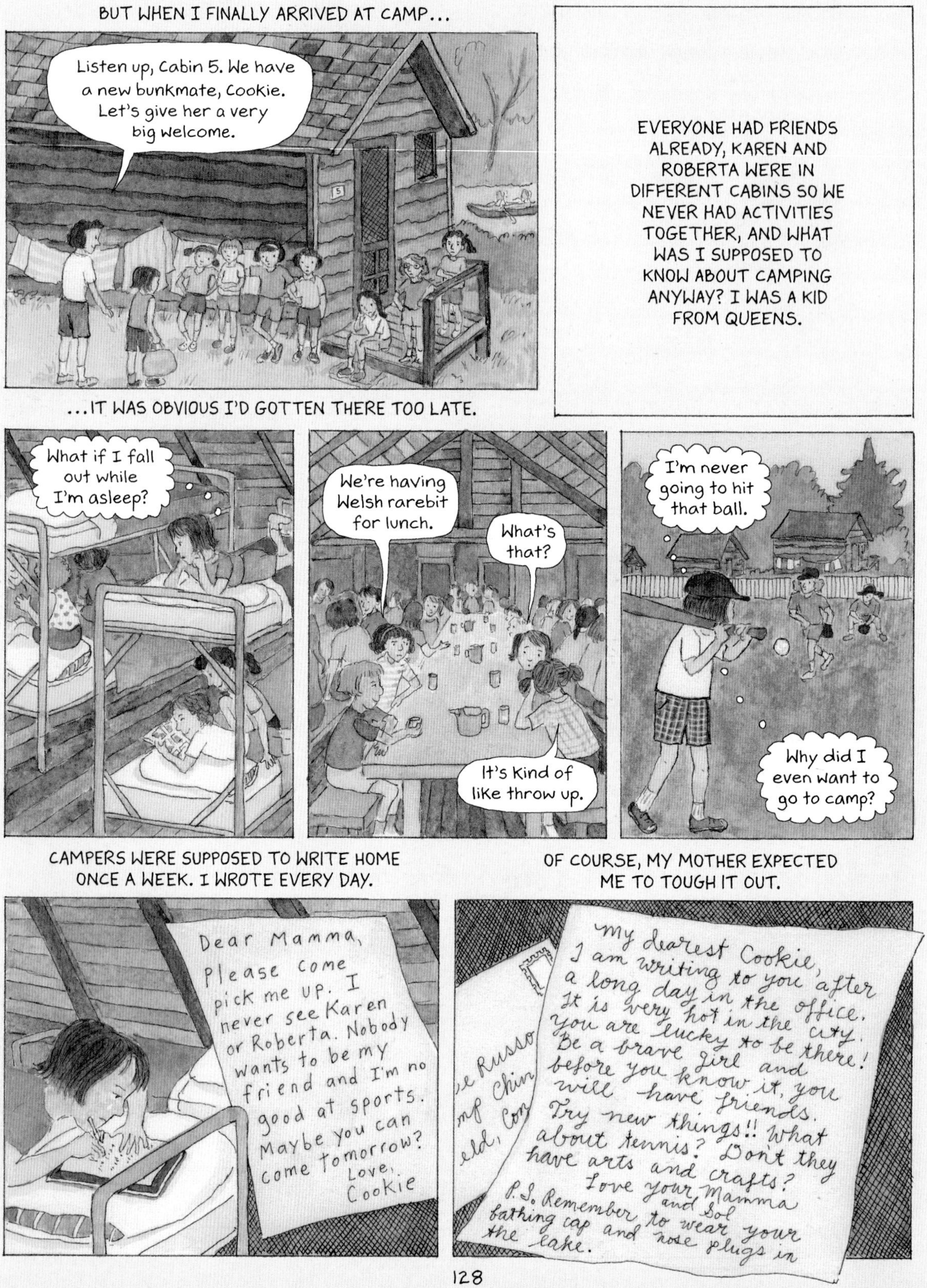
BUT WHEN I FINALLY ARRIVED AT CAMP...
Listen up, Cabin 5. We have a new bunkmate, Cookie. Let's give her a very big welcome.
5
...IT WAS OBVIOUS I'D GOTTEN THERE TOO LATE.
EVERYONE HAD FRIENDS ALREADY, KAREN AND ROBERTA WERE IN DIFFERENT CABINS SO WE NEVER HAD ACTIVITIES TOGETHER, AND WHAT WAS I SUPPOSED TO KNOW ABOUT CAMPING ANYWAY? I WAS A KID FROM QUEENS.
What if I fall out while I'm asleep?
We're having Welsh rarebit for lunch.
What's that?
It's kind of like throw up.
I'm never going to hit that ball.
Why did I even want to go to camp?
CAMPERS WERE SUPPOSED TO WRITE HOME ONCE A WEEK. I WROTE EVERY DAY.
Dear Mamma,
Please come pick me up. I never see Karen or Roberta. Nobody wants to be my friend and I'm no good at sports. Maybe you can come tomorrow?
Love,
Cookie
OF COURSE, MY MOTHER EXPECTED ME TO TOUGH IT OUT.
My dearest Cookie,
I am writing to you after a long day in the office. It is very hot in the city. You are lucky to be there! Be a brave girl and before you know it, you will have friends. Try new things!! What about tennis? Don't they have arts and crafts?
Love your Mamma and Sol
P.S. Remember to wear your bathing cap and nose plugs in the lake.

AND THEN... DIVINE INTERVENTION! ON THE FIRST SUNDAY THERE WAS A TRUCK TO TAKE THE CATHOLIC CAMPERS TO CHURCH IN A NEARBY TOWN.

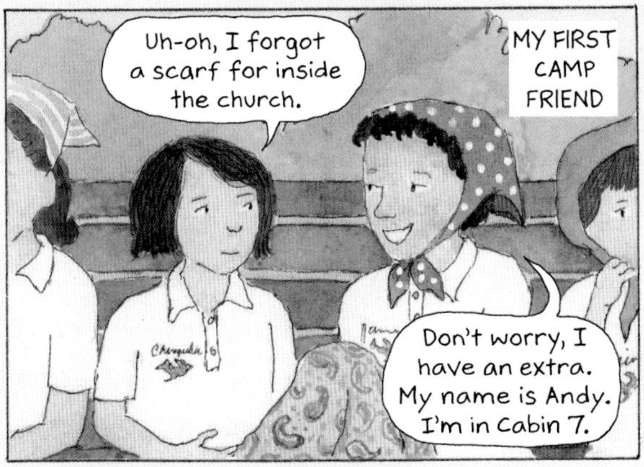
Uh-oh, I forgot a scarf for inside the church.
MY FIRST CAMP FRIEND
Don't worry, I have an extra. My name is Andy. I'm in Cabin 7.

AFTER THAT, THINGS GOT EASIER. I FOLLOWED MY MOTHER'S ADVICE, SMILING A LOT AND EVEN TRYING TO PLAY TENNIS.

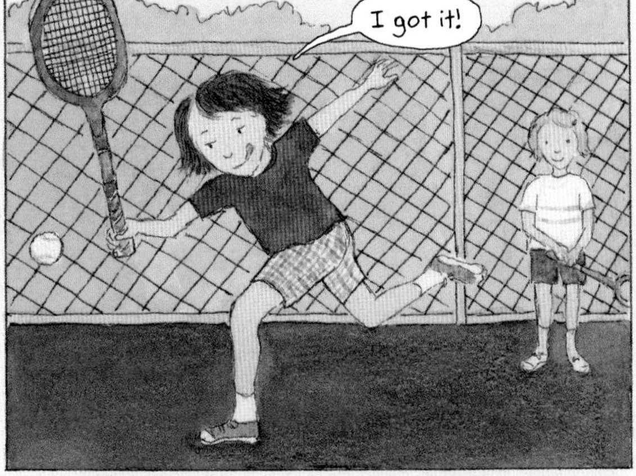
I got it!

BY THE NIGHT OF MY FIRST CAMPFIRE, I REALIZED I NEVER WANTED TO GO HOME.

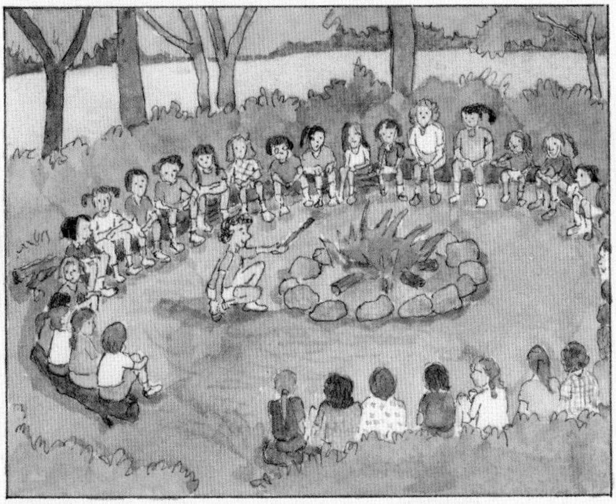

THE LAST DAY OF CAMP CAME TOO SOON. I RELUCTANTLY CLIMBED INTO THE BACK SEAT OF SOL'S RAMBLER.

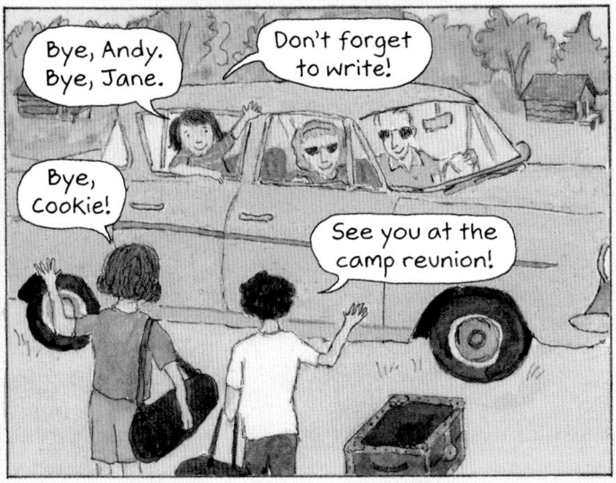
Bye, Andy. Bye, Jane.
Don't forget to write!
Bye, Cookie!
See you at the camp reunion!

AS THE CAR WENDED ITS WAY DOWN ROUTE 7, MY MOTHER BEGAN TO BADGER SOL ABOUT HIS DRIVING...

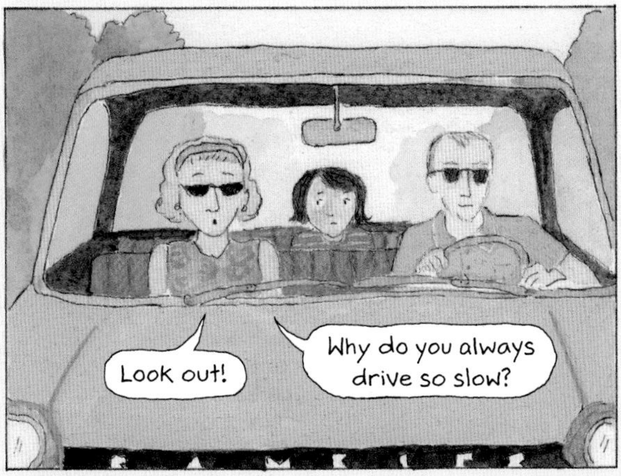
Look out!
Why do you always drive so slow?

...IN BETWEEN CATCHING ME UP ON THE LATEST FAMILY NEWS.

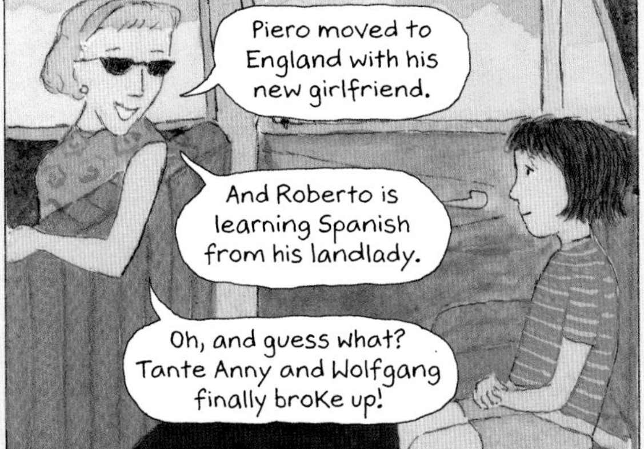
Piero moved to England with his new girlfriend.
And Roberto is learning Spanish from his landlady.
Oh, and guess what? Tante Anny and Wolfgang finally broke up!

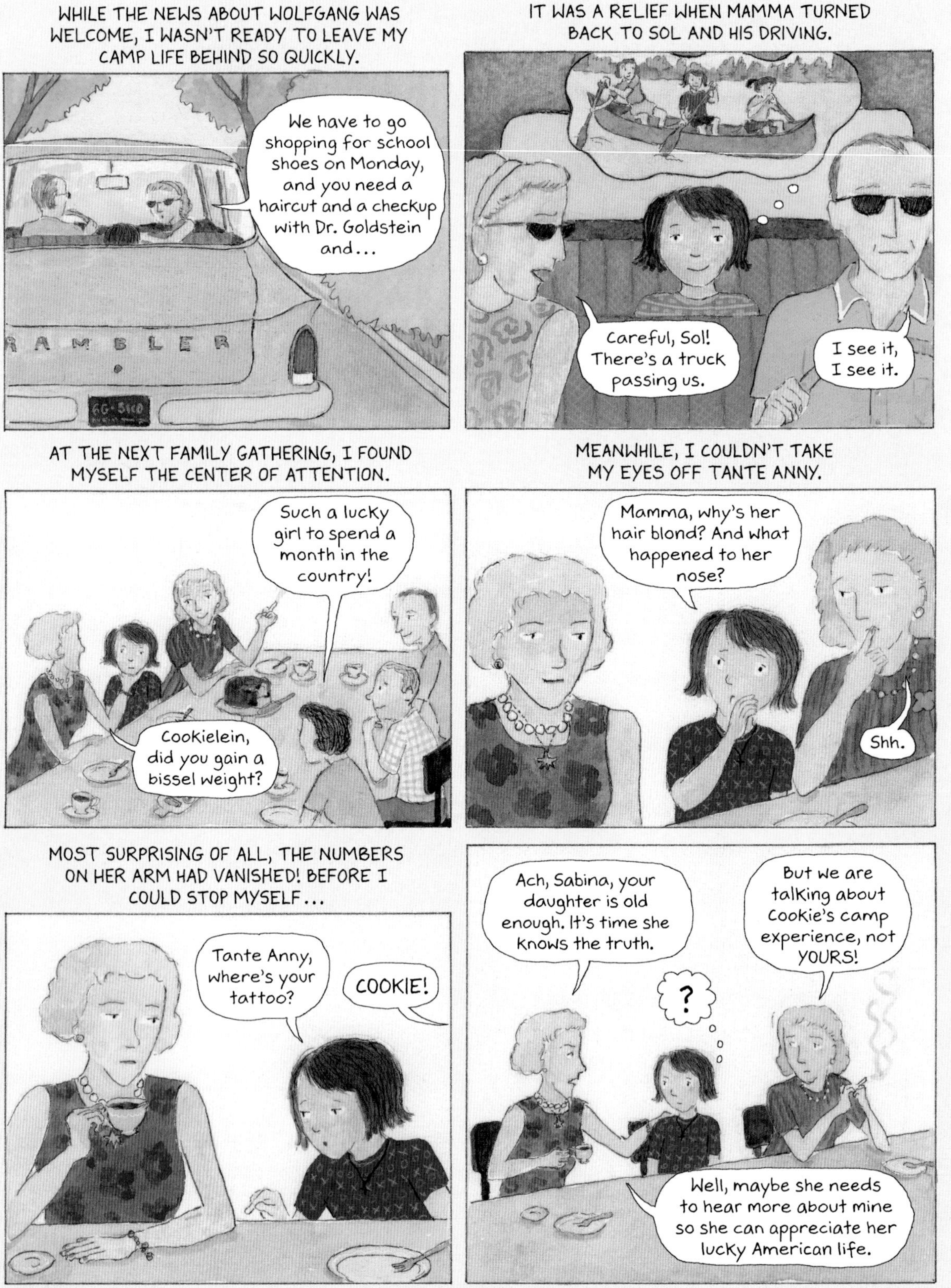
WHILE THE NEWS ABOUT WOLFGANG WAS WELCOME, I WASN'T READY TO LEAVE MY CAMP LIFE BEHIND SO QUICKLY.
We have to go shopping for school shoes on Monday, and you need a haircut and a checkup with Dr. Goldstein and...
RAMBLER
IT WAS A RELIEF WHEN MAMMA TURNED BACK TO SOL AND HIS DRIVING.
Careful, Sol! There's a truck passing us.
I see it, I see it.
AT THE NEXT FAMILY GATHERING, I FOUND MYSELF THE CENTER OF ATTENTION.
Such a lucky girl to spend a month in the country!
Cookielein, did you gain a bissel weight?
MEANWHILE, I COULDN'T TAKE MY EYES OFF TANTE ANNY.
Mamma, why's her hair blond? And what happened to her nose?
Shh.
MOST SURPRISING OF ALL, THE NUMBERS ON HER ARM HAD VANISHED! BEFORE I COULD STOP MYSELF...
Tante Anny, where's your tattoo?
COOKIE!
Ach, Sabina, your daughter is old enough. It's time she knows the truth.
But we are talking about Cookie's camp experience, not YOURS!
?
Well, maybe she needs to hear more about mine so she can appreciate her lucky American life.

"Cookielein, those numbers were burned on my arm when I arrived at Auschwitz, a concentration camp. A concentration camp is nothing like a sleepaway camp.

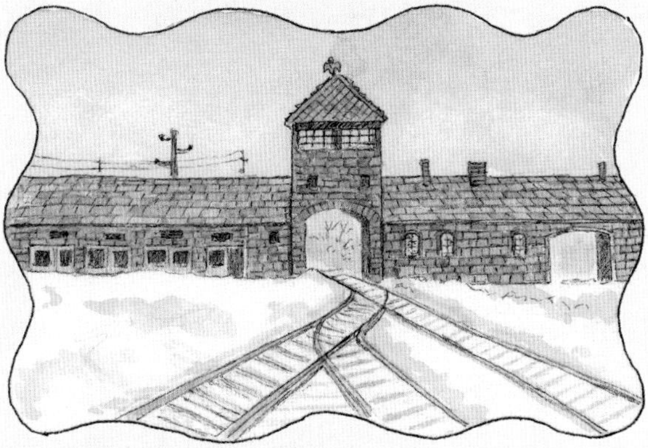

"Before I was sent there, I worked on a farm with my husband and other young Jewish people. We were planning to immigrate to Palestine.

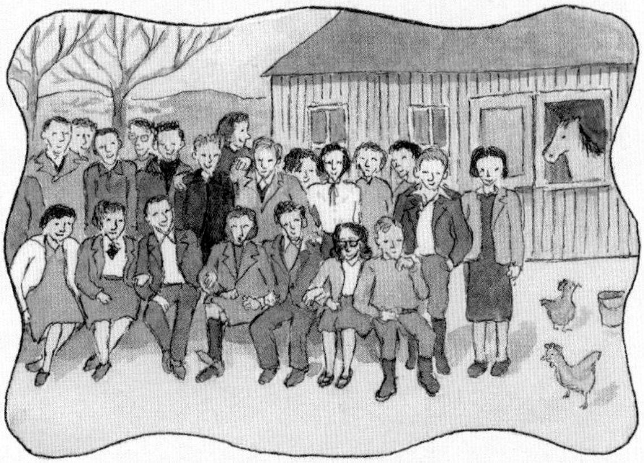

"But then the Nazis rounded us up and crammed us into a cattle car on a train headed to Poland with no food or water.

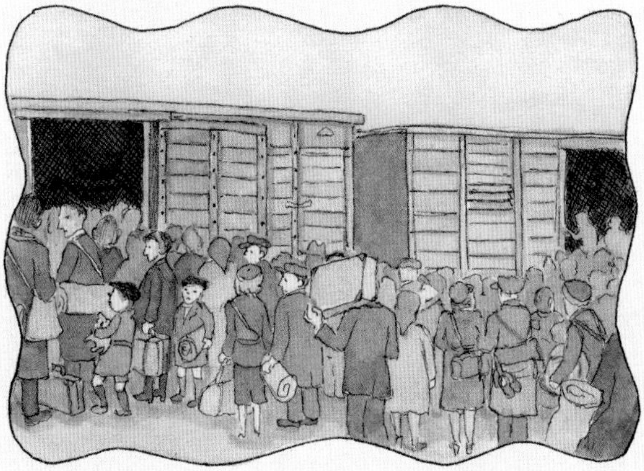

"When the train finally stopped a day later, we were in Auschwitz. SS soldiers were yelling. Dogs were barking.

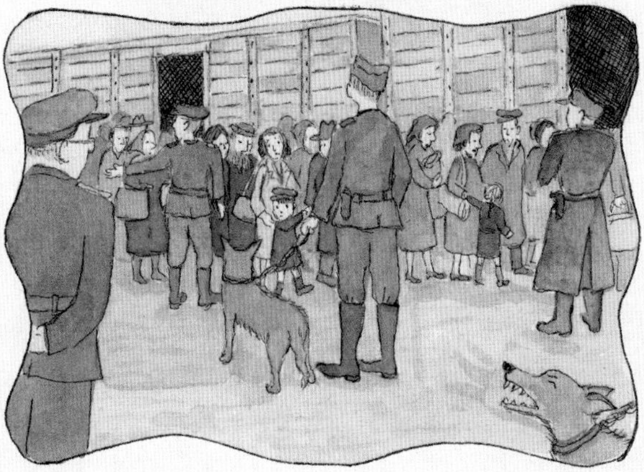

"Right away I was marched with other women to a building where our heads were shaved. We were branded with our numbers and got our uniforms.

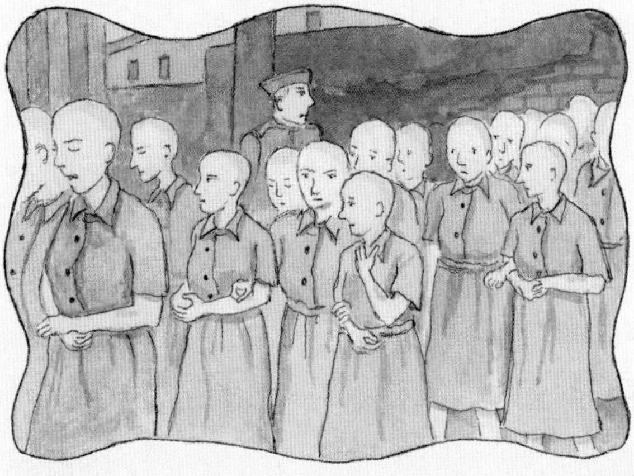

"We were forced to sleep in barracks on concrete bunks. We worked long hours with only watery soup and a little bread to eat.

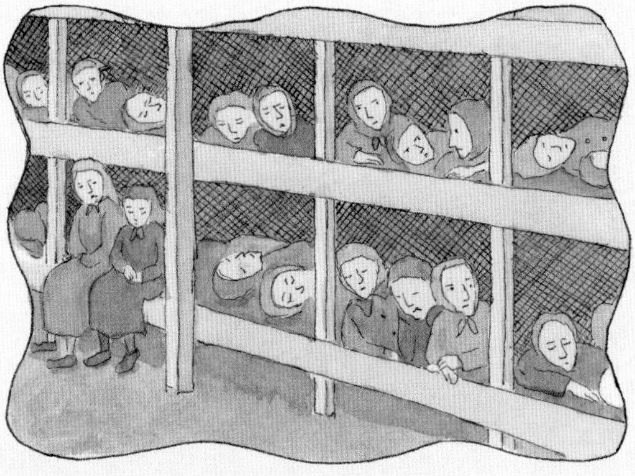

"Luckily for me, I knew how to type and do bookkeeping, so I was selected to work in an office.

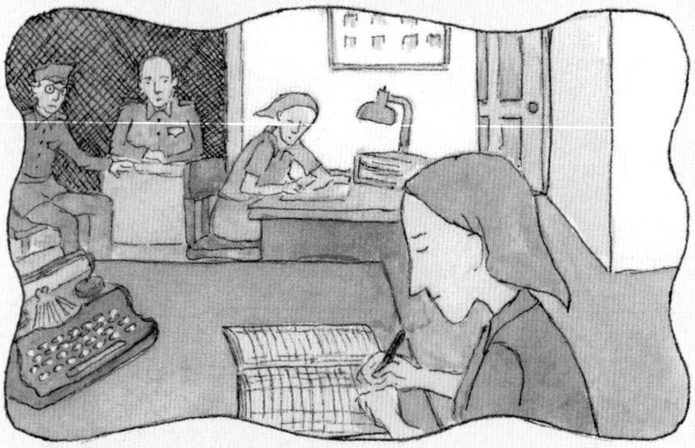

"I kept records of the food eaten by the prisoners. Imagine, the Nazis kept track of such a thing?!

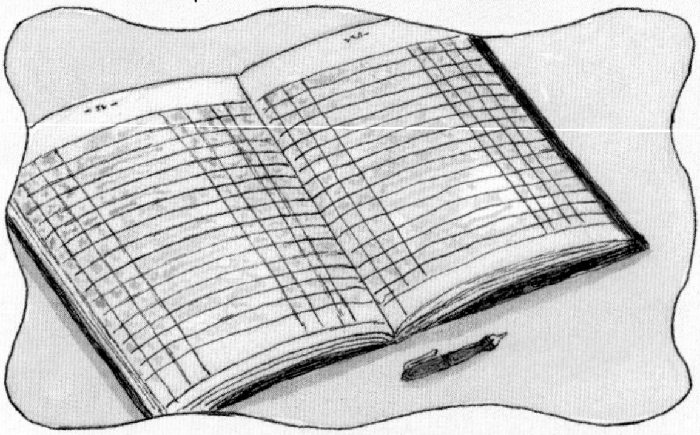

"A year went by and almost another. But then, one cold winter day, we were forced to leave Auschwitz and head west. Now all we had to eat was snow.

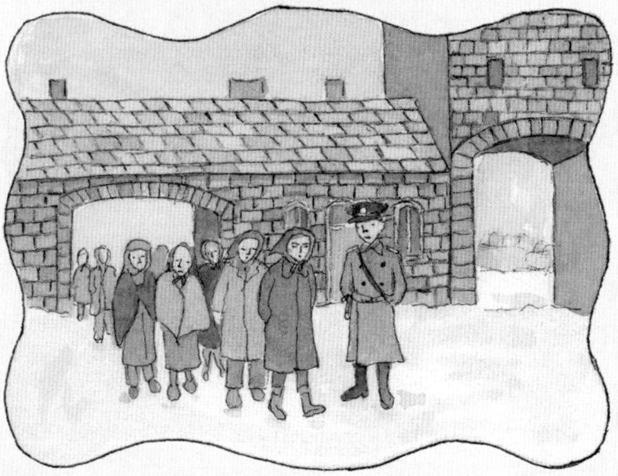

"We moved from one camp to another. During one of our marches, we noticed there were fewer SS men, so a small group of us snuck away to hide in a barn.

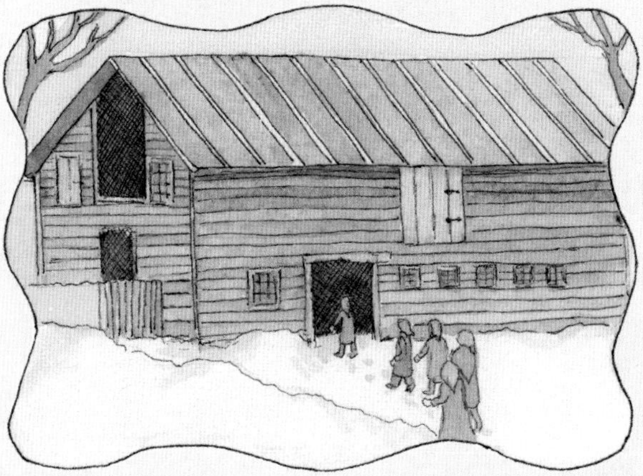

"We saw some American soldiers and found out the war was over. I stayed at a displaced persons camp until I could contact Emmy and get my papers to come to the United States.

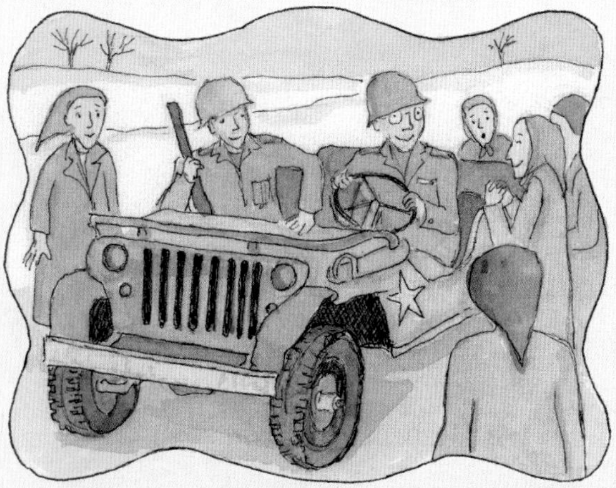

"Your mother was here already. She and Tante Emmy met me at the dock. Later, I learned my dear husband, Heinz, had died in Auschwitz just days before the liberation."

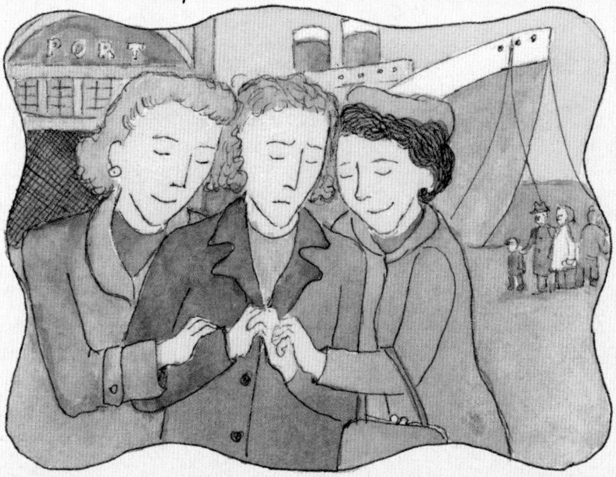
PORT

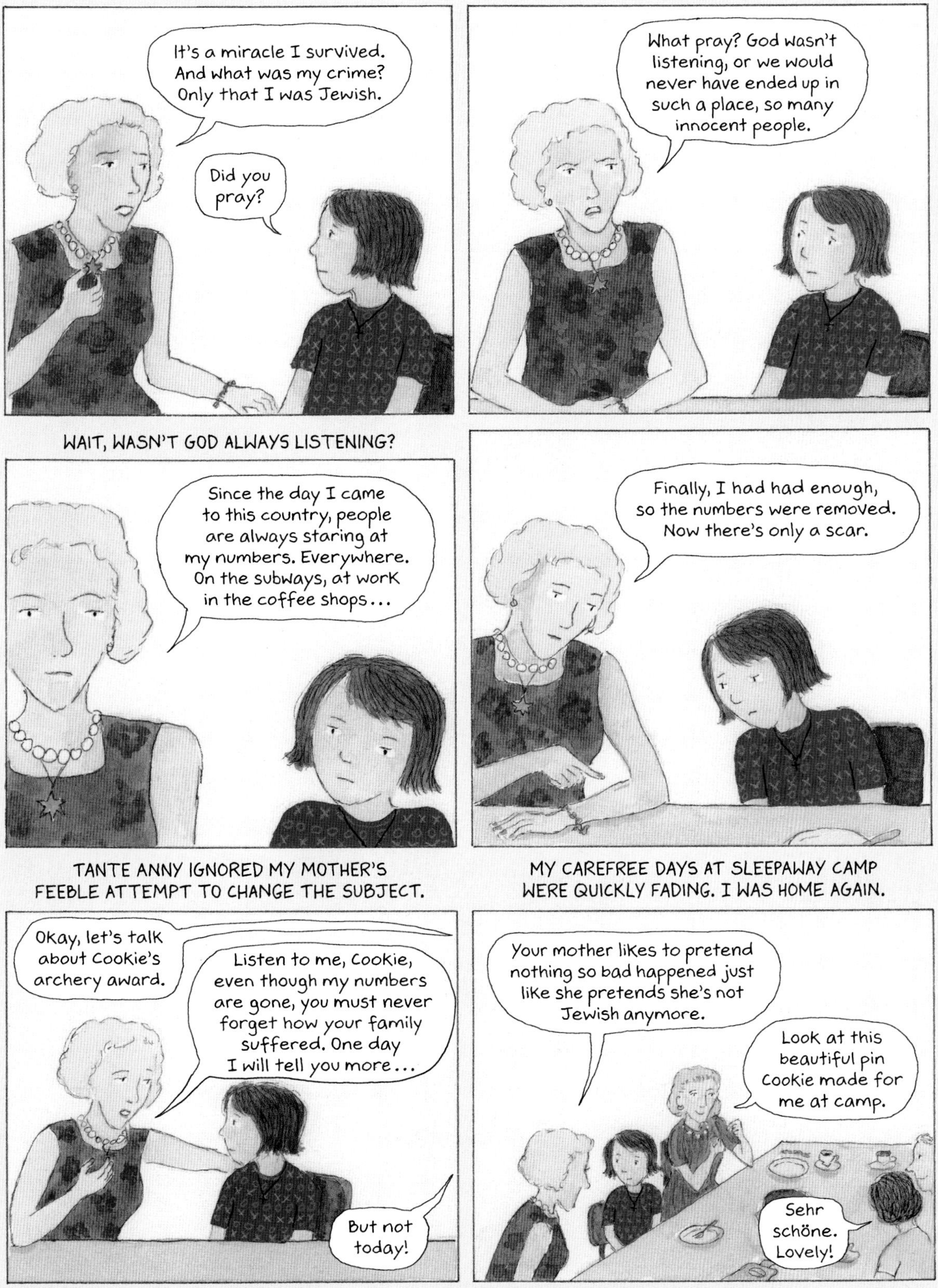
It's a miracle I survived. And what was my crime? Only that I was Jewish.
Did you pray?
What pray? God wasn't listening, or we would never have ended up in such a place, so many innocent people.
WAIT, WASN'T GOD ALWAYS LISTENING?
Since the day I came to this country, people are always staring at my numbers. Everywhere. On the subways, at work in the coffee shops...
Finally, I had had enough, so the numbers were removed. Now there's only a scar.
TANTE ANNY IGNORED MY MOTHER'S FEEBLE ATTEMPT TO CHANGE THE SUBJECT.
MY CAREFREE DAYS AT SLEEPAWAY CAMP WERE QUICKLY FADING. I WAS HOME AGAIN.
Okay, let's talk about Cookie's archery award.
Listen to me, Cookie, even though my numbers are gone, you must never forget how your family suffered. One day I will tell you more...
But not today!
Your mother likes to pretend nothing so bad happened just like she pretends she's not Jewish anymore.
Look at this beautiful pin Cookie made for me at camp.
Sehr schöne. Lovely!

FOURTEEN

A Haircut like Jackie's

1960

MY FIFTH-GRADE TEACHER WAS REPUTED TO BE THE MEANEST TEACHER IN THE SCHOOL.

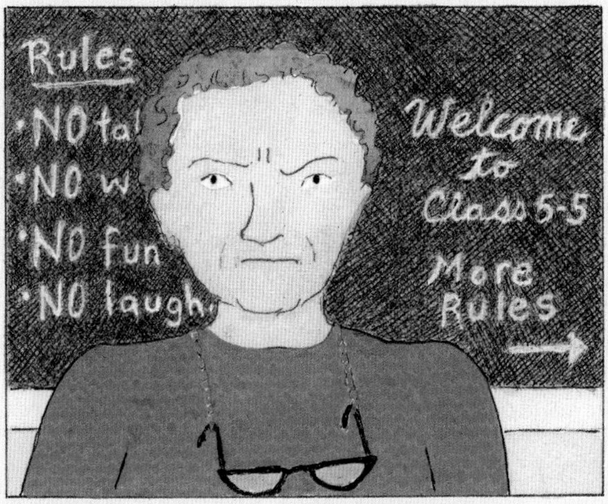
Rules
•NO ta
•NO w
•NO fun
•NO laugh
Welcome to Class 5-5
More Rules

MISS BISHOP ASSIGNED US OUR DESKS, AND I ENDED UP NEXT TO A REPULSIVE BOY NAMED HOWARD G.

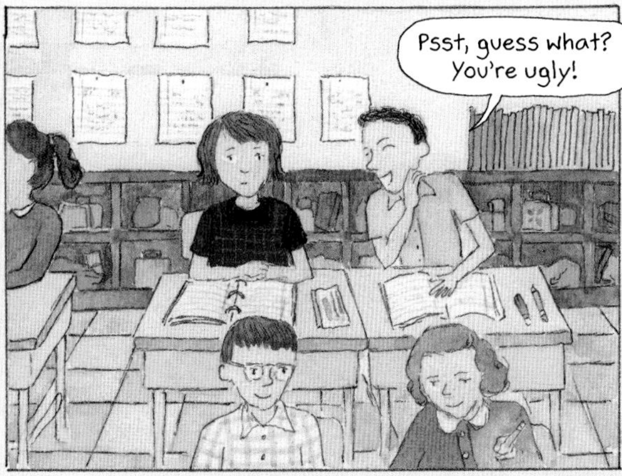
Psst, guess what? You're ugly!

HOWARD DID EVERYTHING HE COULD TO GET ME IN TROUBLE.

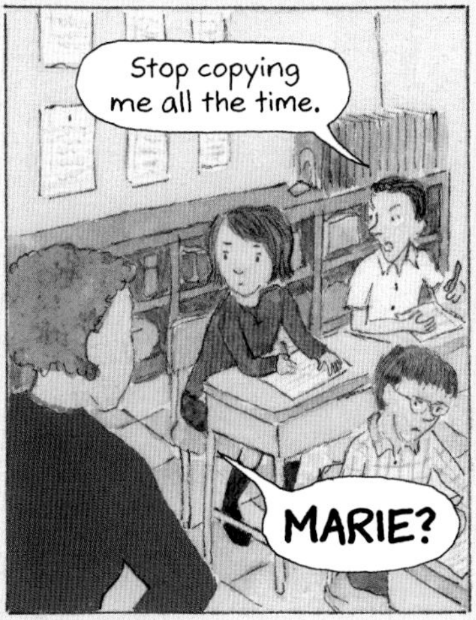
Stop copying me all the time.
MARIE?

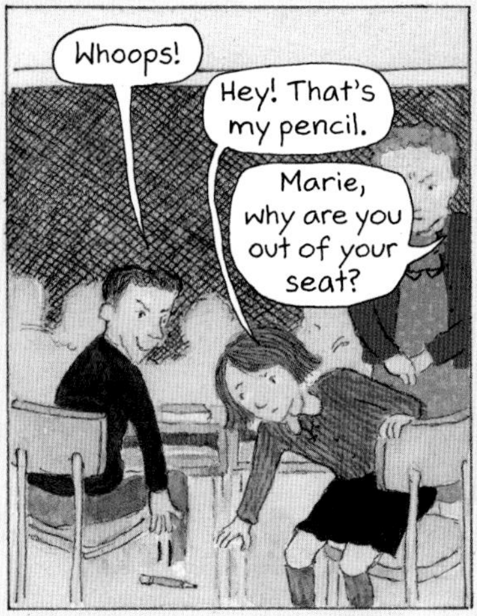
Whoops!
Hey! That's my pencil.
Marie, why are you out of your seat?

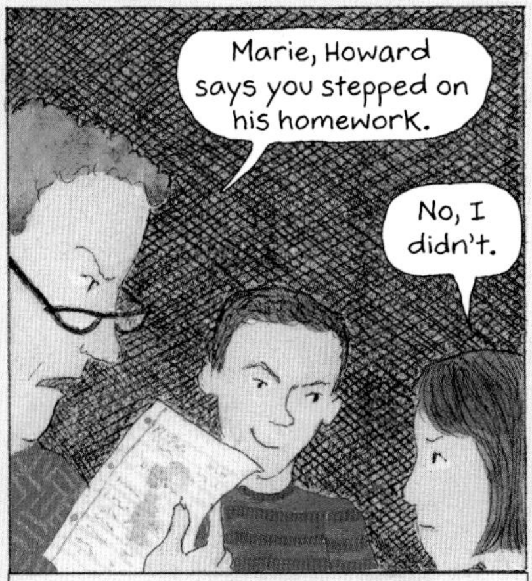
Marie, Howard says you stepped on his homework.
No, I didn't.

IT WAS GOING TO BE A LONG YEAR.

MISS BISHOP HAD A FEW OTHER ROLES AT P.S. 196. SHE MONITORED THE BOYS' BATHROOM TO MAKE SURE NO ONE LINGERED THERE TOO LONG.

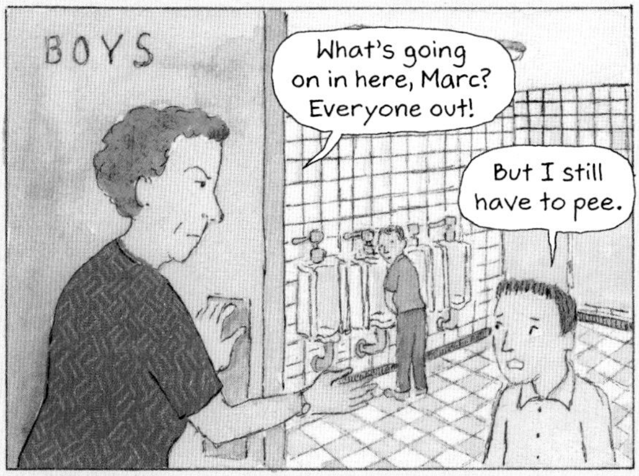
BOYS
What's going on in here, Marc? Everyone out!
But I still have to pee.

AND SHE WAS IN CHARGE OF THE SCHOOL CHORUS. THANKS TO ROBERTO, I LOVED TO SING, SO I DID MY BEST TO IGNORE MISS BISHOP'S CONSTANT SCOWL.

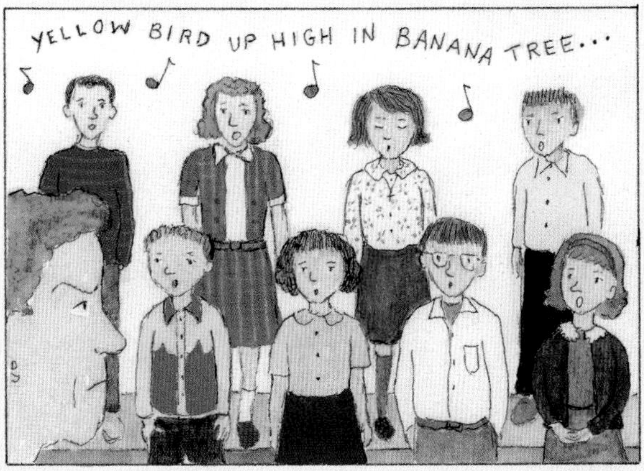
YELLOW BIRD UP HIGH IN BANANA TREE...

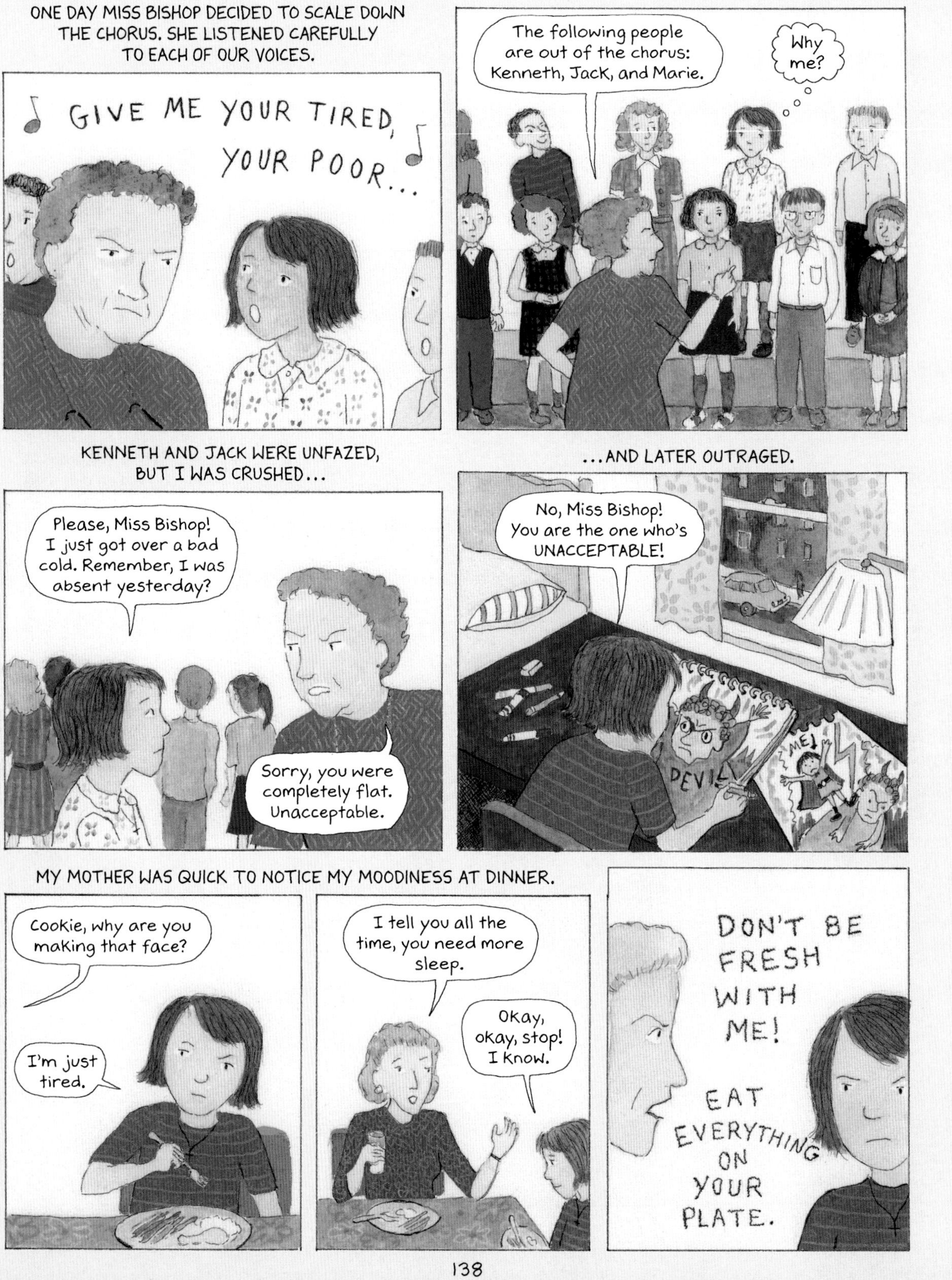
ONE DAY MISS BISHOP DECIDED TO SCALE DOWN THE CHORUS. SHE LISTENED CAREFULLY TO EACH OF OUR VOICES.
GIVE ME YOUR TIRED, YOUR POOR...
The following people are out of the chorus: Kenneth, Jack, and Marie.
Why me?
KENNETH AND JACK WERE UNFAZED, BUT I WAS CRUSHED...
Please, Miss Bishop! I just got over a bad cold. Remember, I was absent yesterday?
Sorry, you were completely flat. Unacceptable.
...AND LATER OUTRAGED.
No, Miss Bishop! You are the one who's UNACCEPTABLE!
DEVIL
ME
MY MOTHER WAS QUICK TO NOTICE MY MOODINESS AT DINNER.
Cookie, why are you making that face?
I'm just tired.
I tell you all the time, you need more sleep.
Okay, okay, stop! I know.
DON'T BE FRESH WITH ME!
EAT EVERYTHING ON YOUR PLATE.

I STARED AT THE SOGGY CANNED ASPARAGUS AND FELT LIKE I WAS GOING TO THROW UP.

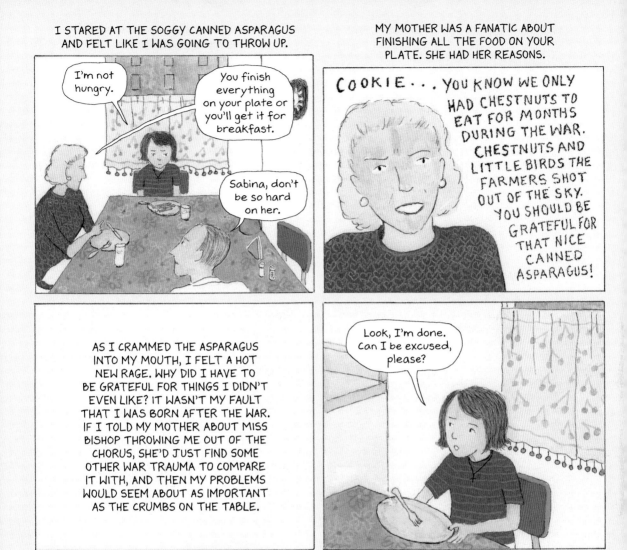

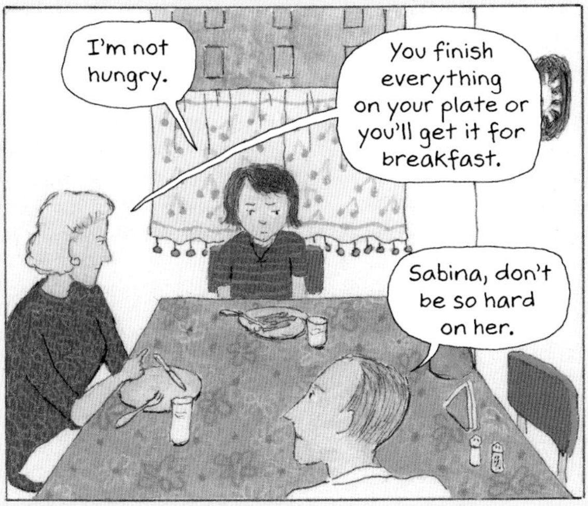
I'm not hungry.
You finish everything on your plate or you'll get it for breakfast.
Sabina, don't be so hard on her.

MY MOTHER WAS A FANATIC ABOUT FINISHING ALL THE FOOD ON YOUR PLATE. SHE HAD HER REASONS.

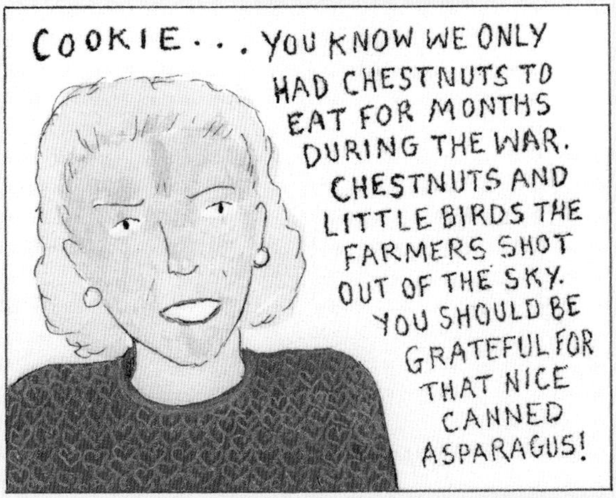
COOKIE... YOU KNOW WE ONLY HAD CHESTNUTS TO EAT FOR MONTHS DURING THE WAR. CHESTNUTS AND LITTLE BIRDS THE FARMERS SHOT OUT OF THE SKY. YOU SHOULD BE GRATEFUL FOR THAT NICE CANNED ASPARAGUS!

AS I CRAMMED THE ASPARAGUS INTO MY MOUTH, I FELT A HOT NEW RAGE. WHY DID I HAVE TO BE GRATEFUL FOR THINGS I DIDN'T EVEN LIKE? IT WASN'T MY FAULT THAT I WAS BORN AFTER THE WAR. IF I TOLD MY MOTHER ABOUT MISS BISHOP THROWING ME OUT OF THE CHORUS, SHE'D JUST FIND SOME OTHER WAR TRAUMA TO COMPARE IT WITH, AND THEN MY PROBLEMS WOULD SEEM ABOUT AS IMPORTANT AS THE CRUMBS ON THE TABLE.

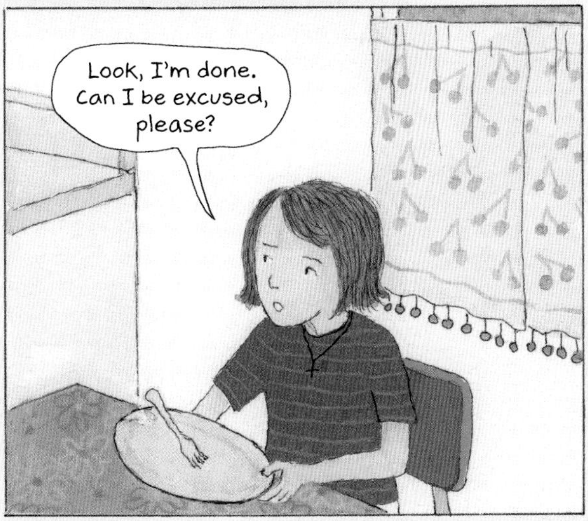
Look, I'm done. Can I be excused, please?

WITH THE SHADOW OF MISS BISHOP HANGING OVER EVERY SCHOOL DAY, I COULDN'T WAIT FOR SATURDAY MORNINGS AND ART LESSONS IN MRS. F.'S ATTIC STUDIO.

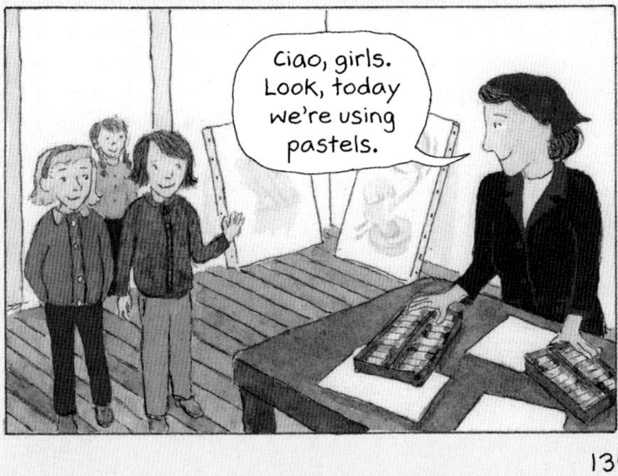
Ciao, girls. Look, today we're using pastels.

ONE WEEKEND SHE TOOK US ON A FIELD TRIP TO THE MUSEUM OF MODERN ART.

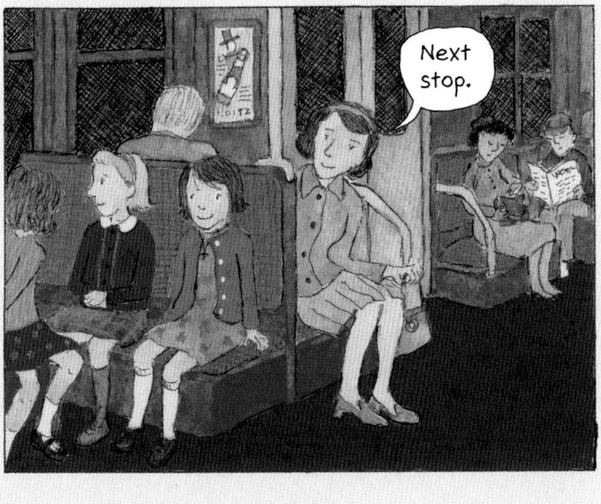
Next stop.

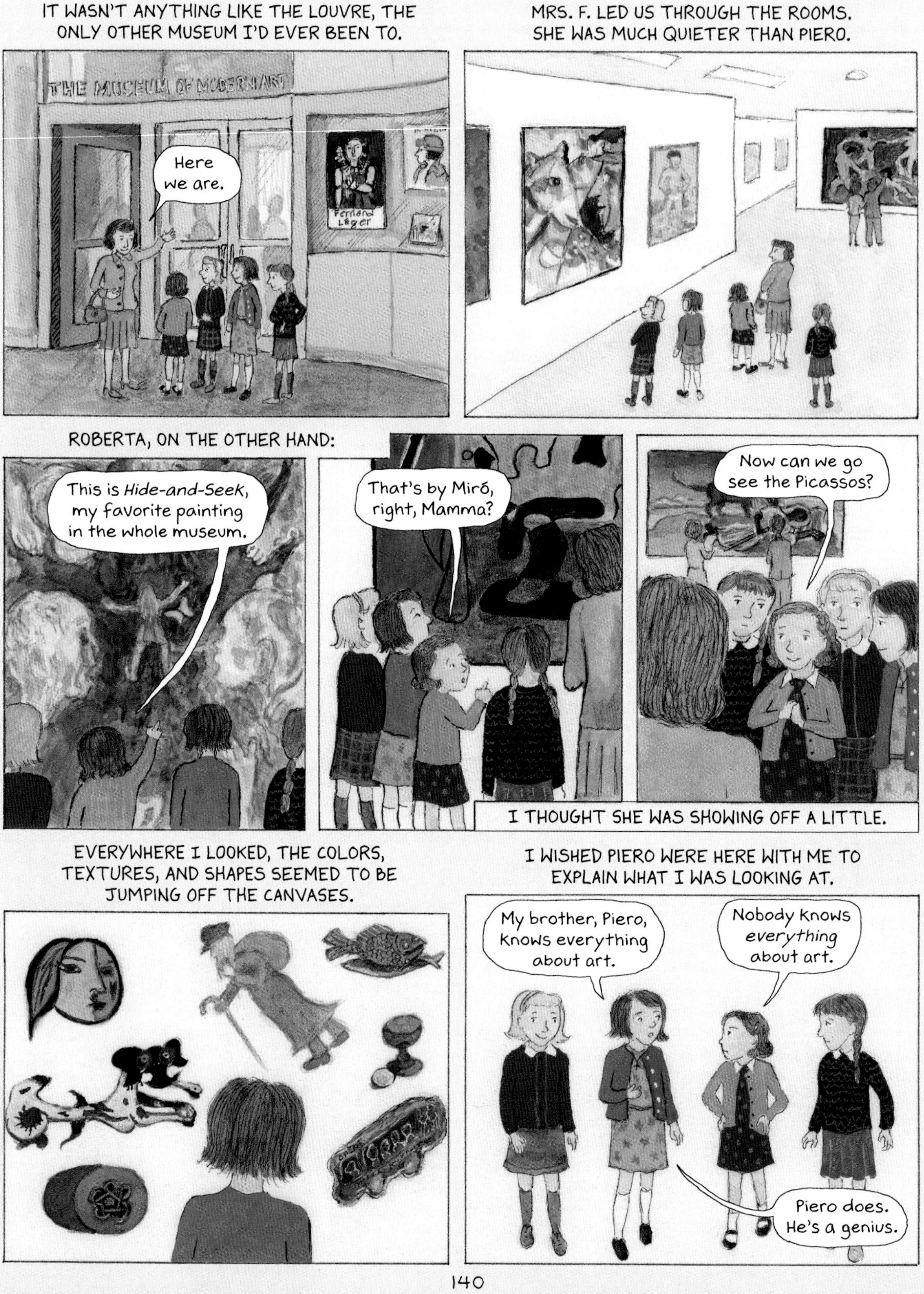
IT WASN'T ANYTHING LIKE THE LOUVRE, THE ONLY OTHER MUSEUM I'D EVER BEEN TO.
THE MUSEUM OF MODERN ART
Here we are.
Fernand Léger
MRS. F. LED US THROUGH THE ROOMS. SHE WAS MUCH QUIETER THAN PIERO.
ROBERTA, ON THE OTHER HAND:
This is *Hide-and-Seek*, my favorite painting in the whole museum.
That's by Miró, right, Mamma?
Now can we go see the Picassos?
I THOUGHT SHE WAS SHOWING OFF A LITTLE.
EVERYWHERE I LOOKED, THE COLORS, TEXTURES, AND SHAPES SEEMED TO BE JUMPING OFF THE CANVASES.
I WISHED PIERO WERE HERE WITH ME TO EXPLAIN WHAT I WAS LOOKING AT.
My brother, Piero, knows everything about art.
Nobody knows *everything* about art.
Piero does. He's a genius.

THEN WE CAME TO A PAINTING THAT STOPPED ME IN MY TRACKS.

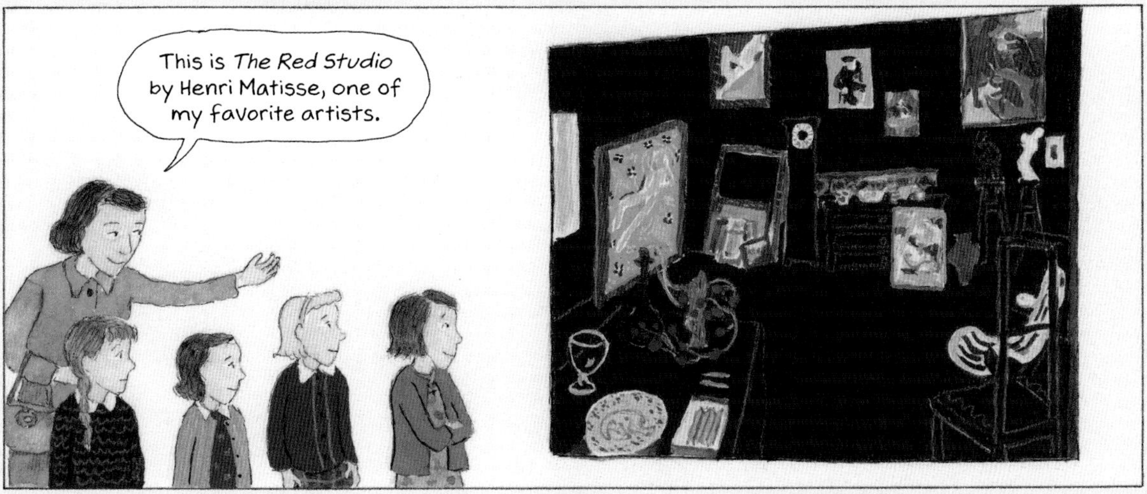
This is *The Red Studio* by Henri Matisse, one of my favorite artists.

WHAT WAS IT ABOUT THIS RED ROOM WITH PAINTINGS ON THE WALLS AND A CLOCK WITH NO HANDS? IT FELT LIKE A SAFE PLACE WHERE NOTHING BAD WOULD EVER HAPPEN—NO ARGUING IN GERMAN, NO STORIES OF WARTIME SUFFERING, NO MISS BISHOP, NO CANNED ASPARAGUS! I LONGED TO STEP INSIDE THIS PERFECT STUDIO AND STAY FOREVER.

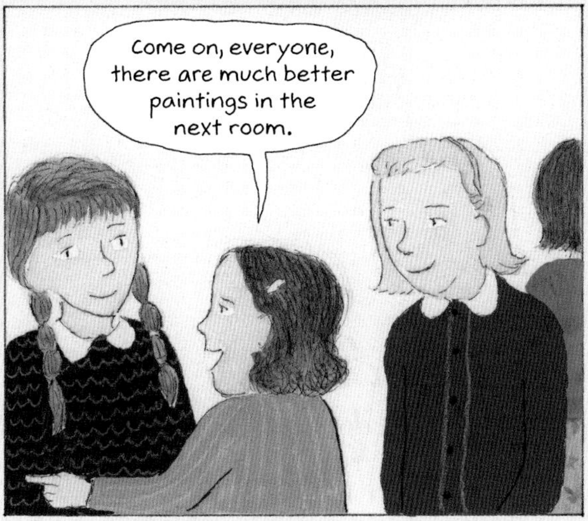
Come on, everyone, there are much better paintings in the next room.

WHILE THE OTHERS FOLLOWED ROBERTA, MRS. F. AND I LINGERED BY THE MATISSE.

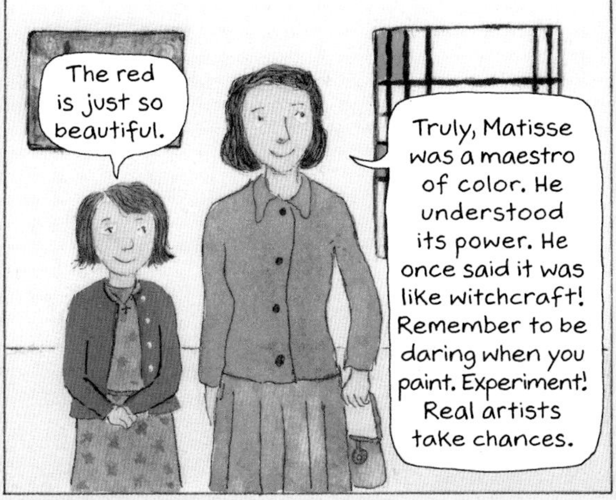
The red is just so beautiful.
Truly, Matisse was a maestro of color. He understood its power. He once said it was like witchcraft! Remember to be daring when you paint. Experiment! Real artists take chances.

TALKING TO MRS. F. WAS ALMOST LIKE TALKING TO PIERO. DID SHE BELIEVE I COULD BECOME AN ARTIST, TOO?

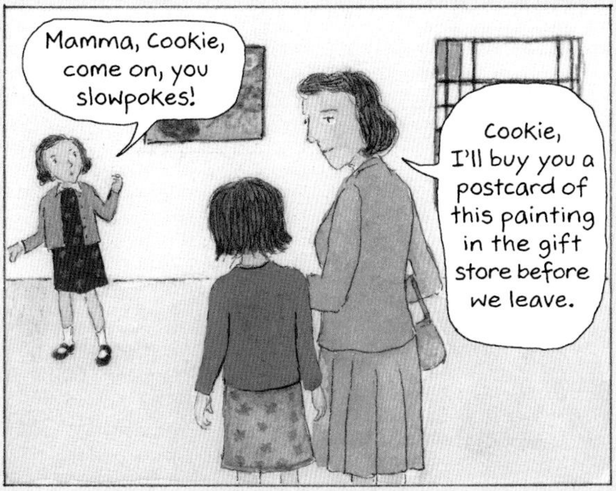
Mamma, Cookie, come on, you slowpokes!
Cookie, I'll buy you a postcard of this painting in the gift store before we leave.

LATER WHEN I GOT HOME, I TAPED THE POSTCARD ON THE WALL NEXT TO MY BED SO I COULD SEE IT EVERY MORNING WHEN I WOKE UP AND EVERY NIGHT BEFORE I TURNED OUT MY LAMP, HOPING I WOULD DREAM ABOUT THE BEAUTIFUL RED STUDIO.

AND SOMETIMES I DID.

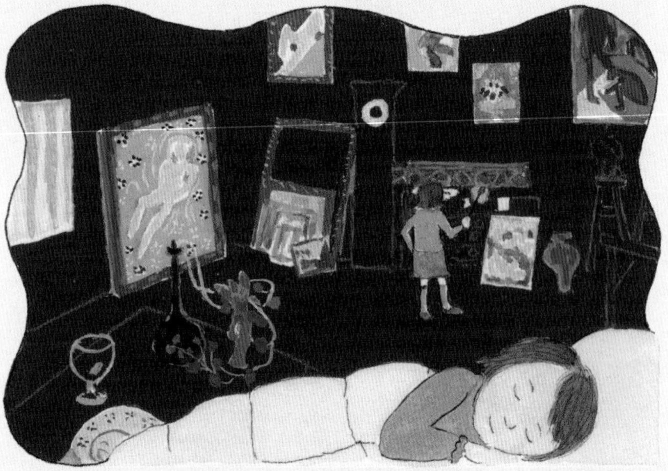

EVEN THOUGH KAREN WASN'T IN MY CLASS ANYMORE, WE STILL SPENT A LOT OF TIME WANDERING AROUND THE NEIGHBORHOOD. ONE DAY WE PASSED A STOREFRONT WITH POSTERS OF JOHN F. KENNEDY IN THE WINDOW.

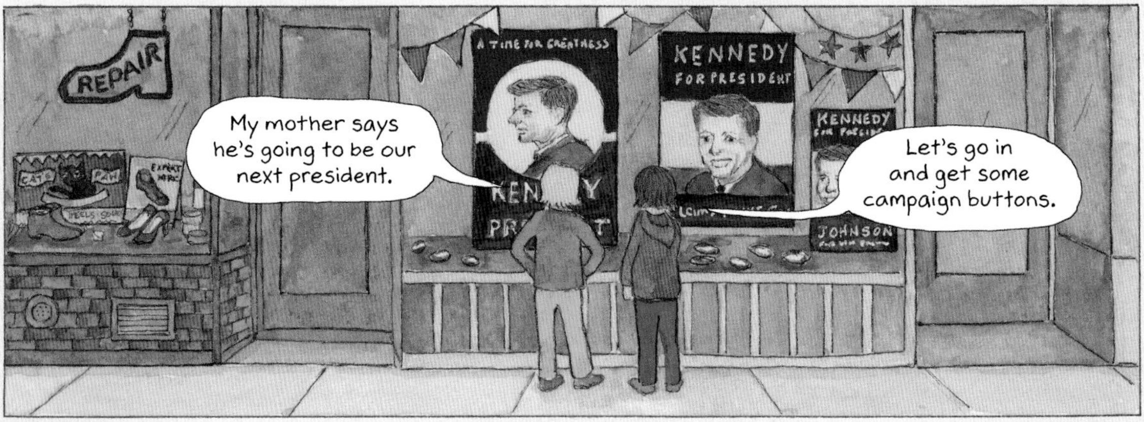
REPAIR
A TIME FOR GREATNESS
KENNEDY
FOR PRESIDENT
KENNEDY
JOHNSON
My mother says he's going to be our next president.
Let's go in and get some campaign buttons.

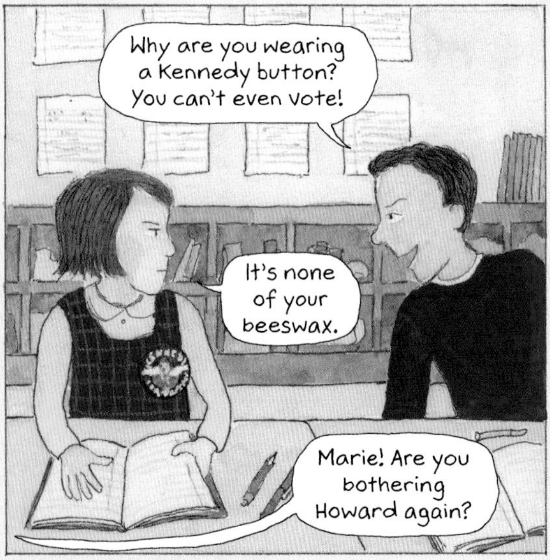
Why are you wearing a Kennedy button? You can't even vote!
It's none of your beeswax.
Marie! Are you bothering Howard again?

WHEN KENNEDY WON THE ELECTION, HE BECAME THE FIRST CATHOLIC AMERICAN PRESIDENT. I WAS SO PROUD THAT I CONTINUED TO WEAR MY CAMPAIGN BUTTON.

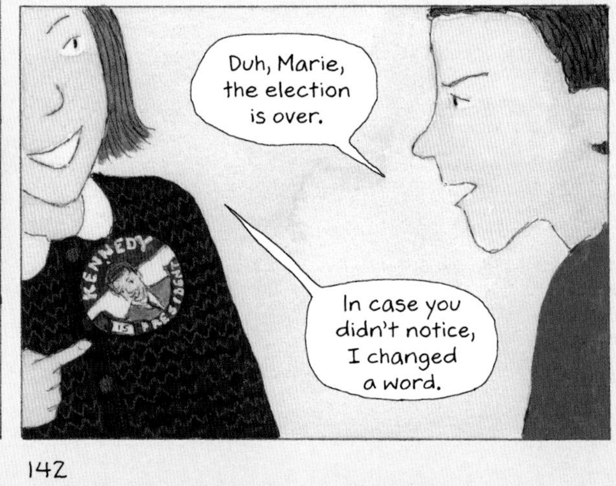
Duh, Marie, the election is over.
KENNEDY
IS
In case you didn't notice, I changed a word.

AT SUNDAY MASS THERE WAS A NEW ELECTRICITY IN THE AIR.

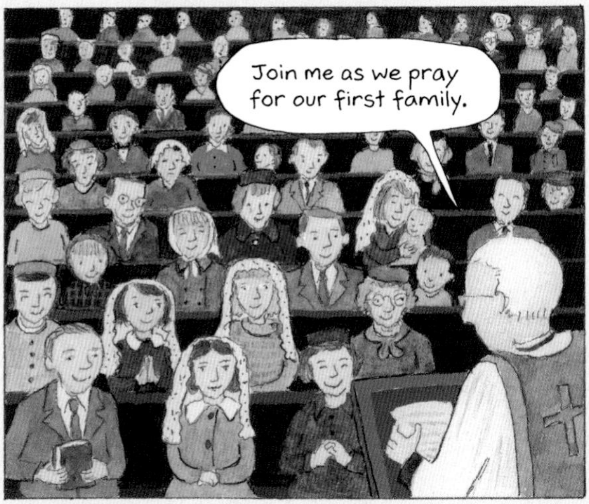
Join me as we pray for our first family.

EVEN MY MOTHER, A DIE-HARD REPUBLICAN, WAS A FAN OF OUR YOUNG PRESIDENT AND HIS GLAMOROUS FIRST LADY, JACKIE.

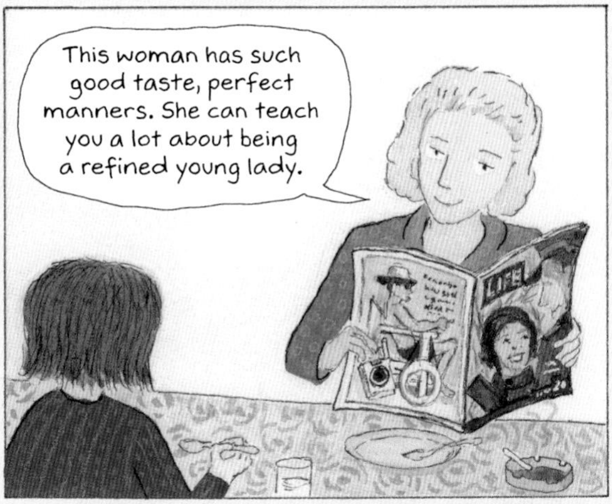
This woman has such good taste, perfect manners. She can teach you a lot about being a refined young lady.

SHE EVEN TOOK ME TO THE BEAUTY PARLOR SO I COULD HAVE A HAIRCUT LIKE JACKIE'S.

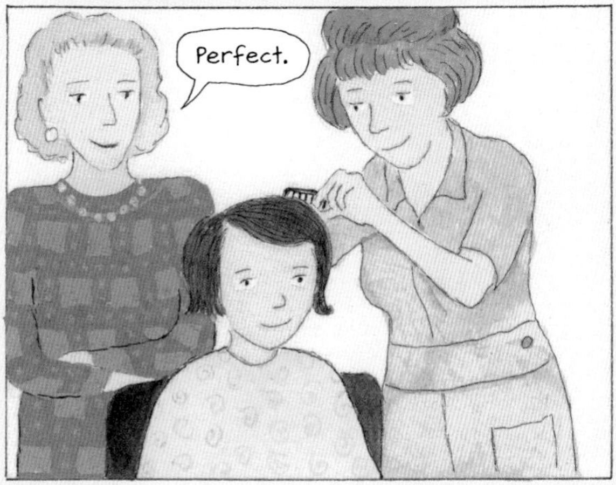
Perfect.

RIDING THIS WAVE OF RENEWED CATHOLIC PRIDE, THE NUN AT MY RELIGIOUS INSTRUCTION CLASS ASKED US IF WE HAD GIVEN ANY THOUGHT TO OUR VOCATIONS.

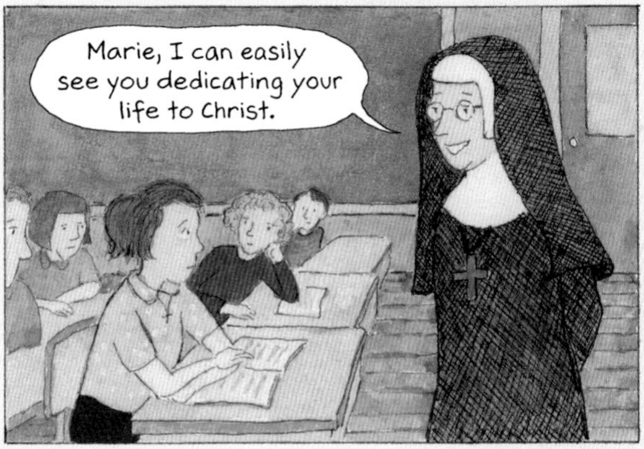
Marie, I can easily see you dedicating your life to Christ.

MY PATH TO ADULTHOOD WAS NOT AS CLEAR AS IT HAD ONCE BEEN. AFTER ALL, IF I BECAME A NUN AND WORE A WIMPLE, NO ONE WOULD BE ABLE TO SEE MY NICE HAIRCUT. WOULDN'T BEING A FIRST LADY LIKE JACKIE BE MORE FUN THAN BEING A NUN? AND WHAT ABOUT LIVING IN A DRAB STONE BUILDING WITH A BUNCH OF OTHER NUNS? WHERE WOULD I PAINT? WOULD I EVEN BE ALLOWED TO HAVE A RED STUDIO IN A CONVENT?

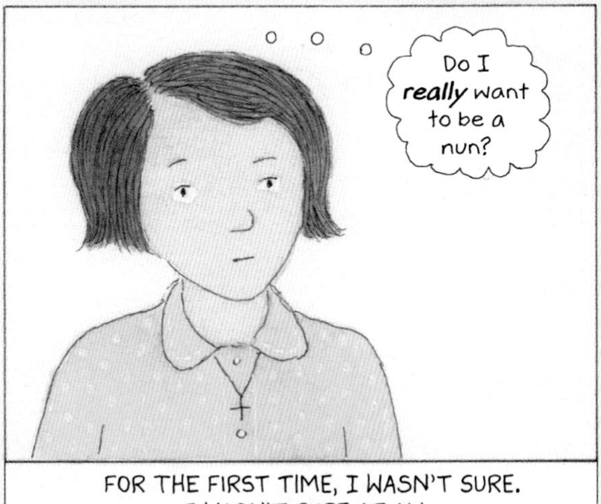
Do I ***really*** want to be a nun?

FOR THE FIRST TIME, I WASN'T SURE. I WASN'T SURE AT ALL.

FIFTEEN

Junior Bridesmaid

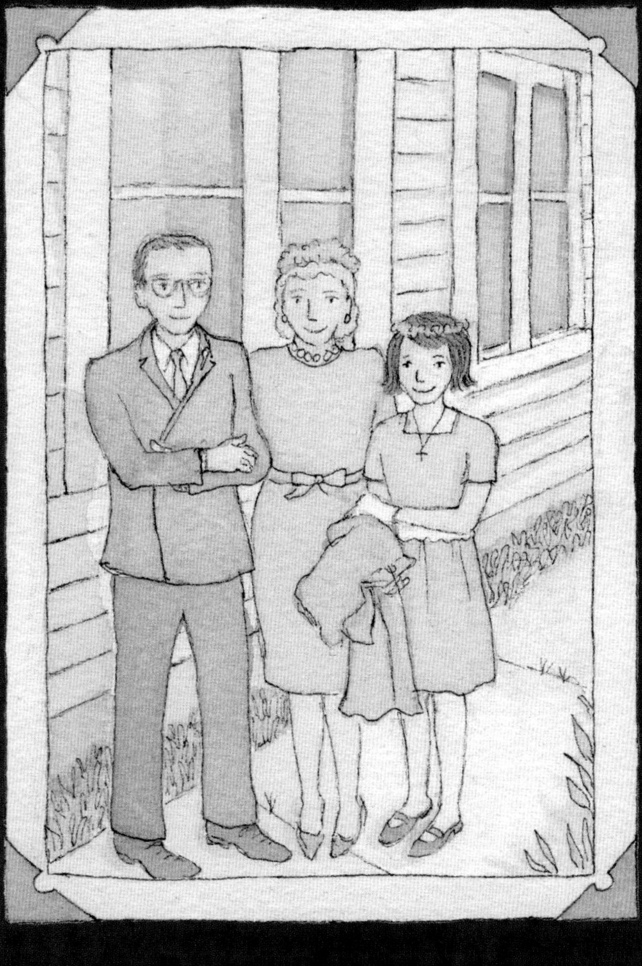

1961-62

BY THE TIME I STARTED SIXTH GRADE, I WAS OFFICIALLY WEARING A TRAINING BRA. I KEPT THIS INFORMATION TO MYSELF. THERE WAS ONE GIRL IN MY CLASS WHO FLAUNTED HER CHANGING BODY. UNLIKE ME, SHE DIDN'T MIND THE EXTRA ATTENTION.

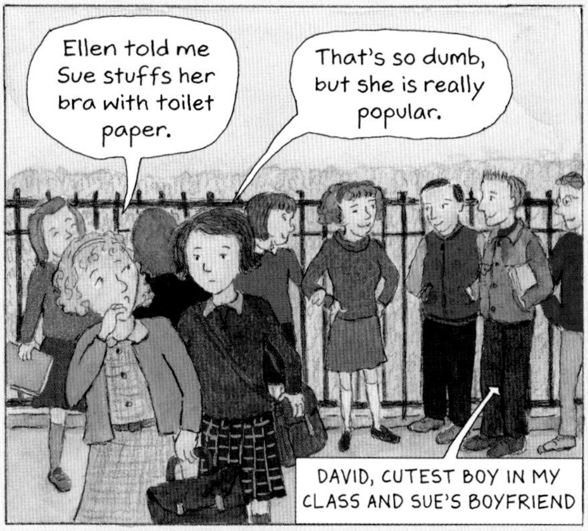
Ellen told me Sue stuffs her bra with toilet paper.
That's so dumb, but she is really popular.
DAVID, CUTEST BOY IN MY CLASS AND SUE'S BOYFRIEND

THE BIG NEWS AT HOME WAS THAT PIERO HAD MARRIED HIS GIRLFRIEND, KATE, IN ENGLAND. MAMMA WAS HAPPY HE WAS FINALLY SETTLING DOWN AND HAD EVEN CUT HIS HAIR.

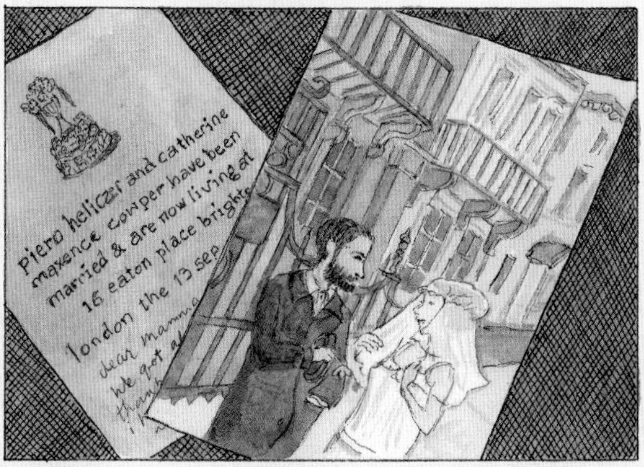
piero heliczer and catherine
maxence cowper have been
married & are now living at
16 eaton place
london the 13 sep
dear mamma

ROBERTO STILL LIKED LIVING IN TEXAS. HE MENTIONED A NEW GIRL IN EVERY LETTER.

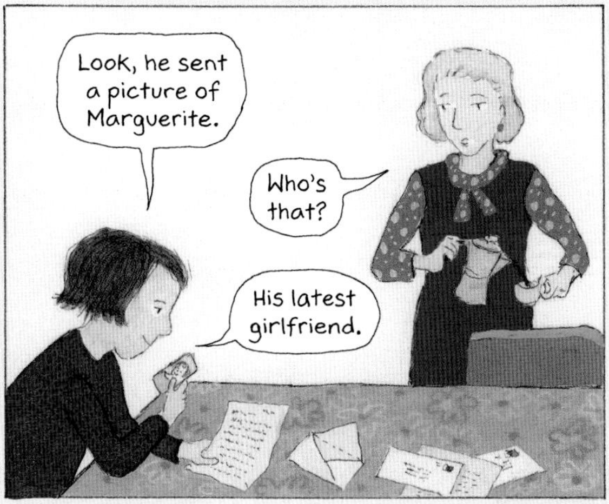
Look, he sent a picture of Marguerite.
Who's that?
His latest girlfriend.

MY MOTHER WAS RELIEVED TO SEE ROBERTO COMING OUT OF HIS SHELL, BECAUSE UNLIKE PIERO, HE HAD ALWAYS BEEN SHY AROUND GIRLS.

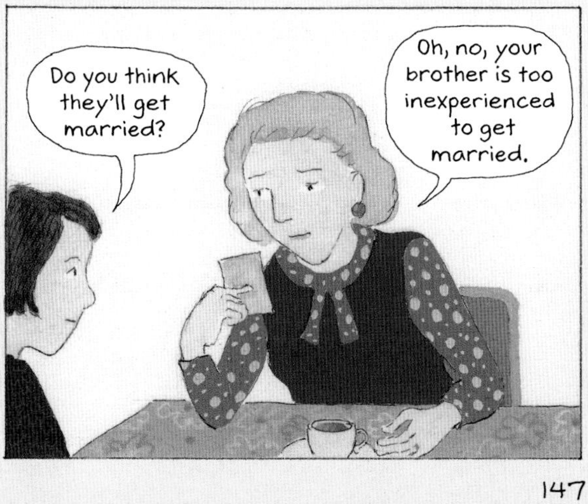
Do you think they'll get married?
Oh, no, your brother is too inexperienced to get married.

SOL'S JOB AT THE REAL ESTATE OFFICE WAS GOING WELL. FOR A WHILE, MY MOTHER WAS IN A PRETTY GOOD MOOD.

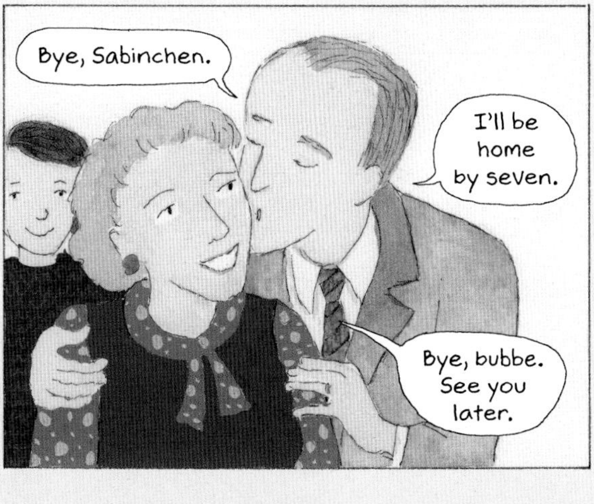
Bye, Sabinchen.
I'll be home by seven.
Bye, bubbe. See you later.

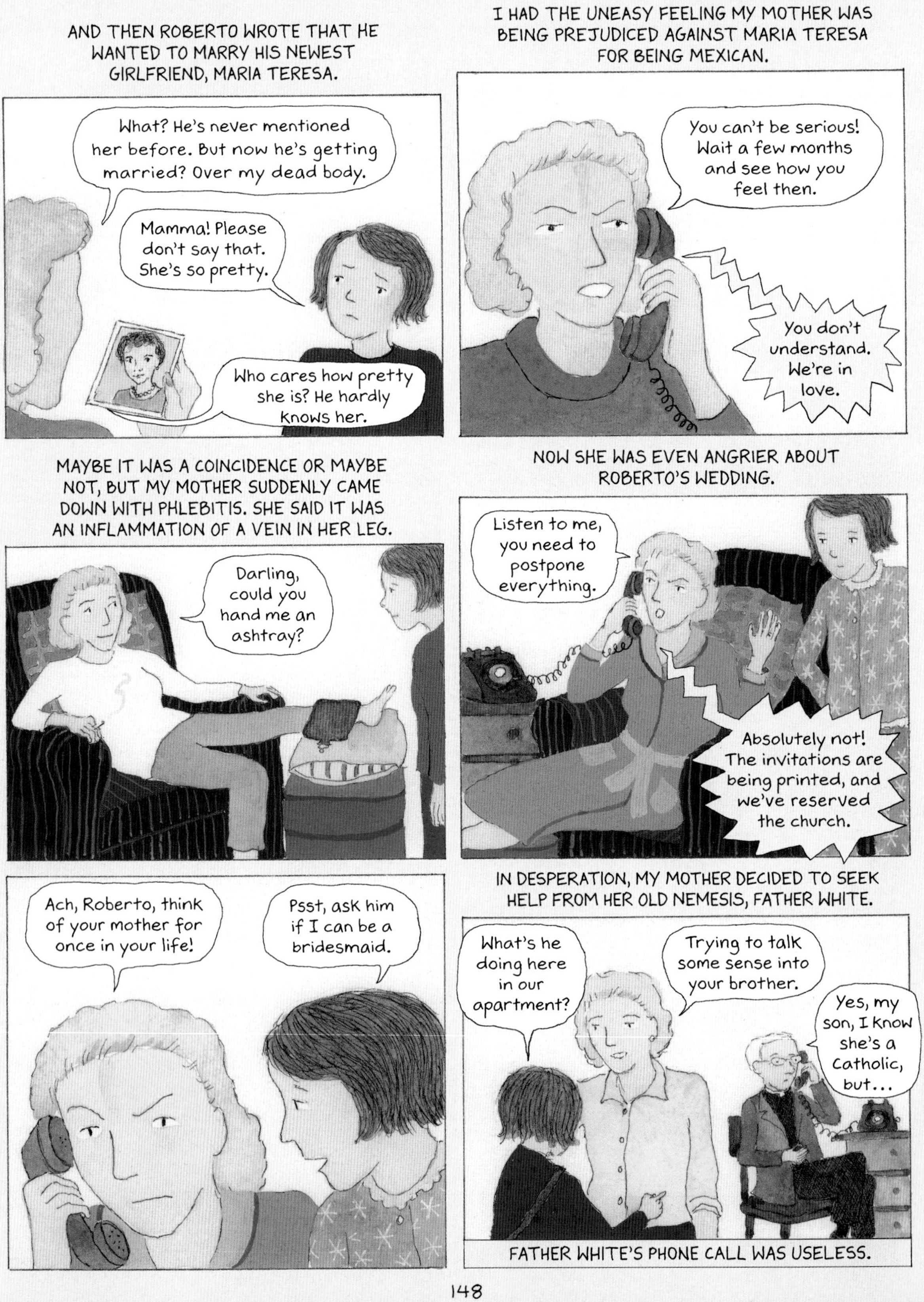
AND THEN ROBERTO WROTE THAT HE WANTED TO MARRY HIS NEWEST GIRLFRIEND, MARIA TERESA.
What? He's never mentioned her before. But now he's getting married? Over my dead body.
Mamma! Please don't say that. She's so pretty.
Who cares how pretty she is? He hardly knows her.
I HAD THE UNEASY FEELING MY MOTHER WAS BEING PREJUDICED AGAINST MARIA TERESA FOR BEING MEXICAN.
You can't be serious! Wait a few months and see how you feel then.
You don't understand. We're in love.
MAYBE IT WAS A COINCIDENCE OR MAYBE NOT, BUT MY MOTHER SUDDENLY CAME DOWN WITH PHLEBITIS. SHE SAID IT WAS AN INFLAMMATION OF A VEIN IN HER LEG.
Darling, could you hand me an ashtray?
NOW SHE WAS EVEN ANGRIER ABOUT ROBERTO'S WEDDING.
Listen to me, you need to postpone everything.
Absolutely not! The invitations are being printed, and we've reserved the church.
Ach, Roberto, think of your mother for once in your life!
Psst, ask him if I can be a bridesmaid.
IN DESPERATION, MY MOTHER DECIDED TO SEEK HELP FROM HER OLD NEMESIS, FATHER WHITE.
What's he doing here in our apartment?
Trying to talk some sense into your brother.
Yes, my son, I know she's a Catholic, but...
FATHER WHITE'S PHONE CALL WAS USELESS.

IT LOOKED LIKE WE WERE GOING TO MISS BOTH MY BROTHERS' WEDDINGS.

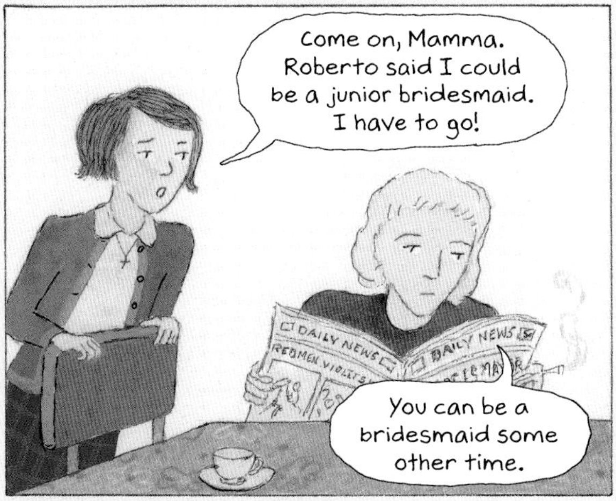

Come on, Mamma. Roberto said I could be a junior bridesmaid. I have to go!
DAILY NEWS
You can be a bridesmaid some other time.

WHEN THE WEDDING INVITATIONS ARRIVED, THEY CAUSED A FAMILY UPROAR.

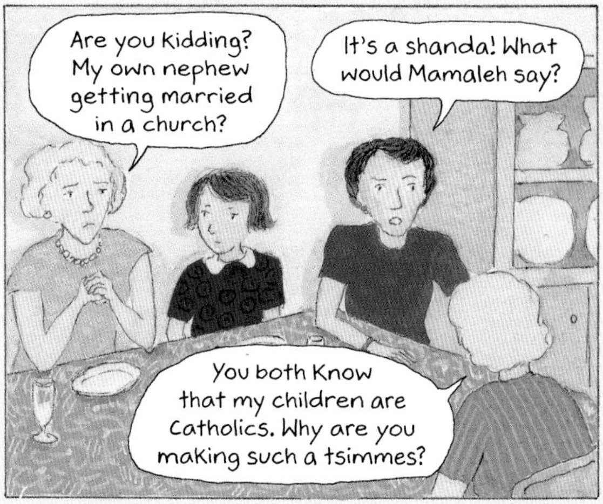

Are you kidding? My own nephew getting married in a church?
It's a shanda! What would Mamaleh say?
You both know that my children are Catholics. Why are you making such a tsimmes?

IN AN EXTRAORDINARY ABOUT-FACE, MAMMA UNEXPECTEDLY JUMPED TO ROBERTO'S DEFENSE.

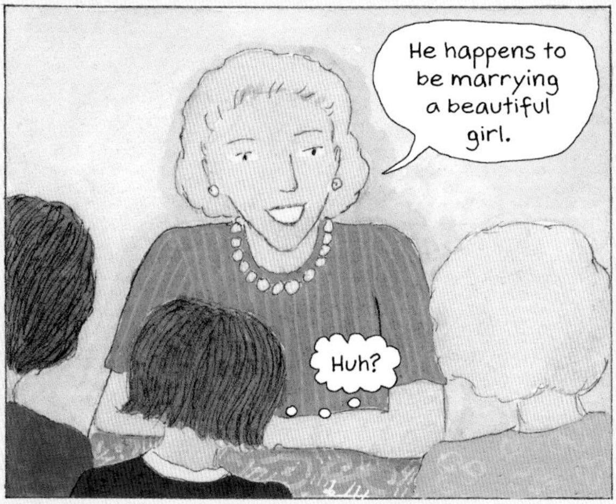

He happens to be marrying a beautiful girl.
Huh?

WAS IT BECAUSE SHE WAS FED UP WITH MY AUNTS' RELENTLESS CRITICISM?

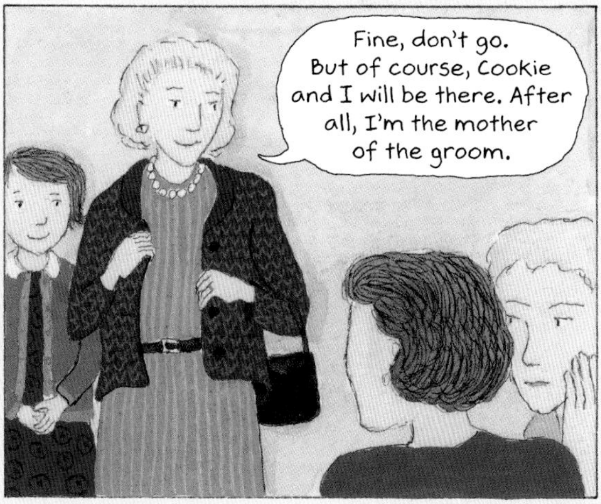

Fine, don't go. But of course, Cookie and I will be there. After all, I'm the mother of the groom.

OR WAS IT THE MEMORY OF HER OWN WEDDING TO JACOB IN ROME, HOW NO ONE IN EITHER OF THEIR FAMILIES HAD BEEN ABLE TO ATTEND?

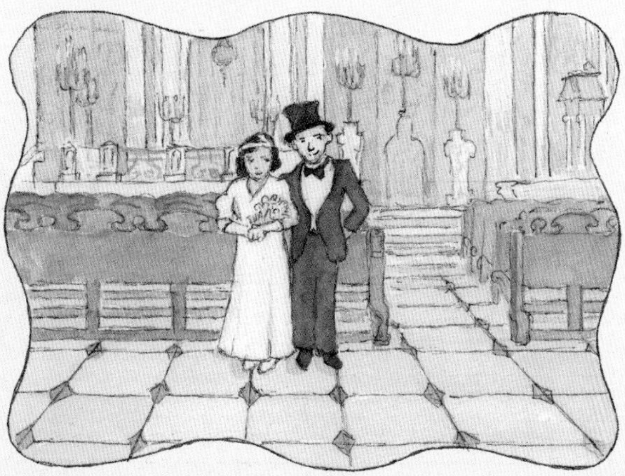

WHATEVER THE REASON, IT DIDN'T MATTER TO ME. I WAS GOING TO BE A JUNIOR BRIDESMAID!

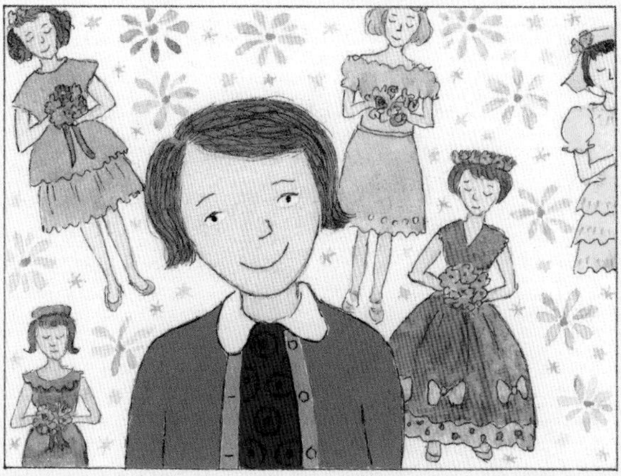

WHEN WE LANDED IN BROWNSVILLE, ROBERTO AND MARIA TERESA WERE WAITING FOR US.

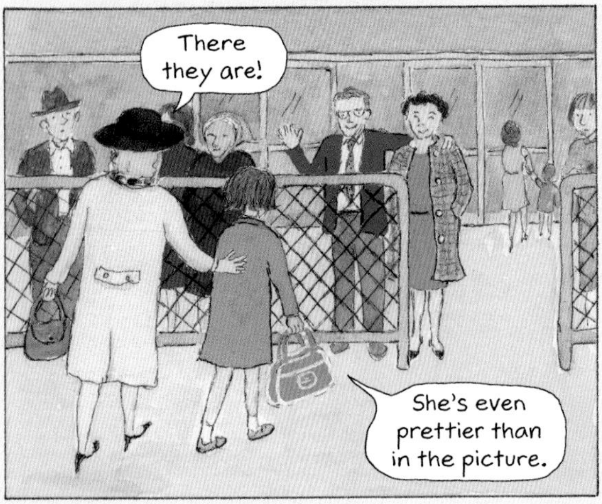
There they are!
She's even prettier than in the picture.

AT FIRST MY MOTHER WAS ON HER BEST BEHAVIOR.

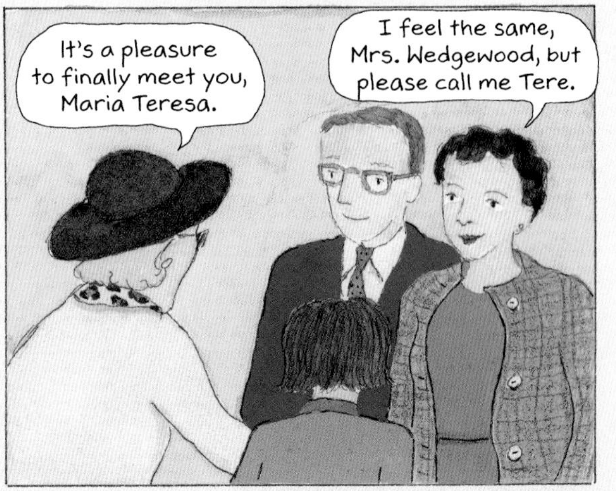
It's a pleasure to finally meet you, Maria Teresa.
I feel the same, Mrs. Wedgewood, but please call me Tere.

THE MOOD CHANGED AS WE DROVE TO TERE'S MOTHER'S HOUSE.

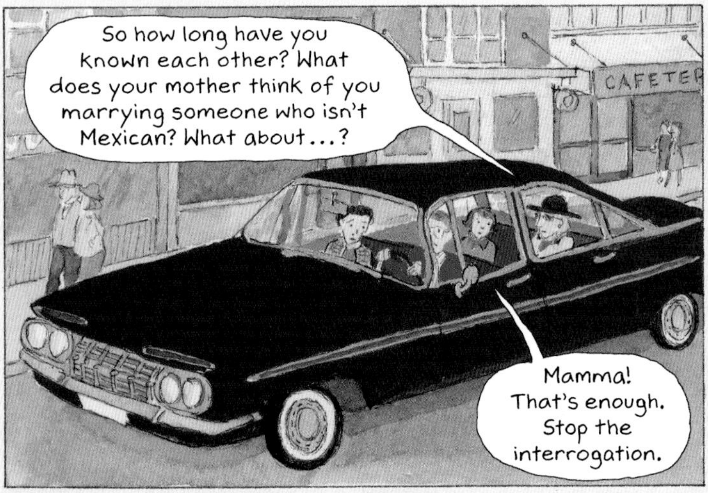
So how long have you known each other? What does your mother think of you marrying someone who isn't Mexican? What about . . . ?
CAFETER
Mamma! That's enough. Stop the interrogation.

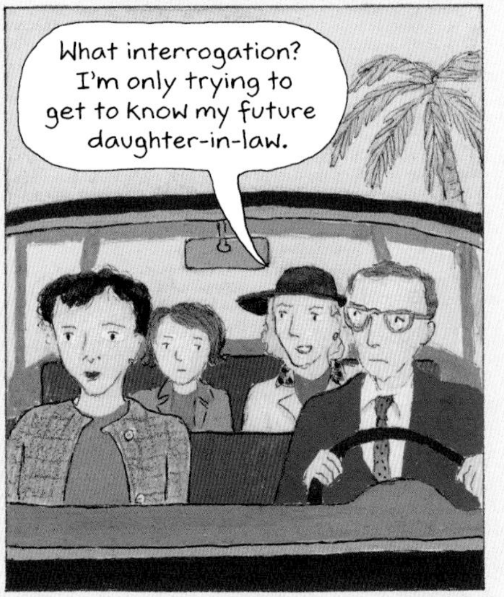
What interrogation? I'm only trying to get to know my future daughter-in-law.

FOR WEEKS MY MOTHER HAD BEEN TELLING ME MEXICAN WOMEN ALL WORE SHAWLS, BRAIDS, AND LONG SKIRTS. BUT SHE WAS COMPLETELY WRONG.

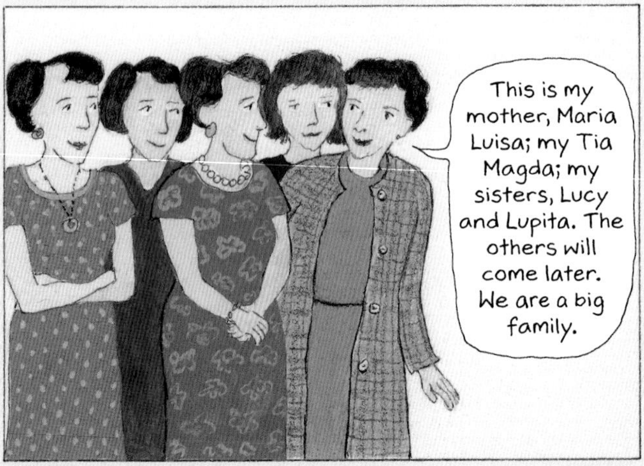
This is my mother, Maria Luisa; my Tia Magda; my sisters, Lucy and Lupita. The others will come later. We are a big family.

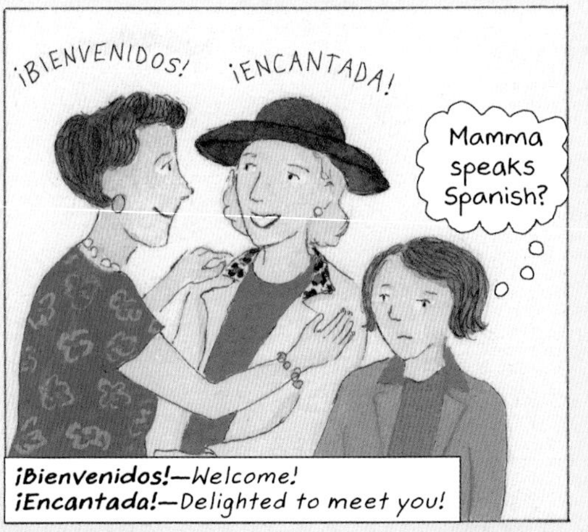
¡BIENVENIDOS!
¡ENCANTADA!
Mamma speaks Spanish?
¡Bienvenidos!—*Welcome!*
¡Encantada!—*Delighted to meet you!*

THE NEXT MORNING ROBERTO AND TERE INVITED ME TO DO SOME LAST-MINUTE ERRANDS WITH THEM.

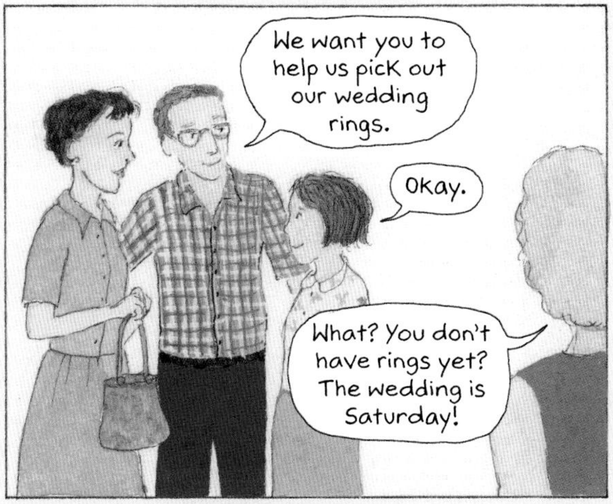
We want you to help us pick out our wedding rings.
Okay.
What? You don't have rings yet? The wedding is Saturday!

I FELT VERY GROWN-UP RIDING AROUND BROWNSVILLE WITH MY BROTHER AND HIS BEAUTIFUL FIANCÉE. EVERYONE SEEMED TO KNOW ABOUT THE BIG WEDDING.

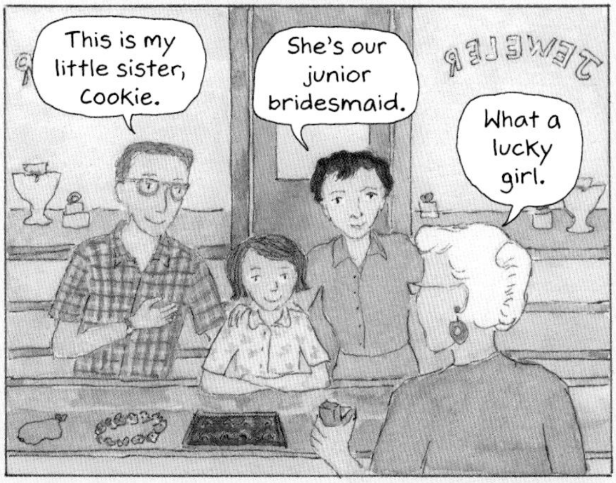
This is my little sister, Cookie.
She's our junior bridesmaid.
What a lucky girl.

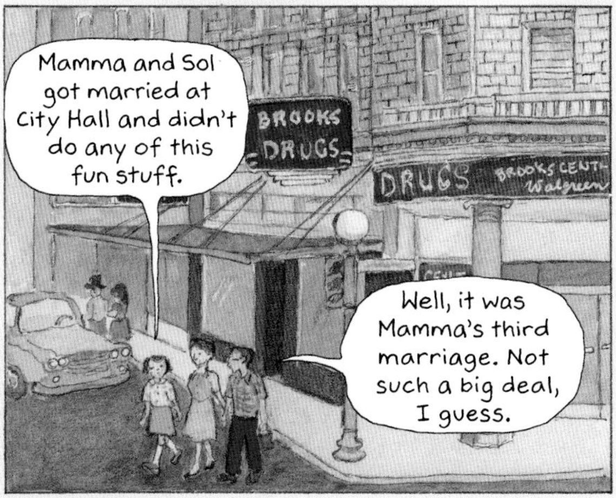
Mamma and Sol got married at City Hall and didn't do any of this fun stuff.
BROOKS DRUGS
DRUGS
Well, it was Mamma's third marriage. Not such a big deal, I guess.

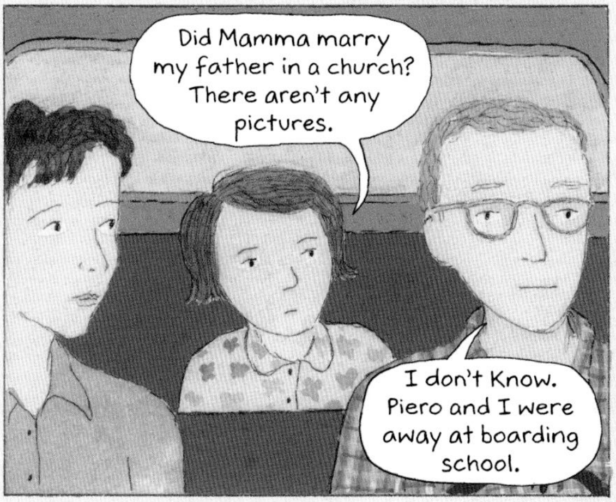
Did Mamma marry my father in a church? There aren't any pictures.
I don't know. Piero and I were away at boarding school.

THE DAY OF THE WEDDING, I GOT UP EARLY TO PREPARE. I HAD AN ARRAY OF NEW FEMININE UNDERGARMENTS TO PUT ON.

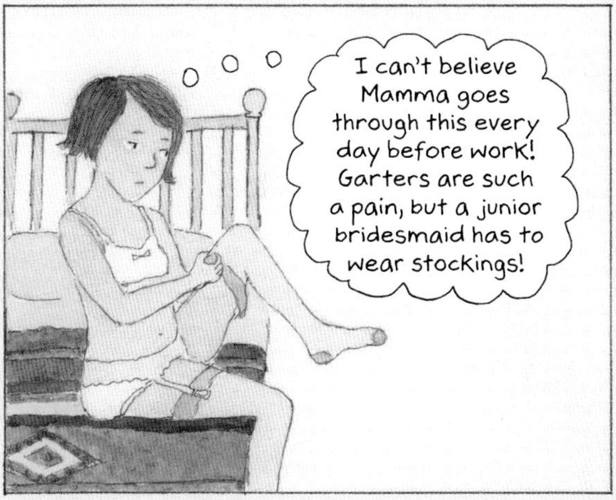
I can't believe Mamma goes through this every day before work! Garters are such a pain, but a junior bridesmaid has to wear stockings!

ROBERTO AND HIS BEST MAN, JACK, CAME TO DRIVE US TO SACRED HEART CHURCH.

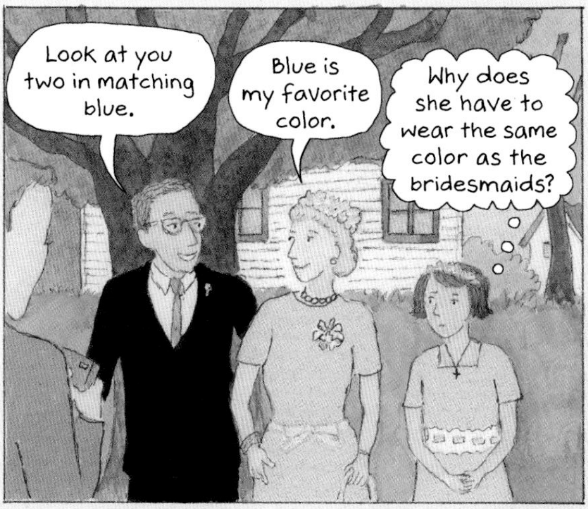
Look at you two in matching blue.
Blue is my favorite color.
Why does she have to wear the same color as the bridesmaids?

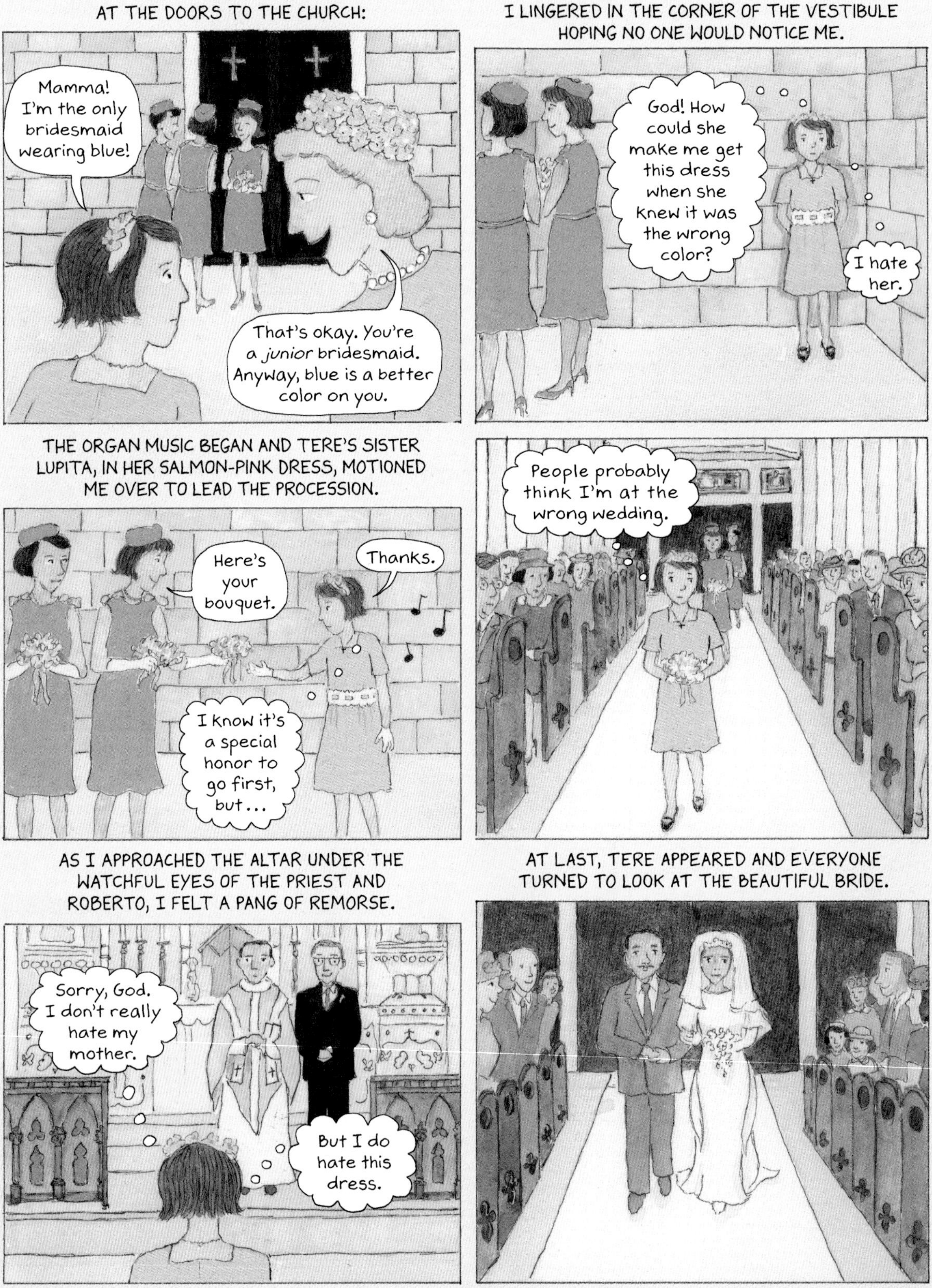
AT THE DOORS TO THE CHURCH:
Mamma! I'm the only bridesmaid wearing blue!
That's okay. You're a *junior* bridesmaid. Anyway, blue is a better color on you.
I LINGERED IN THE CORNER OF THE VESTIBULE HOPING NO ONE WOULD NOTICE ME.
God! How could she make me get this dress when she knew it was the wrong color?
I hate her.
THE ORGAN MUSIC BEGAN AND TERE'S SISTER LUPITA, IN HER SALMON-PINK DRESS, MOTIONED ME OVER TO LEAD THE PROCESSION.
Here's your bouquet.
Thanks.
I know it's a special honor to go first, but...
People probably think I'm at the wrong wedding.
AS I APPROACHED THE ALTAR UNDER THE WATCHFUL EYES OF THE PRIEST AND ROBERTO, I FELT A PANG OF REMORSE.
Sorry, God. I don't really hate my mother.
But I do hate this dress.
AT LAST, TERE APPEARED AND EVERYONE TURNED TO LOOK AT THE BEAUTIFUL BRIDE.

NO ONE WOULD REMEMBER OR CARE ABOUT ANYTHING ELSE. EVEN MY MOTHER WAS DABBING HER EYES WITH A TISSUE. ROBERTO GAZED AT TERE AS IF THEY WERE THE ONLY TWO PEOPLE IN THE CHURCH. SUDDENLY, MY HEART LURCHED FROM AWE TO JEALOUSY.

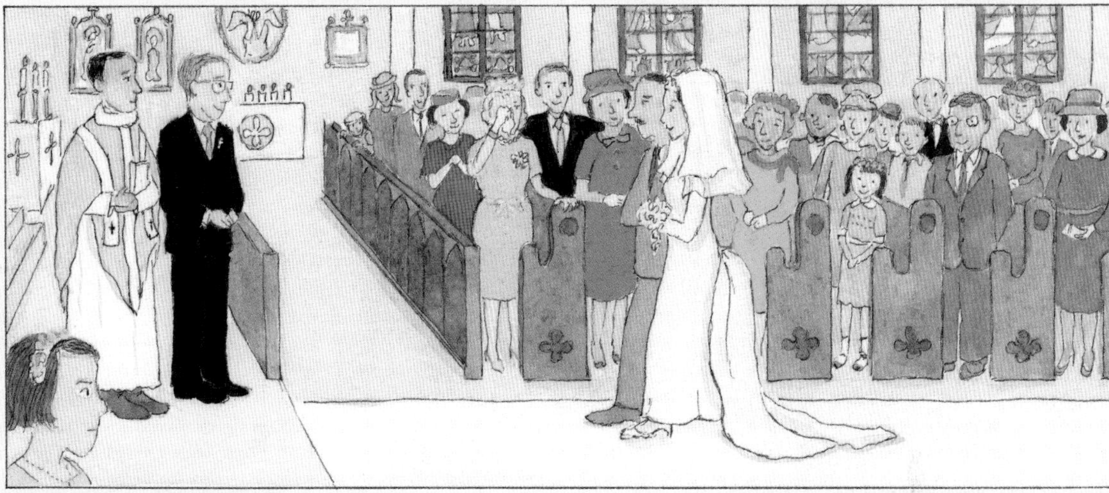

FOR THE FIRST TIME, I REALIZED THAT ROBERTO WAS NEVER COMING HOME TO LIVE WITH US AGAIN.

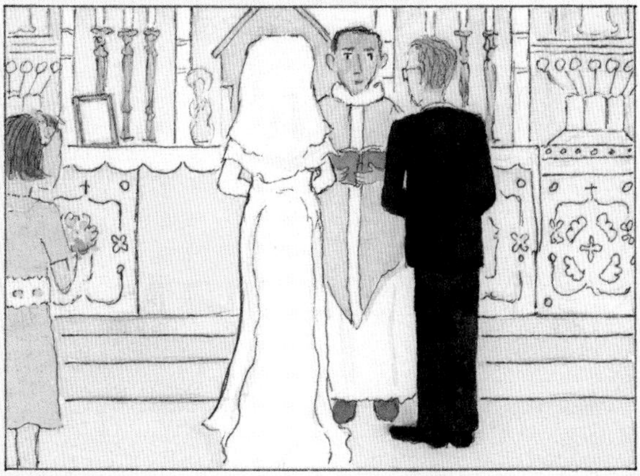

AND NEITHER WAS PIERO.

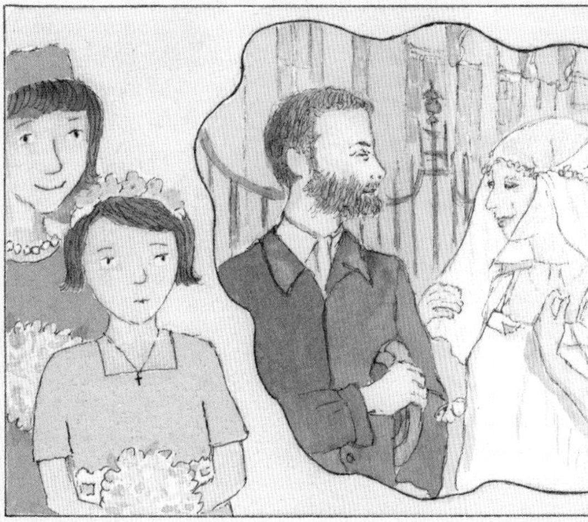

MY BIG BROTHERS HAD FINISHED GROWING UP WHILE I WAS STILL RIGHT IN THE MIDDLE OF IT. THEIR LIVES WERE SEPARATE FROM MINE NOW. MAYBE IN SOME WAY THIS HAD ALWAYS BEEN TRUE. THE FUTURE, MY FUTURE, WAS COMING INTO VIEW. I'D HAVE TO FIGURE OUT HOW TO NAVIGATE MY TEENAGE YEARS AND MAMMA'S SHIFTING MOODS ALL BY MYSELF, AND I COULD ALREADY TELL IT WOULD NOT BE EASY.

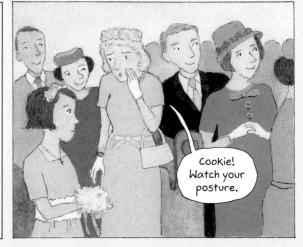

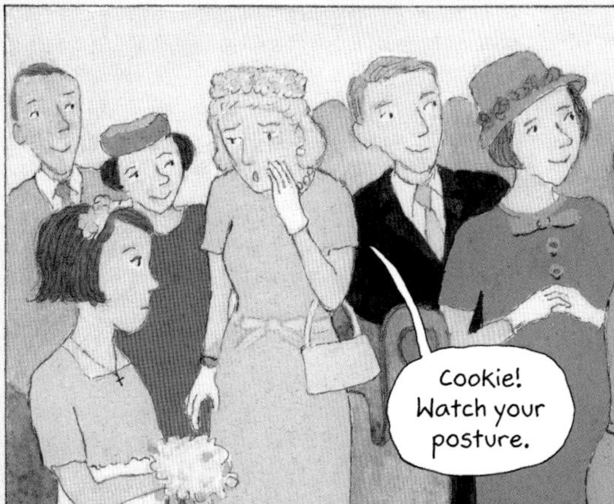
Cookie! Watch your posture.

SIXTEEN

Bernadette

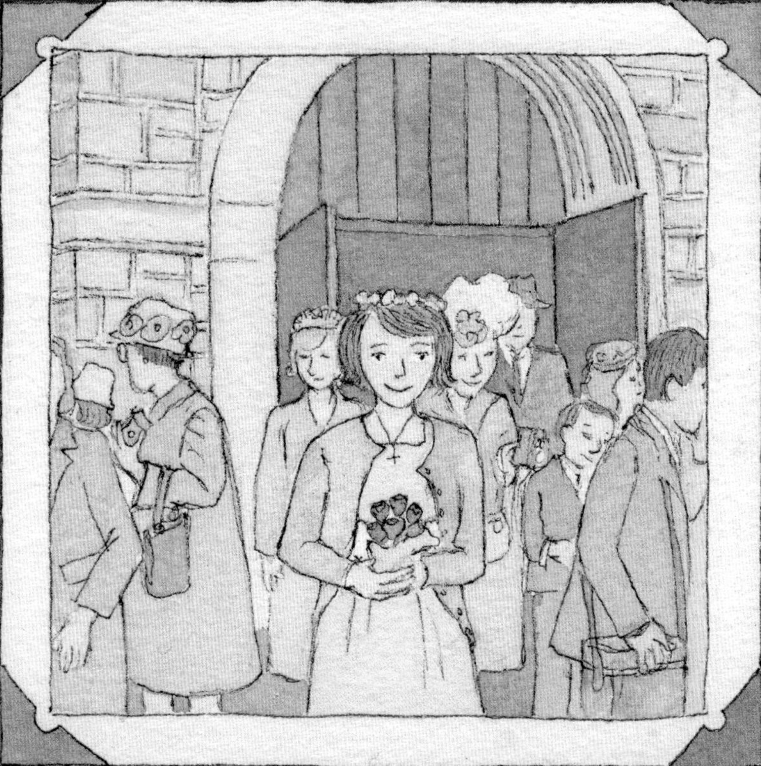

1962-63

AROUND THE TIME THAT ROBERTO AND TERE GOT MARRIED, THE ARMY TRIED TO DRAFT BOTH MY BROTHERS. ONLY ROBERTO ENDED UP REPORTING FOR BASIC TRAINING IN COLORADO. HE WAS LATER STATIONED AT FORT BENNING IN GEORGIA, WHERE HE AND TERE SETTLED INTO A SMALL APARTMENT NEARBY.

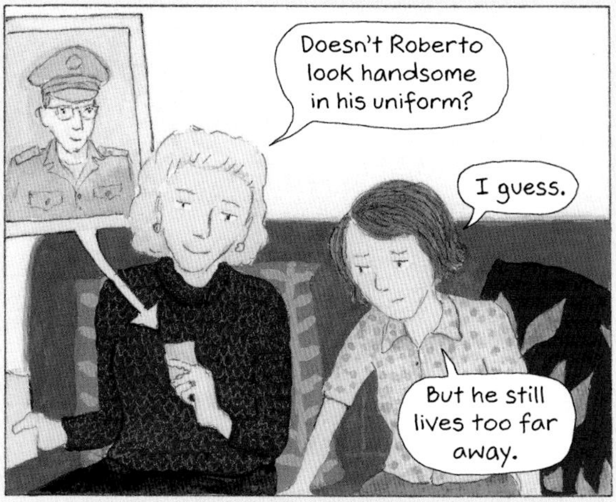
Doesn't Roberto look handsome in his uniform?
I guess.
But he still lives too far away.

PIERO CAME BACK FROM ENGLAND FOR HIS DRAFT INTERVIEW. HE WAS DEEMED PSYCHOLOGICALLY UNFIT.

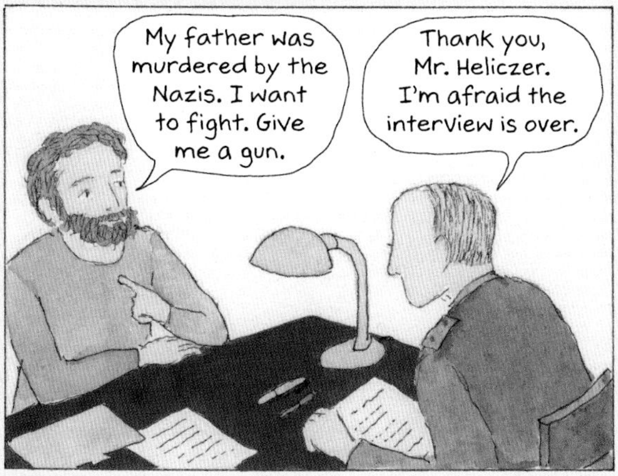
My father was murdered by the Nazis. I want to fight. Give me a gun.
Thank you, Mr. Heliczer. I'm afraid the interview is over.

HE DECIDED TO STAY IN NEW YORK, SO HE SENT FOR KATE. THEY MOVED INTO A TENEMENT ON LUDLOW STREET.

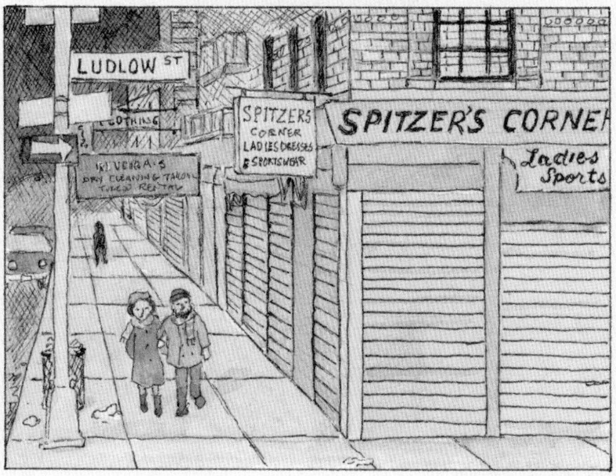
LUDLOW ST
SPITZERS CORNER LADIES DRESSES & SPORTSWEAR
Ladies Sports

MY MOTHER IMMEDIATELY LIKED HER NEW BRITISH DAUGHTER-IN-LAW.

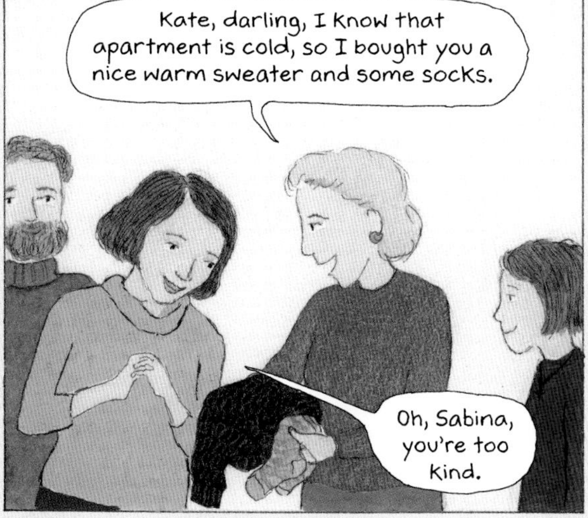
Kate, darling, I know that apartment is cold, so I bought you a nice warm sweater and some socks.
Oh, Sabina, you're too kind.

BUT SHE WAS WORRIED ABOUT HOW PIERO WAS GOING TO SUPPORT HIS NEW WIFE.

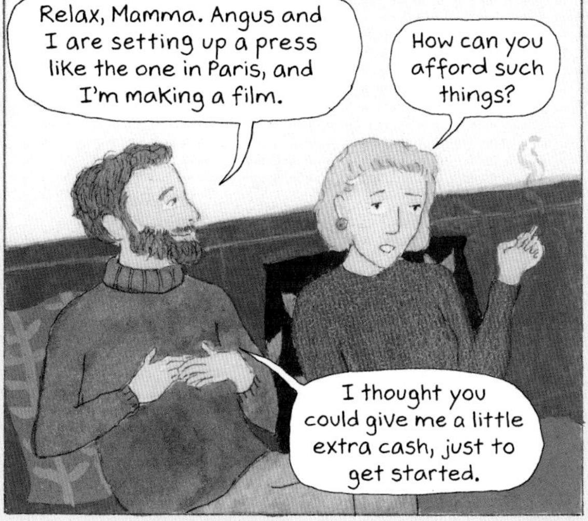
Relax, Mamma. Angus and I are setting up a press like the one in Paris, and I'm making a film.
How can you afford such things?
I thought you could give me a little extra cash, just to get started.

Ach, Piero, you need a job for once. You're a married man.

I have a job! I'm acting in a film by my friend Jack Smith.

DESPITE HER PROTESTS, MY MOTHER ALWAYS ENDED UP GIVING PIERO MONEY.

THANKS, MAMMA.

DOES HE PAY YOU, THIS JACK SMITH? YOU KNOW I CAN'T SUPPORT YOU FOR THE REST OF YOUR LIFE!

I WAS TWELVE AND ABOUT TO START HALSEY JUNIOR HIGH SCHOOL. I HAD PASSED THE TEST TO GET INTO A SPECIAL PROGRAM WHERE I WOULD COMPLETE THE SEVENTH, EIGHTH, AND NINTH GRADES IN ONLY TWO YEARS.

See, you are as smart as your brothers.

Mazel tov, Cookie.

I DIDN'T WANT TO TELL MY MOTHER THAT MY NEW SCHOOL TERRIFIED ME.

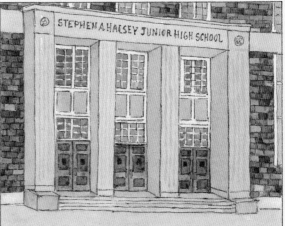

STEPHEN A HALSEY JUNIOR HIGH SCHOOL

IT WAS IN A DIFFERENT NEIGHBORHOOD AND FULL OF TOUGH-LOOKING KIDS.

Wow! How did they get their hair so big?

THE LESS TIME I SPENT THERE, THE BETTER.

Can I get a pass to leave school during lunch period?

Are you kidding? You should be concentrating on your studies, not running around to dirty coffee shops with your friends.

IN A SURPRISE MOVE, KAREN'S MOTHER HAD MADE HER CONVERT TO CATHOLICISM SO SHE COULD ENROLL AT MY OLD SCHOOL, OUR LADY QUEEN OF MARTYRS.

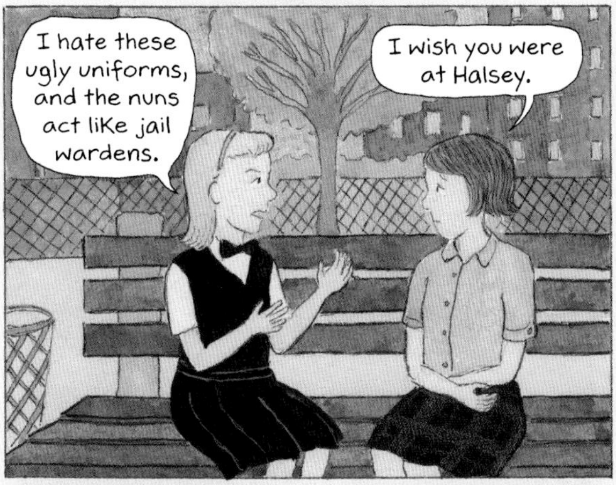
I hate these ugly uniforms, and the nuns act like jail wardens.
I wish you were at Halsey.

WITHOUT KAREN NEARBY AT HALSEY, I WAS TOO POLITE AND SHY.

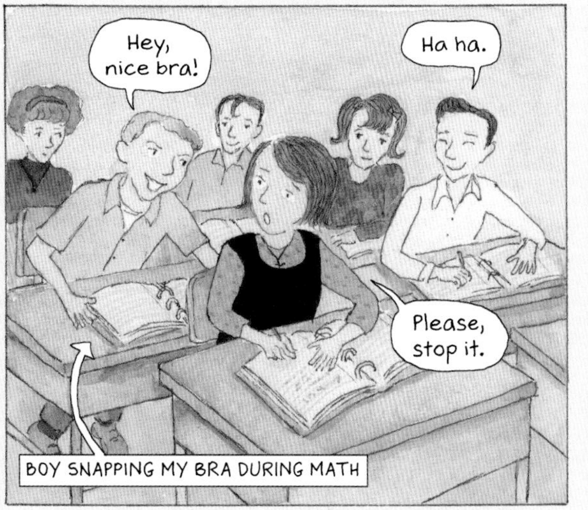
Hey, nice bra!
Ha ha.
Please, stop it.
BOY SNAPPING MY BRA DURING MATH

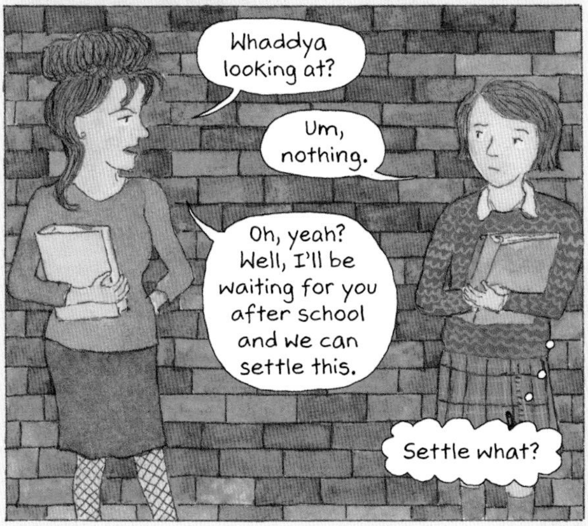
Whaddya looking at?
Um, nothing.
Oh, yeah? Well, I'll be waiting for you after school and we can settle this.
Settle what?

I WAS MORE THAN HAPPY TO SLIP OUT OF SCHOOL EARLY ON WEDNESDAYS TO GO TO RELIGIOUS INSTRUCTION, EVEN THOUGH IT MEANT MISSING PART OF HOME ECONOMICS.

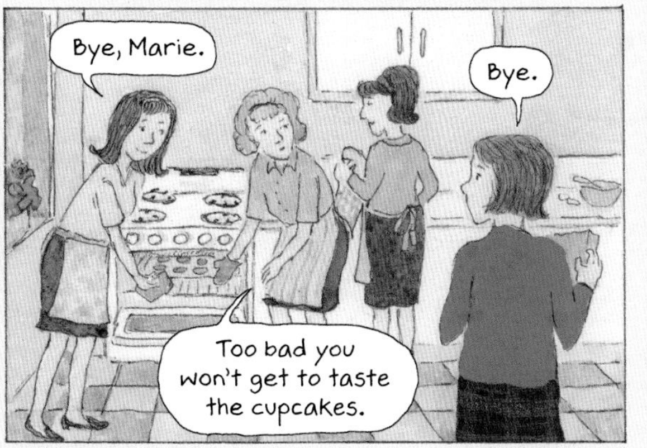
Bye, Marie.
Bye.
Too bad you won't get to taste the cupcakes.

THIS WAS MY LAST YEAR OF RELIGIOUS INSTRUCTION, AND I WAS PREPARING FOR MY CONFIRMATION, A SACRAMENT OF INITIATION AND MATURITY. INITIATION INTO "THE ARMY OF CHRIST."

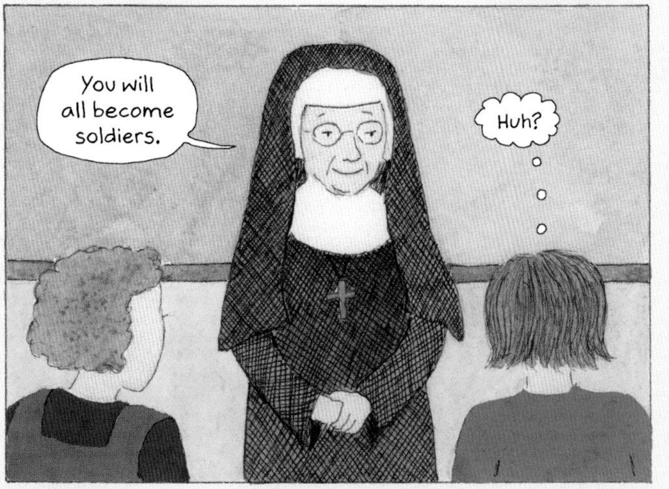
You will all become soldiers.
Huh?

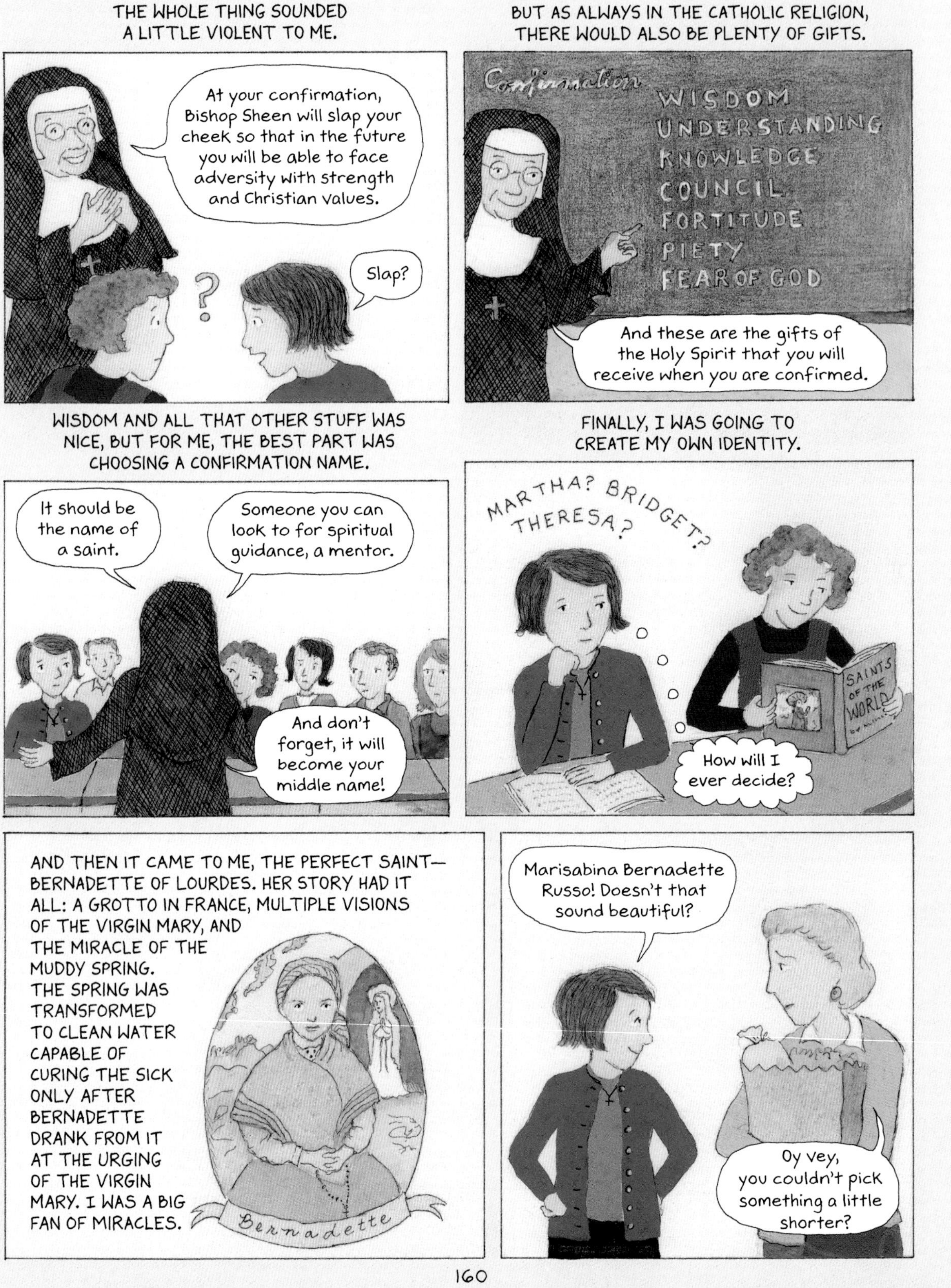
THE WHOLE THING SOUNDED A LITTLE VIOLENT TO ME.
At your confirmation, Bishop Sheen will slap your cheek so that in the future you will be able to face adversity with strength and Christian values.
?
Slap?
BUT AS ALWAYS IN THE CATHOLIC RELIGION, THERE WOULD ALSO BE PLENTY OF GIFTS.
Confirmation
WISDOM
UNDERSTANDING
KNOWLEDGE
COUNCIL
FORTITUDE
PIETY
FEAR OF GOD
And these are the gifts of the Holy Spirit that you will receive when you are confirmed.
WISDOM AND ALL THAT OTHER STUFF WAS NICE, BUT FOR ME, THE BEST PART WAS CHOOSING A CONFIRMATION NAME.
It should be the name of a saint.
Someone you can look to for spiritual guidance, a mentor.
And don't forget, it will become your middle name!
FINALLY, I WAS GOING TO CREATE MY OWN IDENTITY.
MARTHA? BRIDGET? THERESA?
SAINTS OF THE WORLD
How will I ever decide?
AND THEN IT CAME TO ME, THE PERFECT SAINT— BERNADETTE OF LOURDES. HER STORY HAD IT ALL: A GROTTO IN FRANCE, MULTIPLE VISIONS OF THE VIRGIN MARY, AND THE MIRACLE OF THE MUDDY SPRING. THE SPRING WAS TRANSFORMED TO CLEAN WATER CAPABLE OF CURING THE SICK ONLY AFTER BERNADETTE DRANK FROM IT AT THE URGING OF THE VIRGIN MARY. I WAS A BIG FAN OF MIRACLES.
Bernadette
Marisabina Bernadette Russo! Doesn't that sound beautiful?
Oy vey, you couldn't pick something a little shorter?

Mamma, you don't understand. Bernadette had her visions when she was fourteen, just a little older than I am now. Maybe the same thing will happen to me.

Ach, darling, don't talk such nonsense.

DESPITE MY MOTHER'S SKEPTICISM, I WAS CONFIDENT MY NEW NAME WOULD EMPOWER ME.

Ready to settle?

MARISABINA BERNADETTE
UNSTOPPABLE

NOW THAT KAREN WAS A CATHOLIC, WE COULD GO TO CONFESSION TOGETHER ON SATURDAYS, USUALLY MAKING A DETOUR ON THE WAY.

See the kid with the ball? His name is Bobby, and he's in my class. I have a serious crush on him.

What about the one in the black shirt? He's really cute.

That's Chris.

ON SUNDAYS WE WENT TO MASS WITH A RENEWED SENSE OF PURPOSE THAT HAD NOTHING TO DO WITH OUR UPCOMING CONFIRMATIONS.

Let's sit on this side where Bobby's the altar boy.

But Chris is over there.

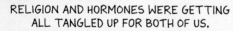

RELIGION AND HORMONES WERE GETTING ALL TANGLED UP FOR BOTH OF US.

AS CONFIRMATION DAY DREW NEAR, I WASN'T SURPRISED THAT NEITHER OF MY AUNTS NOR UNCLE LEO WOULD BE ATTENDING.

A bat mitzvah, now that would be something worth celebrating.

Sabina, the world needs more Jews. Not more Catholics.

IN FACT, NO ONE IN MY FAMILY WAS COMING EXCEPT FOR MY MOTHER. NOT EVEN MY FATHER, WHO WAS A CATHOLIC. ALL HE DID WAS SEND ME FIFTY DOLLARS.

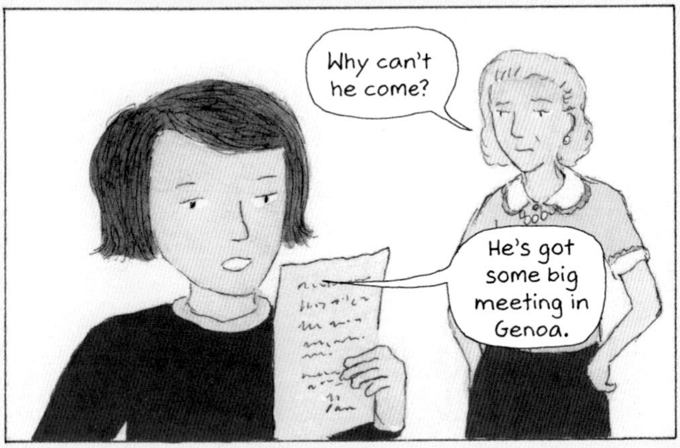

Why can't he come?
He's got some big meeting in Genoa.

AS FOR THE OTHERS:

ROBERTO AND TERE WERE IN GEORGIA ABOUT TO HAVE THEIR FIRST BABY.

PIERO AND KATE HAD TAKEN OFF FOR TANGIERS.

AND SOL WAS WORKING EVERY WEEKEND, EVEN THOUGH HE HADN'T SOLD A HOUSE IN MONTHS.

SENSING MY DISAPPOINTMENT, MAMMA RUSTLED UP A COUPLE OF HER FRIENDS TO JOIN US.

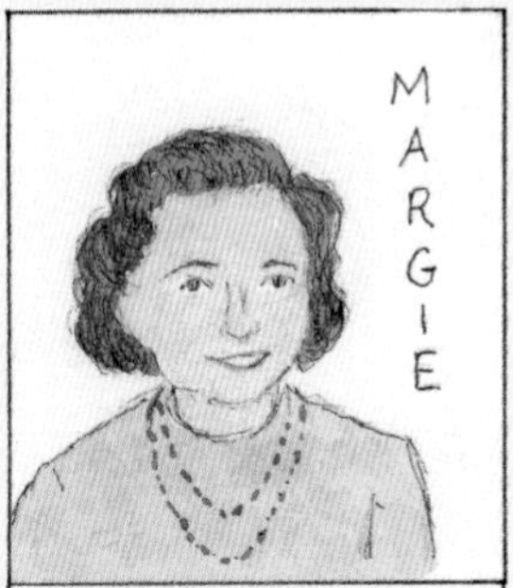

MARGIE

OUR NEIGHBOR IN THE OLD BUILDING. MAMMA'S BEST FRIEND AND A DEVOUT CATHOLIC.

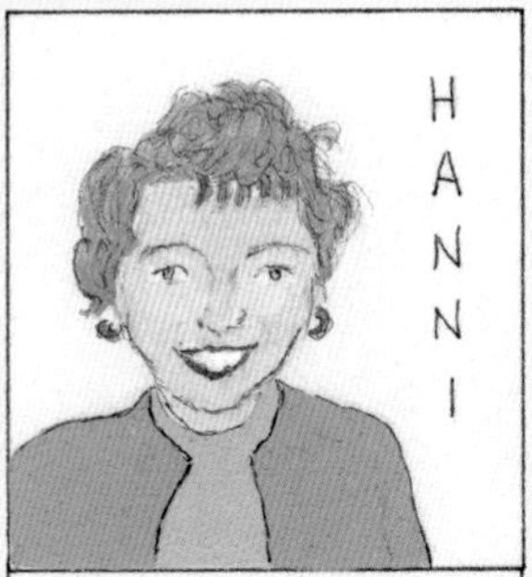

HANNI

MAMMA'S GIRLHOOD FRIEND FROM LEIPZIG. JEWISH, BUT NOT RELIGIOUS.

THEN SHE INSISTED I WEAR MY JUNIOR BRIDESMAID DRESS EVEN THOUGH IT WAS ALREADY A YEAR OLD AND KIND OF SMALL.

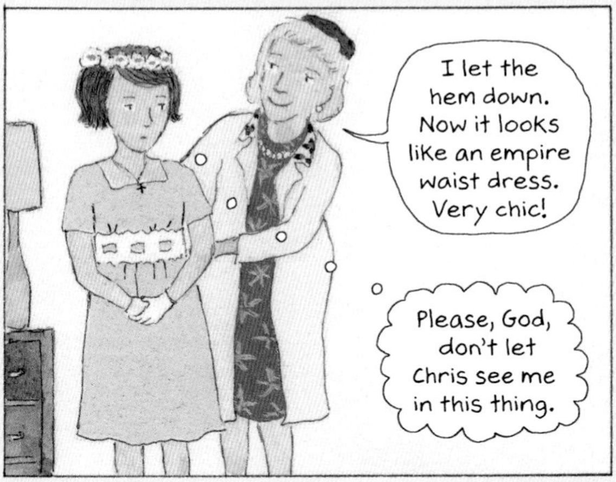

I let the hem down. Now it looks like an empire waist dress. Very chic!
Please, God, don't let Chris see me in this thing.

THE CONFIRMATION MASS WAS LONG AND THE CHURCH HOT. WHEN IT WAS FINALLY MY TURN AT THE ALTAR, I BRAVELY RECEIVED MY SLAP FROM BISHOP SHEEN.

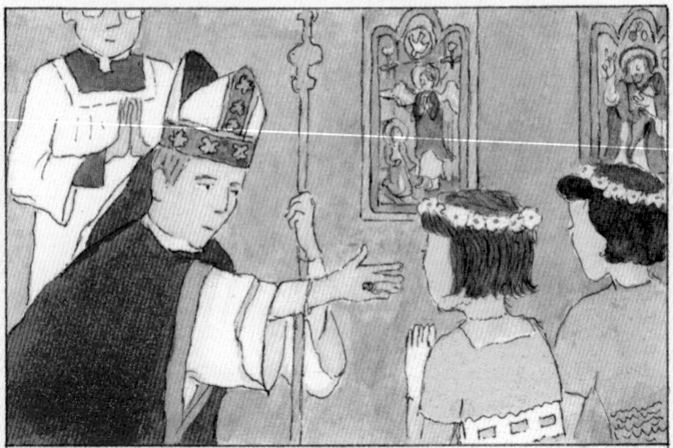

IT DIDN'T HURT AT ALL.

I WAS NOW OFFICIALLY "MARISABINA BERNADETTE RUSSO," A SOLDIER IN THE ARMY OF CHRIST, WHICH SOUNDED PRETTY GROWN-UP TO ME.

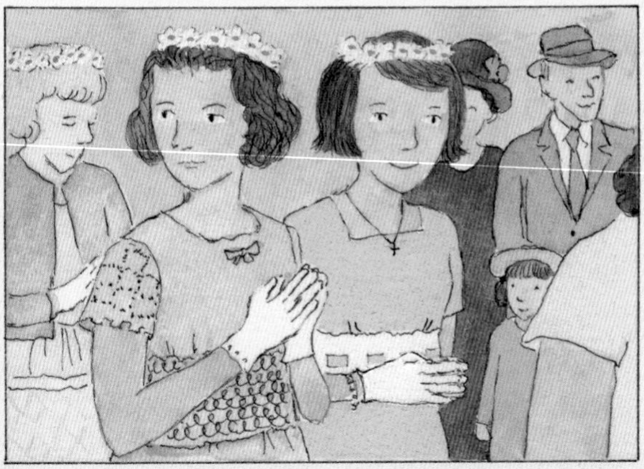

BACK AT THE APARTMENT, MY MOTHER PREPARED A FESTIVE CONFIRMATION LUNCH OF CURED MEATS, BLACK BREAD, PICKLES, AND BEER FOR OUR GUESTS.

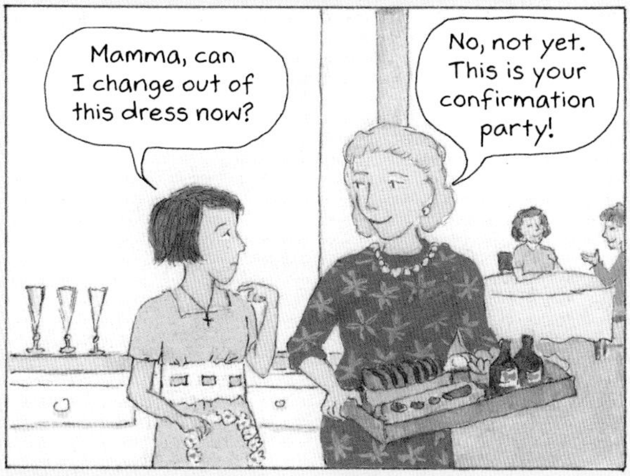
Mamma, can I change out of this dress now?
No, not yet. This is your confirmation party!

AFTER WE ATE, I SLIPPED OUT TO THE TERRACE WHILE MY MOTHER AND HER FRIENDS CONTINUED TO CELEBRATE.

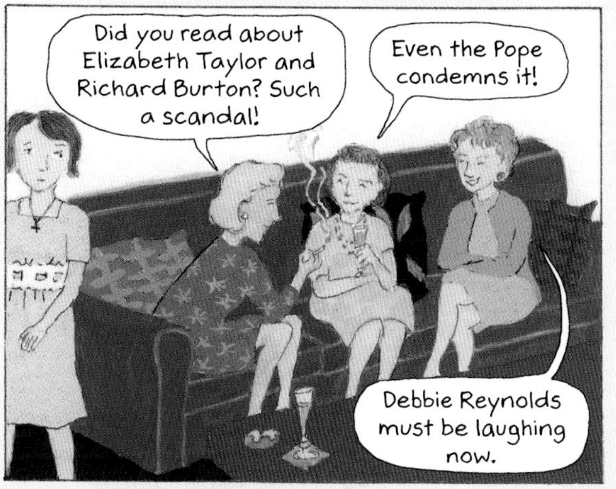
Did you read about Elizabeth Taylor and Richard Burton? Such a scandal!
Even the Pope condemns it!
Debbie Reynolds must be laughing now.

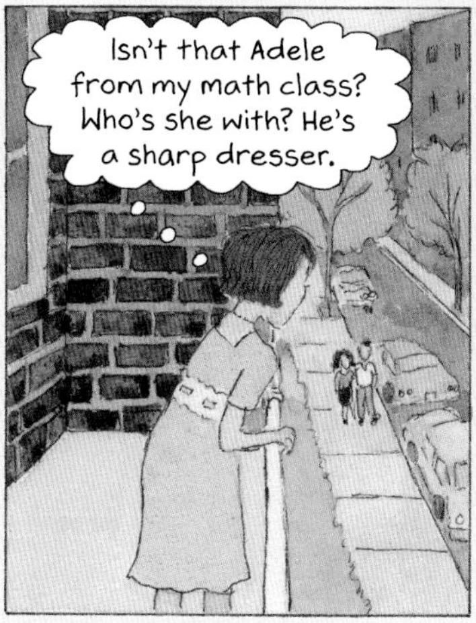
Isn't that Adele from my math class? Who's she with? He's a sharp dresser.

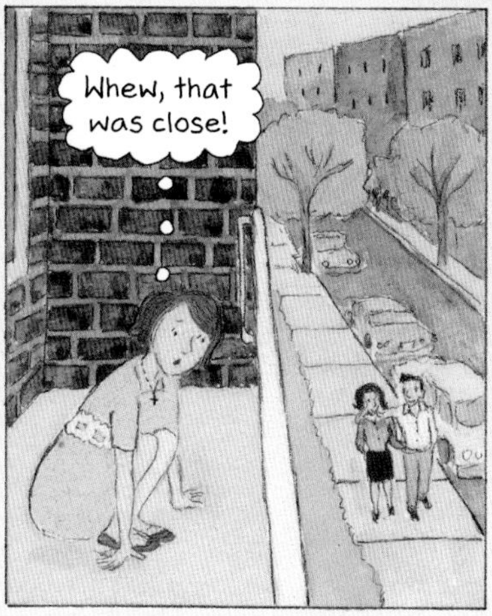
Whew, that was close!

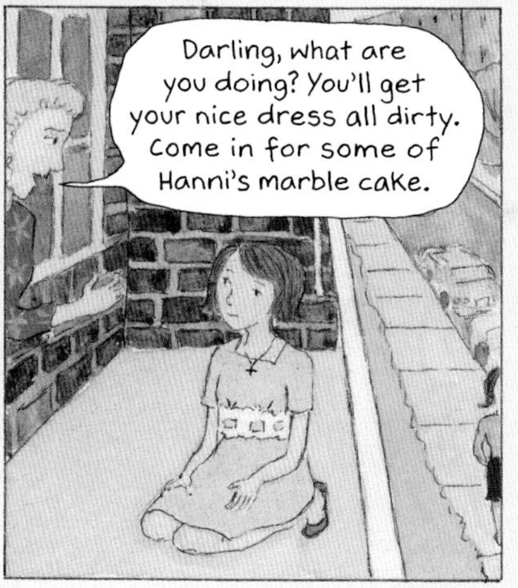
Darling, what are you doing? You'll get your nice dress all dirty. Come in for some of Hanni's marble cake.

THAT EVENING WHEN THE PARTY WAS OVER, I CHANGED OUT OF MY BLUE DRESS AND STUFFED IT IN THE BACK OF MY CLOSET.

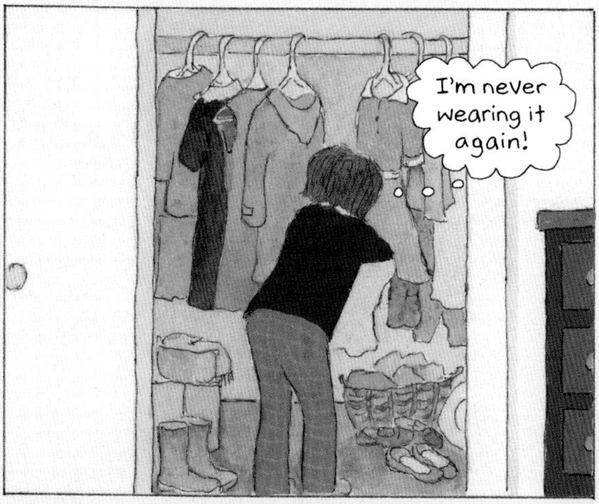
I'm never wearing it again!

I LOOKED AT MY CONFIRMATION CERTIFICATE AND ADMIRED MY NEW NAME.

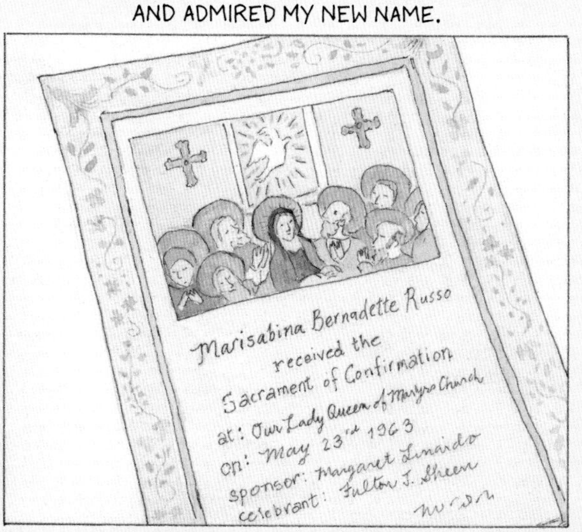
Marisabina Bernadette Russo
received the
Sacrament of Confirmation
at: Our Lady Queen of Martyrs Church
on: May 23rd 1963
sponsor: Margaret Linaido
celebrant: Fulton J. Sheen

BUT THEN I REMEMBERED SOMETHING TANTE ANNY HAD ONCE TOLD ME ABOUT HOW HITLER HAD FORCED ALL THE GERMAN JEWS TO CARRY IDENTITY CARDS WITH THEIR PICTURES AND NAMES AND A BIG RED *J* STAMPED ACROSS ONE PAGE. THIS HAPPENED BEFORE SHE WAS DEPORTED TO AUSCHWITZ.

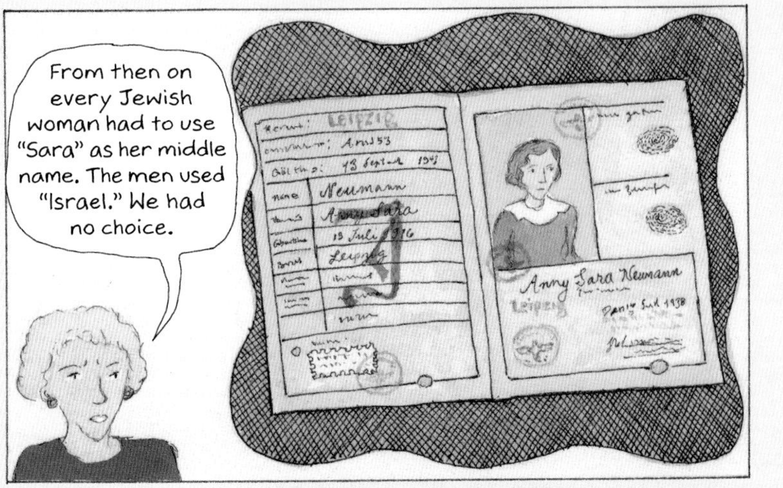
From then on every Jewish woman had to use "Sara" as her middle name. The men used "Israel." We had no choice.
Anny Sara Neumann

"Later we were ordered to wear a Jewish star sewn on our clothes."

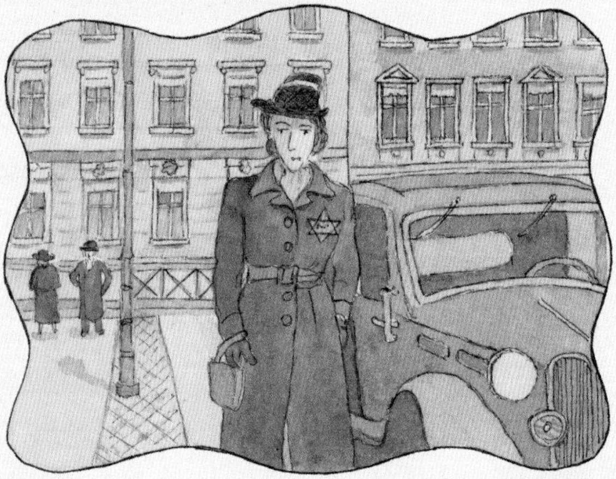

IF GOD WAS TRULY AS MERCIFUL AND JUST AS THE NUNS AND PRIESTS SAID, WHY HAD HE LET ANY OF THAT STUFF HAPPEN? MAYBE TANTE ANNY WAS RIGHT WHEN SHE SAID GOD WASN'T LISTENING?

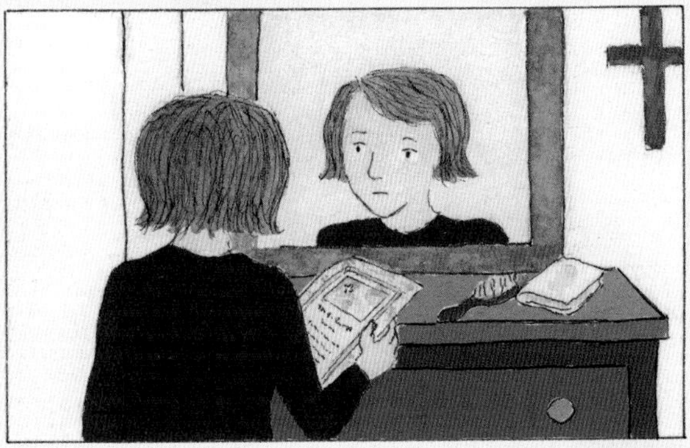

I REALIZED THAT IF THE VIRGIN MARY EVER DECIDED TO APPEAR TO ME IN A VISION, THERE WERE A FEW THINGS WE'D HAVE TO TALK ABOUT BEFORE I AGREED TO BECOME A NUN OR A SAINT.

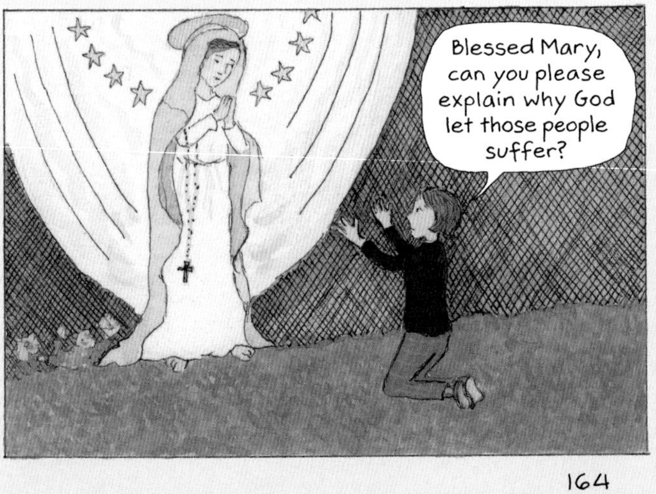
Blessed Mary, can you please explain why God let those people suffer?

AND EVEN IF SHE HAD AN ANSWER, I STILL WASN'T SO SURE I'D BE ABLE TO SAY YES.

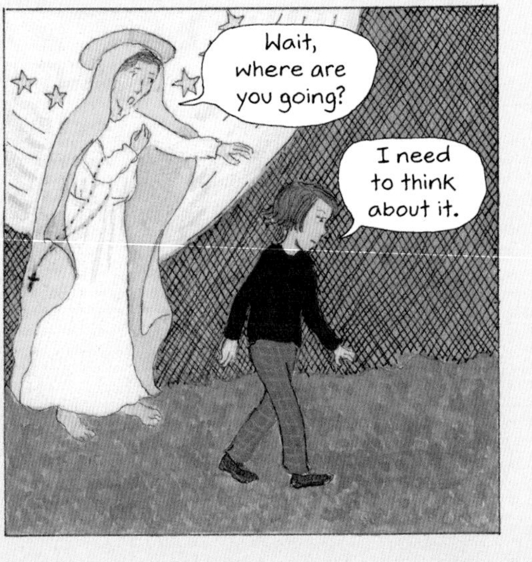
Wait, where are you going?
I need to think about it.

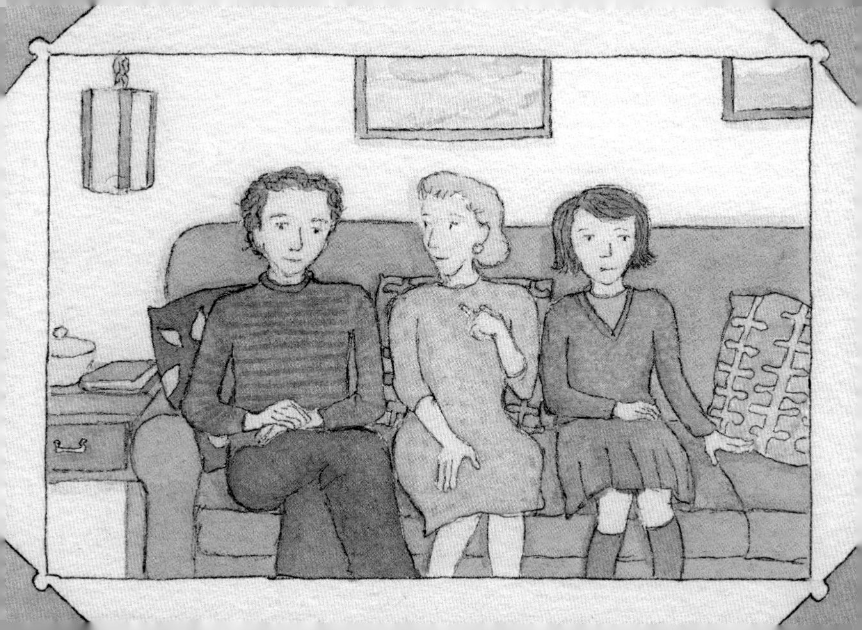

1963-64

BECAUSE OF THE SPECIAL PROGRAM, I WENT STRAIGHT FROM SEVENTH TO NINTH GRADE. ONLY ONE MORE YEAR OF JUNIOR HIGH SCHOOL.

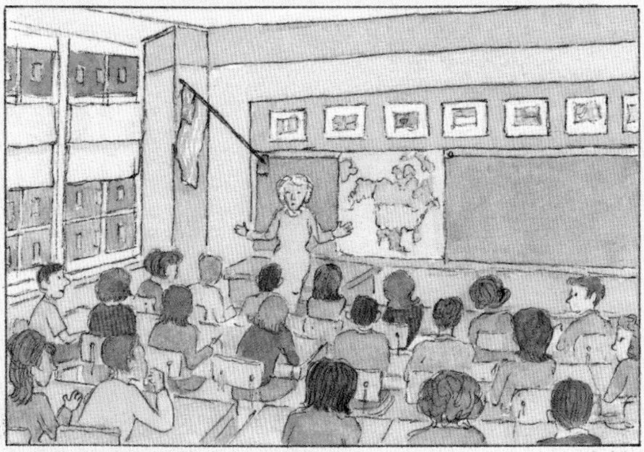

MY NEW BEST FRIEND WAS CAROL, AND SHE WAS A GENIUS. I TRIED NOT TO HOLD IT AGAINST HER.

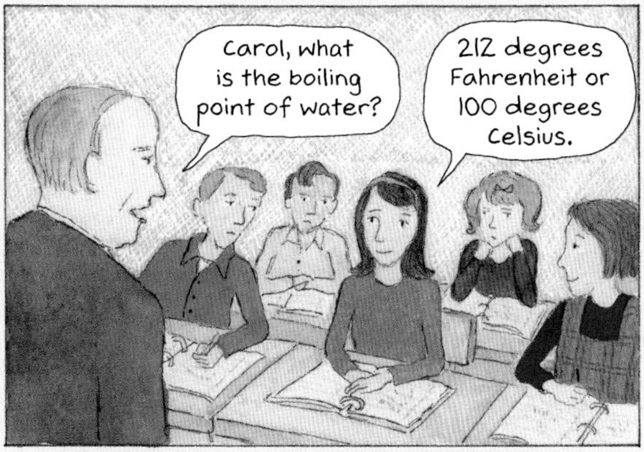
Carol, what is the boiling point of water?
212 degrees Fahrenheit or 100 degrees Celsius.

AFTER SCHOOL, CAROL TOOK BALLET CLASSES IN THE CITY. SHE ALREADY KNEW THAT ONE DAY SHE WOULD BE A BALLERINA.

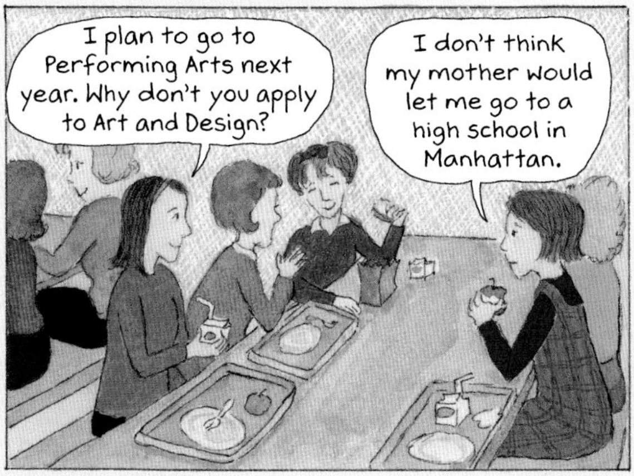
I plan to go to Performing Arts next year. Why don't you apply to Art and Design?
I don't think my mother would let me go to a high school in Manhattan.

BEING CAROL'S FRIEND DID NOTHING TO HELP MY SOCIAL LIFE. BOYS WERE NOT IMPRESSED WITH SMART GIRLS.

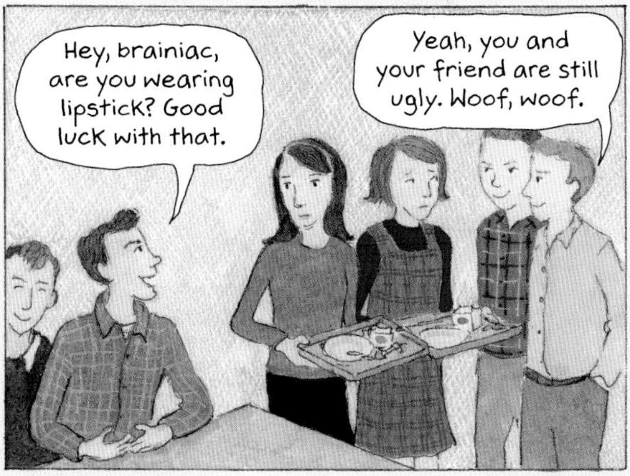
Hey, brainiac, are you wearing lipstick? Good luck with that.
Yeah, you and your friend are still ugly. Woof, woof.

CAROL AND I PRETENDED TO BE IMPERVIOUS. WE HAD OTHER GOALS THAT HAD NOTHING TO DO WITH BOYS, LIKE WRITING A NOVEL.

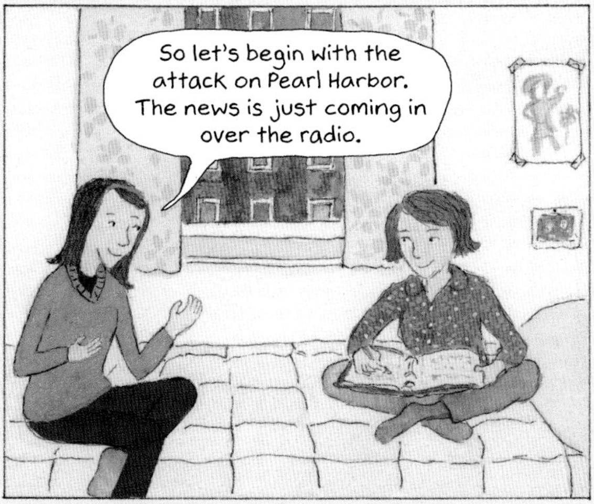
So let's begin with the attack on Pearl Harbor. The news is just coming in over the radio.

WRITING ABOUT WORLD WAR II WAS CAROL'S IDEA. PERSONALLY, I WAS PRETTY SICK OF THE WHOLE SUBJECT, BUT OF COURSE, I DEFERRED TO MY VERY SMART FRIEND.

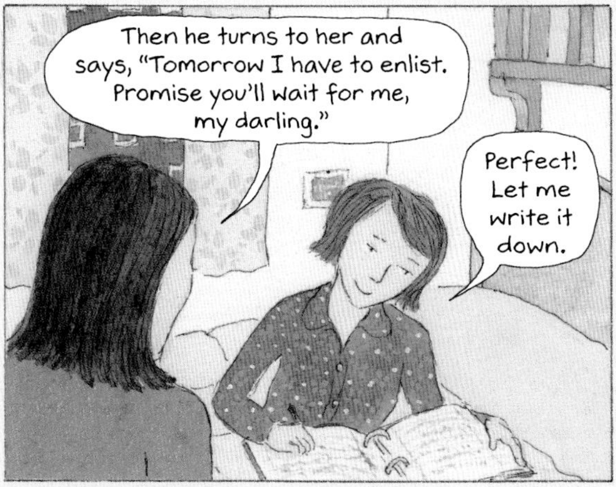
Then he turns to her and says, "Tomorrow I have to enlist. Promise you'll wait for me, my darling."
Perfect! Let me write it down.

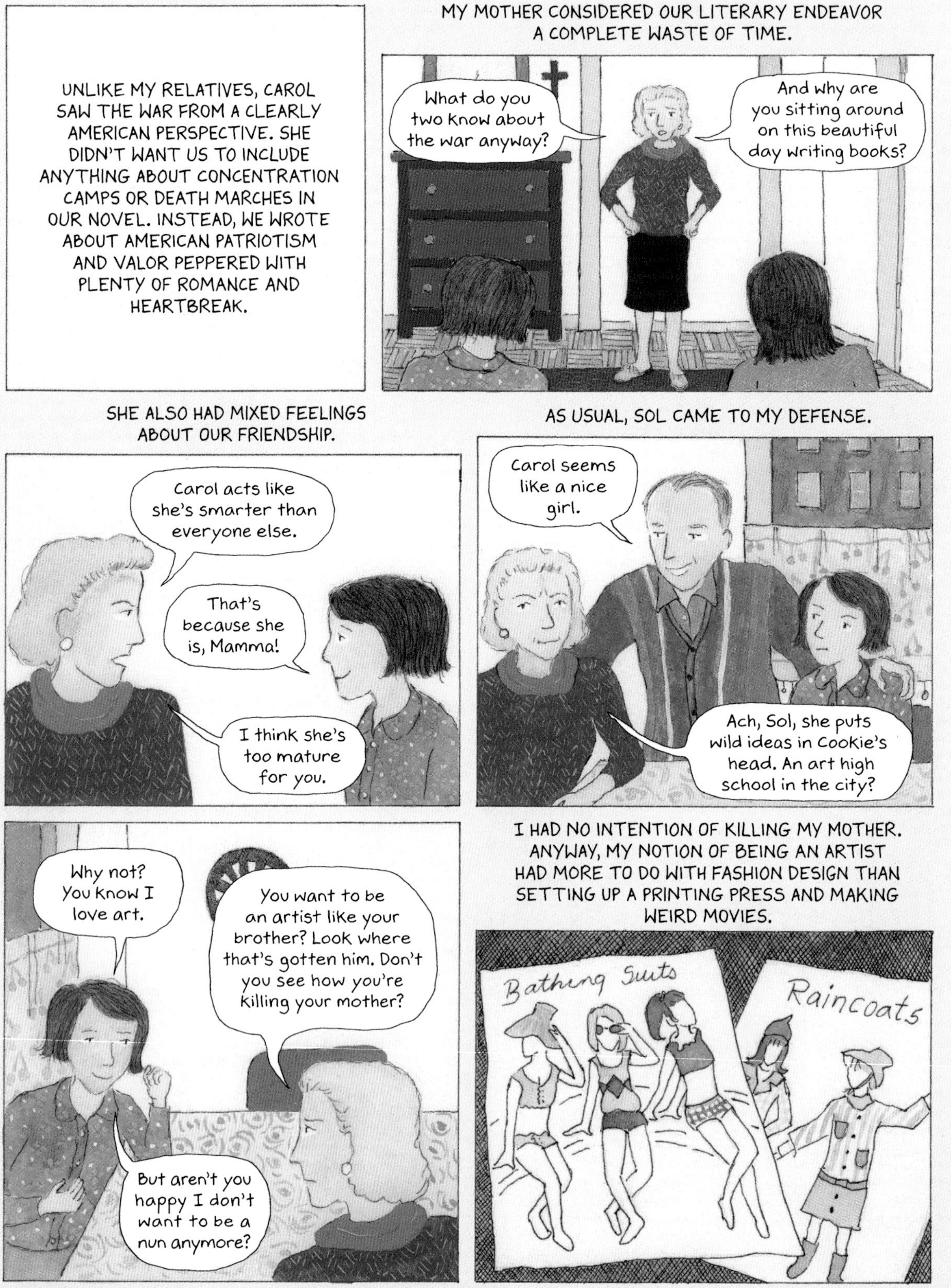
UNLIKE MY RELATIVES, CAROL SAW THE WAR FROM A CLEARLY AMERICAN PERSPECTIVE. SHE DIDN'T WANT US TO INCLUDE ANYTHING ABOUT CONCENTRATION CAMPS OR DEATH MARCHES IN OUR NOVEL. INSTEAD, WE WROTE ABOUT AMERICAN PATRIOTISM AND VALOR PEPPERED WITH PLENTY OF ROMANCE AND HEARTBREAK.
MY MOTHER CONSIDERED OUR LITERARY ENDEAVOR A COMPLETE WASTE OF TIME.
What do you two know about the war anyway?
And why are you sitting around on this beautiful day writing books?
SHE ALSO HAD MIXED FEELINGS ABOUT OUR FRIENDSHIP.
Carol acts like she's smarter than everyone else.
That's because she is, Mamma!
I think she's too mature for you.
AS USUAL, SOL CAME TO MY DEFENSE.
Carol seems like a nice girl.
Ach, Sol, she puts wild ideas in Cookie's head. An art high school in the city?
Why not? You know I love art.
You want to be an artist like your brother? Look where that's gotten him. Don't you see how you're killing your mother?
But aren't you happy I don't want to be a nun anymore?
I HAD NO INTENTION OF KILLING MY MOTHER. ANYWAY, MY NOTION OF BEING AN ARTIST HAD MORE TO DO WITH FASHION DESIGN THAN SETTING UP A PRINTING PRESS AND MAKING WEIRD MOVIES.
Bathing Suits
Raincoats

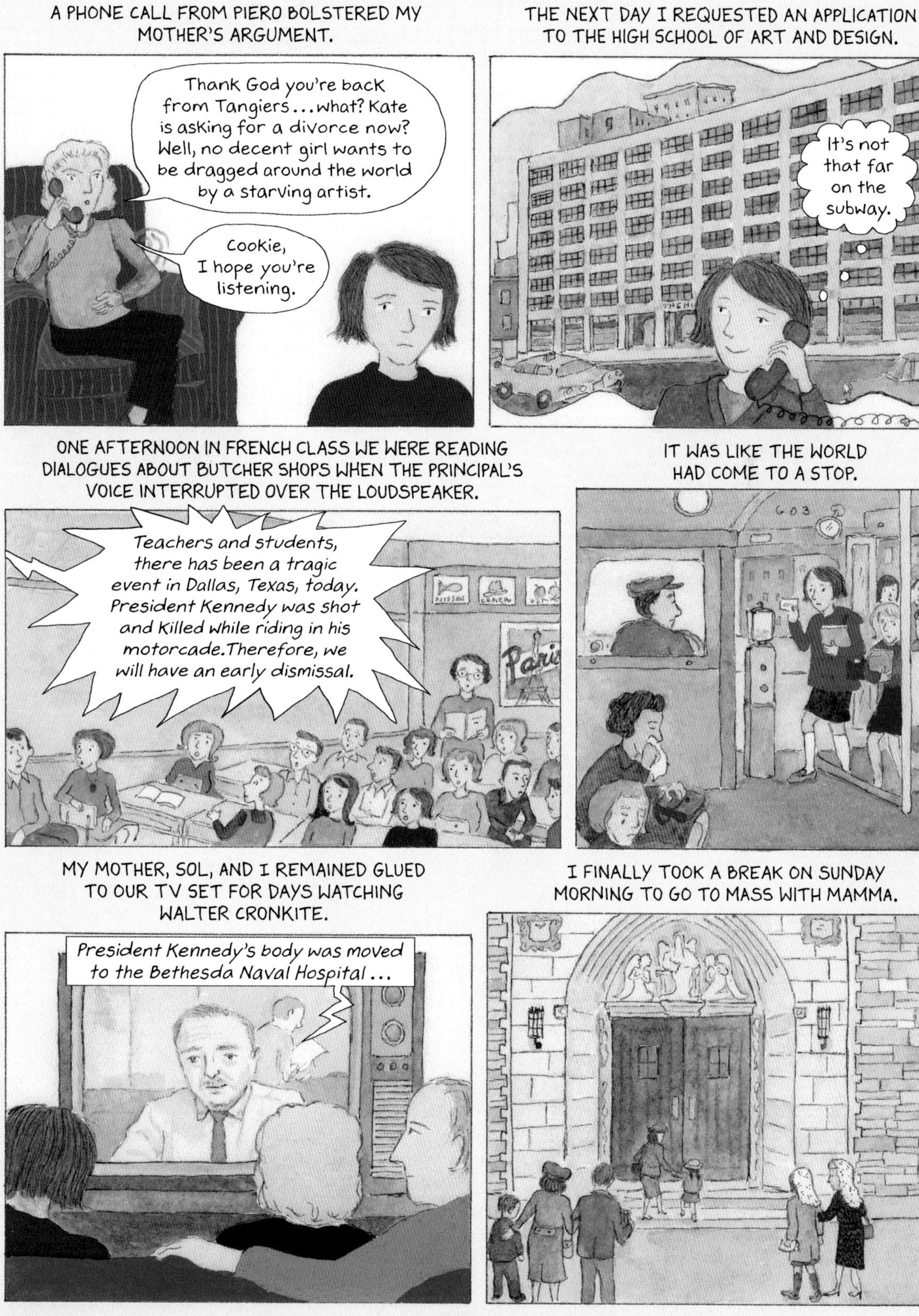
A PHONE CALL FROM PIERO BOLSTERED MY MOTHER'S ARGUMENT.
Thank God you're back from Tangiers . . . what? Kate is asking for a divorce now? Well, no decent girl wants to be dragged around the world by a starving artist.
Cookie, I hope you're listening.
THE NEXT DAY I REQUESTED AN APPLICATION TO THE HIGH SCHOOL OF ART AND DESIGN.
It's not that far on the subway.
ONE AFTERNOON IN FRENCH CLASS WE WERE READING DIALOGUES ABOUT BUTCHER SHOPS WHEN THE PRINCIPAL'S VOICE INTERRUPTED OVER THE LOUDSPEAKER.
Teachers and students, there has been a tragic event in Dallas, Texas, today. President Kennedy was shot and killed while riding in his motorcade. Therefore, we will have an early dismissal.
IT WAS LIKE THE WORLD HAD COME TO A STOP.
MY MOTHER, SOL, AND I REMAINED GLUED TO OUR TV SET FOR DAYS WATCHING WALTER CRONKITE.
President Kennedy's body was moved to the Bethesda Naval Hospital . . .
I FINALLY TOOK A BREAK ON SUNDAY MORNING TO GO TO MASS WITH MAMMA.

NOT ONE TO DWELL ON SAD EVENTS OR INDULGE IN SELF-PITY, MY MOTHER WAS READY FOR WORK ON MONDAY MORNING.

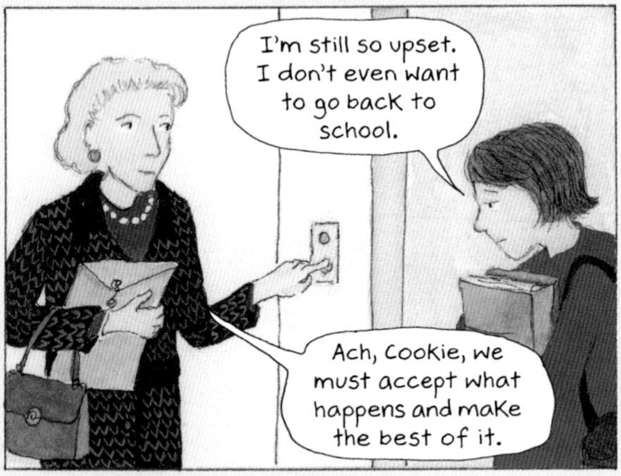
I'm still so upset. I don't even want to go back to school.
Ach, Cookie, we must accept what happens and make the best of it.

FOR MY MOTHER, SENSITIVITY WAS THE WORST CHARACTER FLAW OF ALL.

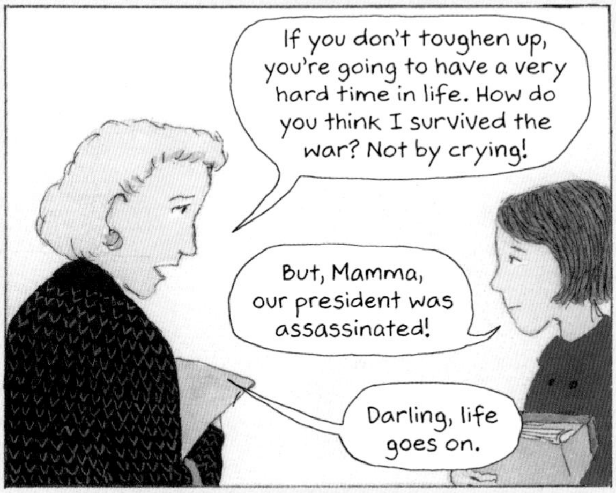
If you don't toughen up, you're going to have a very hard time in life. How do you think I survived the war? Not by crying!
But, Mamma, our president was assassinated!
Darling, life goes on.

AND SO IT DID. KATE LEFT PIERO AND WENT BACK TO ENGLAND. PIERO STARTED SHOWING UP AT OUR APARTMENT MORE AND MORE LOOKING FOR FOOD AND MONEY.

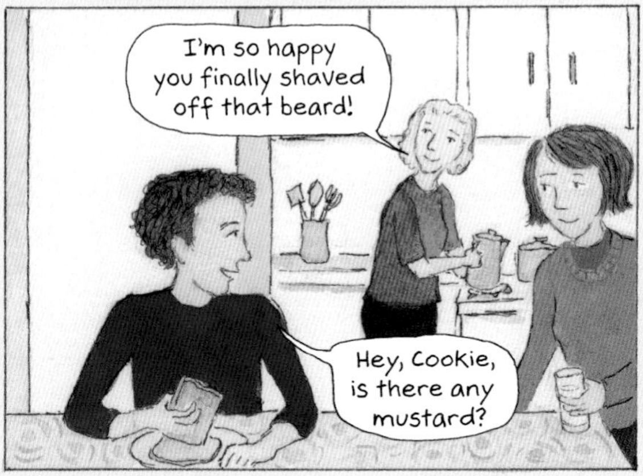
I'm so happy you finally shaved off that beard!
Hey, Cookie, is there any mustard?

ON THE NIGHT OF MY HOLIDAY CONCERT I WAS SURPRISED TO SEE HIM STANDING IN THE SCHOOL LOBBY WITH MAMMA.

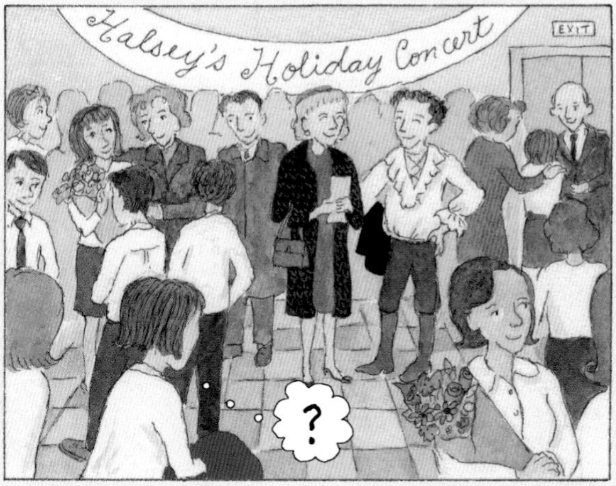
Halsey's Holiday Concert
EXIT
?

FOR THE FIRST TIME I WAS EMBARRASSED BY PIERO AND I WANTED TO GET OUT OF THERE AS QUICKLY AS POSSIBLE.

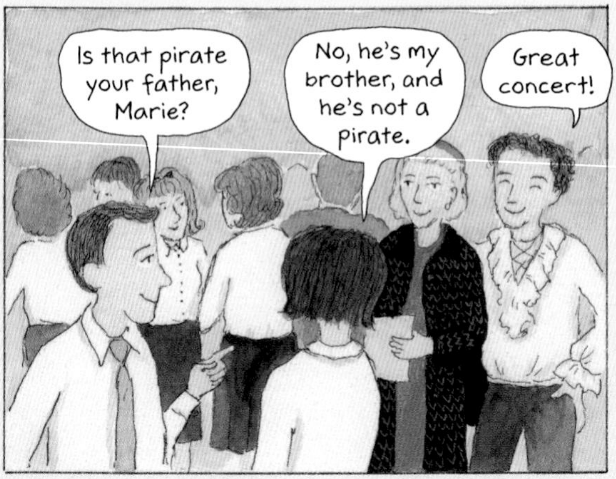
Is that pirate your father, Marie?
No, he's my brother, and he's not a pirate.
Great concert!

WHEN WE WALKED AWAY FROM THE SCHOOL, PIERO COULDN'T STOP TALKING ABOUT ESCARGOTS.

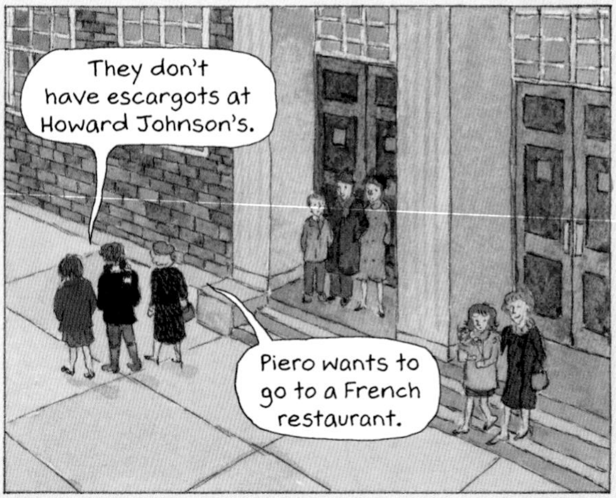
They don't have escargots at Howard Johnson's.
Piero wants to go to a French restaurant.

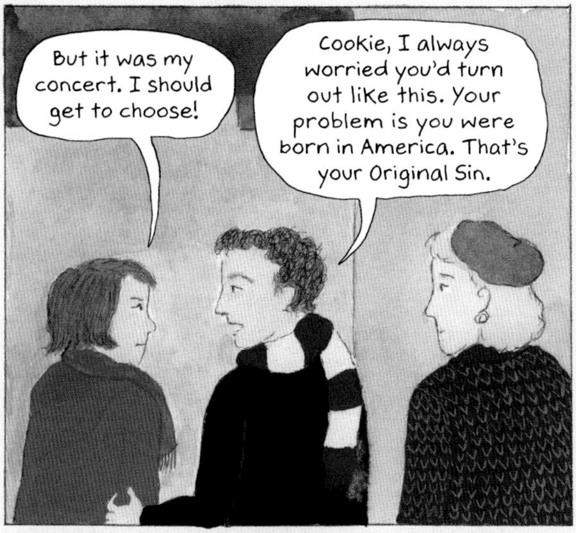
But it was my concert. I should get to choose!
Cookie, I always worried you'd turn out like this. Your problem is you were born in America. That's your Original Sin.

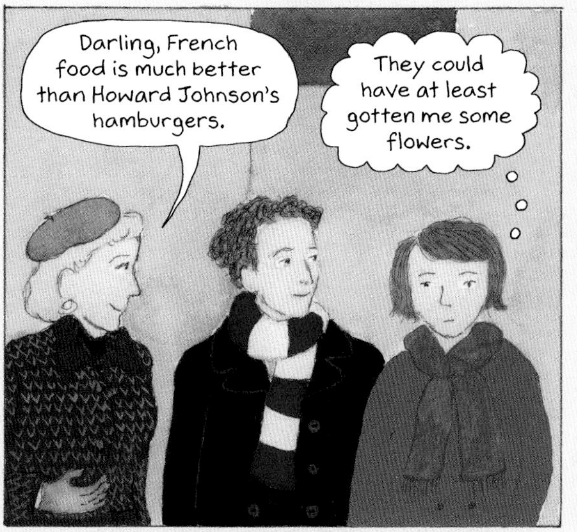
Darling, French food is much better than Howard Johnson's hamburgers.
They could have at least gotten me some flowers.

PIERO TOOK MAMMA'S ARM AND THEY WALKED AHEAD, MY OVERACHIEVING HALF BROTHER AND MY BRAVE LITTLE MOTHER, BONDED IN THEIR EUROPEAN SECRETS OF SURVIVAL.

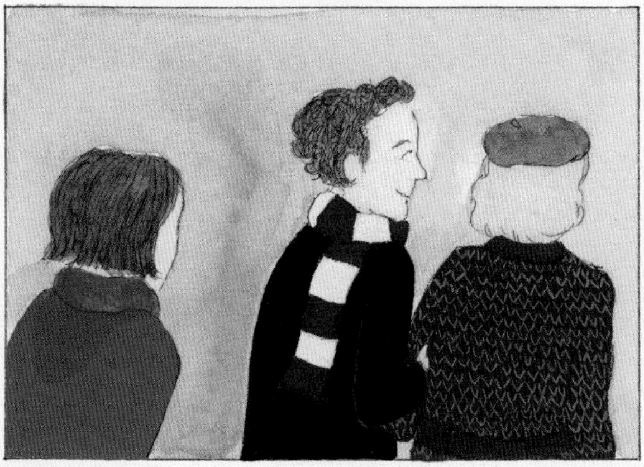

THERE WAS NOTHING FOR ME TO DO BUT TRY TO KEEP UP. NO TIME TO BE SENSITIVE. AFTER ALL, LIFE GOES ON.

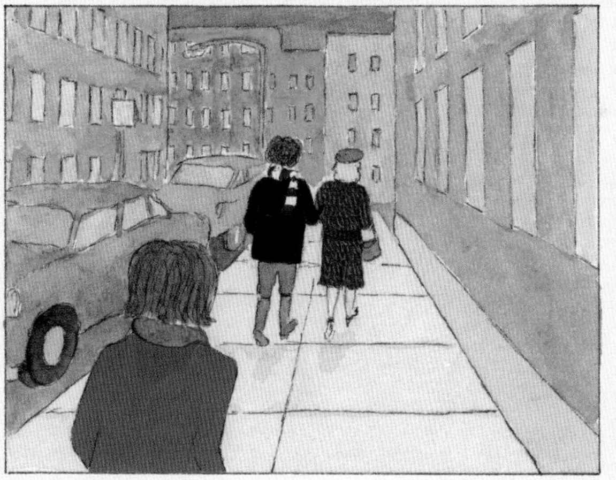

BUT I COULDN'T STOP THINKING ABOUT WHAT PIERO HAD SAID. IF BEING BORN IN AMERICA WAS MY "ORIGINAL SIN," WHAT WAS I SUPPOSED TO DO ABOUT IT? WAS THERE A SPECIAL SACRAMENT I'D NEVER HEARD OF THAT WOULD ABSOLVE IT AND RETURN ME TO A STATE OF GRACE?

OR WOULD IT BE MY BURDEN FOREVER?

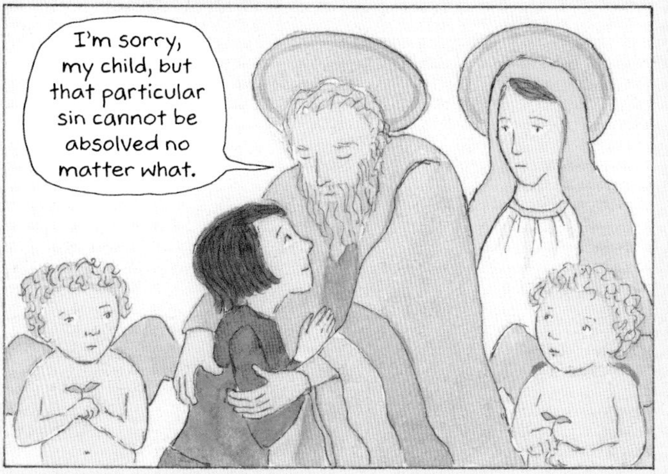
I'm sorry, my child, but that particular sin cannot be absolved no matter what.

EIGHTEEN

Never Stand Next to the Pretty Girls

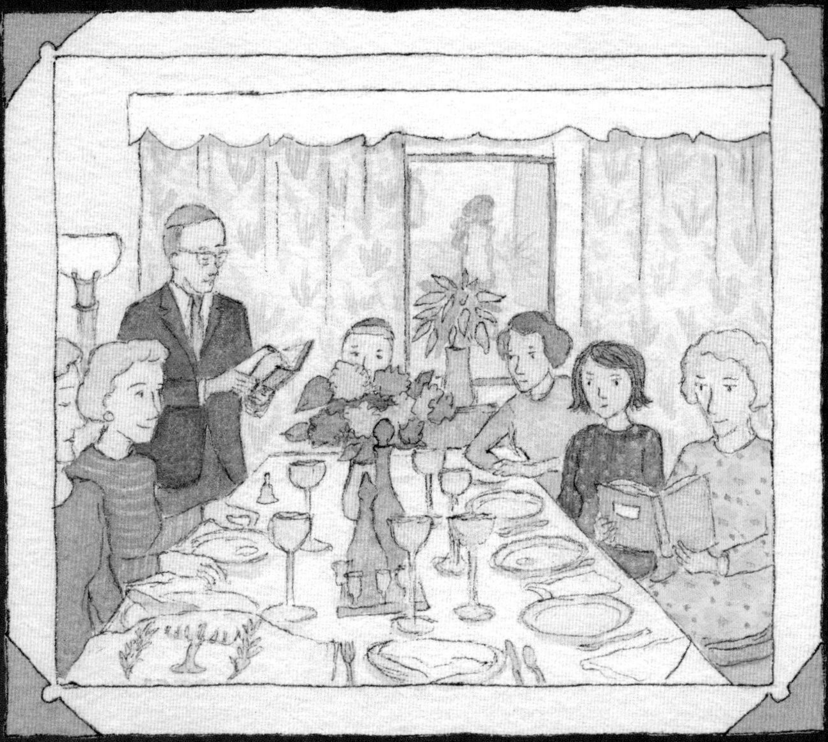

1964-65

SOON AFTER NEW YEAR'S 1964, WHILE PIERO CONTINUED TO MAKE UNDERGROUND FILMS AND WRITE POETRY ON THE LOWER EAST SIDE...

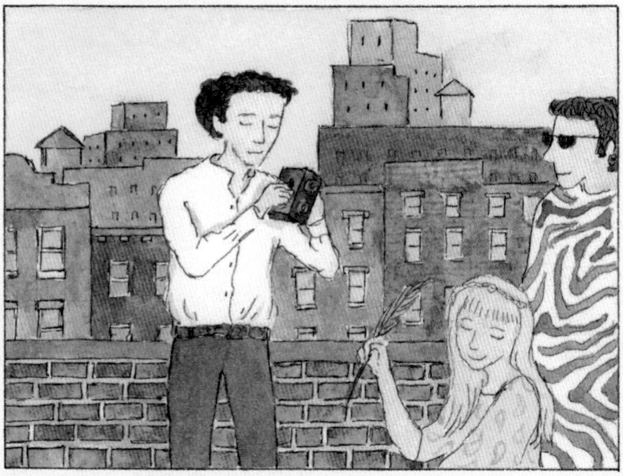

... ROBERTO FOUND A JOB AS AN ENTOMOLOGIST AT IDLEWILD AIRPORT, NEWLY RENAMED JOHN F. KENNEDY INTERNATIONAL AIRPORT, ONLY SEVEN MILES FROM OUR APARTMENT BUILDING.

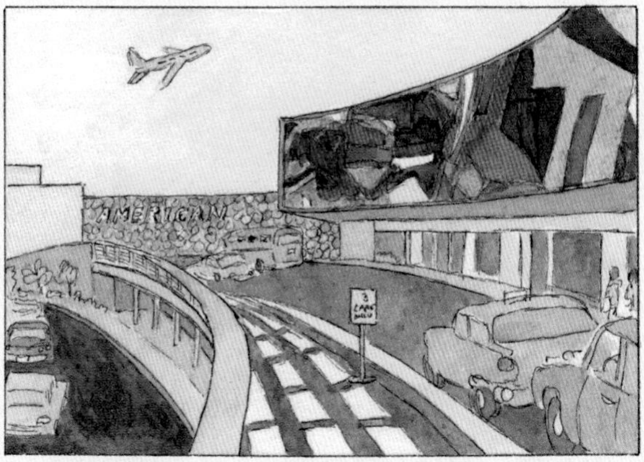

ROBERTO'S JOB—LOOKING FOR INSECTS IN PLANTS AND PRODUCE THAT THE CUSTOMS PEOPLE CONFISCATED FROM FOREIGN TRAVELERS—SEEMED BORING TO ME, BUT IT DID COME WITH A FEW SURPRISING ENCOUNTERS ON THE TARMAC.

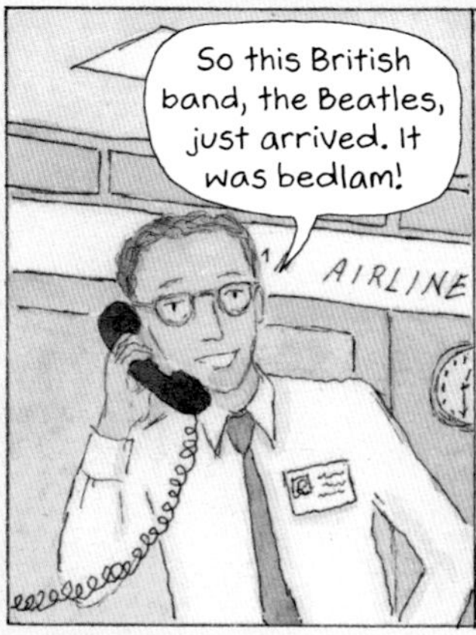
So this British band, the Beatles, just arrived. It was bedlam!
AIRLINE

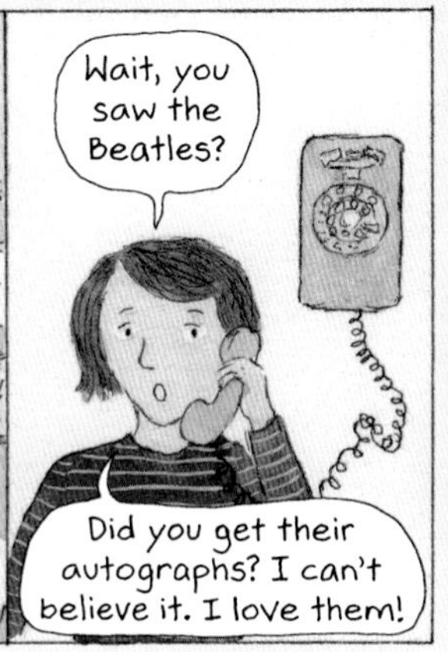
Wait, you saw the Beatles?
Did you get their autographs? I can't believe it. I love them!

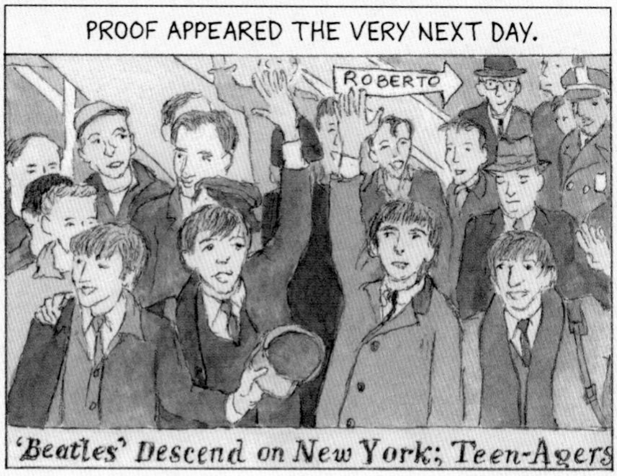
PROOF APPEARED THE VERY NEXT DAY.
ROBERTO
'Beatles' Descend on New York; Teen-Agers

I CLIPPED THE PHOTO FROM THE NEWSPAPER AND BROUGHT IT TO SCHOOL IN A FAILED ATTEMPT TO IMPRESS SOME OF THE POPULAR KIDS.

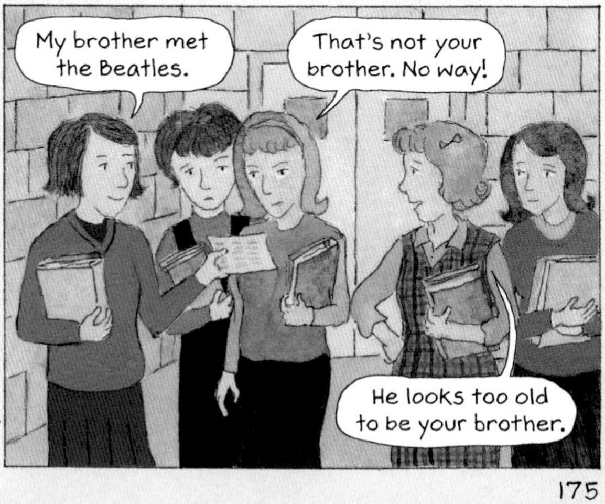
My brother met the Beatles.
That's not your brother. No way!
He looks too old to be your brother.

EVEN CAROL HAD HER DOUBTS.

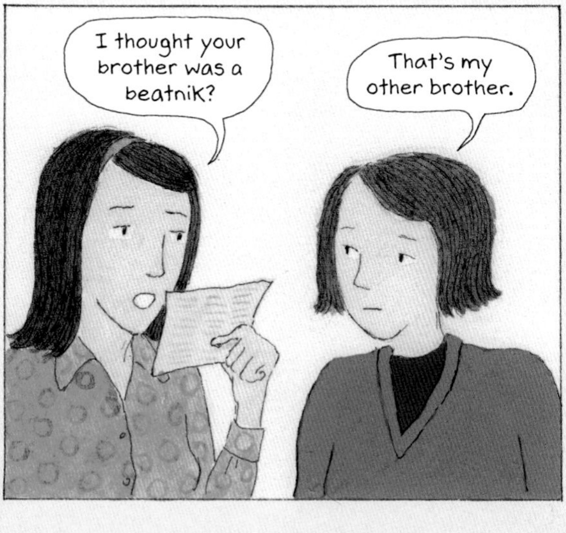
I thought your brother was a beatnik?
That's my other brother.

IN THE SPRING I WAS ACCEPTED TO THE HIGH SCHOOL OF ART AND DESIGN, BUT AS EXPECTED, MY MOTHER REFUSED TO SIGN ON.

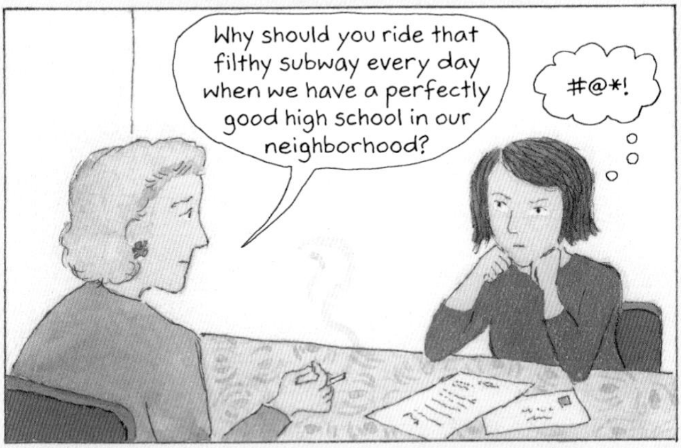
Why should you ride that filthy subway every day when we have a perfectly good high school in our neighborhood?
#@*!

SO CAROL AND I PARTED WAYS AT THE END OF NINTH GRADE. AROUND THE SAME TIME, KAREN'S FAMILY BOUGHT A HOUSE IN THE SUBURBS. POOF! MY TWO BEST FRIENDS WERE GONE BY SEPTEMBER WHEN I STARTED TENTH GRADE AT THE MASSIVE AND INTIMIDATING FOREST HILLS HIGH SCHOOL.

THERE WERE MORE THAN 3,000 STUDENTS IN THREE GRADES ATTENDING CLASS IN TRIPLE SESSIONS. IT MADE HALSEY SEEM ALMOST QUAINT.

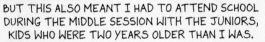

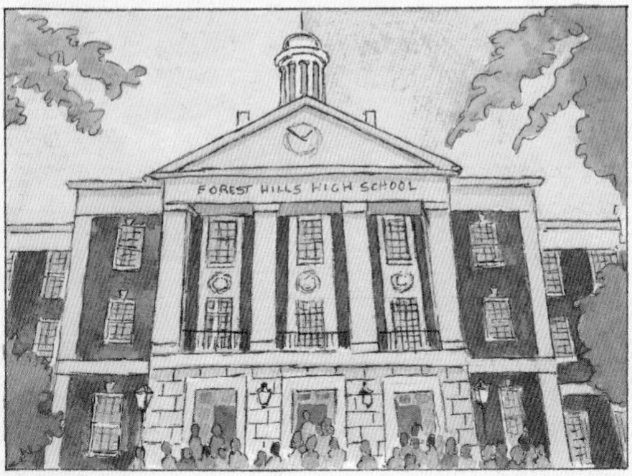
FOREST HILLS HIGH SCHOOL

MY ONE CONSOLATION WAS THAT I HAD GOTTEN INTO A SPECIAL ART PROGRAM. ALONG WITH THE USUAL SUBJECTS, I NOW HAD AN ART CLASS EVERY DAY.

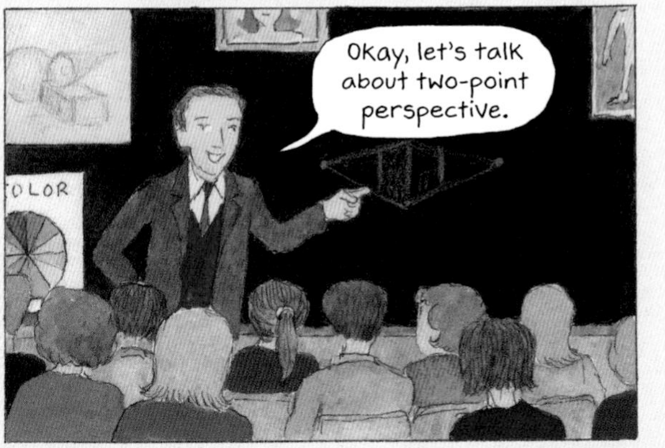
Okay, let's talk about two-point perspective.

BUT THIS ALSO MEANT I HAD TO ATTEND SCHOOL DURING THE MIDDLE SESSION WITH THE JUNIORS, KIDS WHO WERE TWO YEARS OLDER THAN I WAS.

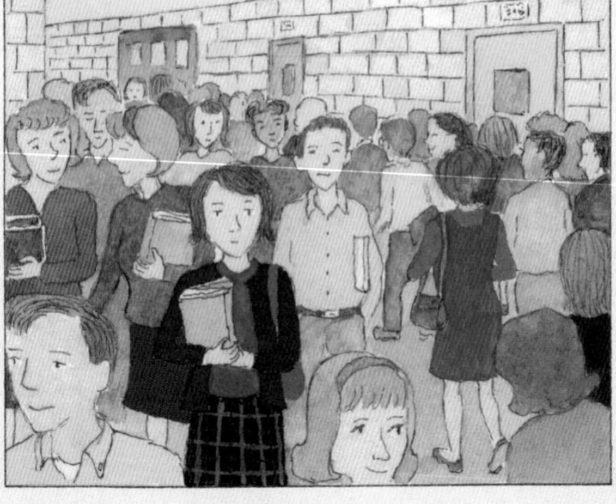

AFTER LONG DAYS OF NAVIGATING THE HALLS AND BOISTEROUS CROWDS, I LOOKED FORWARD TO ALONE TIME IN THE APARTMENT BEFORE MAMMA AND SOL GOT HOME FROM WORK.

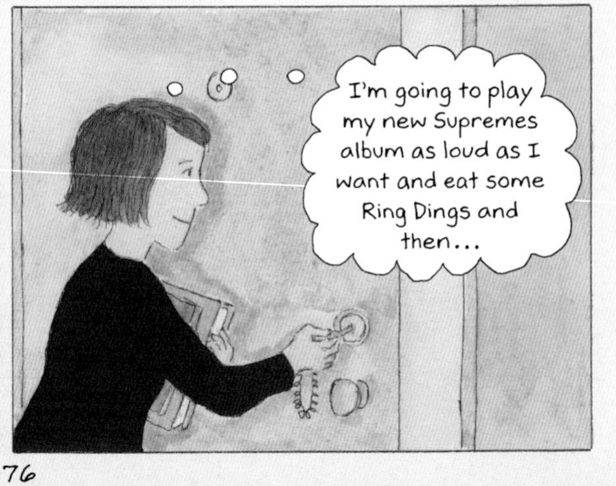
I'm going to play my new Supremes album as loud as I want and eat some Ring Dings and then...

BUT SOMETIMES I FOUND PIERO AND HIS FRIEND ANGUS HAD TAKEN OVER OUR LIVING ROOM.

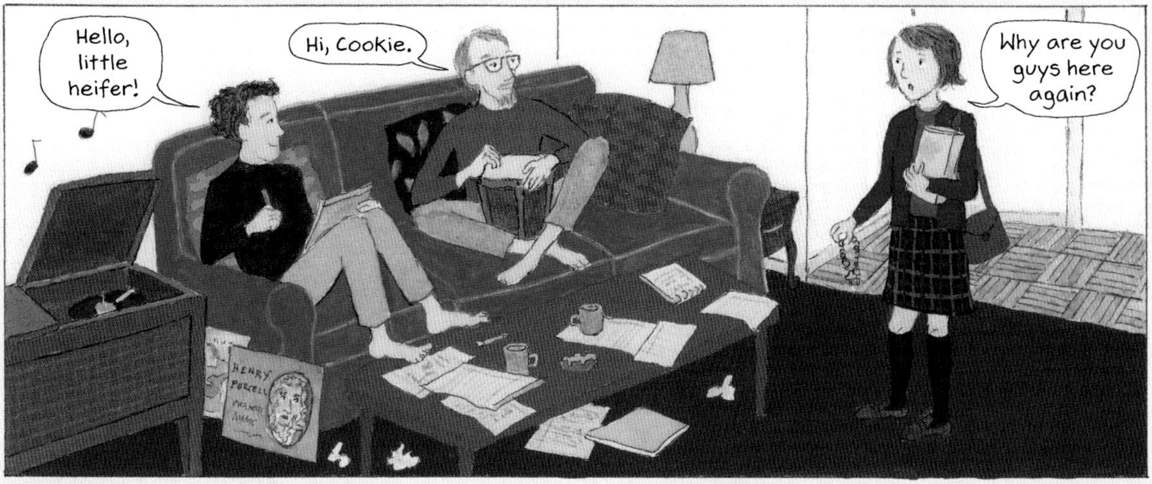
Hello, little heifer!
Hi, Cookie.
Why are you guys here again?
HENRY PURCELL

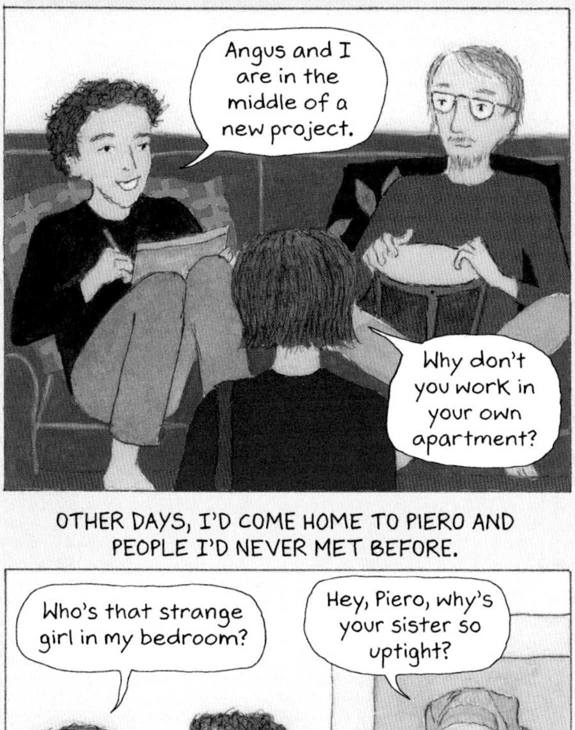
Angus and I are in the middle of a new project.
Why don't you work in your own apartment?

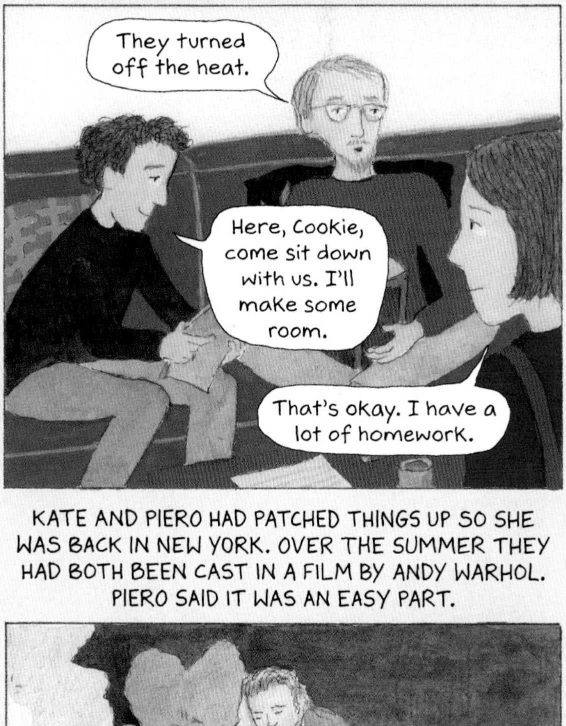
They turned off the heat.
Here, Cookie, come sit down with us. I'll make some room.
That's okay. I have a lot of homework.

OTHER DAYS, I'D COME HOME TO PIERO AND PEOPLE I'D NEVER MET BEFORE.

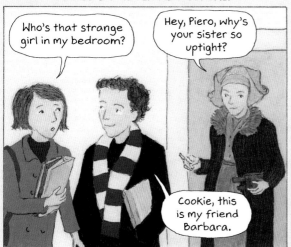

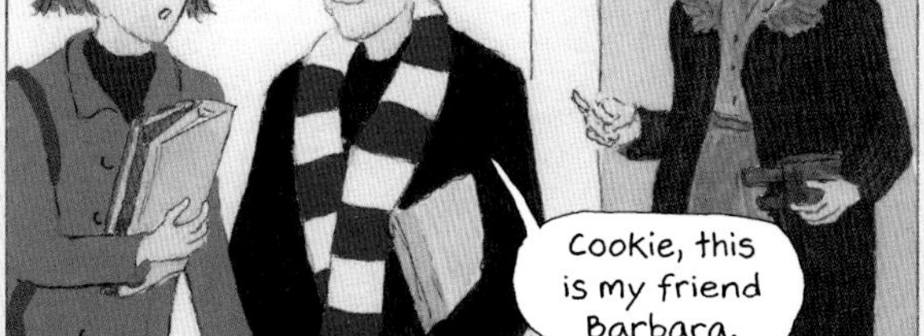
Who's that strange girl in my bedroom?
Hey, Piero, why's your sister so uptight?
Cookie, this is my friend Barbara.

KATE AND PIERO HAD PATCHED THINGS UP SO SHE WAS BACK IN NEW YORK. OVER THE SUMMER THEY HAD BOTH BEEN CAST IN A FILM BY ANDY WARHOL. PIERO SAID IT WAS AN EASY PART.

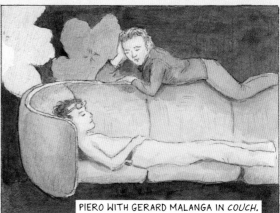

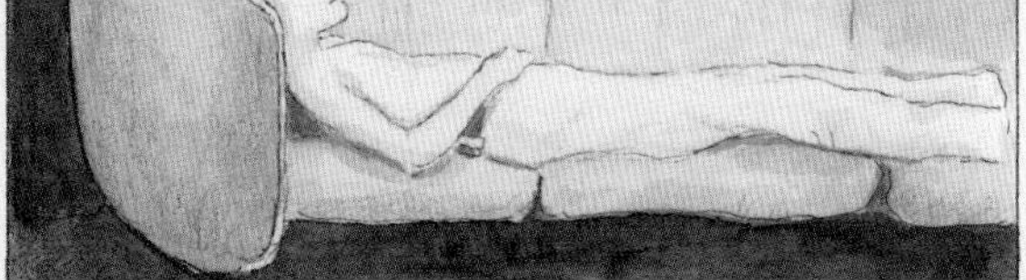
PIERO WITH GERARD MALANGA IN *COUCH*.

SOME EVENINGS MY MOTHER AND SOL WENT TO MANHATTAN FOR ONE OF PIERO'S EVENTS: A POETRY READING, A FILM SCREENING, "A RITUAL HAPPENING." I WAS NEVER ALLOWED TO JOIN IN.

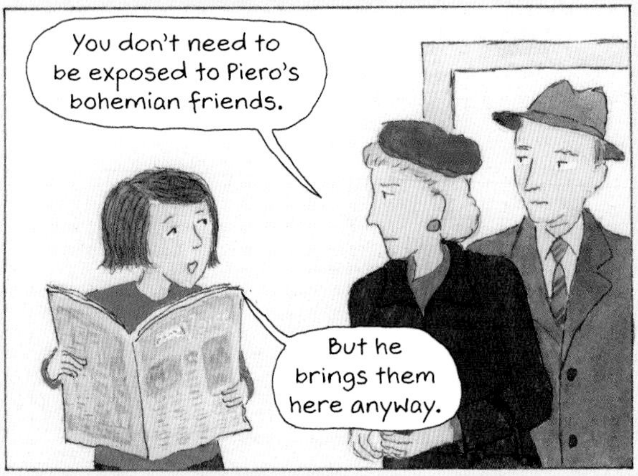
You don't need to be exposed to Piero's bohemian friends.
But he brings them here anyway.

MEANWHILE, MY HIGH SCHOOL SOCIAL LIFE WAS PRETTY MUCH NONEXISTENT. WHEN IT CAME TO BOYS, I DIDN'T KNOW WHERE TO BEGIN.

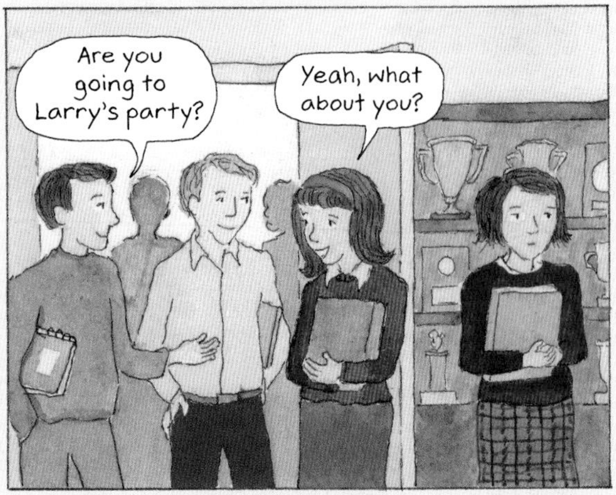
Are you going to Larry's party?
Yeah, what about you?

ONE FRIDAY I DECIDED TO BE BRAVE AND GO TO A SCHOOL DANCE. MAMMA WAS HAPPY TO OFFER ADVICE BASED ON HER OWN SOCIALLY SUCCESSFUL GIRLHOOD IN WEIMAR, GERMANY.

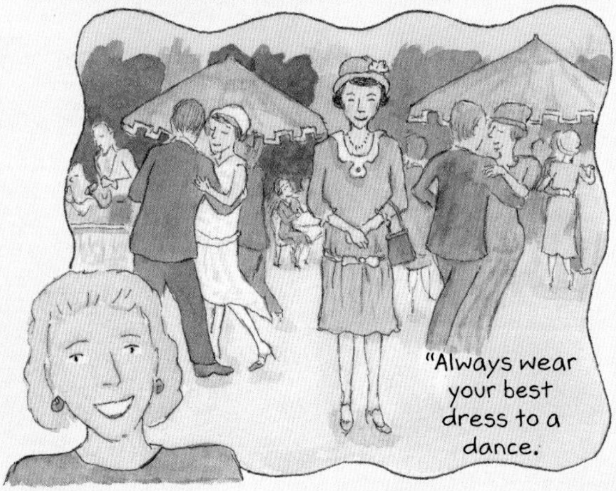
"Always wear your best dress to a dance.

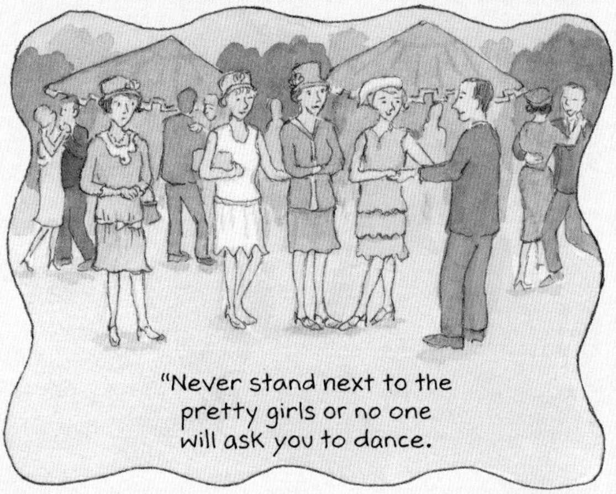
"Never stand next to the pretty girls or no one will ask you to dance.

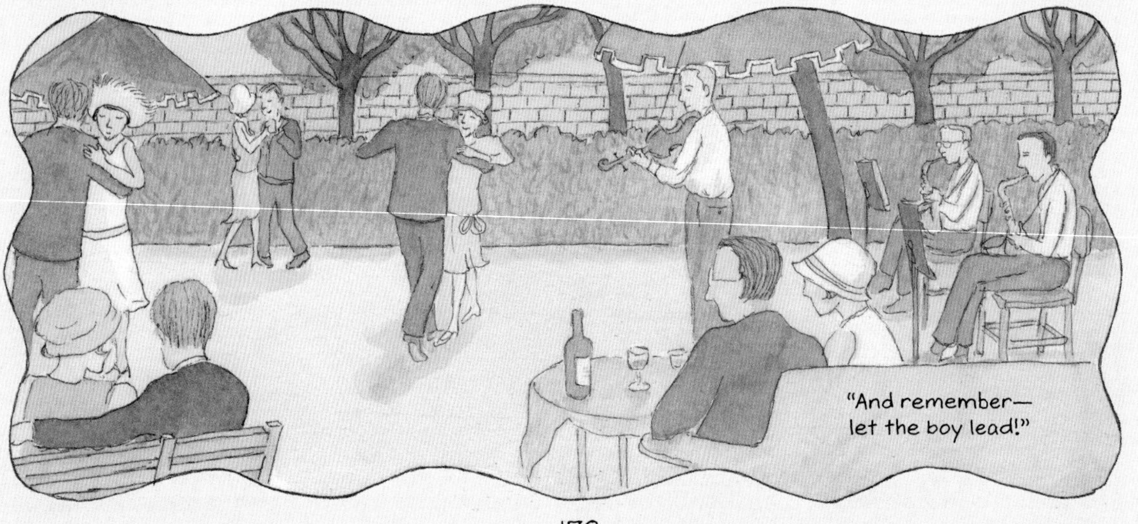
"And remember—let the boy lead!"

UNFORTUNATELY, IN QUEENS IN 1964, NONE OF HER TIPS WERE VERY USEFUL.

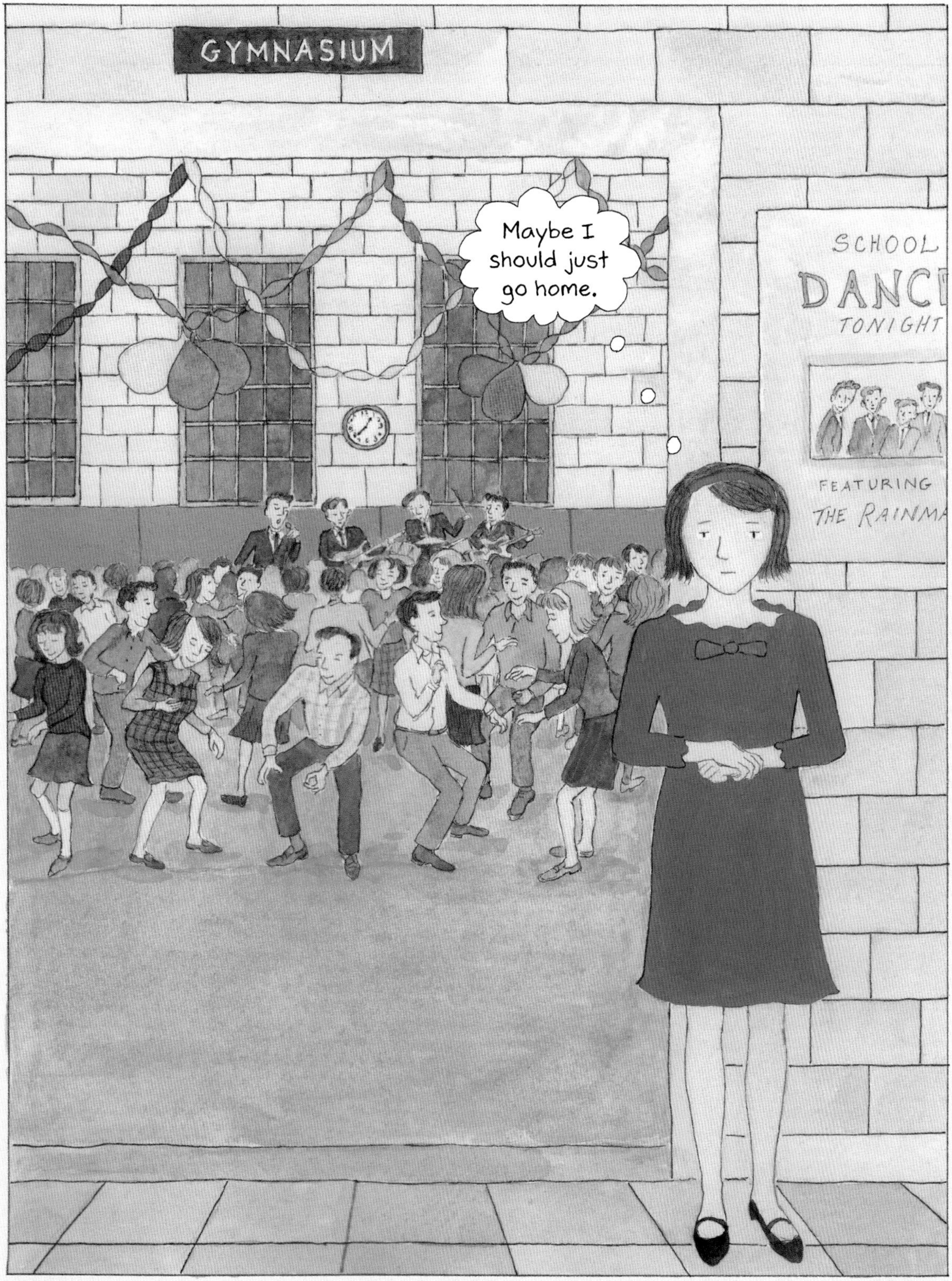
GYMNASIUM
Maybe I should just go home.
SCHOOL
DANC
TONIGHT
FEATURING
THE RAINMA

TO MAKE MATTERS WORSE, I WAS ALSO HINDERED BY ENDLESS FAMILY OBLIGATIONS THAT ALWAYS SEEMED TO TAKE PLACE ON THE WEEKENDS.

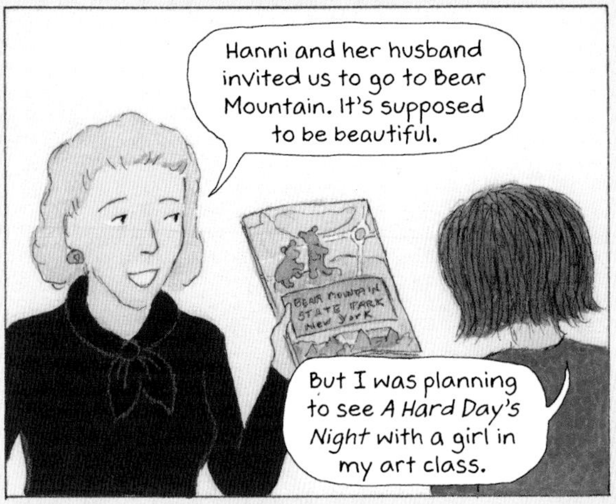
Hanni and her husband invited us to go to Bear Mountain. It's supposed to be beautiful.
BEAR MOUNTAIN STATE PARK NEW YORK
But I was planning to see *A Hard Day's Night* with a girl in my art class.

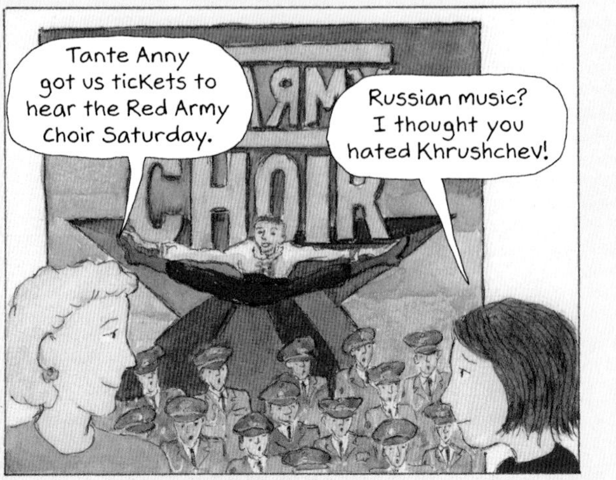
Tante Anny got us tickets to hear the Red Army Choir Saturday.
Russian music? I thought you hated Khrushchev!
CHOIR

ON SUNDAYS WE STILL GATHERED AT TANTE EMMY AND UNCLE LEO'S APARTMENT. I LISTENED TO ENDLESS STORIES ABOUT THE GOOD OLD DAYS BACK IN LEIPZIG. AT LEAST THEY'D FINALLY STOPPED TALKING ABOUT THE WAR ALL THE TIME.

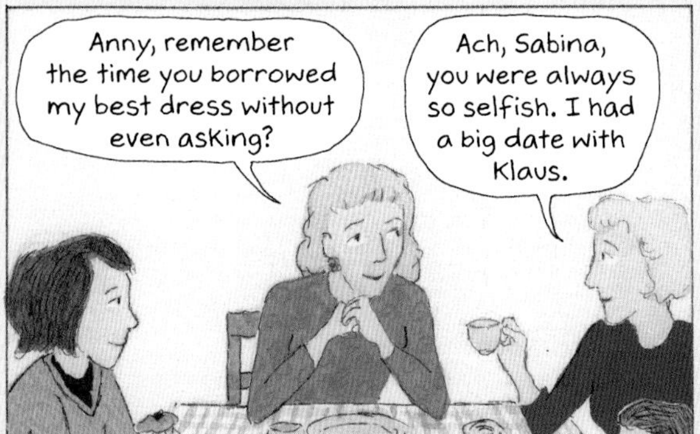
Anny, remember the time you borrowed my best dress without even asking?
Ach, Sabina, you were always so selfish. I had a big date with Klaus.

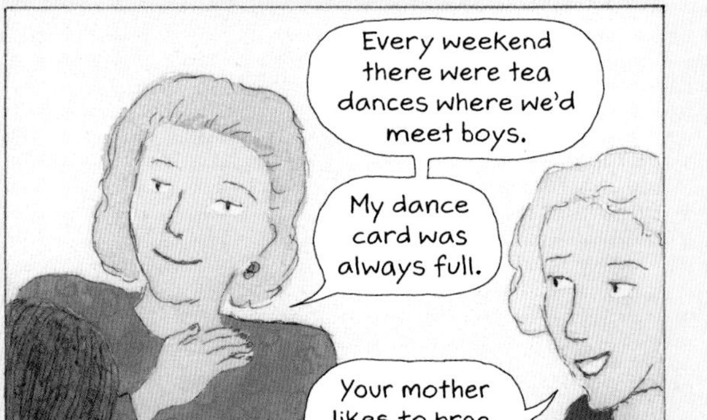
Every weekend there were tea dances where we'd meet boys.
My dance card was always full.
Your mother likes to brag. We were all popular.

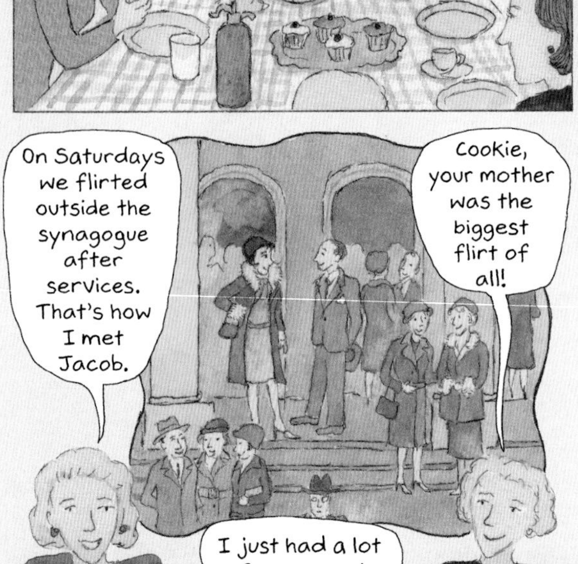
On Saturdays we flirted outside the synagogue after services. That's how I met Jacob.
Cookie, your mother was the biggest flirt of all!
I just had a lot of sex appeal.

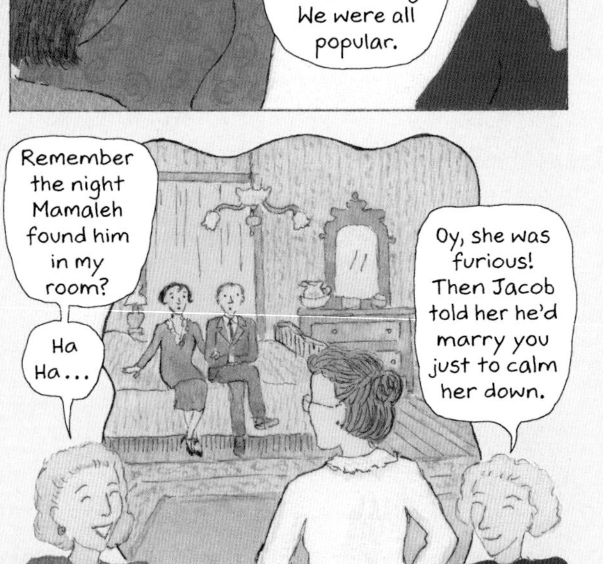
Remember the night Mamaleh found him in my room?
Ha Ha...
Oy, she was furious! Then Jacob told her he'd marry you just to calm her down.

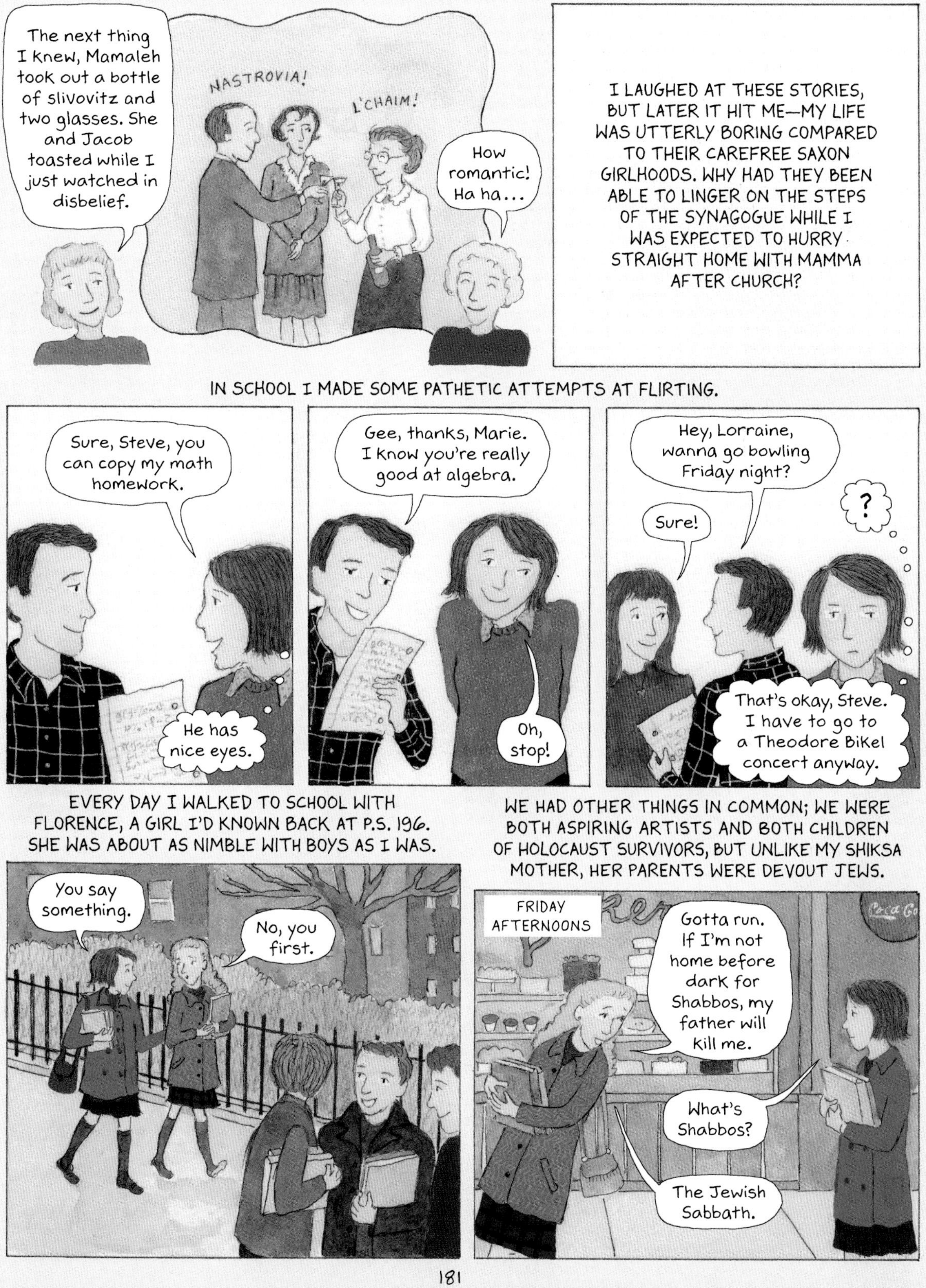
The next thing I knew, Mamaleh took out a bottle of slivovitz and two glasses. She and Jacob toasted while I just watched in disbelief.
NASTROVIA!
L'CHAIM!
How romantic! Ha ha...
I LAUGHED AT THESE STORIES, BUT LATER IT HIT ME—MY LIFE WAS UTTERLY BORING COMPARED TO THEIR CAREFREE SAXON GIRLHOODS. WHY HAD THEY BEEN ABLE TO LINGER ON THE STEPS OF THE SYNAGOGUE WHILE I WAS EXPECTED TO HURRY STRAIGHT HOME WITH MAMMA AFTER CHURCH?
IN SCHOOL I MADE SOME PATHETIC ATTEMPTS AT FLIRTING.
Sure, Steve, you can copy my math homework.
He has nice eyes.
Gee, thanks, Marie. I know you're really good at algebra.
Oh, stop!
Hey, Lorraine, wanna go bowling Friday night?
Sure!
?
That's okay, Steve. I have to go to a Theodore Bikel concert anyway.
EVERY DAY I WALKED TO SCHOOL WITH FLORENCE, A GIRL I'D KNOWN BACK AT P.S. 196. SHE WAS ABOUT AS NIMBLE WITH BOYS AS I WAS.
You say something.
No, you first.
WE HAD OTHER THINGS IN COMMON; WE WERE BOTH ASPIRING ARTISTS AND BOTH CHILDREN OF HOLOCAUST SURVIVORS, BUT UNLIKE MY SHIKSA MOTHER, HER PARENTS WERE DEVOUT JEWS.
FRIDAY AFTERNOONS
Gotta run. If I'm not home before dark for Shabbos, my father will kill me.
What's Shabbos?
The Jewish Sabbath.

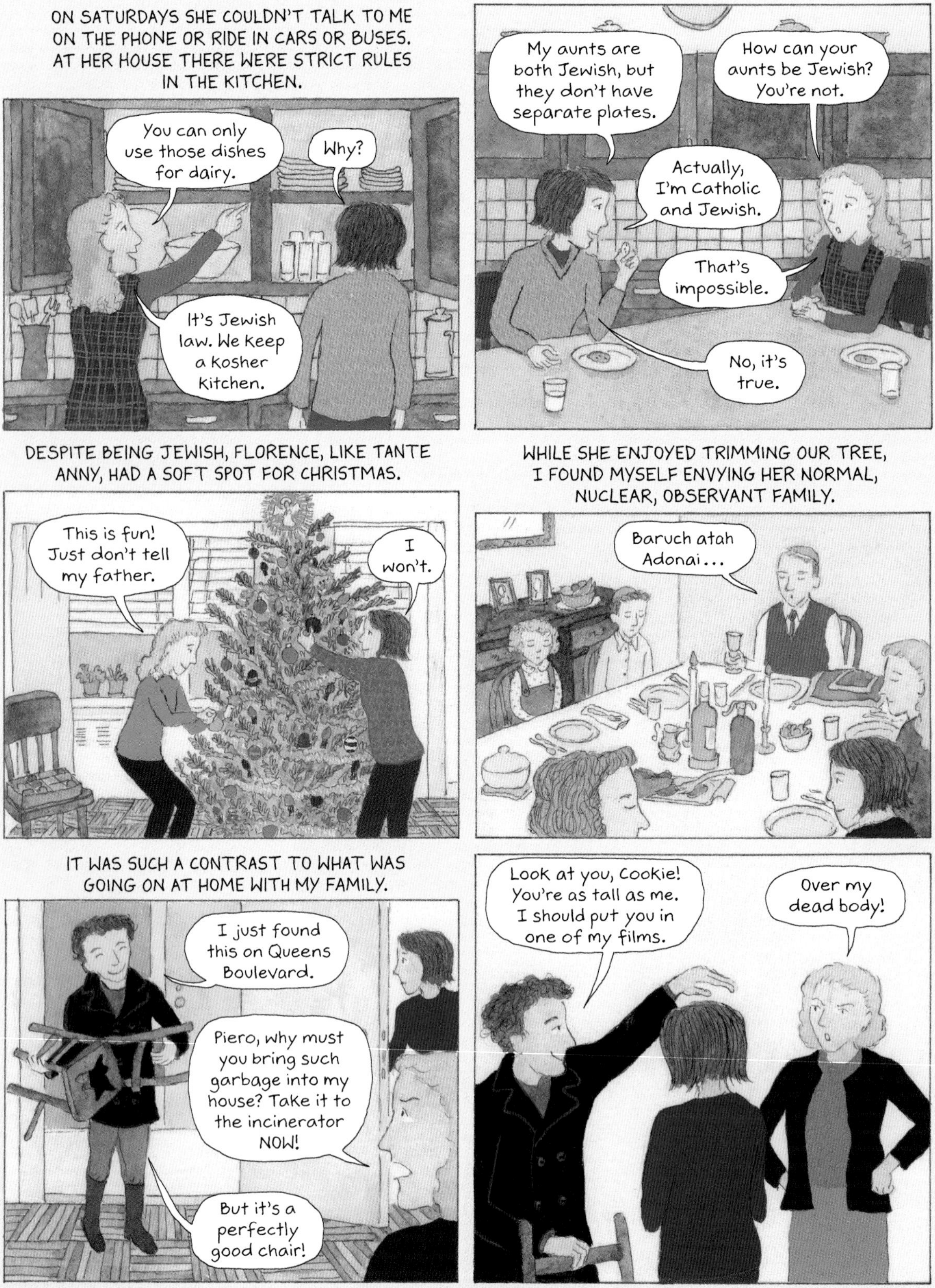
ON SATURDAYS SHE COULDN'T TALK TO ME ON THE PHONE OR RIDE IN CARS OR BUSES. AT HER HOUSE THERE WERE STRICT RULES IN THE KITCHEN.
You can only use those dishes for dairy.
Why?
It's Jewish law. We keep a kosher kitchen.
My aunts are both Jewish, but they don't have separate plates.
How can your aunts be Jewish? You're not.
Actually, I'm Catholic and Jewish.
That's impossible.
No, it's true.
DESPITE BEING JEWISH, FLORENCE, LIKE TANTE ANNY, HAD A SOFT SPOT FOR CHRISTMAS.
This is fun! Just don't tell my father.
I won't.
WHILE SHE ENJOYED TRIMMING OUR TREE, I FOUND MYSELF ENVYING HER NORMAL, NUCLEAR, OBSERVANT FAMILY.
Baruch atah Adonai...
IT WAS SUCH A CONTRAST TO WHAT WAS GOING ON AT HOME WITH MY FAMILY.
I just found this on Queens Boulevard.
Piero, why must you bring such garbage into my house? Take it to the incinerator NOW!
But it's a perfectly good chair!
Look at you, Cookie! You're as tall as me. I should put you in one of my films.
Over my dead body!

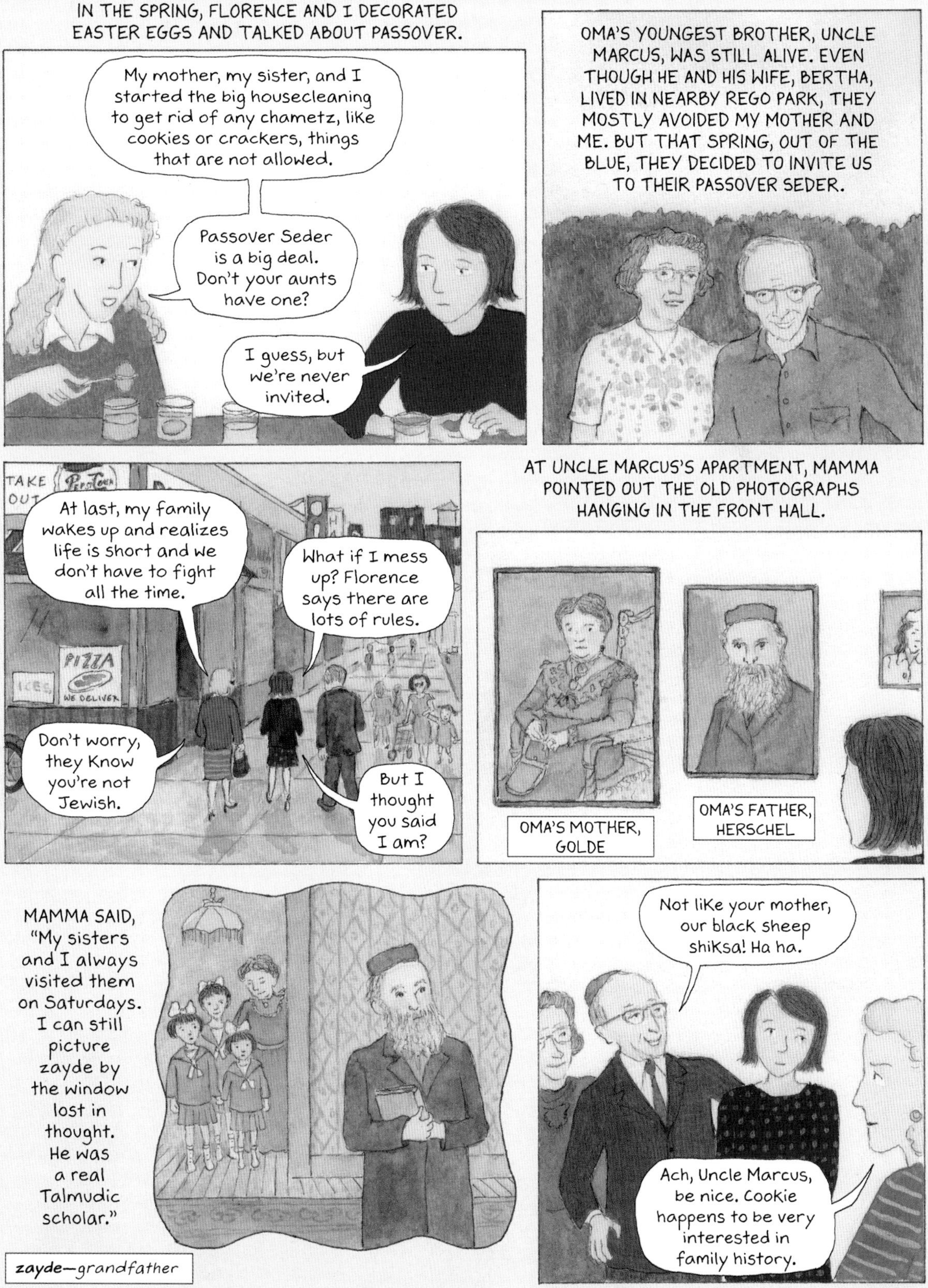
IN THE SPRING, FLORENCE AND I DECORATED EASTER EGGS AND TALKED ABOUT PASSOVER.
My mother, my sister, and I started the big housecleaning to get rid of any chametz, like cookies or crackers, things that are not allowed.
Passover Seder is a big deal. Don't your aunts have one?
I guess, but we're never invited.
OMA'S YOUNGEST BROTHER, UNCLE MARCUS, WAS STILL ALIVE. EVEN THOUGH HE AND HIS WIFE, BERTHA, LIVED IN NEARBY REGO PARK, THEY MOSTLY AVOIDED MY MOTHER AND ME. BUT THAT SPRING, OUT OF THE BLUE, THEY DECIDED TO INVITE US TO THEIR PASSOVER SEDER.
TAKE OUT
PIZZA
ICES
WE DELIVER
At last, my family wakes up and realizes life is short and we don't have to fight all the time.
What if I mess up? Florence says there are lots of rules.
Don't worry, they Know you're not Jewish.
But I thought you said I am?
AT UNCLE MARCUS'S APARTMENT, MAMMA POINTED OUT THE OLD PHOTOGRAPHS HANGING IN THE FRONT HALL.
OMA'S MOTHER, GOLDE
OMA'S FATHER, HERSCHEL
MAMMA SAID, "My sisters and I always visited them on Saturdays. I can still picture zayde by the window lost in thought. He was a real Talmudic scholar."
zayde—grandfather
Not liKe your mother, our black sheep shiksa! Ha ha.
Ach, Uncle Marcus, be nice. Cookie happens to be very interested in family history.

MAMMA WAS RIGHT; I *WAS* INTERESTED IN FAMILY STORIES. THEY WERE LIKE PIECES OF A PUZZLE I NEEDED TO PUT TOGETHER SO I COULD FIGURE OUT WHERE I FIT IN.

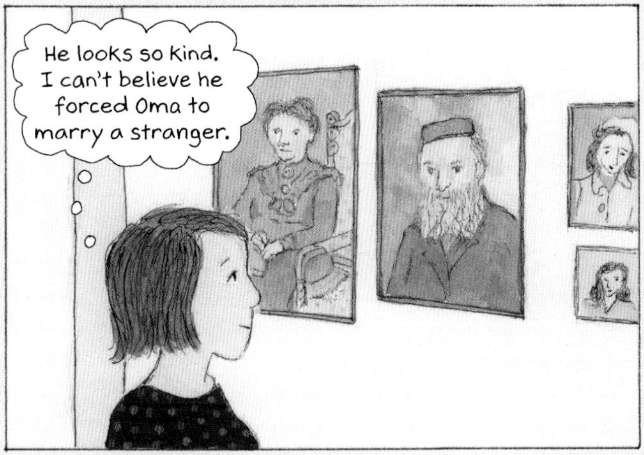
He looks so kind. I can't believe he forced Oma to marry a stranger.

I WAS BEGINNING TO UNDERSTAND THAT BEING JEWISH, MORE THAN ANYTHING, HAD SHAPED THESE STORIES: OMA AND THE RABBI'S SON, THE BOYS ON THE STEPS OF THE SYNAGOGUE, MAMMA AND JACOB ELOPING TO ITALY BECAUSE THE NAZIS BARRED JEWS FROM MEDICAL SCHOOL AFTER 1932.

THE SEDER BEGAN. I HOPED NO ONE WOULD REMEMBER I WAS CATHOLIC.

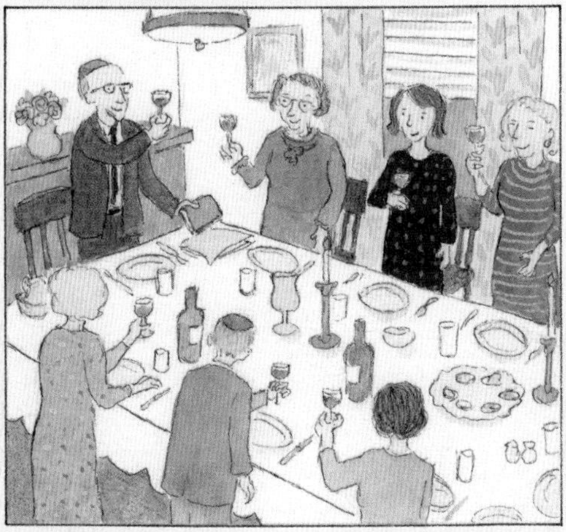

UNCLE MARCUS TOLD A STORY OF FOUR SONS: THE WISE, THE WICKED, THE SIMPLE, AND "THE ONE WHO DIDN'T KNOW HOW TO ASK." SUDDENLY, ALL EYES WERE ON ME.

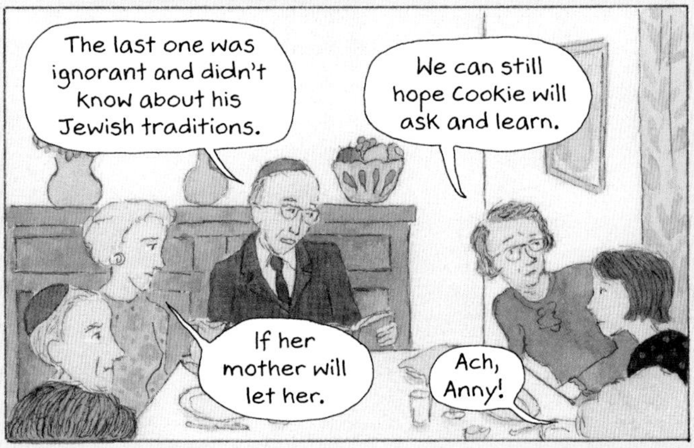
The last one was ignorant and didn't know about his Jewish traditions.
We can still hope Cookie will ask and learn.
If her mother will let her.
Ach, Anny!

THERE WERE BITTER HERBS AND HANDWASHING, WINE AND MATZO. EVERYONE AT THE TABLE, EVEN MAMMA, MOVED IN GRACEFUL SYNCOPATION. IT WAS AS IF THEY ALL SHARED A SECRET MEMORY.

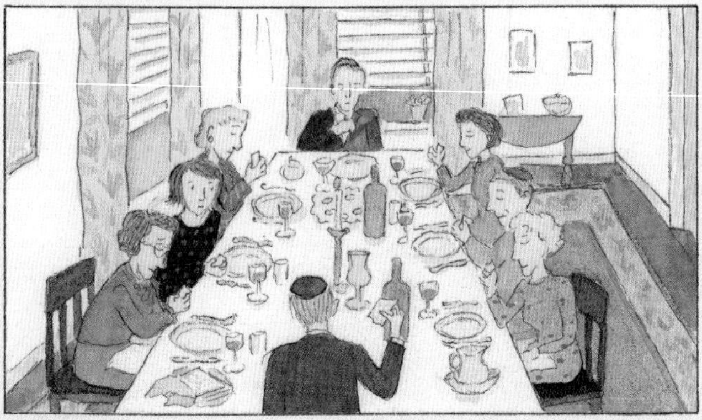

AND OF COURSE, THEY DID. THE ONLY ONE WHO COULDN'T REMEMBER WAS ME.

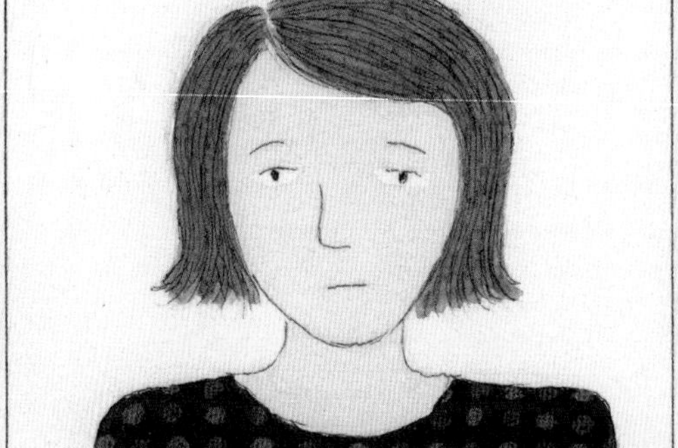

NINETEEN

The Lucky One

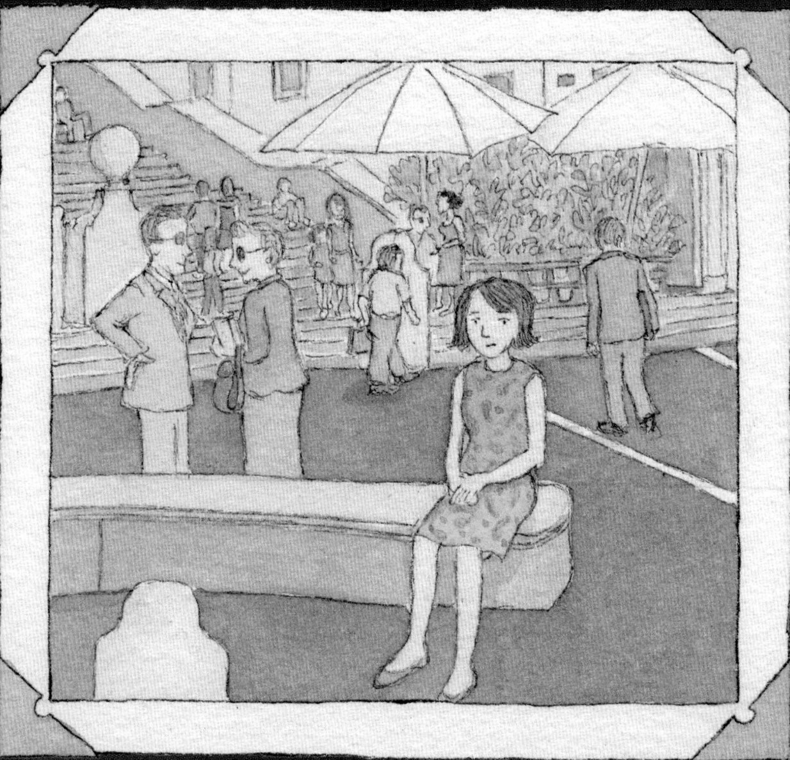

1965

THE SUMMER AFTER TENTH GRADE, MY MOTHER AND I TOOK ANOTHER TRIP TO EUROPE. THIS TIME A STOP IN GENEVA WAS NOT ON OUR ITINERARY. WHILE MY FATHER WAS SENDING HIS CHECKS EVERY MONTH, HIS LETTERS TO ME WERE BECOMING MORE AND MORE SPORADIC. HE SEEMED TO HAVE LOST INTEREST. THAT WAS FINE WITH ME.

TO MY SURPRISE, MAMMA DECIDED THAT OUR FIRST STOP WOULD BE GERMANY.

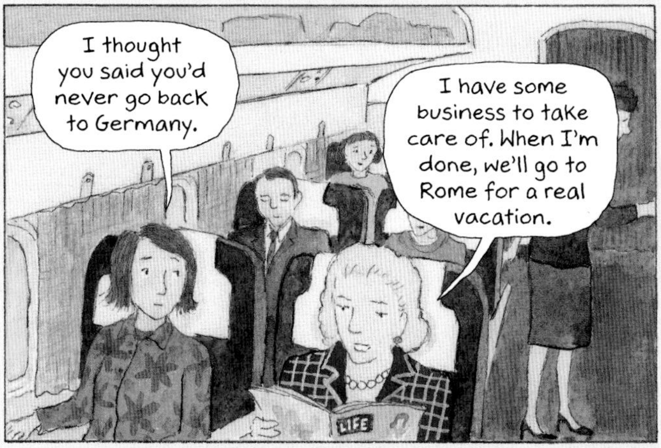
I thought you said you'd never go back to Germany.
I have some business to take care of. When I'm done, we'll go to Rome for a real vacation.
LIFE

AT THE STUTTGART AIRPORT, I WONDERED IF MY MOTHER REGRETTED HER DECISION.

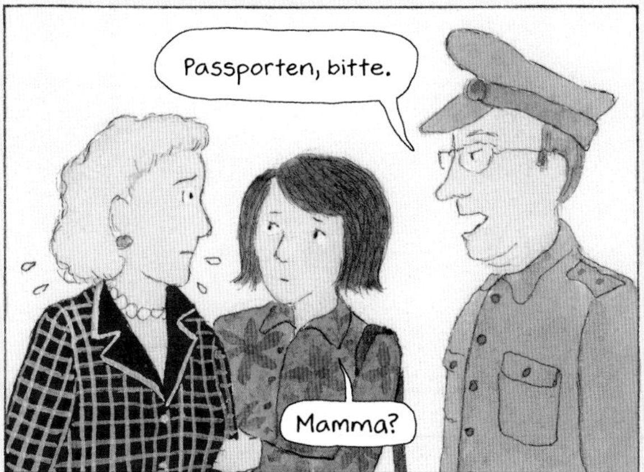
Passporten, bitte.
Mamma?

Passporten, bitte.—*Passports, please.*

BUT THEN WE WERE PICKED UP BY A JOLLY OLD MAN MY MOTHER CALLED "UNCLE NILS." JUST LIKE EVERYTHING IN MY FAMILY, IT WAS A LONG, COMPLICATED STORY.

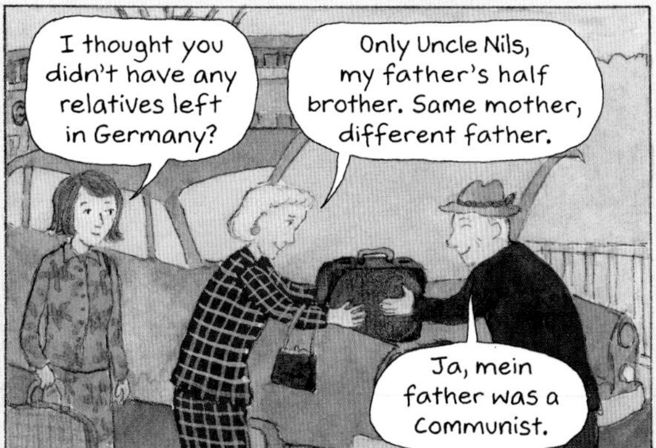
I thought you didn't have any relatives left in Germany?
Only Uncle Nils, my father's half brother. Same mother, different father.
Ja, mein father was a Communist.

THE NEXT DAY, WHILE MAMMA MET WITH A GERMAN LAWYER, I HUNG OUT WITH MY NEW RELATIVES AND THEIR DACHSHUND.

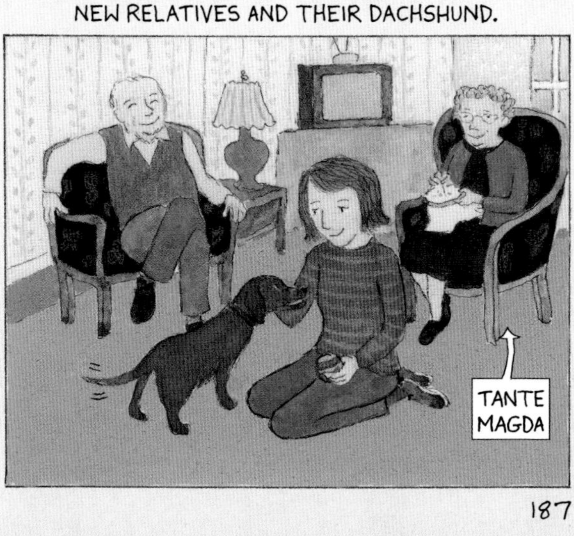
TANTE MAGDA

AT DINNERTIME, MAMMA FINALLY RETURNED. SHE WAS IN A VERY GOOD MOOD.

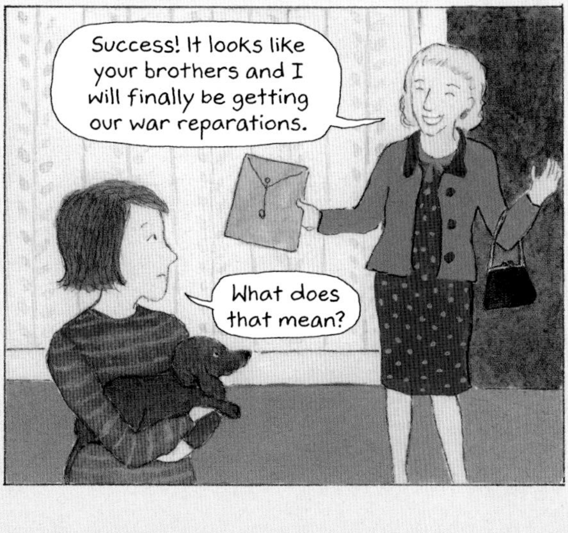
Success! It looks like your brothers and I will finally be getting our war reparations.
What does that mean?

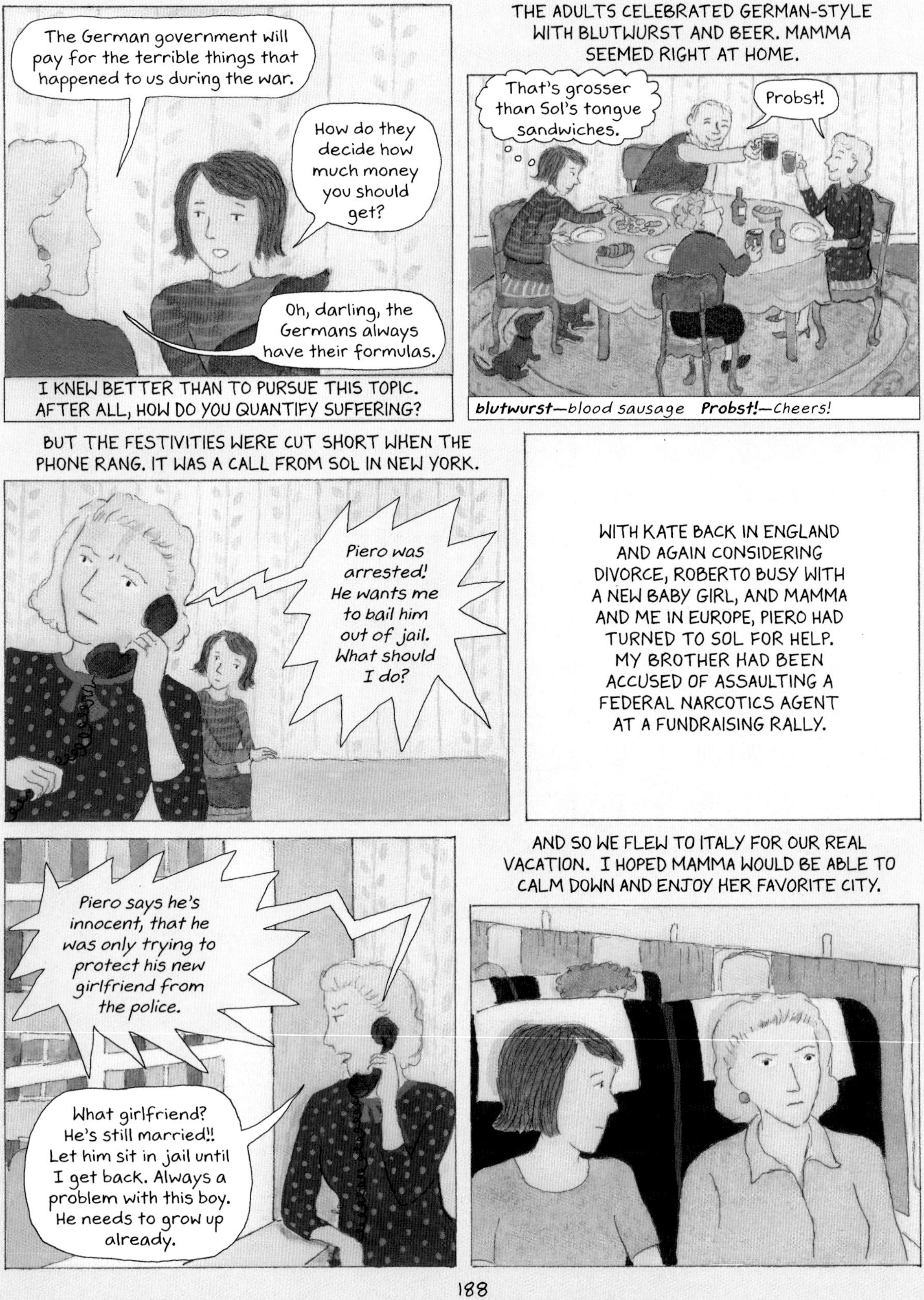
The German government will pay for the terrible things that happened to us during the war.
How do they decide how much money you should get?
Oh, darling, the Germans always have their formulas.
I KNEW BETTER THAN TO PURSUE THIS TOPIC. AFTER ALL, HOW DO YOU QUANTIFY SUFFERING?
THE ADULTS CELEBRATED GERMAN-STYLE WITH BLUTWURST AND BEER. MAMMA SEEMED RIGHT AT HOME.
That's grosser than Sol's tongue sandwiches.
Probst!
blutwurst—blood sausage Probst!—Cheers!
BUT THE FESTIVITIES WERE CUT SHORT WHEN THE PHONE RANG. IT WAS A CALL FROM SOL IN NEW YORK.
Piero was arrested! He wants me to bail him out of jail. What should I do?
WITH KATE BACK IN ENGLAND AND AGAIN CONSIDERING DIVORCE, ROBERTO BUSY WITH A NEW BABY GIRL, AND MAMMA AND ME IN EUROPE, PIERO HAD TURNED TO SOL FOR HELP. MY BROTHER HAD BEEN ACCUSED OF ASSAULTING A FEDERAL NARCOTICS AGENT AT A FUNDRAISING RALLY.
Piero says he's innocent, that he was only trying to protect his new girlfriend from the police.
What girlfriend? He's still married!! Let him sit in jail until I get back. Always a problem with this boy. He needs to grow up already.
AND SO WE FLEW TO ITALY FOR OUR REAL VACATION. I HOPED MAMMA WOULD BE ABLE TO CALM DOWN AND ENJOY HER FAVORITE CITY.

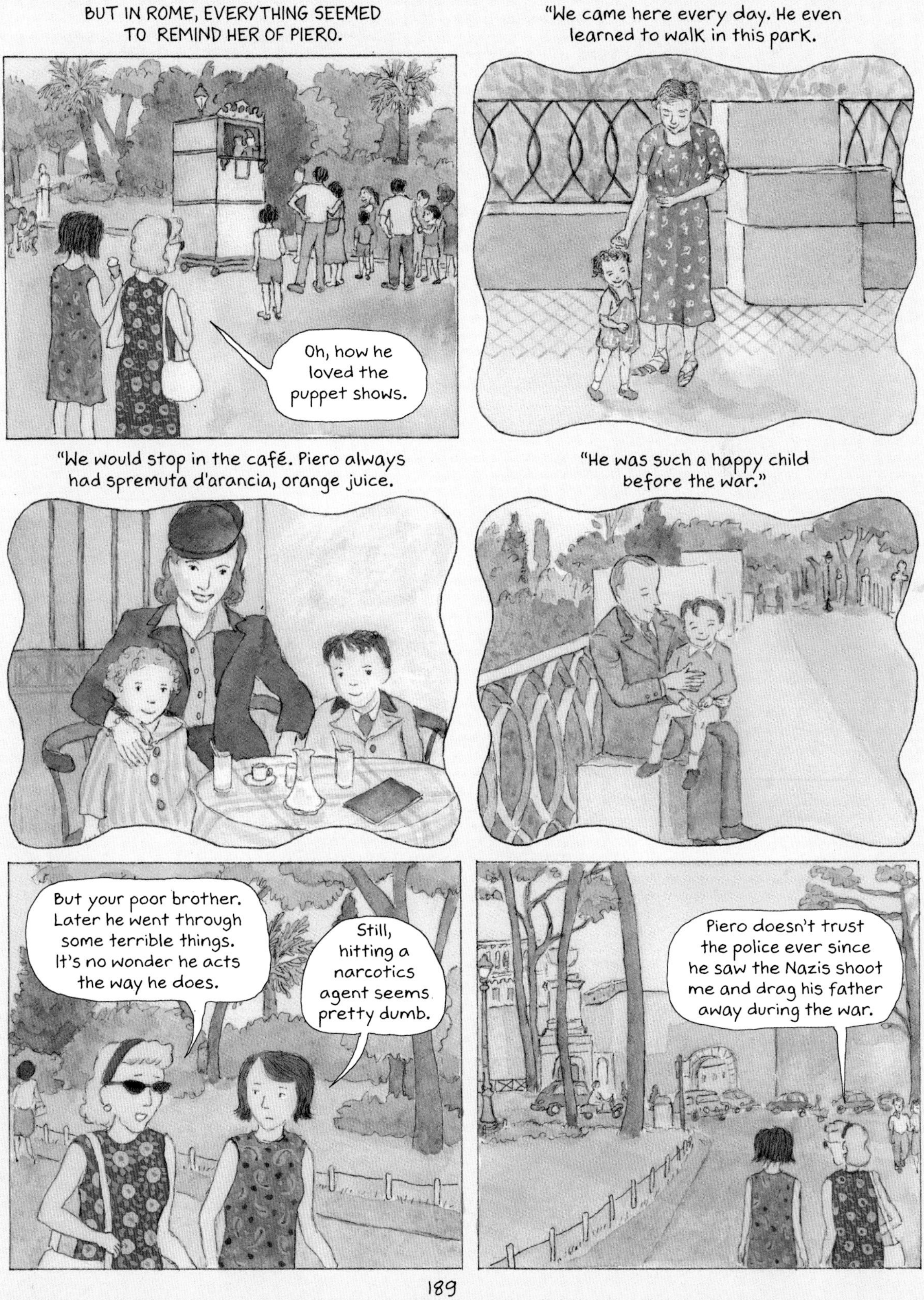
BUT IN ROME, EVERYTHING SEEMED TO REMIND HER OF PIERO.
Oh, how he loved the puppet shows.
"We came here every day. He even learned to walk in this park.
"We would stop in the café. Piero always had spremuta d'arancia, orange juice.
"He was such a happy child before the war."
But your poor brother. Later he went through some terrible things. It's no wonder he acts the way he does.
Still, hitting a narcotics agent seems pretty dumb.
Piero doesn't trust the police ever since he saw the Nazis shoot me and drag his father away during the war.

THEN MY MOTHER TOLD ME A STORY SHE'D NEVER SHARED BEFORE.

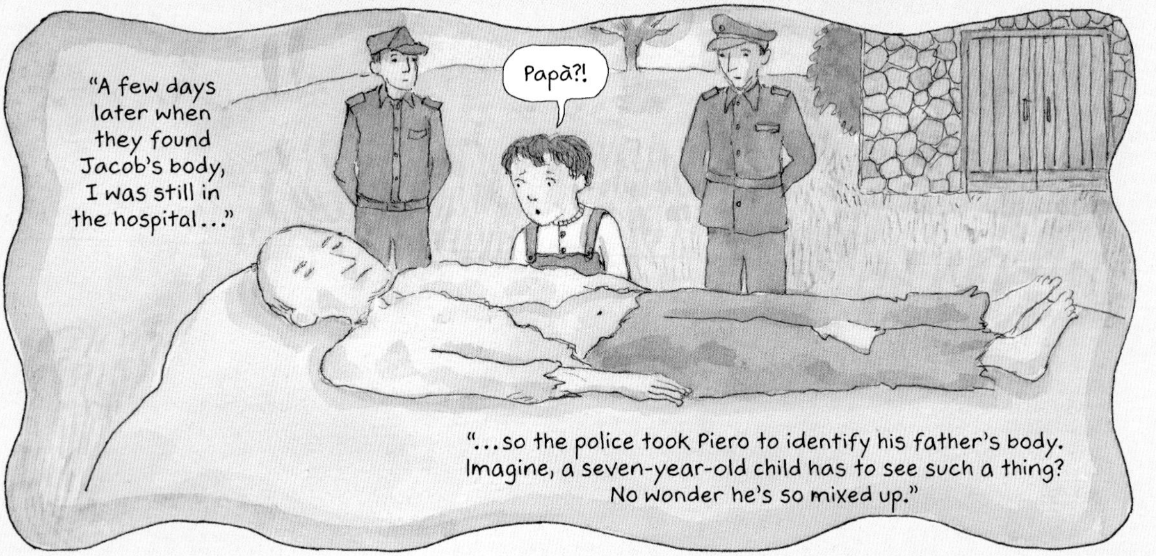
"A few days later when they found Jacob's body, I was still in the hospital..."
Papà?!
"...so the police took Piero to identify his father's body. Imagine, a seven-year-old child has to see such a thing? No wonder he's so mixed up."

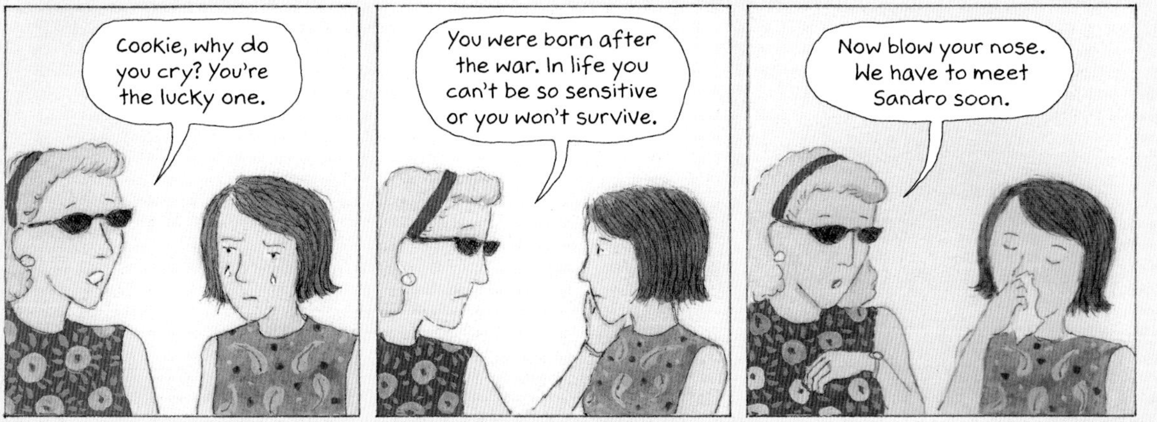
Cookie, why do you cry? You're the lucky one.
You were born after the war. In life you can't be so sensitive or you won't survive.
Now blow your nose. We have to meet Sandro soon.

I KNEW I WAS LETTING MAMMA DOWN WITH MY TEARS. MAYBE IF I'D GONE THROUGH THE WAR LIKE MY BROTHERS I WOULD BE STRONGER. OR MAYBE NOT.

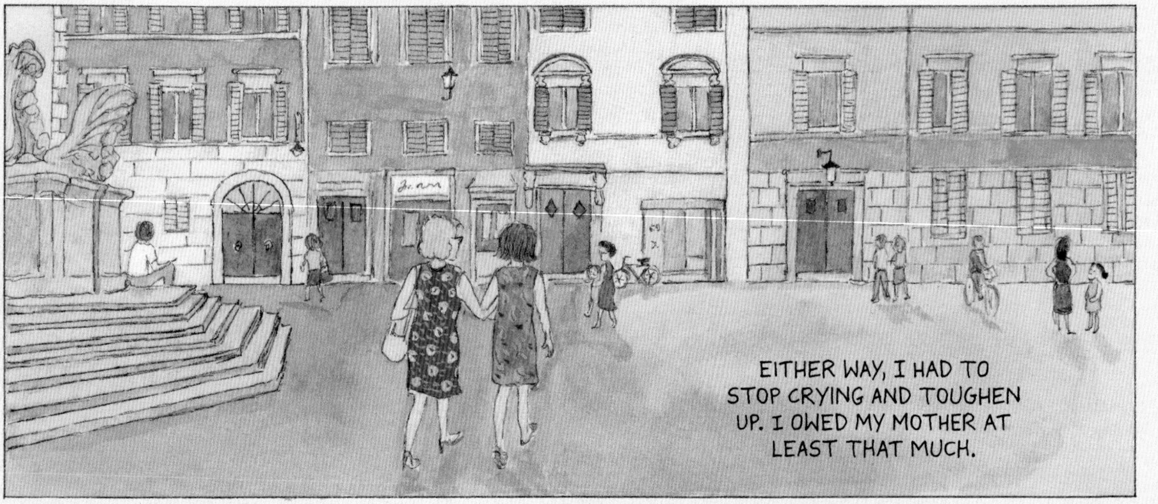
EITHER WAY, I HAD TO STOP CRYING AND TOUGHEN UP. I OWED MY MOTHER AT LEAST THAT MUCH.

TWENTY

And That's the Way It Is

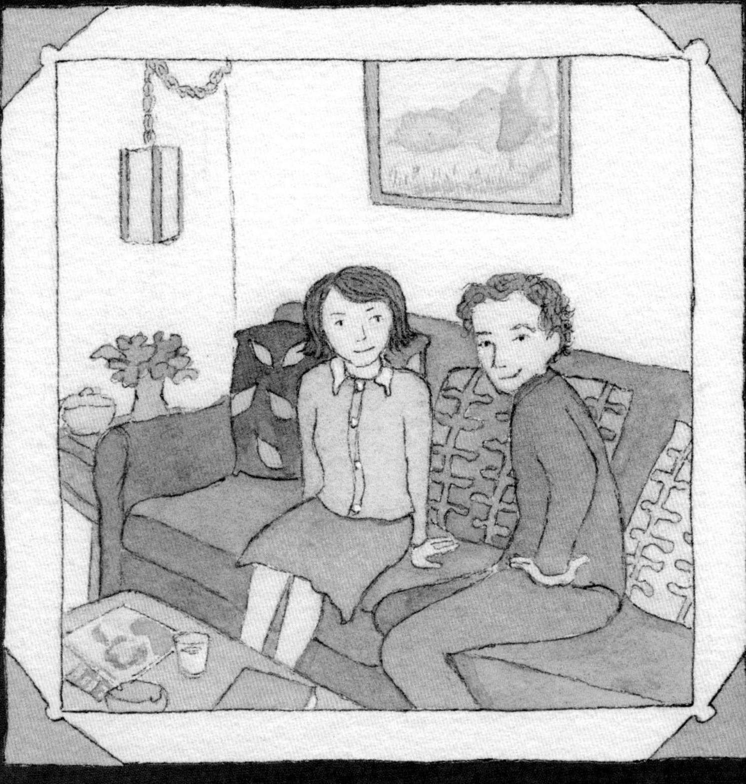

1965

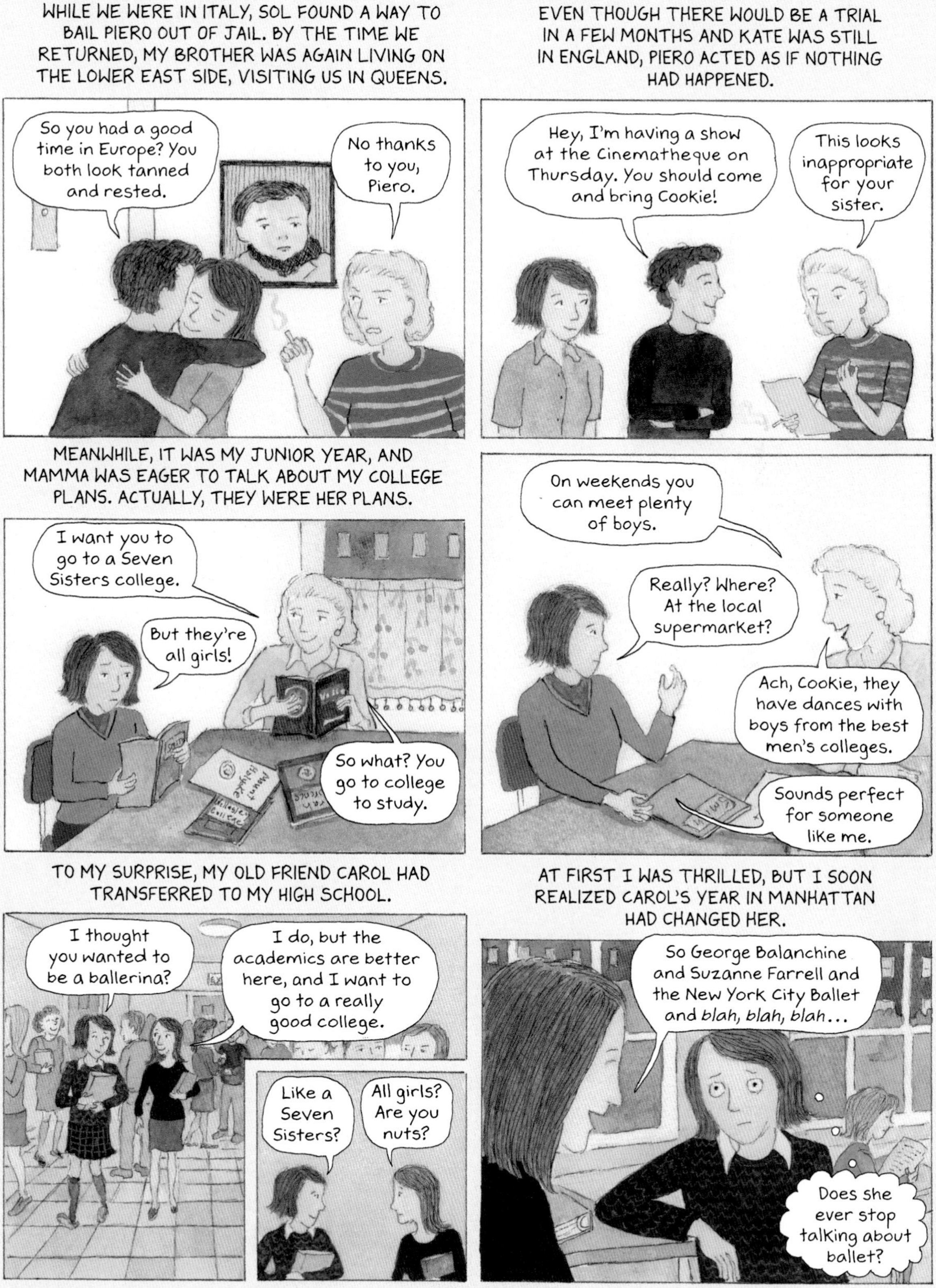
WHILE WE WERE IN ITALY, SOL FOUND A WAY TO BAIL PIERO OUT OF JAIL. BY THE TIME WE RETURNED, MY BROTHER WAS AGAIN LIVING ON THE LOWER EAST SIDE, VISITING US IN QUEENS.
So you had a good time in Europe? You both look tanned and rested.
No thanks to you, Piero.
EVEN THOUGH THERE WOULD BE A TRIAL IN A FEW MONTHS AND KATE WAS STILL IN ENGLAND, PIERO ACTED AS IF NOTHING HAD HAPPENED.
Hey, I'm having a show at the Cinematheque on Thursday. You should come and bring Cookie!
This looks inappropriate for your sister.
MEANWHILE, IT WAS MY JUNIOR YEAR, AND MAMMA WAS EAGER TO TALK ABOUT MY COLLEGE PLANS. ACTUALLY, THEY WERE HER PLANS.
I want you to go to a Seven Sisters college.
But they're all girls!
So what? You go to college to study.
On weekends you can meet plenty of boys.
Really? Where? At the local supermarket?
Ach, Cookie, they have dances with boys from the best men's colleges.
Sounds perfect for someone like me.
TO MY SURPRISE, MY OLD FRIEND CAROL HAD TRANSFERRED TO MY HIGH SCHOOL.
I thought you wanted to be a ballerina?
I do, but the academics are better here, and I want to go to a really good college.
Like a Seven Sisters?
All girls? Are you nuts?
AT FIRST I WAS THRILLED, BUT I SOON REALIZED CAROL'S YEAR IN MANHATTAN HAD CHANGED HER.
So George Balanchine and Suzanne Farrell and the New York City Ballet and *blah, blah, blah*...
Does she ever stop talking about ballet?

BESIDES HER DANCE OBSESSION, CAROL WAS NOW AN EXPERT ON BOYS AND DATING.

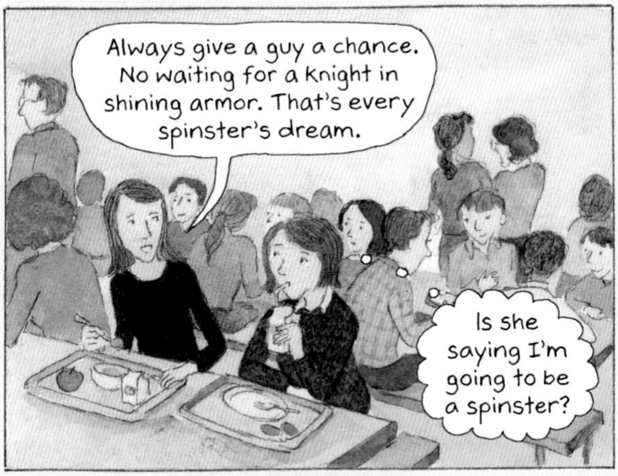
Always give a guy a chance. No waiting for a knight in shining armor. That's every spinster's dream.
Is she saying I'm going to be a spinster?

AS SOON AS I TOLD HER I LIKED A CERTAIN BOY, SHE WOULD START LIKING HIM, TOO.

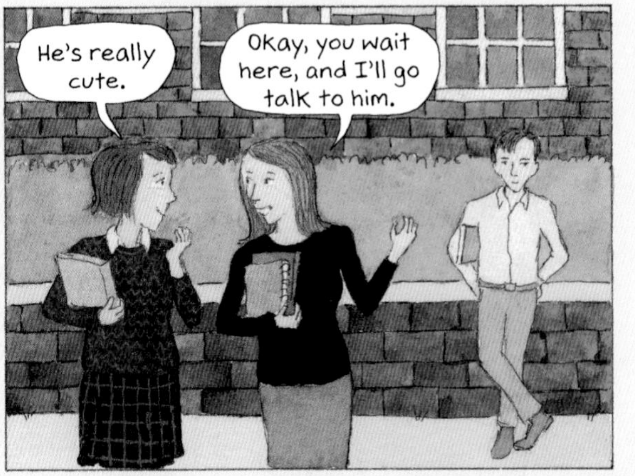
He's really cute.
Okay, you wait here, and I'll go talk to him.

WORST OF ALL, I COULD TELL MY OTHER FRIENDS DIDN'T LIKE HER.

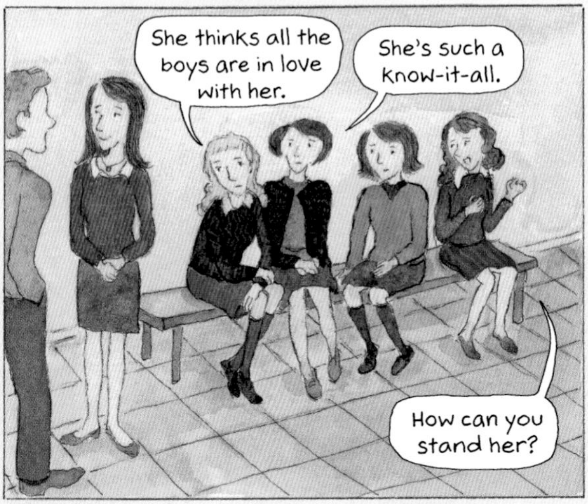
She thinks all the boys are in love with her.
She's such a know-it-all.
How can you stand her?

I MADE A CHOICE AND STARTED TO AVOID CAROL AS MUCH AS POSSIBLE.

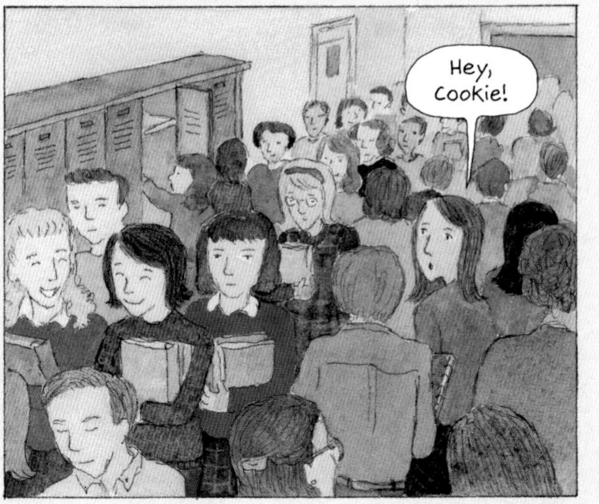
Hey, Cookie!

MEANWHILE, FLORENCE AND I GABBED ON THE PHONE EVERY NIGHT. I TRIED TO FIND SOME PRIVACY IN OUR SMALL APARTMENT.

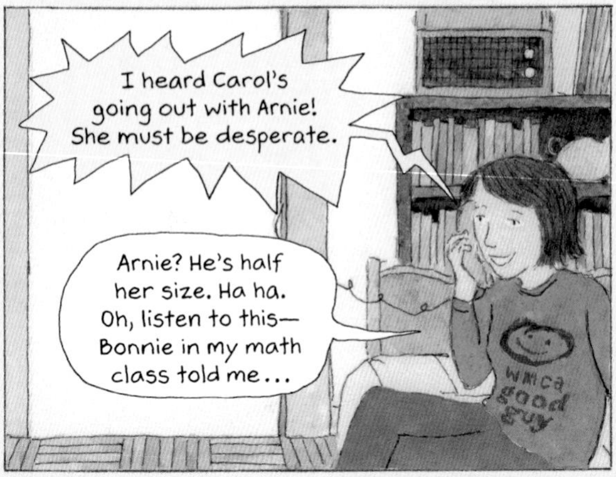
I heard Carol's going out with Arnie! She must be desperate.
Arnie? He's half her size. Ha ha. Oh, listen to this— Bonnie in my math class told me...
WMCA good guy

BUT MY SENSE OF PRIVACY WAS JUST AN ILLUSION.

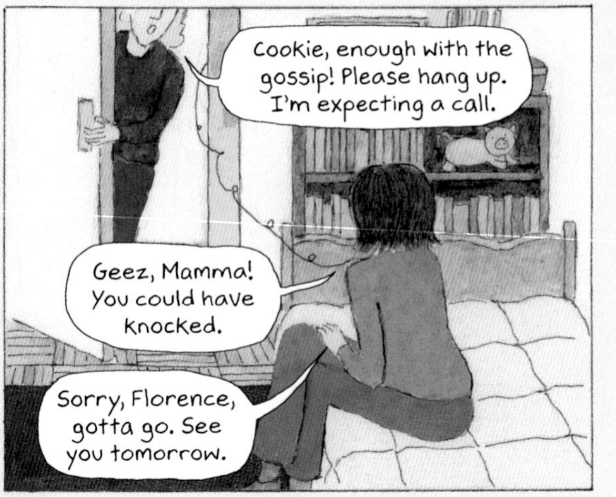
Cookie, enough with the gossip! Please hang up. I'm expecting a call.
Geez, Mamma! You could have knocked.
Sorry, Florence, gotta go. See you tomorrow.

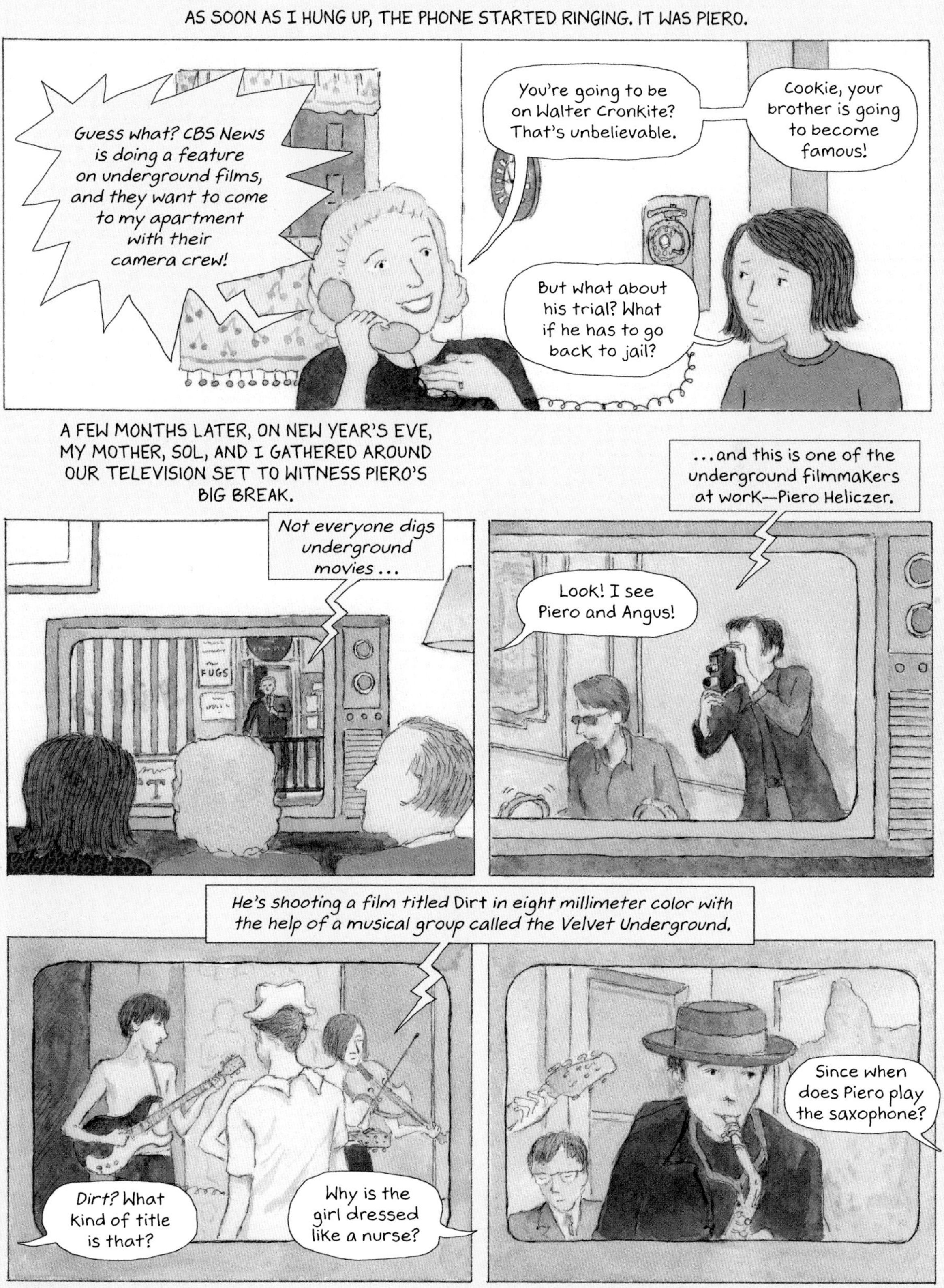
AS SOON AS I HUNG UP, THE PHONE STARTED RINGING. IT WAS PIERO.
Guess what? CBS News is doing a feature on underground films, and they want to come to my apartment with their camera crew!
You're going to be on Walter Cronkite? That's unbelievable.
Cookie, your brother is going to become famous!
But what about his trial? What if he has to go back to jail?
A FEW MONTHS LATER, ON NEW YEAR'S EVE, MY MOTHER, SOL, AND I GATHERED AROUND OUR TELEVISION SET TO WITNESS PIERO'S BIG BREAK.
Not everyone digs underground movies . . .
FUGS
. . . and this is one of the underground filmmakers at work—Piero Heliczer.
Look! I see Piero and Angus!
He's shooting a film titled Dirt in eight millimeter color with the help of a musical group called the Velvet Underground.
Dirt? What kind of title is that?
Why is the girl dressed like a nurse?
Since when does Piero play the saxophone?

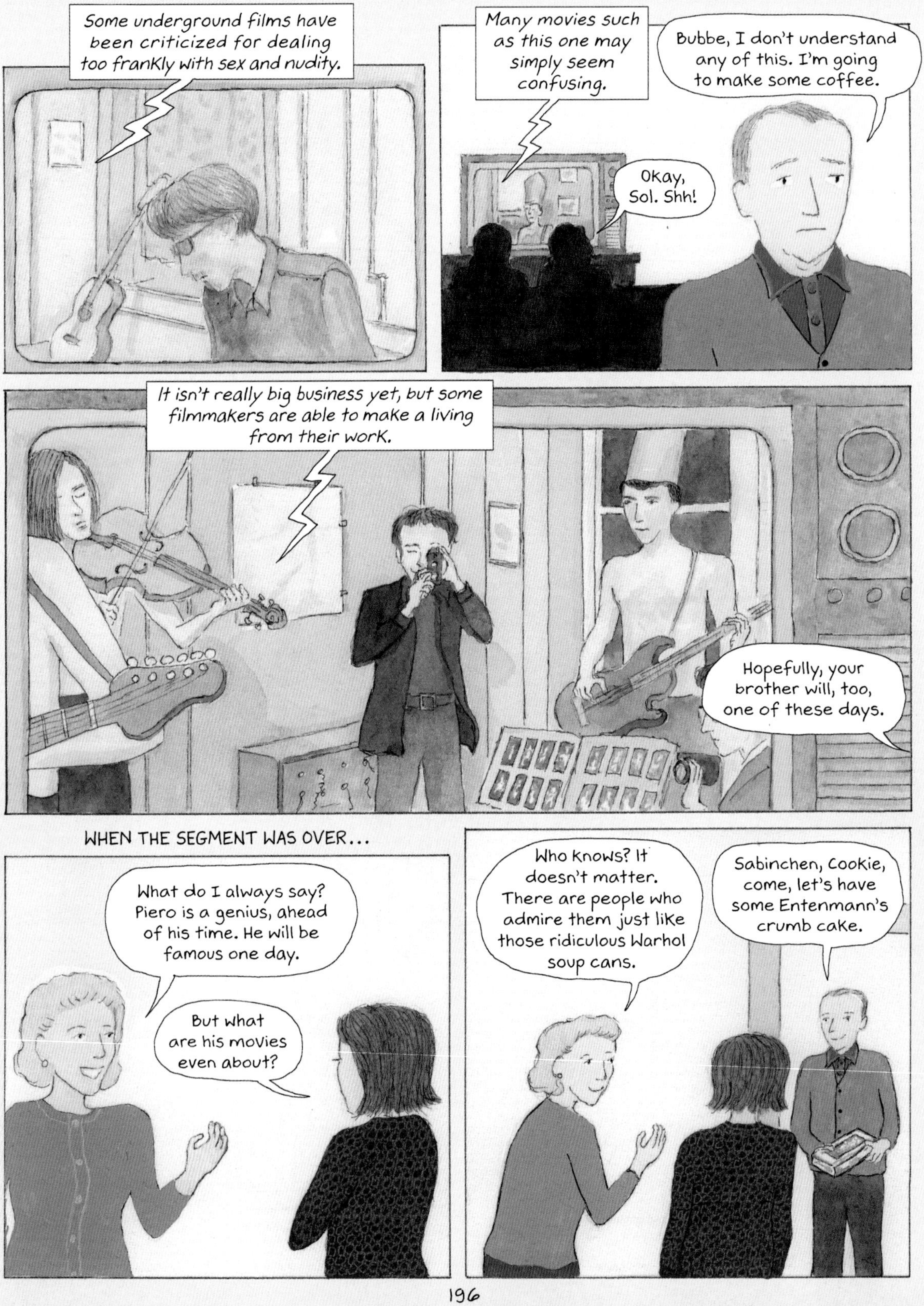
Some underground films have been criticized for dealing too frankly with sex and nudity.
Many movies such as this one may simply seem confusing.
Bubbe, I don't understand any of this. I'm going to make some coffee.
Okay, Sol. Shh!
It isn't really big business yet, but some filmmakers are able to make a living from their work.
Hopefully, your brother will, too, one of these days.
WHEN THE SEGMENT WAS OVER...
What do I always say? Piero is a genius, ahead of his time. He will be famous one day.
But what are his movies even about?
Who knows? It doesn't matter. There are people who admire them just like those ridiculous Warhol soup cans.
Sabinchen, Cookie, come, let's have some Entenmann's crumb cake.

AS I SAT DOWN AT THE KITCHEN TABLE, I HAD THE DISTINCT FEELING I WAS MISSING OUT ON SOMETHING.

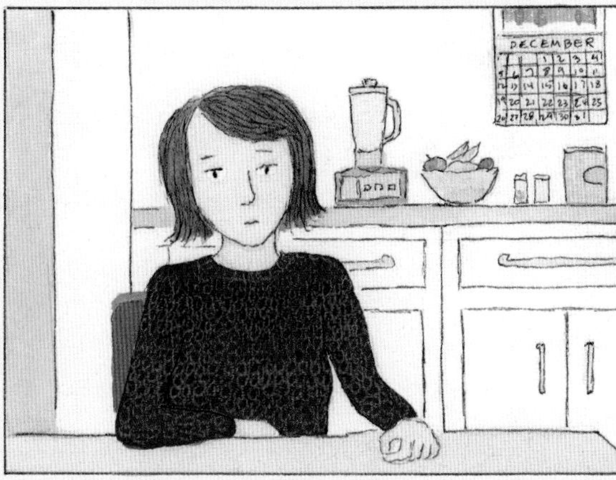
DECEMBER

IT WAS NEW YEAR'S EVE. MY BROTHER WAS ON THE NEWS MAKING STRANGE UNDERGROUND MOVIES. MAMMA AND SOL WERE READY FOR THEIR NIGHTLY KAFFEE UND KUCHEN.

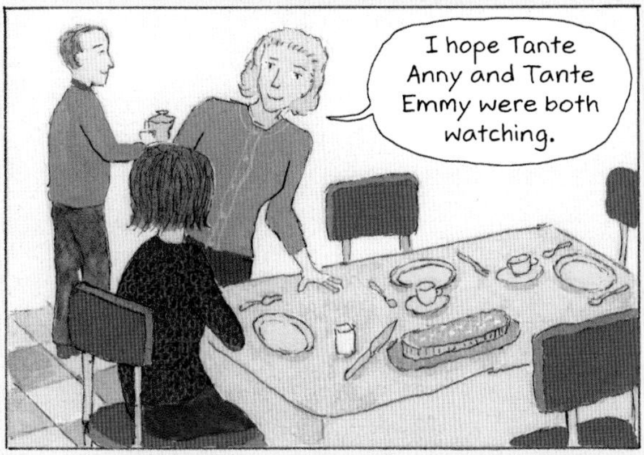
I hope Tante Anny and Tante Emmy were both watching.

BUT WHAT ABOUT ME? I WAS FIFTEEN. WASN'T I SUPPOSED TO BE AT A PARTY LIKE A NORMAL AMERICAN TEENAGER?

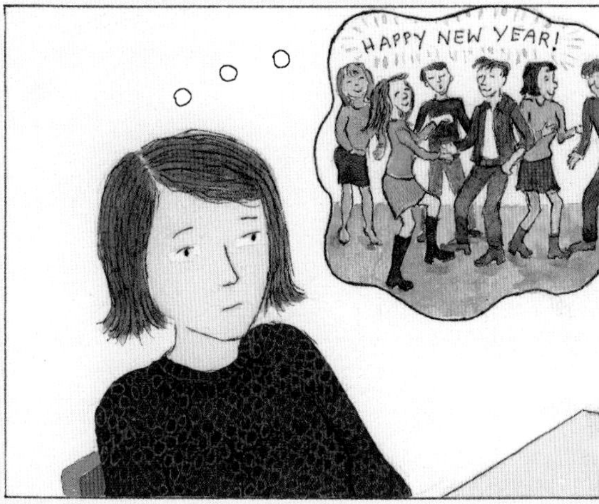
HAPPY NEW YEAR!

THE CBS REPORTER HAD CALLED PIERO'S FILM "SIMPLY CONFUSING." THAT WAS A PRETTY GOOD DESCRIPTION OF MY LIFE.

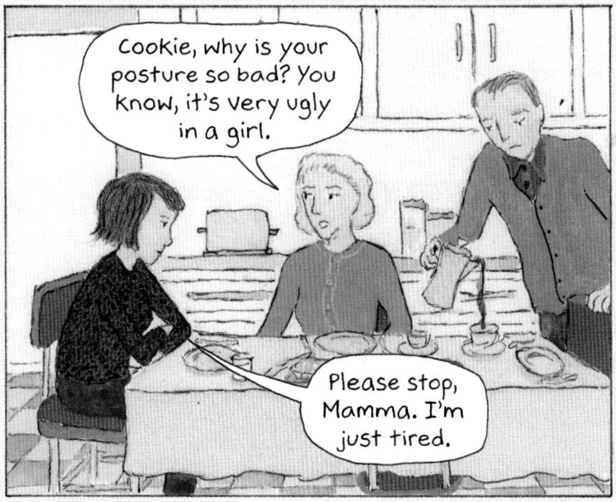
Cookie, why is your posture so bad? You know, it's very ugly in a girl.
Please stop, Mamma. I'm just tired.

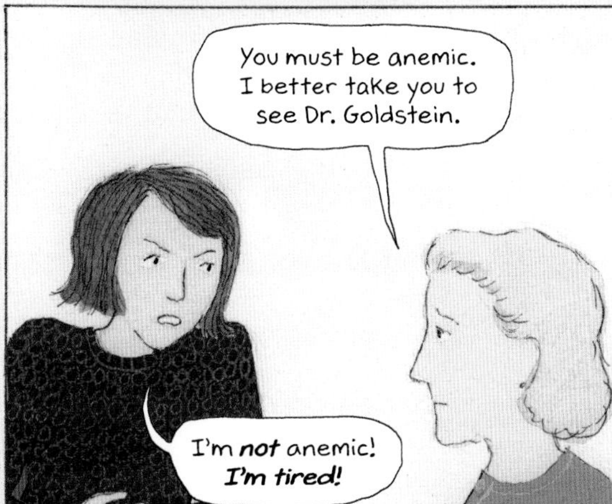
You must be anemic. I better take you to see Dr. Goldstein.
I'm ***not*** anemic! ***I'm tired!***

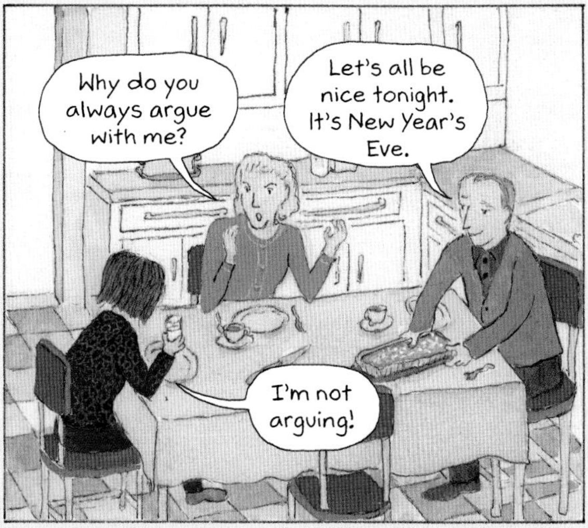
Why do you always argue with me?
Let's all be nice tonight. It's New Year's Eve.
I'm not arguing!

HOW WAS ANY OF THIS FAIR? PIERO DID WHAT HE WANTED AND MAMMA WAS MOSTLY OKAY WITH IT, BECAUSE AFTER ALL, HE WAS A GENIUS, STILL AFFECTED BY WHAT HAD HAPPENED DURING THE WAR.

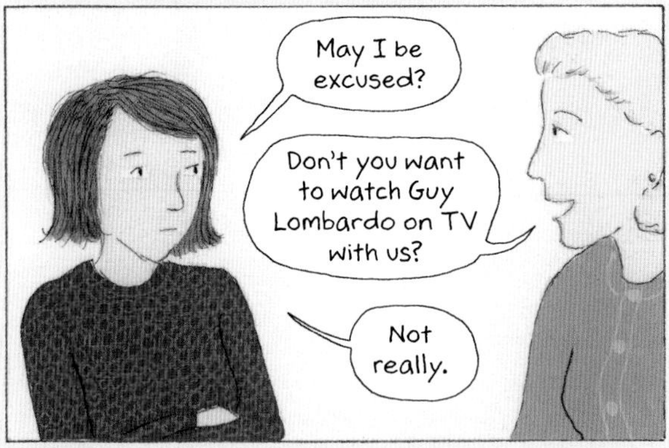
May I be excused?
Don't you want to watch Guy Lombardo on TV with us?
Not really.

MEANWHILE, I WAS EXPECTED TO OBEY AND SUCCEED BECAUSE I WAS THE LUCKY ONE BORN IN AMERICA.

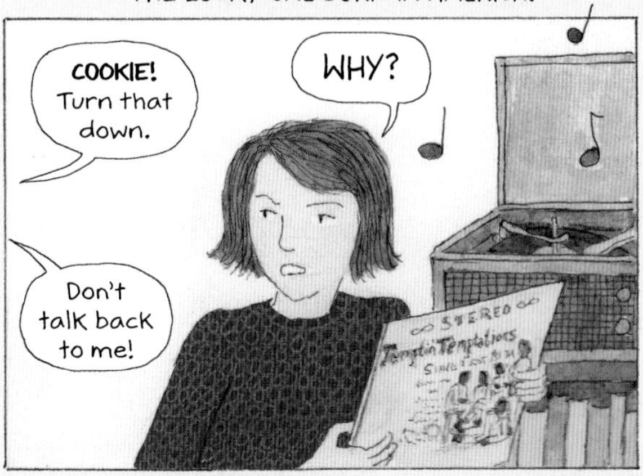
COOKIE! Turn that down.
WHY?
Don't talk back to me!
STEREO

MAYBE MY MOTHER HAD ONCE BEEN DIFFERENT? BEFORE THE WAR? BEFORE MY FATHER LEFT HER? BEFORE I WAS BORN? I WOULD PROBABLY NEVER KNOW, BUT DID IT REALLY MATTER?

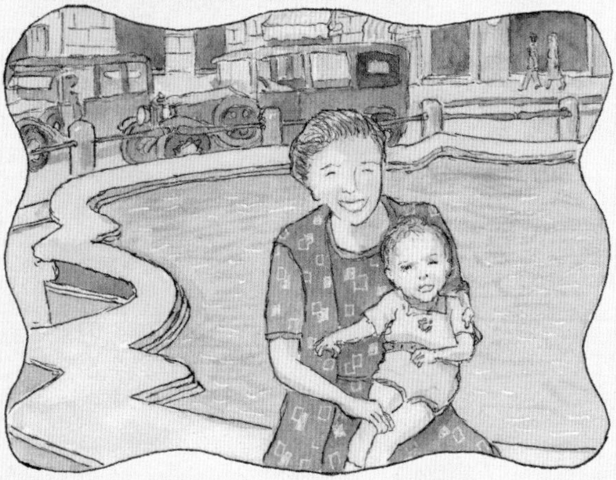

MY GOALS WERE SET: FINISH HIGH SCHOOL, ESCAPE TO COLLEGE, AND THEN KEEP GOING ON A PATH AWAY FROM THIS APARTMENT AND MAMMA'S OLD-WORLD RULES.

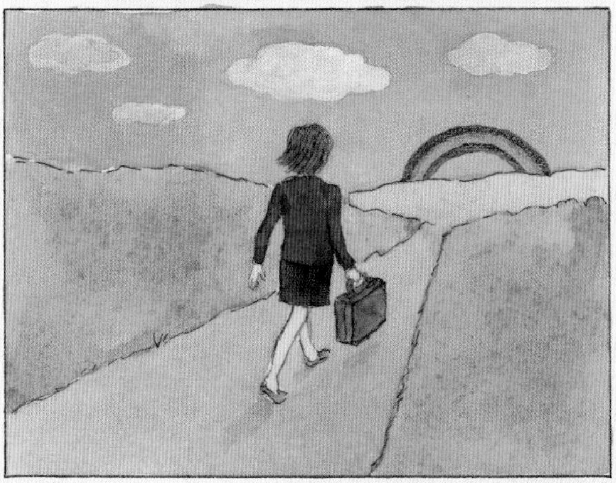

BUT THAT WAS ALL IN THE FUTURE. FOR NOW I'D LISTEN TO MY RECORDS, DRAW WITH THE PASTELS PIERO HAD GIVEN ME FOR CHRISTMAS, AND DAYDREAM ABOUT TOMORROW, THE FIRST DAY OF 1966.

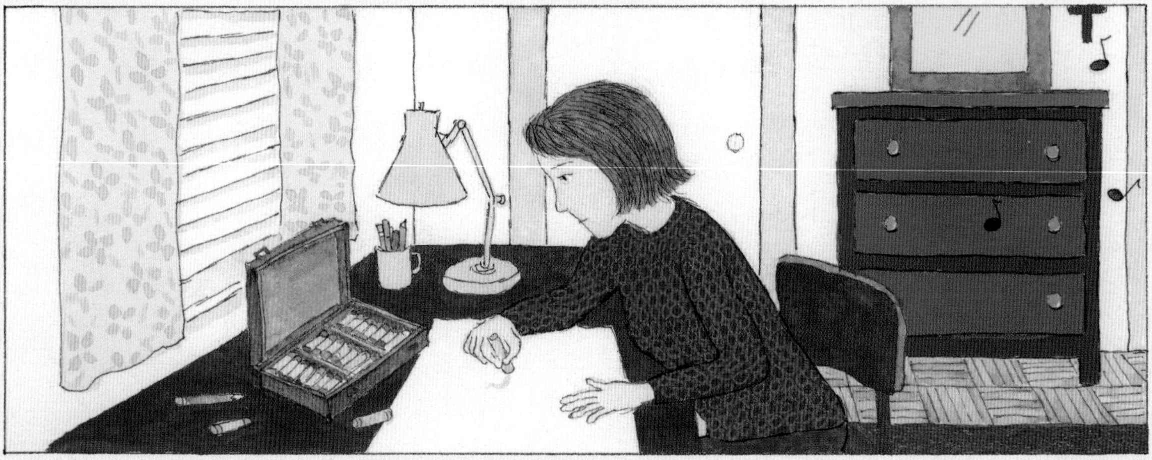

TWENTY-ONE

Maybe Dating Isn't All It's Cracked Up to Be

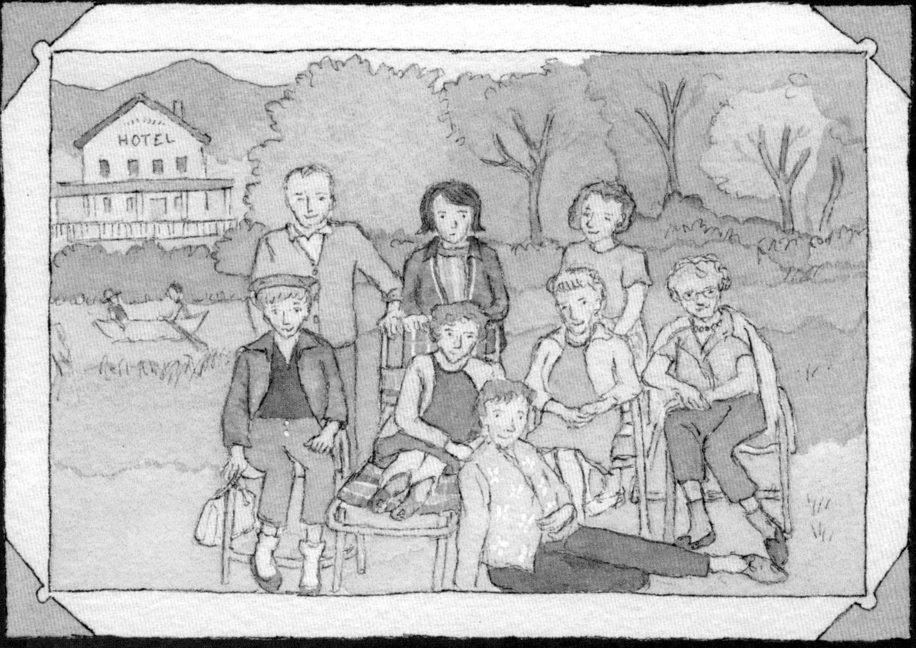
HOTEL

1966

IN THE SPRING, PIERO'S TRIAL BEGAN AND MY MOTHER GOT TIME OFF FROM WORK TO ATTEND. AT DINNER EACH NIGHT, SOL AND I RECEIVED A FULL REPORT.

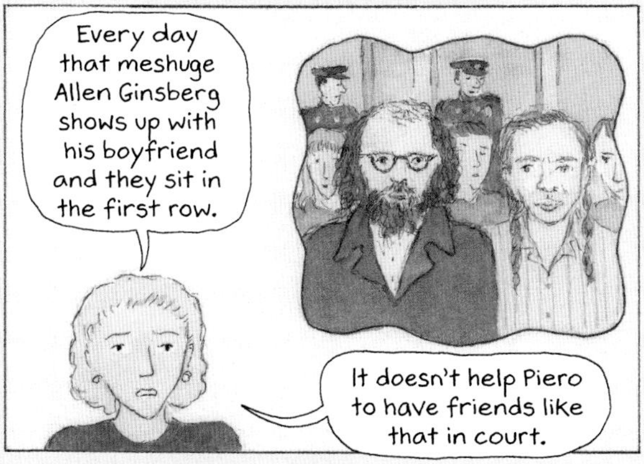
Every day that meshuge Allen Ginsberg shows up with his boyfriend and they sit in the first row.
It doesn't help Piero to have friends like that in court.

SOL HAD RECENTLY SUFFERED A MILD HEART ATTACK, SO ONCE AGAIN HE WASN'T WORKING. MAMMA MOVED SEAMLESSLY FROM BASHING ALLEN GINSBERG TO BASHING SOL.

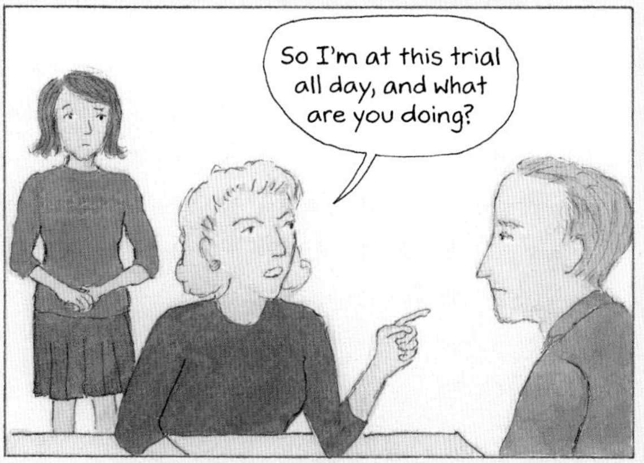
So I'm at this trial all day, and what are you doing?

IT SEEMED A BIT UNREASONABLE TO ME. AFTER SEVEN YEARS OF MARRIAGE, SOL SEEMED TO THINK SO, TOO.

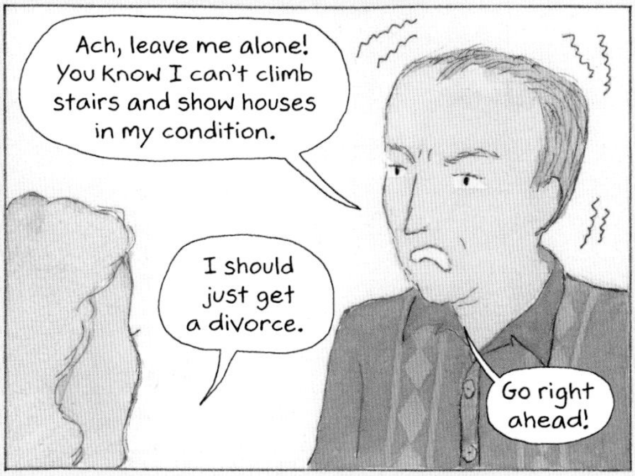
Ach, leave me alone! You know I can't climb stairs and show houses in my condition.
I should just get a divorce.
Go right ahead!

WHEN THE TRIAL FINALLY ENDED, PIERO WAS CONVICTED OF ASSAULT AND GOT TWO YEARS' PROBATION.

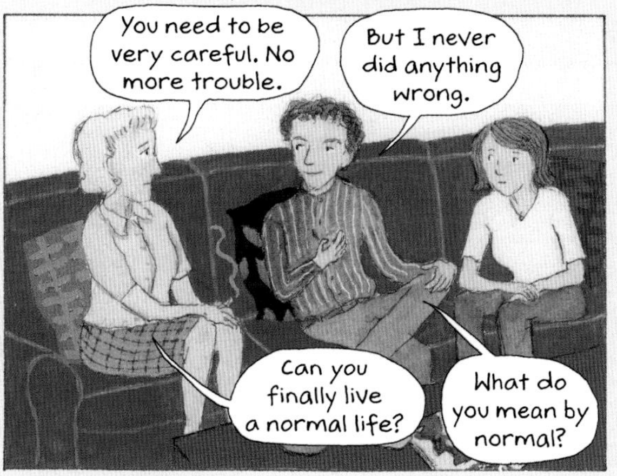
You need to be very careful. No more trouble.
But I never did anything wrong.
Can you finally live a normal life?
What do you mean by normal?

WHILE SOL CONTINUED TO RECOVER, MY MOTHER DECIDED TO TAKE DRIVING LESSONS ON SUNDAY MORNINGS WITH A LOCAL COLLEGE BOY.

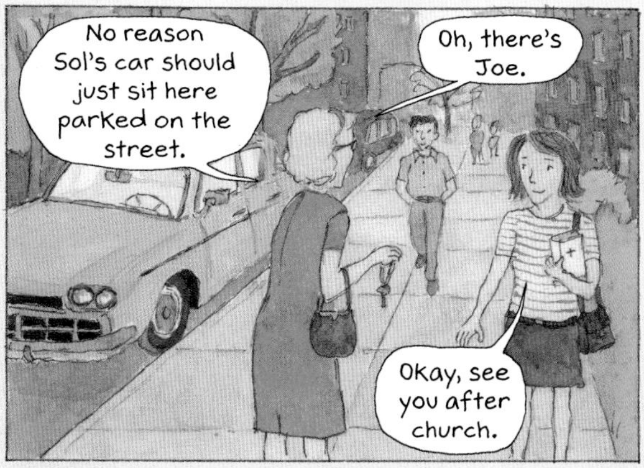
No reason Sol's car should just sit here parked on the street.
Oh, there's Joe.
Okay, see you after church.

SOL AND I BOTH FELT A LITTLE UNEASY, BUT SINCE SHE ALWAYS CAME HOME FROM HER LESSONS SMILING, WE HOPED FOR THE BEST.

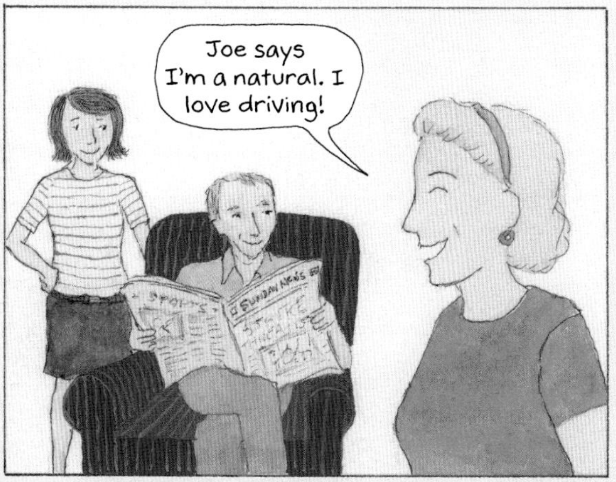
Joe says I'm a natural. I love driving!

AFTER FAILING MANY ROAD TESTS, MY MOTHER FINALLY GOT HER LICENSE. SOL AND I WERE LESS THRILLED THAN SHE WAS.

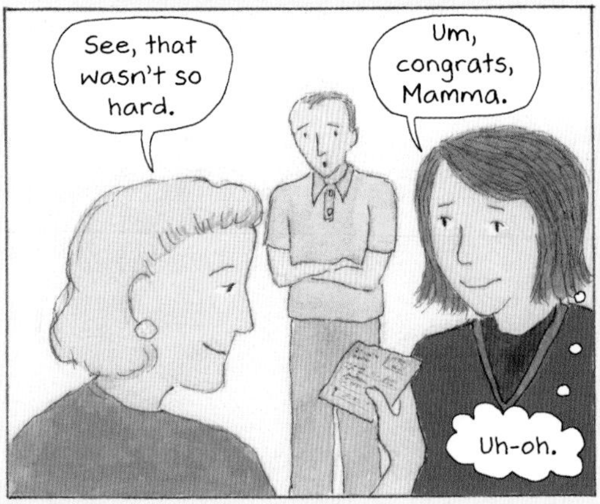
See, that wasn't so hard.
Um, congrats, Mamma.
Uh-oh.

A FEW WEEKS LATER, SHE WAS READY FOR A ROAD TRIP.

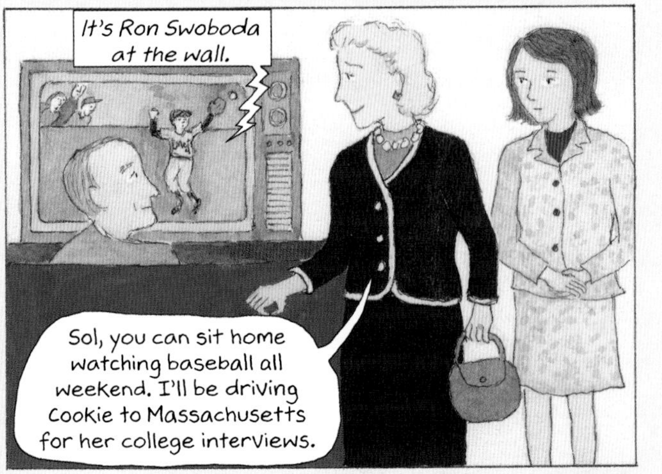
It's Ron Swoboda at the wall.
Sol, you can sit home watching baseball all weekend. I'll be driving Cookie to Massachusetts for her college interviews.

THREE HOURS ALONE IN THE CAR WITH MAMMA AT THE WHEEL? I DREADED EVERY MINUTE.

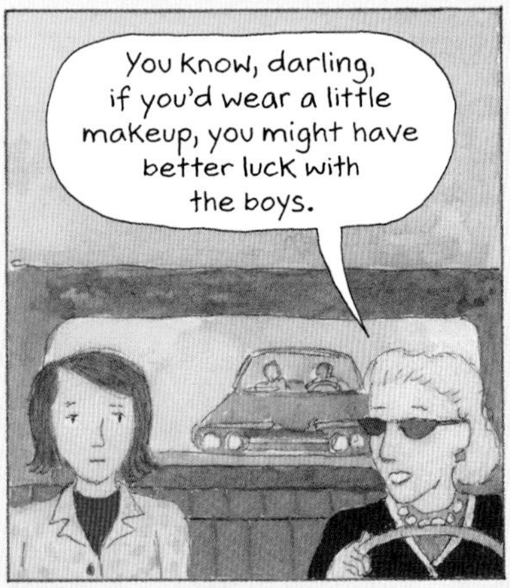
You know, darling, if you'd wear a little makeup, you might have better luck with the boys.

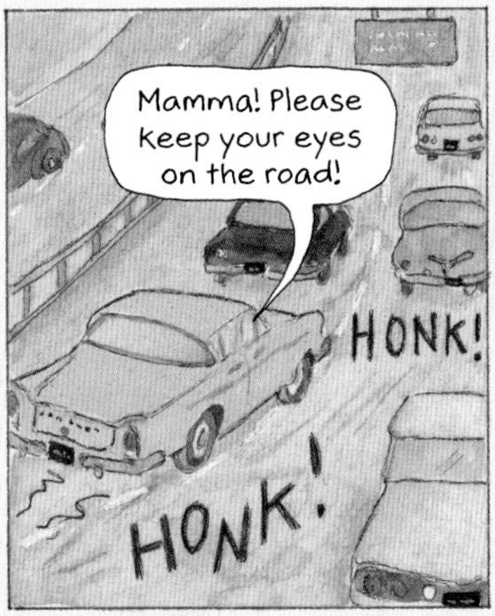
Mamma! Please keep your eyes on the road!
HONK!
HONK!

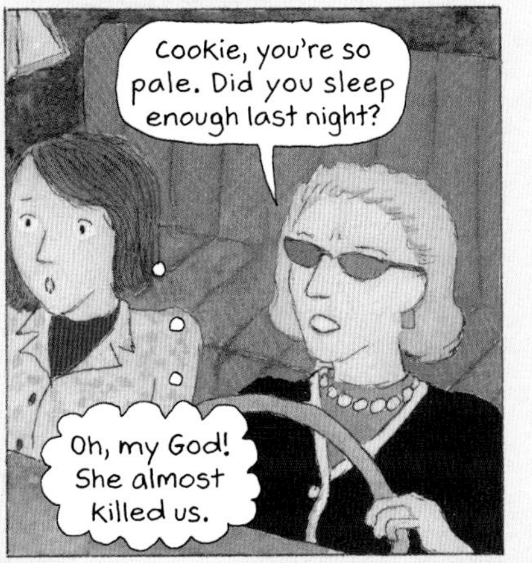
Cookie, you're so pale. Did you sleep enough last night?
Oh, my God! She almost killed us.

NOT A MINUTE TOO SOON, WE PULLED UP TO THE ADMISSIONS BUILDING AT THE FIRST CAMPUS.

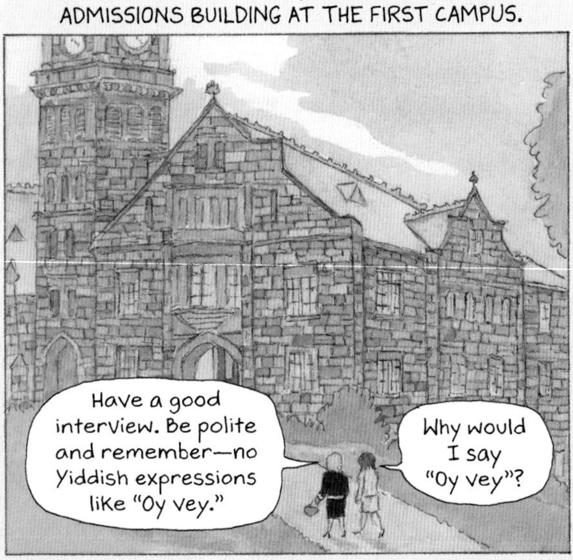
Have a good interview. Be polite and remember—no Yiddish expressions like "Oy vey."
Why would I say "Oy vey"?

I FELT INTIMIDATED BY THE PRIM AND PROPER WOMAN WHO INTERVIEWED ME.

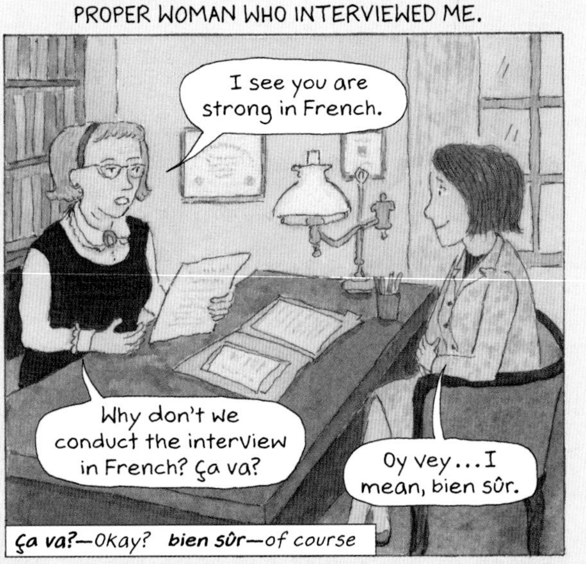
I see you are strong in French.
Why don't we conduct the interview in French? ça va?
Oy vey . . . I mean, bien sûr.

ça va?—*Okay?* ***bien sûr***—*of course*

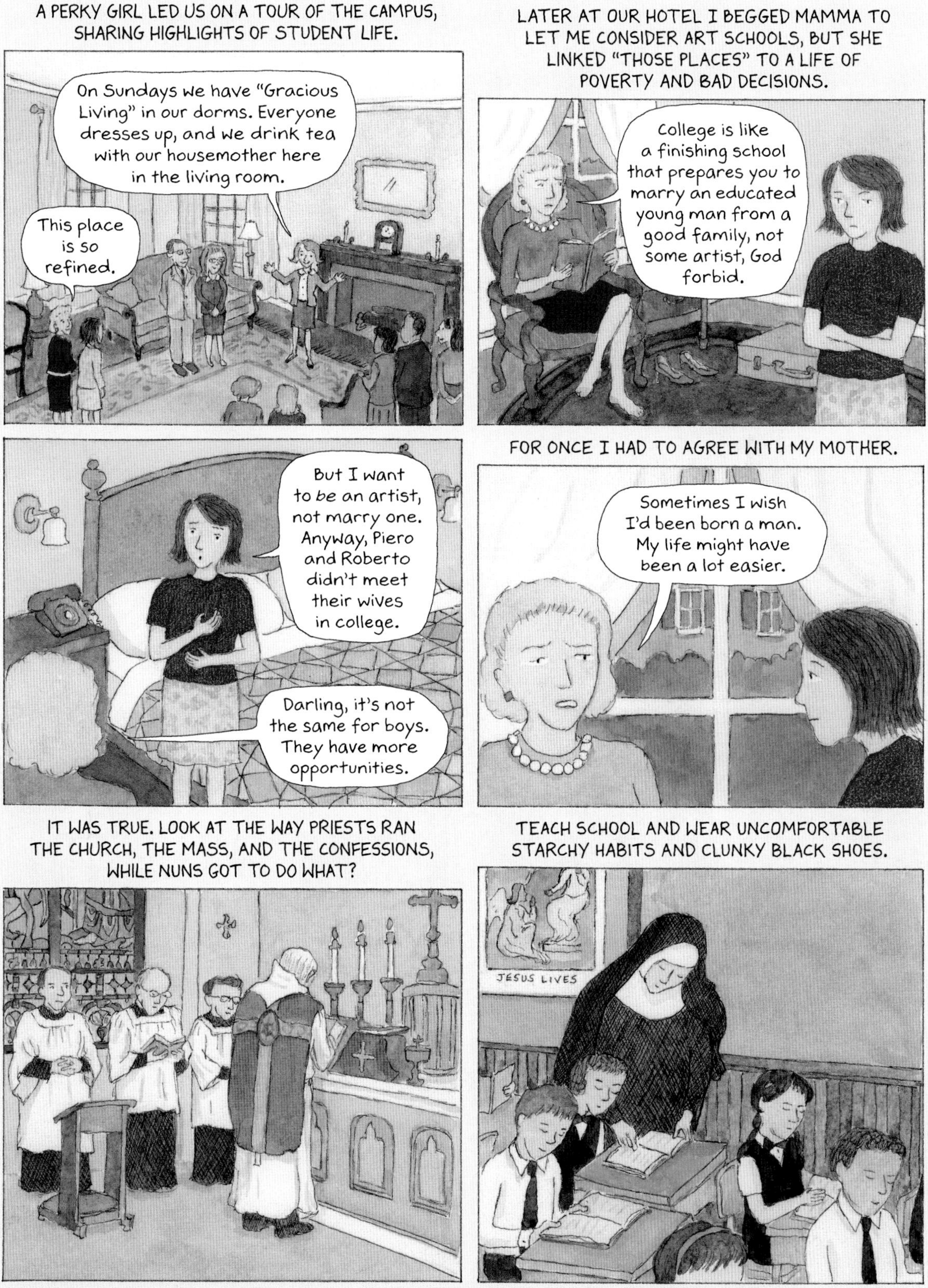
A PERKY GIRL LED US ON A TOUR OF THE CAMPUS, SHARING HIGHLIGHTS OF STUDENT LIFE.
On Sundays we have "Gracious Living" in our dorms. Everyone dresses up, and we drink tea with our housemother here in the living room.
This place is so refined.
LATER AT OUR HOTEL I BEGGED MAMMA TO LET ME CONSIDER ART SCHOOLS, BUT SHE LINKED "THOSE PLACES" TO A LIFE OF POVERTY AND BAD DECISIONS.
College is like a finishing school that prepares you to marry an educated young man from a good family, not some artist, God forbid.
But I want to *be* an artist, not marry one. Anyway, Piero and Roberto didn't meet their wives in college.
Darling, it's not the same for boys. They have more opportunities.
FOR ONCE I HAD TO AGREE WITH MY MOTHER.
Sometimes I wish I'd been born a man. My life might have been a lot easier.
IT WAS TRUE. LOOK AT THE WAY PRIESTS RAN THE CHURCH, THE MASS, AND THE CONFESSIONS, WHILE NUNS GOT TO DO WHAT?
TEACH SCHOOL AND WEAR UNCOMFORTABLE STARCHY HABITS AND CLUNKY BLACK SHOES.
JESUS LIVES

LOOK AT THE NEWSCASTERS ON TV, THE ASTRONAUTS, THE PRINCIPAL OF MY SCHOOL—ALL MEN WHO, LIKE MY TWO BROTHERS, SEEMED TO HAVE A LOT MORE CHOICES IN THEIR LIVES.

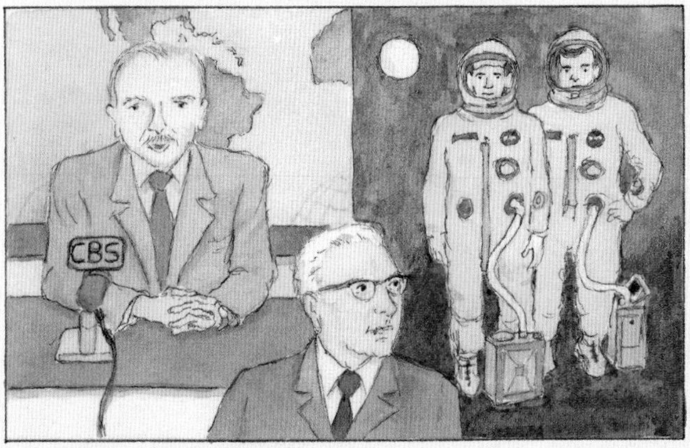
CBS

AND YET, DESPITE MY INCREASING RESENTMENT OF MALE PRIVILEGE, I STILL PINED FOR A BOYFRIEND TO HANG OUT WITH ON SATURDAY NIGHTS.

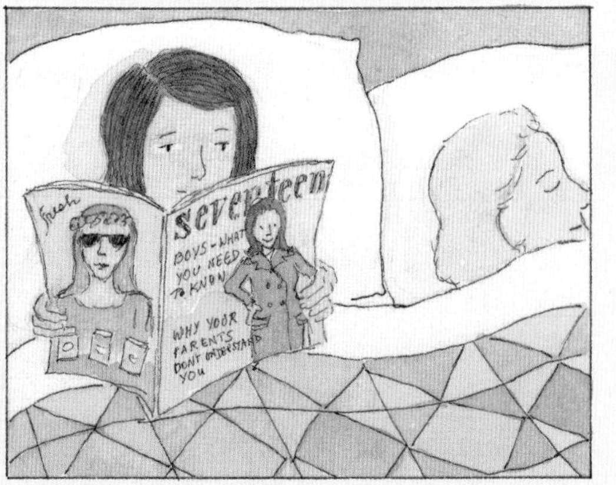
seventeen

MY SIXTEENTH BIRTHDAY WAS APPROACHING, AND THE CLOSEST I'D COME TO A REAL DATE WAS PLAYING PING-PONG WITH A YOUNG POLISH DISHWASHER ONE WEEKEND DURING A FAMILY TRIP TO THE CATSKILLS.

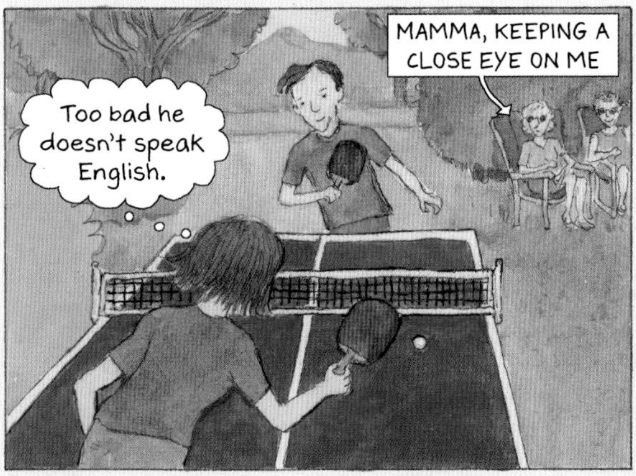
MAMMA, KEEPING A CLOSE EYE ON ME
Too bad he doesn't speak English.

JUST AS I'D ONCE TRIED TO USE ROBERTO'S BRUSH WITH THE BEATLES TO ENHANCE MY SOCIAL STANDING, I NOW DECIDED TO ENLIST PIERO'S HELP.

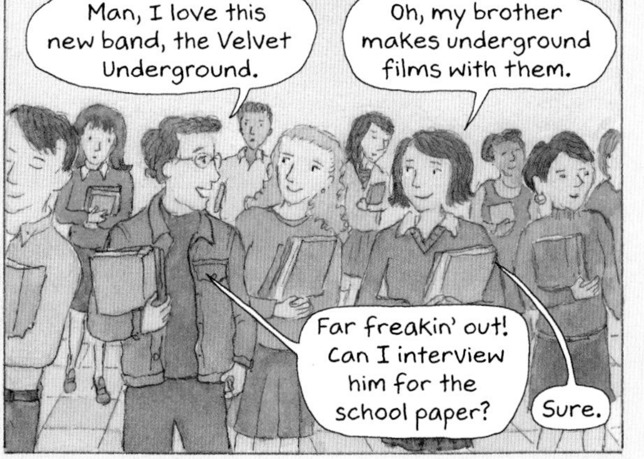
Man, I love this new band, the Velvet Underground.
Oh, my brother makes underground films with them.
Far freakin' out! Can I interview him for the school paper?
Sure.

UNFORTUNATELY, THIS STRATEGY ENDED UP COSTING ME MONEY AND WASTED TIME.

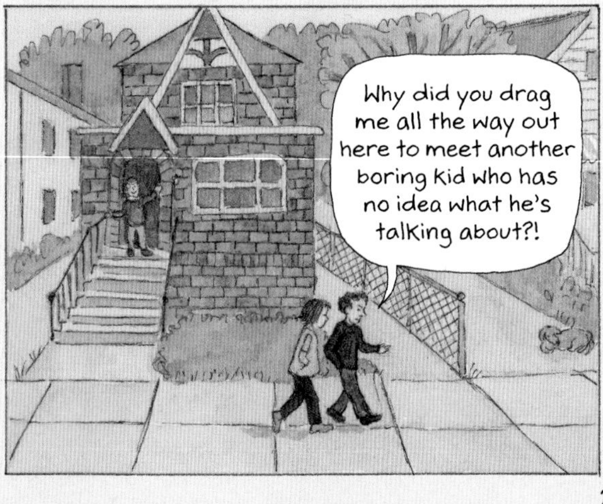
Why did you drag me all the way out here to meet another boring kid who has no idea what he's talking about?!

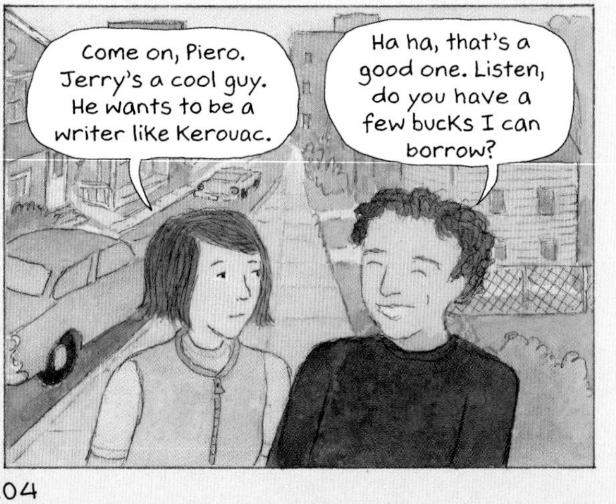
Come on, Piero. Jerry's a cool guy. He wants to be a writer like Kerouac.
Ha ha, that's a good one. Listen, do you have a few bucks I can borrow?

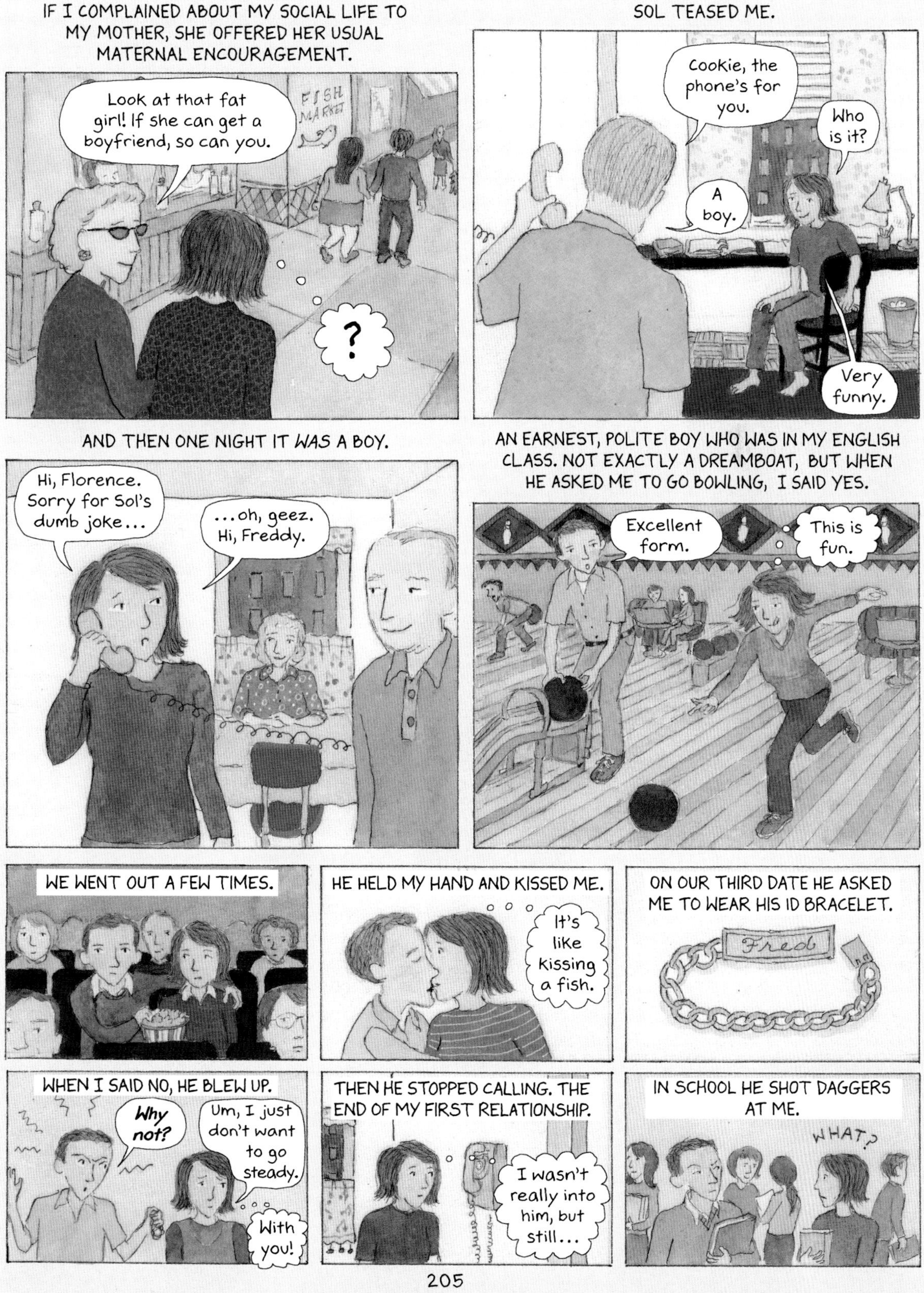
IF I COMPLAINED ABOUT MY SOCIAL LIFE TO MY MOTHER, SHE OFFERED HER USUAL MATERNAL ENCOURAGEMENT.
Look at that fat girl! If she can get a boyfriend, so can you.
FISH MARKET
?
SOL TEASED ME.
Cookie, the phone's for you.
Who is it?
A boy.
Very funny.
AND THEN ONE NIGHT IT *WAS* A BOY.
Hi, Florence. Sorry for Sol's dumb joke...
...oh, geez. Hi, Freddy.
AN EARNEST, POLITE BOY WHO WAS IN MY ENGLISH CLASS. NOT EXACTLY A DREAMBOAT, BUT WHEN HE ASKED ME TO GO BOWLING, I SAID YES.
Excellent form.
This is fun.
WE WENT OUT A FEW TIMES.
HE HELD MY HAND AND KISSED ME.
It's like kissing a fish.
ON OUR THIRD DATE HE ASKED ME TO WEAR HIS ID BRACELET.
Fred
WHEN I SAID NO, HE BLEW UP.
Why not?
Um, I just don't want to go steady.
With you!
THEN HE STOPPED CALLING. THE END OF MY FIRST RELATIONSHIP.
I wasn't really into him, but still...
IN SCHOOL HE SHOT DAGGERS AT ME.
WHAT?

MAYBE DATING WASN'T ALL IT WAS CRACKED UP TO BE.

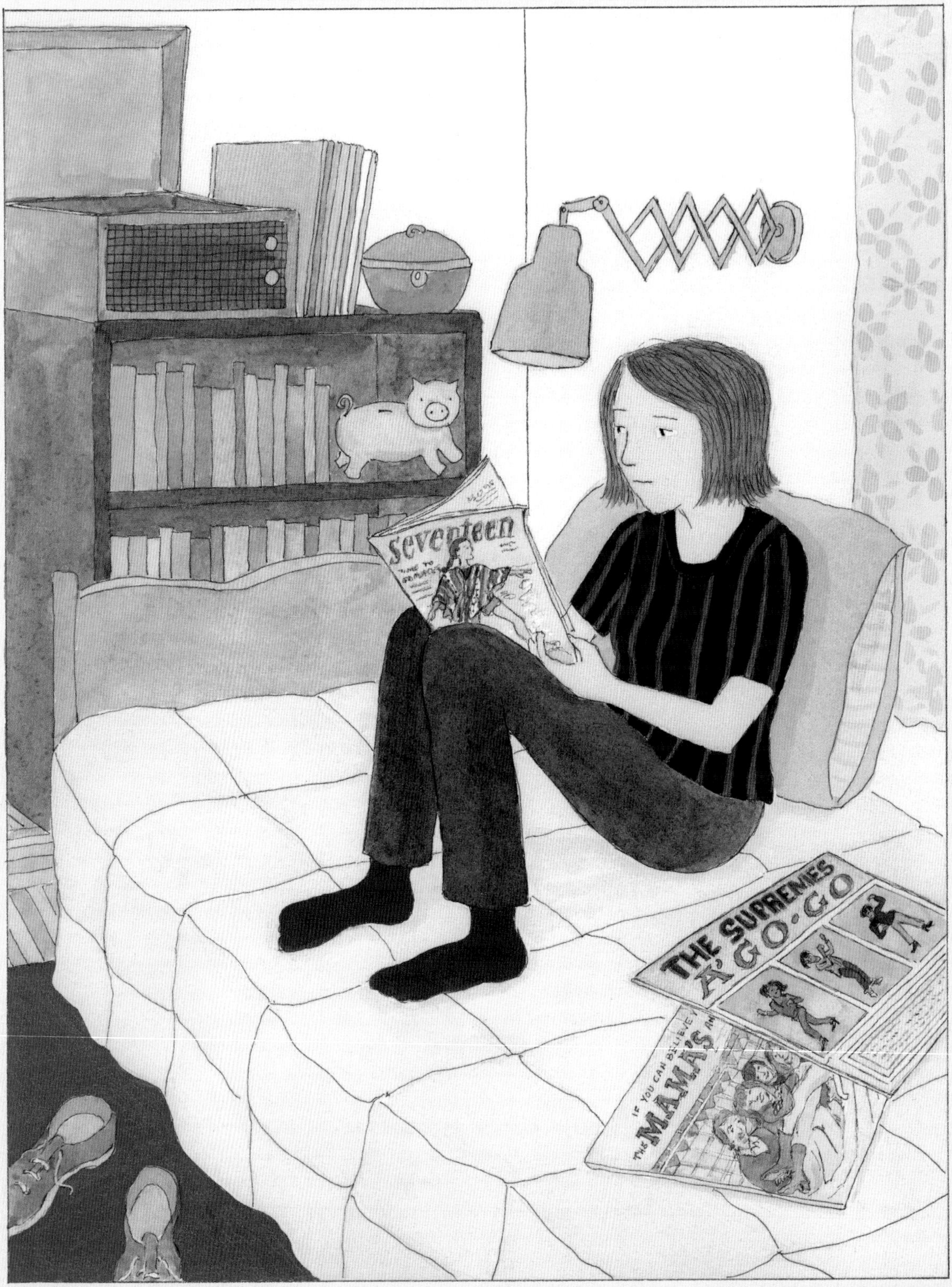
Seventeen
THE SUPREMES
A'GO-GO
IF YOU CAN BELIEVE
THE MAMA'S

TWENTY-TWO

Surprise Party

1966-67

THE FALL OF SENIOR YEAR, I MET WITH MY COLLEGE ADVISER, AN ELDERLY MAN IN A BOW TIE WHO CONSIDERED HIMSELF AN EXPERT ON THE IVIES AND SEVEN SISTERS.

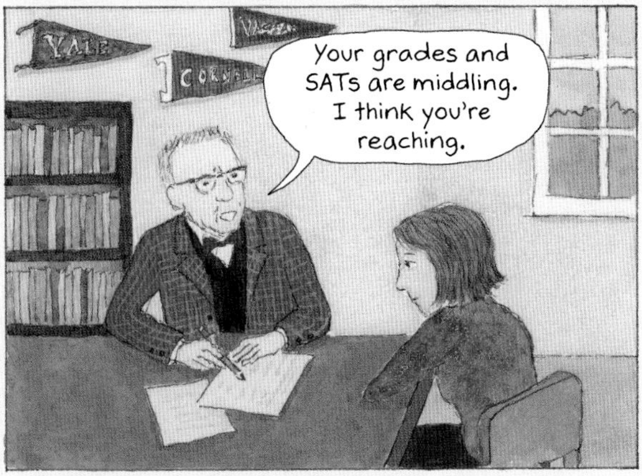
YALE
Your grades and SATs are middling. I think you're reaching.

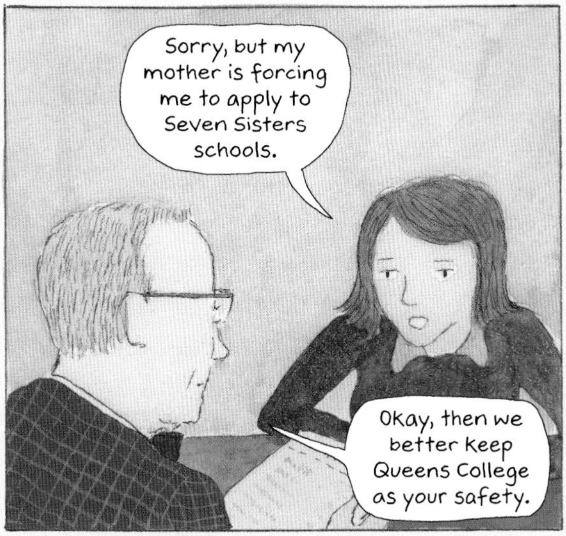
Sorry, but my mother is forcing me to apply to Seven Sisters schools.
Okay, then we better keep Queens College as your safety.

ONCE ALL THE APPLICATIONS WERE MAILED AND FINANCIAL AID APPLIED FOR, THERE WAS NOTHING TO DO BUT WAIT. AND WAIT.

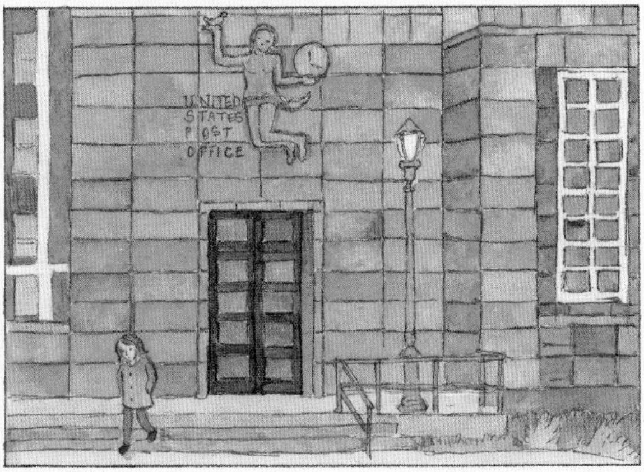
UNITED STATES POST OFFICE

MY MOTHER HAD STOPPED GOING TO CHURCH EXCEPT ON HOLIDAYS BECAUSE THERE WAS A NEW PRIEST FROM THE PHILIPPINES AND SHE COMPLAINED SHE COULDN'T UNDERSTAND A WORD HE SAID IN LATIN OR ENGLISH.

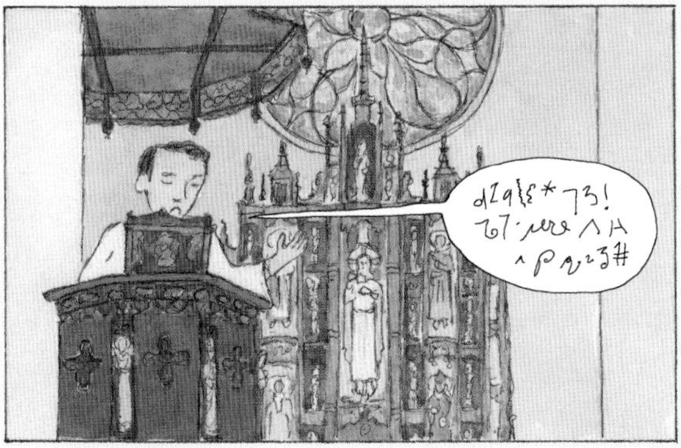

NEITHER COULD I, BUT I LET HIS VOICE BECOME THE WHITE NOISE TO MY SWIRLING THOUGHTS. I PRETENDED TO FOLLOW THE MASS WHILE LOST IN THE FUTURE AND MY PRIVATE PRAYERS.

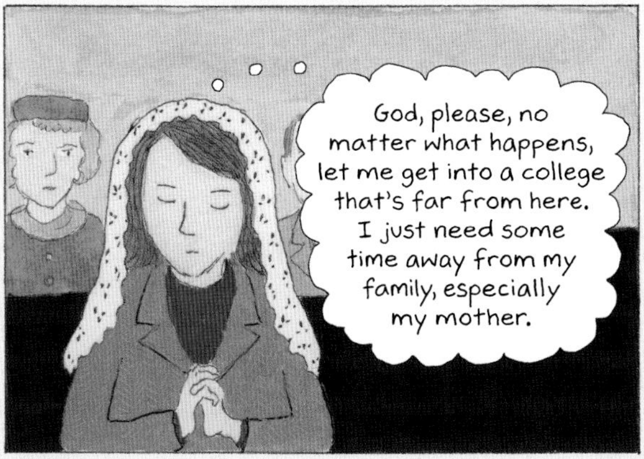
God, please, no matter what happens, let me get into a college that's far from here. I just need some time away from my family, especially my mother.

EVEN THOUGH SOL WAS WORKING AGAIN, THE NIGHTLY ARGUMENTS STARTED TO ESCALATE.

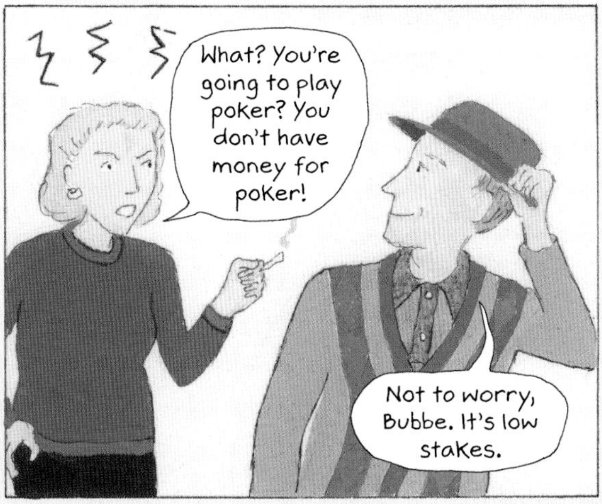
What? You're going to play poker? You don't have money for poker!
Not to worry, Bubbe. It's low stakes.

AT TIMES IT SOUNDED LIKE MAMMA AND SOL WERE FINALLY ON THE VERGE OF DIVORCE.

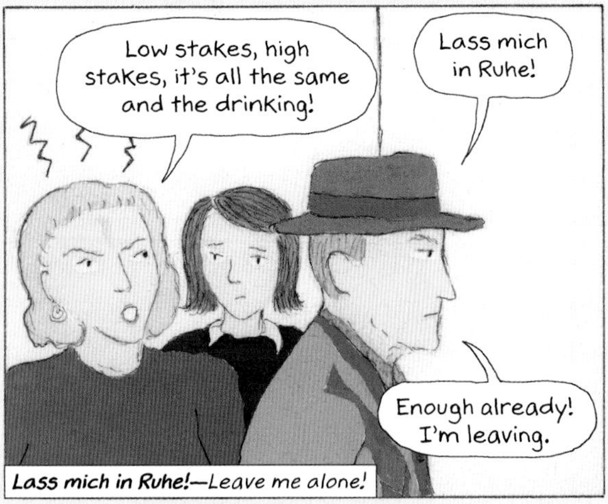
Low stakes, high stakes, it's all the same and the drinking!
Lass mich in Ruhe!
Enough already! I'm leaving.
Lass mich in Ruhe!—Leave me alone!

SOME WEEKENDS WE DROVE OUT TO VISIT ROBERTO AND HIS FAMILY ON LONG ISLAND. I HAD FUN PLAYING WITH MY NIECES.

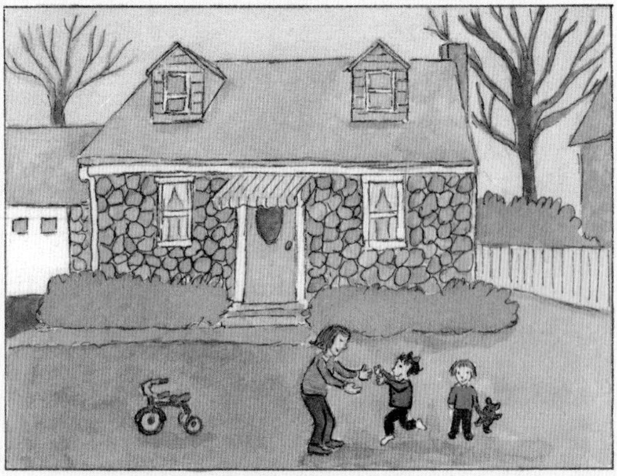

BUT MY MOTHER'S TEMPER WOULD RUIN EVERYTHING.

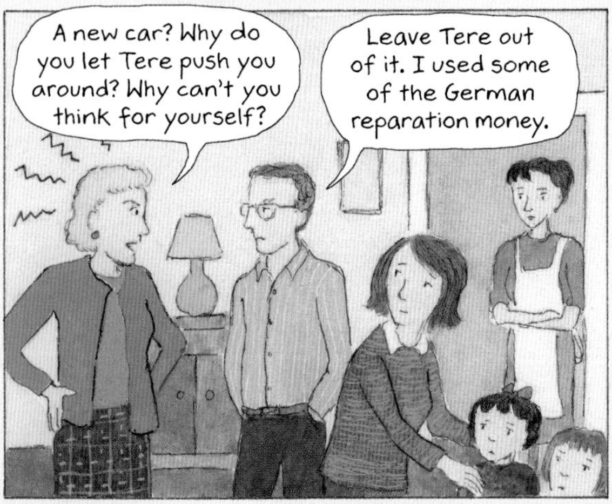
A new car? Why do you let Tere push you around? Why can't you think for yourself?
Leave Tere out of it. I used some of the German reparation money.

ON OTHER WEEKENDS, THERE WERE THE USUAL CONFRONTATIONS WITH PIERO.

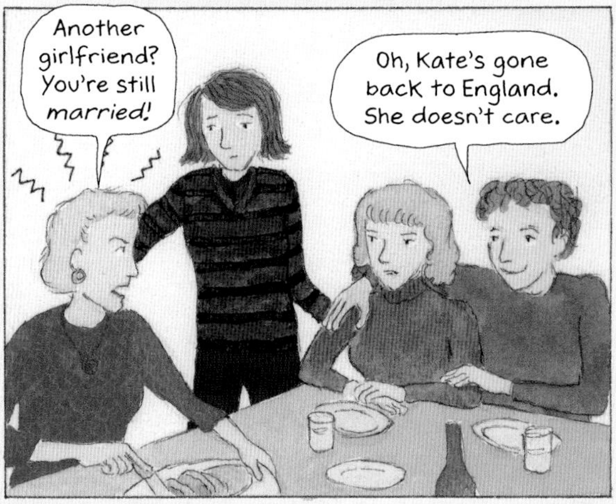
Another girlfriend? You're still *married!*
Oh, Kate's gone back to England. She doesn't care.

I DID EVERYTHING I COULD TO STAY OUT OF MY MOTHER'S WAY.

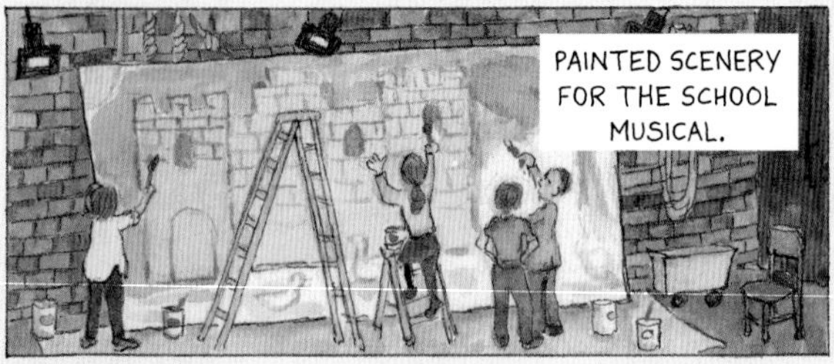
PAINTED SCENERY FOR THE SCHOOL MUSICAL.

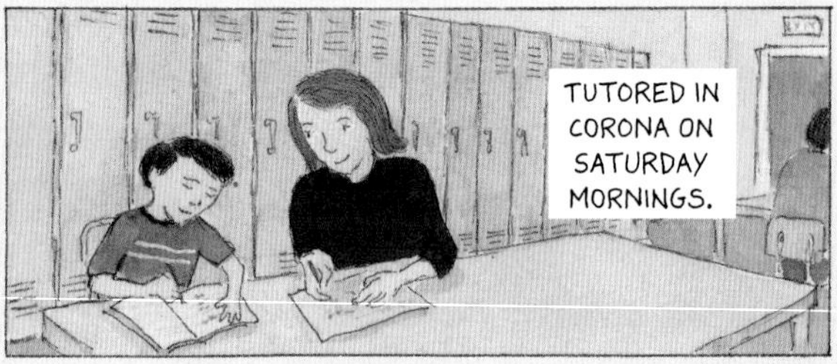
TUTORED IN CORONA ON SATURDAY MORNINGS.

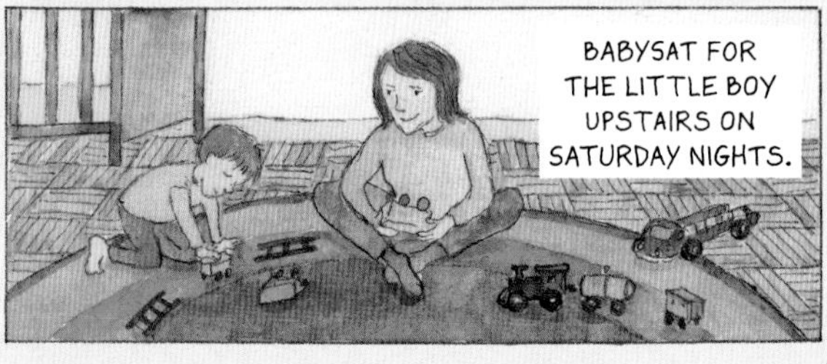
BABYSAT FOR THE LITTLE BOY UPSTAIRS ON SATURDAY NIGHTS.

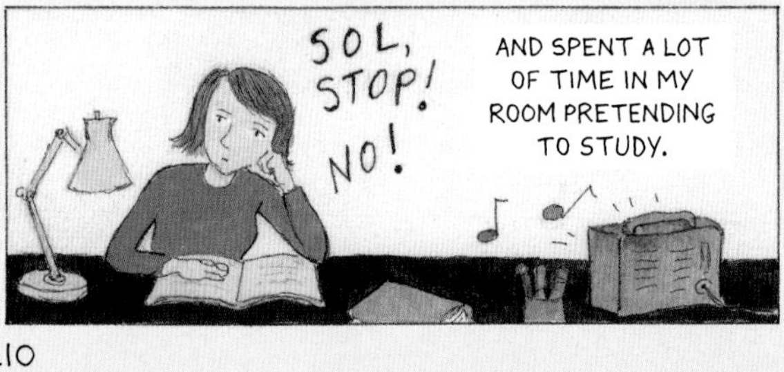
SOL, STOP!
NO!
AND SPENT A LOT OF TIME IN MY ROOM PRETENDING TO STUDY.

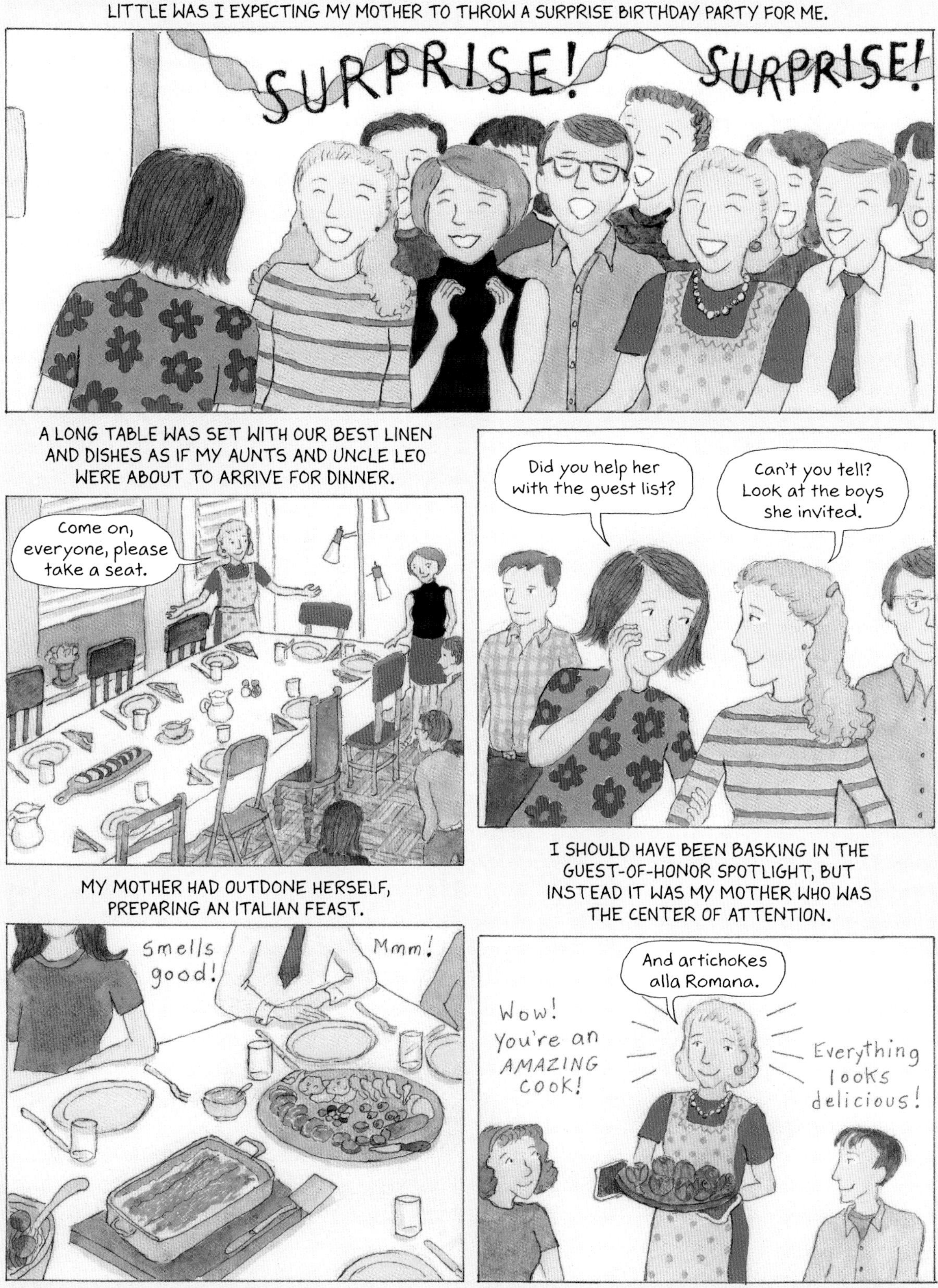
LITTLE WAS I EXPECTING MY MOTHER TO THROW A SURPRISE BIRTHDAY PARTY FOR ME.
SURPRISE!
SURPRISE!
A LONG TABLE WAS SET WITH OUR BEST LINEN AND DISHES AS IF MY AUNTS AND UNCLE LEO WERE ABOUT TO ARRIVE FOR DINNER.
Come on, everyone, please take a seat.
Did you help her with the guest list?
Can't you tell? Look at the boys she invited.
MY MOTHER HAD OUTDONE HERSELF, PREPARING AN ITALIAN FEAST.
Smells good!
Mmm!
I SHOULD HAVE BEEN BASKING IN THE GUEST-OF-HONOR SPOTLIGHT, BUT INSTEAD IT WAS MY MOTHER WHO WAS THE CENTER OF ATTENTION.
And artichokes alla Romana.
Wow! You're an AMAZING cook!
Everything looks delicious!

AFTER DINNER, MAMMA TOOK OFF HER APRON AND JOINED THE PARTY, LEAVING SOL TO WASH ALL THE DISHES.

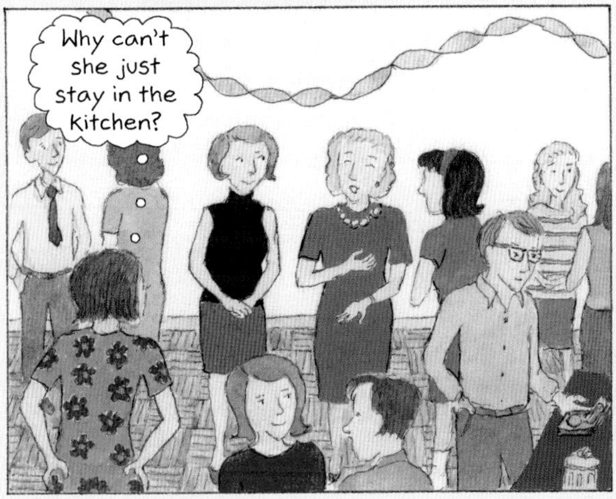
Why can't she just stay in the kitchen?

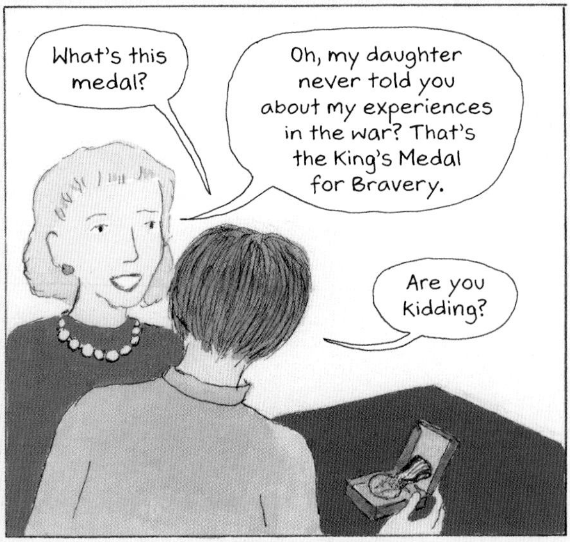
What's this medal?
Oh, my daughter never told you about my experiences in the war? That's the King's Medal for Bravery.
Are you kidding?

I WATCHED IN DISBELIEF AS ALL THE BOYS CROWDED AROUND NOT ME, BUT MY MOTHER. HOW WAS IT POSSIBLE THAT IN ALMOST THREE YEARS OF HIGH SCHOOL I HAD NEVER BEEN ABLE TO ATTRACT THIS KIND OF ATTENTION?

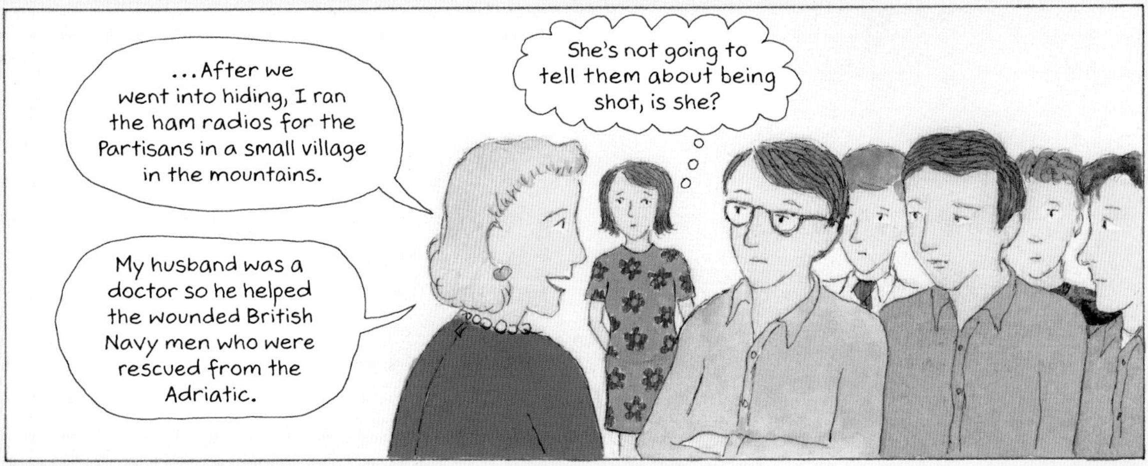
...After we went into hiding, I ran the ham radios for the Partisans in a small village in the mountains.
She's not going to tell them about being shot, is she?
My husband was a doctor so he helped the wounded British Navy men who were rescued from the Adriatic.

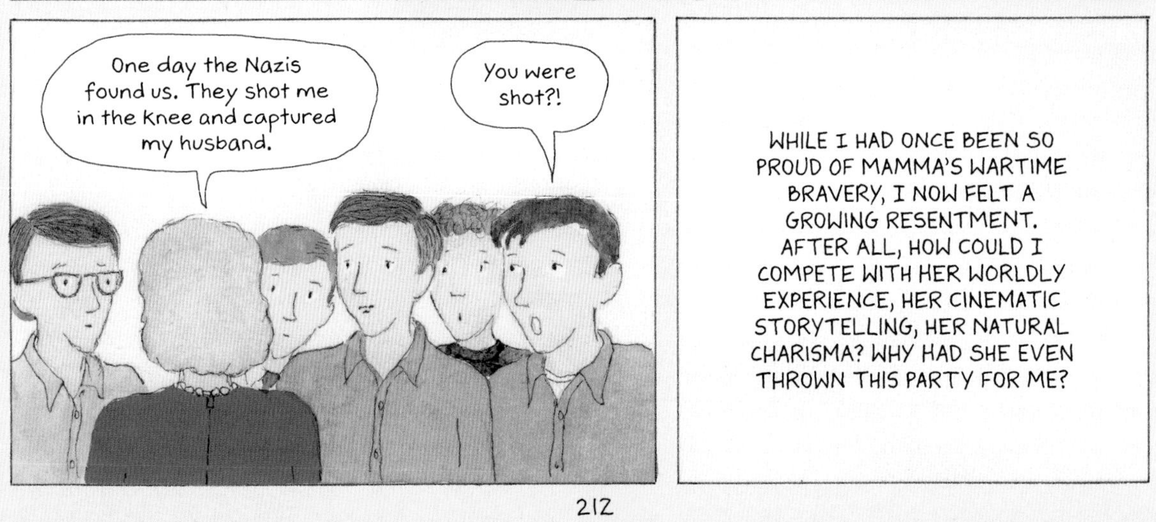
One day the Nazis found us. They shot me in the knee and captured my husband.
You were shot?!

WHILE I HAD ONCE BEEN SO PROUD OF MAMMA'S WARTIME BRAVERY, I NOW FELT A GROWING RESENTMENT. AFTER ALL, HOW COULD I COMPETE WITH HER WORLDLY EXPERIENCE, HER CINEMATIC STORYTELLING, HER NATURAL CHARISMA? WHY HAD SHE EVEN THROWN THIS PARTY FOR ME?

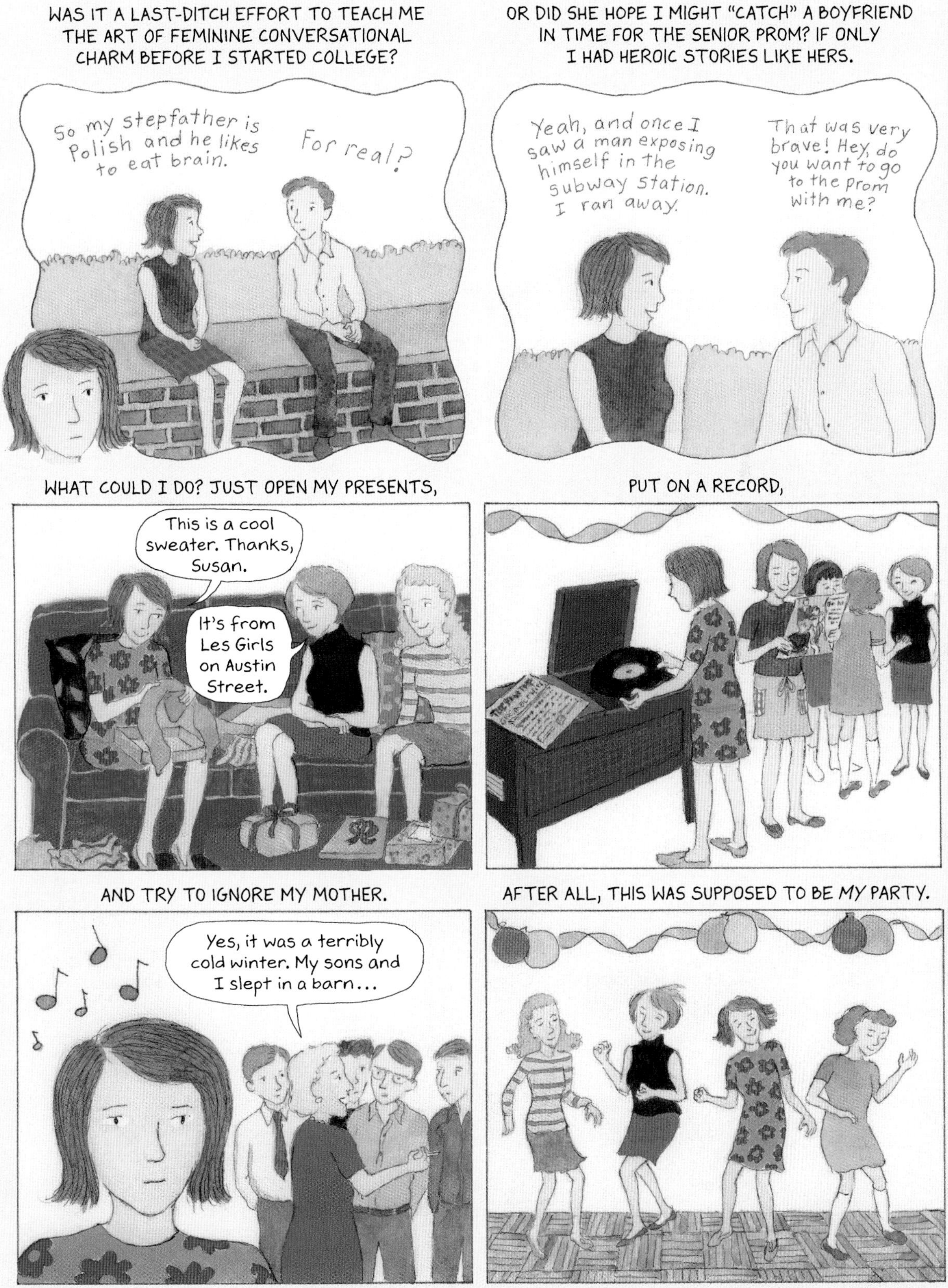
WAS IT A LAST-DITCH EFFORT TO TEACH ME THE ART OF FEMININE CONVERSATIONAL CHARM BEFORE I STARTED COLLEGE?
So my stepfather is Polish and he likes to eat brain.
For real?
OR DID SHE HOPE I MIGHT "CATCH" A BOYFRIEND IN TIME FOR THE SENIOR PROM? IF ONLY I HAD HEROIC STORIES LIKE HERS.
Yeah, and once I saw a man exposing himself in the subway station. I ran away.
That was very brave! Hey, do you want to go to the prom with me?
WHAT COULD I DO? JUST OPEN MY PRESENTS,
This is a cool sweater. Thanks, Susan.
It's from Les Girls on Austin Street.
PUT ON A RECORD,
AND TRY TO IGNORE MY MOTHER.
Yes, it was a terribly cold winter. My sons and I slept in a barn…
AFTER ALL, THIS WAS SUPPOSED TO BE MY PARTY.

TWENTY-THREE

Life Story

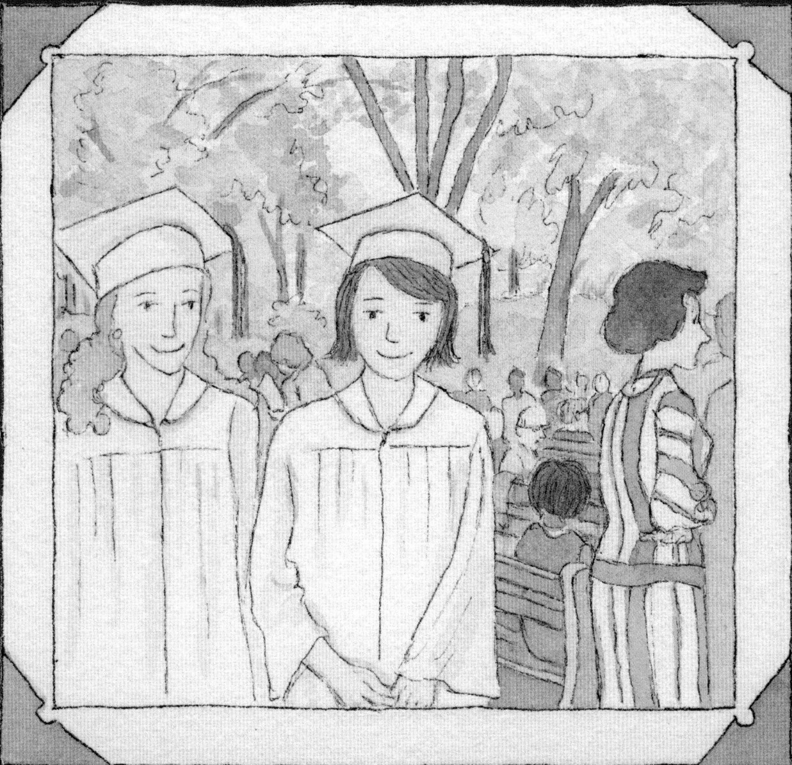

1967

AND THEN THE LETTER ARRIVED, MY ACCEPTANCE TO MOUNT HOLYOKE COLLEGE. MY MOTHER WAS THRILLED.

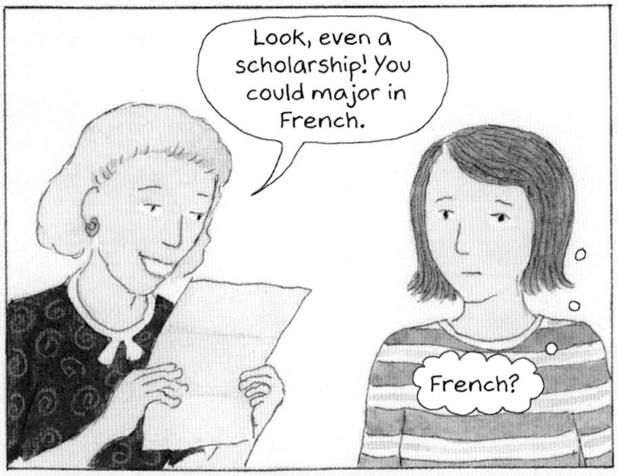
Look, even a scholarship! You could major in French.
French?

AT FIRST MY COLLEGE CHOICE WAS MET WITH SOME DISMAY AMONG MY RELATIVES.

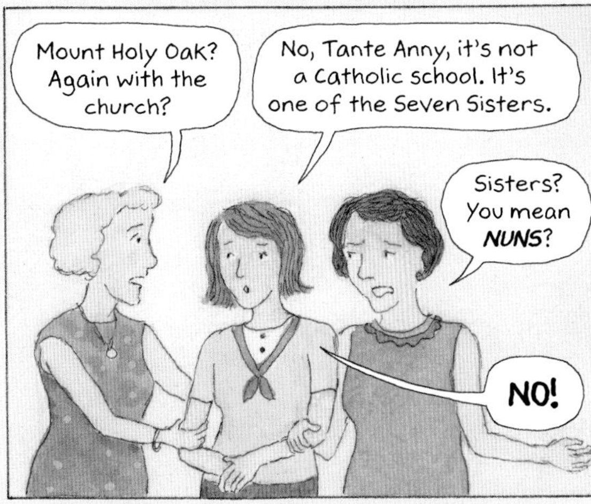
Mount Holy Oak? Again with the church?
No, Tante Anny, it's not a Catholic school. It's one of the Seven Sisters.
Sisters? You mean NUNS?
NO!

ONCE I QUELLED ALL THEIR FEARS, IT WAS TIME FOR A TRADITIONAL FAMILY KAFFEE UND KUCHEN CELEBRATION.

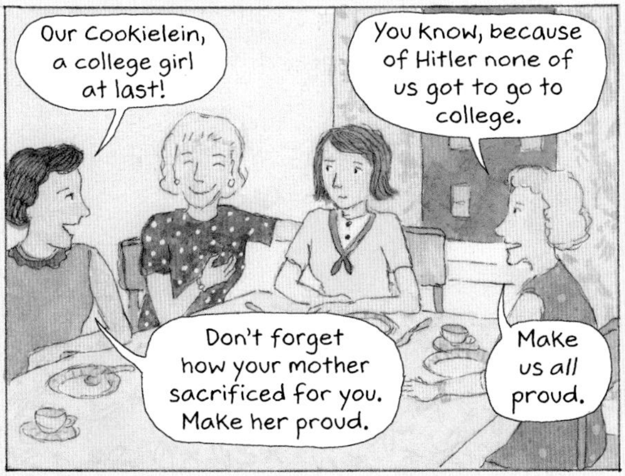
Our Cookielein, a college girl at last!
You know, because of Hitler none of us got to go to college.
Don't forget how your mother sacrificed for you. Make her proud.
Make us all proud.

MY MOTHER SAW MY IMMINENT DEPARTURE AS A CHANCE TO DOWNSIZE TO A ONE-BEDROOM APARTMENT ON THE TOP FLOOR.

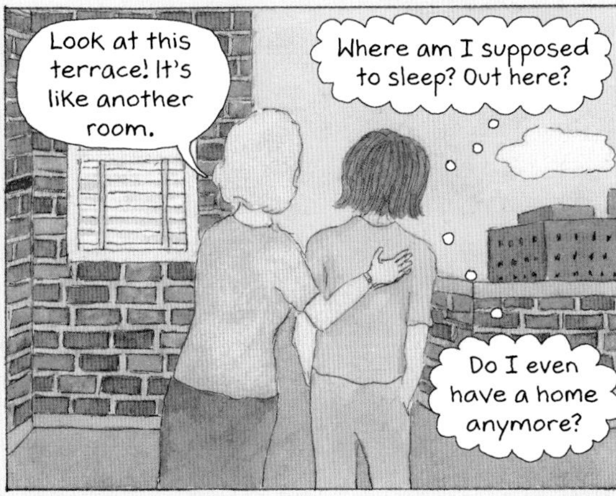
Look at this terrace! It's like another room.
Where am I supposed to sleep? Out here?
Do I even have a home anymore?

EVERY DAY I STUDIED THE MOUNT HOLYOKE CATALOG, WONDERING IF I WAS REALLY GOING TO BE SMART ENOUGH TO FIT IN.

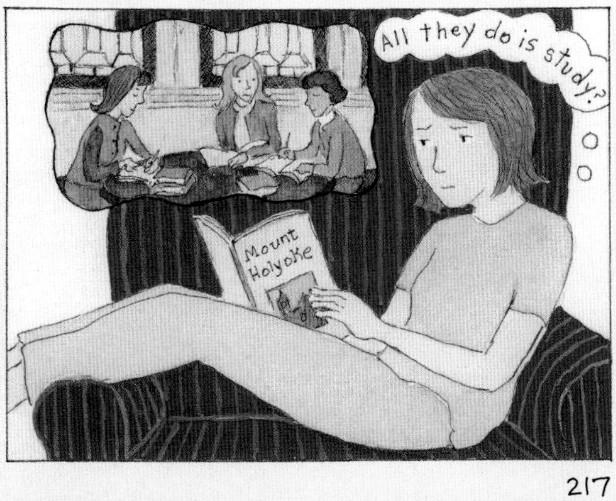
All they do is study?
Mount Holyoke

MOST OF MY FRIENDS WERE GOING TO STATE UNIVERSITIES, COED PLACES THAT PROMISED PARTIES AND FOOTBALL GAMES AND FUN.

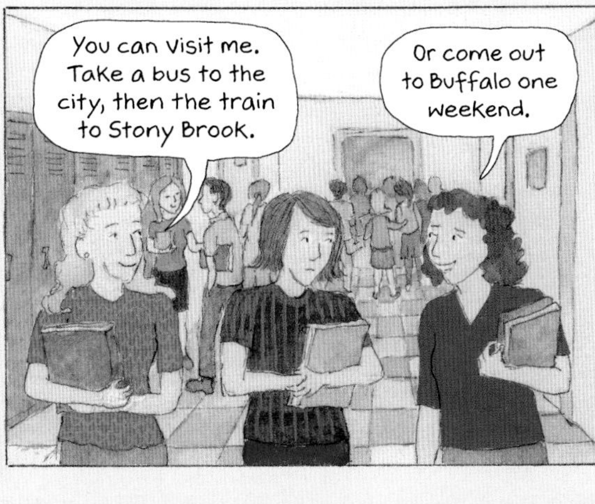
You can visit me. Take a bus to the city, then the train to Stony Brook.
Or come out to Buffalo one weekend.

OUR GRADUATION WAS HELD IN FOREST PARK. I SAT NEXT TO TWO GIRLS I BARELY KNEW. THEY BOTH GIGGLED AND SHREDDED THEIR WRIST CORSAGES DURING THE CEREMONY.

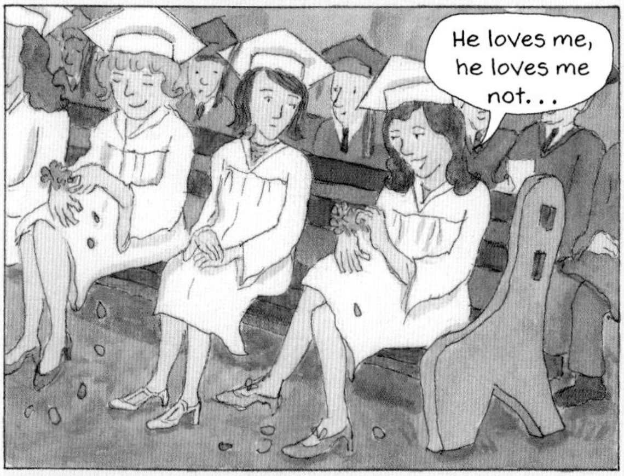
He loves me, he loves me not. . .

LATER WHEN I HANDED IN MY GOWN, I GOT MY DIPLOMA. MY NAME WAS MISSPELLED.

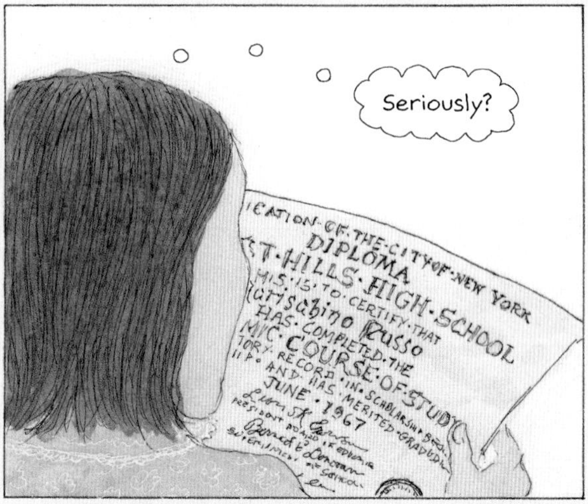
Seriously?
DIPLOMA

I SAID GOODBYE TO MY FAVORITE TEACHERS, AND THAT WAS IT. HIGH SCHOOL WAS OVER.

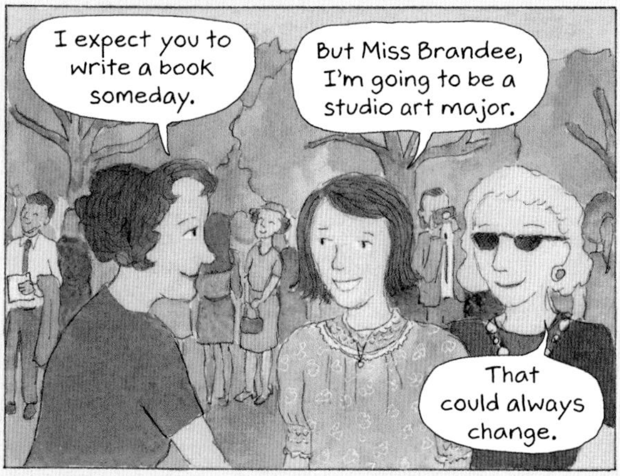
I expect you to write a book someday.
But Miss Brandee, I'm going to be a studio art major.
That could always change.

NOW THE SUMMER LOOMED AHEAD, THE FINAL STRETCH TO FREEDOM. I WORKED TWO JOBS: ONE IN QUEENS, THE OTHER IN THE BRONX. I SPENT A LOT OF TIME ON THE SUBWAY.

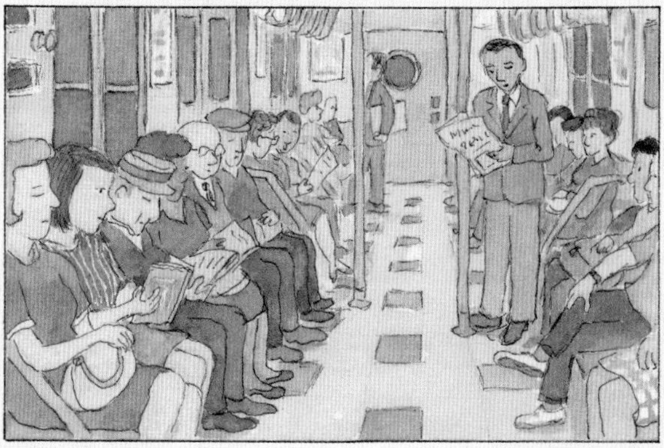

ON A COUPLE OF SATURDAYS, I WENT TO CONFESSION, MORE OUT OF HABIT THAN ANY SPIRITUAL NEED.

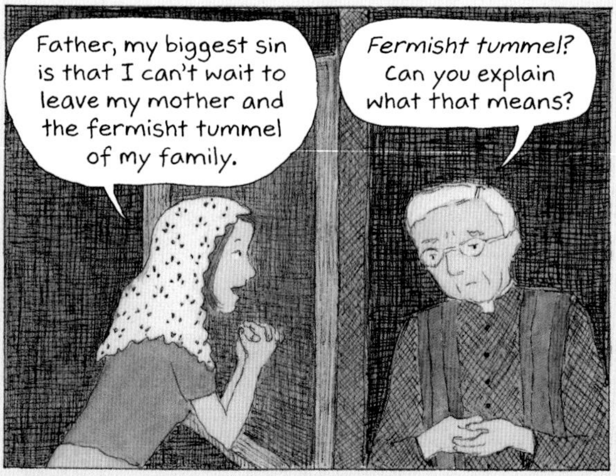
Father, my biggest sin is that I can't wait to leave my mother and the fermisht tummel of my family.
Fermisht tummel? Can you explain what that means?

I DIDN'T PACK MY CRUCIFIX, ROSARY BEADS, OR MISSAL IN MY COLLEGE TRUNK.

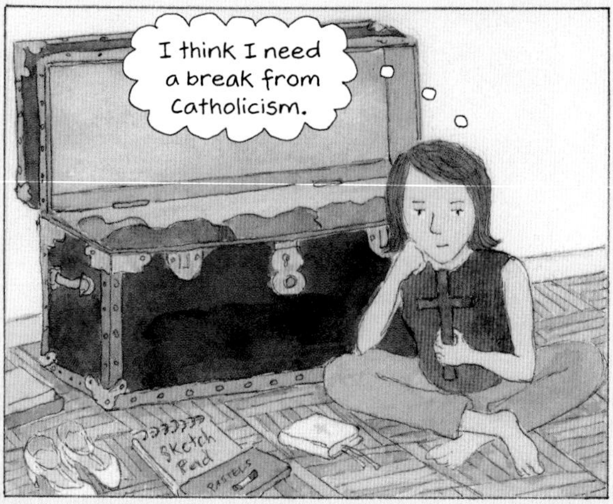
I think I need a break from Catholicism.
Sketch Pad
PASTELS

IN PREPARATION FOR MY DEPARTURE, I SECRETLY SHORTENED ALL MY SKIRTS.

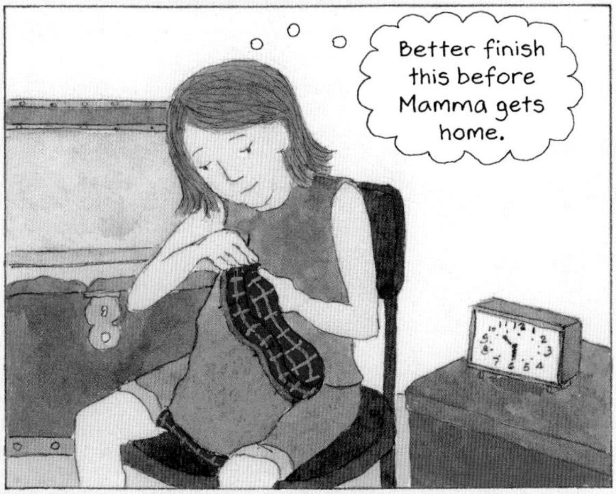
Better finish this before Mamma gets home.

I ALSO REFUSED TO HAVE MY HAIR CUT.

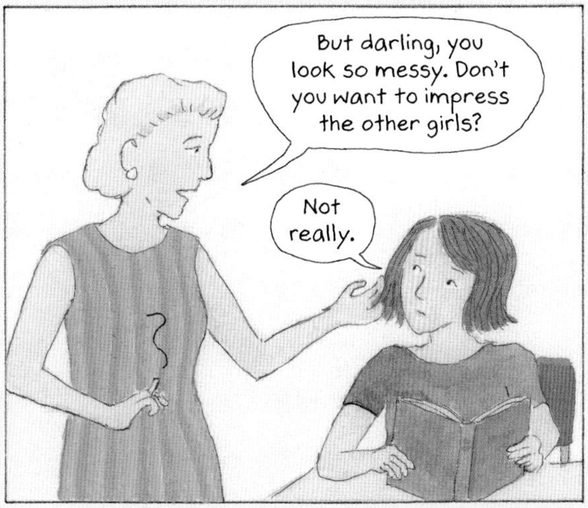
But darling, you look so messy. Don't you want to impress the other girls?
Not really.

MY MOTHER WASN'T HAPPY WHEN I DIDN'T SEEM INTERESTED IN ACCOMPANYING HER TO HAMBURGER EXPRESS FOR LUNCH...

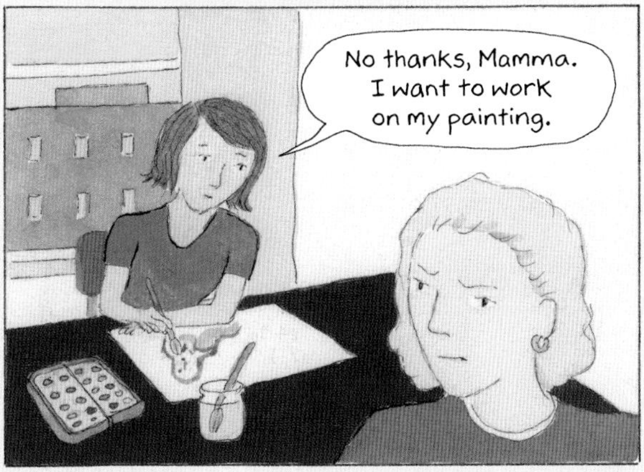
No thanks, Mamma. I want to work on my painting.

...OR WHEN I DISAGREED WITH HER OPINIONS.

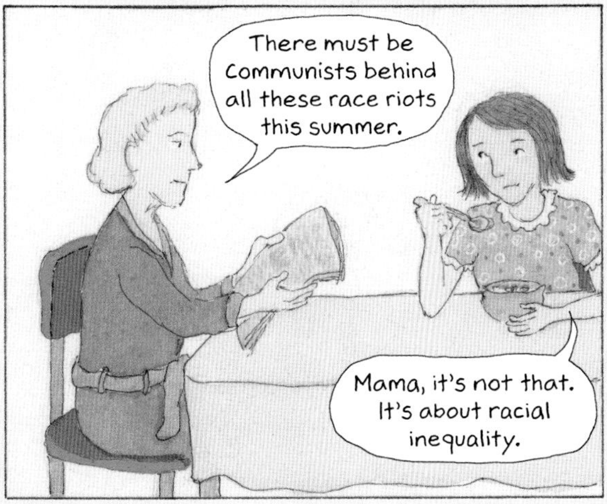
There must be Communists behind all these race riots this summer.
Mama, it's not that. It's about racial inequality.

I SAID GOODBYE TO MY BROTHERS AND REALIZED THAT FOR THE FIRST TIME, I WOULD BE THE CHILD LIVING FARTHEST AWAY FROM MAMMA.

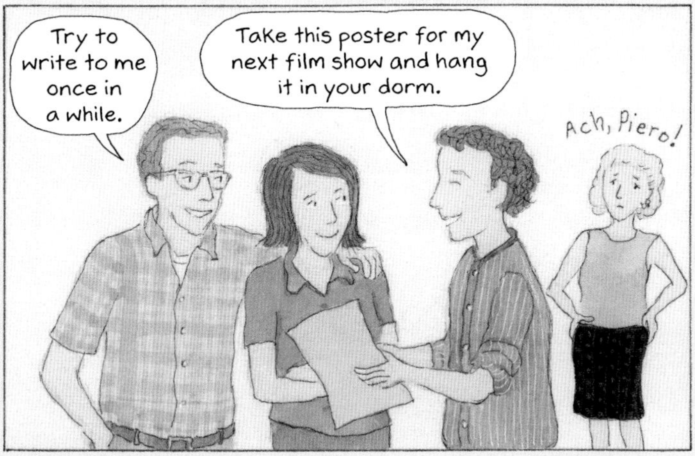
Try to write to me once in a while.
Take this poster for my next film show and hang it in your dorm.
Ach, Piero!

I WAS READY TO GO.

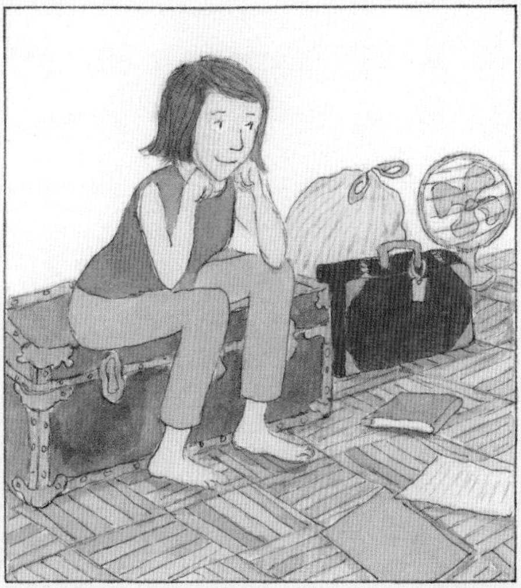

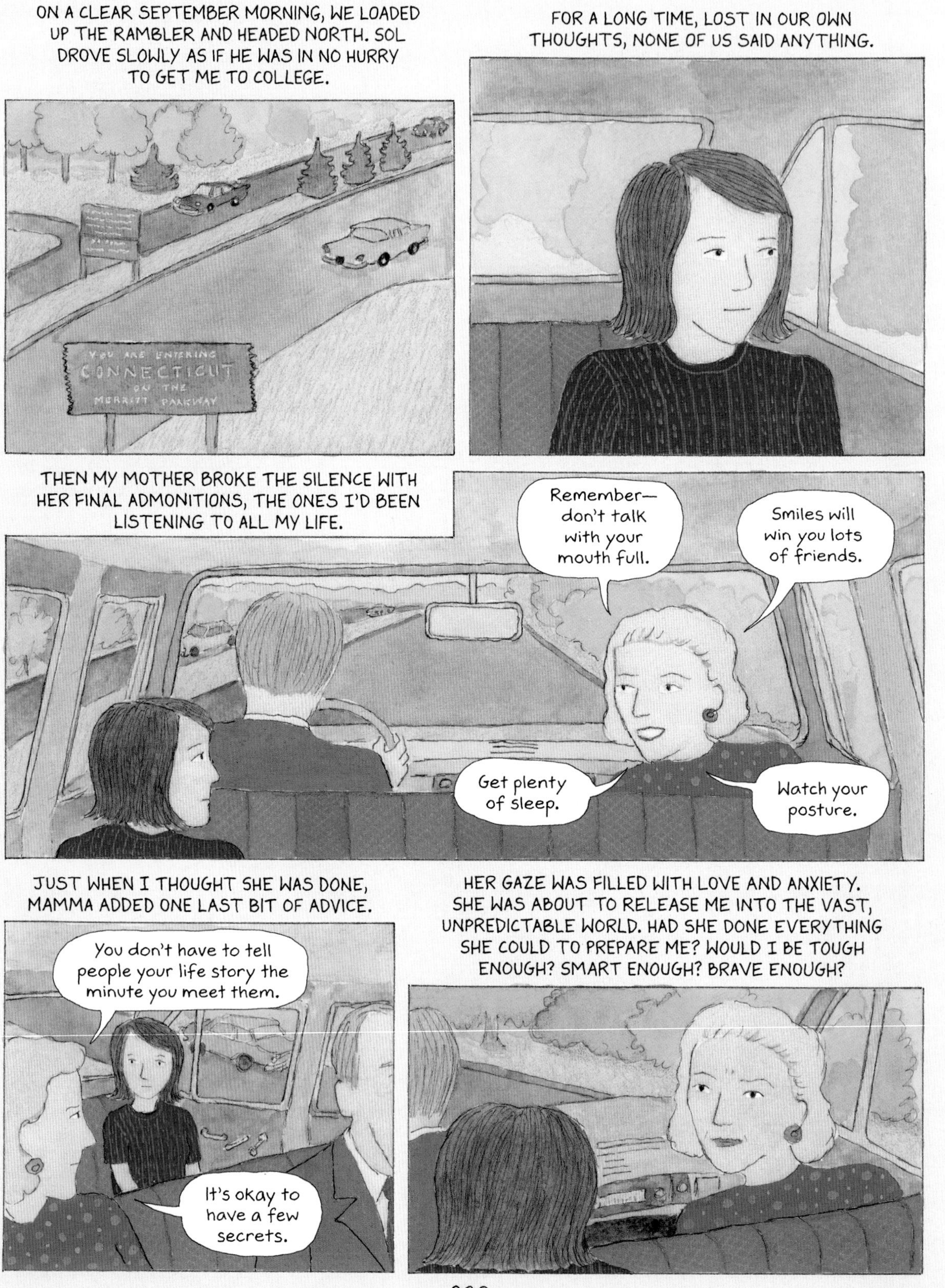
ON A CLEAR SEPTEMBER MORNING, WE LOADED UP THE RAMBLER AND HEADED NORTH. SOL DROVE SLOWLY AS IF HE WAS IN NO HURRY TO GET ME TO COLLEGE.
YOU ARE ENTERING CONNECTICUT ON THE MERRITT PARKWAY
FOR A LONG TIME, LOST IN OUR OWN THOUGHTS, NONE OF US SAID ANYTHING.
THEN MY MOTHER BROKE THE SILENCE WITH HER FINAL ADMONITIONS, THE ONES I'D BEEN LISTENING TO ALL MY LIFE.
Remember—don't talk with your mouth full.
Smiles will win you lots of friends.
Get plenty of sleep.
Watch your posture.
JUST WHEN I THOUGHT SHE WAS DONE, MAMMA ADDED ONE LAST BIT OF ADVICE.
You don't have to tell people your life story the minute you meet them.
It's okay to have a few secrets.
HER GAZE WAS FILLED WITH LOVE AND ANXIETY. SHE WAS ABOUT TO RELEASE ME INTO THE VAST, UNPREDICTABLE WORLD. HAD SHE DONE EVERYTHING SHE COULD TO PREPARE ME? WOULD I BE TOUGH ENOUGH? SMART ENOUGH? BRAVE ENOUGH?

I PROBABLY SHOULD HAVE TRIED TO REASSURE HER THAT I WAS READY FOR MY FUTURE, THAT I LOVED HER AND WAS GRATEFUL FOR HER SACRIFICES, AND THAT YES, ALL THE FAMILY STORIES, THE ONES I HAD GROWN UP WITH, WOULD ALWAYS BE SAFE WITH ME, THE LUCKY ONE BORN IN AMERICA.

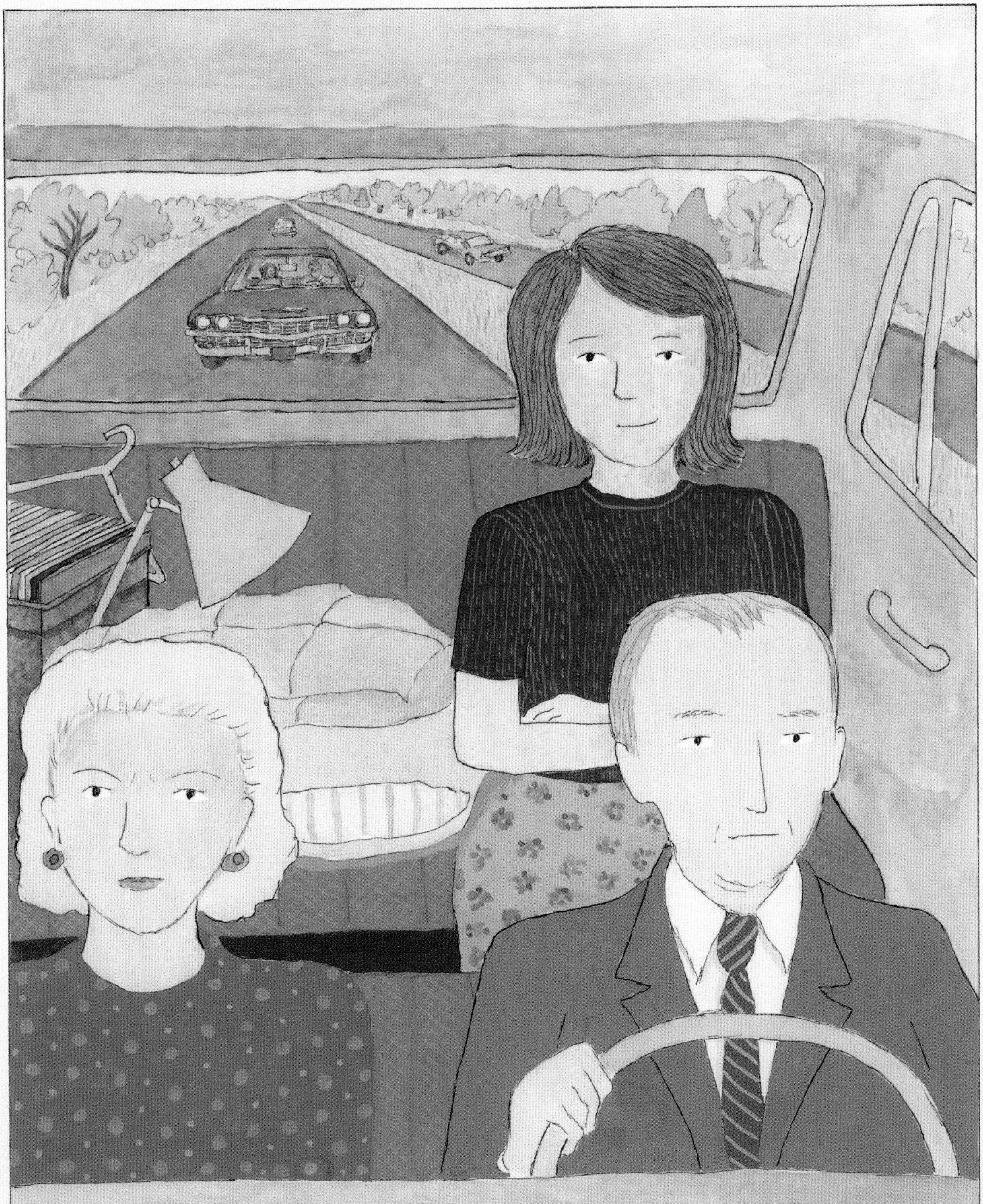

BUT I WAS ONLY SEVENTEEN AND EAGER TO BE ON MY WAY.

Epilogue

When I was nineteen, I dropped out of college to live alone in Florence, Italy. I wanted to get to know my father. He now had an apartment in Rome. How easy it would be for us to spend time together, I thought.

I took Italian classes at a school for foreigners and studied printmaking with an artist I found through the University of Florence. I learned fabric design with another artist. Every day I walked through the streets of Florence in my purple bellbottoms and dark blue cape, trying to be brave.

My father only visited me a handful of times in the six months I lived there. We ate in restaurants, much like the one in Geneva where he had first taken me so many years before. He was formal and guarded, always dressed in a suit and tie. He never explained why he had left my mother when she was pregnant. He never invited me to Rome to meet my aunts and uncle. He never told me that he had another child, a son, who was six years old and lived with his mother in Geneva. He never told me much of anything.

My father did offer belated paternal advice. He stressed the importance of eating a daily green salad and recommended that I return to college, find a boyfriend, and get married. When I came to Rome to surprise him one weekend, he told me to turn around and take the next train back to Florence. He was busy, and he considered it rude of me to just show up unannounced at his doorstep.

Surrounded by Renaissance art in the many churches and museums, I tried to finally discover who I was and where I belonged. I rarely went to mass, but I found solace being inside the churches. I lived on Via Ricasoli and would often walk down that long narrow street to the Accademia Gallery. The world-famous *David* by Michelangelo was the main attraction, but on my first visit I was distracted by one of his unfinished Pietàs nearby. The Virgin and her dying son, Jesus, seemed to be emerging from the stone with a thunderous sadness that matched my own.

I could imagine Michelangelo hammering slowly at the block of marble, trying to discover the secrets of his subjects. Maybe I needed to be just as patient and methodical as I chiseled away at my father's wall of silence. Or maybe one day, like Michelangelo, I would find out that I had run out of time. After all, my father was old already. There was a good chance family secrets would die with him.

When it was almost time for me to return home, I was fluent in Italian. My father told me I spoke very well, but he criticized my "Florentine" accent and told me to work on that. As a going-away gift, he gave me a book about monastic life that he inscribed to "Maria."

Part of the half-title page had been cut away.

As it turned out, I only saw my father once more before he died eleven years later. Despite the distance between us, I never stopped trying to win his approval. I wrote him long letters in Italian. I graduated from Mount Holyoke. My illustrations began to appear in magazines and newspapers that I proudly mailed to him. Just as I'd once been a devout little girl determined to be worthy of God's grace, now in my twenties I did everything I could to be worthy of my father's love. But it never seemed to be enough. Or maybe it was just too late.

One day my mother showed me an old photograph I hadn't seen before. It was mounted on cardboard and carefully saved in a manila envelope. A newborn baby lay still in a crib, his eyes tightly closed. She told me this was my older brother Joseph, who had died three days after birth and only sixteen months before I was born.

"It was the worst thing that ever happened to me," she said. "Worse than anything that happened in the war." My mother, who had relentlessly admonished me all my life to toughen up, now had tears in her eyes. "Your father and I were both devastated. He threw himself into his work, but all I could think of was how much I wanted another child. And then I got pregnant with you."

I wondered if this explained why my father had left her. Had he been afraid of losing another child? Had it been too soon? Or was he so disappointed when I turned out to be a girl that he decided to stay in Europe?

I would never find out. I stared at the tiny face of Joseph and thought I saw a bit of my own likeness. My brother. My full brother! He could have been my comrade sharing the original sin of being born in America. He might have helped me make sense of our Jewish blood and Catholic souls and guilt about being born after the Holocaust. But then I had another thought: If Joseph had lived, would I have been born?

In the end, we can never know everything about our families or the mystery of how we got here. It might just be enough to linger over the photographs and letters, to remember the stories we've heard and pass them on. And one day, when we most need God's grace, we will find it in ourselves, a gift we hadn't noticed before, bestowed by our mishpocheh, those tenacious, loving people who knew we were worthy from the very beginning.

Family Photos

MAMMA AND ME, 1956

The family that raised me—
my mother, my aunts, my
brothers, and my stepfather,
Sol—are all gone now.
These photos are snapshots
we saved in boxes and
occasionally in albums.
They tell their own stories
and help me remember
the people I miss.

PIERO, SABINA, AND ROBERTO, IN ROME AFTER THE WAR, 1945

MICHELE AND SABINA, MY PARENTS, AT A NIGHT CLUB, 1948

SOL AND ME, FATHER-DAUGHTER WEEKEND
AT MOUNT HOLYOKE COLLEGE, 1971

Sol and my mother continued to live
in their top-floor apartment in
Queens, where my mother began her
own import-export business.
Eventually she got a small office in
the city, and Sol occasionally worked
for her. One evening, after taking the
subway home, Sol died in the
apartment of a heart attack.

My mother continued to run her business and travel widely. She eventually moved to Manhattan, a longtime dream. She became active in several Italian American organizations and began speaking at events about her experiences in Italy during World War II, including a conference at the United States Holocaust Memorial Museum. In 1996, she received the title of Cavaliere Ufficiale, one of Italy's highest decorations for public service. A month later, she suffered a severe stroke, and ten months later she died.

credit: Gerard Malanga

PIERO, CAFÉ DE FLORE, PARIS, 1970

PIERO AND ME AT THE PSYCHIATRIC HOSPITAL, 1957

PIERO, ROBERTO, AND ME, 1951

Piero's mental illness became more and more debilitating as the years went on. While he managed to buy a crumbling farmhouse in Normandy with his reparation money and continued for a time to put on film shows and poetry readings in Europe and New York, by the 1980s he was homeless, living on the streets of Manhattan. My mother always tried to help him financially and emotionally, even as it became harder and harder. Piero was in and out of psychiatric hospitals. He married a Dutch woman who made a loving home for him in Amsterdam. Together they had five children. Piero also had three children with other partners. But he continued to be itinerant and often returned to France. In 1993, he died in a motorcycle accident on a French highway.

Roberto and Tere and their daughters moved to California and never lived on the East Coast again. Roberto worked for the U.S. Department of Agriculture for the rest of his career. In 1982, he and my mother took a trip back to Castel di Croce, the village in the Apennine mountains where they had hidden during World War II and where there is a monument to the Partisans—including Jacob—who were killed by the Germans. In 2009, Roberto died in Los Angeles of complications from Parkinson's disease.

TANTE ANNY, PIERO, ROBERTO, AND ME, SUMMER 1951

Tante Emmy and Uncle Leo lived in Washington Heights and continued to host family gatherings until the 1980s when they retired and moved to New Jersey to enjoy "life in the country." Uncle Leo passed away first, and a few years later Tante Emmy died of heart failure.

SABINA, ANNY, AND EMMY WITH OMA ON HER BIRTHDAY, 1958

ROBERTO AND ME AT OUR MOTHER'S APARTMENT, 1985

Tante Anny married a fellow Holocaust survivor from Bratislava. They were happily married and lived in Queens until eventually moving to New Jersey after they both retired. Tante Anny continued to have annual reunions with her friends from Auschwitz who were scattered around the United States. She and her husband were early supporters of the United States Holocaust Memorial Museum.

SABINA, ANNY, AND EMMY, IN VENTNOR, NEW JERSEY, 1992

TANTE ANNY AND SABINA, NEW YORK CITY, 1995

In her later years, she visited many middle schools in New Jersey to share her stories with the students. In 2001, she and I traveled to Leipzig through a German program that arranged for Holocaust survivors to return for a week to their hometowns. Using a walker, Tante Anny guided me to landmarks of her childhood and told me new stories. She died a few years later of an aneurysm. After she died, I found a yellow cloth Jewish star, the one she had once worn sewn to her coat as a young woman, carefully saved in an envelope in a dresser drawer.

ACKNOWLEDGMENTS

When I began this book seven years ago, I had no idea how hard it would be to write and illustrate a graphic memoir. After diving in, I was very lucky to find talented and generous people to show me the way. My gratitude is great.

Of all the lucky breaks, meeting Mark Siegel was one of the luckiest. When I mentioned my fledgling attempt at writing about my life in a graphic book, I was almost embarrassed. He told me to "be brave" and send it to him. Thanks to Mark, my manuscript found its way to Margaret Ferguson, who immediately embraced it. She pushed me to dig deeper and make it better. Wesley Adams took up my project midway and ran with it, helping me to expand both the story and the pictures. How lucky I was to have had not one but two magnificent editors. Likewise, I had the gift of two art directors: first Andrew Arnold, who guided me through early layouts and sketches with enthusiasm and patience, and then Kirk Benshoff, who was just as enthusiastic and patient. Thanks to Kirk's elegant design, my book has a jacket that is eye-catching and beautiful. And kudos to Sunny Lee for envisioning an interior design that flows gracefully from cover to cover.

I thank Andy Clymer for putting me in touch with John Martz, who did such a fine job of creating my font. One of the biggest challenges was writing in German, and I could not have done it without Jens Rekow's generous and meticulous assistance.

Then there are the friends who were my early readers and cheerleaders—Jean Van Leeuwan, Roni Schotter, and Pat Schories. My childhood friends who shared memories and reminded me of things I'd long forgotten—Susan Alter, Florence Steinberger, Marc Levitt, and of course, Karen Kennedy. My artsy girl pals who support and inspire me—Jane Pollak and Liz Alpert Fay. My always-there-for-me friends—Judy Epstein and David Gage. My pal, Suzannah Kincannon, who keeps me laughing. My first editor, mentor, and enduring friend, Susan Hirschman, who could not wait for me to finally complete this book. Here it is, Susan, at last.

I have also been "the lucky one," as my mother used to remind me, because of my family, my beloved and complicated mishpocheh; both the ones who raised me and taught me never to take freedom for granted and the ones who surround me now with their love and encouragement. I am grateful to them all—my children, Hannah, Sam, and Ben; my second daughter, Liz; my grandchildren, Jackson, Travis, Audrey, and Camilla; my nieces, Thérèse, Wynn, and Rose; and my "sister," Patti.

Finally, there is Whitney, my one and my only. He walked into the fermisht tummel many years ago and never looked back. He is the goy my mother adored, the guy I adore evermore. I could not have finished this book without you.